ROYAL AIR FORCE

AIRCRAFT

P1000 - R9999

Compiled by James J Halley

Published by Air-Britain (Historians) Ltd

Registered Office: 12 Lonsdale Gardens, Tunbridge Wells, Kent

Sales Dept: 5 Bradley Road, Upper Norwood, London SE19 3NT

ISBN 0 85130 253 1

Copyright 1996 by James J Halley

Published in Great Britain by

Air-Britain (Historians) Ltd
12 Lonsdale Gardens, Tunbridge Wells, Kent

Correspondence to:

J.J.Halley, 5 Walnut Tree Road,
Shepperton, Middlesex, TW17 ORW
and not to the Tunbridge Wells address

ISBN 0 85130 235 1

Printed by Hollen Street Press
Berwick-upon-Tweed

Blenheims of No.13 Operational Training Unit, with R3607 FV-E in the foreground

This volume is a replacement for the P- and R-series volumes produced in the 1970s and incorporates a large amount of additional information that has come to light over the past twenty years. The opportunity has been taken to expand the 'Fate' column to provide more detail of the circumstances in which an aircraft was written off than was possible in the restricted budgets that applied to the earlier registers.

Additional files have become available in the Public Record Office which had not been found when the original volumes were compiled. Additional details of units have been added where it has been found that the movement records had not been noted with a change of unit. More overseas aircraft have been pinned down to units since the Air Ministry movement cards did not record movements of aircraft once they had been shipped overseas. These have had to be obtained from a variety of secondary sources, including the ever-fallible logbooks. Crews seem to have had difficulty in remembering the serial numbers of the aircraft they had just flown. We can confirm this, having had, on more than one occasion, to go out again to look, having forgotten it in the interval from dispersal to briefing room. Fortunately our eyesight was better in those days, thus reducing the distance one had to walk.

Another problem that remains is that it was normal practice to merely note the aircraft letter. It was then up to the recording officer, or more likely his clerk, to look up the serial that corresponded. Inevitably, this resulted in his using an outdated list so that aircraft serials appeared in the Form 541 that had been replaced, sometimes several times.

The table of Presentation Aircraft has been considerably enlarged and in many cases corrected as the names recorded on various documents in the past were in bad handwriting or completely missed out. Some are still not known but research

is proceeding in this field to connect the names with the identities of the aircraft that carried them.

There are still many areas which remain obscure because of the style of records adopted. The South African Air Force war diaries do not have the same provision as RAF Operations Record Books for recording the serial numbers of their aircraft. As a result, and because all the aircraft with RAF serials used by them were flown in overseas theatres, there are many aircraft which remained unrecorded. Hence, some of the aircraft listed are shown only as 'ME' where it is known that it was shipped to the Middle East but no record has been found in any RAF squadron ORB. Alternatively, it may appear but was recorded with the wrong prefix!

A similar problem exists for training units overseas where a serial is normally recorded only in the event of an accident and, in some units, not even then. The Form 765c (which had to be completed in sextuplicate!) was intended to be passed to various interested parties, including a copy which would end up with the accident investigation branch of the Air Ministry. In the circumstances, it was a great temptation to pass off an accident as an operational loss, which only required a notation on the daily wastage return and did not even require the serial number to be quoted.

We are grateful for the assistance given by the Air Historical Branch over many years, thirty-seven at the last count! Our thanks also to the Public Record Office that has preserved and produced many tons of material.

Our thanks also to the many members of Air-Britain who have contributed to the amendments incorporated after publication of the original volumes and especially to Ray Sturtivant for checking through, and adding to, the tables for this one; also to Malcolm Fillmore for checking the Tiger Moth tables from his voluminous records on the type.

Above: Tornado prototype P5224

Below: Oxford P8833 with ambulance markings

Spitfire P9565 fitted with an experimental long range fuel tank in an effort to increase its range

25 (of 100) Airspeed Oxford IIs delivered by Percival Aircraft between November 1939 and August 1940 to Contract No. 782859/38

P1005 to		
P1054	-	Cancelled
P1070	AAEE/2 FTS/2 FIS/ 2 CFS/4 Gp CF	SOC 20.9.44
P1071	RAFC	Stalled on take-off and spun into ground, Cranwell, 29.12.40
P1072	2 FTS	Destroyed in air raid, Brize Norton, 16.8.40
P1073	5 FTS/3 FTS/ 11 PAFU	To 3735M 23.5.43
P1074	Armstrong-Siddeley/ 14 FTS/Moreton Valence/12 PAFU/ 3 FIS	To 3736M 23.5.43
P1075	2 FTS	Destroyed in air raid, Brize Norton, 16.8.40
P1076	3 FTS/15 FTS/ 2 AGS/1674 CU	SOC 15.2.45
P1077	5 FTS/1 EWS/RAFC/ 2 CFS/15 PAFU	To USAAF 28.1.44
P1078	3 FTS	Hit HT wires in bad visibility Woodchester, Glos., 18.11.40
P1079	RAFC	Engine cut; stalled in forced landing and hit tree near Grantham, Lincs., 4.9.41
P1080	RAFC	Crashed after collision, 15.10.41; NFD
P1081	CFS	Stalled on approach and hit ground, Alton Barnes, 4.2.41
P1082	CFS/RAFC/15 PAFU	SOC 31.5.43
P1083	2 FTS	DBR 6.7.40; NFD
P1084	2 FTS	Destroyed in air raid, Brize Norton, 16.8.40
P1085	RAFC	Swung on take-off; hit ground and undercarriage raised to stop, Barkston LG, 28.9.41
P1086	2 FTS/2 PAFU	Refueller caught fire; aircraft DBF, Southrop, 27.4.42
P1087	16 PFTS	Wing hit ground avoiding Battle landing alongside, Newton, 10.9.41; DBR
P1088	2 FTS	Engine cut; overshot forced landing and hit hedge near Filkins, Glos., 17.10.40
P1089	2 FTS/2 PAFU/ 6 FU/2 FIS/Ingham/ 1687 Flt/Faldingworth/ 1687 Flt/9 AFTS	SS 10.2.56
P1090	2 FTS	DBR 17.5.41; NFD
P1091	15 FTS/14 FTS/ 14 PAFU/Halton	SOC 20.12.44
P1092	15 FTS	Swung on attempted overshoot at night and hit hangar, Weston-on-the-Green, 10.2.42
P1093	15 FTS	Engine cut; wing hit ground in forced landing, Yarnton, Oxon., 21.4.41; DBR
P1094	15 FTS/6 FTS/6 PAFU/ 1655 Flt/16 OTU	SOC 30.5.46
P1095 to		
P1099	-	Cancelled
P1120 to		
P1139	-	Cancelled

200 Handley Page Hampden Is delivered between June 1939 and February 1940 by Handley Page, Radlett, to Contract No. 773239/38

P1145	16 OTU/Cv TB/ 455/5 OTU	SOC 3.1.44
P1146	16 OTU/Cv TB	SOC 9.6.44
P1147	16 OTU/Cv TB/ 5 OTU/1464 Flt	SOC 15.5.44
P1148	16 OTU	Abandoned in bad weather and crashed 1m E of Brackley, Northants., 29.6.41
P1149	16 OTU	Hit by P1302 while taking off, Upper Heyford, 7.2.41
P1150	Cv TB/455/144/415	SOC 10.4.44
P1151	144/14 OTU/Cv TB/ 144/14 OTU/415	Shot down by flak off Brittany coast, 10.4.43
P1152	44/50	Flew into ground at night near Goldsborough, near Whitby, Yorks., 16.11.41, on return from minelaying
P1153	49/455/415	Shot down by flak attacking convoy off Borkum, 28.6.42
P1154	16 OTU/5 OTU	SOC 28.6.44
P1155	14 OTU	Stalled after take-off and dived into ground 1½m NW of Buckminster, Lincs., 27.11.41
P1156	50/455	Missing from attack on German fleet off Dutch coast, 12.2.42
P1157	14 OTU/Cv TB/415	Damaged by flak on night torpedo sweep off Dutch coast and ditched, 18.2.41
P1158	14 OTU/Cv TB/455	SOC 20.12.43
P1159	16 OTU	Crashed in forced landing in bad weather, Denham Golf Course, Bucks., 23.12.41
P1160	CGS/Cv TB/415/ 16 FPP	Collided with Beaufighter NE590 while taxying, Kirkbride, 29.2.44
P1161	1 AAS	Engine cut on bombing practice; crashed in sea 3m N of Mablethorpe, Lincs., 16.8.42
P1162	CGS	Stalled on take-off and crashed 1m SE of Castle Kennedy, 27.7.41
P1163	CGS	Hit trees low flying, Terrington St. Clement, Norfolk, 17.8.42
P1164	144/Cv TB/455/415	SOC 17.2.44
P1165	408	Shot down by night fighter, Winterswyk, Neth., on return from Huls, 28.12.41
P1166	144/50/144/408/ Cv TB/455/3 OAFU	SOC 12.12.43
P1167	16 OTU/14 OTU/ 32 OTU	To Canada 18.8.43 SOC 2.8.44
P1168	14 OTU	Stalled and dived into ground 4m S of Saltby, 9.12.41
P1169	RAE/AAEE/RAE/ AAEE/RAE/Cv TB/ 415/489	SOC 17.2.44
P1170	61	Crashed on landing, Doncaster, 14.10.39
P1171	61/83	Shot down by flak, Kiel, 2.7.40
P1172	144	Missing (Hamburg) 6.9.40
P1173	44	Shot down by Bf 109s, Kristiansand, 12.4.40
P1174	49/16 OTU/5 OTU	Crashed in forced landing in Skye when lost, 16.8.42
P1175	49	Overshot landing, Scampton, 22.4.40, on return from minelaying
P1176	49/14 OTU/1404 Flt	SOC 4.6.44
P1177	49/5 Gp TF/25 OTU/ 16 OTU/Cv TB/ 16 OTU	Flew into ground on landing at night, Weston-on-the-Green, 16.2.42
P1178	83	Shot down by night fighter on raid to Emmerich, 4.6.40
P1179	76/16 OTU	Hit tree on take-off, Upper Heyford, 2.6.40
P1180	76/16 OTU	Hit tree on take-off, Brackley LG, 27.7.40
P1181	76/16 OTU	Engine cut on take-off; crashlanded near Upper Heyford, 25.4.40
P1182	76/16 OTU	Engine cut in circuit; crashlanded, Little Chesterton, near Bicester, 23.12.40
P1183	RAE/83	Shot down by flak, Le Havre, 19.9.40
P1184	16 OTU	Hit tree on night approach, Croughton, 13.9.41
P1185	16 OTU/14 OTU	Missing (Düsseldorf) 1.8.42; believed crashed off Ostend
P1186	14 OTU	Dived into ground ½m N of Pinchbeck, Spalding, Lincs. 26 1.42; cause not known
P1187	44/420	Damaged by flak and attacked by night fighter on return from Stuttgart; crashlanded, Great Bentley, Essex, 5.5.42
P1188	14 OTU/Cv TB/489	Damaged by FW 190s on antishipping sweep and bellylanded, Wick, 3.8.43
P1189	16 OTU/Cv TB/489	Damaged by Ar 196 and ditched off Norwegian coast, 9.4.43
P1194	25 OTU	Engine cut on take-off; crashlanded, Balderton, 27.9.41
P1195	14 OTU	SOC 3.2.44
P1196	14 OTU/5 OTU/ 1402 Flt	SOC 12.4.44
P1197	16 OTU	Overshot landing, hit hut and DBF, Croughton, 25.3.42
P1198	106/144/5 OTU/ 1 TTU	Crashed in sea during practice torpedo drop off Lady Is., Firth of Clyde, 29.4.43
P1199	16 OTU/5 OTU	Collided with Beaufort L9932 on landing, Turnberry, 1.9.42
P1200	16 OTU/Cv TB 32 OTU	To Canada 9.43 Missing on night navex off British Columbia, 18.1.44
P1201	455	Missing (Cologne) 8.11.41
P1202	50	Ran out of fuel on overshoot and crashed 2m E of Skellingthorpe, 1.12.41, on return from Hamburg
P1203	455	Shot down by night fighter near Zwolle, Neth., on return from Essen, 7.4.42
P1204	25 OTU/16 OTU/ 14 OTU/1404 Flt	Hit by Whitley BD276 while parked, St.Eval, 16.7.43
P1205	14 OTU	Lost height and crashed on Grimsthorpe Bombing Range, Lincs., 31.8.42
P1206	49	Shot down by night fighter 13m E of Alkmaar, on return from Bocholt, 8.11.41
P1207	Cv TB/AAEE/ 144/489/455	Ran out of fuel on ASR sortie and ditched off Bridge of Don, Aberdeen, 27.10.43
P1208	16 OTU/Cv TB/455	Yawed after take-off and flew into ground, Wick, 7.10.43
P1209	16 OTU/14 OTU/ 1406 Flt/519	SOC 8.12.43
P1210	16 OTU	Crashed on overshoot, Balderton, 19.6.41
P1211	14 OTU	Dived into ground on approach, Cottesmore, 18.6.41
P1212	408	Stalled on approach and dived into ground 4m N of Coningsby on return from Bremen, 20.10.41

P1213	14 OTU	Control lost after take-off; flew into ground, Cottesmore, 16.3.41
P1214	16 OTU/Cv TB/489	SOC 7.4.44
P1215	14 OTU/CGS/ Cv TB/ATA	SOC 9.6.44
P1216	16 OTU/14 OTU/ TFU/4 OAFU/BTU	Stalled and dived into ground on Braid Fell, Wigtown, 18.1.44
P1217	14 OTU/1402 Flt/517	Crashed on landing on ferry flight, Tollerton, 14.1.44
P1218	408	Missing (Mannheim) 23.10.41
P1219	16 OTU/Cv TB/ 489	Crashed into sea 2m S of Selsey Bill, Sussex, on training flight, 22.7.42
P1220	25 OTU	Overshot landing and hit gun post, Finningley, 30.5.41
P1221	25 OTU/16 OTU	Flew into ground 4m S of Polebrook, 26.3.41
P1222	25 OTU/16 OTU/ 5 OTU	Hit sea and ditched 1m W of Dubh Artach Lighthouse, Argyll, on torpedo practice, 18.1.43
P1223	50/1404 Flt	Ran out of fuel on met flight and crashlanded, Trevose Head, Cornwall, 25.3.43
P1224	RAE/TDU	SOC 22.12.43
P1225	16 OTU	Stalled on landing in fog, Croughton, 9.11.41; DBF
P1226	49	Flew into hill in fog on ferry flight near Branscombe, Devon, 17.3.42
P1227	16 OTU	Overshot landing, Croughton, 14.10.41; DBR
P1228	50/106	Missing (Hamburg) 1.12.41
P1229	16 OTU/Cv TB	SOC 24.1.44
P1230	16 OTU/14 OTU	To RCAF 18.8.43
P1233	25 OTU	Missing on night navex, 19.5.41
P1234	25 OTU	Hit balloon cable in bad visibility and crashed, Weybridge, Surrey, 25.10.41; DBR
P1235	14 OTU/Cv TB	SOC 21.12.43
P1236	25 OTU/Cv TB/455	SOC 3.2.44
P1237	16 OTU/Cv TB/ 144/489/455	SOC 3.1.44
P1238	14 OTU/Cv TB/ RAE/TDU	SOC 3.12.43
P1239	50/420	Shot down by night fighter off Terschelling on return from Essen, 13.4.42
P1240	14 OTU	Engine cut; crashed in forced landing, Little Bytham, Lincs., 8.4.41
P1241	14 OTU	Engine cut; crashed in forced landing 2m from Cottesmore, 15.1.41
P1242	14 OTU/1 AAS	SOC 16.12.43
P1243	14 OTU/Cv TB/ 5 OTU/455/5 OTU/ 1 TTU	SOC 20.1.44
P1244	16 OTU/455/408	Missing (Kassel) 28.8.42
P1245	25 OTU/Cv TB/455	To Russian Navy, 12.10.42
P1246	16 OTU/Cv TB/ 455/RAE/455	Suffered structural damage and hydraulics failed; crashlanded near Leuchars, 17.11.43; DBR
P1247	16 OTU	Stalled on night overshoot, Croughton, 16.4.42
P1248	25 OTU	Hit balloon cable and crashed, Concord Park, Sheffield, 19.4.41
P1249	14 OTU/Cv TB	SOC 28.6.44
P1250	76/16 OTU/CGS/ Cv TB/144	Shot down by flak attacking shipping off Norway, 13.12.42
P1251	76/16 OTU	Engine cut after take-off from Upper Heyford; crashlanded, Fritwell, Oxon., 5.5.40
P1252	1 AAS	To GI airframe 24.11.41
P1253	106/61	Ran out of fuel returning from Cologne and flew into ground, Great Wratting, Suffolk, 2.3.41
P1254	106/14 OTU/	SOC 20.2.44
P1255	106/BTU	SOC 18.9.44
P1256	106	Crashed during night training at Misson, Yorks., 27.9.40; possibly mistook Q-site for airfield
P1257	16 OTU/455/420/ Cv TB/489	Missing on shipping sweep off Norwegian coast, 13.4.43
P1258	106/5 Gp TF/25 OTU/ 489/Cv TB/455/415	Shot down by night fighter during shipping sweep off Dutch coast, 16.8.43
P1259	106	Shot down by flak while mine-laying in Elbe Estuary, 19.9.40
P1260	7	Flew into Snaefell, Isle of Man, in cloud on navex, 1.1.40
P1261	7/16 OTU/5 OTU	2134M NTU; to 3098M 17.9.43
P1265	7/16 OTU/14 OTU/ 1402 Flt	Missing from met. flight off NW Ireland, 8.9.43
P1266	7/16 OTU	Engine cut on night navex; crashlanded, Babdown Farm, 1.8.40
P1267	76	Hit tree during forced landing in bad visibility near Princes Risborough, Bucks., 11.12.39
P1268	76/16 OTU	Undershot at night and hit bowser, Upper Heyford, 21.6.40
P1269	76/16 OTU	Overshot and hit hangar, Upper Heyford, 24.7.41
P1270	76	Stalled on take-off and flew into ground, Upper Heyford, 4.3.40
P1271	76/16 OTU	Broke up in dive 3m W of Gloucester, 8.10.40
P1272	TDU/14 OTU/455	Missing (Hamburg) 1.12.41
P1273	14 OTU/Cv TB/144	Damaged by fighters on flight to North Russia and crashlanded near Petsamo, 4.9.42
P1274	185/14 OTU	Control lost on night overshoot; crashed 2m NNE of Cottesmore, 10.5.40
P1275	185/14 OTU	Hit trees on night approach, Cottesmore, 29.5.40
P1276	185/14 OTU	Engine cut on night take-off; control lost and flew into ground, Cottesmore, 7.12.40
P1277	14 OTU	Overshot night landing, Saltby, 2.5.42
P1278	14 OTU	Stalled after engine cut on take-off and crashed 1m SE of Cottesmore, 17.7.41
P1279	185	Undercarriage collapsed on landing, Cottesmore, 24.2.40; to 1857M, later 3097M and 3447M
P1280	14 OTU	Undercarriage collapsed on landing, Cottesmore, 12.6.40; to 2108M
P1281	14 OTU	Stalled on night take-off and crashed, Cottesmore, 1.6.40
P1282	14 OTU/Cv TB/ 415/TDU	SOC 17.2.44
P1283	14 OTU	Failed to take-off; hit building, Cottesmore, 3.3.41
P1284	16 OTU/Cv TB/5 OTU	Crashed in forced landing while lost and short of fuel 10m S of Letterkenny, Eire, 28.10.42; interned
P1285	16 OTU	Overshot landing and hit truck, Upper Heyford, 1.9.41

P1286	14 OTU/Cv TB/415	SOC 17.2.44
P1287	25 OTU/Cv TB/455	To Russian Navy, 12.10.42
P1288	16 OTU	Crashed on landing at night, Kidlington, 25.2.41
P1289	14 OTU	Hit Anson R3386 on landing, Cottesmore, 15.7.41
P1290	106	Shot down by flak while minelaying in Oslofjord, 8.11.41
P1291	25 OTU/16 OTU/ 14 OTU/1401 Flt	Engine cut on met flight; ditched in North Sea, 18.7.43
P1292	14 OTU	Failed to take-off and hit hedge, Cottesmore, 23.2.41
P1293	14 OTU/1404 Flt	Crashed in bad weather on met flight 1½m E of St.Mawgan, 23.7.43
P1294	14 OTU	Dived into ground out of cloud, Llynclyn, Salop., 30.10.41
P1295	144	Missing (Huls) 29.12.41
P1296	16 OTU/Cv TB/ TDU/415	SOC 24.5.44
P1297	25 OTU/16 OTU	Spun into ground, Trismore, Oxon., 20.4.42; cause not known
P1298	14 OTU	Overshot and hit truck, Cottesmore, 25.3.42
P1299	25 OTU/16 OTU	Spun into ground, Locking, Somerset, 6.4.42
P1300	14 OTU/1 AAS/ 5 AOS/1 AAS	SOC 15.12.43
P1301	14 OTU	Collided with P4303 near Saltby, 12.9.41
P1302	16 OTU	Collided with P1149 on landing, Upper Heyford, 7.2.41
P1303	106/5 Gp TF/ 25 OTU/14 OTU	Dived into ground during single-engined practice 5m N of Cottesmore, 29.4.42
P1304	106	Hit trees on approach to Finningley and crashed near Bawtry, 21.12.40
P1305	14 OTU	Dived into ground out of cloud, Sharnbrook,. Beds., 19.8.40
P1309	14 OTU	Overshot and hit pillbox, Cottesmore, 7.7.40
P1310	185/14 OTU/49/ Cv TB/415/455	SOC 27.12.43
P1311	106 32 OTU	To Canada 9.43 SOC 30.4.44
P1312	14 OTU/Cv TB/ 5 OTU/415	SOC 4.6.44
P1313	CGS/Cv TB/415	SOC 17.2.44
P1314	CGS/49/420/408/ Cv TB/1402 Flt	Swung on landing and broke back, Aldergrove, 25.3.43
P1315	CGS	Destroyed in air raid, Sutton Bridge, 13.5.41
P1316	14 OTU	Caught fire on ground, Saltby, 14.2.42; DBR
P1317	50	Damaged by flak and engine cut on approach, Hemswell, 27.8.40 on return from Leipzig
P1318	49	Missing from raid on rail targets in Rhineland, 26.5.40
P1319	49	Missing (minelaying) 26.4.40
P1320	106	Dived into ground on night training flight, Pickencote, 4m N of Stamford, Lincs., 25.11.40
P1321	106/50	Damaged by flak, Castrop-Rauxel, and crashlanded on beach near Happisburgh, Norfolk, 26.7.40
P1322	106/44/25 OTU/ 16 OTU/14 OTU	SOC 7.2.44
P1323	61/49/16 OTU	Stalled and dived into ground 3m S of Upper Heyford, 12.9.41
P1324	44	Undercarriage collapsed in forced landing on return from minelaying, Brackley LG, 2.10.40; to 2261M
P1325	44	Missing from bombing rail targets near La Fère, 12.6.40
P1326	144	Hit by flak, M-Gladbach, and abandoned, 11.5.40
P1327	50	Overstressed in dive on return from minelaying, 1.8.40; to 2214M
P1328	144	Control lost and flew into ground in snow-storm, Willingham, Lincs., 1.2.41
P1329	50	Missing (Hannover) 27.6.40
P1330	50/SF Farnborough/ AAEE/5 AOS/1 AAS	SOC 17.2.44
P1331	44	Undercarriage damaged on take-off for anti-minelaying patrol; crashlanded at Waddington, 24.4.40
P1332	Hendon/16 OTU	Hit ground in snow-storm, Conington, Hunts., 4.2.41
P1333	49	Crashlanded near Breda on return from Merseburg, 17.8.40
P1334	83	Undershot landing at Scampton on return from Gelsenkirchen, 30.8.40
P1335	Hendon/14 OTU/ Cv TB/489	SOC 25.3.44
P1336	106	Hit balloon cable near Coventry and crashed at Caenby, Lincs., 24.5.40
P1337	106/5 Gp TF/455/ 489	Missing from attack on German fleet off Dutch coast, 12.8.42
P1338	44	Missing (Bremerhaven) 12.9.40
P1339	44/1 AAS	SOC 17.1.44
P1340	44	Hit balloon cable and crashed in River Orwell off Harwich on return from Emmerich, 4.6.40
P1341	16 OTU/106	Shot down by flak near Esbjerg on return from Hamburg, 16.1.42
P1342	14 OTU	Stalled on approach and belly-landed at Cottesmore, 9.2.41
P1343	14 OTU	Overshot forced landing in fog and hit trees, Wittering, 22.10.40
P1344	14 OTU/Cv TB/144	Crashed near Petsamo on flight to Russia, 4.9.42
P1345	16 OTU/14 OTU/ Cv TB/5 OTU	SOC 25.5.44
P1346	185/14 OTU/ Cv TB/455	SOC 5.5.44
P1347	49	Hit by flak, Stettin, and eventually crashed in Brittany, 5.9.40
P1348	83	Hit by flak, Hamburg, and crashed near Stade, 6.6.40
P1349	1 AAS	SOC 14.1.44
P1350	RAE/16 OTU	Engine cut; stalled and spun into ground, Fritwell, Oxon., 15.5.41
P1351	RAE/14 OTU	Control lost after take-off from Saltby; crashlanded, 5.5.42
P1352	14 OTU/16 OTU/ Cv TB/5 OTU	Hit rising ground on take-off at night 3½m SW of Long Kesh, 5.3.43
P1353	14 OTU/1401 Flt/521	SOC 23.12.43
P1354	144/83	Ran out of fuel on return from Berlin and ditched off Grimsby, 26.8.40
P1355	83/5 BGS/1401 Flt/521	SOC 22.12.43
P1356	50/16 OTU/ Cv TB/144/489	SOC 26.3.44

200 Armstrong Whitworth Albemarles delivered between October 1940 and March 1943 by A.W.Hawksley, Hucclecote, to Contract No. 816726/38 (replaced by B40671/39)
P1362 - P1401 Mk.I Ser.I; P1402 - P1501 Mk.I Ser.II;
P1502 - PP1659 Mk.I Ser.III

P1360	Mkrs/RAE & AAEE	Prototype. Control lost when part of wing broke away during speed trials; crashlanded, Crewkerne, Somerset, 4.2.41; DBF
P1361	AAEE & Mkrs/AFEE	Second prototype; to 3370M 21.9.42
P1362	AAEE & Mkrs	SOC 30.11.42
P1363	Mkrs & RAE/42 OTU	To 4450M 1.1.44
P1364	Mkrs/TFU/Mkrs/ 297/Hurn	SOC 19.8.47
P1365	AAEE/297/296/297/ 296/22 HGCU	SOC 12.2.45
P1366	AFEE	SOC 19.8.47
P1367	HGCU/297/296/297	SOC 4.5.45
P1368	AAEE	Engine cut; stalled on approach to forced landing and spun into ground, Shalbourne, Berks., 28.2.42; DBF
P1369	RAE, Mkrs & AAEE/ 295	SOC 19.8.47
P1370	295	SOC 4.10.45
P1371	305 FTU/570	SOC 4.10.45
P1372	AAEE/511/42 OTU	SOC 29.11.45
P1373	521/296/42 OTU	SOC 22.3.45
P1374	305 FTU/ 297/295	Failed to maintain height with Horsa in tow and crashlanded 1½m W of Harwell, 6.6.44
P1375	AAEE/296/511/ 42 OTU	SOC 23.4.47
P1376	TDU/296/297	SOC 23.4.47
P1377	295	SOC 9.3.45
P1378	161/511/42 OTU/ 297/42 OTU	SOC 22.3.45
P1379	305 FTU/ 297/295/570/HGCU	SOC 19.8.47
P1380	296/297/296/ 21 HGCU	SOC 19.8.47
P1381	Thruxton/297	Brakes failed while taxying at Welford and undercarriage raised to stop, 24.9.44; DBR
P1382	HGCU/296	Engine cut; ditched near Pantellaria, 24.9.43
P1383	297/296/297/ 22 HGCU	SOC 23.4.47
P1384	297/296/297/42 OTU	NFT
P1385	305 FTU/295	Landed without brakes; swung off runway, hit ditch and undercarriage collapsed, Harwell, 30.3.44
P1386	AFEE	Parachute dummy caught on tail; crashlanded near Ringway, 3.6.42; DBR
P1387	297/296/22 HGCU	SOC 4.1.45
P1388	297/296/22 HGCU	SOC 9.8.45
P1389	296	Hit by Kittyhawk FR851 while parked, Grottaglie, 18.9.43. SOC 10.10.45
P1390	161/295	
P1391	297/296/23 HGCU	SOC 9.2.45
P1392	297/296/ORTU	SOC 19.8.47
P1393	AFEE	Brakes failed on landing, Hartfordbridge, 4.3.43; DBR
P1394	RAE/296/297/ 22 HGCU	SOC 12.2.45
P1395	297/295/297/ 22 HGCU	SOC 24.3.45
P1396	297/296/295	SOC 22.10.44
P1397	295	SOC 9.2.45
P1398	297	Overshot landing into gully, Broadwell, 10.4.44
P1399	297	SOC 26.11.45
P1400	511/42 OTU/297	Missing on SOE flight, 28.7.44
P1401	RAE/296/297/296	Engine cut on air test; crashed near Goubrine, Tunisia, 14.10.43
P1402	AFEE	SOC 26.3.45
P1403	305 FTU/ORTU	SOC 19.8.47
P1404	296/295	Nosewheel collapsed on landing, Netheravon, 8.5.44; DBR
P1405	271/296/297	Spun into ground 2m N of Stoney Cross, 10.10.43; cause not known
P1406	AAEE	Mk.IV prototype; SOC 6.9.45
P1407	271/301 FTU/511	SOC 19.8.47
P1408	1406 Flt	SOC 25.10.44
P1409	1404 Flt/279/ 27 OTU/161/297/ 22 HGCU	SOC 6.1.47
————	SF Netheravon/	
P1430	296/297/296/295	SOC 10.2.46
P1431	CCDU	Engine cut; bellylanded 1½m NE of Tain, 21.10.42
P1432	297/296/22 HGCU	SOC 12.2.45
P1433	511	Missing, presumed ditched 105m W of Tarifa, Spain, 10.8.43
P1434	1406 Flt/CCDU/ 296	Engine lost power and cut out on overshoot; dived into ground, Hurn, 6.12.43; DBF
P1435	Hartfordbridge/ 296	Engine cut; overshot landing, Long Marston, 23.9.44; DBR
P1436	Netheravon/502/ 1404 Flt/295	SOC 27.3.45
P1437	AAEE/296	Hit by flak during paratroop drop and ditched off Catania, Sicily, 13.7.43
P1438	Netheravon/AFEE/ TFU/Netheravon/ Bristols	SOC 30.7.45
P1439	CGS/296	SOC 19.8.47
P1440	HGCU/296	Glider too high on take-off in dust and pulled up tail of tug; crashlanded, Goubrine, 22.7.43
P1441	296/570	SOC 10.4.45
P1442	1404 Flt/Netheravon/ 296/297/42 OTU	Missing (Normandy) 6.6.44
P1443	HGCU/296	Engine cut; DBR in heavy landing, Froha, Algeria, 17.6.43
P1444	HGCU/296	Missing after towing Hadrian to Sicily, 14.7.43
P1445	HGCU/295	SOC 29.11.45
P1446	296	Missing after dropping SAS over Northern Sicily, 12.7.43
P1447	27 MU	Engine failed; lost height and bellylanded, Ellerdine Grange, near High Ercall, 11.1.43
P1448	305 FTU/ORTU	SOC 27.1.45
P1449	301 FTU/511	SOC 19.8.47
P1450	-	SOC 17.8.44
P1451	1 FTU/511	Crashed in sea after night take-off, Gibraltar, 21.11.42
P1452	PTS	To 4804M 12.5.44
P1453	1 FTU/301 FTU/511	SOC 19.8.47
P1454	BOAC	SOC 17.8.44
P1455	2 OAPU/305 FTU	Lost en route to USSR 10.3.43
P1456	-	SOC 7.1.45
P1457	-	SOC 23.4.47
P1458	511/42 OTU	SOC 29.11.45
P1459	BDU/13 OTU	Hit by Blenheim Z7361 while parked, Bicester, 21.12.42; DBR
P1460	BDU/13 OTU/297/ 22 HGCU	SOC 21.6.47

P1461	BDU/27 OTU/297/ 296/295	SOC 29.11.45
P1462	296/297	Flew into high ground descending for para drop near Alton, Hants., 21.12.43
P1463	AFEE/296/ 42 OTU	Hit HT wires on take-off; crashlanded, Ashbourne, 30.3.44; presumed flaps raised too soon; DBF
P1464	297/296/ORTU	SOC 22.3.45
P1465	297	SOC 19.8.47
P1466	297/296	Sank back on take-off and hit ground while towing Horsa to Sicily, Goubrine 2, 13.7.43
P1467	296/42 OTU	SOC 23.4.47
P1468	296	Tyre burst on take-off; DBR on landing, Telergma, 5.8.43
P1469	296	SOC 19.8.47
P1470	296/42 OTU/22 HGCU	SOC 19.8.47
P1471	296/297/296/297	SOC 7.11.45
P1472	511/42 OTU	Tyre burst on landing and engine torn out, Ashbourne, 11.6.44
P1473	301 FTU	SOC 1.9.44
P1474	296	Tyre burst on landing and undercarriage collapsed, Goubrine 2, 31.7.43
P1475	511	SOC 19.8.47
P1476	305 FTU/ORTU	SOC 19.8.47
P1477	305 FTU	To Russia 10.3.43
P1478	297	Missing on ferry flight; believed shot down by enemy aircraft, 23.8.43
P1479	Mkrs	SOC 28.8.44
P1500	511	SOC 19.8.47
P1501	296	Missing from supply drop 10m S of Périgueux, 9.8.44
P1502	42 OTU	SOC 20.2.45
P1503	305 FTU	Built as Mk.II. Flew into hill, Fearnen, near Kenmore, Perthshire, 29.5.43; DBF; cause not known
P1504	305 FTU	SOC 25.10.45
P1505	-	SOC 29.11.45
P1506	AAEE/ORTU	SOC 16.3.45
P1507	305 FTU	SOC 19.8.47
P1508	305 FTU/9 FP	Overshot landing and undercarriage raised to stop, Cambridge, 23.12.43; not repaired and SOC 9.8.44
P1509	-	SOC 19.8.47
P1510	511/296/22 HGCU	SOC 12.2.45
P1511	297	SOC 29.11.45
P1512	296/ORTU	SOC 19.8.47
P1513	AFEE/42 OTU	SOC 23.10.44
P1514	511/42 OTU	SOC 23.4.47
P1515	296	SOC 3.8.44
P1516	296	Missing on transport flight between Gioia and Goubrine, 1.10.43
P1517	296	SOC 19.8.47
P1518	296/42 OTU	SOC 25.11.44
P1519	42 OTU	Overshot landing, swung and undercarriage collapsed, Ashbourne, 7.8.44; DBR
P1520	511	SOC 5.12.45
P1521	296	Missing after towing Hadrian to Sicily, 13.7.43
P1522	HGCU/296	Collided with P1552 on overshoot, Goubrine, 8.7.43; DBF
P1523	AAEE/Mkrs/RAE	SOC 5.10.44
P1524	296/511/42 OTU	SOC 23.4.47
P1525	296	SOC 14.10.44
P1526	AFEE/296	Ran into hole while taxying, Goubrine 2, 4.9.43; DBR

P1527	296	Tyre burst on landing; swung and undercarriage collapsed, Froha, 11.6.43
P1528	296	Failed to climb on take-off; forcelanded, hit ditch and undercarriage collapsed 3m N of Tafaraoui, 18.9.43
P1529	HGCU	SOC 19.8.47
P1550	296/297/296	SOC 5.12.45
P1551	296/297/42 OTU	SOC 22.3.45
P1552	296	Damaged beyond repair when hit by P1522 while parked, Goubrine 2, 8.7.43
P1553	HGCU/296	Missing on transport flight between Goubrine and Gioia, 7.10.43; presumed ditched
P1554	42 OTU	Hit house on night approach, Ashbourne, 18.12.44
P1555	-	SOC 24.8.44
P1556	511	Engine cut; ditched 6m E of Gibraltar, 30.4.43
P1557	296/570	SOC .45
P1558	ATA	SOC 27.2.45
P1559	ORTU	SOC 19.8.47
P1560	42 OTU	SOC 1.1.45
P1561	511	SOC .45
P1562	305 FTU	To Russia 25.4.43
P1563	42 OTU/9 FP	Hit hedge on take-off and crashlanded, Ashbourne, 15.6.44; DBF
P1564	511/ATA	SOC 27.10.44
P1565	511	Undercarriage retracted after landing, Blida, 21.4.43; DBR
P1566	42 OTU	SOC 23.10.44
P1567	305 FTU	To Russia 3.3.43
P1568	305 FTU/3 OADU/ATA	SOC 5.10.45
P1569	305 FTU	SOC 1.9.44
P1590	305 FTU	To Russia 15.3.43
P1591	305 FTU/3 OADU/ ATA	Nosewheel collapsed in heavy landing, White Waltham, 8.8.44; DBR
P1592	42 OTU	Undercarriage collapsed after landing, Ashbourne, 26.4.44
P1593	ORTU	Spun into ground in bad weather near Peterhead, Aberdeenshire, 10.7.44; DBF
P1594	305 FTU/3 OADU/ATA	SOC 6.4.45
P1595	305 FTU	To Russia 25.4.43
P1596	42 OTU	SOC 23.10.44
P1597	ORTU	SOC 19.8.47
P1598	305 FTU/3 OADU/ 42 OTU	SOC 3.1.45
P1599	-	SOC 25.10.44
P1600	38 MU	Undercarriage collapsed after landing, Llandow, 9.8.44; DBR
P1601	-	SOC 3.12.44
P1602	-	SOC 22.8.44
P1603	-	SOC 16.8.44
P1604	ORTU	SOC 19.8.47
P1605	ORTU	Both engines cut on approach; crashlanded, Cottesmore, 28.7.44
P1606	42 OTU	Engine cut on approach; lost height and undershot; undercarriage collapsed, Hethel, 21.11.44
P1607	42 OTU	SOC 20.2.45
P1608	ORTU	SOC 19.8.47
P1609	-	SOC 24.8.44
P1630	-	SOC 1.9.44
P1631	ORTU	SOC 19.8.47
P1632	ORTU	SOC 19.8.47
P1633	ORTU	SOC 19.8.47
P1634	AAEE	SOC 29.11.45
P1635	42 OTU/ORTU	SOC 19.8.47

P1636	305 FTU	To Russia 31.3,43
P1637	305 FTU	To Russia 31.3.43
P1638	305 FTU	To Russia 25.4.43
P1639	305 FTU/2 APS/ORTU	SOC 19.8.47
P1640	305 FTU	To Russia 4.4.43
P1641	305 FTU/3 OADU/ ORTU	SOC 7.12.45
P1642	305 FTU	To Russia 12.4.43
P1643	ORTU	Undercarriage leg broke off on landing; swung off runway, Harwell, 6.9.44; DBR
P1644	305 FTU/3 OADU/ ATA	Undercarriage leg collapsed on landing, White Waltham, 15.8.44; DBR
P1645	305 FTU	To Russia 27.4.43 and lost in transit
P1646	DH Props	Reversing prop research; SOC 9.7.46
P1647	305 FTU	To Russia 12.4.43
P1648	ORTU	SOC 19.8.47
P1649	-	SOC 19.8.47
P1650	305 FTU/3 OADU/ATA	SOC 31.5.45
P1651	42 OTU/297/ 22 HGCU	Undercarriage leg collapsed on landing and engine torn out, Fairford, 8.1.45
P1652	ORTU	SOC 19.8.47
P1653	42 OTU/570/ATA	SOC 29.11.45
P1654	305 FTU/3 OADU/ATA	SOC 5.6.45
P1655	ORTU	SOC 19.8.47
P1656	42 OTU/295	SOC 14.2.46
P1657	ATA	SOC 5.6.45
P1658	305 FTU/3 OADU/ATA	SOC 7.11.45
P1659	42 OTU	Brakes failed; ran down slope and undercarriage raised to stop, Ashbourne, 12.9.44

*   *   *   *   *   *   *   *   *   *

70 Westland Lysander Is and IIs delivered between September and December 1939 by Westlands, Yeovil to Contract No. 611814/37
Mk.Is to P1699; remainder Mk.IIs

P1665	1 SAC/41 OTU/ 58 OTU	Hit by Spitfire P7748 while parked, Balado Bridge, 31.5.43; DBR
P1666	Cv to Mk.III/ 1481 Flt/27 OTU	SOC 23.7.43
P1667	204 Gp CF/CF Lydda/ Levant CF	Crashed in forced landing near Lydda, 25.5.43
P1668	10 OTU/Cv to Mk.III/12 OTU	Crashed in forced landing, Chipping Warden, 9.3.43
P1669	16/28/20	Engine cut; undershot forced landing on to rough ground, Maungdaw, 24.2.43; DBR
P1670	613/28	Overshot landing at Fatehgarh, 14.4.42
P1671	613/1 SAC/7 AACU/ Netheravon/7 AACU/ 1492 Flt/3 RAFRS/ 2 AAPC	SOC 12.1.44
P1672	2	Bombs exploded on landing, Bekesbourne, 22.5.40
P1673	16/231	DBR in gale, Newtownards, 21.11.40
P1674	16/239/India	
P1675	16/239/613/20/ 1 IAF/4 IAF	Crashed in forced landing 70 m NE of Hyderabad, 24.3.43
P1676	451	Crashed at Giarabub, Libya, 5.10.41; NFD
P1677	614/India	SOC 31.7.44
P1678	16/28/20	SOC 31.7.44
P1679	WDCF	Crashed in forced landing in sand-storm near Mersa Matruh, 19.11.42

P1680	5 OTU/Talbenny/Cv to TT.III/8th AAF	SOC 4.1.44
P1681	Cv to TT.III/53 OTU/ SF Farnborough/ 53 OTU	SOC 20.7.43
P1682	Cv to TT.III/1483 Flt/4 AAPC/1628 Flt/1631 Flt	SOC 25.10.43
P1683	Cv to TT.III/RAE/ 1 AGS	Crashed in forced landing, Braunton Burrows, Devon, 4.1.42
P1684	16/277/116	To 3929M 7.43
P1685	16	Damaged by Hurricane during supply drop on Calais and crashlanded, Hawkinge, 27.5.40
P1686	2/28	Bombs fell off on take-off and destroyed aircraft at LG near Mingaladon, 17.2.42
P1687	16	Crashed in forced landing, Banwell, Somerset, 18.9.40; to 2234M
P1688	2/6 AACU/11 Gp CF/ 287/1489 Flt/ 60 OTU/3 APC	SOC 25.8.43
P1689	26	Shot down off Dunkerque, 29.5.40
P1690	614/7 AACU/India	Lost 15.7.42; NFD
P1691	13/1 SAC/41 OTU/ 8 AACU	Blown over in gale, Weston Zoyland, 4.6.43
P1692	613	Hit truck on approach and crashed, Netherthorpe, 6.9.40
P1693	613/1487 Flt	
P1694	110 RCAF/613/ 1 IAF	Crashed on landing, Manzai, 13.11.41
P1695	110 RCAF/26/ 6 AACU/12 Gp AAC Flt/288/Cv to TT.III/ 1487 Flt/60 OTU/ 3 APC	To 3951M 7.43
P1696	110 RCAF/613/India	Lost 15.7.42; NFD
P1697	110 RCAF/26/1 SAC/ 1441 Flt/1483 Flt/ 8 AACU	SOC 15.9.43
P1698	110 RCAF/26/1 SAC/ 41 OTU/53 OTU	SOC 11.8.43
P1699	4/241/6 AACU	DBR 6.5.41; NFD
P1711	4	Crashed on ferry flight en route to Aspelaere ALG, 14.5.40
P1712	4/241/28/20	SOC 31.7.44
P1713	13/8 AACU/FE	To FFAF
P1714	2/26/6 AACU/ 12 Gp AAC Flt	Crashed on overshoot, Digby, 21.11.41
P1715	9 AGS/9 OAFU/2 AGS	SOC 23.10.43
P1716	Cv to TT.III/ 1487 Flt	SOC 25.8.43
P1717	ME	SOC 1.12.43
P1718	Cv to TT.III/ 1483 Flt/21 OTU	SOC 23.10.42
P1719	Cv to TT.III/ 7 AGS	Flew into ground at Kenfig Hill, Glam., 12.2.42
P1720	16	Missing from tactical recon- naissance off Gravelines, 28.5.40
P1721	2	Presumed lost in France
P1722	2	Presumed lost in France
P1723	2/BP/20	Temp. fitted with mock-up of BPA Mk.III turret then to India; NFT
P1724	613	Engine cut; crashlanded, Scothern, Lincs., 16.9.40
P1725	13/7 AACU/13 Gp AAC Flt/1441 Flt/ 2 AAPC	SOC 12.1.44
P1726	26/1 SAC/41 OTU/ CF White Waltham	SOC 18.5.43

Lysander II

P1727	2/28/20	SOC 31.7.44
P1728	Mkrs/AAEE as TT.III	To RCAF 14.12.41 as No.1578
P1729	112 RCAF/1 SAC/ 41 OTU/53 OTU	To 3973M 7.43
P1730	416 Flt/110 RCAF/ 7 AACU/289/1489 Flt/16 APC	SOC 12.1.44
P1731	416 Flt/110 RCAF/ 614/6 AACU/6 Gp TTF/6 AACU	Hit balloon cable and crashed in Belfast Lough near Sydenham, 30.4.42
P1732	416 Flt/110 RCAF/ 613/20	Crashed on landing, Chakulia, 3.5.42
P1733	4/8 AACU/12 Gp AAC Flt/288/51 OTU/2/1495 Flt/ 2 AAPC	SOC 12.1.44
P1734	4/241/20	Destroyed in air raid, Dinjan, Assam, 25.10.42
P1735	-	To FFAF Chad 24.8.40
P1736	-	To FFAF Chad 24.8.40
P1737	267	Crashed in forced landing 2m N of Helwan, 5.3.42
P1738	-	To FFAF Chad 24.8.40
P1739	55/113	SOC 1.11.43
P1740	6	Shot down by Bf 109 near Halfaya Pass, Western Desert, 26.5.41
P1741	Cv to TT.III/1488 Flt	SOC 25.10.43
P1742	2/268/India	SOC 9.8.42
P1743	110 RCAF/Cv to TT. III/1483 Flt/4 AAPC/ 1628 Flt/1631 Flt	SOC 15.1.44
P1744	Cv to TT.III/8 AGS	SOC 13.7.43
P1745	CFS/26	Overshot landing at W.Malling, 27.6.40

* * * * * * * * *

Six Percival Vega Gull IIIs delivered in November 1938 by Percival Aircraft, Luton, to Contract No. 812425/38

P1749	24	Destroyed in air raid, Hendon, 8.10.40
P1750	24	Engine cut on take-off; hit pile of bricks, Hendon, 12.7.40
P1751	24	DBR by enemy aircraft, Coulommiers, 16.5.40
P1752	24	Swung and undercarriage collapsed in forced landing in bad weather, Wentworth Golf Course, Surrey, 13.1.40
P1753	24	Hit pile of earth while landing in mist, Hendon, 13.10.39; DBR
P1754	24/9 Gp CF	SOC 20.11.44

* * * * * * * * *

Two G.A.L. 38s to Specification S.23/37 built by General Aircraft, Hanworth, to Contract No. 790401/38

P1758	Mkrs	Not delivered
P1761	-	Not completed

* * * * * * * * *

Two D.H.89A Dragon Rapides delivered in November 1938 by de Havilland, Hatfield, to Contract No. 808642/38

P1764	24	DBR by enemy aircraft, Coulommiers 16.5.40
P1765	24	SOC 4.4.40

* * * * * * * * *

Two Fairey Barracuda prototypes to Spec. S.24/37 built by Fairey, Hayes, to Contract No. 777067/38

P1767	Mkrs	Retained by Faireys
P1770	Mkrs & RAE	DBR during pilotless catapult launch, Farnborough, 4.9.41

* * * * * * * * *

12 Folland 43/37 test-bed aircraft delivered to DTD in 1940 by Folland Aircraft, Hamble, under Contract No. 953635/38

P1774	Napier/Bristols	Sabre III, Centaurus I; Crashed 14.9.44
P1775	Bristols	Hercules VIII, Centaurus IV; Crashed 18.9.44
P1776	Napier/Bristols	Sabre I, Centaurus I; Crashed 28.8.44
P1777	Napier/Bristols	Sabre I, Centaurus I
P1778	Napier/Bristols/ R-R	Sabre I, Centaurus I; Griffon. SOC 27.3.45
P1779	Bristols/Napier	Hercules XI, Sabre I; Crashed 14.9.44
P1780	Bristols/Napier	Hercules XI, Sabre I,V,VIII
P1781	Bristols/ Centaurus Flt	Centaurus IV. Crashed on take-off, Heston, 28.4.44
P1782	Bristols	Hercules XI
P1783	Bristols	Hercules XI
P1784	Bristols	Hercules XI; SOC 5.3.45
P1785	Bristols	Hercules XI

* * * * * * * * *

200 Airspeed Oxford Is and IIs delivered between September 1939 and April 1940 by Airspeed, Portsmouth, to Contract No. 777546/38
Mk.II to P1860; Mk.I P1861 onwards

P1800	2 FTS	Stalled and flew into ground descending out of cloud, Burford, Oxon., 11.12.39
P1801	2 FTS	All three destroyed
P1802	2 FTS	in air raid,
P1803	2 FTS	Brize Norton, 16.8.40
P1804	2 FTS/15 FTS/RAFC/ 15 PAFU/3 PAFU/ 38 Gp CF	SOC 30.9.44
P1805	-	Delivered direct to RCAF
P1806	2 FTS	Flew into ground on approach to night landing, Southrop, 2.2.41
P1807	5 FTS	Stalled and dived into ground in bad visibility, Tetbury, Glos., 29.11.39
P1808	3 FTS/6 FTS/ 6 PAFU/3 FIS/ATA	SOC 29.8.46
P1809	5 FTS/11 FTS/ 15 FTS/15 PAFU/ 18 PAFU	SOC 15.12.44
P1810	3 FTS	Crashed in night landing, South Cerney, 12.10.41; DBF
P1811	5 FTS/11 FTS/ 2 FIS/2 AGS/ 51 OTU/Holme	SOC 13.6.44
P1812	-	Delivered direct to RCAF
P1813	3 FTS	Engine cut after take-off; hit wall and crashlanded 1½m SE of South Cerney, 3.8.41
P1814	3 FTS/RAFC/2 CFS/ 2 AGS/7 AACU/577/ 288	SS 23.6.49
P1815	3 FTS	Engine cut; undershot forced landing at night and hit tree 1m E of South Cerney, 20.10.39
P1816	3 FTS/2 FIS/ RAFC/2 CFS	Lost power on approach to forced landing while lost at night; bellylanded 1m SSE of Waddington, 5.2.41

12

Serial	Units	Fate
P1817	3 FTS	Crashed on night training flight ½m N of Cirencester, Glos., 3.3.40; cause not known
P1818	3 FTS/1 OTU/ 11 PAFU/ATA	SOC 8.1.46
P1819	-	Delivered direct to RCAF; no record of receipt
P1820	3 FTS/CFS/3 FIS/ 1691 Flt/Middleton St. George/6 Gp CF	SOC 12.4.46
P1821	3 FTS	Collided with P1955 and crashed near South Cerney, 3.8.40
P1822	RAFC/1691 Flt	SOC 23.6.44
P1823	3 FTS	Hit trees on night approach, South Cerney, 8.3.40
P1824	8 FTS/5 FTS/ 14 FTS/12 FTS/ 16 OTU/3 FIS	SOC 11.5.44
P1825	8 FTS/14 FTS/ 14 PAFU	To Admiralty 6.1.44
P1826	-	Delivered direct to RCAF; no record of arrival
P1827	RAFC	Overshot landing and hit hut, Cranwell, 12.1.40; DBR
P1828	RAFC	Undershot night landing and hit tree, Barkston LG, 23.3.41
P1829	14 FTS/16 PFTS/ 2 FIS/2 Gp CF	SOC 12.5.44
P1830	14 FTS	Hit hedge in forced landing, Holtsmere End, near Hemel Hempstead, Herts., 18.11.40
P1831	14 FTS	Crashed 17.2.41; NFD
P1832	14 FTS/3 FTS	Swung on approach to flare path and hit wall; stalled and crashed, Bibury, 6.3.41
P1833	-	Diverted to RCAF
P1834	14 FTS	Collided with P8827 and crashed near Cranfield, 20.8.40
P1835	14 FTS/14 PAFU	To 4115M 9.43
P1836	RAFC/2 FTS/12 PAFU/11 PAFU/ 30 OTU/Glosters	SOC 2.5.46
P1837	RAFC/15 FTS/2 FTS	Destroyed in air raid, Brize Norton, 16.8.40
P1838	RAFC/6 FTS/6 PAFU	Hit ground avoiding another aircraft after take-off, Chipping Norton, 7.7.42
P1839	RAFC	Crashed 13.12.40; NFD
P1840	-	Delivered direct to RCAF; no record of arrival
P1841	15 FTS/2 FTS	Destroyed in air raid, Brize Norton,16.8.40
P1842	15 FTS/2 FTS	Crashed in forced landing, Stoney Stanton, near Hinckley, Leics., 26.12.41
P1843	15 FTS/2 FTS	Destroyed in air raid, Brize Norton, 16.8.40
P1844	15 FTS/15 PAFU/ ATA	SOC 4.8.44
P1845	11 FTS	Flew into The Wrekin in bad visibility, Salop., 7.11.39
P1846	-	Delivered direct to RCAF
P1847	11 FTS/2 FIS/ 2 CFS	Control lost on overshoot; stalled and hit ground, Dalcross, 18.11.41
P1848	11 FTS	Landed on top of P1929, 11.10.40; DBR
P1849	11 FTS	Hit tree while overshooting forced landing in bad visibility, Chaddesley Corbett, near Kidderminster, Worcs., 25.4.40; DBR
P1860	11 FTS/1 FIS/6 PAFU	SOC 21.6.44

Serial	Units	Fate
P1861	RAFC/1447 Flt/ 2 FIS/20 PAFU/ 21 PAFU	SOC 28.11.46
P1862	11 FTS/11 PAFU	Dived into ground on attempted overshoot at night, Wheaten Aston, 23.5.42; DBF
P1863	-	Delivered direct to RCAF
P1864	Mkrs RAE & AAEE/ 14 PAFU	Mk.III prototype, later cv to Mk.V. SOC 28.10.44
P1865	RAFC/2 FTS/6 PAFU	To 3612M 18.1.43
P1866	RAFC	Hit ridge on take-off and stalled, West Freugh, 22.1.40
P1867	RAFC/16 PFTS	Hit house in attempted forced landing in bad weather, Wold Road, Hull, Yorks., 6.12.42
P1868	RAFC/6 FTS/ 14 PAFU/12 PAFU	Crashlanded on decoy airfield while lost near Hemswell, 12.10.42
P1869	15 FTS	Dived into ground after take-off, Windrush, 6.8.40
P1870	-	Delivered direct to RCAF
P1871	15 FTS	Failed to reach flying speed on take-off; stalled while clearing wall, Dyce, 8.2.40
P1872	15 FTS/2 FTS/ 21 PAFU	SS 3.9.47
P1873	15 FTS/RAFC/6 FTS/ 6 AACU/20 PAFU/ 11 PAFU	SOC 30.1.45
P1874	15 FTS	Lost height after night take-off and hit trees, Windrush, 30.7.40
P1875	RAFC/5 OTU/ 14 PAFU	SOC 30.6.50
P1876	RAFC/11 FTS/ Dalcross/1447 Flt	To 4347M 18.11.43
P1877	-	Delivered direct to RCAF
P1878	2 FTS/11 FTS/ 6 AACU/577/288/ 289/4 Del Flt	Engine cut; lost height and bellylanded, Edzell, 17.7.45
P1879	2 FTS	SOC 27.4.42
P1880	2 FTS/11 FTS/ 11 PAFU/14 PAFU	SOC 11.8.44
P1881	RAFC	Lost elevator on take-off; stalled and dived into ground, Cranwell, 16.5.41; DBF
P1882	RAFC/1447 Flt/10 RS	To 4346M 18.11.43
P1883	2 FTS	Destroyed in air raid, Brize Norton, 16.8.40
P1884	-	Direct to RCAF
P1885	2 FTS	Destroyed in air raid, Brize Norton, 16.8.40
P1886	8 FTS	Destroyed in air raid, Montrose, 25.10.40
P1887	8 FTS/11 FTS/ 11 PAFU/2 FIS	SOC 18.9.44
P1888	8 FTS/14 FTS/ 15 FTS	Sideslipped into ground in forced landing while lost 5m S of Hereford, 22.6.41
P1889	8 FTS/RAFC/ 11 PAFU	Collided with V4222 in cloud, Gailey Cross Roads, Staffs., 21.7.43
P1890	15 FTS	Collided with N6326 near Charlbury, Oxon., 9.7.40
P1891	5 FTS/2 FTS/ 15 FTS/15 PAFU	Engine cut; lost height and hit tree in forced landing ½m W of South Collington, Worcs., 24.3.42; DBF
P1892	3 FTS/3 PAFU/ 691/17	SS 20.2.56
P1893	15 FTS/2 FTS	Collided with Oxford on approach, Brize Norton, 31.3.41
P1894	15 FTS/RAFC/ 11 FTS/2 CFS/ 2 AGS/ATA/15 PAFU	To R.Neth AF 14.8.46

Serial	Units	Fate
P1895	15 FTS/RAFC/3 GTS/ BOAC/605/63 Gp CF	SOC 21.10.49
P1896	15 FTS	Hit hedge on take-off after forced landing, Cross in Hand, Lutterworth, Leics., 11.6.40
P1897	5 FTS/3 FTS/5 OTU/ 2 OTU/1 OTU	SS 18.8.50
P1898	5 FTS/3 FTS/ 3 PAFU/20 PAFU	SOC 4.1.45
P1899	15 FTS/RAFC/ 11 PAFU/6 PAFU	SOC 15.11.44
P1920	Mkrs & RAE/6 FTS	Crashed in attempted forced landing while lost in bad weather near Rochdale, Lancs., 9.2.42
P1921	5 FTS/3 FTS	Stalled on take-off due to frost on wings, South Cerney, 8.11.40; DBR
P1922	15 FTS/2 FTS	Abandoned when control lost in cloud near Brize Norton, 15.2.41
P1923	14 FTS/2 FTS/ 6 AACU/577/ 21 PAFU/12 PAFU	SOC 29.6.45
P1924	3 FTS/6 AACU/ 18 PAFU	SOC 22.9.44
P1925	3 FTS/2 FTS/ 3 PAFU/21 PAFU	SOC 18.2.46
P1926	14 FTS/CCDU/ 20 PAFU	Engine cut on overshoot; crashlanded 1m N of Weston-on-the-Green, 6.3.45
P1927	14 FTS	Crashed 11.7.41; DBF
P1928	11 FTS/11 PAFU	Stalled on night overshoot and dived into ground, Yeaton Peverey, 2m NE of Montford Bridge, Salop., 19.7.42
P1929	11 FTS/11 PAFU/ 21 PAFU	SOC 17.5.46
P1930	2 FTS	Dived into ground on night navex in blizzard, Boughton Heath, Moreton-in-Marsh, Glos. 7.12.41
P1931	2 FTS	Destroyed in air raid, Brize Norton, 16.8.40
P1932	2 FTS/3 FTS/ 15 PAFU/14 PAFU/ 21 PAFU	SOC 30.3.45
P1933	11 FTS	Lost height after night take-off and hit tree, Shawbury, 8.4.40
P1934	11 FTS	Sold to Airspeed 2.7.47
P1935	8 FTS/2 FTS/3 FTS/ 20 PAFU/15 PAFU	SOC 18.10.45
P1936	8 FTS/11 FTS	To 3734M 14.5.43
P1937	8 FTS/3 FTS/ 15 FTS/RAFC	Hit trees on approach, Barkston LG, 6.9.41; DBF
P1938	8 FTS/11 FTS	Abandoned in spin near Shawbury, 30.7.41
P1939	4 FTS	Damaged at Habbaniya and SOC 6.7.41
P1940	4 FTS/Iraq CF	SOC 29.3.45
P1941	2 FPP	Overshot landing in fog and hit tree, Sealand, 10.1.40; DBR
P1942	4 FTS/Iraq CF/ 4 FTS	Flew into ground in sand-storm 10m W of Jebel Saman, Iraq, 13.6.41
P1943	4 FTS/70 OTU	Brake jammed while taxying; swung and hit Blenheim BA260, Nakuru, 29.7.42
P1944	-	To RNZAF direct as NZ255
P1945	4 FTS	SOC 21.6.41
P1946	4 FTS/70 OTU	Failed to climb on take-off and hit trees, Gil Gil, 4.8.42
P1947	4 FTS/70 OTU	Hit cables on overshoot and crashlanded, Eastleigh, Nairobi, 3.7.42; DBR
P1948	4 FTS/70 OTU	SOC 6.45
P1949	4 FTS/70 OTU	SOC 1.11.43
P1950	4 FTS	SOC 28.9.44
P1951	8 FTS/3 FTS/ 2 FIS/3 PAFU/ECFS/ 15 PAFU/21 PAFU	SOC 29.11.45
P1952	3 FTS	Crashed after collision near South Cerney, 1.6.41
P1953	-	To RNZAF as NZ257
P1954	8 FTS/14 FTS	DBR 5.8.41; NFD
P1955	3 FTS	Collided with P1821 and crashlanded, 3.8.40
P1956	5 FTS/3 FTS/ 11 FTS	Hit by P1934 while parked, Shawbury, 27.6.41
P1957	5 FTS/3 FTS/3 FIS	To R.Hellenic AF 1.4.47
P1958	5 FTS/14 FTS	Hit by N6375 while parked, Cranfield, 28.5.41; DBR
P1959	5 FTS/RAFC/2 FTS/ 2 PAFU/18 PAFU/ 38 Gp CF/1555 Flt	SOC 19.3.47
P1960	8 FTS/5 FTS/ 14 FTS	Engine cut; hit hedge in forced landing, Rearsby, 27.11.40
P1961	8 FTS	Hit house on take-off due to ice on wings, Montrose, 1.3.40; DBR
P1962	8 FTS/14 FTS/2 FTS/ 3 FTS/ECFS/16 PFTS	SOC 6.10.44
P1963	-	Direct to RNZAF as NZ253
P1964	11 FTS/2 FTS	Spun into ground near Tew, Oxon., 12.5.40; cause not known
P1965	11 FTS/2 FTS	Destroyed in air raid, Brize Norton, 16.8.40
P1966	11 FTS/2 FTS/ 14 PAFU	To Belgian AF 12.6,47
P1967	14 FTS	Crashed at Barton-in-the-Clay, Beds., 8.10.41; cause not known
P1968	14 FTS/14 PAFU/ 19 PAFU/1 PAFU/ 21 PAFU	SOC 29.11.45
P1969	RAFC/16 PFTS/12 PAFU/3 FIS/20 PAFU	SOC 16.1.45
P1980	RAFC	Undershot night approach and hit huts, Cranwell, 29.5.40
P1981	RAFC/Gosport/ 42 OTU	SOC 20.12.44
P1982	RAFC/15 FTS/8 AACU	SOC 30.7.46
P1983	-	Direct to RNZAF as NZ258
P1984	-	To Iran AF as No 801
P1985	3 FTS/3 GTS/BOAC	SOC 4.12.43
P1986	14 PTS/2 FIS/3 PAFU/ 19 PAFU/21 PAFU	SOC 8.8.44
P1987	3 FTS/42 OTU/ 20 PAFU	Collided with HN853 and lost tail near Kidlington, 14.3.44
P1988	3 FTS/3 PAFU	Failed to take-off and under-carriage raised to stop, South Cerney, 19.3.42
P1989 to P1992	-	Direct to RNZAF as NZ261 to NZ264
P1993	-	Direct to Iranian AF as 802; impressed into RAF; NFT
P1994	RAFC/6 FTS/6 PAFU	To 3616M
P1995	RAFC/CFS/7 FIS	Flew into high ground at night near Imber, Wilts., 13.3.43
P1996 to P2001	-	Direct to RNZAF as NZ265 to NZ270
P2002	-	Direct to Iran AF as No 803
P2003	-	Direct to RNZAF as NZ259
P2004 to P2009	-	Direct to RNZAF as NZ271-276
P2030 to P2044	-	Direct to RNZAF as NZ277-280, 260, 281-290 respectively
P2045 to P2059	-	Direct to RNZAF as NZ1201 to 1215

75 Handley Page Hampden Is delivered between February and July 1940 by English Electric, Preston, to Contract No. 952962/38

P2062	AAEE/14 OTU	Control lost on approach, Woolfox Lodge, 31.3.41
P2063	49/144	Missing from intruder over Norway, 23.11.42
P2064	7/14 OTU/408/ Cv TB/415	SOC 11.4.44
P2065	16 OTU/455/ Cv TB/415	Caught fire refuelling, Thorney Island, 26.2.43
P2066	16 OTU	Stalled in forced landing SW of Wroxton Heath, Banbury, Oxon., 27.3.41
P2067	16 OTU/14 OTU 32 OTU	To Canada 9.43 SOC 30.4.44
P2068	49	Engine cut after take-off from Scampton for training flight; crashlanded, Welton Cliff Farm, 19.6.41
P2069	16 OTU/4 FPP	Engine cut on ferry flight; crashed on approach, Upper Heyford, 7.8.40
P2070	50	Ran out of fuel on return from Berlin and crashlanded, Lautersheim, 26.8.40
P2071	106	Abandoned on air test 3m NNW of Market Drayton, Salop., 23.12.40
P2072	14 OTU	Hit hill in bad visibility near Richmond, Yorks., 5.10.40
P2073	106/408/Cv TB/ 5 OTU	To 4348M 20.11.43
P2074	14 OTU/Cv TB/ 144/5 OTU	SOC 20.12.43
P2075	14 OTU/455/Cv TB/ 5 OTU/1 TTU	SOC 16.12.43
P2076	14 OTU	Undershot single-engined landing, Cottesmore, 15.12.41;
P2077	44	Damaged by flak, Bernburg, and crashlanded near Ouisthuizen, Neth., 14.8.40
P2078	16 OTU/Cv TB/455	Missing from sweep off Norway, 11.12.42
P2079	144	Abandoned out of fuel on return from Munich 5m from Hemswell, 9.11.40
P2080	144/16 OTU/Cv TB/ 144/489/455	SOC 20.2.44
P2081	144/25 OTU/ 16 OTU	Hit trees on approach, Chipping Warden, 14.2.42
P2082	61	Crashed in Kiel Canal while minelaying in Kiel Bay, 6.11.40
P2083	106/5 Gp TF/106	Crashed in forced landing, Wellesbourne Mountford, on return from minelaying off Brest, 27.5.41
P2084	CGS/Cv TB/144/ 489	Missing from shipping sweep off Skagerrak, 20.5.43
P2085	16 OTU/455	Swung on landing and undercarriage collapsed, Wigsley, 11.3.42, on return from Essen
P2086	16 OTU/4 FPP	Engine cut on approach; crashlanded, Honeybourne, 7.8.40
P2087	44	Shot down by flak near Krefeld, 7.9.40
P2088	61/14 OTU	Stalled on approach, Cottesmore, 17.6.41
P2089	61	Ran out of fuel on return from Bordeaux and crashlanded near Lyme Regis, Dorset, 20.8.40
P2090	61	Damaged by flak, Kiel, and crashlanded, Oresund, Sweden, 27.9.40
P2091	16 OTU/415/489/ 5 OTU	Dived into sea off Rillane Castle, Ayrshire, 22.12.42
P2092	14 OTU	Shot down by enemy aircraft, Little Bytham, Lincs., 8.4.41
P2093	50/1 AAS	SOC 17.2.44
P2094	144/50/420	Hit by Lancaster L7581 while parked, Waddington, 20.5.42
P2095	49/25 OTU/455/ Cv TB/455	To Russian Navy, 12.10.42
P2096	83	Crashed on approach from training flight 1m E of Scampton, 27.9.40
P2097	83	Crashed on return from Lorient, Appleford Bridge, near Abingdon, 28.12.40
P2098	106	Missing (minelaying off Brest) 28.12.40
P2099	106	Crashed in forced landing, Uffingham, Rutland, 17.5.41
P2100	16 OTU/455/ 5 OTU	Flew into hill 2m SW of Maybole, Ayrshire, 19.7.42
P2110	16 OTU	Swung on take-off, Upper Heyford, 7.8.40; DBF
P2111	49/25 OTU	Missing on navex; presumed ditched in Bristol Channel, 12.6.41
P2112	49/14 OTU	Stalled on approach, Saltby, 8.12.41
P2113	16 OTU/25 OTU/ Cv TB/16 FPP	Crashlanded, Tod Brow, 1m W of West Newton, Cumberland, 20.10.43
P2114	16 OTU	Flew into ground due to icing, 8m W of Abingdon, 5.1.41
P2115	16 OTU	Wing broke off recovering from dive, Charlton-on-Otmoor, Oxon., 7.4.41
P2116	14 OTU	Shot down by night fighter 2m N of Deventer returning from Cologne, 31.5.41
P2117	144	Engine lost power on return from Brest; bellylanded at Boscombe Down, 24.8.40; to 2270M
P2118	14 OTU/1406 Flt/ 519	Flew into hills in bad weather on ASR mission, Ben Loyal, Sutherland, 26.8.43
P2119	14 OTU/Cv TB/415	SOC 3.2.44
P2120	14 OTU/16 OTU	Spun into ground, Saxilby, Lincs., 16.5.42
P2121	44	Shot down by flak while bombing barges, Antwerp, 18.9.40
P2122	144/Cv TB/144	To Russian Navy 12.10.42
P2123	44	Ran out of fuel returning from Berlin and ditched off Cromer, Norfolk, 1.9.40
P2124	50	Ran out of fuel returning from Berlin and ditched off Scarborough, Yorks., 26.8.40
P2125	83	Swung on take-off for Cologne, hit hedge and crashlanded, Scampton, 27.11.40; DBR
P2126	83/Cv TB/ 455	Damaged in air raid, Pachenga, 27.9.42 and left in N.Russia
P2127	14 OTU/12 MU	Crashed on approach during air test, Little Bampton, Cumberland, 20.10.41
P2128	14 OTU	Undercarriage collapsed on landing, Scampton, 31.7.41
P2129	106/16 OTU/ 14 OTU	Crashed after flare ignited 1m SE of Cottesmore, 1.8.42 SOC 20.2.44
P2130	AAEE/1407 Flt	SOC 20.2.44
P2131	16 OTU	Engine cut; overshot landing, Upper Heyford 8.8.40; to 2177M
P2132	16 OTU	Overshot night landing and hit house, Brackley LG, 23.8.40

P2133	16 OTU/Cv TB/489	To Canada 9.43
	32 OTU	SOC 27.4.44
P2134	49	Flew into high ground on night navex, Haigh, near Wakefield, Yorks., 29.9.40
P2135	49	Stalled off turn after take-off on transit flight, Scampton, 31.8.40
P2136	44/1 AAS	Control lost on approach, Manby, 7.2.43
P2137	44	Shot down by flak, Hasenheide, near Berlin, 21.10.40
P2138	83/16 OTU/14 OTU/ 1402 Flt/BTU	SOC 18.9.44
P2139	16 OTU/25 OTU/ 16 OTU/25 OTU/ 14 OTU/1402 Flt	SOC 29.11.43
P2140	16 OTU	Undercarriage collapsed on landing, Upper Heyford, 12.10.40
P2141	16 OTU	Hit by L6027 while parked, Upper Heyford, 13.1.41
P2142	44/16 OTU	Engine cut; abandoned near Tusmore Park, Oxford, 10.2.42
P2143	49	Ran out of fuel and crashed, Andover, returning from Bordeaux, 17.10.40
P2144	61	Engine cut on return from Düsseldorf; crashlanded, East Dereham, Norfolk, 3.6.41
P2145	49/16 OTU/455	Stalled on approach and spun into ground on training flight, Crail, 16.7.42

* * * * * * * * * *

One Miles Magister I delivered from store in June 1939 by Blackburn Aircraft, to Contract No. 602395/37

P2150	4 ERFTS/5 EFTS	Spun into ground during aerobatics, South Godstone, Surrey, 3.5.40

* * * * * * * * * *

150 Fairey Battle Is delivered between June and October 1939 by Fairey, Heaton Chapel, to Contract No. 768880/38

P2155	-	To RCAF 21.8.39 as 1301
P2156	88	To RCAF 27.10.40 as 1750
P2157	5 Gp TTF/ Driffield TTF	To RAAF 21.3.42
P2158	5 Gp TTF/Driffield TTF/5 Gp TF/241	SOC 19.11.43
P2159	88	Engine cut; bellylanded and hit hedge 2m N of Lardglass, N.Ireland, 20.3.41; to 2556M
P2160	88	Presumed lost in France 6.40
P2161	226	Crashed near La Chapelle-Moutils, Seine et Marne, during attack on enemy troops in battle area, 13.6.40
P2162	12	Shot down by Bf 109s while attacking enemy tanks near Poix, 7.6.40
P2163	103	Presumed lost in France 6.40
P2164	-	To RCAF 15.3.40 as 1621
P2165	-	To RCAF 11.3.41 as 1936
P2166	-	To RAAF 4.4.40
P2167	-	To RAAF 21.3.40
P2168	-	To RAAF 18.4.40
P2169	-	To RAAF 21.3.40
P2170	-	To RCAF 21.3.40 as 1624
P2171	-	To RCAF 21.8.39 as 1302
P2172	-	To RCAF 21.8.39 as 1303
P2173	-	To RCAF 21.8.39 as 1304

P2174	12	To SAAF 9.41
P2175	12	SOC 17.8.41
P2176	12/105	Abandoned in France 6.40
P2177	12/15/105/142	To SAAF 29.3.41 as 950
P2178	12	To SAAF 10.9.41
P2179	12/150	To SAAF 5.41 as 928
P2180	12/15/226	Destroyed on evacuation, Reims, 16.5.40
P2181	12	To SAAF 2.3.42
P2182	12/150	Shot down near Douzy attacking bridges, Sedan, 14.5.40
P2183	12/150/218	Shot down near Nouvion-sur-Meuse, Ardennes, while attacking columns near Bouillon, 12.5.40
P2184	12/150	Presumed lost in France 6.40
P2185	-	To RCAF 21.8.39 as 1305
P2186	-	To RCAF 21.8.39 as 1306
P2187	-	To RCAF 21.8.39 as 1307
P2188	142/63/12 OTU	To RCAF 2.4.41 as 1909
P2189	142/218	Presumed lost in France 6.40
P2190	142/105	Damaged attacking troop columns near Luxembourg, 10.5.40; believed abandoned while under repair
P2191	142/103	Shot down by Bf 109 near Sedan, 14.5.40
P2192	142/218	Presumed lost in France 6.40
P2193	142/103	Crashed near Sensenruth, Luxembourg, while attacking column near Bouillon, 10.5.40
P2194	142	Presumed lost in France 6.40
P2195	142	Missing 14.5.40; NFD
P2196	-	To RCAF 21.8.39 as 1308
P2197	-	To RCAF 21.8.39 as 1309
P2198	-	To RCAF 21.8.39 as 1310
P2199	142/1 FTS	To RCAF 13.6.41 as 2058
P2200	142/226/105	Shot down by ground fire near Luxembourg, 10.5.40
P2201	142/218	Shot down on reconnaissance near Kreilsheim, 20.4.40
P2202	105/218/88	Shot down over St.Vith while attacking troop columns near Bouillon, 11.5.40
P2203	105/63/218	Crashed at Troisvierges, Luxembourg, while attacking troop columns, 11.5.40
P2204	105/12	Shot down by flak, Veldwezelt, while attacking bridges near Maastricht, 12.5.40
P2233 to P2242	-	To RCAF 21.8.39 as 1311, 1317, 1312, 1313, 1318, 1314, 1319, 1315, 1316 and 1320
P2243	105/12	Damaged attacking troop columns near Luxembourg, 10.5.40 and crashlanded, Piennes; to 2483M 31.5.40
P2244	226/150	Flew into ground on night bombing practice near St. Hilaire-le-Grand, Marne, 31.3.40
P2245	226/63/1 AACU/ Abingdon/Bicester	To RAAF 4.6.41
P2246	226/142	Damaged by Bf 109s and crash-landed after attack on bridges near Sedan, 14.5.40
P2247	105/88	Abandoned when lost on reconnaissance, Pont-sur-Yonne, Yonne, 27.3.40
P2248	105	Presumed lost in France 6.40
P2249	105/218/142	Missing from attack on troop columns near St. Vith, 11.5.40
P2250	226/105	Control lost at night; spun into ground, Champigneul, Marne, 31.3.40

16

P2251	226/63/88	Shot down near Bercheux, Luxembourg, while attacking troop columns near Bouillon, 11.5.40
P2252	226/106/5 Gp TTF	To RCAF 17.3.41
P2253	226/106	Undercarriage collapsed in forced landing in bad weather, Sigglesthorne Grange, Catfoss, 16.1.40; DBR
P2254	226/63/226	Forcelanded near Brussels and abandoned, 13.5.40
P2255	226/15/226	Destroyed on evacuation, Reims, 16.5.40
P2256	226/103	Hit tree on ranges at St. Hilaire-le-Grand, Marne, 27.3.40
P2257	226/63/12 OTU	To RCAF 8.3.41 as 1888
P2258	105/88	Abandoned on evacuation, Les Grandes Chapelles, 21.5.40
P2259	105/63/12 OTU	To RCAF 27.10.40 as 1778
P2260	105/Mildenhall/ 207/3 Gp TTF	Control lost in cloud; dived into ground, Gosberton, Lincs., 26.2.40
P2261	105/88	Shot down near St.Vith while attacking troop columns near Bouillon, 11.5.40
P2262	40/12	To RCAF 23.6.41 as 2023
P2263	88/RAE	To RAAF 13.3.42
P2264	218	To RAAF 5.1.42
P2265	105/226	Crashed on night training flight near Calais, 7.4.40
P2266	150/4 BGS/RAE	SOC 8.8.43
P2267	52/105/226	Missing (Sedan) 14.5.40
P2268	52/12 OTU/88	SOC 13.10.43
P2269	52/12 OTU	Hit by AA fire while lost on navex, Portsmouth; abandoned and crashed, Ryde, Isle of Wight, 3.6.40
P2270	52/12 OTU	Undershot night landing; stalled and DBR, Benson, 19.7.40; to 2143M, later RCAF A164
P2271	52/12 OTU	Abandoned after control lost at night, South Moreton, 3m SW of Benson, 5.8.40; DBF
P2272	63/12 OTU	Engine cut; bellylanded and hit tree, Burrow Corner, near Tiverton, Devon, 21.7.40; to 2159M
P2273	63/12 OTU	Control lost after night take-off from Benson; dived into ground, Ewelme, Oxon., 8.4.40; DBF
P2274	63	Hit trees on high ground in bad visibility descending from cloud, Checkendon, Berks., 3.11.39
P2275	63/12 OTU	SOC 29.5.40
P2276	150/4 BGS	To RAAF 28.2.42
P2277	AAEE/CFS/2 BGS/ 5 FTS/1 FTS	Undershot landing; hit tree and overturned, Shrewton, 25.10.41; DBF
P2278	103/4 BGS/4/ 1472 Flt	SOC 10.3.44
P2300	105/304	To RAAF 15.1.41
P2301	1 AOS/9 BGS	To RCAF 12.12.41 as 2115
P2302	142	To RCAF 13.3.41 as 1900
P2303	103	To RCAF 12.12.41 as 2114
P2304	103 31 BGS	To Canada 4.5.41 SOC 16.2.45
P2305	103	To RAAF 11.3.41
P2306	103	To RCAF 21.12.40 as 1998
P2307	103	To SAAF 5.2.41 as 936
P2308	103/12	To RCAF 26.2.41 as 1861
P2309	300	To RCAF 5.2.41 as 1851
P2310	142	SOC 4.9.40
P2311	103/12 31 BGS	To Canada 10.4.41 SOC 16.2.45

P2312	103/150/18 OTU	To RCAF 11.3.41 as 1934
P2313	88	Blew up on take-off, Les Grandes Chappelles, 29.5.40
P2314	103	Presumed lost in France, 6.40
P2315	218/103	Damaged attacking Ju 87s near Poix and forcelanded near Paris, 8.6.40; abandoned
P2316	8 AOS/8 BGS	Engine cut; bellylanded and hit wall 10m NE of Evanton, 20.5.40
P2317	W Freugh/4 BGS/ 3 FTS/4 BGS	To RAAF 5.1.42
P2318	8 AOS/8 BGS	To RCAF 19.4.41 as 1949
P2319	AASF	To RCAF 12.12.41 as 2116
P2320	98/88	To RCAF 21.2.41 as 1869
P2321	142	To SAAF 11.7.41
P2322	3 AOS/1 AAS	To SAAF 17.1.43 later RAAF
P2323	3 AOS/1 AAS	To SAAF 2.3.43
P2324	218	Missing (Sedan) 14.5.40
P2325	142	To RCAF 2.3.41 as 1876
P2326	218	Hit by flak and abandoned, St.Vith, 11.5.40
P2327	150/142	Stalled at night on air test; sank into ground in bad visibility, Binbrook, 22.10.40
P2328	103	Crashed near Gasny, Eure, during attack on enemy columns near Vernon, 10.6.40
P2329	142	To RCAF 7.4.41 as 1946
P2330	98	Missing 26.5.41
P2331	226/12	To RCAF 27.4.41 as 1981
P2332	12	Damaged attacking bridges near Maastricht and crashed, Vroenhoven, 12.5.40
P2333	142	Shot down by Bf 109 during attack on bridges, Sedan, 14.5.40
P2334	150	Destroyed in air raid, Ecury-sur-Coole, 11.5.40
P2335	226	Shot down, 14.6.40; NFD
P2336	150	Missing from attack on columns near Neufchateau, 12.5.40
P2353	226	To Belgian AF after forced landing near Brussels after attacking columns SW of Breda, 13.5.40
P2354	88	To RAAF 3.1.43
P2355	88	Damaged in air raid, Mourmelon, 10.5.40, and abandoned
P2356	88	Missing at night over battle area, 23.5.40
P2357	103	Missing from attack on German columns near Luxembourg, 10.5.40
P2358	12 OTU/AAEE/12 OTU 31 BGS	To Canada 10.4.41 SOC 11.1.43
P2359	4 FPP	Engine cut on take-off for ferry flight to 142 Squadron; undercarriage collapsed on landing, Aston Down, 12.5.40
P2360	218	Missing (Sedan) 14.5.40
P2361	-	To RCAF 2.2.40 as 1665
P2362	5 BGS/12 FTS/ 16 PFTS/309/ 231/104 OTU	SOC 28.4.44
P2363	5 BGS/1 FTS	To RAAF 8.11.42
P2364	-	To RAAF 2.5.40
P2365	-	To RAAF 11.5.40
P2366 to P2369	-	To RCAF 2.2.40 as 1653, 1647, 1646 and 1654

*   *   *   *   *   *   *   *   *   *

100 Miles Magister Is delivered between March and June 1939 by Philips & Powis, Woodley, to Contract No. 778435/38

Serial	Units	Fate
P2374	23 ERFTS/24 EFTS/B-P	SOC 15.3.45
P2375	219	Spun into ground, Bolton-on-Swale, 13.3.40
P2376	152/19 MU	Crashed in forced landing near Knaresborough, Yorks., 16.3.40
P2377	267/41 SAAF	SOC 26.4.41
P2378	38/12 SOP/238	SOC 1.12.43
P2379	WDCF	Destroyed by enemy action 6.5.41
P2380	Finningley/Avro/Napier/GAL	SOC 31.10.44
P2381	AAEE/16 EFTS/ME	SOC 31.12.46
P2382	HQ Flt AASF	Crashed 24.10.39; presumed left in France
P2383	HQ Flt AASF/218	Destroyed in air raid, 23.5.40
P2384	SF Northolt/141/52 OTU/2 FIS/14 PAFU	To 4513M 2.44
P2385	219	Hit HT cable during AA co-operation, Piercebridge, near Darlington, 6.8.40
P2386	Malta	Destroyed in air raid, 5.42
P2387	SF Wyton/Coningsby/ATA	
P2388	SF Wyton/ATA/RAE	Sold 8.5.50; to G-AMBM
P2389	SF Andover/331/201 Gp CF	SOC 26.4.45
P2390	71 OTU	SOC 1.3.44
P2391	SF Ismailia/71 OTU	SOC 1.9.43
P2392	219/607	Crashed on take-off, Sherburn-in-Elmet, 9.10.40
P2393	113/CFWD/204 Gp CF/Adv.Salvage Unit	Crashed near Benghazi, 7.12.43
P2394	103	Presumed lost in France 5.40
P2395	219	Hit by incendiary bomb and burnt out, Tangmere, 11.5.41
P2396	33/112	Burnt on evacuation, El Adem, 4.41
P2397	33/204 Gp CF/213/206 CU	SOC 31.5.45
P2398	33/TURP/208/CFWD/70 OTU	SOC 17.4.41
P2399	108	SOC 1.9.43
P2400	274/252 Wg	Hit wires and crashed near Cairo, 6.10.41
P2401	39	Flew into ground in bad visibility 10m NE of Cairo, 15.2.41
P2402	3 BGS/CF Woodley/3 BGS/ATA	Crashed 28.6.41; NFD
P2403	4 AOS/4 BGS/15 EFTS/2 FIS/17 SFTS/7 OAFU/7 EFTS	SOC 10.12.47
P2404	5 ATS/9 BGS/241/15 EFTS/8 EFTS/10 FIS	Sold 15.11.46; to G-AJZH
P2405	6 ATS/10 BGS/10 AOS/10 OAFU	To 4111M 9.46
P2406	8 ATS/8 BGS/5 EFTS/16 EFTS/3 EFTS/HGCU/3 EFTS/ATA	Sold 11.3.46 to Argentina
P2407	1 AACU/Rootes	To 5355M 7.45
P2408	1 AACU/ATA	Sold 28.11.46; to G-AIZT
P2409	1 AACU/15 EFTS/21 EFTS/ATA	Sold 20.5.46 to Argentina
P2410	1 AACU	DBR 20.11.41; NFD
P2426	30 EFTS/16 EFTS/Bottesford/ATA	Sold 18.3.46 to Argentina
P2427	8 EFTS/5 EFTS/FPP/24 EFTS/ATA	Sold 3.5.49; to G-ALUX
P2428	24 EFTS/8 EFTS/10 FIS/5 GTS	Sold 26.2.48; to G-AKMS
P2429	30 EFTS/16 EFTS	Sold 13.5.46 to Argentina
P2430	30 EFTS/16 EFTS	Hit tree in circuit, Ashbourne, 15.10.40
P2431	SF Hucknall/2 SAC/42 OTU/Llanbedr	Ditched after engine failure on take-off, Llanbedr, 22.5.44
P2432	8 EFTS/15 EFTS	Crashed in forced landing 2m NNW of Annan, Dumfries, 15.3.41
P2433	6 EFTS/16 EFTS	Crashed in forced landing, Galley Common, Nuneaton, Warks., 5.3.41
P2434	1	NFT 26.3.40; presumed lost in France 5.40
P2435	AASF	Lost in France 5.40
P2436	43/FPP/ATA/155 Wg	Sold 21.11.46; to G-AITT
P2437	Stoke Orchard/268/24 EFTS/16 EFTS	Dived into ground near Derby, 25.3.42
P2438	AASF	Lost in France 5.40
P2439	247	Crashed in forced landing near Roborough, 21.5.41
P2440	Stoke Orchard/268/24 EFTS/111	SOC 25.2.44
P2441	242/219	Crashed in forced landing, Barnham Court, Sussex, 10.10.41
P2442	1 AOS/5 AOS/5 EFTS/CFS/16 EFTS/5 GTS	SOC 27.5.44
P2443	1 AACU/132/ME	SOC 29.6.44
P2444	1 AACU/11 EFTS/157	SOC 13.6.44
P2445	SF Aboukir/253 Wg/202 Gp CF/3 RAAF/267	NFT; PSOC 1.1.47
P2446	6 Gp CF/107/110/16 EFTS/ECFS	SOC 3.8.44
P2447	1 FP/268	Spun into ground near Bury St. Edmunds, 2.11.40
P2448	2 FP/SFP	Stalled on take-off, Kemble, 7.2.41
P2449	SF Aboukir/253 Wg 202 Gp CF/450/263 Wg	Crashed into aircraft pen on landing, Dekheila, 14.2.42
P2450	CF Heliopolis/SF Aboukir/CF Heliopolis/267	SOC 15.6.41
P2451	SF Aboukir/CF Heliopolis	Crashed 1.12.39; NFD
P2452	SF Aboukir/CF Heliopolis/71 OTU	DBR 5.7.41 by enemy action; NFD
P2453	CF Heliopolis/267/127	SOC 31.5.45
P2454	Eastchurch/Brize Norton/10 FTS/Ternhill/5 FTS/8 EFTS	Hit tree on approach. Waltham St.Lawrence, 1.10.41
P2455	Eastchurch/Ternhill/5 FTS/8 EFTS/10 FIS/51 Gp CF	Sold 29.4.49
P2456	CF Andover	Flew into ground 4m S of Andover, 29.11.39
P2457	SAC/24 EFTS/ATA	Sold 27.5.48
P2458	HAD/13 MU/2 SAC/1526 Flt/7 FIS	SOC 25.3.44
P2459	W.Raynham/Wyton/ATA/71/334/ATA	Sold 6.5.46 to Argentina
P2460	2 STT/5 FTS/30 MU	DBR in gale, Sealand, 5.12.40
P2461	2 STT/9 BGS/24 EFTS/453/Drem/488	SOC 22.7.44
P2462	2 STT/8 EFTS/10 FIS/HQ FTC/ATA	Sold 22.9.47 to Thailand
P2463	2 STT/12 FTS/11 EFTS	SOC 7.2.44
P2464	2 STT/5 FTS/456	Spun into ground, Winterslow, Wilts., 23.5.43
P2465	32/15 FTS/M.Wallop/51 OTU/72	Sold 18.3.46

P2466	32/141/2 EFTS/	
	6 FIS	DBR 28.1.42
P2467	29/85	Destroyed in air raid, Croydon, 31.8.40
P2468	29/15 EFTS/2 FPP	Flew into ground in bad weather on ferry flight, Raffles, near Carlisle, 13.1.42
P2469	25/602/Drem/406	DBR 7.9.41; NFD
P2470	25/15 FTS	DBR 15.5.41; NFD
P2493	65/46/15 EFTS/ 21 EFTS/24 EFTS/ 11 EFTS	Sold 3.5.49; to G-ALUW
P2494	65/91/253/257/FIU	SOC 31.1.45
P2495	151	Hit house while low flying, Goring-on-Thames, Oxon., 4.8.39
P2496	151/18 OTU/92/615/ 32 MU	Blown over on take-off, Manston, 28.4.42
P2497	1/87	Crashed during aerobatics, 15.3.40
P2498	1	Damaged in flying accident 3.40 and abandoned at Chateau Bougon, 6.40
P2499	64/72/74/2 FIS/ 105 OTU/1381 CU/ RAE	Sold 28.6.50
P2500	64/68/2 FIS/ 14 PAFU/2 FIS	Sold 24.2.49; to G-ALIO
P2501	73/611	Hit tree on take-off from field, Woodend Farm, Fife, 18.4.42
P2502	73/24/SF Yeadon/ 15 EFTS	DBR in forced landing on navex, 5.6.41
P2503	66/242/6 FIS/ 4 FIS/6 FIS/2 EFTS	Sold 18.3.46 to Argentina
P2504	66/607	Sold 27.5.46 to Argentina
P2505	23	Crashed in forced landing, Hill Farm, Thorney, Hunts., 8.5.40
P2506	23/16 EFTS/3 EFTS	Sold 6.12.46; to G-AIZK
P2507	79/Warmwell/ATA	To U-0272 at Mkrs
P2508	79	Dived into ground during aerobatics, Garlinge (sic), France, 2.1.40
P2509	111/141/Ayr	Hit wires and crashed near Ayr, 11.12.41
P2510	85	Lost in France 5.40

* * * * * * * * * *

18 Wellington IAs delivered in December 1939 and January 1940 by Vickers, Weybridge, to Contract No. 781439/36 to replace RNZAF aircraft

P2515	37	Missing from leaflet raid, 24.3.40
P2516	37/15 OTU/ 26 OTU	Swung on take-off and hit excavator, Lossiemouth, 18.5.42
P2517	37/Hendon/Yeadon/ 149/3 Gp TF	To 2794M 22.11.41
P2518	Mkrs/Cv DWI/ 1 GRU/RAE/3 GRU/ OADF/1 GRU	Engine cut; crashlanded, Kilo 30, 9.2.42; DBR
P2519	214/15 OTU/305/ 27 OTU/303 FTU/ 1 OADU/FE	SOC 29.3.45
P2520	9	Missing from attempted strike on battle-cruisers N of Bergen, 12.4.40
P2521	Cv DWI/1 GRU/ 138/161/303 FTU/ 1 OADU/FE	Cv to Mk.XV; SOC 26.4.45
P2522	Cv DWI/1 GRU/RAE/ 3 GRU/AFEE/24	SOC 10.3.43
P2523	9/15 OTU	Crashed 15.10.40; NFD

P2524	115	Shot down by Bf 110s off Sylt, 7.4.40
P2525	37/214/311/ 15 OTU	SOC 25.3.44
P2526	38	Abandoned in fog while lost on return from Heligoland, Melton Constable, Norfolk, 21.2.40
P2527	149/215/11 OTU/ 20 OTU/280	SOC 14.7.44
P2528	149/215/11 OTU/ CGS/303 FTU/ 1 OADU/FE	SOC 26.4.45
P2529	214/15 OTU	Failed to become airborne and hit fence, Harwell, 6.11.40
P2530	214	Ran out of fuel on approach; forcelanded in field; hit ditch and undercarriage collapsed, Stradishall, 31.8.40 on return from Berlin
P2531	214/305/CGS	SOC 16.4.43
P2532	214/12 OTU/ 30 OTU	SOC 19.11.44

* * * * * * * * * *

1000 Hawker Hurricane Is delivered between November 1939 and July 1940 by Glosters, Hucclecote (to P3264) and Hawkers, Brooklands and Langley, (remainder) to Contract No. 962371/38

P2535	85	Lost in France 5.40
P2536	607	Missing 18.5.40
P2537	79	Lost in France 5.40
P2538	85/87	Lost in France 5.40
P2539	73	Lost in France 5.40
P2540	87	Crashed 2.3.40; to 4 RSU 10.5.40; NFT
P2541	73	Lost in France 5.40
P2542	43/73	Shot down by Bf 109s over Tonbridge, Kent, 14.9.40
P2543	43/73	Lost in France 5.40
P2544	274/71 OTU	Engine cut; overshot forced landing, Ismailia, 6.6.41; to 2636M 8.41
P2545	1/73	Lost in France 5.40
P2546	1	Lost in France 5.40
P2547	85	Lost in France 5.40
P2548	87/5 OTU/55 OTU	Overturned in forced landing while lost, Hunningham, near Leamington Spa, Warks., 12.12.40
P2549	501	Shot down by Bf 110s, Chilham, Kent, 18.8.40
P2550	56/242	Shot down near Cambrai, 23.5.40
P2551	85	Lost in France 5.40
P2552	85	Crashed on landing, Seclin, 5.4.40
P2553	615	Lost 31.5.40; NFD
P2554	615	Lost in France 5.40
P2555	43/85	Lost in France 5.40
P2556	56/3 RAAF/274/ 73/71 OTU	SOC 27.4.44
P2557	213/17/85	Crashed in sea while attacking He 111 off Felixstowe, 12.7.40
P2558	213/17/6 OTU/ 56 OTU/9 FTS	Engine caught fire in air; abandoned, Leighterton, Glos., 28.8.41
P2559	17	Missing 1.7.40
P2560	Mkrs/6 OTU/605	Damaged by Bf 109s and abandoned off North Foreland, 15.11.40; crashed, Tilmanstone, Kent
P2561	607	SOC 5.6.42
P2562	43/87/1/87	Lost in France 5.40

Serial	Units	Fate
P2563	85/43/85	Crashed in forced landing near Lille/Seclin, 2.3.40; cause not known
P2564	607/615	Missing from interception near Vitry, 12.5.40
P2565	607/9 FTS/55 OTU	SOC 21.11.44
P2566	607/7 OTU	Stalled off turn and dived into ground, Brynsfoot, Holywell, Cornwall, 19.6.40; DBF
P2567	607/615	Lost in France 5.40
P2568	17/601	Missing over Dunkerque, 28.5.40
P2569	73	Lost in France 5.40
P2570	73/263/258/43/ 59 OTU/41 OTU	SOC 22.5.44
P2571	615/607	Missing 11.5.40
P2572	615/607	Lost in France 12.5.40
P2573	607	Lost in France 12.5.40
P2574	607	Lost in France 11.5.40
P2575	73/312/55 OTU/ 8 FTS/2 FIS/5 PAFU/ 1623 Flt/691	SOC 23.5.44
P2576	43/73	Crashed at Sierck, 23.4.40
P2577	615	Lost in France 5.40
P2578	615/1 RCAF/231	Crashed 10.9.42; NFD
P2579	43/73/615	Lost in France 5.40
P2580	615	Lost in France 5.40
P2581	615	Shot down by Bf 109 near Folkestone, 15.8.40
P2582	615	Lost in France 5.40
P2583	615	Lost in France 5.40
P2584	ME	NFD
P2614	261	Damaged by CR.42s on approach to Hal Far and crashlanded, 9.7.40; DBR
P2615	607	Lost in France, 10.5.40
P2616	607	Missing 12.5.40
P2617	615/607/1 RCAF/ MSFU/9 FTS/8 FTS/ 9 FTS/9 OAFU	To museum aircraft
P2618	615/607	Lost in France 5.40
P2619	615/607	Lost in France 5.40
P2620	615	Lost in France 5.40
P2621	615/607	Lost in France 5.40
P2622	615	Lost in France 5.40
P2623	261	Shot down by CR.42 over Malta, 13.7.40
P2624	33	SOC 26.5.41
P2625	-	NFT
P2626	4 FPP	Tipped up taxying on soft ground, Ussel, and destroyed on evacuation, 19.5.40
P2627	274	Forcelanded 30m W of Mersa Matruh, 17.12.40; NFT
P2628	33/274	Believed aircraft damaged when taxied over filled-in shell crater, Bardia, 10.1.41; NFT
P2629	261	Missing after chasing Ju 87 over Valletta, 19.1.41
P2630	79/5 OTU/55 OTU/ 8 FTS/RAFC/ 59 OTU/5 PAFU	SOC 12.2.45
P2631	253	Shot down, 30.8.40; SOC 1.9.40; NFD
P2632	46	Lost aboard *Glorious* 8.6.40
P2633	46	Lost aboard *Glorious* 8.6.40
P2634	79	Lost in France 5.40
P2635	79	Lost in France 5.40
P2636	229	Missing while detached to France, 29.5.40; NFD
P2637	504	NFT
P2638	3 RAAF/274/73/ 80/208	Shot down by Bf 109s returning from tactical reconnaissance mission, El Imayed, 24.7.42
P2639	274/80	Missing 21.1.41
P2640	33/73/94/274/ 71 OTU	Engine cut; bellylanded, Ekheib, 31.7.42; DBR
P2641	274/80/94	Destroyed in air raid, Malta, 18.9.41
P2642	-	
P2643	80/274/ADU	Undercarriage jammed; belly-landed, Sidi Haneish, 19.4.41
P2644	4 FPP	Ran into bomb crater on landing; undercarriage leg broken off, Marignane, 8.6.40; abandoned
P2645	261	Shot down by Bf 109 in sea off Malta, 7.3.41
P2646	33/274/208/40 SAAF	Engine cut; forcelanded, LG.75, 21.6.42; believed abandoned
P2647	73/1 RCAF/213/ 52 OTU	SOC 29.12.41
P2648	ME	NFT
P2649	73/1	Lost in France 5.40
P2650	ME	NFT
P2651	274	Engine cut; bellylanded 30m SW of Gazala and abandoned, 30.1.41
P2652	274	Ditched off Malta on ferry flight, 22.2.41
P2653	261	Dived into sea off Malta, 22.3.41; presumed shot down by Bf 109
P2672	4 FPP	Engine cut; crashed on approach to forced landing near Westbury-on-Severn, Salop., 20.5.40
P2673	213/85	Shot down by Bf 109s near Kenley, 1.9.40
P2674	229/253/229/ 17/55 OTU	To Mk.II BV171
P2675	CFF	Lost in France 5.40
P2676	CFF	Lost in France 5.40
P2677	56/151/46/253	Shot down by Bf 109; abandoned and crashed, Denton, near Newhaven, Sussex, 29.9.40
P2678	73/1/	Lost 1.9.40; NFD
P2679	245/605/59 OTU	To 3314M 5.43
P2680	607	Shot down by Bf 109s, East Peckham, Kent, 9.9.40
P2681	245/238/59 OTU/ 55 OTU/9 FTS/116/ 245/87/55 OTU	SOC 27.5.44
P2682	145/43/8 FTS	Damaged 7.5.41; cv to Mk.II DG641 during repair
P2683	87	Lost in France 5.40
P2684	601	Damaged by enemy aircraft over Brussels, 18.5.40; NFT and SOC 10.7.40
P2685	46	Engine cut; hit post in forced landing near Derby, 24.7.40
P2686	1/303	Hit by return fire from Bf 110s and abandoned near Penshurst, Kent, 6.9.40
P2687	87	Lost in France 5.40
P2688	1/615/56 OTU	Damaged 22.4.42; NFT
P2689	1/73	Shot down near Sedan, 14.5.40
P2690	56/609	Damaged by fighters over Portland and abandoned off Whitenose, Dorset, 13.8.40
P2691	501	SOC 4.9.40
P2692	56	Shot down near Southend, 13.8.40
P2693	607/3/17/59 OTU	Bounced on landing, stalled and crashed, Crosby, 10.2.42
P2694	1	Lost in France 5.40
P2695	73	Lost in France 5.40
P2696	601/145	Engine cut; crashlanded, Haywards Heath Golf Club, 25.10.40; DBF

Above: Oxford P1864, the prototype Mk.III, flying on one engine

Below: Lysander II P9073 of No.6 Squadron in desert surroundings

Above: Waco ZVN P6330 was purchased to provide experience with tricycle undercarriages

Below: Vega Gull P1754 awaiting delivery to No. 24 Squadron at Hendon

Serial	Units	Fate
P2697	607	Lost in France 5.40
P2698	79	Overshot landing in fog at night and hit dispersal pen, Biggin Hill, 23.6.40
P2699	CFF	To 1 RSU 16.5.40; abandoned in France 5.40;
P2700	CFF	Missing 1.6.40; NFD
P2701	85	Shot down over Belgium, 11.5.40
P2713	607	Lost in France 5.40
P2714	CFF	Destroyed by enemy action in France and SOC 30.5.40
P2715	79/310/1 SAC/ 41 OTU/ACC CF/ 41 OTU	SOC 31.3.46
P2716	85	Damaged by return fire from Do 17 and abandoned off Harwich, 11.7.40
P2717	605/302/56 OTU/ MSFU/59 OTU	To 5054M 3.3.45
P2718	79	Lost 28.8.40; NFD
P2719	79	Lost 28.8.40; NFD
P2720	145	Damaged by Bf 109 and crash-landed near Ventnor, Isle of Wight, 7.11.40
P2721	213	Shot down by Bf 109s in sea off Dunkerque, 28.5.40
P2722	85/257	To 3085M 5.5.42
P2723	145	Missing, believed shot down by Bf 110s while attacking Ju 88s near Dunkerque, 27.5.40
P2724	32/306/17	Collided with P2874 during practice attack near Elgin, 8.7.41
P2725	504	Damaged by return fire from Do 17 over London and rammed it; abandoned and crashed, Chelsea, London, 15.9.40
P2726	CFF	To 1 RSU 18.5.40; presumed lost in France 5.40;
P2727	32	Destroyed by enemy action, 2.6.40; NFD
P2728	Gosport/607	Shot down by Bf 109s, Goudhurst, Kent, 9.9.40
P2729	229	Lost while detached to France, 5.40
P2730	242	Shot down near Cambrai, 23.5.40
P2731	610/213	To Admiralty 3.41
P2732	242	Shot down near Dunkerque, 31.5.40
P2751	1	Wing hit ground in circuit in bad visibility near Wittering, 3.11.40
P2752	302	Shot down by Bf 109s over Chatham; abandoned and crashed, Stoke, Kent, 15.10.40
P2753	601	Shot down by Bf 109 off St. Catherine's Point, Isle of Wight, 26.7.40
P2754	17/615/317/11 Gp AAC Flt/287/286 59 OTU/56 OTU	Collided with V6913 during dummy attack and crashed, Maryton Farm, near Montrose, 27.4.43
P2755	32	Shot down by Bf 109 off Dover, 25.8.40
P2756	79	Abandoned on fire near Chilverton Elms, Kent, 7.7.40; believed attacked by Spitfires
P2757	CFF	Lost in France 5.40
P2758	CFF	Lost in France 5.40
P2759	CFF	Lost in France 5.40
P2760	501	Damaged by Bf 109s over Ashford and blew up, Chilham, Kent, 15.9.40
P2761	CFF	To 1 RSU 10.5.40; presumed lost in France 5.40
P2762	17	Crashed 12.7.40; NFD
P2763	213	Missing from patrol over Dunkerque, 31.5.40
P2764	229/615	Missing from patrol near Abbeville, 22.6.40; believed shot down by return fire from He 111s
P2765	605	Hit by return fire from He 111s and abandoned, Kingsley, Hants., 9.9.40
P2766	213	Shot down near Portland, 25.8.40
P2767	249/242	Lost 9.6.40 in France
P2768	615	Shot down by fighters, Morden Park golf course, Surrey, 18.8.40
P2769	249/242/79	SOC 30.9.40
P2770	145	Shot down by Bf 109s, Ashey Down, 2m W of Brading, Isle of Wight, 7.11.40
P2792	213	Missing from patrol over Dunkerque, 28.5.40
P2793	615/501	Shot down by return fire from He 111 over Maidstone, Kent, 13.9.40
P2794	6 OTU/17	Crashed in forced landing, Monkton, near Manston, 11.11.40
P2795	32/310/255/ 55 OTU	Hit P3718 while landing, Usworth, 5.12.41
P2796	73	Damaged by Bf 110 and abandoned, Boxley, Kent, 11.9.40
P2797	CFF	Lost in France 5.40; 1 RSU 16.5.40 and presumed abandoned
P2798	87	Abandoned after engine failure at night near Marshfield, Glos., 23.10.41
P2799	5 OTU/55 OTU/ MSFU/615/56 OTU	Crashed 14.2.43; NFD
P2800		Lost in France 5.40; believed on ferry flight
P2801	615	Shot down by Bf 109s, Seal, Kent, 21.8.40
P2802	213	Missing, presumed shot down in Channel off Bognor, Sussex, 12.8.40
P2803	73	Missing 24.5.40
P2804	73	Shot down near Conflans, 10.5.40
P2805	Tangmere/85/43/ 55 OTU/56 OTU	Undercarriage retracted prematurely on take-off; sank back on to runway, Kinnell, 22.3.43
P2806	Tangmere/85/242	Shot down by Bf 109s off Sheerness, Kent, 5.11.40
P2807	4 FPP	Crashed in forced landing on ferry flight 10m N of Juvincourt, 12.5.40
P2808	Tangmere	Lost in France 5.40
P2809	242	Missing while escorting Blenheims to Cambrai, 23.5.40; presumed shot down by Bf 110s
P2810	1/73	Burnt on evacuation, 16.5.40
P2811	1/73	Shot down near Poilcourt, 11.5.40
P2812	73	Shot down near Namur, 14.5.40
P2813	73	Crashed on landing, Reims, 14.5.40 and burnt
P2814	501/213/229/56 OTU/ ATA/Zeals	To 3954M 9.43
P2815	73/229	Shot down by Bf 109s, Ightham, Kent, 30.9.40

P2816	CFF	Lost in France 5.40
P2817	213	Shot down in sea off Dunkerque, 28.5.40
P2818	85	Missing from patrol over Belgium, 15.5.40
P2819	87	Lost in France 5.40
P2820	73/1	Lost in France 5.40
P2821	85	Shot down by Bf 109 over Belgium, 13.5.40
P2822	1/6 OTU/56 OTU/ 9 Gp CF/59 OTU	Abandoned after engine fire 2½m NE of Milfield, 28.7.43
P2823	87	Cv to Mk.II BV161 12.40
P2824	85	Missing from patrol over Belgium, 16.5.40
P2825	3	Lost in France 6.40
P2826	87/151/43/MSFU/ 318/59 OTU/5 PAFU	SOC 24.5.44
P2827	145/238/85/ 32/315	Engine cut on approach; hit fence, Speke, 7.7.41; DBR
P2828		Lost in France 5.40
P2829	55 OTU	Damaged 3.8.41; cv to Mk.II DR355 during repair
P2830	607	Lost in France 5.40
P2831	242	Hit by return fire from Do 17 and abandoned near Caterham, Surrey, 9.9.40
P2832	7 OTU/55 OTU/ 56 OTU	Engine cut on overshoot; hit tree and crashed, Tealing, 13.5.42
P2833		Lost in France 5.40
P2834	213	Shot down in sea off Dunkerque, 28.5.40
P2835	605/257/5 FTS	Damaged 21.7.41 and cv to Mk.II DR353 during repair
P2836	245/238	Damaged by Bf 110 near Kenley and abandoned, Pembury, Kent, 15.9.40
———		Missing, presumed shot down in Channel off Bognor, Sussex, 12.8.40
P2854	242/32/213	SOC 17.6.44
P2855	87/308/79/ 59 OTU/2 TEU	Shot down near Namur, 5.40
P2856	73	SOC 27.5.44
P2857	263/258/615/ MSFU/53 OTU	Lost in France 5.40
P2858		To 4685M 20.3.44
P2859	504/3/17/20 OTU/ 55 OTU/RN	SOC 28.8.44
P2860	504/3/Sumburgh/ 17/1/55 OTU/ME	Engine cut on approach; ditched off Sumburgh, 23.7.40
P2861	504/3/232	Collided with Hudson P5152 on take-off, Wick, 23.7.40
P2862	3/504/3	Damaged 18.8.41; cv to Mk.II DR368 during repair
P2863	3/56/8 FTS	Engine cut; bellylanded 4m SE of Elgin, 20.5.41
P2864	3/Sumburgh/17	SOC 17.5.44
P2865	504/253/87/286/ 1623 Flt/691	Damaged by fighters over Bournemouth and crashlanded, 30.9.40
P2866	234/56	Destroyed by enemy action, 3.6.40
P2867	501	Lost in France 5.40
P2868	CFF	NFT
P2869	73/253/9 FTS/ ECFS/ME/RATG	Lost in France 5.40; 1 RSU 16.5.40 and presumed abandoned
P2870	CFF	Spun into ground out of cloud, Cambridge, 26.9.41
P2871	Kenley/615/ 56 OTU	Shot down by Bf 110 off Portland, Dorset, 15.8.40
P2872	87	
P2873	CFF	Lost in France 5.40
P2874	Kenley/17	Collided with P2724 during practice attack near Elgin, 8.7.41
P2875	73	Shot down by Bf 109s over Thames Estuary, 6.9.40
P2876	229	Missing while detached to France, 27.5.40
P2877	229/253/229/1/ 59 OTU	Engine cut; stalled on approach to forced landing, Cleator, Cumberland, 26.6.42
P2878	242/615	Damaged by enemy aircraft over Portsmouth; abandoned and crashed, Warrendown, Forest Side, Hants., 26.8.40
P2879	85/229	Damaged by Bf 109 near Westcliffe, Essex, and abandoned; crashed at Hoo, Kent, 23.9.40
P2880	1	Missing 25.5.40; believed hit by flak on patrol
P2881	Tangmere/225/32/ 55 OTU	Engine cut; crashlanded, Gretna, Dumfriesshire, 10.7.43
P2882	56	Broke away from formation in low cloud; flew into tree on high ground and dived into ground, West Horsley, Surrey, 17.6.40
P2883	253/52 OTU/245/ME	SOC 30.9.43
P2884	229/111/242	Damaged by Bf 109s and abandoned, Lidmore, Sussex, 15.9.40
P2885	229/111	Damaged by fighters near Abbeville and crashlanded in France, 6.6.40
P2886	229/111	To Admiralty 11.1.42
P2887	5 OTU/55 OTU/ 1 AACU/1608 Flt/595	SOC 17.6.44
P2888	229/111	Damaged by Bf 110 over Felixstowe and abandoned, 31.8.40
P2900	607	Shot down by Bf 110s in sea off Swanage, Dorset, 1.10.40
P2901	229/253/9 FTS/ 1/55 OTU	Engine cut; crashlanded, Lessonhall, Cumberland, 23.7.42
P2902	245	SOC 10.8.40
P2903	303/501	Collided with V6806 over Cranbrook and crashed, Staplehurst, Kent, 25.10.40
P2904	607/17/331	Cv to Mk.II DR357 8.41
P2905	605/17	Missing 6.7.40
P2906	245/59 OTU/ 55 OTU	Swung on landing and hit R4123, Usworth, 9.3.42
P2907	CFF	Lost in France 5.40
P2908	504/133	Damaged 20.8.41 and cv to Mk.II DR369 during repair
P2909	3/232/55 OTU/ 71 OTU	SOC 1.4.44
P2910	234/56	Crashed near Boscombe Down; presumed collided with V7569, 23.11.40
P2911	3/232	To GI airframe 5.3.41; to 3192M 18.7.42
P2912	607/1401 Flt/ME	SOC 27.4.44
P2913	245/9 FTS/9 PAFU/ 17 SFTS	To 3838M 25.11.43
P2914	245/8 FTS/ 9 FTS/ECFS	SOC 26.6.44
P2915	263/258/Digby/ 56 OTU/ME	SOC 28.8.44
P2916	263/501/605	Damaged by Bf 109 and abandoned, Staplehurst, Kent, 26.10.40
P2917	263	Engine cut; overshot forced landing and hit hedge 1½m SSW of Tranent, E.Lothian, 20.7.40; DBF

P2918	145/302/56 OTU/ME	SOC 28.8.44
P2919	7 OTU/615/56 OTU/ 9 FTS/ECFS/7 PAFU/ 7 FTS	SOC 9.6.47
P2920	601/238/59 OTU	Crashed 11.11.41; NFD
P2921	32/315/245/MSFU	To Admiralty 10.1.42
P2922	56	Shot down by Bf 109 in Channel off Calais, 13.7.40
P2923	85	Missing from interception over North Sea, 18.8.40
P2924	145/111/145	Damaged by Bf 109s near Ventnor and abandoned, Birdham, Sussex, 7.11.40
P2946	238/253	Shot down by Bf 109s, Crundale, Kent, 2.9.40
P2947	238	Ditched on convoy escort S of Isle of Wight, 8.8.40
P2948	238/5 OTU/55 OTU/ MSFU	Hit vehicle on take-off, Gibraltar, 23.12.42
P2949	238/601/59 OTU/ 239/ME	SOC 28.8.44
P2950	238	Damaged by return fire from Do 17 and crashlanded, Southdown, Dorset, 13.7.40
P2951	145	Shot down by fighters off Swanage, Dorset, 11.8.40
P2952	145	Missing, presumed shot down by Bf 109s near Dunkerque, 1.6.40
P2953	73/310	To Admiralty 5.41
P2954	213/302	Shot down by fighters, Battlesbridge, Essex, 15.9.40
P2955	145	Missing, believed shot down by Bf 109 off Isle of Wight, 8.8.40
P2956	145	Hit windsock during night take-off and crashlanded, Tangmere, 25.6.40
P2957	145	Missing from convoy escort S of Isle of Wight, 8.8.40
P2958	111/85/253	Damaged by fighters and abandoned over Channel, 26.9.40
P2959	501	Lost in France 6.40
P2960	253/257	Damaged by Bf 109s over Thames Estuary and abandoned, Eastchurch, Kent, 23.9.40
P2961	242	Missing from ground attack mission near Gravelines, 12.1.41
P2962	73/242	Shot down over Thames Estuary, 7.9.40; believed crashed at Theydon Bois, Essex
P2963	615	To Admiralty 10.11.41
P2964	501	Lost in France 6.40
P2965	46	Crashed in forced landing, Fyfield, Essex, 17.12.40
P2966	615	Shot down by Bf 109s, Robsacks Wood, near Sevenoaks, Kent, 18.8.40
P2967	242	Shot down by Bf 109s near Milstead, Kent, 27.9.40
P2968	32/151/46/ 9 FTS/9 PAFU	To instr. airframe 11.43 for Irish Air Corps as 107
P2969	CFF	Lost in France 6.40
P2970	56	Damaged by return fire from Do 17s and abandoned 10m N of Margate, Kent, 12.8.40
P2971	1 RCAF	Damaged by Bf 109s and abandoned, Staplehurst, Kent, 31.8.40
P2972	6 OTU/17/52 OTU	To Admiralty 16.10.41
P2973	Tangmere	Lost in France 6.40
P2974	85/315/56 OTU/FE	SOC 1.45
P2975	73/85/52 OTU	Engine cut; bellylanded 1½m S of Aldbourn, Wilts., 24.8.41; cv to Mk.II DR372
P2976	242	Dived into sea in cloud on patrol 5m NE of Winterton, Norfolk, 20.8.40; cause not known
P2977	CFF	SOC 1.7.40; believed DBR in air raid, 6.40
P2978	238	Shot down by fighters 2m E of Weymouth, Dorset, 11.8.40
P2979	238/229/111/ 59 OTU	To 3087M 5.5.42
P2980	1	Ran out of fuel on night patrol; overshot forced landing and hit trees, Withyham, near Tunbridge Wells, Kent, 24.8.40
P2981	257	Shot down by Bf 109s off St.Catherine's Point, Isle of Wight, 8.8.40
P2982	55 OTU	Dived into field out of cloud 1m W of Kirkpatrick, Dumfries, 22.9.42
P2983	238/5 FTS/245/ 288/55 OTU	SOC 22.5.44
P2984	73/32	Abandoned in fog after engine failure on night patrol over Hayling Island, Hants., 16.1.41
P2985	56/111/303	Shot down by Bf 109 over Gillingham, Kent, and abandoned, North Benfleet, Essex, 5.9.40
P2986	242 6/40 501	To Admiralty 4.41; retd and SOC 30.3.43
P2987	3/504/85/32/87/ 52 OTU/55 OTU/ 56 OTU/1 TEU/2 TEU	SOC 1.6.44
P2988	263/56/249	Damaged by Bf 110s over Rochester and abandoned, Rainham, Kent, 2.9.40
P2989	238/RAE/AFDU/312/ 607/402/151 OTU	Bounced on landing and undercarriage collapsed, Risalpur, 1.3.44; SOC 30.6.44
P2990	263	Undershot night landing and hit hedge, Grangemouth, 31.7.40; DBR
P2991	263	Hit obstruction in forced landing while lost on night interception, Carstairs Junction School, Lanark, 13.7.40
P2992	263/258/615/302/ 56 OTU/331/56 OTU/ 55 OTU/527	DBR in accident 29.7.44; NFD
P2993	3/504/1 RCAF/ 9 FTS/55 OTU/ RAF Rayak	To FFAF in ME; SOC 28.8.44
P2994	605/17/46	To Admiralty 16.1.41
P2995	249	Engine cut after night take-off from Church Fenton; hit wires and crashed in Copmanthorpe Wood, Yorks., 16.7.40
P3020	3	To Admiralty 5.41; to 4505M 20.1.44
P3021	3/504/112 RCAF/ Digby/52 OTU	Dived into ground out of cloud, Washing Pool Hill, Almondsbury, Glos., 31.10.41
P3022	605	Shot down by Bf 109s off Dungeness, 12.10.40
P3023	17/232/55 OTU	Damaged 31.5.41; cv to Mk.II DR342 during repair
P3024	46	Damaged by fighters and abandoned, South Fambridge, Essex, 3.9.40
P3025	17/56/111	Damaged by Bf 109 over Channel and abandoned, Newchurch, Kent, 7.9.40
P3026	46/145/315/303/ FAA/59 OTU/ 63 OTU/4 TEU	2689M NTU; SOC 27.5.44

25

P3027	17	Engine cut on take-off; crash-landed, Debden, 17.9.40
P3028	56/56 OTU	Damaged in accident 17.8.41 and SOC 22.12.41
P3029	111	Damaged by enemy aircraft and crashed, Brenchley, Kent, 16.8.40
P3030	46/601/55 OTU	Engine cut; bellylanded 1m S of Felton, Northumberland, 27.3.42
P3031	46/607/55 OTU/ 59 OTU	Hit tree on approach at night, Brunton, 23.1.43
P3032	253	Believed shot down by return fire from Ju 88, Kingsnorth, Kent, 6.9.40
P3033	17/260/607/55 OTU/ 56 OTU/2 TEU	SOC 23.6.44
P3034	73/242/111/59 OTU/87/55 OTU	Engine cut; bellylanded, White Close Farm, Weatherall, Cumberland, 14.10.42
P3035	6 OTU/79	Hit Chance light on overshoot at night, Pembrey, 15.2.41
P3036	6 OTU/32	To Admiralty 14.12.41
P3037	229	Abandoned during patrol over Kent, 30.9.40; cause not known
P3038	229	Damaged by enemy aircraft near Biggin Hill and abandoned, 11.9.40
P3039	229/312/56 OTU/ 55 OTU	Spun into ground ½m N of Edderside, Cumberland, 27.5.43; cause not known
P3040	501	Damaged, believed by return fire from Ju 87s, and abandoned, Hawkinge, 15.8.40
P3041	501/1 RCAF/247	Dived into ground at night 4m SW of St.Dennis, Cornwall, 24.2.41
P3042	1/8 FTS	To Admiralty 17.9.42
P3043	56	Missing, presumed shot down off Harwich, Essex, 16.8.40
P3044	1	Missing from patrol, 3.9.40
P3045	1	Burnt on evacuation, Nantes, 18.6.40
P3046	111/59 OTU	SOC 29.12.41
P3047	1	Damaged by Bf 109s and abandoned over sea near Harwich, Essex, 15.8.40
P3048	308/79/59 OTU	To Admiralty 14.9.42
P3049	242/257	Shot down by fighters, Spitend Point, Isle of Sheppey, Kent, 7.9.40
P3050	79	Damaged by Bf 109 and crash-landed, Hawkhurst, Kent, 31.8.40; DBF
P3051	3 FPP	Crashed on take-off, Orleans/Bricy, 13.6.40
P3052	46	Damaged by fighters and abandoned, Hawkwell, Essex, 4.9.40
P3053	46	Damaged by Bf 109s near Maidstone and crashlanded, Meopham Green, Kent, 8.9.40
P3054	5 OTU/55 OTU	Engine cut; bellylanded on to road, Sheraton Hall Farm, near Castle Eden, Co. Durham, 18.8.41
P3055	249/56/5 FTS	Collided with P3668 during combat practice and crashed near Newport, Salop., 9.1.42
P3056	310	To Admiralty 7.41
P3057	249/213	Damaged 17.12.40; 2136M NTU; cv to Mk.II BV169 during repair
P3058	257	Missing, presumed shot down by Bf 109s off St.Catherine's Point, Isle of Wight, 8.8.40
P3059	501	Shot down by Bf 109s over Canterbury, Kent, 18.8.40
P3060	46/73/85/52 OTU/ 56 OTU	Hit cable of drifting balloon and crashlanded 1m S of Balminning, Fife, 7.1.43
P3061	242/17/52 OTU	To Admiralty 9.9.42
P3062	46	Crashed after collision near Ancaster, Lincs., 13.1.41
P3063	46	Damaged by return fire from Do 17 and abandoned, Canewdon, Essex, 3.9.40
P3064	46	Missing near Southend, 3.9.40; believed crashed in R. Crouch
P3065	151/9 FTS	Engine cut; hit tree in attempted forced landing, Seagry, near Hullavington, Wilts., 26.10.41
P3066	46	Crashed on landing on return from patrol, Stapleford, 3.9.40
P3067	46	Shot down over Thames Estuary, 27.9.40; NFD
P3068	1 RCAF	Damaged by return fire from Do 17s near Maidstone and crashed on landing, Northolt, 1.9.40; cv to Mk.II DG615
P3069	1 RCAF/310/306	Hit tree on approach at night, Buntingsdale SLG, 23.2.41
P3080	1 RCAF	Damaged by Bf 109 over Tunbridge Wells, Kent, and abandoned, 15.9.40
P3081	1 RCAF	Damaged by Bf 109s and abandoned near Northolt, 9.9.40
P3082	501	Shot down by Bf 109 off Cherbourg, 20.7.40
P3083	501/247/SFP	Flew into high ground in cloud on ferry flight, Rodney Stoke, Somerset, 24.12.40
P3084	501	Hit by return fire from Do 17s and crashed off Portland, 12.7.40
P3085	302	Collided with V6923 and abandoned, Chobham, Surrey, 29.10.40
P3086	302/112 RCAF/ 52 OTU/56 OTU/ 5 PAFU	SOC 3.1.45
P3087	242	Damaged, probably by Bf 110, and crashed, Caterham, Surrey, 9.9.40
P3088	242/249/56	Damaged, believed by Bf 110, near Portland, and abandoned, 30.9.40
P3089	242/303/306/52 OTU/ 59 OTU/7 PAFU	SOC 16.11.44
P3090	242	To Admiralty 4.41
P3091	213	SOC 31.8.41
P3092	213/79	To Admiralty 9.1.42
P3093	87/260/55 OTU/ 316/56 OTU	Collided with W9178 during practice dogfight and crashed near Sutton Bridge, 17.9.41
P3094	46	Crashlanded after dogfight, Staplecross, Kent, 11.9.40; DBF
P3095	3/32/59 OTU/ 63 OTU/4 TEU	SOC 22.5.44
P3096	238	Shot down, probably by return fire from Ju 88s, and abandoned near Tunbridge Wells, Kent, 11.9.40
P3097	245/43/55 OTU/ 46/121	Dived into ground 2m NW of Scampton, 21.6.41; cause not known
P3098	238	Shot down by Bf 109s over Solent, 26.9.40
P3099	245	Crashed on landing, Aldergrove, 9.11.40; DBF

P3100	79/316/56 OTU/ 2 TEU	SOC 17.6.44
P3101	245/289	Engine cut; ditched off Burnt-island, Fife, 8.12.41
P3102	501	Shot down by Bf 109s over Hawkinge; abandoned and crashed, Acrise, Kent, 29.8.40
P3103	79	Cv to Mk.II DR340 during overhaul, 5.41
P3104	232/MSFU/59 OTU	Undershot and hit trees on approach, Brunton, 9.1.44
P3105	17/111	Missing, presumed shot down off Margate, Kent, 11.8.40
P3106	17/111/9 FTS	Damaged 20.8.41; cv to Mk.II DR370 during repair
P3107	605	Crashed on patrol in bad visibility near S.Norwood, London, 14.10.40; possibly hit balloon cable
P3108	607	Shot down by Bf 109s off Selsey, Sussex, 28.9.40
P3109	615	Shot down by Bf 109s off Dover, 14.8.40
P3110	73	Shot down attacking Ju 88s and abandoned, West Hanningfield, Essex, 5.9.40
P3111	615	To Admiralty 21.4.41; to 4503M 28.1.44
P3112	32/315/303/225/ 56 OTU	Missing on training flight; presumed ditched off E Scottish coast, 25.7.43
P3113	213	Lost 5.9.40 but no mention in 213 Sqn ORB; OK on 3.9.40
P3114	46/229/56 OTU	To Admiralty 16.10.41
P3115	253	Damaged by return fire from Ju 88s and abandoned, Cudham, Surrey, 31.8.40
P3116	607/59 OTU	Rolled recovering from dive and dived into cottage, Kingsfield House, Penton, Cumberland, 7.5.42; DBF
P3117	607	Shot down by Bf 109, Goudhurst, Kent, 9.9.40
P3118	87	Ran out of fuel on night patrol and abandoned, Knaphill, near Woking, Surrey, 1.11.40
P3119	151/501/FAA/RAE	To 3585M 2.3.43
P3120	302/303	Destroyed in air raid, Northolt, 6.10.40
P3121	79/59 OTU	Damaged 3.7.41; cv to Mk.II DR350 during repair
P3122	79	Flew into ground on firing range, Pembrey, 24.2.41
P3123	249/56	Missing from patrol over Calais, 5.2.41
P3124	238/229	Damaged by Bf 109s and abandoned near Stockbury, Kent, 15.10.40
P3140	501/43	Damaged by Bf 109; abandoned and crashed in sea off Felpham, Sussex, 19.7.40
P3141	501	Shot down by Bf 109s 4m NW of Dover, 24.8.40
P3142	310/43/55 OTU/ MSFU	Engine cut due to fuel starvation; undershot forced landing, hit bank and overturned, Courtauld Factory, near Flint, 23.10.41
P3143	310	Engine cut; abandoned on training flight and crashed in river near Ely Station, Cambs. 16.10.40
P3144	263/32	Damaged by Bf 109 near Dover; abandoned and crashed, Hougham, Kent, 19.7.40
P3145	263/1 RCAF/213/ 56 OTU/247/55 OTU	Crashed on approach, Usworth, 28.11.41
P3146	263/32/9 FTS/ 55 OTU	Collided with drogue cable during firing practice and crashed near Cummertrees, Dumfries, 5.5.43
P3147	111/32	Caught fire during combat and abandoned near Horsmonden, Kent, 18.8.40
P3148	310/SFP/55 OTU/ India	SOC 12.44
P3149	87/1449 Flt	To Admiralty 17.9.42
P3150	85	Shot down by Bf 109 and crashed, Kenley, 1.9.40
P3151	615/85/504/133/ 52 OTU/55 OTU/1/ 247/1622 Flt/667	SOC 18.5.44
P3152	151	To Admiralty 9.4.41
P3153	56	Damaged by return fire from Do 17s; crashlanded, 21.8.40; DBF
P3154	607/249/56	Damaged by enemy aircraft near Yeovil and abandoned, Alton Pancras, Somerset, 7.10.40
P3155	145	Shot down by return fire from Hs 126 10m S of Hastings, Sussex, 1.8.40
P3156	310/9 FTS/55 OTU/ 59 OTU/5 PAFU	SOC 3.1.45
P3157	310/AAEE	SOC 23.3.45
P3158	615	Destroyed in air raid, Kenley, 18.8.40
P3159	310	Shot down by Bf 109s, Wennington, near Romford, Essex, 31.8.40
P3160	615	Missing; presumed shot down in sea off Dover, 14.8.40
P3161	615/607/232/56 OTU/ 43/32/56 OTU	Flew into ground during practice attack 6m ENE of Forfar, Angus, 19.2.43
P3162	111/253/303/71/ 56 OTU	Crashed after collision with W9114, Terrington St.John, Lincs., 2.6.41
P3163	145	Missing from convoy escort off Isle of Wight, 8.8.40; presumed shot down by Bf 110
P3164	145/247/52 OTU/ 59 OTU/5 PAFU	Taxied into flare, Chetwynd, 27.8.44 and DBR
P3165	245	To Admiralty 30.3.42
P3166	85	Shot down by Bf 110 over Tunbridge Wells; abandoned and crashed, Goudhurst, Kent, 31.8.40
P3167	145	Shot down by Bf 109 5m S of Bembridge, Isle of Wight, 27.10.40
P3168	17/260/253	To Admiralty 15.2.42
P3169	1/9 FTS/71 OTU	SOC 26.9.44
P3170	1/79/1/59 OTU	Crashed in sea near Doone Bay, Kirkcudbright, 21.6.42
P3171	32	Damaged by Bf 109s near Dover, 14.8.40; SOC on return
P3172	1	Damaged by Bf 110 and crashlanded, Sandown Golf Course, Isle of Wight, 11.8.40; DBF
P3173	1	Hit by AA fire over Portsmouth; abandoned and crashed, Chidham, Sussex, 16.8.40
P3174	213	Shot down by Bf 109s near Pluckley, Kent, 17.10.40
P3175	257	Shot down by Bf 110, Walton-on-the-Naze, Essex, 31.8.40
P3176	238/17/52 OTU/ 55 OTU	Bellylanded while lost and hit tree, Garstang, Lancs., 4.1.43
P3177	238	Shot down by Bf 109 over Portland, Dorset, 13.8.40

P3178	238/9 FTS/5 FTS/ 286/59 OTU/5 PAFU	SOC 3.1.45
P3179	43	Shot down by Bf 109, Hove, Sussex, 30.8.40
P3200	87/213	Shot down by Bf 109s off Portland, 25.8.40
P3201	46	Shot down near Sheerness, 8.9.40; believed crashed near Maidstone
P3202	43	Damaged by enemy aircraft and abandoned; crashed, Bosham, Sussex, 26.8.40
P3203	79	Damaged by return fire from He 111 and abandoned over Irish Sea, 29.9.40
P3204	238/73	Shot down by fighters near Burnham, Essex, 5.9.40
P3205	32/302/56 OTU	Flew into ground in forced landing at night while lost, Wells-on-Sea, Norfolk, 22.5.41; DBF
P3206	302/151/504/303/ MSFU/2 TAF CF	SOC 17.11.44
P3207	242/55 OTU	Bellylanded at Usworth, 11.4.41; cv to Mk.II DG631
P3208	238/501	Shot down by Bf 109, Sturry, Kent, 18.8.40
P3209	17/73/312/56 OTU	Engine cut on take-off; bellylanded ½m E of Sutton Bridge, 21.11.41
P3210	56 OTU	Flew into sea on approach in bad weather 2m off Donna Nook, 19.6.41
P3211	79/9 FTS/55 OTU/ 74 OTU	SOC 1.3.44
P3212	229/317/11 Gp AAC Flt/116	Flew into ground with jammed controls at Greenford, Middlesex, 14.2.42
P3213	253	Damaged by Bf 109 over Dungeness and abandoned, 30.8.40
P3214	43/238/59 OTU	Crashed 15.9.41; NFD
P3215	87	Damaged by Bf 109s near Portland and crashlanded, Abbotsbury, Dorset, 15.8.40
P3216	43	Damaged by return fire from Ju 87 and crashlanded, Selsey, Sussex, 16.8.40; repaired and cv to Mk.II BV174
P3217	302/79/303/8 FTS	Engine cut; undershot forced landing and hit fence; undercarriage torn off, Bucksburn, Aberdeen, 2.1.42
P3218	242/52 OTU/ 59 OTU/5 PAFU	SOC 23.10.44
P3219	238/5 FTS	Engine cut; hit tree in forced landing, Cheswardine, Cheshire, 14.6.41; DBF
P3220	43	Shot down by return fire from He 111s near West Wittering, Sussex, 26.8.40
P3221	145/1 RCAF/56 OTU	Crashed 15.5.41; NFD
P3222	238	Shot down by Bf 109 off Weymouth, Dorset, 11.8.40
P3223	238	Cv to Mk.II DG614 3.41
P3224	73	Shot down by fighters, North Fambridge, Essex, 5.9.40
P3225	87/1 RCAF/213/ 56 OTU	SOC 29.12.41
P3226	73	Shot down by BF 109s over Thames Estuary, 23.9.40
P3227	229/501/79/317/ 55 OTU	Caught fire in air and crashed attempting to forceland ½m W of Kirtlebridge, Dumfries, 15.6.42
P3228	601/59 OTU	Engine cut; crashlanded 1m N of Kingstown, Carlisle, 27.11.41
P3229	1/59 OTU	To Admiralty 31.3.42
P3230	601/64/59 OTU	Engine cut; bellylanded and slid into sea, Ruthwell, Dumfries, 20.8.41
P3231	615	Missing from ground attack mission to Blankenberge, 15.2.41; believed shot down by Bf 109s near Vlissingen
P3232	601	Damaged by enemy aircraft near Winchester and abandoned, Durley, Hants., 15.8.40
P3233	-	To SAAF 20.8.40
P3234	73	Shot down by Bf 109s near Billericay, Essex, 7.9.40
P3250	- 71 OTU	To SAAF 10.40; retd to RAF; Overshot landing and undercarriage collapsed, Ismailia, 29.6.43
P3251	-	To SAAF 20.8.40
P3252	-	To SAAF 10.40 as 294
P3253	-	To SAAF 10.40 as 289
P3254	-	To SAAF 10.40 and used by 2 SAAF and 1564 Flt
P3255	3/Sumburgh/17/257/ 59 OTU	Stalled in bad weather and spun into ground in circuit, Cark, 21.9.42
P3256	3/17/55 OTU	Engine cut; bellylanded 2m SW of Morpeth, Northumberland, 14.8.41; cv to Mk.II DR365 during repair
P3257	-	To SAAF 10.40 as 291
P3258	-	To SAAF 20.8.40
P3259	-	To SAAF 20.8.40
P3260	3	Flew into ground during slow roll at low level near Castletown, 19.10.40
P3261	3/5 FTS	Crashed 1.8.41; NFD
P3262	-	To SAAF 10.40 as 293
P3263	501/4 FPP/ SFP	Engine caught fire on take-off; lost height and crashed, Kemble, 17.4.41
P3264	87/238/79	Engine cut; ditched 5m S of Pembrey, 27.4.41
P3265	Rotol/229/145/ 32/87/17/55 OTU/ 182/198	SOC 27.3.45
P3266	242	Shot down in sea by flak off Boulogne, 24.5.40
P3267	43/213	Dived into ground in snow storm, Risby Park, 3½m SSW of Beverley, Yorks., 31.12.40; presumed loss of control
P3268	242/7 OTU/6 OTU/310/ 312/9 FTS/55 OTU	SOC 15.1.45
P3269	Mkrs	Merlin trials; to 3388M 12.10.42
P3270	501	SOC 18.8.40 as missing in France
P3271	242/4 FPP	Spun into ground after shooting down Ju 88 near Aston Down, 25.7.40
P3272	242	Shot down in sea by flak off Boulogne, 24.5.40
P3273	151/112 RCAF/402/ 9 FTS/32/MSFU/India	To GI airframe 4.10.44
P3274	73	Missing from patrol, 24.5.40
P3275	151	Hit by return fire from Do 17 off Orfordness, Suffolk, and ditched, 12.7.40
P3276	1	Damaged by Bf 109s and crashed near Tonbridge, Kent, 1.9.40

P3277	CFF	Lost in France 5.40
P3278	CFF	Lost in France 5.40
P3279	4 FPP	Taxied into bomb crater, Reims/ Champagne, 14.5.40; abandoned
———		
P3300	CFF	Lost in France 5.40
P3301	151	To Admiralty 4.41
P3302	151	Shot down by Bf 109s off North Foreland, Kent, 12.8.40
P3303	151	Shot down off Dunkirk by Bf 109s, 29.5.40
P3304	151	Shot down by Bf 109s off Ramsgate, Kent, 12.8.40
P3305	151/607	Stalled and crashed during dummy attack 2½m NE of Grangemouth, 15.11.40
P3306	151	Collided with V7432 in formation and abandoned near Waddington; 24.9.40
P3307	151/263/258/615/ 302/56 OTU	Engine cut; bellylanded 2m NE of Sutton Bridge, 14.8.41; cv to Mk.II DR364 during repair
P3308	605/312/55 OTU	Engine cut; undershot bellylanding and hit bank, Horden, Co.Durham, 30.4.41
P3309	151/46/121/253/ 56/56 OTU/2 TEU	SOC 17.7.44
P3310	151	Damaged by return fire from Do 17s and abandoned off Christchurch, Hants., 14.8.40
P3311	56	Ditched on patrol off Dunkerque, 27.5.40
P3312	151	Damaged by return fire from Ju 88 and abandoned near Shoeburyness, Essex, 31.8.40
P3313	151	Hit by fire from He 111 off Cherbourg and abandoned 18.6.40
P3314	145/263/1 RCAF/ 213/56 OTU	Destroyed in air raid, Sutton Bridge, 12.5.41
P3315	151	Shot down by flak, Amiens, 8.6.40
P3316	151	Hit ground during slow roll at low altitude, North Weald, 24.7.40
P3317	87/1449 Flt	SOC 11.6.42
P3318	3/1/111/607/ 17/331/55 OTU	Flew into high ground in bad weather 1m E of Waskerley Park Reservoir, Co.Durham, 11.11.41
P3319	151	Collided with P3323 over Strait of Dover and crashed, 25.5.40
P3320	151/9 FTS	To Admiralty 30.10.41
P3321	151	Abandoned off Dunkirk, 29.5.40
P3322	151	Shot down by Bf 109 off Calais, 28.6.40
P3323	151	Collided with P3319 over Strait of Dover and crashed, 25.5.40
P3324	151	Missing from attack on He 111s over Channel N of Charbourg, 18.6.40
———		
P3345	87/55 OTU	To 4861M
P3346	Tangmere	Lost in France 6.40
P3347	501	Believed abandoned in Jersey, 20.6.40
P3348	610/213	Missing from patrol off Portland, Dorset, 13.8.40
P3349	501/238	Engine cut; bellylanded, Picket Piece, 3m NE of Andover, Hants., 28.11.40; DBF
P3350	610/213	SOC 16.9.40; NFD
P3351	73/32/71/55 OTU	Cv to Mk.II DR393 1.42
P3352	Tangmere	Presumed lost in France 6.40
P3353	32	Shot down by Bf 109s near Le Tréport, 8.6.40
P3354	213	Missing 28.5.40
P3355	56	Missing, presumed shot down by Bf 110s near Gravelines, 27.5.40
P3356	56	SOC 21.9.40
P3357	253/43	Engine cut; hit ditch in forced landing, Chirnside, Berwick, 31.10.40; to 3254M 4.41
P3358	601	Damaged by return fire from Ju 87 and landed on fire, Tangmere, 16.8.40; DBR
P3359	253	Control lost in rainstorm; crashed at Irby-on-Humber, Lincs., 10.7.40
P3360	17	Missing, pres. shot down by Bf 109 near Abbeville, 6.6.40
P3361	213	Missing from patrol over Dunkerque, 31.5.40
P3362	213/17/601/MSFU/ 59 OTU/41 OTU	SOC 18.5.44
P3363	601	Shot down by Bf 109s, Brenchley, Kent, 6.9.40
P3364	CFF	Presumed lost in France 6.40
P3380	615/87/56 OTU/ 55 OTU/3 TEU	Hit by AG278 while parked, Annan, 20.6.44; DBR
P3381	145	Shot down by Bf 109 S of Isle of Wight, 8.8.40
P3382	601	Damaged by Bf 109s and abandoned near Sutton Valence, Kent, 6.9.40
P3383	601/303/253	Flew into ground 2m E of Warbister, Rousay, Orkneys, 12.6.41; cause not known
P3384	56	Hit by return fire from Bf 110 and crashlanded, Meopham, Kent, 2.9.40; to 5 S of TT as serviceable aircraft; to 3228M 18.7.42
P3385	245/605/59 OTU/ 55 OTU/607/55 OTU/ 328/32/MSFU	Flew into hill in cloud, Blaenau Ffestiniog, Caernarvon, 9.8.42
P3386	43/1 FPP	Hit HT cable in bad visibility and overturned, Abbotsley, Hunts., 16.3.41; DBF
P3387	Tangmere/87	Hit by return fire from Ju 88 and crashed in sea off Selsey Bill, 13.8.40
P3388	Tangmere	SOC 25.12.40
P3389	605/55 OTU	Engine cut on approach; crashlanded, Usworth, 29.8.41
P3390	Tangmere	Presumed lost in France 5.40
P3391	145	Shot down S of Isle of Wight, 12.8.40
P3392	242	Shot down by Bf 110s while escorting Blenheims near Cambrai, 23.5.40
P3393	601/8 FTS/84 Gp CF	SOC 26.9.44 for spares
P3394	87/MSFU/59 OTU	Engine cut; abandoned 3m off Dunstanburgh, Northumberland, 8.9.43
P3395	1/55 OTU/5 FTS	Bellylanded in error and hit gun position, Ternhill, 24.3.42
P3396	501/1/59 OTU/7 PAFU	SOC 16.11.44
P3397	501/52 OTU/56 OTU/ 2 TEU	SOC 17.6.44 as spares
P3398	73/85	To Admiralty 4.41
P3399	6 OTU/111/308	Hit balloon cable and dived into ground, Whitley, Coventry, 16.10.40
P3400	145	Damaged by Bf 109 and ditched off Selsey, Sussex, 11.7.40

Serial	Units	Fate
P3401	79	Damaged by Bf 109s and ditched off Rye, Sussex, 27.6.40
P3402	85/601	Hit car on approach and crash-landed, Exeter, 25.11.40; cv to Mk.II BV160 during repair
P3403	Tangmere	Presumed lost in France 6.40
P3404	87	Collided with another Hurricane and crashed near Exeter, 24.10.40; DBF
P3405	17	SOC 26.9.40
P3406	1/59 OTU	Collided with V6954 and abandoned 2m E of Cummertrees, Dumfries, 13.5.42
P3407	501	Lost in France; believed shot down 30m NE of Betheniville
P3408	85/306/257/55 OTU/ 9 FTS/9 PAFU/247/32/ 56 OTU/1 TEU/2 TEU	SOC 17.7.44
P3409	85	Collided with L1889 while taxying, Martlesham Heath, 13.8.40; DBR
P3410	3/17	To 2749M 15.10.41
P3411	3/232/5 FTS/59 OTU	Dived into ground our of cloud 2m NE of Acklington, 14.1.43
P3412	253	Cv to Mk.II DG613 3.41
P3413	3/232/238/607/ 17/55 OTU	Engine cut; bellylanded, Castletown, Co. Durham, 11.12.41
P3414	3/504	Shot down off Weymouth, Dorset, 30.9.40; NFD
P3415	3/504/151/8 FTS	Lost at sea en route to Middle East, 11.42
P3416	3/5 OTU/55 OTU/ 9 FTS/9 PAFU	To Irish Air Corps 12.43 as 108
P3417	17/501	Shot down by Bf 109s, Ulcombe, Kent, 28.9.40
P3418	-	To 1 RSU 18.5.40; presumed lost in France 5.40
P3419	213	Shot down off Dunkerque, 31.5.40
P3420	87	Abandoned in spin after control lost at night, Stockwood, Bristol, 29.12.40
P3421	501/249/56	Shot down by Bf 109s and crashed, Worgret, 1m W of Wareham, Dorset, 10.10.40
P3422	229	Crashed 8.2.41; DBF; NFD
P3423	43/605	Shot down by Bf 109s 5m SW of Dunkerque, 27.5.40
P3424	213	Missing from patrol over Dunkerque, 31.5.40
P3425	607/43/607	Engine cut; ditched 5m E of Dunbar, E.Lothian, 11.4.41
P3426	Tangmere	Presumed lost in France 5.40
P3427	Tangmere	Presumed lost in France
P3428	245	Hit cables low flying and crashed, Ballymena, Antrim, 26.6.41; DBF
P3429	504/3/501/46	Abandoned after elevator controls failed and crashed in AM Works Dept, Ashford, Kent, 30.11.40
P3448		Presumed lost in France 5.40
P3449	232/55 OTU	Damaged 12.8.41; cv to Mk.II DR362 during repair
P3450	501	SOC 21.6.40 as lost in France
P3451		Presumed lost in France 5.40
P3452	CFF/5 OTU/308/ 79/SF Sydenham/1 FPP	Ditched on ferry flight, Sydenham - Abingdon, in Red Wharf Bay, Anglesey, 26.1.42
P3453	501	Lost in France 5.40
P3454	3/17/59 OTU	Collided with V7136 and crashed 2m W of Belford, Northumberland, 27.4.43
P3455		Lost in France 5.40
P3456	73/229/245/ 9 FTS/ECFS	3629M NTU; SOC 7.3.45
P3457	253	Abandoned in spin after control lost at night 5m E of Prestwick, 7.8.40
P3458	607/111/3 FPP/ 111/5 OTU/55 OTU/ 56 OTU	Stalled and spun into ground inverted, Broomknow Farm, Berwickshire, 7.6.43
P3459	229/111/85/71	Engine cut; crashlanded near Kirton-in-Lindsey, Lincs., 1.1.41
P3460	601/32/71/55 OTU	To Admiralty 28.8.41
P3461	32/79	Shot down on patrol by own aircraft, 8.7.40
P3462	238/43/55 OTU/ 59 OTU/5 PAFU	SOC 23.9.44
P3463	229/249/601/121/ 59 OTU	Flew into hill in bad visibility 4m SW of Langholm, Dumfries, 6.2.42
P3464	43	Damaged by Bf 110 and abandoned, 9.7.40; DBF
P3465	87	To 3213M 18.7.42
P3466	43/59 OTU/253/ MSFU/RAE	SOC 16.11.44
P3467	85/242/55 OTU/ MSFU	Ditched after operational launch, 1.6.42
P3468	43	Shot down by fighters 10m S of Isle of Wight, 8.8.40
P3469	85/274	Missing, presumed shot down by Bf 109s during attack on Maleme, Crete, 25.5.41
P3470	73/1/111	Flew into hills on ferry flight in bad visibility 10m NW of Edzell, 5.12.40
P3471	1	Hit by return fire from He 111s and crashlanded near Brighton, 19.7.40
P3472	17	Missing, pres. shot down by Bf 109s near Abbeville, 6.6.40
P3473	56	Damaged by Bf 109s and crashlanded, Courtsend, near Foulness, Essex, 26.8.40
P3474	213	SOC 21.11.40
P3475	229/9 FTS/RAFC/ 6 FTS/56 OTU/ 253/59 OTU	Collided with V7173 and crashed Elwick, Northumberland, 14.7.43
P3476	17	Shot down by fire from Ju 88 over Dunkirk, 1.6.40
P3477	17	Shot down by Bf 109 near Dunkerque, 3.6.40
P3478	56	Hit by Belgian AA on patrol and abandoned, 27.5.40
P3479	56	Damaged during attack on Bf 110 and crashed near Faversham, Kent, 13.8.40
P3480	213	SOC 28.6.40
P3481	32	Damaged by Bf 109s and crashed near Lyminge, Kent, 24.8.40
P3482	17	Engine caught fire; crashed in wood near Elsenham, Essex, 15.7.40; DBF
P3483	605/17	Missing, believed shot down by Bf 109s near Douai, 26.5.40
P3484	601	Shot down near Abbeville, 7.6.40
P3485	242/Speke/ Northolt/87	Missing on ground-attack mission outside Dieppe, 19.8.42
P3486	601	Missing over Dunkerque, 27.5.40
P3487	615	Destroyed in air raid, Kenley, 18.8.40
P3488	229/253	Destroyed in air raid, Kenley, 18.8.40

P3489	229/253/229	Missing while detached to France, 29.5.40
P3490	601	Shot down near Abbeville, 7.6.40
P3491	501	SOC 21.6.40 as lost in France
P3492	229/253/229	Missing while detached to France, 31.5.40
P3515	111/242/257/ 56 OTU/151 OTU	Flew into ground on low flying exercise near Campbellpur, NWFD, 13.4.44
P3516	145/501	Shot down near Ashford, Kent, 6.9.40; believed crashed near Kempston Manor, Hothfield
P3517	145	Crashlanded in bad visibility, Wickham, Hants., 15.7.40; to 2121M 7.40
P3518	32/257	Shot down by Bf 109 over Ingatestone; abandoned and crashed, Galleywood, Essex, 3.9.40
P3519	87	Stalled off turn at low altitude and dived into ground near Yeadon, 1.6.40; DBF
P3520	87	Lost in France 5.40
P3521	145	Engine cut and caught fire after landing, Tangmere, 8.12.40; cv to Mk.II BV167 during repair
P3522	32/213	Flew into hill in cloud, Calbergh Moor, Yorks., 10.1.41
P3523	145	Missing, believed shot down by Bf 110s while attacking Ju 88s near Dunkerque, 27.5.40
P3524	238/111/59 OTU/ 318/59 OTU/7 PAFU	SOC 4.10.44
P3525	87/56/46	Stalled off turn and spun into ground on patrol near Stapleford, Essex, 11.9.40; DBF
P3526	Tangmere	Lost in France 5.40
P3527	6 OTU/43/87/ 55 OTU	Engine cut; bellylanded near Durham, 8.8.41
P3528	6 OTU	Engine cut; stalled on approach to forced landing, Needham Hall, Wisbech, Cambs., 15.8.40; DBF
P3529	238/151	Missing from patrol over Amiens, 7.6.40
P3530	238/111/247	To Admiralty 28.8.41
P3531	43	Shot down by Bf 109s and abandoned off Selsey Bill, 19.7.40
P3532	CFF	Lost in France 5.40
P3533	CFF/46	Lost in France 5.40
P3534	32/504/1 RCAF	Damaged by return fire from He 111s over Tunbridge Wells; abandoned and crashed, Lakestreet Manor, Mayfield, Sussex, 11.9.40
P3535	CFF	Lost in France 5.40
P3536	17	Shot down on patrol by AA fire, Chatham, and abandoned, Rochester, Kent, 13.10.40
P3537	253	Engine cut; crashlanded, Gains Hill, Kent, 17.10.40
P3538	253/302	Shot down by Bf 109 on patrol, Mayfield, Sussex, 8.11.40
P3539	17/232	Engine cut; overturned in forced landing near Elgin, Moray, 25.4.41; cv to Mk.II DG634 during repair
P3540	CFF	Abandoned at Merville and captured, 5.40
P3541	CFF	Lost in France 5.40
P3542	501	SOC 21.6.40 due to enemy action
P3543	CFF	Missing 1.6.40
P3544	501/303/96/ 55 OTU/MSFU	To 3583M 2.3.43
P3545	145	Shot down by Bf 110 over convoy off St.Catherines Point, Isle of Wight, 8.8.40
P3546	CFF	To 1 RSU 10.5.40 and presumed abandoned
P3547	56	Hit by return fire from Do 17 over Manston and crashlanded near Whitstable, Kent, 16.8.40; DBF
P3548	229/111	Ran out of fuel after intercepting Do 17s and crashed near Boyton, 6m E of Woodbridge, Suffolk, 11.8.40
P3549	245/52 OTU/ 59 OTU/55 OTU	Control lost; spun into ground 3m S of Lochmaben, Dumfries, 26.3.43
P3550	32	Shot down near Ypres, 23.5.40
P3551	253/303/71/ 55 OTU	Engine cut; bellylanded on approach, Usworth, 1.6.41; cv to Mk.II DR343 during repair
P3552	253	Missing on patrol near Douai, 21.5.40
P3553	229	Shot down off Dunkerque, 31.5.40
P3554	32/56/213/607	Damaged by Bf 109s near Swanage and abandoned, Aldingbourne, Dorset, 5.10.40
P3574	607	Shot down by Bf 109s while attacking Do 17s over Mayfield, Goudhurst, Kent, 9.9.40
P3575	43/605	Damaged by return fire from He 111s near Arras; forcelanded and burnt, 22.5.40
P3576	234/249	Damaged by Bf 110s near Southampton and abandoned, 16.8.40
P3577	245/303	Shot down by Bf 109s over Thames Estuary, 15.9.40
P3578	257	NFT 1.8.40
P3579	56/249	Shot down by Bf 109 near Dover, 10.1.41
P3580	605/247	Spun into ground at night on approach ½m NE of Roborough, 3.3.41
P3581	605	Shot down by Bf 109s 5m SW of Dunkerque, 27.5.40
P3582	605/501	Damaged by return fire from Ju 87s near Folkestone and abandoned, 15.8.40
P3583	605/312	Engine cut; bellylanded, Cregneish, Isle of Man, 3.5.41; DBR
P3584	85	Stalled off turn during practice dogfight and spun into ground 1m W of Debden, 31.5.40
P3585	605/213/303/ 253/TFU/RAE	SOC 9.2.45
P3586	CFF	Lost in France 5.40
P3587	56	Damaged during combat and crashlanded, Hawkinge, 13.8.40
P3588	605/229/9 FTS	SOC 14.4.42 for spares; to 2850M
P3589	CFF	Damaged 11.6.40 and presumed abandoned
P3590	CFF	Lost in France 6.40
P3591	79	Shot down by Bf 109s over Channel, 27.6.40
P3592	79	To GI airframe 11.3.41; to 3214M 18.7.42
P3593	87	Ran out of fuel on night patrol and ditched off Torquay, Devon, 11.4.41

P3594	87/151/56/249	Caught fire while attacking He 111 over Channel and abandoned near Canterbury, Kent, 7.9.40
P3595	6 OTU/111	Shot down by Bf 109s while attacking Do 17s near Margate, Kent, 11.8.40
P3596	87	Dived into ground soon after night take-off, Hullavington, 25.7.40; DBF
P3597	46/247/MSFU/ 59 OTU	To 5044M; SOC 16.12.46
P3598	87/308/Northolt/ 56 OTU/2 TEU	SOC 21.11.44
P3599	238	Shot down by fighters off Poole, Dorset, 1.10.40
P3600	111/5 FTS/71 OTU	Spun into ground 20m S of Carthago, 9.4.43
P3601	257	Damaged during attack on Ju 88 off Selsey Bill, 15.8.40; SOC 11.10.40
P3602	245/59 OTU/55 OTU	Bellylanded while lost in bad weather, Wear Head, Co. Durham, 27.9.41; DBF
P3603	229/9 FTS	Hit ground recovering from spin on approach, Babdown Farm, 24.3.41
P3604	501	Lost in France 6.40
P3605	607/501/229/ 9 FTS/56 OTU/ 1 TEU/2 TEU	SOC 1.6.44
P3606	263/607/55 OTU	Engine cut; bellylanded 4m W W of Seaham Harbour, Co. Durham, 16.7.41
P3607	3/5 FTS	Took off in coarse pitch from Chetwynd; stalled and crashed, Culeston Common, 26.11.41
P3608	504/3/232	Collided with W9204 and crashed, Grantown-on-Spey, Moray, 20.3.41
P3609	245/79/253/79/ 59 OTU/55 OTU	Stalled and spun into ground on approach, Usworth, 26.10.41
P3610	253	Engine cut; crashed in forced landing in wood, Nonington, Kent, 3.9.40
P3611	238	Shot down by Bf 109s over Shaftesbury and abandoned near Mere, Wilts., 5.10.40
P3612	56/312	Bounced on take-off, swung and crashed, Penrhos, 22.2.41
P3613	59 OTU/55 OTU/ 1 AAS/5 FTS	To 3591M 2.3.43
P3614	504/133/59 OTU	Engine cut; undershot landing and hit fence, Milfield, 1.2.43
P3615	234/249	Damaged by Bf 109s and abandoned, Linton, Kent, 25.10.40
P3616	234/249	Shot down by fighters over Southampton, 16.8.40
P3617	238	Shot down on convoy escort off Isle of Wight, 8.8.40
P3618	238	Engine cut; crashlanded, Stockbridge, Hants., 14.11.40
P3619	6 OTU/56 OTU	SOC 1.8.44
P3620	257/MSFU/59 OTU	Collided with P3104 during dummy attack and crashed, Fenwick, Northumberland, 7.8.42
P3621	6 OTU/310/402/289	SOC 15.1.45
P3622	257	Damaged by Bf 109s over Channel and crashlanded, Hawkinge, 28.7.40; DBR
P3623	257/17/253/ 59 OTU	Dived into ground, Westlington, Bucks., 21.9.41; presumed due to anoxia
P3640	238/79/307/Northolt/ 56 OTU/2 TEU	SOC 30.10.44
P3641	257/213/607/121/ 55 OTU/TFU/India	
P3642	257	Forcelanded on transit flight to Hendon, 16.9.40; cv to Mk.II BV166 during repair
P3643	257	Shot down over Detling, 23.9.40
P3644	6 OTU/310/255/ 55 OTU	Engine cut; bellylanded and hit fence near Stagshow, Northumberland, 24.10.41
P3645	303	DBR in taxying accident, Northolt, 9.8.40
P3646	501	Damaged by Bf 109s near Dover and abandoned, Lydden, Kent, 31.7.40
P3647	73/1 RCAF	Shot down by Bf 110s, Hever, Kent, 27.9.40
P3648	-	SOC 13.2.41
P3649	85/32	SOC 22.11.40
P3650	605/151/71/ 56 OTU/2 TEU	SOC 17.7.44
P3651	501	SOC 15.8.40; NFT after serving with 501 Sqn in 5.40
P3652	111	Damaged by Bf 110s over Thorney Island and crashlanded, Hawkinge, 15.8.40
P3653	1/501	Hit balloon cable and spun into ground, Patchway, Bristol 21.2.41
P3654	501/5 OTU/ 55 OTU/307	To Admiralty 6.9.42
P3655	234/56	Damaged by Bf 109s off Bournemouth and crashed, 30.9.40
P3656	234/56/504/133/ 56 OTU/1449 Flt	Forcelanded on training flight, St.Mary's, 8.3.43; to 4012M 5.7.43
P3657	245	Dived into Lough Neagh, Ulster, 21.10.40; cause not known
P3658	263/258/Northolt/ Hatfield/55 OTU	Abandoned after control lost, during aerobatics, Wark-on-Tyne, Northumberland, 22.3.42
P3659	79/9 FTS	Stalled on approach and undercarriage collapsed, Castle Combe, 15.6.41; DBR
P3660	249/56	Spun into ground during practice dogfight 1m NW of High Post, Wilts., 15.9.40
P3661	234/79	Control lost in searchlight beam; crashed in sea 3½m off Linney Head, Pembs., 4.4.41
P3662	257	Shot down by enemy aircraft near Portsmouth, 12.8.40; details not known
P3663	111/303/96/8 FTS	Spun into sea on approach, Montrose, 9.9.41
P3664	3/232/71/55 OTU	Flew into high ground in snowstorm, Sunniside, Whickham, Co. Durham, 10.2.42
P3665	607/43/55 OTU	Dived into ground, Low Pittington, Co. Durham, 15.9.41; cause not known
P3666	6 OTU	Undercarriage jammed; bellylanded at Sutton Bridge, 6.6.40
P3667	607/56/249	To Admiralty 5.6.42
P3668	607/5 FTS	Hit P3055 during dummy attack and crashed near Newport, Salop., 9.1.42
P3669	6 OTU/111	Taxied into gun position and tipped up; abandoned, Dreux, 8.6.40

P3670	1 RCAF/213/232	Cv to Mk.II DG646 5.41
P3671	6 OTU/111	Collided with Do 17 off Folkestone and lost wing; abandoned, 10.7.40
P3672	1 RCAF/501/253/ 615/402/52 OTU	Engine cut; undershot belly-landing 10m E of Debden, 1.7.41
P3673	17	Shot down by Bf 109s, Ingrave, Essex, 3.9.40
P3674	245	Control lost during exercise; stalled at low altitude and crashed, Newton Stewart, Co. Tyrone, 6.8.41
P3675	607/601/59 OTU	To Admiralty 9.9.42
P3676	6 OTU/111/79	Damaged by Bf 110s over Biggin Hill and crashed, Surbiton, Surrey, 4.9.40
P3677	32/605	Shot down by Bf 109 near Brasted, Kent, 7.10.40
P3678	253	Damaged by Bf 109 and crash-landed in flames, Falmer, Sussex, 1.12.40
P3679	32/504/133/ 52 OTU/56 OTU	Hit by machine gun fire in error during camera-gun practice and abandoned near Arbroath, Angus, 1.7.42
P3680	Tangmere	Lost in France 6.40
P3681	601	Damaged by return fire from He 111 and caught fire; abandoned and crashed, Cranmore, Isle of Wight, 11.7.40
P3682	Tangmere	Lost in France 6.40
P3683	242	Burnt on evacuation, Nantes, 18.6.40
P3684	242/1	Hit balloon cable at night and abandoned, Finsbury Park, London, 19.8.40
P3700	238/303	Damaged by Bf 109 over Beachy Head and abandoned, Poynings, Kent, 9.9.40
P3701	17/111	To Admiralty 9.1.42; became 4576M 25.2.44
P3702	238/249/56/ 52 OTU/55 OTU	Crashed 7.8.41; NFD
P3703	238	Stalled avoiding hill while emerging from cloud and dived into ground, West Tedworth, Wilts., 5.7.40
P3704	257/145	Caught fire and crashed 1m S of Chichester, Sussex, 30.11.40
P3705	257/55 OTU/ 56 OTU/55 OTU	SOC 3.1.45
P3706	257/46	To Admiralty 28.12.41
P3707	257/310/ME	SOC 1.4.44
P3708	257	Shot down by Bf 110; abandoned and crashed, Foulness, Essex, 18.8.40
P3709	257/601	Collided with V6917 off Exmouth, Devon, 25.10.40
P3710	229/FAA/MSFU	Swung on landing and under-carriage collapsed, Gibraltar, 13.4.43
P3711	609/607/55 OTU	SOC 27.5.44
P3712	229/96/55 OTU/ 8 FTS	Engine cut; hit pole attempting to forceland, Main Road, Lunan Bay, Angus, 3.11.41
P3713	253/79/316/ 56 OTU/59 OTU	SOC 23.5.44
P3714	253/501/56 OTU	Engine cut on take-off; belly-landed 1m N of Sutton Bridge, 28.5.41; cv to Mk.II DR341 during repair
P3715	238/242/247/8 FTS/ 17 PAFU/59 OTU	Dived into ground near Belford, Northumberland, 29.6.43; cause not known
P3716	229/79/5 FTS/ 59 OTU/5 PAFU	SOC 3.1.45
P3717	238/253/257/43/ 55 OTU/8 FTS	Undercarriage collapsed in heavy landing, Montrose, 25.6.41; cv to Mk.II DR348 during repair
P3718	55 OTU	Hit by P2795 while parked, Usworth, 20.10.41
P3719	242/5 OTU/111	To Admiralty 5.41
P3720	3 RAAF/274/229	Shipped to Iran as No.252
P3721	274/Air Ftg School/1 METS	SOC 31.3.43
P3722	274/3 RAAF/274	Destroyed on evacuation, El Adem, 22.4.41
P3723	274/71 OTU	SOC 1.3.44
P3724	33	Shot down by CR 42 near Mersa Matruh, 31.10.40
P3725	33/3 RAAF/274/71 OTU/ 74 OTU/ADU	Engine cut on overshoot; spun into ground, Wadi Natrun, 27.1.42
P3726	33/3 RAAF/70 OTU	Ground-looped while taxying and undercarriage collapsed, Ismailia, 15.4.41; DBR
P3727	33/71 OTU	SOC 23.12.43
P3728	33	Crashlanded in Western Desert, 10.12.40; NFD
P3729	33/238/274	Shot down by Bf 109 on convoy escort, 15.7.41
P3730	418 Flt/261/ 73 OTU/Aden Def Flt	SOC 1.12.43
P3731	418 Flt/261/127	Shot down by D.520 on patrol over Deir-es-Zor, Syria, 3.7.41
P3732	Abbotsinch/ 418 Flt/33	SOC 30.5.41; pres. lost in Greece
P3733	418 Flt/261	Shot down by Bf 109s in sea off Malta, 12.2.41
P3734	33/274	Crashed 11.2.44
P3735	501/601	Caught fire after attacking Bf 109 and abandoned near Gravesend, 31.8.40
P3736	145/MSFU/FAA/ 59 OTU/5 PAFU	SOC 1.1.45
P3737	605	Damaged by Bf 109s and spun avoiding trees during forced landing, Marks Cross, Sussex, 26.10.40
P3738	Wick/232	Stalled on approach and wing hit ground, Castletown, 22.9.40; DBR
P3739	151/56 OTU	Dived into ground, Walpole St. Andrews, Norfolk, 9.3.42; cause not known
P3755	87	Hit tree in circuit at night 1½m ENE of Windrush LG, 19.12.40; DBR
P3756	46/607	Cv to Mk.II DG612
P3757	1 RCAF/43/9 FTS/ RAFC/6 FTS/USAAF Hendon/24	NFT 28.8.43
P3758	73	Damaged by own AA fire and abandoned 5m NW of Beverley, Yorks., 25.8.40
P3759	245/607/312	Overshot landing and hit pile of sand, Jurby, 16.6.41; cv to Mk.II DR349 during repair
P3760	17	Missing, presumed shot down by Bf 110s off Orfordness, Suffolk, 11.8.40
P3761	245/263/258/5 FTS	Engine cut; crashlanded on flarepath, Ternhill, 12.9.41; recat as DBR and SOC 29.12.41
P3762	245	Sent for overhaul 13.2.41 and SOC 12.6.41
P3763	33/3 RAAF	Destroyed on evacuation, El Adem, 22.4.41

Serial	Units	Fate
P3764	238	Shot down by Bf 109 off Isle of Wight, 13.8.40
P3765	33/3 RAAF/71 OTU	Engine cut; crashlanded, Moascar Camp, 26.6.41; DBR
P3766	238	Damaged by Bf 109 and abandoned 15m S of Swanage, Dorset, 20.7.40
P3767	238/263/501/213/ 1 RCAF/257/401	Crashed in forced landing 1m N of Digby, 2.5.41
P3768	4 FPP	Engine cut in circuit; stalled and crashed, Sealand, 14.8.40
P3769	7 OTU/5 OTU/ 55 OTU/1 AAS	SOC 19.7.45
P3770	3/504	Shot down by fighters 3m W of Dymchurch, Kent, 11.9.40
P3771	3/79/59 OTU/56 OTU	Hit HT cable on low flying exercise and crashed, Broom Brae Wood, Fife, 28.5.43
P3772	3/504/232/55 OTU	Flew into ground in cloud when lost, Lockton Low Moor, near Levisham, Yorks., 19.5.41
P3773	3/17	To Admiralty 25.11.41
P3774	3/504/56 OTU	Engine cut; bellylanded in field, Gedney Drove, near Holbeach, Lincs., 17.1.42; DBR
P3775	257/43/59 OTU/ 56 OTU/41 OTU	SOC 18.5.44
P3776	257/601/MSFU/318/ 59 OTU/63 OTU/ 3 TEU	SOC 18.5.44
P3777	79/247/56 OTU/ 55 OTU	SOC 14.12.44
P3778	17	Taken on unauthorised flight by non-pilot; crashed near Quendon, Newport, Essex, 27.6.40; DBF
P3779	242	Burnt on evacuation, Nantes, 18.6.40
P3780	17/501/151/213	Damaged by Bf 110 and abandoff Selsey Bill, Sussex, 11.9.40
P3781	43	Shot down by enemy aircraft 10m S of Isle of Wight, 8.8.40
P3782	1	Dived into ground, Chart Sutton, Kent, 3.9.40; cause not known
P3783	601	Missing from interception off Portland, Dorset, 11.8.40
P3784	43/249/56/52 OTU	To Admiralty 1.11.41
P3785	73/302/56 OTU	Caught fire in air and dived into ground, Holbeach, Lincs., 17.4.41
P3786	43	Shot down by Bf 109s near Ashford and abandoned, Warehorn, Kent, 2.9.40
P3787	56/151	Shot down in sea off Ramsgate, Kent, 30.6.40
P3788	17/112 RCAF/52 OTU/ 55 OTU/41 OTU	SOC 12.6.44
P3789	238/213	Missing from interception off Portland, Dorset, 11.8.40
P3802	238/253	Damaged by Bf 109 and crashlanded near Maidstone, Kent, 30.8.40
P3803	501	Missing, presumed shot down by Bf 109s near Ramsgate, Kent, 12.8.40
P3804	238/253	Shot down by Bf 109s, Stone, near Faversham, Kent, 14.9.40
P3805	238/MSFU/56 OTU	SOC 18.5.44
P3806	151	Damaged by Bf 109 and abandoned over Thames Estuary, 9.7.40
P3807	151/419 Flt/9 FTS	Engine cut on approach; bellylanded, Babdown Farm, 27.5.41; DBR
P3808	501	Shot down by Bf 109 over Dover, 26.7.40; may have been hit by own AA
P3809	79/43/56 OTU	Dived into ground, Friday Bridge, 6m S of Wisbech, Cambs., 13.12.41
P3810	79/312	To 3257M 18.7.42
P3811	AAEE/615	Forcelanded on Dungeness on return from escort mission, 10.2.41; cv to Mk.II DG644 5.41 during repair
P3812	302/306/52 OTU/ 56 OTU/59 OTU/ 7 PAFU	SOC 13.7.44
P3813	242/151	Abandoned out of fuel in bad weather on night patrol near Market Harborough, 16.1.41
P3814	242/303/253	To Admiralty 29.10.41; became 4559M 3.4.44
P3815	242/501	Shot down over Canterbury and crashed, Rayhams Farm, Whitstable, Kent, 18.8.40
P3816	501/46	Shot down by fighters over Chatham, Kent, Kent, 18.9.40
P3817	Takoradi	Swung on landing and ran into pipes, Lagos, 26.9.40
P3818	33/3 RAAF	Engine cut; crashlanded in desert 20m S of Gazala, 8.4.41; destroyed by Army as salvage impracticable
P3819	501/238	Shot down by fighters off Portland, Dorset, 11.8.40
P3820	501	Shot down by Bf 109 over Ashford and crashed, Bethersden, Kent, 17.9.40
P3821	33/274	Flew into ground during practice attack near Burg el Arab, 10.3.41
P3822	33/3 RAAF/274/451	SOC 21.3.42
P3823	238	Shot down by Bf 109s on convoy escort S of Isle of Wight, 8.8.40
P3824	33	Missing from reconnaissance near Sidi Barrani, 10.12.40
P3825	RAE/ADU	Crashed near Takoradi, 2.10.40
P3826	208	Destroyed on evacuation, El Adem, 22.4.41
P3827	605/422 Flt/1 AACU/ 1608 Flt/1616 Flt	SOC 18.12.44
P3828	605	Damaged by Bf 109s and abandoned, Lamberhurst, Kent, 28.9.40
P3829	7 OTU/607	To Admiralty 4.41; became 4561M 24.2.44
P3830	238	Damaged by Bf 110 and abandoned near Newport, Isle of Wight, 26.9.40
P3831	501/601/59 OTU	Abandoned after cowling came off 1½ m E of Gretna Green, Dumfries, 12.4.41
P3832	605	Shot down by Bf 109 off French coast, 24.9.40
P3833	238/96/SF Northolt/ 55 OTU/87/43/ 56 OTU/India	SOC 31.7.44
P3834	249	Hit by return fire from Ju 88 and crashed, Dallington, Sussex, 27.9.40
P3835	245/315/303	To 2694M 29.9.41
P3836	238	Shot down by Bf 109s over Solent, 28.9.40
P3854	7 OTU/85/257/ 56 OTU	Believed damaged in air raid, Sutton Bridge, 2.5.41; not repaired and SOC 2.8.41

P3855	249/56/52 OTU/ 55 OTU	Flew into hill while lost in bad weather 2m S of Langholm, Dumfries, 6.12.42
P3856	7 OTU/5 OTU/ 55 OTU	Engine cut; abandoned near Castletown, Co.Durham, 12.10.41
P3857	7 OTU/5 OTU/ME	SOC 29.3.45
P3858	1 RCAF	Shot down by Bf 109s; abandoned and crashed, Broomfield, Kent, 31.8.40
P3859	1 RCAF	Damaged by fighters over Thames Estuary and abandoned, 18.9.40
P3860	607	Collided with L1728; abandoned near Slindon, Sussex, 7.10.40
P3861	249/9 FTS/Northolt	SOC 5.3.45
P3862	249/56/52 OTU/1/ 55 OTU/41 OTU	SOC 30.5.44
P3863	73/247/56 OTU/286/ 1454 Flt/286/ 9 PAFU/41 OTU	SOC 12.6.44
P3864	242/RAE/242/73/ 85/52 OTU	Dived into ground near Bishops Stortford, Herts., 30.4.41; presumed due to anoxia
P3865	43/73	Shot down by Bf 109s, Teynham, Kent, 15.9.40
P3866	249/56/257	Shot down by enemy aircraft on night weather test 4m NE of Duxford, 5.5.41; DBF
P3867	302	Hit by Spitfire at dispersal, Westhampnett, 14.2.41; DBR
P3868	249/17/73/52 OTU/ 5 FTS/MSFU	Spun into ground, Holywell, Flint, 13.9.42
P3869	1 RCAF	Shot down by return fire from Do 17s; abandoned near Gravesend, 31.8.40
P3870	249/56	To Admiralty 4.41
P3871	151/79	Collided with another aircraft on patrol, 12.1.41
P3872	1 RCAF/302	Crashed in forced landing in bad visibility, Nutwood Farm, Thames Ditton, Surrey, 18.10.40
P3873	1 RCAF	Shot down by Bf 109 and abandoned, Smarden, Kent, 5.10.40
P3874	1 RCAF	Shot down by return fire from Do 215 over North Weald; crashed at Little Bardfield, Essex, 26.8.40
P3875	111	Shot down by Bf 109s over Thames Estuary, 2.9.40
P3876	1 RCAF	Shot down by Bf 109s over Tunbridge Wells, Kent, 15.9.40
P3877	79/302/52 OTU	To Admiralty 7.41
P3878	17	Damaged by Bf 109 and abandoned off Chatham, Kent, 24.9.40
P3879	32/56	Shot down by Bf 109s off Dover, 29.7.40
P3880	111/260/56 OTU/ 59 OTU	Flew into ground during low flying exercise and broke up, Micklethwaite, Yorks., 9.9.41
P3881	263/258/615/ 5 AOS/59 OTU	Crashed in forced landing near Silloth, 4.5.42; DBR
P3882	151	DBR 27.9.40; NFD
P3883	1 RCAF/56 OTU/ FAA/MSFU	Engine cut on met flight; ditched off Gibraltar, 19.11.42
P3884	601/71/56 OTU/ATA	To 4262M 10.43
P3885	601	Shot down off Portland, 11.8.40
P3886	601/1/59 OTU/ MSFU/253/India	SOC 28.9.44
P3887	310	Damaged by return fire from Do 17s and abandoned near Maldon, Essex, 26.8.40
P3888	310/312/56 OTU	Hit HT cables while low flying and crashed, Ladybank, Fife, 11.7.42
P3889	310	Collided with P3707 and crashed near Duxford, 29.10.40
P3890	257/303	Shot down by Bf 109s; abandoned and crashed, Selstead, Kent, 7.9.40
P3891	17/308	Crashed in forced landing while lost 2½m S of Halesowen, Birmingham, 10.11.40
P3892	17/303	Shot down by Bf 109s, Stowting, Kent, 5.10.40
P3893	257	Damaged by Bf 109 and abandoned, Bobbingworth, Essex, 29.10.40
P3894	17/52 OTU	Engine cut; hit tree on approach, Debden, 23.6.41
P3895	85	Rolled during low aerobatics and spun into ground, Castle Camps, 22.7.40
P3896	145	Damaged by Bf 109s and abandoned, Guestling, Sussex, 12.10.40
P3897	1	Control lost when dazzled by searchlight; abandoned in spin, Lacey Green, Bucks., 27.8.40
P3898	145/229/9 FTS/ 9 PAFU/56 OTU/ 7 PAFU	SOC 16.11.44
P3899	145/1 RCAF/96	Crashed in sea after night take-off, Squires Gate, 28.12.42
P3900	32/87/145/17/ 52 OTU/55 OTU	Missing over North Sea, 12.12.41; apparently tried to shoot down loose barrage balloon
P3901	615/303/253/ 55 OTU	Flew into Manwitch Fell, Cumberland, 28.4.43; believed iced up in cloud
P3902	249/56/52 OTU/232/ 59 OTU	Flew into high ground in bad visibility, Haggy Hill, near Langholm, Dumfries, 16.3.42
P3903	43	Damaged by Bf 109s near Ashford and crashlanded, Old Romney, Kent, 2.9.40
———		
P3920	238/1 RCAF	Shot down by Bf 109s on bomber escort to Abbeville, 5.2.41
P3921	253	Damaged by Bf 109s and abandoned near Woldingham, Surrey, 30.8.40
P3922	17/111	Missing, believed shot down by Bf 109 off Margate, Kent, 11.8.40
P3923	302/5 FTS	Undercarriage collapsed in forced landing while lost, Abbots Bromley LG, 8.8.41; DBR
P3924	302/245	To Admiralty 5.41
P3925	56/302	To Admiralty 5.41
P3926	145/316/FPP/ MSFU/55 OTU	SOC 18.5.44
P3927	302	Caught fire in air and hit hedge in forced landing, Wheel, near Beverley, Yorks., 17.8.40; DBR
P3928	232	Undercarriage raised during take-off on scramble, Elgin, 26.2.41; cv to Mk II DR363 during repair

P3929	607/SDF Christchurch/ TFU/1449 Flt/13 Gp CF/ 59 OTU/5 PAFU	SOC 3.1.45
P3930	302	Both crashed in forced landings
P3931	302	in bad visibility, Kempton Park, Middx., 18.10.40
P3932	302/306/256/315/303	Damaged 9.8.41; SOC 22.12.41
P3933	607/302	Crashed near Leconfield, 24.8.40
P3934	302/312/56 OTU/ MSFU	Lost at sea due to enemy action, 2.6.42; NFD
P3935	302/8 FTS	Hydraulic fluid caught fire; abandoned near Brechin, Angus, 27.7.41
P3936	263/32/315	Ran out of fuel and ditched in Irish Sea, 27.3.41
P3937	607/121/55 OTU/ 56 OTU/1 TEU/2 TEU	SOC 18.5.44
P3938	79/306	Engine cut; crashed in forced landing, Bratton LG, 8.12.40; DBF
P3939	302/303	Damaged by Bf 109s over Dartford, Kent, and abandoned, 15.9.40
P3940	151	Damaged by Bf 110s near Southend and abandoned, Battlesbridge, Essex, 18.8.40
P3941	151	Shot down by Bf 109s off Dymchurch, Kent, 15.8.40
P3942	111	Shot down by Bf 109s off North Foreland, Kent, 11.8.40
P3943	111	Damaged by return fire from Do 17s near Kenley; abandoned on fire, Tatsfield, Kent, 18.8.40
P3944	111	Shot down by Bf 110s over Selsey Bill; abandoned and crashed, Sidlesham, Sussex, 15.8.40
P3960	310	Damaged by return fire from Do 17s over Clacton; abandoned and crashed, Goldsands, near Southminster, Essex, 26.8.40
P3961	111/85/Kirton-in-Lindsey/Northolt/ Hucknall/5 PAFU	Engine cut; undershot forced landing and overturned, Chetwynd, 23.10.44; DBR
P3962	607	Missed flarepath, skidded and hit bowser, Usworth, 20.12.40; DBR
P3963	1 RCAF	Damaged, believed by return fire from Do 17s, over Biggin Hill and abandoned, Shipbourne, Kent, 1.9.40
P3964	43	Abandoned and crashed in sea off Selsey Bill, 20.7.40; cause obscure
P3965	85/605/312/ 55 OTU/8 FTS	Engine cut on take-off, Montrose, 29.12.41; DBR
P3966	85	Shot down by Bf 109; abandoned and crashed, Pitsea Marshes, Essex, 26.8.40
P3967	3 RAAF/6	Shot down by Bf 109s over Western Desert, 24.6.41
P3968	33	Shot down by CR 42s near Mersa Matruh, 31.10.40
P3969	33/71 OTU/261	Destroyed in air raid, Takali, 28.9.41
P3970	33	Engine cut on approach; crashlanded, Paramythia, 24.2.41
P3971	43	Damaged by return fire from Ju 88 over Emsworth, Hants., 15.8.40; destroyed in air raid while under repair, Tangmere, 16.8.40
P3972	43	Damaged by return fire from He 111s over Petworth and abandoned, Cocking Down, Sussex, 13.8.40
P3973	43	Collided with Bf 109 5m S of The Needles, Isle of Wight and crashed in sea, 21.7.40
P3974	257/303	Shot down by Bf 109; abandoned and crashed near Wilmington, Kent, 6.9.40
P3975	257/303	To Admiralty 3.41
P3976	274	Missing from ground attack mission 3m W of Bardia, 13.12.40
P3977	3 RAAF/274	Missing intercepting Ju 87s over front line, 17.6.41
P3978	274/71 OTU/ 73 OTU/FF Aden	NFT
P3979	87/213/MSFU	To Admiralty 30.3.42
P3980	274/3 RAAF/33/ 73/3 RAAF	Engine cut; forcelanded near Gazala, 7.4.41; destroyed on evacuation
P3981	32/229/56 OTU/ 1441 Flt/316/ 55 OTU	SOC 11.7.44
P3982	3	Control lost; dived into ground 1m E of Scrabster, Caithness, 18.11.40
P3983	312/56 OTU/331	To 2747M 10.41
P3984	238	Shot down by fighters and abandoned near Corfe Castle, Dorset, 10.10.40

* * * * * * * * * *

P3991 - P4039; P4061 - P4095; P4123 - P4169; P4191 - P4232; P4253 - P4279		Swordfish for Royal Navy to Contract No. 962679/38

Note: These blocks were originally allocated to 200 Oxfords to Contract No. 777546/38 but re-allotted;

RAF use

P4016	Spotter Unit Seletar/ 4 AACU	
P4019	4 AACU	
P4021	Spotter Unit Seletar/ 4 AACU	
P4023		
P4026	Spotter Unit Seletar/ 4 AACU	
P4027	Spotter Unit Seletar/ 4 AACU	
P4028	Spotter Unit Seletar/ 4 AACU	
P4030	Spotter Unit Seletar/ 4 AACU	
P4068	Spotter Unit Seletar/ 4 AACU	
P4148	9 PAFU	SOC 30.12.44
P4155	9 PAFU	SOC 10.11.44
P4198	9 PAFU	SOC 30.12.44
P4263	9 PAFU	Crashed 3m S of Newburgh, Fife, 21.2.44

* * * * * * * * * *

120 Hampden Is built by English Electric, Preston, and delivered between February and August 1940 to Contract No. 773239/38

P4285	50/44	Engine cut; hit trees on approach, Coningsby, on return from Kassel, 9.9.41

P4286	50/44	Crashed at Oosterhout, Neth. on return from Breda, 16.5.40		P4320	16 OTU	Control lost on approach, Upper Heyford, 1.9.41
P4287	50	Abandoned over Germany on return from Hamburg, 9.9.40		P4321	49/1 AAS	Bellylanded at Manby, 13.4.43
P4288	50	Engine cut on approach; crashlanded 2m ENE of Waddington, 9.7.40		P4322	49	Missing from minelaying off Brest; believed ditched 10m S of Sidmouth, Devon, 6.1.41
P4289	50	Crashed after engine failure on approach to Waddington, Coleby Grange, 8.6.40		P4323	16 OTU/106	Shot down by flak while minelaying, Heligoland Bight, 24.2.42
P4290	44	Ditched out of fuel off Lowestoft, Suffolk on return from Stettin, 6.9.40		P4324	61	Forcelanded out of fuel, Vlieland, Neth., 27.8.40 on return from Merseburg; salvaged and test flown by *Luftwaffe*
P4291	144	Missing (Merseburg) 17.8.40		____		
P4292	16 OTU	Engine cut during night training; rolled and dived into ground, Weston-on-the-Green, 7.12.40		P4335	61	Missing (Salzbergen) 13.8.40; presumed ditched
P4293	AAEE	Crashlanded after engine failure, Andover, 23.3.40 ; SOC 7.6.40		P4336	61	Shot down by flak near Krefeld-Uerdingen while attacking Ruhr railways, 10.6.40
P4294	76/16 OTU	Stalled on approach on night training to Upper Heyford, Tusmore Park, 5.8.40		P4337	61/5 OTU	To 2169M; SOC 17.9.43
				P4338	61/144/AAEE	SOC 21.4.44
P4295	76/16 OTU	Stalled landing at night, Brackley LG, 4.6.40		P4339	61	Collided with L4138 on take-off for training flight, Cottesmore, 13.6.40
P4296	76/16 OTU/1 AAS	SOC 3.2.44		P4340	83	Shot down by flak near Mesum, 5m SE of Rheine on return from Dortmund-Ems Canal, 13.8.40
P4297	76/16 OTU	Stalled while circling school, Iwerne Minster, Blandford, Dorset, 13.6.40		P4341	61	Hit by flak near Amsterdam, on return from Geestacht, and crashed off Dutch coast, 30.6.40
P4298	61/25 OTU	Stalled on approach, Finningley, 30.8.41				
P4299	49	Missing (Düsseldorf) 5.2.41		P4342	61/25 OTU	Crashed on air firing practice off Bridlington, Yorks., 6.8.41
P4300	14 OTU	Missing on night navex, 30.6.41; presumed ditched		P4343	61	Shot down by flak during low level attack on Wilhelmshaven, 21.7.40
P4301	16 OTU	Crashed at night, Charlton, Oxon., while trying to locate Croughton, 23.10.41		P4344	61	Hit by flak and crashed near Jever airfield returning from Wilhelmshaven, 21.7.40
P4302	106/25 OTU	Dived into ground on night overshoot, Balderton, 16.9.41		P4345	144	Hit balloon cable and crashed into flour mill, Felixstowe, 13.6.40, on return from attack on communications targets
P4303	14 OTU	Collided with P1301 near Saltby, 12.9.41				
P4304	49/Cv TB/489	Missing from daylight sweep off Norway, 14.5.43; last seen with port engine on fire		P4346	61	Hit by flak, Schwerte, and crashed, Jollenbeck, 22.6.40
P4305	49	Shot down by flak while minelaying and crashed in Kiel Canal, 27.6.40		P4347	144/Cv TB/489/16 FPP	Taxying accident at Kirkbride, 2.12.43; NFD
				P4348	144/16 OTU	Spun into ground, Upper Heyford, 1.3.42
P4306	14 OTU/420/Cv TB/415	SOC 28.4.44		P4349	61	Crashlanded short of fuel in fog, Gayton, near Kings Lynn, Norfolk, 8.6.40, on return from Hannover; to 2157M
P4307	7/14 OTU	Engine cut on take-off, Cottesmore, 4.5.41				
P4308	14 OTU	Crashed after control lost, Oakham, Rutland, 27.9.40		P4350	49	Ditched off Calais on return from Stettin, 6.9.40
P4309	7/14 OTU	Overshot landing at Cottesmore, 13.6.40		P4351	49	Ditched 10m E of Skegness out of fuel on return from Kiel, 5.8.40
P4310	44	Missing (Soest) 13.6.41				
P4311	7/14 OTU	Stalled in forced landing, Kidwelly, Carmarthen, 17.9.40		P4352	44	Ditched in North Sea when returning from minelaying in Great Belt, 4.7.40
P4312	7/14 OTU/Cv TB/144/489/455	SOC 7.2.44		P4353	44	Engine cut on take-off for air test, Waddington, 25.8.40
P4313	7/14 OTU	Flew into hill in bad visibility ½m E of Laxey, Isle of Man, 27.3.41		P4354	AAEE	Collided with Buffalo AS430 and crashed, Bowerchalke, 12m SW of Salisbury, Wilts., 22.10.40
P4314	7/14 OTU/106	Engine cut on night training; crashed 1m S of Finningley, 3.1.41				
P4315	7/14 OTU/Cv TB/415/489	SOC 8.4.44		P4355	61	Shot down by flak during attack on communications targets near Rheine, 21.6.40
P4316	TDU/14 OTU	Dived into ground after take-off, Cottesmore, 21.6.41		P4356	61	Shot down by flak near Rotterdam on raid on Geestacht, 30.6.40
P4317	25 OTU/14 OTU/489	SOC 18.4.44		P4357	61	Engine cut; ditched on air firing practice off Skipsea, Yorks., 5.8.40
P4318	106/25 OTU/16 OTU/14 OTU	Flew into hill in cloud, Arkengathdale Moor, Yorks., 16.8.42				
P4319	16 OTU	Spun into ground after night take-off 1m SW of Upper Heyford, 10.10.41				

P4358	61	Shot down by flak during low-level attack, Wilhelmshaven, 21.7.40
P4359	144	Engine cut in bad weather; abandoned, Taversham, Norfolk, 9.2.41, on return from Mannheim
P4360	144	Missing from attack on barge lift on Mitteland Canal at Rothensee, 22.8.40
P4361	144	Shot down by flak, Kiel, 5.7.40
P4362	144	Missing (minelaying in Elbe) 6.10.40
P4363	144	Missing (minelaying off Heligoland) 24.6.40
P4364	144	Crashlanded after engine failure near Scampton on ferry flight, 19.6.40; DBR; to 2140M
P4365	144	Crashed on return from Merseburg, Hemswell, 17.8.40; cause not known
P4366	144	Shot down by flak, Kessel, 8m SW of Venlo, during raid on Wanne-Eickel, 12.7.40
P4367	144	Damaged by flak, Wilhelms-haven, and ditched 90m E of Skegness, Lincs., 21.7.40
P4368	144	Crashed in Ysselmeer on return from Homberg, 10.8.40
P4369	144/25 OTU/ Cv TB/TDU	SOC 17.1.44
P4370	144	Shot down by night fighter, Wynandsrade, on return from Ludwigshaven, 3.9.40
P4371	44	Crashed off Pas-de-Calais after bombing invasion barges, Calais, 11.9.40
P4372	44	Shot down by flak, Gelsen-kirchen, 30.8.40
P4373	44/25 OTU/ 16 OTU/Cv TB/144	Shot down by ships' flak off SW Norway on sweep, 13.12.42
P4374	44	Undercarriage collapsed on landing on ferry flight, Radlett, 2.9.40
P4375	44	Hit balloon cable over Hamburg and crashed, 28.7.40
P4376	83	Returned with engine failure from Hannover and crashed 4m E of Scampton, 3.8.40
P4377	106/49	Missing (minelaying off Frederikshaven) 7.8.40
P4378	144	Stalled on overshoot and dived into ground, West Raynham, 6.9.40, on return from Hamburg
P4379	61	Missing (Salzbergen) 13.8.40
P4380	83	Ditched out of fuel off Grimsby, Lincs., on return from Berlin, 26.8.40
P4381	83	Developed stabilised yaw and hit tree 1m E of Fiskerton, 3.11.40; DBR
P4382	50	Missing on practice operational flight near Vlieland, 11.8.40
P4383	50	Ditched 32m E of Flamborough Head returning on one engine from minelaying off Fehmarn, 1.8.40
P4384	49	Crashed near Abingdon on return from Bordeaux, 28.12.40; cause not known
P4389	50	Lost height after take-off for air test, Lindholme, 18.6.41
P4390	61	Shot down by flak, Nordhorn, 8.7.40, during raid on Dortmund-Ems Canal

P4391	144/14 OTU	Blew up 1m NE of Akeman Street RLG, 28.8.41 on night training flight
P4392	83	Abandoned over Lincoln while lost in bad weather, 28.9.40, on return from Lorient
P4393	44	Crashed on landing on ferry flight, Waddington, 9.7.40; believed control runs incorrectly fitted
P4394	144	Control lost in cloud after engine failure; crashed, Wainfleet, Lincs., 2.3.41
P4395	50/14 OTU/Cv TB/ 5 OTU/1 TTU	SOC 16.12.43
P4396	61	Damaged by flak; believed ditched 20m NW of Heligoland on return from Hamburg, 14.11.40
P4397	61	Hit by X2911 on ground, Hemswell, 24.9.40
P4398	61/83/106	Missing (Munster) 29.1.42
P4399	61	Control lost in thunderstorm; crashed near Dartford, Kent, on return from Cologne, 31.7.41
P4400	61/25 OTU/ 44/420	Shot down by fighters while bombing battlecruisers off Belgian coast, 12.2.42
P4401	61/Cv TB	SOC 17.2.44
P4402	83	Abandoned 2½m NNW of Louth out of fuel on return from Munich, and crashed 4m W of Hemswell, 9.11.40
P4403	49	Overshot landing and hit hedge, St.Eval, 4.4.41, on return from minelaying off Lorient
P4404	49	Crashlanded after flak damage during attack on airfields in Northern France, 7.12.40; DBR
P4405	61	Crashed at Oulton, Norfolk, 10.2.41, on return from Wilhelmshaven
P4406	44	Shot down by flak while mine-laying, Lorient, 28.7.41
P4407	144	Abandoned near Wittering after engine/fuel trouble on return from Le Havre, 30.11.40
P4408	50	Crashed in North Sea during air-sea rescue sortie, 15.8.41
P4409	49/50	Swung on take-off on training flight and undercarriage coll-apsed, Lindholme, 1.4.41; DBR
P4410	83	Hit by flak; presumed ditched on return from Dortmund-Ems Canal, 13.8.40
P4411	50	Overshot single-engined land-ing, Docking, 1.10.40, on return from Berlin
P4412	83/25 OTU	Lost control and crash-landed, Balderton, 29.8.41
P4413	106	Engine cut; overshot landing, Pocklington, 16.9.41, on return from Hamburg
P4414	44/106	Missing from night intruder, Cologne-Koblenz, 22.2.42; presumed ditched
P4415	44/1 AAS/144	To Russian Navy, 12.10.42
P4416	49	Missing, believed ditched on return from Berlin, 26.8.40
P4417	50	Missing (Cologne) 6.10.40
P4418	61/14 OTU/Cv TB	SOC 24.1.44

*　　*　　*　　*　　*　　*　　*　　*　　*　　*

P4420-P4469; P4478-P4500;
P4521-P4561; P4575-P4613;   Cancelled Anson Is to Contract
P4627-P4673   No. 766119/38

* * * * * * * * *

110 De Havilland Queen Bees delivered between February and May 1939 by De Havilland, Hatfield, to Contract No. 962680/38

P4677	4 AACU	Lost in evacuation, Singapore, 1.42
P4678	4 AACU	Lost in evacuation, Singapore, 1.42
P4679	1 AACU & PAU	Dived into ground, Aberporth, 5.9.41
P4680	1 AACU & PAU/ 1618 Flt	Crashed on landing, Cleave, 4.4.43
P4681	4 AACU	Lost in evacuation, Singapore, 2.42
P4682	1 AACU	Refused signals and crashed in sea off Cleave, 6.9.40
P4683	4 AACU	Lost in Singapore, 1.42
P4684	1 AACU	Shot down off Watchet, 22.7.40
P4685	1 AACU & PAU/1621 Flt/1620 Flt/PAU/ 1618 Flt/PAU	SOC 8.1.45
P4686	2 AACU/PAU/ 1 AACU	Crashed in sea off Aberporth, 3.1.41
P4687	PAS	Hit trees on piloted take-off from forced landing near Marlow, Bucks., 22.7.39
P4688	1 AACU	Crashed in forced landing near Manorbier, 14.8.39
P4689	3 AACU	Ditched off Malta, 29.12.39
P4690	PAS	Crashed in forced landing near Shillington, 23.5.39 (piloted)
P4691	1 AACU	Crashed 24.10.39
P4692	3 AACU	Ditched off Malta, 26.12.39
P4693	3 AACU	Damaged by AA and crashed on approach, Malta, 23.12.39
P4694	3 AACU	SOC 5.4.41
P4695	2 AACU/PAU/1 AACU	Crashed in sea, 2.2.41
P4696	1 AACU	SOC 2.10.40
P4697	1 AACU	Aerial shot away; crashed near Bradworthy, Devon, 24.4.40
P4698	1 AACU	Crashed in sea off Burrow Head, 11.8.39
P4699	1 AACU	Crashed on take-off, Kidsdale, 31.10.39 (piloted)
P4700	1 AACU & PAU	Crashed in sea off Manorbier, 5.3.43
P4701	1 AACU & PAU	Shot down off Burrow Head, 25.2.41
P4702	1 AACU & PAU	Shot down off Aberporth, 2.1.41
P4703	1 AACU	Hit by AA; forcelanded in sea and sank off Burrow Head, 23.2.40
P4704	PAS/1 AACU	Swung and hit trees on take-off, Kidsdale, 12.4.40
P4705	PAS/1 AACU	Shot down off Manorbier, 10.7.40
P4706	1 AACU & PAU	Crashed in sea off Cleave, 27.3.42
P4707	PAS/1 AACU	Hit by AA and crashed in sea off Cleave, 10.4.40
P4708	PAS/3 AACU	SOC 31.3.43
P4709	PAS/3 AACU	Bounced on landing, Hal Far, 13.3.40; to Admiralty
P4710	PAS/1 AACU	Shot down in sea off Burrow Head, 26.4.40
P4711	PAS/1 AACU	Crashed in forced landing near Llangybi, Cardigan, 18.12.41
P4712	PAS/1 AACU	Shot down near Kidsdale, 11.10.41

P4713	PAU/1 AACU	Shot down by rockets off Aberporth, 17.12.40
P4714	PAU/1 AACU	Crashed near Cleave, 17.4.41
P4715	3 AACU	To Admiralty; SOC 31.3.43
P4716	1 AACU	Lost height and hit lake on approach, Cleave, 8.7.40
P4747	PAU & 1 AACU	Crashed in sea off Manorbier, 27.6.41
P4748	3 AACU	SOC 31.3.43
P4749	PAU & 1 AACU	Shot down off Burrow Head, 13.2.42
P4750	PAU & 1 AACU	Crashed in sea 2m N of Bude, Cornwall, 7.3.42
P4751	PAU/1 AACU	Crashed in sea off Cleave, 25.2.42
P4752	PAU/1 AACU	Shot down off Burrow Head, 3.2.41
P4753	PAU/3 AACU	SOC 31.3.43
P4754	PAU/1 AACU	Shot down off Burrow Head and sank, 6.5.40
P4755	PAU/1 AACU	Crashed on landing off Burrow Head and sank, 30.5.40
P4756	PAU/1 AACU	Hit hut on landing, Kidsdale, 9.5.40
P4757	PAU & 1 AACU	Crashed on approach, Towyn, 16.4.42
P4758	PAU/1 AACU	Control lost in bad weather; crashed 20m S of Burrow Head, 10.12.40
P4759	PAU/1 AACU	Crashed in sea off Ty Croes, Anglesey, 16.4.42
P4760	PAU/3 AACU	SOC 31.3.43
P4761	PAU & 1 AACU/1618 Flt/PAU/1621 Flt	Crashed in forced landing near Cardigan, 7.2.43
P4762	PAU/1 AACU	Glided into sea and sank off Burrow Head, 24.5.40
P4763	PAU/1 AACU	Failed to answer signals and crashed on landing, Kidsdale, 3.6.40
P4764	PAU/1 AACU	Crashed at Langtree, Devon, 10.7.42
P4765	PAU/1 AACU	Crashed in sea off Tonfanau, 23.6.41
P4766	PAU/1 AACU	Shot down off Burrow Head, 3.2.41
P4767	PAU & 1 AACU	Crashed near Newborough Warren, Anglesey, 22.10.41
P4768	PAU/1 AACU	Shot down off Manorbier, 4.9.40
P4769	PAU/1 AACU	Shot down off Cleave, 19.8.42
P4770	PAU/1 AACU	Hit by AA; engine cut; landed off Burrow Head and sank, 3.7.40
P4771	PAU/1 AACU	Shot down off Ty Croes, 26.1.42
P4772	PAU & 1 AACU	Crashed at Sandy Cove, Cornwall, 19.6.42
P4773	PAU/1 AACU	Crashed on landing, Aberporth, 12.1.41
P4774	PAU/1620 Flt	Sold 4.9.47
P4775	PAU/1 AACU	Shot down at Ty Croes, 5.5.41
P4776	PAU/1 AACU	Shot down off Aberporth, 9.3.41
P4777	PAU & 1 AACU	Crashed in forced landing near Aberporth, 26.2.41
P4778	PAU/1 AACU	Shot down off Manorbier, 7.8.40
P4779	PAU/1 AACU	Shot down off Burrow Head, 7.6.40
P4780	PAU & 1 AACU	Shot down off Weybourne, 12.12.41
P4781	PAU/1 AACU	Radio contact lost; crashed at Perunain near Swansea, 23.1.41

P4788	PAU/1620 Flt/Mona	SOC 26.4.45
P4789	PAU & 1 AACU	Shot down at Ty Croes, 1.8.42
P4790	PAU/1 AACU	Crashed on landing, Aberporth, 21.11.41
P4791	PAU/1 AACU	Crashed off Burrow Head, 25.3.42
P4792	PAU/1 AACU	Crashed on landing, Weybourne, 17.11.41
P4793	PAU/1 AACU	Presumed crashed in sea off Anglesey, 23.9.41
P4794	PAU & 1 AACU	Crashed on landing, Aberporth, 25.7.42
P4795	PAU/1 AACU	Crashed in sea off Towyn, 2.11.41
P4796	PAU/1 AACU	Shot down in Cardigan Bay, 19.6.42
P4797	PAU & 1 AACU	Crashed off Aberporth, 26.9.42
P4798	PAU/1 AACU	Crashed near Kidsdale, 16.10.41
P4799	PAU/1 AACU	Crashed off Burrow Head, 23.2.42
P4800	PAU/1 AACU	Shot down off Burrow Head, 15.8.40
P4801	PAU/1 AACU	Shot down off Aberffraw, Anglesey, 26.2.41
P4802	PAU/1 AACU	Crashed on landing off Manorbier, 25.10.40
P4803	PAU/1 AACU	Shot down off Aberporth, 19.7.41
P4804	PAU/1 AACU	Shot down off Aberporth, 4.9.41
P4805	PAU/1 AACU/1620 Flt	Crashed in sea off Anglesey, 18.2.43
P4806	PAU & 1 AACU/1618 Flt	Crashed on landing, Cleave, 7.3.43
P4807	PAU/1 AACU	Shot down off Burrow Head, 12.7.41
P4808	PAU/1 AACU	Crashed 2m N of Cleave, 27.3.42
P4809	PAU/1 AACU	Shot down off Tonfanau, 1.11.41
P4810	PAU/1 AACU/1620 Flt	Sold 23.11.46
P4811	PAU/1 AACU	Shot down at Ty Croes, 14.8.41
P4812	PAU/1 AACU	Dived into sea off Burrow Head, 18.8.41
P4813	PAU/2 AACU/1 AACU/PAU/1 AACU	Crashed on landing, Weybourne, 2.7.41
P4814	PAU/1 AACU	Crashed in sea off Aberporth, 13.1.41
P4815	PAU & 1 AACU	Crashed after launch, Manorbier, 5.7.41
P4816	PAU/1 AACU	Shot down off Anglesey, 2.5.41
P4817	PAU & 1 AACU	Crashed on approach, Towyn, 23.3.42
P4818	PAU/1 AACU	Shot down off Burrow Head, 25.9.40
P4819	PAU/1 AACU	Shot down off Aberporth, 9.1.41
P4820	PAU/1 AACU	Crashed on approach, Cleave, 23.8.42
P4821	PAU/1 AACU	Spun into sea off Cleave, 2.10.40
P4822	PAU/1 AACU	Sank after landing off Burrow Head, 7.3.41

* * * * * * * * * *

70 Bristol Blenheim IVs delivered between August and October 1939 by Bristols, Filton, to Contract No. 774679/38

P4825	600/248/51 OTU/12 PAFU	SOC 16.6.44
P4826	139	Shot down by Bf 109 near Maastricht, 12.5.40
P4827	139/114	Shot down by Bf 109s 10m SSW of Sedan, 14.5.40
P4828	82	Shot down, Neufchatel-Hardelot, Pas-de-Calais, during raid on Hesdin, 22.5.40
P4829	RAE/600/248/2 SAC/6 OTU/42 OTU	To 4172M 12.9.43
P4830	RAE/233/SD Flt, Christchurch	Engine cut; control lost avoiding house, hit tree and spun into ground 3m S of Salisbury, Wilts., 17.9.40
P4831	RAE/601/248/Dyce/254/404/132 OTU/2 FP	Undercarriage retracted in error after landing, Cosford, 29.7.43; to 3992M
P4832	RAE/AAEE/SD Flt, Christchurch	Ditched on calibration flight 24m SSW of Worth Matravers, Dorset, 17.7.41
P4833	RAE/29/235/1 AGS	SOC 21.1.44
P4834	RAE/SD Flt	Damaged by return fire while shooting down He 111 off Dutch coast and crashlanded, Martlesham Heath, 12.5.40; DBF
P4835	RAE/29/235/143/489/143	Tyre burst on take-off; swung and undercarriage collapsed, Limavady, 23.5.42; DBR
P4836	RAE/23/235	Overshot landing at night and hit ditch, North Coates, 17.4.40
P4837	600/248	Collided with L9455 during practice attack on Beaufort and crashed in sea off Thorney Island, 20.5.40
P4838	82	Shot down by Bf 109 near Laon on raid on Gembloux, 17.5.40
P4839	82/90/17 OTU/TFU/17 OTU/13 OTU	Both engines cut; crashlanded in field 1½m N of Hutton Cranswick, 13.6.43
P4840	82/107/105	Collided with another Blenheim over Homs and crashed, 22.9.41
P4841	82	Both engines cut after take-off; crashlanded, Upper Heyford, 10.10.39
P4842	82	Shot down by fighters on reconnaissance to Heligoland and Elbe areas, 27.2.40
P4843	82	Missing on reconnaissance over NW Germany, 7.7.40
P4844	RAE/23/235	Lost height in turn at night and dived into ground in circuit, Bircham Newton, 8.5.40
P4845	RAE/29/235/272/404	Overshot forced landing and hit wall while lost in bad visibility 5m N of Dyce, 14.11.41
P4846	RAE/600/SD Flt Christchurch/TFU/AFEE	SOC 15.8.44
P4847	RAE/604/248/Dyce/248/404	To 3980M 23.7.43
P4848	RAE/SD Flt Perth	Flew into hill in bad visibility on ferry flight, Kirbyshire, N. Wales, 8.11.39
P4849	RAE/64/236/9 AOS/5 AOS	SOC 8.5.44
P4850	RAE/64/236/53	Missing from attack on *Admiral Hipper* in Brest, 11.3.41
P4851	82	Missing (Gembloux) 17.5.40
P4852	82	Missing (Gembloux) 17.5.40; crashed at Pancy-Courtecon, Aisne.
P4853	82	Engine cut on air firing practice; lost height on approach, struck wires and cartwheeled, Cleave, 10.9.39

Above: Lysander II P1676 at Dekheila in 1941

Below: Hurricane I P3675 of No.601 Squadron

41

Above: Albemarle P1362 at Boscombe Down in January 1942

Below: Whitley V P5018, ZA-Q of No.10 Squadron, at Leeming

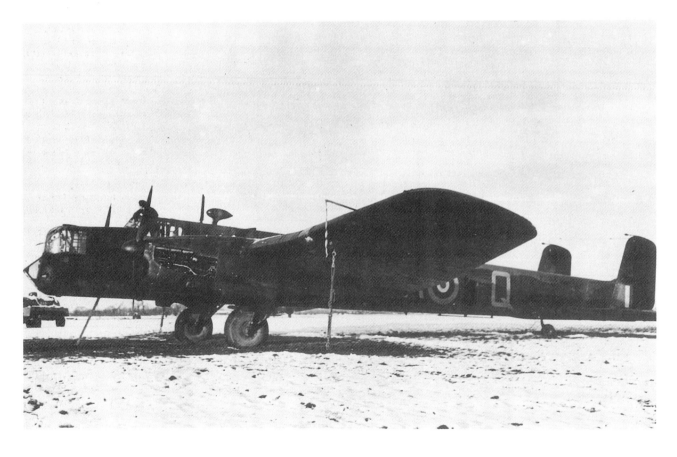

P4854	82	Missing (Gembloux) 17.5.40
P4855	82	Dived into ground after control lost in cloud 5m S of Swaffham, Norfolk, 8.4.40
P4856	107/57/13 OTU	Spun into ground near Bicester, 26.12.41
P4857	107	Lost in France 5.40
P4858	110/18/110/17 OTU/ 9 AOS/1 AOS/1 OAFU	Engine cut on take-off; dived into ground, Wigtown, 15.6.42
P4859	110	Shot down on reconnaissance by Bf 110s 125m N of Terschelling, 10.1.40
P4860	110/139	Flew into sea in Waddenzee off Wierum during shipping sweep off Delfzyl, 8.5.41
P4861	82	Both engines cut on take-off; hit hedge and undercarriage torn off, Weston Zoyland, 18.9.39
P4862	82	Engine cut on take-off; belly-landed at Kirtlington, Oxon., 10.10.39; DBR
P4863	82/6	Engine cut; forcelanded with undercarriage unlocked 68m WNW of Wadi Halfa, 12.12.41; DBR
P4864	107	SOC 6.5.40; NFD
P4898	82	Missing (Gembloux) 17.5.40
P4899	RAE	SOC 27.5.44
P4900	35/OATU/OADU/34	SOC 14.10.44
P4901	-	Lost in France 6.40
P4902	25/17 OTU	Stalled on night navex and spun into ground near N. Crawley, Bucks., 7.8.40; DBF
P4903	82	Missing (Gembloux) 17.5.40
P4904	82	Shot down by Bf 109s, Lappion, Aisne, en route to Gembloux, 17.5.40
P4905	82/107/40/107	Shot down by Bf 109, Bettenhoven, 15m WNW of Liège en route to Maastricht, 12.5.40
P4906	107/RAE/107	Missing (Stavanger) 18.4.40
P4907	35/17 OTU	Caught in downdraught and dived into sea on night navex, Tremadoc Bay, North Wales, 24.5.40
P4908	40	Hit by flak during raid on Chartres airfield and ditched off Cherbourg, 15.8.40
P4909	40	Damaged by flak and crash-landed 2m ESE of Béthune during attack on enemy troops near Boulogne, 23.5.40
P4910	-	To G-AFXD for R.Hellenic AF
P4911	-	To G-AFXE for R.Hellenic AF
P4912	35/40/35/101	Stalled on training flight and spun into ground 5m NW of Oxford, 6.6.40; DBF
P4913	40	Shot down by fighters 11m NE of Mons during raid on Dinant, 15.5.40
P4914	107	Shot down by Bf 109, Bierset, 6m W of Liège, en route to Maastricht, 12.5.40
P4915	-	To G-AFXF for R.Hellenic AF
P4916	-	To G-AFXG for R.Hellenic AF
P4917	40	Hit by flak and crashlanded during attack on enemy troops near St.Valery, 6.6.40; destroyed to avoid capture
P4918	40/105/5 AOS	Engine cut on approach; stalled and hit ground, Jurby, 28.7.42
P4919	107	Hit by flak, Gravelines, and crashlanded on return, 2.6.40; DBR
P4920	40	Shot down 3m ESE of Marquise, Pas-de-Calais, during attack on enemy troops near Rety, 25.5.40
P4921	-	To G-AFXH for R.Hellenic AF
P4922	-	To G-AFXI for R.Hellenic AF
P4923	139	Shot down by Bf 109s, Herstal-Rhées, Liège, returning from Maastricht, 12.5.40
P4924	107	Damaged by Bf 109s during attack on Stavanger/Sola and bellylanded, Lossiemouth, 17.4.40; DBR
P4925	107	Damaged by flak attacking enemy tanks near Boulogne and ditched in English Channel, 22.5.40
P4926	139	Crashed in sea off Argèles-sur-Mer, Pyrenées Orientales, 14.3.40
P4927	40	Missing from attack on enemy troops near St.Valery, 6.6.40

* * * * * * * * * *

164 Armstrong Whitworth Whitley V delivered between April and August 1940 by Armstrong Whitworth, Coventry, to Contract No. 751547/38

P4930	19 OTU	SOC 7.6.41
P4931	10 OTU	Missing (Essen) 17.9.42
P4932	19 OTU/10 OTU	SOC 26.4.45
P4933	102	Abandoned out of fuel near Maltby, Yorks., while lost on return from Lunen, 19.10.40
P4934	51	Ditched in bad weather on return from Cologne off Durham coast, 27.2.41
P4935	10	Missing (Berlin) 7.9.40; presumed ditched on return
P4936	102	Missing (Berlin) 15.11.40
P4937	10/78	Abandoned when lost on return from Bremen near South Molton, Devon, 4.1.41
P4938	77/19 OTU/10 OTU	SOC 28.2.46
P4939	10 OTU	Stalled on take-off and dived into ground ½m NW of Abingdon, 29.4.41
P4940	10 OTU	Hit RT cables in bad visibility in circuit, Kingston Bagpuize; crashed at Hinton, Oxon., 5.6.41
P4941	58/78/10 OTU/42 OTU	SOC 29.8.44
P4942	77/10 OTU	Overshot landing and undercarriage collapsed, Abingdon, 1.10.41
P4943	BATDU/58	Missing (Hamburg) 7.11.40
P4944	BATDU/10 OTU	Missing (Bremen) 25.6.42
P4945	102	Destroyed in air raid, Driffield, 15.8.40
P4946	10	Missing (Bremen) 9.5.41
P4947	77	Crashlanded in bad visibility on return from Brest, Waddington, 4.4.41; DBF
P4948	77	Missing (Frankfurt) 30.6.40
P4949	DH Props/TFU	SOC 4.12.43
P4950	78	Missing (Lorient) 29.12.40
P4951	58/42 OTU	SOC 19.4.45
P4952	10	Abandoned out of fuel 3m W of Bellingham and crashed on Watch Crags, Northumberland, 15.10.40 on return from Stettin
P4953	10/10 OTU	Engine cut on take-off; hit trees and crashlanded, Abingdon, 28.3.42

43

P4954	10	Crashed near Abbeville attacking enemy troop concentrations, 12.6.40
P4955	10	Hit by flak and crashed near Zevenbergen, Neth. on return from Jena, 17.8.40
P4956	10/10 OTU	Overshot landing, Kidlington, 12.7.42
P4957	10	Flew into hill in cloud 3m from Slaggyford, Northumberland, 30.10.40, on return from Magdeburg
P4958	10/78	Crashed on take-off for Lorient, Linton-on-Ouse, 2.12.40; DBF
P4959	10	Caught fire on ground, Leeming, 27.10.40; DBR
P4960	10	Hit trees in forced landing and crashed, Ampton Park, Bury St. Edmunds, Suffolk, 20.6.40, on return from Antwerp
P4961	10	Abandoned after engine failure on return from Berlin 5m SSW of Harleston, Suffolk, 21.12.40
P4962	10/10 OTU	Undercarriage collapsed on landing, Stanton Harcourt, 1.5.44
P4963	10	Crashed in forced landing in fog, Battisford, Suffolk, 4.6.40, on return from Homberg; DBR
P4964	78	Missing (Sterkrade) 2.10.40; crashed Hummelo, 13m E of Arnhem
P4965	10	Damaged by fighter over Turin and lost engine; ditched attempting to land on beach, Dymchurch, Kent, 14.8.40 and DBR
P4966	10	Engine cut; ditched 20m off Spurn Head en route to Antwerp, 15.9.40
P4967	10	Bellylanded short of fuel 5m ESE of Northallerton, Yorks., on return from Berlin, 4.9.40
P4968	51	Missing (Zchornewitz) 20.8.40
P4969	51/77/1502 BATF/10 OTU/19 OTU	Crashed in forced landing after engine failure, Lossiemouth, 9.1.43
P4970	51/PTS/296	SOC 27.9.45
P4971	51/3 OTU/1 OTU	Crashed after take-off 1m E of Silloth, 16.7.41
P4972	51	Undershot landing at Dishforth on return from Magdeburg, 30.10.40
P4973	51	Ditched off Dutch coast on return from Berlin, 5.9.40
P4974	51	Abandoned over sea while lost on return from Bremen, 12.2.41
P4980	51	Missing (Jülich/Rheydt) 22.5.40
P4981	51	Abandoned out of fuel near Grimethorpe, Yorks., on return from Bremen, 12.2.41
P4982	51	Hit balloon cable and crashed, Langley, Bucks., 15.8.40, on return from Bordeaux
P4983	51	Missing (Gelsenkirchen) 12.8.40
P4984	51	Ran out of fuel on return from Stettin and crashed in forced landing near St.Osyth, Essex, 29.11.40
P4985	51/77/19 OTU	SOC 12.1.44
P4986	51	Missing (Bohlen) 17.8.40
P4987	51/24 OTU	SOC 17.5.44
P4988	58/2 BATF/1502 BATF/10 OTU/24 OTU	SOC 22.2.44
P4989	77/102/10 OTU	Crashed in forced landing, Horton, near Chipping Sodbury, Glos., 20.4.43
P4990	10	Shot down during raid on Sesto Calende, Valera, 27.8.40
P4991	58	Missing (Düsseldorf) 3.6.41
P4992	77	Missing (Antwerp) 19.9.40; presumed ditched
P4993	10	Hit balloon cable and crashed, Weybridge, Surrey, 14.10.40, on return from Le Havre; DBF
P4994	10	Hit house after take-off for training flight; stalled and crashed, Leeming, 22.12.40
P4995	102	Ditched 50 m NW of Innistrahull Lighthouse, Ulster, during convoy patrol, 7.10.40
P4996	51/78	Flew into hills 3m E of Craig, Ross & Cromarty, 27.2.41 on return from Cologne
P4997	10 OTU	Engine lost power; crashed in forced landing, Swanton Morley, 23.12.43
P4998	19 OTU	Hit trees on overshoot, Elgin, 20.3.42
P4999	10 OTU	Undershot landing and hit tree, Abingdon, 23.3.41
P5000	19 OTU	SOC 31.5.45
P5001	10	Ditched on return from Milan off North Foreland, Kent, 5.11.40
P5002	58	Abandoned out of fuel on return from Berlin off Hornsea, Yorks., 31.8.40
P5003	58/19 OTU/81 OTU	SOC 28.6.45
P5004	77/10 OTU	Ditched in North Sea on return from Bremen, 26.6.42
P5005	102/78/19 OTU	Flew into Burgie Hill, Moray, on approach to Lossiemouth, 15.6.42
P5006	19 OTU	Dived into ground out of cloud on navex, Ben Aigen, Moray, 24.9.40
P5007	51	Missing (Gelsenkirchen) 20.7.40; crashed at Ibbenburen
P5008	58	Shot down by night fighter, Groenlo, Neth., on return from Hamm, 19.9.40
P5009	10 BGS	Flew into high ground in bad visibility on ferry flight near Loch Enoch, Kirkcudbright, 27.11.40
P5010	502	Hit obstruction on runway on take-off and crashlanded, Limavady, 5.3.41
P5011	51	Failed to take-off for training flight and overshot into road, Dishforth, 3.9.40
P5012	102	Shot down by night fighter off Egmond on return from Berlin, 16.12.40
P5013	51	Abandoned while short of fuel on return from Bremen, Hatfield, Yorks., 12.2.41
P5014	19 OTU/102	Missing (Essen) 4.7.41
P5015	19 OTU/102/10 OTU	Engine cut on navex; crashed on landing, Stanton Harcourt, 23.4.44
P5016	10	Missing (Bremen) 28.6.41
P5017	77	SOC 4.9.40; possibly damaged in air raid, Kemble, 14.8.40
P5018	10	Missing (Duisburg) 1.7.41
P5019	BADU/AAEE/10 OTU/24 OTU/19 OTU/24 OTU/19 OTU	SOC 26.4.45

Serial	Units	Fate
P5020	51/19 OTU/24 OTU	SOC 10.6.44
P5021	51	Damaged by flak, Berlin, and ditched 120m E of Firth of Forth, 9.9.40
P5022	102	DBR in air raid, Driffield, 15.8.40
P5023	77/10 OTU	Hit tree in bad visibility and crashed, Eaton, Berks., 24.10.41
P5024	10 BGS/9 AGS/ 7 AGS/19 OTU	SOC 29.11.45
P5025	419 Flt	Crashed on landing, Stradishall, 11.10.40
P5026	78	Missing (Stettin) 29.11.40
P5027	51	SOC 20.2.44
P5028	58	SOC 31.5.45
P5029	419 Flt/1419 Flt/ 138 ____	Ditched off Beachy Head after engine cut due to fuel shortage on SOE mission to France, 23.10.42
P5040	10 OTU	Engine cut; crashed in forced landing near Witney, Oxon., 9.12.42
P5041	502	Crashed into hills near Campbeltown, Argyll 23.1.41
P5042	77	Missing (Bremen) 11.9.40; crashed, Venebrugge, Neth.
P5043	19 OTU	Undershot landing at Lossiemouth 18.5.42
P5044	77	Hit balloon barrage and crashed 1m SE of Eastleigh, Hants., 5.8.40, on return from Bordeaux
P5045	502	Crashed in Galway Bay, Eire, on return from patrol, 12.3.41
P5046	102/77	Hit by flak, Berlin, and ditched in North Sea, 24.9.40
P5047	AAEE/109/10 OTU	Crashed at Windrush Farm, Oxon., 18.5.41
P5048	10	Missing (Hamburg) 11.5.41
P5049	77/3 OTU/1 OTU/ 3 OTU	SOC 28.6.45
P5050	502	Missing from patrol off Ushant, 4.2.42
P5051	502/1 OTU/3 OTU	Missing, presumed ditched in North Sea, 13.3.42
P5052	502/3 OTU	Hit roof of RAF College on approach, Cranwell, 18.3.42; DBR
P5053	AAEE/109/10 OTU	SOC 25.2.44
P5054	502	Ditched on anti-submarine sweep off Downhill, Londonderry, 18.11.40
P5055	10	Missing (Bremen) 28.6.41
P5056	77	DBR in air raid, Driffield, 15.8.40
P5057	AAEE/109/10 OTU	Flew into Caerne Hill, Montgomery, 9.5.42
P5058	58	Ditched in Humber off Scunthorpe, Lincs., on return from Plzen, 21.10.40
P5059	502	Ditched on training flight 2m E of Kinloss, 23.10.41
P5060	51	Missing (Bremen) 4.1.41
P5061	502/53	SOC 15.10.44
P5062	502/612/19 OTU	SOC 26.4.45
P5063	502/1 OTU/3 OTU	SOC 31.5.41
P5064	502	Crashed after take-off 2m E of Kinloss, 5.11.40
P5065	502/1 OTU/3 OTU/ 42 OTU	SOC 15.12.44
P5070	612	Flew into mountain near Dunbeith, Caithness, on return from anti-submarine patrol, 1.5.41
P5071	612	Crashed on approach, Dyce, 18.2.41
P5072	19 OTU/102	Ditched in North Sea returning from Duisburg, 21.11.40
P5073	102	Attacked by enemy aircraft after take-off from Linton-on-Ouse for Berlin, and crashed, Tholthorpe, 24.10.40
P5074	102	Damaged by own AA returning from Turin and abandoned out of fuel 4m N of Midhurst; crashed at Elstead, Sussex, 24.11.40
P5075	19 OTU	Ditched in Loch Ryan, 26.9.42; cause not known
P5076	58/19 OTU	Engine seized on night navex; crashlanded, Old Meldrum, Aberdeenshire, 7.7.41; DBF
P5077	102	Missing (minelaying off Le Havre) 28.11.40
P5078	502/3 OTU	SOC 8.2.45
P5079	10 OTU	SOC 19.4.45
P5080	612/19 OTU	SOC 27.9.45
P5081	502/3 OTU/19 OTU	SOC 31.5.45
P5082	102	Ditched 20m E of Aberdeen on return from Bremen, 29.10.40
P5083	612/3 OTU	Missing presumed ditched in North Sea, 9.3.42
P5084	10 BGS	SOC 18.4.44
P5085	10 OTU/19 OTU	SOC 15.11.40
P5086	10 OTU/19 OTU	SOC 26.4.45
P5087	10 OTU	Missing, presumed ditched in Irish Sea, 14.3.41
P5088	10 OTU/19 OTU	Crashed on overshoot, Kinloss, 3.11.40; to 2332M
P5089	58	Ditched out of fuel on return from Plzen 2m off Sheringham, Norfolk, 21.10.40
P5090	502	Crashed into mountain 1m W of Balquhidder, Perthshire, on return from convoy escort, 24.11.40
P5091	102/77	Flew into high ground on return from Hanau ½m W of Snape, Yorks., 9.10.40
P5092	19 OTU/102/ 19 OTU	Photoflash exploded and aircraft broke up 3m SE of Lossiemouth, 26.5.42
P5093	502/1 OTU/3 OTU	SOC 19.4.45
P5094	10	Overshot landing on return from Ostend and ran on to road, Leeming, 9.9.40
P5095	51	Ditched in Humber north of Scunthorpe, Lincs., on return from Plzen, 21.10.40
P5096	502	Hit air raid shelter on take-off and forcelanded, Wick, 4.2.41
P5097	58/102	Damaged by flak over Berlin and crashlanded near Kings Lynn, Norfolk, 14.11.40
P5098	58	Hit Lysander R9100 on landing after aborting raid on Boulogne, Linton-on-Ouse, 23.12.40; DBF
P5099	10 OTU/19 OTU	Caught fire when flare fouled tail unit; abandoned over Spey Bay, 13.3.42
P5100	10 OTU/RR/10 OTU/24 OTU	Hit trees on overshoot, Badsey, Worcs., 31.8.42
P5101	10 OTU/19 OTU	Hit trees on overshoot, Forres, 22.2.42
P5102	102/3 OTU/10 OTU/ 24 OTU/19 OTU	Hit trees on take-off, Forres, 2.10.44
P5103	19 OTU	Dived into ground, Ardestie, Dundee, 21.10.41
P5104	Mkrs/AAEE	SOC 27.9.45

P5105	51/78/19 OTU	Hit bridge attempting to ditch at night in River Dee 2m W of Ballater, Aberdeen, 16.11.42
P5106	51	Shot down by night fighter 1m W of Weert, Neth., on return from Ludwigshafen, 10.5.41
P5107	19 OTU/502/3 OTU/24 OTU	SOC 17.5.44
P5108	51	Crashedlanded on sandbank off Pilsum on return from Cologne, 2.3.41
P5109	10	Ditched in North Sea on return from Warnemünde, 12.9.41
P5110	-	SOC 12.9.40; possibly damaged in air raid, Kemble, 14.8.40
P5111	Hendon/77	Hit building on landing, Abingdon, 28.12.40, on return from Bordeaux
P5112	51	Ditched in North Sea on return from Düsseldorf, 8.12.40

* * * * * * * * * *

50 Lockheed Hudson Is delivered between March and July 1940 by Lockheed, Burbank, to Contract No. 791587/38

P5116	220/407/PRU/6 OTU/1 OTU	Overshot landing at Silloth, 26.10.41
P5117	233	Abandoned in bad weather near Scremerston, Berwick, 5.10.40
P5118	1 OTU/269/1 OTU/5 OTU	SOC 7.44
P5119	1 OTU/269/6 OTU/1 OTU/5 OTU	SOC 17.12.43
P5120	206	Hit ridge on approach; bounced, stalled and undercarriage collapsed, Bircham Newton, 20.6.40
P5121	269/1 OTU/269/1 OTU/ATA/Newmarket	SOC 17.7.44
P5122	224/6 OTU/ATA	SOC 28.6.45
P5123	233	Forcelanded at Sligo, Eire, on return from convoy patrol, 25.1.41; to Irish Air Corps, 13.4.42 as No.91
P5124	220	Ran out of fuel returning from patrol and crashlanded on beach 1m N of Hayle, Cornwall, 7.11.40; to 2429M
P5125	1 OTU/269/PRU/220/1 OTU/301 FTU/1 FU	SOC 9.7.44
P5126	1 OTU/269/1 OTU/ATA	SOC 7.7.44
P5127	220	Swung after take-off and dived into ground 1m from Thornaby, 11.6.40; bombs exploded
P5128	1 OTU/269	Missing on patrol 8.2.41
P5129	1 OTU/269	Missing on patrol 28.9.40
P5130	1 OTU/269	Lost 26.10.40; NFD
P5131	1 OTU/269	Shot down by flak over Trondheim, Norway, 11.6.40
P5132	269	Missing 24.10.40
P5133	206	Stalled after steep turn; hit ground and blew up, Syderstone, Norfolk, 5.8.40
P5134	1 OTU	Stalled on approach, Scorton, 9.6.43
P5135	220	Crashed in sea off Hartlepool, Co.Durham, 4.12.40
P5136	224/233/1 OTU	Crashed on overshoot, Kirkbride, 31.1.42
P5137	206/PRU/220/1 OTU/1444 Flt/1 OTU	SOC 19.4.45

P5138	1 OTU/6 OTU/1 OTU/ATA	SOC 9.5.44
P5139	FDU/220/1 OTU	SOC 29.11.45
P5140	206/1 OTU/ATA/1 OTU/ATA	SOC 14.5.45
P5141	206/220/608/6 OTU/1 OTU	SOC 9.4.45
P5142	1 OTU	Turned after night take-off and dived into sea, Solway Firth, 29.11.40
P5143	206/1 OTU/ATA	SOC 28.4.45
P5144	1 OTU	Swung on landing and wrecked, Silloth, 4.9.40
P5145	AAEE & MAEE	Trials aircraft; to 4555M 2.44
P5146	220	Missing on patrol, 2.4.41
P5147	269/1 OTU/269/1 AAS/1 OTU	Missing on diversion raid for Bremen, 26.6.42
P5148	269/1 OTU/206/1 OTU	Damaged while taxying, Thornaby, 23.9.43
P5149	320/1 OTU/Benson/Melton Mowbray	SOC 28.12.44
P5150	220/1 OTU	SOC 29.11.45
P5151	220	Engine cut on return from patrol; lost height and ditched off Redcar, Yorks., 16.1.41
P5152	269/1 OTU/269	Collided with Hurricane P2863 on take-off, Wick, 23.7.40
P5153	269/1 OTU/206	Crashed on landing on return from convoy patrol and bombs exploded, Bircham Newton, 6.8.40
P5154	1 OTU	SOC 2.6.42
P5155	1 OTU	Swung and undercarriage collapsed in heavy landing, Silloth, 2.8.41; DBF
P5156	233/1 OTU	SOC 1.12.44
P5157	220	Destroyed in air raid Thornaby, 6.6.40
P5158	220/6 OTU/5 OTU	To 4466M 1.44
P5159	224/6 OTU/1 OTU	Crashed on landing, Thornaby, 31.5.43
P5160	PDU/PRU/1 OTU	Engine cut; forcelanded on sandbank and overtaken by tide, Solway Firth, 3.5.42
P5161	269/224/1 OTU	Ditched off Jurby Head, Isle of Man, 14.4.42
P5162	206	Missing from ASR search for Hampdens off Texel, 4.7.40
P5163	SAAF/267/CF W.Africa	NFT
P5164	SAAF/267	Engine cut; hit obstacle and crashed near Abbassia, Cairo, 5.10.41; DBF
P5165	-	Sunk in Pacific on delivery

* * * * * * * * * *

40 Hawker Hurricane X built by Canadian Car and Foundry and delivered between March and August 1940 to Contract No. 964753/38

P5170	AAEE/5 FTS/RAE	To 5054M; SOC 4.7.45
P5171	85/71/56 OTU	Crashed in forced landing near Swaffham, Norfolk, 24.5.41
P5172	253/402/52 OTU/287/59 OTU/1 TEU/5 PAFU	SOC 23.9.44
P5173	208/1 METS/74 OTU	SOC 1.11.43
P5174	ME	Lost 20.4.41; NFD
P5175	79	Cv to Mk.II BV159
P5176	274/3 RAAF	Ran out of fuel and forcelanded in desert near Gazala East; burnt as enemy nearby, 7.4.41

P5177	79	Missing from interception over Irish Sea, 29.9.40
P5178	79	Forcelanded in Eire, 29.9.40; to Irish Air Corps, 7.10.40
P5179	253/288	Engine cut on take-off; crash-landed, Duxford, 28.7.42; DBR
P5180	1 RCAF/303/59 OTU	To Admiralty 28.8.41
P5181	253	Crashed in forced landing, Charing, Kent, 5.9.40; NFD
P5182	151	To Admiralty 1.10.41
P5183	151/229/111/ 56 OTU/MSFU	Forcelanded on sandbank in Mersey, 28.10.41; to 2807M 12.41
P5184	253	Shot down by Bf 109s, Bredgar, Kent, 14.9.40
P5185	253	Shot down, probably by return fire from Do 17s, over Dungeness, 1.9.40
P5186	151/605/257	Missing in cloud while intercepting Ju 88 off Happisburgh, Norfolk, 24.2.41
P5187	111/5 OTU/1/RAE/ 63 OTU/4 TEU	SOC 14.12.44
P5188	43/145/56 OTU/ MSFU	Engine cut; forcelanded on sandbank, Hilbury Is., 13.3.42
P5189	213/6 OTU/501	Shot down by Bf 109 off Hastings, Sussex, 28.11.40
P5190	151/56 OTU/59 OTU	Ran short of fuel while lost and bellylanded, Castlemilktown, Ulster, 7.41; cv to Mk.II DG623 during repair
P5191	43/245	To 3252M 7.42
P5192	85/71/56 OTU	Engine cut; bellylanded 3m N of Wolferton, Norfolk, 4.4.41
P5193	501	Crashed near Cranbrook, Kent, 25.10.40; believed damaged by enemy aircraft
P5194	501/247/263/247/ MSFU/1624 Flt/567	SOC 22.12.44
P5195	56	Overturned in forced landing while lost, New Leake, near Boston, Lincs., 18.3.41; to Mk.II DG620 3.41
P5196	258/260/59 OTU/ 55 OTU/9 PAFU/ 56 OTU/2 TEU/ 81 OTU/1665 HCU	SOC 18.9.44
P5197	1/79/59 OTU/43	Engine cut; abandoned 1m E of Chathill, Northumberland, 16.5.42
P5198	213/1 RCAF/ 56 OTU	Swung on landing and overturned, Tealing, 6.10.42
P5199	1/55 OTU	Forcelanded at Marske, Yorks., 10.4.41; to DG632
P5200	501	Shot down by Bf 109s over Maidstone, Kent, 11.9.40
P5201	615/504	Dived into sea out of cloud, Dawlish, Devon, 14.7.41
P5202	213/247/56 OTU/ 287/India	To GI airframe 10.44
P5203	32	To Admiralty 4.41
P5204	79	Cv to Mk.II BV170
P5205	607	Damaged by enemy aircraft and abandoned, Kaylthorpe, Isle of Wight, 26.9.40
P5206	151/56/249/258/ 9 FTS	To Admiralty 30.1.42
P5207	79/229/245	To 3272M 11.41
P5208	601/504/52 OTU	Collided with V7572 and abandoned 3m W of Dunmow, Essex, 21.7.41
P5209	46/317/56 OTU/ MSFU/55 OTU/ 41 OTU	SOC 18.5.44

Two Hawker Typhoon prototypes delivered in November 1940 and July 1941 respectively by Hawker, Kingston, to Contract No. 815124/38

P5212	AAEE/Northolt/AAEE	SOC for static tests
P5216	Makers & AAEE/ Rotol	SOC 25.2.45

* * * * * * * * * *

Two Hawker Tornado prototypes delivered in December 1942 and August 1941 respectively by Hawker, Kingston, to Contract 815124/38

P5219	Makers	SOC 25.8.43
P5224	RR/AAEE/RAE	SOC 20.9.44

* * * * * * * * * *

50 Fairey Battle Is delivered between September and November 1939 by Fairey, Heaton Chapel, to Contract No.768880/38

P5228	-	To RCAF 19.4.40 as 1652
P5229	12	Shot down near Pouru-St.Rémy, Ardennes during attack on bridges near Sedan, 14.5.40
P5230	18 OTU	To SAAF 24.7.41
P5231	12	Abandoned in France 6.40
P5232	150	Shot down attacking Sedan bridges, 14.5.40
P5233	226	To RCAF 29.8.41 as 2067
P5234	226	To RAAF 27.8.41
P5235	150	Missing from night intruder mission over enemy troops, 20.5.40
P5236	150/12	To RCAF 8.3.41 as 1885
P5237	103/12	To RCAF 27.8.41 as 2108
P5238	142	Damaged by enemy aircraft, Laon, 19.5.40 and abandoned at Chateau Bougon
P5239	-	To RAAF 21.3.40
P5240	266/245/142	To RAAF 2.3.41
P5241	-	To RAAF 29.3.40
P5242		To RAAF 18.4.40
P5243		To RAAF 4.4.40
P5244	266	Engine cut after take-off; force-landed and hit ditch, Sutton Bridge, 17.1.40; DBR
P5245	-	To RCAF 20.4.40 as 1662
P5246	266	To SAAF 2.7.40 as 923
P5247	-	To RAAF 1.3.40
P5248	266/Exp Flt Martlesham Heath/420 Flt/CGS/ Warmwell	SOC 10.12.44
P5249	-	To RAAF 18.4.40
P5250	266/234	To RCAF 18.10.40 as 1760
P5251	266/245	To SAAF 15.7.41
P5252	-	To RCAF 2.4.41 as 1937
P5270	-	To RCAF 22.5.41 as 1958
P5271	-	To RCAF 17.5.41 as 1963
P5272	-	To RCAF 25.4.41 as 1977
P5273	-	To RAAF 4.6.41
P5274	-	To RCAF 11.3.41 as 1918
P5275	-	To RAAF 3.4.41
P5276	-	To RCAF 10.6.41 as 2033
P5277	2 AACU	SOC 10.3.44
P5278	-	To RCAF 2.4.41 as 1864
P5279	-	To RCAF 25.4.41 as 1950
P5280	-	To RCAF 3.4,41 as 1940
P5281	-	To RCAF 11.4.41; passed on to RAAF
P5282	-	To RCAF 2.4.41 as 1938
P5283	88/239	Engine cut; undershot forced landing, Watchlaw, Northumberland, 25.7.42; DBR
P5284	-	To RCAF 1.4.41 as 1975

P5285	-	To RCAF 19.8.41 as 2080
P5286	-	To SAAF 12.4.41 but lost at sea en route
P5287	-	To RCAF 29.3.41 as 1911
P5288	2/26/1472 Flt	SOC 13.10.43
P5289	-	To RAAF 1.10.40
P5290	-	To RCAF 8.8.41 as 2059
P5291	-	To RCAF 4.41 as 2013
P5292	-	To RCAF 27.9.40 as 1721
P5293	-	To RCAF 28.10.40 as 1764
P5294	-	To RCAF 4.41 as 2045

*   *   *   *   *   *   *   *   *   *

80 Hampden Is built by Canadian Associated Aircraft and delivered between September 1940 and August 1941 to Contract No. 965794/38

Up to P5337 assembled by Quebec Group and remainder by Ontario Group

P5298	5 BGS/5 AOS/32 OTU	SOC 2.8.44
P5299	-	SOC 23.4.42
P5300	5 BGS/1 AAS	SOC 14.1.44
P5301	5 BGS/Cv TB/415	Missing on shipping sweep, 26.7.43
P5302	5 AOS/Cv TB/455	SOC 3.2.44
P5303	16 OTU	Spun into ground near Leamington on navex, 1.11.41
P5304	16 OTU/Cv TB/455	Flew into mountain in transit to Russia, Arvastuotter, Sweden, 4/5.9.42
P5305	16 OTU	Undershot night approach and hit trees, Brackley LG, 22.7.41
P5306	-	SOC 23.4.42
P5307	-	SOC 23.4.42
P5308	16 OTU	Flew into hill during bombing practice, Corble Farm, Brill, Bucks., 29.9.41
P5309	16 OTU/Cv TB/ 5 OTU/415	SOC 27.2.44
P5310	16 OTU	Control lost after prop fell off; crashed 5m SE of Aberayron, Card., 17.10.41
P5311	25 OTU/14 OTU/ Cv TB/1404 Flt	SOC 20.12.43; poss to 3075M
P5312	25 OTU/14 OTU	Missing (Bremen) 26.6.42; crashed off Borkum
P5313	16 OTU/5 OTU	Swung on take-off, Turnberry, 24.7.42
P5314	16 OTU	Shot down by intruder 4m NE of Upper Heyford, 20.9.41
P5315	16 OTU/Cv TB/415	To Russian Navy, 12.10.42
P5316	-	Collided with Tiger Moth N5447 near Hooton Park, 24.7.41
P5317	-	SOC 18.5.44
P5318	16 OTU	Flew into hill at night near Wigginton Church, Bloxham, Oxon., 22.10.41
P5319	16 OTU	Control lost after engine failure at night; crashed near Bourton-on-the-Water, Glos., 26.2.42
P5320	14 OTU/455	SOC 10.3.44
P5321	44/408/14 OTU	Collided with Halifax W1013 near March, Cambs., on return from Cologne, 31.5.42
P5322	83/14 OTU	Missing (Düsseldorf) 1.8.42
P5323	106/Cv TB/455	Ran out of fuel and crashed, Kandalashka, 5.9.42
P5324	83/49	Shot down by flak or fighters during attack on German battle fleet, 12.2.42
P5325	455	Missing (minelaying off Lorient) 3.4.42
P5326	455	Engine cut on take-off on air test; dived into ground, Wigsley, 12.3.42
P5327	455/Cv TB	SOC 1.4.44
P5328	455	Crashed at Folly Farm, Haddenham, Bucks., on return from minelaying off La Rochelle, 3.1.42; cause not known
P5329	455	Control lost when prop came off on ferry flight; crashed, Watchfield, 2m E of Highbridge, Somerset, 25.3.42
P5330	106/420	Shot down by night fighter on return from Rostock 4m SSE of Assens, Fyn, Denmark, 25.4.42
P5331	144/Cv TB/5 OTU	Stalled on turn after take-off, Long Kesh, 14.7.43
P5332	44/420	Shot down by night fighter in Ijsselmeer, during raid on Bremen, 3.7.42
P5333	16 OTU/5 OTU/ 1402 Flt	SOC 19.11.43
P5334	408/1406 Flt/ 519	Missing on met flight over North Sea due to engine failure, 25.8.43
P5335	50/144/Cv TB/489	SOC 17.2.44
P5336	-	To Canada
	32 OTU	SOC 2.8.44
P5337	124 RCAF	Crashed on ferry flight near Dugald, Manitoba, 24.11.42
P5338	AAEE/TDU/RAE	SOC 20.6.46
P5339	5 BGS/1 AAS	SOC 17.2.44
P5340	1 AAS	SOC 9.6.44
P5341	CGS/Cv TB/1 TTU	Engine cut; crashed off Dunure, Firth of Clyde, 16.8.43
P5342	-	SOC 24.3.42
P5343	CGS/Cv TB/415	SOC 20.2.44
P5344	14 OTU/1404 Flt/517	SOC 9.1.44
P5345	16 OTU	Landed on Anson R9668, Upper Heyford, 13.10.41
P5346	16 OTU	Flew into ground during low-level night bombing practice, Otmoor ranges, Oxon., 3.4.42
P5386	16 OTU	Dived into ground on night bombing exercise 2m E of Chalgrove, Oxon., 6.11.41
P5387	16 OTU/14 OTU/ Cv TB/489	SOC 22.3.45
P5388	16 OTU	Swung on take-off and hit L4202, Upper Heyford, 20.4.42
P5389	Cv TB/5 OTU	SOC 16.12.43
P5390	16 OTU/Cv TB/489/455	SOC 19.12.43
P5391	16 OTU	Overshot landing at Towyn, 3.10.41; DBR
P5392	408	Dived into ground, Newfarm, Longdown, Hants., 15.12.41 on return from Cherbourg
P5393	83	Collided on ground with AE374, Scampton, 14/15.12.41
P5394	16 OTU/Cv TB/415	Ditched after engine failure, Padstow Harbour, Cornwall, 28.10.42, after torpedo strike in Bay of Biscay
P5395	1406 Flt/519	SOC 13.4.44
P5396	3 FPP	Dived into ground on overshoot, Burtonwood, 7.11.41
P5397	16 OTU/14 OTU	Collided with AE192 1m NW of Market Deeping, 30.7.42
P5398	14 OTU	Crashed at night, Whittle Farm, Brockhampton, Glos., 7.4.42; cause not known
P5399		To Canada 5.42
	32 OTU	Swung on take-off and undercarriage collapsed, Patricia Bay, BC, 16.9.43; DBR

P5400	-	To Canada 5.42
	32 OTU	Swung on take-off and broke back, Patricia Bay, 5.8.42
P5421	-	To Canada 5.42
	32 OTU	Undershot night approach and hit obstruction, Patricia Bay, 27.7.43
P5422	-	To Canada 5.42
	32 OTU	SOC 2.8.44
P5423	-	To Canada
	32 OTU	SOC 2.8.44
P5424	-	To Canada 5.42
	32 OTU	Overshot landing at Patricia Bay, 10.11.43; DBR
P5425	-	To Canada 11.41
	32 OTU	SOC 2.8.44
P5426	-	To Canada 5.42
	124 RCAF	Dived into ground on approach 3m NE of Rockcliffe, Ottawa, 29.5.42
P5427	-	To Canada 4.42
	32 OTU	Abandoned after control lost near Patricia Bay, 31.7.43
P5428	-	To Canada 5.42
	32 OTU	Stalled on landing and crash-landed, Patricia Bay, 24.10.42; to RCAF and SOC 2.8.44
P5429	-	To Canada 11.41
	32 OTU	Hit by P5428 while parked, Patricia Bay, 5.9.43; DBR
P5430	-	To Canada 5.42
	32 OTU	SOC 26.5.44
P5431	-	To Canada 5.42
	32 OTU	Engine cut in circuit; lost height and crashlanded, Brentwood, near Patricia Bay, 24.2.43
P5432	-	To Canada 5.42
	32 OTU	Swung on landing and ground-looped, Patricia Bay, 2.12.42; to RCAF and SOC 2.8.44
P5433	-	To Canada 5.42
	32 OTU	Dived into sea during low flying exercise, Saanich Inlet, Vancouver Island, 14.3.43
P5434	-	To Canada 5.42
	32 OTU	Swung on take-off, hit mound and crashlanded, Patricia Bay, 26.4.43; DBF
P5435	-	To Canada 5.42
	32 OTU	To GI airframe A386 16.3.44
P5436	-	To Canada 11.42
	32 OTU	Developed stabilised yaw after torpedo drop; ditched in Saanich Inlet, Vancouver Island, 15.11.42; salvaged for preservation

*   *   *   *   *   *   *   *   *   *

Five (of 140) Airspeed Queen Wasps delivered in April 1940 by Airspeed, Portsmouth, to Contract No. 968560/38

P5441	PAS/RAE/PAU	SOC 27.7.43
P5442	PAU	SOC 27.7.43
P5443	PAU	
P5444	PAU	SOC 27.7.43
P5445	1 AACU/PAU	Crashed in sea, 15.9.42
P5446 to		
P5450	-	Not completed
P5551 to		
P5480	-	Cancelled
P5496 to		
P5525	-	Cancelled
P5546 to		
P5565	-	Cancelled

P5571-P5620		50 Lockheed Hudsons for RAAF to Contract No. 971221/38

*   *   *   *   *   *   *   *   *   *

Five Airspeed Envoy IIIs delivered in November 1939 by Airspeed, Portsmouth, to Contract No. 967144/38

P5625	Northolt/15 Gp CF/ 17 Gp CF/Gosport/ Turnhouse	SOC 8.4.43
P5626	1 EWS/10 FTS/ Cranwell/24/ Limavady/Turnhouse/ Gosport/R-R	Sold 30.1.46; became G-AHAC
P5627	16 Gp CF/Gosport	SOC 4.7.42
P5628	27 Gp CF/Napiers	SOC 5.6.44
P5629	Turnhouse/Leuchars	SOC 29.7.43

*   *   *   *   *   *   *   *   *   *

Seven Percival Q.6s delivered in June 1939 by Percival Aircraft, Luton, to Contract No. 963632/38

P5634	Northolt/Benson/ Halton/Hendon	Sold 20.5.46; to G-AHTB
P5635	24	DBR in air raid, Hendon, 8.10.40
P5636	24/PDU/Heston/15 Gp CF/Tiree	SOC 14.8.44
P5637	Ternhill/8 EFTS/ Northolt/Heston/ 61 OTU/ADGB CF/ Northolt	Sold 29.4.46; to G-AHOM
P5638	Gosport/Northolt/ 24/Halton	To Admiralty 6.6.43
P5639	Andover/61 OTU/ Andover/Northolt/ Speke/MCS	Sold 20.5.46; to G-AHTA
P5640	267	
P5641	-	Apparently not delivered

*   *   *   *   *   *   *   *   *   *

P5646-P5720		Walrus Is delivered to Admiralty to Contract No. B974377/39

RAF use

P5650	1680 Flt	SS 21.5.47
P5658	276	Sold 23.1.47
P5663	275/278/MAEE	SS 26.3.47
P5667	293	SOC 14.3.46
P5669	Med	SOC 29.8.46
P5696	283	NFT
P5712	ME	SOC 23.8.45
P5718	ME	SOC 31.5.44

*   *   *   *   *   *   *   *   *   *

Four Curtiss Condors purchased from International Air Freight under Contract No.961733/38 in September 1939 for E & WS, Yatesbury but found to be unairworthy

P5723	-	Ex G-AEWD; SOC 11.9.39
P5724	-	Ex G-AEZF; SOC 11.9.39
P5725	-	Ex G-AEWE; SOC 11.9.39
P5726	-	Ex G-AEWF; SOC 11.9.39

*   *   *   *   *   *   *   *   *   *

28 D.H. Queen Bees delivered in June and July 1939 by De Havilland, Hatfield, to Contract No. 962680/38

P5731	PAU/1 AACU	Shot down near Aberporth, 3.10.41

49

P5732	PAU/1 AACU	Shot down off Ty Croes ranges, Anglesey, 1.8.41
P5733	PAU/1 AACU	Dived into ground Aberporth, 17.10.41
P5734	PAU/1 AACU	Shot down off Aberporth, 20.7.41
P5735	PAU/1 AACU	Crashed off Aberporth, 18.9.41
P5736	1 AACU/PAU/1 1 AACU	Shot down off Aberporth, 8.4.41
P5737	PAU & 1 AACU/1618 Flt/1620 Flt	Crashed near Bodorgan, 5.8.43
P5738	PAU/1 AACU	Control lost; crashed off Ty Croes, 20.8.41
P5739	2 AACU/1 AACU	Shot down off Cleave, 2.7.40
P5740	2 AACU/1 AACU	Shot down off Cleave, 17.6.40
P5741	PAU & 1 AACU	Shot down in sea off Aberporth, 20.1.42
P5742	PAS/1 AACU	Landed in sea off Manorbier and DBR during salvage, 14.10.40
P5743	PAS/1 AACU/PAU	Dived into ground 3m N of St.Athan, 2.1.41
P5744	PAS/1 AACU	Shot down off Burrow Head, 4.9.40
P5745	PAU & 1 AACU	Crashed in sea off Aberporth, 14.2.42
P5746	PAU & 1 AACU	Shot down off Burrow Head, 26.2.42
P5747	PAS/1 AACU	Radio control lost in cloud; crashed in sea off Manorbier, 4.12.40
P5748	PAU/1 AACU	Engine cut; crashed off Cleave, 23.9.40
P5749	PAU & 1 AACU	Crashed on landing, Aberporth, 5.8.42
P5767	1 AACU	Spun into ground, 13.10.39
P5768	1 AACU	Shot down in sea, 28.9.39
P5769	2 AACU/PAU/1 AACU	Shot down in sea off Aberffraw, Anglesey, 22.2.41
P5770	2 AACU/PAU & 1 AACU/1621 Flt	Crashed on landing, Aberporth, 23.1.43
P5771	1 AACU/PAU/1 AACU	Crashed in sea off Manorbier, 16.6.42
P5772	PAS/1 AACU	Hit wall in forced landing in fog while piloted, Trawsfynydd, N.Wales, 19.2.40
P5773	PAS/1 AACU	Stalled near Kidsdale and crashed, 7.3.40
P5774	1 AACU	DBR in heavy landing, Kidsdale, 12.1.40
P5775	1 AACU	Shot down off Burrow Head, 19.10.39

*   *   *   *   *   *   *   *   *   *

Airspeed Envoy purchased from North-East Airways in November 1938 under Contract No. 968450/39

P5778	EWS/9 FTS	Ex G-ADBA; to GI use, 11.12.39

*   *   *   *   *   *   *   *   *   *

200 North American Harvard Is delivered between August 1939 and June 1940 by North American Aviation, Inglewood, to Contract No. 791588/38

P5783	6 FTS/15 FTS 22 SFTS	To S Rhodesia 2.41; SOC 31.3.44
P5784	6 FTS	Turned after night take-off and dived into ground 3m E of Woodstock, Oxon., 14.3.40; DBF
P5785	6 FTS/71 OTU	SOC 31.8.44

P5786	6 FTS 22 SFTS	To S Rhodesia 3.41; SOC 9.8.44
P5787	1 FTS/6 FTS 22 SFTS	To S Rhodesia 4.41; SOC 6.6.45
P5788	1 FTS/6 FTS	Hit ground during low flying exercise, Haselton, near Cheltenham, 19.8.40
P5789	1 FTS/10 FTS	To S Rhodesia 15.2.41; SOC 4.8.45
P5790	1 FTS/2 FTS 20 SFTS	To S Rhodesia 2.41; SOC 30.9.44
P5791	1 FTS	Collided with N5792 during formation practice and crashed, Collingbourne Kingston, 5m NE of Netheravon, 23.9.39
P5792	1 FTS	Collided with N5791 during formation practice and crashed, Collingbourne Kingston, 5m NE of Netheravon, 23.9.39
P5793	15 FTS	Undershot landing, stalled and hit hedge, Bibury, 5.8.40
P5794	15 FTS 22 SFTS/20 SFTS	To S Rhodesia 15.2.41; SOC 30.11.44
P5795	14 FTS/15 FTS 20 SFTS	To S Rhodesia 4.41;
P5796	14 FTS/15 FTS 22 SFTS	To S Rhodesia 15.2.41; SOC 5.4.45
P5797	1 FTS 20 SFTS	To S Rhodesia 16.8.40; SOC 31.8.44
P5798	14 FTS/15 FTS 20 SFTS	To S Rhodesia 2.41; SOC 31.3.42
P5799	14 FTS 20 SFTS/22 SFTS	To S Rhodesia 3.1.40; SOC 2.11.45
P5800	14 FTS/15 FTS/ME	NFT 31.12.41
P5801	14 FTS	Dived into ground, Alves, Moray, 18.12.39; cause not known
P5802	14 FTS/15 FTS	To S Rhodesia 4.41
P5803	14 FTS/15 FTS	Broke up in air during aerobatics near Upper Heyford, 18.9.40
P5804	14 FTS 20 SFTS	To S Rhodesia 3.11.40; Swung on night take-off on to rough ground, Cranborne, 16.6.41; DBR
P5805	14 FTS/15 FTS 22 SFTS	To S Rhodesia 4.41; DBR in accident, 28.5.42; NFD
P5806	14 FTS/15 FTS	SOC 21.11.40
P5807	14 FTS	Undershot forced landing while lost in bad weather; hit hedge and overturned near Northampton, 18.4.40
P5808	14 FTS/15 FTS	To S Rhodesia 2.41; SOC 4.12.43
P5809	14 FTS 22 SFTS	To S Rhodesia 11.4.41; SOC 31.10.44
P5810	- 20 SFTS	To S Rhodesia 3.11.40; Stalled and spun into ground, Senale, S Rhodesia, 5.6.42
P5811	14 FTS/15 FTS	To S Rhodesia 1.41; SOC 2.11.45
P5812	14 FTS/41 OTU	SOC 14.5.45
P5813	14 FTS	Engine cut; hit trees in forced landing, North Crawley, Bucks., 31.5.40
P5814	15 FTS 22 SFTS	To S Rhodesia 22.2.41; Crashed near Gwelo, 15.2.43; cause not known
P5815	15 FTS 20 SFTS	To S Rhodesia 12.40; Crashed at Hillsode, S Rhodesia, 12.5.43
P5816	15 FTS/14 FTS 20 SFTS	To S Rhodesia 3.11.40; SOC 7.5.43
P5817	15 FTS/14 FTS	Collided with N4638 near Bozeat, Northants., 10.6.40

Serial	Units	History
P5818	15 FTS/41 OTU	SOC 10.10.44
P5819	15 FTS 22 SFTS	To S Rhodesia 1.41; SOC 13.5.42
P5820	15 FTS	Ran away backwards down hill after forced landing and hit wall, Ambergate near Birkenhead, Cheshire, 8.1.40; DBR
P5821	15 FTS 22 SFTS	To S Rhodesia 22.2.41; SOC 2.11.45
P5822	15 FTS/14 FTS/ 15 FTS 20 SFTS	To S Rhodesia 8.1.41; SOC 5.2.45
P5823	14 FTS/15 FTS 22 SFTS	To S Rhodesia 9.4.41; SOC 31.10.44
P5824	14 FTS/15 FTS/ Upavon 20 SFTS	To S Rhodesia 6.41; SOC 2.11.45
P5825	14 FTS/15 FTS	To S Rhodesia 3.41
P5826	14 FTS/15 FTS 20 SFTS	To S Rhodesia 20.2.41; Dived into ground near Salisbury, S Rhodesia, 6.4.42; cause not known
P5827	14 FTS/15 FTS	To S Rhodesia 15.2.41; SOC 30.9.43
P5828	15 FTS	Flew into ground on night approach 1½m S of Weston-on-the-Green, 23.11.40; DBF
P5829	15 FTS/14 FTS/ 15 FTS	To S Rhodesia 2.41; SOC 30.11.44
P5830	2 Cam Unit/PRU	To S Rhodesia 4.41; SOC 9.8.44
P5831	15 FTS 22 SFTS	To S Rhodesia 3.41; SOC 2.11.45
P5832	15 FTS	To S Rhodesia 5.41
P5833	15 FTS 22 SFTS	To S Rhodesia 22.2.41; Crashed on navex, Fort Victoria, SR, 13.4.44
P5834	15 FTS 22 SFTS/20 SFTS	To S Rhodesia 2.41; SOC 31.12.43
P5835	6 FTS 22 SFTS	To S Rhodesia 6.41; Missing near Sonambula, SR, 12.6.44
P5836	2 FTS 22 SFTS	To S Rhodesia 22.2.41; SOC 5.3.45
P5837	2 FTS/1 FPP/ATA	SOC 23.5.44
P5838	2 FTS/15 FTS	To S Rhodesia 2.41
P5839	6 FTS	To S Rhodesia
P5840	6 FTS 22 SFTS	To S Rhodesia 22.2.41 SOC 30.12.43
P5841	6 FTS	Stalled while low flying and spun into ground, Tingewick, Bucks., 8.6.40
P5842	6 FTS	Stalled off turn over Otmoor bombing range and spun; hit ground recovering, Islip, Oxon., 18.5.40
P5843	15 FTS/ME	SOC 15.1.42
P5844	15 FTS	To S Rhodesia 15.2.41; SOC 2.11.45
P5845	15 FTS 22 SFTS/20 SFTS	To S Rhodesia 19.2.41; SOC 15.5.44
P5846	15 FTS 22 SFTS	To S Rhodesia 20.2.41; SOC 3.4.44
P5847	15 FTS 20 SFTS	To S Rhodesia 6.41; SOC 5.3.45
P5848	15 FTS	Hit chimney; rolled, hit tree and crashed near Fochabers, Moray, 9.1.40
P5849	15 FTS 20 SFTS	To S Rhodesia 4.41; SOC 31.12.43
P5850	6 FTS	Stalled off turn and dived into ground, Kingham Hill, Oxon., 27.8.40
P5851	6 FTS 22 SFTS	To S Rhodesia 3.41; Abandoned when lost in cloud on navex, Que Que, S Rhodesia, 24.3.42
P5852	6 FTS 22 SFTS	To S Rhodesia 15.2.41; SOC 31.7.44
P5853	6 FTS 20 SFTS	To S Rhodesia 22.1.41; SOC 30.9.44
P5854	15 FTS 22 SFTS	To S Rhodesia 2.41; SOC 7.5.43
P5855	6 FTS 20 SFTS	To S Rhodesia 3.11.40; NFT
P5856	6 FTS 20 SFTS	To S Rhodesia 3.11.40; Ran out of fuel; stalled and crashed, Gadzema, SR, 17.2.41
P5857	10 FTS 20 SFTS	To S Rhodesia 3.11.40; SOC 2.11.45
P5858	10 FTS/15 FTS 20 SFTS	To S Rhodesia 2.41; SOC 2.11.45
P5859	1 FTS/15 FTS/ FPP/ATA	SOC 17.3.44
P5860	1 FTS/41 OTU	SOC 25.4.44
P5861	1 FTS/10 FTS 20 SFTS	To S Rhodesia 3.11.40; Stalled after night take-off and hit ground, Cranborne, 27.2.41
P5862	12 Gp Pool	Stalled emerging from cloud and spun into ground, Aston Down, 26.1.40
P5863	1 FTS/6 FTS/ 15 FTS 20 SFTS	To S Rhodesia 4.41; Collided with N7001 and damaged, 29.5.42; SOC 11.8.42
P5864	12 Gp Pool/5 OTU	Stalled off low turn and spun into ground, Winforton, Hereford, 9.4.40
P5865	609/242/609/615/ 609/15 FTS 22 SFTS	To S Rhodesia 3.41; SOC 5.4.45
P5866	603/Turnhouse/401/ 61 OTU/41 OTU/587	SOC 26.6.45
P5867	602/Coltishall/ATA	SOC 17.3.44
P5868	152/242/141 20 SFTS	To S Rhodesia 3.11.40; Crashed on Inkomo bombing range, 1.10.42; cause not known
P5869	12 Gp Pool/5 OTU/ 61 OTU/41 OTU	SOC 7.5.45
P5870	12 Gp Pool/5 OTU	Engine cut on approach; undershot, hit wall and overturned, Aston Down, 8.6.40
P5871	12 Gp Pool	Spun into ground, Oakridge, near Chalford, Glos., 21.11.39; cause not known
P5872	12 Gp Pool/5 OTU/ 55 OTU/52 OTU/ 61 OTU/41 OTU	SOC 10.9.44
P5873	6 FTS/15 FTS	To S Rhodesia 22.2.41; SOC 5.2.45
P5874	6 FTS	To S Rhodesia 22.1.41; SOC 9.8.44
P5875	6 FTS/15 FTS 22 SFTS	To S Rhodesia 4.3.41; SOC 2.11.45
P5876	- 20 SFTS	To S Rhodesia 10.8.40; Lost wing in dive, Inkomo bombing range, 25.8.41
P5877	2 FTS/15 FTS 22 SFTS	To S Rhodesia 2.41; SOC 31.10.44
P5878	2 FTS/15 FTS	To S Rhodesia 5.41; SOC 9.8.44
P5879	6 FTS	To S Rhodesia 2.41; Damaged and SOC 7.1.42
P5880	6 FTS 20 SFTS	To S Rhodesia 2.41; Crashed at Estes Mazoe, SR, 12.8.41

Serial	Units	Remarks
P5881	6 FTS, 22 SFTS	To S Rhodesia 22.2.41; DBR 11.6.41
P5882	10 FTS	To S Rhodesia 3.11.40 SOC
P5883	10 FTS, 22 SFTS/20 SFTS	To S Rhodesia 2.1.41 Crashed on Inkoma bombing range, S Rhodesia, 5.1.43
P5884	10 FTS	Turned and lost height after take-off from Ternhill; flew into ground, Wollerton, 4.7.40; DBF
P5885	15 FTS/14 FTS/15 FTS	Stalled off turn after take-off and spun into ground near Brockworth, Glos., 9.9.40
P5886	15 FTS, 22 SFTS/20 SFTS	To S Rhodesia 22.2.41; SOC 30.11.44
P5887	15 FTS, 22 SFTS/20 SFTS	To S Rhodesia 25.1.41; SOC 2.7.45
P5888	15 FTS/71 OTU	SOC 1.1.44
P5889	15 FTS, 22 SFTS	To S Rhodesia 2.41; Crashed at Thornhill, SR, 20.10.41
P5890	15 FTS	Stalled recovering from dive and spun; hit ground, Farley Mount, Hants., 20.5.40; DBF
P5891	10 FTS/15 FTS, 22 SFTS	To S Rhodesia 19.2.41; SOC 31.1.43
P5892	15 FTS, 22 SFTS/20 SFTS	To S Rhodesia 6.41; DBR in accident, 13.1.42; NFD
P5893	15 FTS/71 OTU	
P5894	2 FTS/15 FTS	To S Rhodesia 2.41; SOC
P5895	2 FTS, 22 SFTS	To S Rhodesia 2.41; SOC 17.8.43
P5896	10 FTS, 20 SFTS	To S Rhodesia 3.11.40; Crashed during night flying at Hatfield, SR, 20.8.41
P5897	2 FTS/3 FPP/ATA	SOC 29.3.45
P5898	2 FTS/15 FTS, 20 SFTS	To S Rhodesia 2.41; SOC 30.11.43
P5899	2 FTS/15 FTS, 22 SFTS	To S Rhodesia 4.3.41; SOC 9.8.44
P5900	2 FTS/15 FTS, 22 SFTS	To S Rhodesia 15.2.41; SOC 20.11.45
P5901	2 FTS/15 FTS	Control lost after night take-off; crashed in wood 1½m N of Windrush, 25.7.40; DBF
P5902	15 FTS/14 FTS/15 FTS	To S Rhodesia 3.41; SOC 5.1.45
P5903	2 FTS/15 FTS	To S Rhodesia 3.41; SOC 30.9.43
P5904	14 FTS/15 FTS, 22 SFTS	To S Rhodesia 15.2.41; SOC 1.9.43
P5905	14 FTS/15 FTS, 22 SFTS/20 SFTS	To S Rhodesia 2.41; SOC 2.2.44
P5906	14 FTS/15 FTS/1 FPP/ATA	SS 9.2.49
P5907	15 FTS/10 FTS	To S Rhodesia 15.8.40; SOC 30.11.43
P5908	6 FTS, 22 SFTS	To S Rhodesia 25.1.40; SOC 2.11.45
P5909	-, 20 SFTS	To S Rhodesia 7.8.40; DBR 23.1.41
P5910	-, 20 SFTS	To S Rhodesia 16.8.40; Crashed near Inkomo bombing range, SR, 9.12.40
P5911	6 FTS/ATA	SOC 17.3.44
P5912	6 FTS, 22 SFTS	To S Rhodesia 29.1.41; SOC 2.11.45
P5913	6 FTS	To S Rhodesia 25.1.41; SOC 31.7.44
P5914	6 FTS, 20 SFTS/33 FIS	To S Rhodesia 3.11.40; SOC 9.8.44
P5915	3 FPP/ATA	SOC 17.3.44
P5916	-, 20 SFTS	Delivered to S Rhodesia; SOC 15.12.41
P5917	-, 20 SFTS/22 SFTS	Delivered to S Rhodesia; SOC 2.11.45
P5918	-, 20 SFTS/22 SFTS	Delivered to S Rhodesia; Crashed, 26.5.41
P5919	-, 20 SFTS	Delivered to S Rhodesia; Damaged 5.11.42 and SOC
P5920	-, 20 SFTS	Delivered to S Rhodesia; SOC 5.3.45
P5921	-	Direct to SAAF as 1302
P5922	-, 20 SFTS	Delivered to S Rhodesia; Crashed 10m NE of Marandellas, SR, 14.9.44; DBR
P5923	-	Delivered to S Rhodesia; SOC 7.6.43
P5924	-, 20 SFTS	Delivered to S Rhodesia; SOC 15.3.42
P5925	-	Delivered to S Rhodesia; SOC 4.5.45
P5926	-, 20 SFTS	Delivered to S Rhodesia; SOC 31.8.44
P5927	-, 20 SFTS	Delivered to S Rhodesia; Crashed at Greendale, SR, 26.2.43
P5928	-	Delivered to S Rhodesia; NFT
P5929	-, 20 SFTS	Delivered to S Rhodesia; Collided with N7191 and crashed, New Martinsthorpe LG, 8.3.43
P5930	-, 20 SFTS	Delivered to S Rhodesia; Crashed at Goromonzi, SR, 17.12.40
P5931	-	Delivered to S Rhodesia; SOC 3.10.42
P5932	-	Delivered to S Rhodesia; SOC 18.7.40
P5933	-, 20 SFTS/22 SFTS	Delivered to S Rhodesia; DBR in accident, 2.9.43; NFD
P5934	-, 20 SFTS	Delivered to S Rhodesia; SOC 5.3.45
P5935	-, 20 SFTS	Delivered to S Rhodesia; NFT
P5936	-, 20 SFTS	Delivered to S Rhodesia; SOC 29.2.44
P5937	-, 20 SFTS	Delivered to S Rhodesia; SOC 31.7.44
P5938	-, 20 SFTS	Delivered to S Rhodesia; SOC 30.10.44
P5939	-, 20 SFTS	Delivered to S Rhodesia; Crashed on take-off, Cranborne, 25.3.41
P5940	-, 20 SFTS	Delivered to S Rhodesia; Damaged 7.12.43 and SOC
P5941	-, 20 SFTS	Delivered to S Rhodesia; DBR in accident, 7.12.43
P5942	-, 20 SFTS	Delivered to S Rhodesia; SOC 9.6.42
P5943	-, 20 SFTS	Delivered to S Rhodesia; Spun into ground near Cleveland Dam, SR, 14.10.40
P5944	-, 20 SFTS	Delivered to S Rhodesia; SOC 23.10.41
P5945	-, 22 SFTS/20 SFTS	Delivered to S Rhodesia; SOC 4.5.45
P5946	-	Delivered to S Rhodesia; SOC 30.11.43
P5947	-, 22 SFTS/20 SFTS	Delivered to S Rhodesia; NFT
P5948	-, 22 SFTS	Delivered to S Rhodesia; Crashed at Ruwa, Salisbury, SR, 14.11.41
P5949	-, 20 SFTS	Delivered to S Rhodesia; DBR in accident, 24.7.41

P5950	-	Delivered to S Rhodesia;
	20 SFTS	DBR 13.3.42; SOC 5.6.42
P5951	-	Delivered to S Rhodesia;
	20 SFTS	Crashed on sewage farm,
		Salisbury, SR, 20.6.41; SOC
		23.3.42
P5952	-	Delivered to S Rhodesia;
	20 SFTS	Stalled on landing and over-
		turned, Cranborne, 5.10.40
P5953	-	Delivered to S Rhodesia;
		SOC 30.11.43
P5954	-	Delivered to S Rhodesia;
	20 SFTS	Crashed 35m SW of
		Marandellas, SR, 16.12.43
P5955	-	Delivered to S Rhodesia;
	20 SFTS	SOC 30.11.43
P5956	-	Delivered to S Rhodesia;
	20 SFTS	SOC 31.12.43
P5957	-	Delivered to S Rhodesia;
	20 SFTS	DBR in accident, 28.1.41
P5958	-	Delivered to S Rhodesia;
	20 SFTS	Crashed 19m from Salisbury,
		S Rhodesia, 26.7.43; DBR
P5959	-	Delivered to S Rhodesia;
	20 SFTS	NFT
P5960	-	Delivered to S Rhodesia;
		SOC 2.11.45
P5961	-	Delivered to S Rhodesia;
	20 SFTS	DBR 15.4.41
P5962	-	Delivered to S Rhodesia;
	20 SFTS	Crashed during aerobatics,
		Headlands, SR, 15.3.44; DBR
P5963	-	Delivered to S Rhodesia;
	20 SFTS	Crashed at Marandellas,
		Salisbury, SR, 3.10.40
P5964	-	Delivered to S Rhodesia;
	20 SFTS	Crashed, Glenforest Farm, near
		Salisbury, SR, 11.11.40
P5965	-	Delivered to S Rhodesia;
	20 SFTS	SOC 6.3.41
P5966	-	Delivered to S Rhodesia;
	20 SFTS	To GI airframe 8.11.42
P5967	-	Delivered to S Rhodesia;
	20 SFTS	NFT
P5968	-	Delivered to S Rhodesia;
	20 SFTS	NFT
P5969	-	Delivered to S Rhodesia;
	20 SFTS	SOC 5.1.45
P5970	-	Delivered to S Rhodesia;
	20 SFTS	NFT
P5971	-	Delivered to S Rhodesia;
	20 SFTS	SOC 14.7.44
P5972	-	Delivered to S Rhodesia;
	20 SFTS	Collided with P5977 and
		crashed, Ruwa, SR, 5.10.40
P5973	-	Delivered to S Rhodesia;
	20 SFTS/22 SFTS	NFT
P5974	-	Delivered to S Rhodesia;
	20 SFTS	SOC 30.11.43
P5975	-	Delivered to S Rhodesia;
	22 SFTS	SOC 4.8.45
P5976	-	Delivered to S Rhodesia;
	20 SFTS	NFT
P5977	-	Destroyed to S Rhodesia;
	20 SFTS	Collided with P5972 and
		crashed, Ruwa, SR, 5.10.40
P5978	-	Delivered to S Rhodesia;
	20 SFTS	SOC 5.3.45
P5979	-	Delivered to S Rhodesia;
	20 SFTS	SOC 21.9.41
P5980	-	Delivered to S Rhodesia;
	20 SFTS	SOC 14.7.44
P5981	-	Delivered to S Rhodesia;
	20 SFTS	Crashed at Riverside Farm, 9m
		NE of Norton, SR, 15.12.41

P5982	-	Delivered to S Rhodesia;
	20 SFTS	SOC 31.8.44

*   *   *   *   *   *   *   *   *   *

Eight Percival Vega Gull IIIs delivered between March and July 1939 by Percival, Luton, to Contract No. 976895/39

P5986	-	To Admiralty 24.5.39
P5987	-	To Admiralty 24.5.39
P5988	Andover/S of Photog/	
	White Waltham/ACC	
	CF/613/AEAF CF/	
	SHAEF CS	SOC 14.3.45
P5989	24/Hucknall/24/510	SOC 6.2.45; to G-AHET
P5990	24/Halton/8 EFTS/	
	FTC CF/ATA	SOC 27.11.44
P5991	24/SF Northolt	Engine cut on take-off; crash-
		landed, Hendon, 15.5.40
P5992	24	To G-AFVI for Air Attaché,
		Lisbon, 16.6.39
P5993	24/Northolt	SOC 9.11.43

*   *   *   *   *   *   *   *   *   *

One Percival Proctor I delivered in January 1940 by Percival, Luton, to Contract No. 975967/39

P5998	DH/Mkrs/1 SS	SOC 8.7.43

*   *   *   *   *   *   *   *   *   *

P5999- 6037		Proctor IAs delivered direct to
P6050- 6079		Admiralty to Contract
P6101- 6113		No.975967/39
except:		
P6062	Mkrs/RAE/Mkrs	Sold 4.4.46

*   *   *   *   *   *   *   *   *   *

140 Percival Proctor Is delivered between May 1940 and August 1940 by Percival Aircraft, Luton, to Contract No. 975967/39

P6114	267	DBR by enemy action, 6.5.41
P6115	CF Heliopolis/	Hit obstacle on landing, Barce,
	CF Cyrenaica/CFWD	3.4.41; SOC 30.5.41, possibly
		having been abandoned on
		evacuation of airfield
P6116	CF Heliopolis/	
	267/Malta ASR & CF	SOC 2.45
P6117	CF Heliopolis/204	
	Gp CF/173	SOC 27.11.44
P6118	CF Helopolis/267/	Swung on landing and tipped
	173	up, Lydda, 17.8.42; DBR
P6119	CF Heliopolis/267	SOC 1.11.41
P6120	CF Heliopolis/267	SOC 30.7.42
P6121	CF Heliopolis/	
	CF Lydda	SOC 15.2.42
P6122	CF Heliopolis/CFWD/	
	173/267/173/MECS	SOC 30.11.44
P6123	CF Heliopolis/267	SOC 6.45
P6124	CF Heliopolis/267	Destroyed on evacuation,
		El Adem, 22.4.41
P6125	CF Heliopolis/173/	Swung on take-off to avoid
	267/173	Spitfire and undercarriage
		collapsed, Helwan, 17.8.42;
		SOC 31.12.42
P6126	CF Heliopolis/203	
	Gp CF/173/267/MECS	SOC 29.3.45
P6127	CF Heliopolis/117	SOC 31.1.43
P6128	CF Heliopolis/117/203	
	Gp CF/CF Khartoum/	
	Iraq & Persia CF	SOC 1.11.45

P6129	24/510/St.Athan	Pilot's harness jammed control column on take-off; aircraft turned and hit ground, St.Athan, 18.6.45
P6130	Northolt/ATA/2 SS/ 25 Gp CF/Ternhill/ 25 Gp CF	Sold 10.7.46
P6131 to P6145		Proctor IAs delivered
P6166	-	direct to
P6167	-	Admiralty
P6168	Ternhill/Perth/2 SS/ BW Flt/4 RS/6th TAD USAAF/NFDW/FIDS	Sold 14.1.46; to G-AHLW
P6169	Ternhill/8 EFTS/13/ 26/Gatwick/84 Gp CF	To USAAF 31.1.44
P6170	Halton/Perth/2 SS/ BW Flt/1 EFTS/2 RS/42 OTU	Sold 18.1.46; to G-AHAZ
P6171	10 FTS/Cranwell/ Perth/2 SS/BW Flt/ 2 RS/Grove	SOC 22.10.44
P6172	S Cerney/3 FTS/ 2 EWS/1 SS/2 SS/ BW Flt/2 RS/4 RS	Sold 17.9.46; to G-AIKH
P6173	Wick/18 Gp CF/PTS/ ACC CF/83 Gp CF/ Grove/Ballykelly	Sold 25.11.46; to G-AIIP
P6174	613/4/Clifton/ Coltishall/1 RS/OATS	Sold 30.8.46; to G-AIEX
P6175	614/24 EFTS	SOC 29.12.42
P6176	225	Destroyed in air raid, Kenley, 20.8.40
P6177	16/13/4 SS/4 RS/HP	Sold 23.3.46; G-AHDH
P6178	110 RCAF/4	DBR 14.12.42; SOC 11.1.43
P6179	Andover/ATA/24/ 510/MCS/Andover/ 52 Base HQ	Sold 9.9.46; to G-AIKI
P6180	Benson/12 OTU/ Halton/2 SS/2 RS/ 4 RS	SOC 14.7.45
P6181	Benson/12 OTU/ Halton/1 STT/1 EFTS/ FTC CF/38 Gp CF	SOC 12.7.45
P6182	Wyton/Swanton Morley/ FRU/85 Gp CF/301	Sold; to G-AGYC
P6183	Wyton/Perth/2 SS/ BW Flt/4 RS/38 Gp CF	Sold 2.7.46; to G-AHVH
P6184	3 Gp CF/2 SS/2 RS/ Halton/2 RS/Grove	SOC 4.12.44
P6185	Linton/2 SS/2 RS/ BW Flt/1 EFTS	Sold 14.6.46; to G-AHUX
P6186	Grantham/12 FTS/2 SS/ 2 RS/BW Flt/1 EFTS	Sold 9.10.46; to G-AIHH
P6187	6 Gp CF/ATA/Halton/ 1 EFTS	Sold 25.2.46; to G-AHFU
P6188	10 Gp CF/SF Colerne/ 2 RS	Sold 28.1.46; to G-AGYA
P6189	10 Gp CF/16/TFPP/ 41 OTU/Old Sarum/ Grove	Sold 10.5.46; to G-AHMS
P6190	SF Northolt/2 SS/2 RS/ 16 Gp CF	Sold 18.1.46; to G-AHFX
P6191	Hucknall/ATA/2 SS/ 2 RS/BW Flt/Tain	Sold 8.9.46; to G-AILP
P6192	Woolsington/2 SS/2 RS/ BW Flt/1 RS/CF White Waltham/4 RS	Sold 17.5.46; to G-AHTC
P6193	13 Gp CF/2 SS/ 2 RS/SF Clifton	Caught fire starting up, Clifton 29.7.43; DBR
P6194	15 Gp CF/24/USAAC/ 510/2 RS/83 Gp CF/ PAU	Sold 23.2.46; to G-AHDI
P6195	Leuchars/2 SS/BW Flt/Grove	Sold 18.6.46; to G-AHUY
P6196	Farnborough/S of Photography/2 SS/BW Flt/Heston/24 Gp CF	Sold 11.9.46; to G-AIKG
P6197	Halton/Perth/2 SS/ Halton/4 RS/Madley	Sold 17.1.46; to G-AGWV
P6198	Abingdon/ATA	Collided with Spitfire P9425, Boscombe Down, 5.11.41; SOC 5.6.42
P6199	Abingdon/ATA/4 SS/ 4 RS/Heston	SOC 11.10.44
P6200	Abingdon/24/510/ Hendon	Sold 18.1.46; to G-AHFY
P6226	Woodley/8 EFTS/2 SS/BW Flt	Sold 23.5.46; to G-AHMX
P6227	Woodley/8 EFTS/ Perth/2 SS/4 RS/ Grove/TCDU/ GCI Flt Harwell	Sold 7.10.46; to G-AIEV
P6228	Grantham/12 FTS/ Perth/2 SS/BW Flt/ 1 EFTS/SHAEF CS/ BAFO CW	Forcelanded on bad weather and ground-looped to avoid bank near Fuhlsbüttel, 21.9.45
P6229	12 FTS/1 SS/1 RS	Spun into ground avoiding Blenheim, Warren Farm, near Grantham, 2.2.44
P6230	1 AACU/S of Photography/ATA/ 10 OTU/SF Abingdon	Sold 2.9.46; to G-AILN
P6231	Northolt/ATA/27 OTU/93 Gp CF	Sold 24.1.46; to G-AGYB
P6232	1 SS/BW Flt/ 2 TAF CF	Destroyed in air raid, Melsbroek, 1.1.45
P6233	Wyton/Perth/2 SS/ Yeadon/51 Gp CF/ 2 RS/23 Gp CF	Sold 27.8.47; to G-AKVV
P6234	1 SS	Spun into ground off turn on approach, Cranwell, 7.2.41
P6235	1 SS/ADGB CF	Sold 26.6.46; to G-AHVI
P6236	1 SS	To 4811M; SOC 15.7.47
P6237	1 SS/4 SS/4 RS/ 1 EFTS/38 Gp CF/ Rivenhall/Tarrant Rushton	Sold 7.10.46; to G-AJLS
P6238	1 SS/1 RS/2 TAF CF/ BAFO CS	SOC 31.8.45
P6239	1 SS/2 SS/2 RS/BW Flt	To 4800M 10.9.45
P6240	309/2 SS/Thornaby	To Czech AF 15.7.46
P6241	SF Northolt/23 OTU/ Pershore/MCCS	Tyre burst on take-off; over-turned on landing, Andover, 17.3.45
P6242	1 SS/84 Gp CF/MCCS/ 24 Gp CF	Sold 25.11.46; to G-AIYH
P6243	2 SS/BW Flt/Locking	Sold 10.3.47; to G-AJGD
P6244	Hucknall/Perth/20 Wg/ 2 SS/BW Flt/1 EFTS/ 2 TAF CF	Failed to become airborne on and hit obstruction, A.82 Rouvres, 20.10.44
P6245	Abingdon/Perth/2 SS/ ATA/2 SS/BW Flt/ Yatesbury/1 EFTS	Sold 8.6.46; to G-AHTN
P6246	2 SS/BW Flt	Sold 7.10.46; to G-AIEE
P6247	1 SS	Hit HT cables low flying, Kirby-le-Thorpe, Lincs. 10.6.42
P6248	8 MU/2 SS/2 RS/ BW Flt/510	Sold 10.9.46; to G-AIHE
P6249	1 SS/4 RS	Collided on approach with LZ738 and crashed, Madley, 6.11.43
P6250	Sydenham/Belfast CF/RAE	Sold 11.2.46
P6251	2 SS/1 SS/2 RS	Sold 18.1.46; to G-AGZL
P6252	Sydenham/Belfast CF/10 Gp CF/219/ Horsham St.Faith/ 1 ADF	Sold 10.5.46; to G-AIIK

54

P6253	2 SS	Spun into ground in bumpy weather near Calne, Wilts., 29.7.41
P6254	2 SS/1 SS/24/510/ Hendon/Northolt/FCCS	SOC 19.6.45
P6255	1 SS/1 EFTS/23 Gp CF	SOC 18.5.45
P6256	225/16	Crashed on take-off, Roborough, 9.6.41; DBF
P6257	2 SS/BW Flt/2 RS	Undershot landing and hit hedge, Yatesbury, 19.8.43; DBR
P6258	2 SS/BW Flt/1 EFTS	Sold 18.6.46; to G-AHVB
P6259	Leuchars/2 RS/4 RS	Sold 18.1.46; to G-AGZM
P6260	2 SS/1 SS	Sold 10.7.46; to G-AHUW
P6261	2 SS/2 RS/BW Flt	To 4496M 10.9.45
P6262	2 SS/4 SS/ADGB CF	Sold 18.1.46; to G-AHFW
P6263	2 SS	Spun into ground on approach, Yatesbury, 28.2.41
P6264	2 SS/2 RS//BW Flt/ 4 RS	Sold 23.2.46; to G-AHDJ
P6265	2 SS/BW Flt/Grove	SOC 6.10.44
P6266	2 SS	Spun into ground during aerobatics near Calne, Wilts., 16.5.42
P6267	2 SS/1 EFTS/ Castletown/13 Gp CF	Sold 31.1.46; to G-AHAB
P6268	4 SS/4 RS/1 RS/ 12 Gp CF	Sold 17.6.46; to G-AHUZ
P6269	2 SS/10 Gp CF/ 1 EFTS/24 Gp CF	Sold 14.5.46; to G-AHMG
P6270	2 SS/1 SS/1 RS	To 4786M
P6271	Watchfield/2 EWS/ 1 SS/CF Woodley/ CNS	Sold 13.6.46; to G-AHTV
P6272	2 EWS/2 SS/BW Flt	SOC 20.9.43
P6273	2 SS/2 RS	Sold 10.5.46; to G-AHMR
P6274	8 MU	Flew into hill in bad visibility, Hilcot Wood, Colesbourne, Glos., 23.10.40
P6275	Watchfield/2 EWS/ 1 SS	Stalled at low altitude in bad visibility and dived into ground, Leasingham, Lincs., 10.7.41
P6301	Watchfield/2 EWS/ 1 SS	Crashed when control column came loose on take-off, Cranwell, 19.12.40
P6302	Watchfield/2 EWS/ 1 SS/2 SS/BW Flt/2 RS	Hit tree on take-off, Wroughton, 10.4.43; DBF
P6303	1 SS/4 FPP	Engine cut; crashlanded, Blackwaterfoot, Arran, 22.2.44; DBR
P6304	1 SS/1 RS	Collided with HM313 while taxying, Cranwell, 27.10.43; DBR
P6305	1 SS/1 EFTS/2 RS/ 29 Gp CF	Sold 24.5.46; to G-AHMW
P6306	1 SS/1 RS	Wing hit ground on landing, Cranwell, 8.5.43; DBR
P6307	2 SS	Spun into ground off turn 1m S of E.Avebury, Wilts., 21.4.41
P6308	614/1 SS/2 Gp CU/34 Wg	SOC 6.7.45
P6309	2 SS/Vickers	Sold 5.9.46; to G-AIEC
P6310	1 SS	Spun into ground off turn, Cranwell, 2.8.41
P6311	2 SS/1 SS/ATA/BDU	SOC 19.5.43
P6312	2 SS/BW Flt/1 RS	Sold 5.9.46; to G-AIIW
P6313	2 SS/3 PAFU/ 23 Gp CF	Abandoned out of fuel while lost, Cheale, Lincs., 19.10.46
P6314	2 SS/1 SS	Spun into ground off turn, Cranwell, 7.2.42; DBF
P6315	Watchfield/2 SS/ 1 SS/1 EFTS/ECFS/ Keevil	Sold 20.6.46; to G-AHVC
P6316	1 SS/ATA/FTC CF/ 1 EFTS	Sold 10.10.46; to G-AIEF
P6317	614/225/Macmerry/ Turnhouse/Kenley	SOC 28.12.43
P6318	ATA/BW Flt/ATA/ 2 Del Flt/Northolt	SOC 11.9.44
P6319	225/41 OTU/241 8th USAAF/4 RS	Sold 10.9.46; to G-AIIJ
P6320	13/26/171	Lost power on take-off and hit tree, Elstree, 4.7.42
P6321	225/24/8th USAAF	SOC 14.5.44
P6322	2 SS/Halton/2 SS/ Halton	Sold 4.10.46; to G-AIED

* * * * * * * * * *

Miles M.15 prototype to Specification T.1/37 built by Philips & Powis to Contract No. 678259/37

P6326	Mkrs	Flown under makers registration U-0234; not delivered to RAF

* * * * * * * * * *

Waco ZVN delivered in March 1939 by Waco Aircraft, Troy, Ohio, to Contract No. 977169/39

P6330	RAE	Tricycle undercarriage trials. Nose-wheel collapsed while landing and aircraft overturned, Farnborough, 22.8.40

* * * * * * * * * *

100 Miles Magister Is delivered between June and September 1939 by Philips & Powis, Woodley, to Contract No. 778435/38

P6343	85/607	Lost in France 5.40
P6344	74/54/124	Sold 26.2.48; to G-AKMM
P6345	74	Hit HT wires and crashed, Rayleigh, Essex, 7.11.39; stored and became 5361M 7.45
P6346	46/Hucknall/24 EFTS/2 FIS	To Turkey 12.5.43
P6347	229/46/Pembrey/ PRU	Hit balloon cable and crashed, Langley, Bucks. 8.10.40
P6348	213	Hit trees in forced landing, Stoneyburn, W.Lothian 6.5.41
P6349	213/23/605	Crashed 19.9.44; NFD
P6350	41/219	Flew into ground, Tunstall, Catterick 12.11.39
P6351	87/73/ME	NFT
P6352	17/20 OTU/17	SOC 13.10.42
P6353	17/5 OTU/118/5 ERFTS/CFS/2 FIS	Stalled on approach near Laurencekirk, Kincardine, 8.12.42
P6354	56/N.Weald	Damaged in air raid and SOC 10.10.40
P6355	72/406/ Abingdon/406	To U-0262 at Mkrs
P6356	19/ATA	Sold 25.3.46 to Argentina
P6357	3/Kenley	Destroyed in air raid, 20.8.40
P6358	54	Hit tree while low flying, Upminster, Essex 15.3.40
P6359	43/3	Crashed after take-off, Inverness, 9.7.40
P6360	43/3/ME	SOC 31.12.46
P6361	Fairey/ME	SOC 31.12.46
P6362	32 MU	Dived into ground, Worth Matravers LG, Dorset, 14.9.40
P6363	St.Athan/130/ Bottesford/ATA	DBR 25.6.44
P6364	St.Athan	Hit HT cable in bad visibility 4 m E of St.Athan, 23.4.40
P6365	St.Athan/303	

Serial	Units	Remarks
P6366	16 EFTS/8 EFTS/ 4 FIS/6 FIS/2 EFTS/ 3 EFTS	Sold 1.10.48; G-AICD
P6367	29 ERFTS/30 EFTS/ 16 EFTS/3 EFTS/ 10 FIS	Sold 4.11.46; to F-BDPH
P6368	29 ERFTS/30 EFTS/ 16 EFTS/2 FIS	Dived into ground near Gourdon, Kincardine 8.8.43
P6369	8 EFTS/10 FIS	Sold 10.3.47 to Thailand
P6370	15 EFTS/Polish FTS/ 16 EFTS/Halton	To 4047M
P6371	15 EFTS/ATA	SOC 7.12.44; later to Argentina
P6372	5 EFTS/16 EFTS/ATA	Hit Spitfire R7261 on take-off, Thame, 14.2.45
P6373	16 EFTS/3 EFTS/ATA	To Portuguese AF 27.11.44
P6374	8 EFTS/21 EFTS/ 6 PAFU	Sold 24.6.47; to G-ALGK
P6375	15 EFTS	SOC 23.7.40; NFD
P6376	8 EFTS/10 FIS	Sold 25.3.46
P6377	24/601	Blown over on take-off from forced landing, Sidford, Devon, 6.12.40
P6378	Bristols/15 EFTS/ 7 FIS	To 4774M 5.44
P6379	267/74 OTU	SOC 1.1.47
P6380	Hucknall/R-R/ Rotol/Mkrs	To U-0259 at Miles; later G-AGVW
P6381	16 EFTS/3 EFTS/ HGCU/21 HGCU	Engine cut; crashlanded, Hanney Road, Berks., 28.12.44; DBR
P6382	16 EFTS/3 EFTS	Sold 10.3.47; to G-AJRS
P6396	24 EFTS/15 EFTS/ 21 EFTS	To Portuguese AF 24.8.44
P6397	Northolt/71	Crashed during low aerobatics, North Weald, 28.8.41
P6398	Northolt/15 EFTS/ 29 EFTS/5 GTS	SOC 27.5.44
P6399	612/Ouston	
P6400	612/Marham/99/ Colerne/2 FIS	Crashed in practice forced landing, Laurencekirk, Kincardine, 11.4.43
P6401	612/Leconfield/ 485/129/Skeabrae	SOC 28.6.45
P6402	612/Woolsington/ Ouston/13 Gp CF/ BLEU	Sold 1.5.50; to G-AMBP
P6403	Northolt/N.Weald	Crashed at North Weald, 15.8.39; NFD
P6404	Northolt/Biggin Hill/24 EFTS/2 FIS	Crashed in forced landing, Stracathro, 10.5.42
P6405	Northolt	Sold 6.3.46
P6406	8 EFTS/10 FIS	SOC 25.2.44
P6407	23 ERFTS/24 EFTS/ 21 EFTS/8 OAFU/ FTC CF	Sold 5.12.47; to G-AKJV
P6408	23 ERFTS/24 EFTS/ 416/7 FIS	Hit HT wires and crashed near Collingbourne Kingston, Wilts., 7.1.44
P6409	23 ERFTS/24 EFTS/ 16 EFTS	SOC 21.11.44
P6410	23 ERFTS/24 EFTS/ 60 OTU/485/7 FTS/ SPTU/ECFS	Sold 14.11.46; to G-AKGS
P6411	23 ERFTS/24 EFTS/ 68/Church Fenton	Sold 23.8.46; to G-AIDP
P6412	15 EFTS/5 EFTS/24 EFTS/2 FIS/9 PAFU	Sold 18.6.46 to Argentina
P6413	15 EFTS/8 EFTS/ 15 EFTS/7 FIS	Dived into ground low flying near Chinton, Wilts., 19.10.42
P6414	-	To Irish Air Corps 7.6.40 as No.76
P6415	16 EFTS/310/4 FIS	Flew into high ground in low cloud, Therfield, near Royston, Cambs., 16.11.41
P6416	Linton/4 Gp CF/266	Sold 6.5.46 to Argentina
P6417	16 EFTS	Sold 11.3.46 to Argentina
P6418	-	To R.Egyptian AF direct
P6419	16 EFTS	Sold 10.3.47; to G-AJRV
P6420	8 EFTS/FTC CF/ 8 EFTS/Mkrs/Fairey/ Syerston	Sold 22.12.47; G-AKMZ NTU
P6421	Pembrey/16 EFTS/ 17 SFTS/21 PAFU	Sold 8.6.48; to G-AKKW
P6422	-	To Irish Air Corps 7.6.40 as No.77
P6423	5 EFTS/8 EFTS/ 10 FIS/141	Sold 26.11.46; to F-BDPD
P6424	15 EFTS/8 EFTS/ 7 FIS/2 FIS/604	To Irish Air Corps 24.8.44 as No.127
P6436	15 EFTS/8 EFTS	Crashed on overshoot, Woodley, 14.9.41
P6437	15 EFTS	Crashed while low flying, Hollee, Dumfries, 23.7.40
P6438	15 EFTS/8 EFTS/ 10 FIS	Sold 15.11.46; to G-AIUF
P6439	Watton/Horsham St.Faith/5 EFTS/ CFS/ECFS/29 EFTS	Sold 1.11.46; to F-BDPG
P6440	-	To Irish Air Corps 7.6.40 as No.74
P6441	8 EFTS/10 FIS	Sold 20.11.46; to F-BDPA
P6442	16 EFTS/CF Amman	SOC 10.1.46
P6443	Feltwell/ATA	Sold 10.3.47 for parts
P6444	18/83/16 EFTS	DBR 17.3.42; NFD
P6445	57/6 EFTS/8 EFTS/ 21 EFTS/7 FIS	SOC 7.7.44
P6446	605/2 FIS/18 PAFU/ FTC CF/10 FIS/ 7 FIS/CFS	Sold 8.6.48; to G-AKKS
P6447	16 EFTS	Collided with P6373 and crashed, Hilton, Derby, 8.5.42
P6448	8 EFTS/21 EFTS	Sold 25.3.46 to Argentina
P6449	16 EFTS/234/ Warmwell/234/118/ 104 MU	SOC 20.9.45
P6450	16 EFTS	Crashed in forced landing 1m S of Banbury, Oxon., 8.12.40
P6451	16 EFTS/4 FIS/ 22 EFTS	Sold 8.4.46 to Argentina
P6452	24 EFTS/15 FTS/ 21 EFTS	To Turkey 14.6.43
P6453	24 EFTS/8 EFTS/ 24 EFTS	Spun into ground near Luton, 5.3.41
P6454	16 EFTS/F-BFTS/ 5 EFTS/CFS/2 FIS	SOC 7.2.44
P6455	Wyton/ATA/RCCS	Sold 12.5.50
P6456	Wyton/8 EFTS/ 5 EFTS/Denham/ 21 EFTS/AAEE/778/ 4/43 OTU/ECFS	Sold 11.7.46
P6457	Mildenhall/3 Gp CF	Sold 27.5.46; to LV-XRP
P6458	Abingdon/81	Lost in France 5.40
P6459	3/257	Hit anti-glider pole in forced landing, Brentwood, Essex, 18.10.40
P6460	111	Crashed in forced landing, Exted Farm, Kent, 2.7.42; DBR
P6461	Filton/16 EFTS	Crashed 6.2.41; NFD
P6462	Mildenhall/149	Blown over on take-off, Cleave, 8.11.39
P6463	213/Tangmere/1	Crashed near Arundel, Sussex, 1.11.41; NFD
P6464	Wyton/82/Lossiemouth/ ATA/Halton	Sold 11.3.46
P6465	SF Gosport/16 Gp CF/ 125	SOC 19.8.44
P6466	24 EFTS/25 Gp CF/604/ 174/264/142 Wg/264	SOC 20.2.45

200 Fairey Battle Is delivered between November 1939 and May 1940 by Fairey, Heaton Chapel, to Contract No. 768880/38
(from P6616 built as Battle Trainers)

Serial	Unit	Fate
P6480	-	To RCAF 28.5.41 as 1969
P6481	-	To RAAF 15.1.41
P6482	226/88	SOC 29.6.43
P6483	-	To RAAF 24.3.41
P6484	-	To RAAF 3.4.41
P6485	-	To RCAF 25.4.41 as 1953
P6486	-	To RCAF 29.8.41 as 2071
P6487	-	To SAAF 9.7.41
P6488	-	To RCAF 27.8.41 as 2093
P6489	-	To RAAF 15.1.41
P6490	-	To RCAF 5.41 as 2038
P6491	3 SGR	To SAAF 16.2.41 as 943
P6492	-	To RCAF 28.11.40 as 1814
P6493	-	To RCAF 11.4.41
P6494	-	To RCAF 28.11.40 as 1834
P6495	-	To Canada 4.5.41
P6496	-	To RCAF 27.9.40 as 1719
P6497	-	To RCAF 26.9.40 as 1726
P6498	-	To RCAF 25.4.41 as 1984
P6499	-	To RAAF 25.3.41
P6500	-	To RCAF 11.3.41 as 1928
P6501	-	To SAAF 29.3.41 as 951
P6502	-	To RCAF 26.9.40 as 1712
P6503	-	To RAAF 3.1.41
P6504	-	To RCAF 29.3.41 as 1912
P6505	-	To RCAF 19.4.41 as 1945
P6506	-	To SAAF 11.7.41
P6507	-	To RCAF 23.3.41 as 1916
P6508	-	To RCAF 17.5.41 as 1964
P6509	-	To RAAF 3.4.41
P6523	-	To RCAF 11.3.41 as 1925
P6524	-	To RCAF 22.5.41 as 1957
P6525	-	To RCAF 5.41 as 2043
P6526	-	To RCAF 22.5.41 as 1959
P6527	-	To RCAF 5.41 as 2040
P6528	-	To RCAF 24.5.41
P6529	-	To SAAF 15.6.41
P6530	-	To RCAF 6.3.41 as 1853
P6531	-	To RAAF 3.4.41
P6532	-	To RCAF 24.5.41
P6533	-	To SAAF 11.7.41
P6534	-	To RCAF 5.41 as 2007
P6535	-	To RCAF 2.3.41 as 1893
P6536	-	To RAAF 25.3.41
P6537	-	To RCAF 17.5.41 as 1965
P6538	-	To RCAF 27.10.40 as 1779
P6539	-	To RCAF 8.10.40 as 1736
P6540	-	To RCAF 5.2.41 as 1857
P6541	-	To Canada 10.4.41
	31 BGS	SOC 26.2.44
P6542	-	To RCAF 8.3.41 as 1887
P6543	-	To RCAF 8.3.41 as 1883
P6544	-	To RCAF 26.9.40 as 1710
P6545	-	To RCAF 3.4.41 as 1926
P6546	-	To RCAF 9.10.40 as 1717
P6547	-	To RCAF 8.3.41 as 1889
P6548	-	To RCAF 27.4.41 as 1980
P6549	-	To SAAF 29.6.41 as 978
P6550	-	To RCAF 22.5.41 as 1960
P6551	-	To RCAF 24.5.41
P6552	-	To RCAF 5.2.41 as 1840
P6553	-	To RCAF 5.2.41 as 1855
P6554	-	To RCAF 29.3.41 as 1915
P6555	-	To SAAF 29.3.41 as 955
P6556	-	To RCAF 14.10.41 as 1742
P6557	-	To RCAF 26.9.40 as 1709
P6558	-	To RCAF 25.4.41 as 1979
P6559	-	To RCAF 5.2.41 as 1854
P6560	SGR	To SAAF 5.2.41 as 934
P6561	-	To SAAF 16.2.41 as 941
P6562	-	To Canada 13.5.41
	31 BGS	SOC 23.5.44
P6563	-	To RCAF 31.3.44 as 1952
P6564	-	To Canada 10.4.41
	31 BGS	SOC 27.4.43
P6565	-	To RCAF 11.6.41 as 2000
P6566	-	To RCAF 1.4.41 as 1976
P6567	-	To RCAF 21.2.41 as 1867
P6568	150/142	To RCAF 13.3.41 as 1920
P6569	301	To RCAF 16.12.40
P6570	98	Engine cut in circuit; crash-landed in bog, Kaldadarnes, 14.9.40
P6571	12/Binbrook	Engine cut; crashed in forced landing on Wainfleet Sands, Lincs., 11.7.41
P6572	142/15 EFTS/1 PFTS/16 PFTS/239	SOC 11.3.44
P6596	-	To SAAF 2.7.40 as 925
P6597	12	Missing (Boulogne) 20.8.40
P6598	226	Crashed 2m NW of Vernon, Eure, during attack on bridge, 11.6.40
P6599	88	To RCAF 28.11.40 as 1832
P6600	142	To Fairey 22.9.40; SOC 26.9.40
P6601	226	Lost formation in bad weather and flew into high ground descending in cloud 4m SW of Cushendall, C.Antrim, 22.10.40
P6602	150/142	To RAAF 3.4.41
P6603	613/142	To 2209M 16.9.40
P6604 to		
P6613	-	To R.Hellenic AF 11.12.39
P6614	1 FTS	Control lost on night take-off; dived into ground, Shrewton, 11.11.41
P6615	-	To R. Hellenic AF 21.3.40
P6616	15 EFTS/Hucknall/16 PFTS	To 3312M 5.8.42
P6617	7 FTS/CFS/2 BGS/1 FTS/3 AGS	SOC 14.7.44
P6618	7 FTS/1 FTS/3 AGS/Mona	SOC 14.7.44
P6619	7 FTS/1 FTS/3 AGS	SOC 23.8.44
P6620	11 FTS	To Canada 5.1.41
P6621	11 FTS/1 FTS	SOC 19.11.43
P6622	11 FTS/1 FTS	To RAAF 7.4.42
P6623	12 FTS/16 PFTS	To 3557M 6.2.43
P6624	12 FTS/7 FTS/TFPP/3 AGS	SOC 30.6.43
P6625	12 FTS/1 FTS/12 FTS/16 PFTS	SOC 9.9.44
P6626	12 FTS/16 PFTS/3 AGS	SOC 19.11.43
P6627	12 FTS/16 PFTS/1 FTS/3 AGS	SOC 23.8.44
P6628	12 FTS/16 PFTS/29 MU	SOC 30.9.44
P6629	12 FTS/16 PFTS	SOC 14.7.44
P6630	12 FTS/16 PFTS	Stalled in practice forced landing, Grange Farm, Hockerton, Newark, Notts., 24.6.41
P6631	12 FTS/16 PFTS	To RAAF 5.12.41
P6632	7 FTS/1 FTS/3	Engine cut; forcelanded in lake and overturned, Cults Loch, Castle Kennedy, 9.11.42
P6633	7 FTS/1 FTS	To RCAF 19.12.41 as 2120
P6634	7 FTS/1 FTS	SOC 14.7.44
P6635	12 FTS/1 FTS/3 AGS	SOC 16.10.42
P6636	12 FTS	Engine lost power on approach to forced landing while lost; hit trees, Cossington, Leics., 21.12.40
P6637	15 EFTS/Hucknall/16 PFTS/1600 Flt/1603 Flt	SOC 11.9.43

P6638	12 FTS/16 PFTS/	
	1609 Flt	SOC 7.5.43
P6639	15 EFTS/16 PFTS	To RCAF 21.12.41 as 2118
P6640	7 FTS/16 PFTS	To 3317M 8.42
P6641	7 FTS/16 PFTS/	
	3 AGS	3903M NTU; SOC 23.8.44
P6642	7 FTS	To RAAF 27.9.41
P6643	7 FTS/ATA/1609 Flt	SOC 30.6.43
P6644	7 FTS/PRU/1 PRU/	Collided with Botha L6173 on
	3 AGS	approach, Castle Kennedy, 26.8.42
P6645	7 FTS/1 FTS/ATA	3899M NTU; SOC 10.3.44
P6663	7 FTS	To RCAF 24.7.41 as 2053
P6664	7 FTS/1 FTS	To RAAF 21.1.42
P6665	11 FTS/1 FTS	To RCAF 19.12.41 as 2121
P6666	11 FTS/10 BGS/	
	10 AOS/4 AGS	SOC 30.6.43
P6667	11 FTS/2 BGS	SOC 16.10.43
P6668	11 FTS/1 FTS/	
	16 PFTS	SOC 22.9.43
P6669	11 FTS/1 FTS/3 AGS	SOC 21.1.44
P6670	11 FTS	To RCAF 8.10.40
P6671	11 FTS/1 FTS	SOC 12.5.41
P6672	11 FTS	To RCAF 3.10.40
P6673	11 FTS/1 FTS	Undershot night approach and hit tent, Shrewton 1.1.41; to 2545M for RCAF as GI airframe A125
P6674	12 FTS	Shot down by enemy aircraft, Stroxton, near Harlaxton, 21.4.41; DBF
P6675	12 FTS	Control lost after take-off; dived into ground on night training flight near Harlaxton, 27.4.40
P6676	12 FTS/9 BGS	SOC 19.11.43
P6677	12 FTS/1 FTS	To RAAF 5.12.41
P6678	1 FTS/304/16 PFTS	To 3310M 5.8.42
P6679	1 FTS/16 PFTS	SOC 14.9.43
P6680	12 FTS/1 FTS	Bellylanded in error, Shrewton, 8.11.41; not repaired; to 2934M
P6681	1 FTS/16 PFTS/	
	1 FTS/231	SOC 23.8.44
P6682	12 FTS/1 FTS/	
	1600 Flt	SOC 23.8.44
P6683	12 FTS/1 FTS	SOC 14.9.43
P6684	12 FTS/1 FTS	To RCAF 7.2.42 as 2129
P6685	12 FTS/Burtonwood/	
	305/307/256/59 OTU	SOC 30.6.43
P6686	12 FTS	Hit high ground while low flying 2m N of Melton Mowbray, 11.6.41
P6687	12 FTS/302/308/	
	SF Baginton/1 FTS	To 2933M 11.2.42
P6688	12 FTS/1 FTS	SOC 23.8.44
P6689	1 FTS	To RCAF 1.4.41 as 1974
P6690	1 FTS	SOC 22.9.43
P6691	1 FTS/16 PFTS	To RCAF 24.12.41 as 2133
P6692	Polish OTU/18 OTU	To RCAF 8.8.41 as 2060
P6718	Polish OTU/18 OTU/	
	3 AGS/Mona	SOC 19.11.43
P6719	Polish OTU/18 OTU/	
	3 AGS	SOC 11.7.44
P6720	1 FTS	To RAAF 17.12.41
P6721	18 OTU/16 PFTS	SOC 8.9.43
P6722	1 FTS/3 AGS	SOC 23.8.44
P6723	1 FTS/304/16 PFTS	SOC 22.9.43
P6724	11 FTS	To Canada 1.10.40
	31 SFTS	SOC 9.8.41
P6725	1 FTS/310/12 OTU/	
	1 FTS	SOC 8.9.43
P6726	1 FTS	Bellylanded in error, Netheravon, 18.7.40; to 2144M 7.40
P6727	1 FTS/1609 Flt/	
	1606 Flt	To 3910M 15.7.43
P6728	1 FTS	SOC 1.12.42

P6729	1 FTS	To RAAF 17.12.41
P6730	11 FTS	To Canada 1.12.40
	31 SFTS	SOC 20.10.41
P6731	11 FTS	To RCAF 8.10.40
P6732	98/17/Andover	To RCAF 10.4.41
P6733	11 FTS/12 FTS/1 FTS/	
	309/1 AACU/1600 Flt/	
	1603 Flt	SOC 11.9.43
P6734	11 FTS	To RCAF 1.12.40
P6735	11 FTS/1 FTS/	
	16 PFTS	To 3311M 5.8.42
P6736	11 FTS/1 FTS/3 AGS/	
	Mona	SOC 19.11.43
P6737	11 FTS/1 FTS	To RCAF 19.12.41 as 2123
P6750	CFS/1 FTS	To RCAF 19.12.41 as 2119
P6751	12 FTS/16 PFTS	SOC 29.9.42
P6752	CFS/2 BGS/1 FTS	SOC 15.1.45
P6753	CFS	Engine cut on night approach; hit bank and undercarriage collapsed, Jurby, 14.6.40
P6754	CFS/7 FTS/1 FTS	Failed to recover from divebombing attack on range and hit ground, Pepperbox Hill ranges, Wilts., 28.10.41
P6755	98/12 OTU/16 PFTS	SOC 12.9.43
P6756	98/4 FPP	Engine cut; overshot forced landing into trees, E. Lockinge, Wantage, Berks., 13.6.40
P6757	98/1 FTS/2 AGS	SOC 14.7.44
P6758	98/3 FPP/1 FTS/	
	2 AGS	SOC 14.7.44
P6759	98/12 OTU/103/	
	12 OTU/1 FTS/3 AGS	SOC 14.7.44
P6760	98/3 FPP	To RCAF 10.6.41 as 2001
P6761	98/12 OTU/142/2	
	RCAF/ATA	To SAAF 31.12.42
P6762	98/12 OTU	To RAAF 27.9.41
P6763	98/12 OTU/16 PFTS	3161M NTU; to 3559M 2.43
P6764	6 BGS/7 BGS/1 FTS	Flew into Town Quarry, Weston-super-Mare, in bad visibility, 25.1.41; DBF
P6765	12 FTS/1 FTS	SOC 23.8.44
P6766	12 FTS	Overshot forced landing while lost and hit railway embankment near Hubberts Bridge, 3m W of Boston, Lincs., 29.12.40
P6767	12 FTS/1 FTS/3 AGS	SOC 16.10.43
P6768	12 FTS/1 FTS	SOC 19.11.43
P6769	12 FTS	Engine cut; overshot forced landing and hit gun post, Harlaxton, 7.4.41

* * * * * * * * * *

Four De Havilland Hornet Moth seaplanes purchased from de Havilland Canada, Downsview, three in July 1939 and one (P6788) in November 1939, to Contract No. 974735/39

P6785	MAEE	To Admiralty; new aircraft
P6786	-	To Admiralty direct;
P6787	-	All three second-hand
P6788	-	aircraft

* * * * * * * * * *

75 Airspeed Oxford IIs delivered between November 1939 and June 1940 by de Havilland to Contract No. 980423/38

P6795	2 FTS/14 FTS/14 PAFU/	
	3 PAFU/USAAF	SOC 14.5.44
P6796	2 FTS/14 FTS	Crashed in forced landing 3m S of Baldock, Herts., 11.4.41
P6797	2 FTS	Destroyed in air raid, Brize Norton, 16.8.40

P6798	2 FTS/2 PAFU/ 11 PAFU/18 OTU/ 1655 MTU/NTU/139	Sold 23.6.49
P6799	2 FTS	Destroyed in air raid, Brize Norton, 16.8.40
P6800	2 FTS/14 PAFU/ 11 PAFU	Hit high ground while low flying, Worlds End, Denbigh, 30.1.44
P6801	5 FTS/11 FTS/ 60 OTU/51 OTU/AFDU/ ATA/512/132 OTU	Sold 23.6.49
P6802	5 FTS/11 FTS/2 FTS/ 2 PAFU/ATA	SOC 9.5.46
P6803	5 FTS	Crashed in forced landing, Tarporley, Cheshire, 17.1.40
P6804	5 FTS/RAFC/ 15 PAFU	Hit tree on low flying exercise, 1m SW of Kirmington, 5.6.42; DBF
P6805	5 FTS/14 FTS/ 14 PAFU	Crashed near Ossington, 23.3.42; NFD
P6806	5 FTS/11 FTS/ATA/ 17 SFTS/456	SOC 13.1.47
P6807	3 FTS	Overshot flarepath and sank into ground on attempted overshoot, Bibury, 23.12.40
P6808	3 FTS/16 PAFU	Engine cut on take-off; overshot runway into ditch, Newton, 10.11.42
P6809	RAFC/1 Cam Unit/ 1690 Flt	Wing caught fire on approach; DBR after landing, Harlaxton, 13.9.45
P6810	CFS/7 FIS/3 FIS/ 1508 Flt/62 OTU	Crashed 30.10.44; NFD
P6811	RAFC	Flew into radio mast and crashed, Daventry, 15.8.41
P6812	CFS/7 FIS/3 FIS/ 3 PAFU	SOC 30.5.44
P6813	CFS/6 FTS/6 PAFU	Hit trees on approach in bad weather, Little Rissington, 3.11.42
P6814	CFS	Hit trees on take-off from Upavon due to ice on wings; crashed, Rowde, Cleeve, Wilts., 17.12.40
P6815	CFS/11 FTS	Collided with N6295 on approach, Shawbury, 18.7.41
P6816	RAFC/1 SS	To 2839M 1.42
P6817	RAFC/16 PFTS/116	SOC 5.7.44
P6818	RAFC/2 FTS/2 PAFU/ 9 Gp CF	SOC 14.12.43
P6819	RAFC/16 PFTS	To USAAF 22.6.44
P6831	- 21 SFTS	To S Rhodesia 18.3.41 DBR in accident, 25.4.41
P6832	- 21 SFTS	To S Rhodesia 18.3.41; SOC 5.1.45
P6833	-	To S Rhodesia SOC 5.2.45
P6834	- 21 SFTS	To S Rhodesia 27.3.40 SOC 3.1.42
P6835	- 21 SFTS	To S Rhodesia 27.3.40 SOC 31.3.44
P6836	-	To S Rhodesia SOC 8.2.45
P6837	- 21 SFTS	To S Rhodesia SOC 13.7.44
P6838	- 21 SFTS	To S Rhodesia SOC 5.1.45
P6839	- 21 SFTS	To S Rhodesia 1.4.40 SOC 7.1.43
P6840	-	To S Rhodesia PSOC
P6841	- 23 SFTS	To S Rhodesia SOC 5.2.45
P6842	-	To S Rhodesia PSOC

P6843	-	To S Rhodesia 1.4.40 SOC 1.3.43
P6844	-	To RNZAF as NZ1229
P6845	- 21 SFTS	To S Rhodesia 1.4.40 Crashed and DBF, 28.2.41
P6846	-	To RNZAF as NZ1230
P6847	- 20 SFTS	To S Rhodesia Flew into trees and crashed, 20.10.40
P6848	-	To RNZAF as NZ1231
P6849	- 21 SFTS	To S Rhodesia Damaged 27.8.42; SOC 8.12.42
P6850	-	To RNZAF as NZ1232
P6851	-	To RNZAF as NZ1233 12.4.40
P6852	- 20 SFTS	To S Rhodesia SOC 9.9.40
P6853	-	To RNZAF as NZ1234
P6854	-	To S Rhodesia NFT
P6855	- 21 SFTS/24 CAOS/ 21 SFTS	To S Rhodesia SOC 30.9.44
P6856	- 20 SFTS	To S Rhodesia Crashed at Nelson Farm, Wetza, SR, 3.9.40
P6857	- 21 SFTS	To S Rhodesia 1.6.40 NFT
P6858	- 21 SFTS	To S Rhodesia SOC 1.3.43
P6859	- 21 SFTS	To S Rhodesia SOC 8.3.45
P6860	-	To RNZAF as NZ1235 24.7.40
P6861	- 21 SFTS	To S Rhodesia 7.5.40 SOC 8.9.44
P6862	-	To RNZAF as NZ1236 26.8.40
P6863	-	To RNZAF as NZ1237 24.7.40
P6864	- 21 SFTS	To S.Rhodesia 1.6.40 Hit by Harvard, Thornhill, 23.8.43; SOC 27.2.44 as BER
P6865	-	To RNZAF as NZ1238
P6866	- 21 SFTS	To S Rhodesia SOC 5.2.45
P6867	- 21 SFTS/23 SFTS	To S Rhodesia 30.7.40 SOC 30.9.44
P6868	- 21 SFTS	To S Rhodesia 1.6.40 SOC 17.8.43
P6869	-	To RNZAF as NZ1239 26.7.40
P6870	-	To RNZAF as NZ1240 16.5.40
P6871	-	To RNZAF as NZ1241
P6872	-	To RNZAF as NZ1242
P6873	- 21 SFTS	To S Rhodesia SOC 31.7.44
P6874	-	To RNZAF as NZ1243
P6875	-	To RNZAF as NZ1244 16.5.40
P6876	-	To RNZAF as NZ1245
P6877	- 21 SFTS/CFS	To S Rhodesia SOC 17.10.45
P6878	-	To RNZAF 30.8.40 but tf to RAAF
P6879	-	To S Rhodesia 6.6.40 PSOC
P6880	-	To RNZAF as NZ1246

*   *   *   *   *   *   *   *   *   *   *

62 Bristol Blenheim IVs delivered between September 1939 and January 1940 by Bristols, Filton, to Contract No. 774679/38

P6885	114	Lost in France 5.40
P6886	21	Damaged by Bf 109 near Dixmude and bellylanded at Watton, 29.5.40

Serial	Units	History
P6887	21	Engine cut after take-off from Watton for reconnaissance; hit tree and crashed near Griston, 31.3.40
P6888	21	Misjudged approach and bounced; swung and undercarriage collapsed, Bircham Newton, 3.12.39
P6889	110	Shot down near Attigny during attack on Sedan bridges, 14.5.40
P6890	21	Damaged by Bf 109, Sedan, and belly-landed, Watton, 14.5.40
P6891	-	To G-AFXJ for RHAF
P6892	-	To G-AFXK for RHAF
P6893	82	Missing (Gembloux) 17.5.40
P6894	82/107	Crashed at Cavillon, Somme, during attack on Amiens, 10.7.40
P6895	82	Shot down by Bf 109s near Veenhuizen on return from Dortmund-Ems Canal, 2.7.40
P6896	SAC/2 SAC/6 OTU/ 56 OTU	Hit HT cables and undercarriage retracted on landing, Valley, 1.7.41
P6897	-	To G-AFXL for RHAF
P6898	-	To G-AFXM for RHAF
P6899	SAC	SOC 13.1.40
P6900	SAC/2 SAC/6 OTU/ CGS/1 AGS	SOC 10.1.44
P6901	40	Shot down by flak near Voorberg during attack on Ypenburg airfield, 10.5.40
P6902	139	Missing attacking enemy columns near Monthermé, Ardennes, 15.5.40
P6903	-	To G-AFKN for RHAF
P6904	-	To G-AFXO for RHAF
P6905	35/101	Crashlanded and exploded 1m from Swaffham returning from shipping sweep, 25.9.40
P6906	35/101/13 OTU	SOC 15.8.43
P6907	35/108/13 OTU	To 2541M 20.12.40
P6908	35/101/235	Missing from patrol, 11.8.41
P6909	235	Hit tree low flying in bad weather near Detling, 29.5.40
P6910	82	Missing (Forêt de Gault) 13.6.40; crashed at Courgivaux, Marne
P6911	15/264/15	Shot down by flak near Münsterbilzen during attack on Maastricht bridges, 12.5.40
P6912	15/264/15	Shot down by flak, Kattevennen, near Genk, during attack on Maastricht bridges, 12.5.40
P6913	15/264/104/15	Shot down near St.Inglevert attacking troop columns near Calais, 26.5.40
P6914	15/264/15	Shot down by flak at Gellick during attack on Maastricht bridges, 12.5.40
P6915	82	Damaged by Bf 109s on reconnaissance to Abbeville, 7.6.40; SOC on return
P6916	53	Destroyed in air raid, believed at Metz, 10.5.40
P6917	15/264/15	Shot down near Landrecies, Nord, during raid on roads near Le Cateau, 18.5.40
P6918	35	Engine cut on take-off; stalled and dived into ground, Upwood, 6.4.40
P6919	35/17 OTU	SOC 5.9.42
P6920	114	Missing (N.France) 14.5.40
P6921	104/13 OTU	To 3438M
P6922	53/59	Crashed on take-off, Poix, 5.4.40 and abandoned in France 6.40
P6923	114	Missing (Forêt de Gault) 13.6.40
P6924	101	Missing (Cherbourg) 18.7.40
P6925	101/110/82	Missing (Forêt de Gault) 13.6.40
P6926	53/59	Missing on reconnaissance, 13.5.40
P6927	CFS/5 AOS/1 AAS	SOC 10.6.44
P6928	53/57	Missing from night intruder, 26.8.40
P6929	104	Undershot night landing and hit bomb dump, Bicester, 27.3.40; DBR
P6930	57	Crashed near Vlijtingen on reconnaissance over Belgium, 13.5.40
P6931	57/53/18/139/ OADU/244	Tyre burst on take-off; swung and undercarriage collapsed, Sharjah, 26.10.42; DBR
P6932	57	Missing (Le Cateau) 18.5.40
P6933	57/53/18	Shot down during attack on barges by Bf 109s in Scheldt 6m NW of Vlissingen, 16.7.40
P6934	18	Hit trees on overshoot ½m W of Gt. Massingham, 28.11.40
P6950	254	Ditched on patrol, 6.7.40
P6951	ME	NFT 17.6.40; believed intended for RCAF
P6952	248	Shot down by return fire from enemy aircraft off Norwegian coast, 20.10.40
P6953	101	Ran out of fuel returning from Mannheim and abandoned over Fairlight, near Hastings, Sussex, 16.12.40
P6954	21	Collided with L1342 on take-off and crashed, Swanton Morley, 28.7.41
P6955	101	Missing (Boulogne) 8.9.40
P6956	235	Spun into ground out of cloud, Docking, Norfolk, 26.5.40
P6957	235	Shot down by Bf 109 off Egmond on reconnaissance over Zuyder Zee, 27.6.40
P6958	235	Shot down by Bf 109 on reconnaissance, Ouderkerk aan de Amstel, 27.6.40
P6959	218/17 OTU	Dived into ground out of cloud, Hine Heath, Stanton, Salop., 3.1.42
P6960	218	To Admiralty 22.5.44
P6961	Mkrs & AAEE/1 AGS	SOC 10.1.44

*   *   *   *   *   *   *   *   *

114 Westland Whirlwind Is delivered between June 1940 and December 1941 by Westlands, Yeovil, to Contract No. 980384/39

Serial	Units	History
P6966	25/263	Tyre burst on take-off and aircraft damaged; abandoned near Stenhousemuir, Stirlingshire, 7.8.40
P6967	25/263/RAE/137	To 3497M 9.4.43
P6968	263	Collided with P6999 and crashed near Bath, 9.10.41
P6969	263	Missing from attack on Ar 196 12m S of Start Point, Devon, 8.2.41; cause not known
P6970	263	Crashed 10m NW of Barfleur on ground-attack mission, 6.11.41; cause not known
P6971	263/137/263	SOC 14.7.44

Above: The predecessor of the Catalina, Consolidated 28-5 P9630. The prefix N was the US civil aircraft identification letter
applied for ferrying purposes

P 6326
Below: The Miles M.15 prototype P6316

Above and below: The General Aircraft GAL.38 fleet shadower in its single and triple-tailed forms

P6972	263/137	SOC 30.9.44	P7003	263	Dived into ground out of cloud near Wool, Dorset, 21.9.42; cause unknown
P6973	263	SOC 25.10.43			
P6974	263	Damaged by flak during shipping strike, Cherbourg; bellylanded at Warmwell, 24.10.43	P7004	263	Tyre burst on take-off, Pembrey; hit mound on landing, swung and undercarriage collapsed, Fairwood Common, 14.3.42
P6975	263	Flew into high ground descending in cloud on ferry flight, Bovey Tracey, Devon, 29.12.40	P7005	263/137	Missing from ground attack mission to Neufchatel, 2.3.43
P6976	263/137	Wing hit ground on landing, Manston, 1.5.43; DBR	P7006	263	Flew into ground while low flying near Chepstow, Mon., 29.5.41; DBF
P6977	263/137	Bellylanded at Coltishall, 10.11.41; DBR	P7007	263	SOC 30.9.44
P6978	263	Flew into high ground descending in cloud on ferry flight near Bovey Tracy, Devon, 29.12.40	P7008	263	Took avoiding action and slats opened in tight turn; tailplane broke off and wing detached near Aldermaston, Berks., 30.4.41
P6979	263	Missing from attack on ships in Cherbourg harbour, 24.10.43	P7009	263	Returned short of fuel from attack on Lannion airfield and abandoned 5m S of Eddystone lighthouse, 29.9.41
P6980	AAEE/263	Dived into sea while firing on sea marker 1½m off Burnham-on-Sea, Somerset, 12.12.40	P7010	263	Missing from attack on ships off Brest, 14.4.43; presumed shot down by flak
P6981	263/137/263	Blown aside by gust on landing, Warmwell, 1.8.43; DBF	P7011	263/137/263	SOC 30.9.44
P6982	263/137	SOC 30.9.44	P7012	137/263	SOC 30.9.44
P6983	263/137/263	SOC 14.7.44	P7013	263	SOC 4.11.43
P6984	263	Abandoned after engine failure, Middlemore, S.Devon, 19.1.41	P7014	263	Took off in coarse pitch and hit trees, Warmwell, 8.10.42
P6985	263	SOC 24.3.41	P7015	263	Engine caught fire during attack on Morlaix airfield, 30.10.41; failed to return
P6986	263/137/263/ 137/263	Missing from attack on ships in Cherbourg harbour, 24.10.43	____		
			P7035	137/263	Shot down by Bf 109 in sea off Morlaix on ground-attack mission, 23.7.42
P6987	263	Hit by flak attacking convoy off St.Brelade; dived into sea 45m SW of Jersey, Channel Islands, 7.12.42	P7036	137	Spun off turn during dogfight with Spitfire and crashed on White Horse Common, North Walsham, Norfolk, 9.3.42; DBF
P6988	263	Radio failed returning from convoy patrol; engine cut attempting to foreland while lost and spun into ground, Portreath, 14.3.41; DBF	P7037	263/137/263	SOC 30.9.44
			P7038	137/263	Caught fire on ground, Charmy Down, 3.1.42; DBR
P6989	263	Presumed damaged by return fire from Do 17 off Lizard; crashed near Helston, Cornwall, 1.4.41	P7039	263	Both tyres burst in heavy landing; overturned, Fairwood Common, 7.3.42
P6990	263/SF Colerne/263	SOC 9.12.43	P7040	263	SOC 30.9.44
P6991	263	Lost power on take-off; hit tree and crashlanded 2m W of Warmwell, 9.2.43	P7041	263	Brakes failed; taxied into dispersal pen, Fairwood Common, 2.4.42; DBR
P6992	263	Broke up in air during roll after part of aircraft detached, Wittering, 20.4.41	P7042	263	Damaged by Bf 109s and abandoned 5m off Cherbourg, 4.9.41
P6993	263/137	Engine cut on return from night intruder to Rue; bellylanded 1m N of Sandwich, Kent, 22.6.43	P7043	263	Missing on ground-attack mission to Valognes, 7.11.42
P6994	263	To USAAF 4.6.42	P7044	263	Crashed after control lost in cloud near Coleford, Glos., 14.12.41; DBF
P6995	263	Missing from night intruder mission, 17.4.43; believed crashed near St.Lô	P7045	263	Stalled on approach; spun into ground, Filton, 12.6.41
P6996	263/R-R	DBR 5.9.41; NFD	P7046	263/137/263	SOC 14.7.44
P6997	AAEE/AFDU/137/263	SOC 30.9.44	P7047	137/263	Engine cut in circuit at night on return from shipping strike; undershot approach, hit obstruction and stalled, Tangmere, 8.10.43; DBF
P6998	263/137	Damaged by flak near Abbeville and crashlanded at Lympne, 22.12.42; DBR			
P6999	263	Collided with P6968 over Bath and crashed, 9.10.41	P7048	137	Sold to Westlands, 1944, and became G-AGOI
P7000	263	Hit by flak and dived into sea attacking convoy off Sark, 15.6.43	P7049	137	Bounced on landing and props hit ground on return from patrol, Matlask, 27.6.42; DBR
P7001	263	Hit ground during attack on enemy headquarters, Quineville, near Lestre, Manche, 10.9.41	P7050	137	Missing while escorting destroyers off Belgian coast, 12.2.42; presumed shot down
P7002	263/137	Flew into sea in flat calm and ditched off Deal, Kent, 14.4.43			

P7051	263/137	Hit ridge on take-off; stalled and hit ground; engine caught fire, Manston, 18.1.43; SOC as BER
P7052	263	Hit by flak, La Haye du Puits, and ditched off Cap de Carteret, 12.2.43
P7053	137	Collided with another Whirlwind during formation practice and lost part of tail; crashed near Englishcombe, Somerset, 28.10.41
P7054	137/263/137	Missing, presumed shot down by flak near Poperinghe, 23.1.43
P7055	137/263	SOC 30.9.44
P7056	263/SF Colerne/ 137/263	SOC 14.10.43
P7057	137/263	Undercarriage leg collapsed in heavy landing, Warmwell, 7.5.43; DBR
P7058	137	Missing, presumed shot down by flak from train near Thielt, 25.4.43
P7059	263	Hit by flak attacking convoy and abandoned off Querqueville, 22.5.43
P7060	137/263	Shot down in sea off Morlaix by Bf 109 on ground-attack mission, 23.7.42
P7061	263/137	Collided with P7102 while taxying on wet grass, Manston, 13.1.43; DBR
P7062	137/263	Hit trees during practice attack and spun into ground near Wroughton, 19.2.43
P7063	137	Missing from night attack on ships off Gravelines, 18.5.43
P7064	137	Hit by flak on ground attack mission and ditched off Boulogne, 31.10.42
P7089	263	Hit by flak from convoy off Guernsey, 23.5.43; SOC on return as not worth repair
P7090	137/263/SF Colerne/263	Missing from night intruder to Caen, 19.4.43
P7091	137	Ditched 26m S of Lizard Point on return from strike on Landerneau, 30.10.41
P7092	137/263	SOC 22.1.44
P7093	137	Missing while escorting destroyers off Belgian coast, 12.2.42; presumed shot down by Bf 109s
P7094	137/263	Ran out of fuel on return from attack on convoy off Barfleur and abandoned near Swanage, Dorset, 15.5.43
P7095	137	Hit by flak, Doullens, and failed to return, 23.1.43
P7096	137/263	Hit ridge on landing and wheel torn off, Warmwell, 10.9.43; DBR
P7097	137/263/3 FP	Swung off runway into soft ground, Hawarden, 8.1.44; not repaired
P7098	137/263	SOC 22.1.44
P7099	263	Missing from shipping strike off Ouistreham, 18.4.43
P7100	263	SOC 30.9.44
P7101	137	Hit by Lysander N1249 while parked, Matlask, 30.6.42; DBR
P7102	137/263	SOC 30.9.44
P7103	137	Lost wing during aerobatics 1m N of Aylsham, Norfolk, 4.5.42
P7104	137	Engine cut; landed on bad ground and undercarriage collapsed, Manston, 30.3.43; DBR
P7105	137/263	Shot down by flak attacking convoy off St.Brelade, 7.12.42
P7106	137	Missing while escorting destroyers off Belgian coast; presumed shot down by Bf 109s, 12.2.42
P7107	137	Missing as for P7106, 12.2.42
P7108	263	SOC 30.9.44
P7109	137	Missing from ground-attack mission to Etaples, 31.10.42
P7110	263	Engine cut on ferry flight; crashlanded on approach, Warmwell, 13.7.43; DBF
P7111	137/263	SOC 11.1.44
P7112	263	Blown over by gust on landing and wing hit ground; overturned, Fairwood Common, 14.3.42
P7113	263	Shot down by flak during attack on Morlaix airfield, 23.9.43
P7114	263/137	Hit P7119 on night take-off, Manston, 19.2.43; DBF
P7115	137	Hit by flak near Le Touquet and abandoned over Channel, 31.10.42
P7116	263/SF Colerne	SOC 1.5.43
P7117	263	Missing from night intruder mission; believed shot down by flak near Airel, 17.4.43
P7118	137	Believed caught fire due to glycol leak; abandoned near Sheringham, Norfolk, 29.5.42
P7119	137	Hit by P7114 taking off while waiting on flare-path, Manston, 19.2.43; DBF
P7120	263	Bellylanded in error, Warmwell, 28.10.42; DBR
P7121	137	Hit ground during dive-bombing practice, Manston, 16.4.43
P7122	137	Flew off on reciprocal after shooting down Blenheim in error; presumed ditched 20m NE of Cromer, Norfolk, 27.5.42
P7123 to P7128	-	Cancelled
P7158 to P7177	-	Cancelled
P7192 to P7221	-	Cancelled
P7240 to P7269		Cancelled

*   *   *   *   *   *   *   *   *   *

1,000 Supermarine Spitfire IIAs delivered between June 1940 and July 1941 by Castle Bromwich Aircraft Factory to Contract No. 981687/39

Mk.IIB indicated by *; some built as Mk.VA/VB as shown

P7280	AAEE/403/54/403/ 457/61 OTU/5 PAFU/ 61 OTU	Spun into ground out of cloud, Crickheath Farm, near Oswestry, Salop., 15.9.44
P7281	612/611/41/54/616/ 412/417/53 OTU/ 57 OTU/61 OTU	SOC 23.1.44
P7282	611/41	Shot down by fighters, Postling, Kent, 30.10.40
P7283	611/41/54/234/152/ 5 PAFU/17 SFTS/ 7 PAFU/10 AGS	SOC 18.6.45

P7284	611/41/54/315/308/ 610/3 Del Flt	Spun into ground in circuit, Valley, 24.11.41
P7285	266/603	Shot down by Bf 109s 16m E of Dover, 8.11.40
P7286	152/266/603/234/ 66/152	Overshot landing into fence, Swanton Morley, 16.9.41; DBR and SOC 10.11.41
P7287	266/603/65/122/ Cv VA/2 US	To Admiralty 3.5.44
P7288	266/603/111/610/ 340/58 OTU/53 OTU	To 4409M 30.11.43
P7289	266/603/Drem/19/ 331/58 OTU/61 OTU/ CGS	Hit ground low flying 3m N of Long Sutton, Lincs., 9.9.43; DBF
P7290	611/421 Flt/Middle Wallop/154/AFDU/ 57 OTU	To Admiralty 4.8.43
P7291	611/64	DBR in air raid, Martlesham Heath, 11.5.41
P7292	611/74/66/609	Shot down by Bf 109 while escorting ASR Lysander off Dover, 4.6.41
P7293	65/616/130/61 OTU/ 131/61 OTU/52 OTU/ 53 OTU	Collided with P7826 and crashed, Scotton Common, near Blyton, Lincs., 16.11.43
P7294	266/603/41/145/417/ 52 OTU/53 OTU	Overshot landing and under-carriage torn off; hit wall, Kirton-in-Lindsey, 26.6.44
P7295	266/603/65/ 61 OTU	Flew into hill in cloud, Cadair Bronwen, 2m SSE of Llandrillo, Merioneth, 14.12.42
P7296	266/234/64/504/ 57 OTU	SOC 8.3.45
P7297	266/603/Cv VA/ 602/71/350/USAAF/ 53 OTU/61 OTU	SOC 21.11.44
P7298	611	Caught fire over Croydon, possibly hit by AA; abandoned and crashed, Weybridge, Surrey, 11.9.40
P7299	54/66/610/41/54/ 234/19/Cv VA/66	Hit by P7304 while parked, Portreath, 26.2.42; DBR
P7300	611/41/54	Shot down by Bf 109s near Maidstone, Kent, 3.3.41
P7301	611/41/19/AAEE/ 1687 Flt	NFT 21.11.44
P7302	611/41	Shot down by Bf 109 off Dungeness, 20.2.41
P7303	611/66/421 Flt	Shot down by Bf 109s over Hawkinge and crashed near Newchurch, Kent, 11.10.40
P7304	611/152/234/266/ 234/66/61 OTU	Collided with P7444 and crashed near High Ercall Salop., 22.8.43
P7305	611/303/609	Shot down by Bf 109s near Ramsgate, Kent, 9.5.41
P7306	74	Damaged by Bf 109s over Chatham and abandoned, Blacketts Marshes, Tonge, Kent, 27.11.40
P7307	266/603/421 Flt/ 65/308/154/61 OTU	Collided with BM140 and crashed, Hayes, Middlesex, 17.3.42
P7308	74/54/308/71/Cv VA/ 133/421/164/602/ 61 OTU	SOC 11.44
P7309	266/603	Damaged by Bf 109s over Hastings; abandoned and crashed near Brede, Sussex, 25.10.40
P7310	266/74/609/41/145/ 417/53 OTU/58 OTU/ 1 TEU	SOC 16.8.44
P7311	266/603	Collided with Spitfire P7315 on landing, Drem, 17.12.40
P7312	74	Damaged by Bf 109 and crashlanded, Stanford, Kent, during interception off Dover, 1.11.40
P7313	266	Shot down by return fire from He 111 and abandoned over Billericay, 11.9.40
P7314	611/41/611/308	Missing, presumed ditched in Channel, 5.7.42
P7315	266/603/41/145/417/ 52 OTU/53 OTU	SOC 6.11.44
P7316	74/41/145/19/Cv VA	To Admiralty 1.9.42
P7317	421 Flt/234	Collided with P7779 over Channel and crashed, 13.5.41
P7318	19/1401 Flt/53 OTU/ 57 OTU	SOC 1.3.45
P7319	421 Flt/152/130/ 53 OTU	Caught fire and abandoned near St.Athan, 24.9.42
P7320	611/41/145/417/ 53 OTU/CGS	SOC 2.11.44
P7321	611/65/Cv ASR IIC/277	Lost 28.9.43; NFD
P7322	611/41	Damaged by Bf 109s and abandoned off Dungeness, 20.2.41
P7323	611	Crashed in forced landing while lost, Cooksey Green near Bromsgrove, Staffs., 11.10.40
P7324	266/603/111/Cv VA/ 81/165/167/521/ 8 OTU/61 OTU	SOC 22.8.44
P7325	266/603/41/145/19/ 331/61 OTU/57 OTU/ Cv ASR.IIC/277	SOC 25.7.44
P7326	611/41	Missing on patrol, 10.12.40; NFD
P7327	266/603/616	Missing, presumed shot down by Bf 109s on sweep, 25.6.41
P7328	266/603/74	Shot down by Bf 109s off Dungeness, 27.3.41
P7329	74	Collided with P7373 during practice attack, Coltishall, 8.10.40
———		
P7350	266/603/616/64/ CGS/57 OTU	SS 8.7.48 but preserved in BoBMF; G-AWIJ NTU
P7351	421 Flt/91	Damaged by Bf 109s and ditched off Sandgate, Kent, 20.4.41
P7352	74/234/64/403/54/ 403/131/57 OTU	Broke up in dive and crashed near Brunton, 19.4.43; believed due to oxygen failure
P7353	74/41/154/417/ 52 OTU	Engine cut; bellylanded in field, Brockhampton, Glos., 15.7.42
P7354	612/611/41/54/501/ 504/58 OTU/2 TEU/ CGS	SOC 2.11.44
P7355	74/611/403/131/ 61 OTU	Hit crashed Oxford L9703 on landing, swung and hit snow-bank; overturned, Tatenhill, 2.3.44
P7356	74/611/Northolt/ 61 OTU	Abandoned when engine caught fire near Stafford, 2.10.43
P7357	19/331/58 OTU/ 53 OTU	SOC 24.4.45
P7358	421 Flt/19/504/ 58 OTU/FLS	NFT 30.6.44
P7359	603/Turnhouse/64/ 66/19/331/58 OTU/ Cv ASR.IIC/277/ 1696 Flt	To store 9.12.44; NFT
P7360	74	Shot down by Bf 109s near Hollingbourne, Kent, 17.10.40
P7361	74/610/130/306/303/ 306/308/315/61 OTU/ 58 OTU/57 OTU	NFT 3.12.44

P7362	74	Abandoned on patrol 1½m SE of Southwold, Suffolk, 23.9.40; cause not known	P7422	19/234/131	SOC 18.11.41
P7363	74/W.Malling/66	Crashed after high speed stall at low altitude 1m NW of Gull Rock, Portreath, 20.3.42	P7423	19	Shot down by Bf 109, London Road, Chelmsford, Essex, 29.10.40
P7364	74	Damaged by Bf 109s and abandoned; crashed, Hadlow Place, near Tonbridge, Kent, 22.10.40	P7424	66/610/130	Crashed after control lost in low cloud, Rosemeray, Morvah, Cornwall, 3.7.41; DBF
P7365	266/603	Shot down by Bf 109s, Chartham Hatch, Kent, 25.10.40	P7425	19	Abandoned after control lost during aerobatics, Albury, Herts., 31.7.41
P7366	74/19/331/61 OTU/ 58 OTU/61 OTU/ Cv ASR.IIC/276	SOC 25.7.44	P7426	74	Shot down by Bf 109s and abandoned, Cowden, Kent, 20.10.40
P7367	74/41/145/19/53 OTU	SOC 14.8.44	P7427	19/1402 Flt/ 58 OTU/2 TEU	Abandoned after control lost 1m S of Dunfermline, Fife, 17.2.44
P7368	74/611/403/54/403/ 457/57 OTU/AFDU	Dived into ground, Hardwicke, Cambs., 2.2.44	P7428	19/74	Damaged 31.3.41; SOC 17.5.41; NFD
P7369	611	Stalled on landing and undercarriage collapsed, Ternhill, 28.9.40	P7429	19	Abandoned after collision with another Spitfire during formation practice near Fowlmere, 24.3.41
P7370	74	Damaged by fighters over Maidstone; abandoned and crashed, Coxheath, Kent, 20.10.40	P7430	19/71/401/154/ 61 OTU	Engine cut; crashlanded near Mostyn, Flintshire, 29.1.43
P7371	611/41/54	Dived into sea off Calais on sweep, 9.3.41; cause not known	P7431	74	Shot down by Bf 109s, South Nutfield, Surrey, 22.10.40
P7372	19/121/340/53 OTU	Collided with P8193 and crashed near Pontypool, Glam., 9.11.42	P7432	19/610/501/504/ 58 OTU/CF Inverness/ 58 OTU/FLS	SOC 17.8.44
P7373	74	Collided with P7329 during practice attack, Coltishall, 8.10.40	P7433	66/91/501/504/ 58 OTU	Throttle lever broke; overshot forced landing and hit hedge, Aberuthven, Perth, 22.6.42
P7374	611/41/616/485/ 130/61 OTU/52 OTU/ 5 PAFU/17 SFTS/CGS	SOC 30.11.44	P7434	19/308/315/610/ 342/53 OTU/57 OTU	SOC 1.6.45
P7375	611/41	Shot down by Bf 109s, Stanford, Kent, 30.10.40	P7435	19/65/616	Abandoned out of fuel and crashed in sea 1m S of Hove, Sussex, 23.6.41
P7376	611/72/74/350/277	SOC 2.6.45	P7436	603/609	Abandoned over Channel on sweep, 21.5.41
P7377	19/91/19/64/611/ 331/58 OTU/53 OTU	SOC 20.8.45	P7437	66	Damaged in air raid, Exeter, 20.5.41; NFT
P7378	421 Flt/91/501/ 350/58 OTU/ Northolt/53 OTU	Engine cut; hit P8641 during emergency down-wind landing, Llandow, 4.4.43	P7438	145/485/403/ 457/57 OTU	Hit by Spitfire EP114 while parked, Kirton-in-Lindsey, 15.10.44
P7379	19	Missing on sweep; presumed shot down by Bf 109s, 19.4.41	P7439	603	Shot down by Bf 109, Waltham, Kent, 27.10.40
P7380	19/234/52 OTU/ 61 OTU	Engine cut; crashlanded 8m SE of Chester, 18.7.43			
P7381	19/74	Shot down by Bf 109 on patrol over Channel, 19.4.41	P7440	66/609/118/501/152/ CGS/17 SFTS/9 PAFU/ 10 AGS	SOC 18.6.45
P7382	421 Flt/501/504/ 58 OTU/FLS/CFE	SOC 26.3.45	P7441	66/421 Flt	Shot down by Bf 109s near Ashford and crashed, Coldbridge, Kent, 12.10.40
P7383	421 Flt/54	Missing, believed after engine failure on patrol off Clacton, 20.4.41	P7442	611/41/145/403/54/ 403/154/61 OTU/ 53 OTU	Crashed near Cambridge, Glos., 12.12.42; believed due to throttle failure
P7384	64/19/331/58 OTU/ CGS	Tyre burst on take-off; swung and overturned, Catfoss, 25.4.44	P7443	611/41/54	Shot down by Bf 109 near Calais while escorting Blenheims, 26.2.41
P7385	74/303/64/611/ 52 OTU/SF Digby	SOC 9.2.45	P7444	421 Flt/66/485/312/ 416/61 OTU/CGS	SOC 2.11.44
P7386	74	Damaged by Bf 109s near Dover and abandoned over Sandwich Bay, 14.11.40	P7445	421 Flt/66/64/ 403/457	Crashed in sea 4m W of Peel, Isle of Man, 29.11.41; presumed control lost in cloud
P7387	603	Collided with He 111 near Faversham, Kent, and crashed near Teynham, 21.11.40	P7446	66/222/308/130/ 133/134/61 OTU/ 2 TEU/58 OTU/ 57 OTU	SOC 22.3.45
P7388	603/111/123/331/ 58 OTU/53 OTU/CGS/ 5 PAFU	SOC 28.6.45	P7447	66/118/616/412/ Cv VA/USAAF/332/ 349/61 OTU	Took off in coarse pitch; bounced and undercarriage leg collapsed, Heston, 19.7.41; DBR
P7389	603/64/611/340/ 53 OTU/CGS	To repair 22.2.44; NFT	P7448	611/41/65/234/ 501/152/57 OTU	Engine lost power and cockpit filled with smoke; abandoned 3m S of Alnwick, Northumberland, 12.7.44
P7420	19	Hit tree in forced landing near Kersey, Suffolk, 15.11.40			
P7421	19/131/57 OTU/CGS	SOC 12.9.44			

<u>P7449</u>	603	Damaged on patrol; dived into ground, Broomfield, near Leeds Castle, Kent, 29.11.40
P7490	66/609/65/122/154/ Cv ASR.IIC/278/277	SS 8.7.48
P7491	66	Collided with P7492 and crash-landed, Dormansland, near Edenbridge, Kent, 28.11.40
P7492	66	Collided with P7491 and abandoned, Stonehurst Farm, Dormansland, Kent, 28.11.40
P7493	66/145	Crashed after collision with P7737 over Tangmere, 21.5.41
P7494	74/611/308/315/ 610/123/CGS/ 53 OTU/AAEE/ SHAEF CS	SOC 15.5.45
P7495	-	SOC 29.11.40
P7496	603/Turnhouse/64/ CGS	SOC 2.11.44
P7497	421 Flt/66/421 Flt	SOC 9.1.41
P7498	421 Flt/610/130/ 501/Cv VA/601/ 421/164	Hit by L1031 while parked, Skeabrae, 14.8.42
P7499	421 Flt	Shot down by Bf 109s, Sholden, near Deal, Kent, 27.11.40
P7500	66/64/Northolt/308	Missing from sweep to St. Omer, 17.7.41
P7501	74/610/19/234/306/ 308/52 OTU/61 OTU	Ran out of fuel and bellylanded in field near Market Drayton, Salop., 27.12.43; NFT
P7502	74/602/313/457	Spun into ground near Ramsey, Isle of Man, 5.12.41
P7503	421 Flt/611/308/ 315/306/303/306/ 52 OTU/SF Northolt/ 53 OTU/7 PAFU/1 AGS	Taxied into bowser, Pembrey, 11.4.45; SOC as BER
P7504	66/72/74/53 OTU	Collided with P8592 and crashed near Cowbridge, Glam., 5.7.42
P7505	66/91/118/403/54/ 403/54/133/601/ 421/164/602/Cv PR XIII/4	SOC 28.3.45
P7506	74	Shot down by Bf 109s off Dungeness, 12.3.41
P7507	41	Hit balloon cable in bad visibility and crashlanded, Dagenham, Essex, 1.11.40; DBR
P7508	41/54/234/131/ 61 OTU	Swung on landing, Montford Bridge, 4.8.44; DBR
<u>P7509</u>	603/19/234/350/ 52 OTU	Spun into Severn near Chepstow, 23.7.42
P7520	66	Hit by Bf 109 and abandoned off Boulogne, 11.2.41
P7521	66/609/RAE/7 PAFU/ 1 AGS/10 AGS	SOC 18.6.45
P7522	66/65	Wing came off recovering from dive 4m SW of Binbrook, 13.9.41
P7523	74	Damaged by Bf 109 during interception near Dover and crashlanded, Biggin Hill, 1.11.40
P7524	66/303/452/610/ 126/61 OTU/ 52 OTU/CGS	SOC 2.11.44
P7525	66	Bellylanded short of fuel, Tatsfield Corner, Kent, 29.11.40
P7526	74	Shot down by Bf 109s, Elmsted, Kent, 27.10.40
P7527	74/308/57 OTU/ 13 OTU	SOC 30.12.44
P7528	603/111	Missing, presumed shot down by Bf 109s near Hazebrouck, 19.8.41
P7529	603/111/403/ 457/57 OTU	Crashed on landing, Eshott, 11.12.42
P7530	65/CGS	Collided with Wellington P9228 during practice attack and crashed 1m N of Lakenheath, Suffolk, 13.8.43
P7531	421 Flt/91	Abandoned on shipping reconnaissance and crashed in sea off Ramsgate, Kent, 24.4.41; cause not known
P7532	19/Cv VA/81/165/ 167/61 OTU	
P7533	66/610/130/133/ 134/57 OTU	Caught fire and abandoned, Parkside, Birkenhead, 14.10.42
P7534	421 Flt	Crashed on landing, Hawkinge, 6.12.40
P7535	19	Dived into ground after take-off, Duxford, 22.2.41
P7536	74/611/308	Missing from escorting bombers to Lille, 2.7.41
P7537	74	Shot down by Bf 109 near Gravelines on bomber escort mission, 6.5.41
P7538	66/609/306/303/ 306/308/315/ 53 OTU/57 OTU	Undershot landing and hit fence; bellylanded, Eshott, 14.8.44
P7539	66	Dived into ground near Tonbridge, Kent, 27.10.40
P7540	66/609/266/312	Wing hit water in flat calm while low flying, Loch Doon, near Trum, Wigtown, 25.10.41
P7541	66	Shot down by Bf 109s near Dover, 14.2.41
P7542	74/Biggin Hill/ 609/616	To Orfordness 18.7.41
P7543	603/234/306/308/ 350/52 OTU	Crashed in cloud 1m NE of Babdown Farm, 17.10.42
P7544	41/266/19/313/ 417	Hit by P7983 while parked, Charmy Down, 6.1.42; DBR
P7545	19	Shot down by Bf 109 off Southend, 5.11.40
P7546	603/303/1401 Flt	Dived into ground, E.Wretham, 26.2.43
P7547	19	Missing, pres. shot down by Bf 109 near Montreuil, 21.7.41
P7548	41/152/234/131/ 57 OTU/ADGB CS	SOC 1.4.45
P7549	603/41/131/57 OTU	Collided with P7598 and crashed, High Kinnoton, Flint, 16.8.42
P7550	603	Crashed in snowstorm, Grantshouse, Berwickshire, 31.12.40
P7551	72/74	Missing from night interception of Ju 88 off St.David's Head, Pembs., 26.11.41
P7552	603	Flew into ground in snowstorm, Nigg Bay, Aberdeen, 17.1.41
P7553	611/308/74/416/ 61 OTU/58 OTU/ 53 OTU	Crashed in forced landing near Kirton-in-Lindsey, Lincs., 22.4.44
P7554	234/Middle Wallop/ 610/61 OTU/58 OTU/ 53 OTU	Engine cut; bellylanded in field near Kirton-in-Lindsey, 22.4.44; DBR
P7555	64	Shot down by Bf 109s near Calais while escorting Blenheims, 13.3.41
P7556	222/501/130	Spun into ground, Portreath, 14.8.41
P7557	74/54/Middle Wallop/ 152/52 OTU/53 OTU/ 57 OTU	SOC 8.3.45

P7558	41/64/74/61 OTU/	
	58 OTU/17 SFTS	SOC 20.12.44
P7559	74	DBR in air raid, 20.5.41 and
		SOC 26.5.41 NFD
P7560	19/131	Abandoned in spin when control
		lost avoiding hill in cloud, Dale
		Head Farm, Harpur Hill,
		Derbyshire, 22.11.41
P7561	74	Damaged by Bf 109 and stalled
		in attempted forced landing,
		Detling, 10.1.41; DBR
P7562	64/54/452	Missing on sweep, 11.7.41
P7563	91/501/133/134/	Engine lost power; bellylanded
	53 OTU	1m S of Llantwit Major, Glam.,
		30.5.42; DBR
P7564	603/111/401/57 OTU	Throttle broke; crashlanded,
		Beeches Farm, near Hawarden,
		21.8.42; DBR
P7565	91	Damaged by Bf 109s and crash-
		landed 2m N of Hawkinge,
		4.4.41
P7566	19/603/485/121/	
	340/58 OTU/FLS	SOC 13.8.44
P7567	303/452/312/Ayr/	
	57 OTU/17 SFTS/5	
	PAFU	SOC 11.5.45
P7568	66	Shot down by Bf 109s over
		Boulogne, 11.2.41
P7569	234	Shot down by Bf 109 while
		escorting Beauforts off
		Cherbourg, 17.6.41
P7590	41/303/452	Missing on sweep to Gosnay;
		presumed shot down by Bf 109s
		near Béthune, 9.8.41
P7591	74/41/313/AFDU	Engine cut; hit wires in forced
		landing ¼m E of Sessay Stn.
		Yorks., 27.1.44
P7592	74/145/308/123/	
	53 OTU/52 OTU/	
	SF Northolt	SOC 1.45
P7593	421 Flt/FPP	Lost wing and dived into
		ground, Leek, Cheshire,
		17.11.40
P7594	266/485	Missing while escorting
		Blenheims to Lille, 7.8.41
P7595	610/130/411/121/	
	340/53 OTU/V-A	SOC 27.12.44
P7596	610	Missing 5.3.41; presumed shot
		down by Bf 109s over Channel
P7597	603	Hit Hurricane on take-off,
		Drem, 16.2.41
P7598	421 Flt/609/111/	Collided with P7549 and
	131/57 OTU	crashed, High Kinnerton, Flint
		16.8.42
P7599	234/Middle Wallop/	
	501/504/58 OTU/	
	2 TEU/FLS	SOC 26.1.45
P7600	66/609	Stalled on landing and
		undercarriage collapsed, West
		Malling, 13.5.41; DBR
P7601	421 Flt/602/313/	
	154/61 OTU/52 OTU/	
	57 OTU	SOC 30.12.44
P7602	66/609/313/417/	
	53 OTU/61 OTU/	
	57 OTU	SOC 1.6.45
P7603	145/266/411/121/	
	340/CGS/5 PAFU/	
	17 SFTS/5 PAFU	SOC 28.6.45
P7604	421 Flt/64/611/	
	52 OTU/53 OTU/CGS	SOC 2.11.44
P7605	64/145/485/610/	
	61 OTU/52 OTU/	
	Cv ASR.IIC/277	To AST 16.5.44; NFT
P7606	611/315/308	Missing escorting Blenheims
		to Hazebrouck, 29.8.41
P7607	611/66/130/66/	Hit ground recovering from dive
	52 OTU/53 OTU	½m W of Abergerdin, Glam.,
		23.4.43; DBF
P7608	603/111/Hornchurch/	Collided with P8079 and
	57 OTU/61 OTU	crashed, Maesbrook, Salop.,
		27.4.44
P7609	611/64/61 OTU	Engine cut; bellylanded,
		Bagley Marsh, Salop., 1.2.43
P7610	41/54/71/401/302/	Undercarriage leg collapsed on
	417/58 OTU	landing, Balado Bridge,
		24.9.43; DBR
P7611	421 Flt/266/457/	Undercarriage collapsed while
	61 OTU	taxying, Rednal, 17.7.44; DBR
P7612	41/54/Middle Wallop/	
	234/152/57 OTU	SOC 30.12.44
P7613	610/308/315/610/	
	350/ECFS/5 PAFU	SOC 28.6.45
P7614	74	Flown to AST 21.3.41; SOC
		30.4.41
P7615	91	Shot down by Bf 109s,
		Beinden, near Hawkinge,
		26.4.41; DBF
P7616	91/609/616/234/19/331/	
	58 OTU/61 OTU/276	SOC 25.7.44
P7617	19	Abandoned in cloud, Claxton,
		6m SE of Norwich, 21.4.41
P7618	32/74	Missing from patrol, 24.2.41
P7619	41/19/234/Cv VA/	
	1402 Flt/61 OTU/	
	1 FTS ATA	SOC 21.9.45
P7620	19/234/350/52 OTU/	Engine cut; bellylanded, Black
	58 OTU	Hall Farm, 4m NW of Stirling,
		21.7.43; DBR
P7621	145/609/485/152/	
	485/65/122/131/CGS	SOC 2.11.44
P7622	616/66/118/403/54/	Dived into ground low flying
	403/122/154/61 OTU	near Bettisfield, Salop., 14.6.42
P7623	74/602/412/61 OTU/	
	58 OTU/53 OTU	SOC 21.11.44
P7624	41/145	Crashed when control lost
		during low aerobatics ½m S of
		Catterick, 4.11.41; DBF
P7625	66/609/111/331/	
	58 OTU/57 OTU	SOC 26.4.44
P7626	64/452/485/65/122/	
	154/61 OTU/57 OTU	SOC 8.5.46
P7627	91/501/133/CGS/	
	61 OTU/17 SFTS/	
	5 PAFU	SOC 28.6.45
P7628	611/308/504/CGS/	
	Cv ASR.IIC/277/CGS	SOC 2.11.44
P7629	611/308/Cv VA/5 FG	
	Eglinton/61 OTU	SOC 12.44
P7660	66/Biggin Hill/602/	
	313/417/53 OTU/	
	AFDU/1695 Flt	SOC 12.44
P7661	AAEE/R-R/Cv VA/	Wrinkled wing recovering from
	AAEE/61 OTU	dive, 30.6.44; SOC 23.8.44 as
		DBR
P7662	65/616	Crashed near Worthing, Sussex,
		10.3.41; believed due to anoxia
P7663	64/234/130/152/	Undershot landing, hit ground
	53 OTU	and stalled, Hibaldstow, 15.1.44
P7664	421 Flt/501	Crashed 1.8.41; NFD
P7665	65	Shot down by Bf 109s near
		St.Omer, 5.2.41
P7666	41/54	Damaged by Bf 109s and
		abandoned off Harwich, 20.4.41
P7667	74/65/122/131/	Engine cut; overturned in forced
	61 OTU/53 OTU	landing, Faldingworth, 15.4.44
P7668	66/609/19/234/133/	
	134/58 OTU/CGS	SOC 1.6.45

Spitfire IIA   Spitfire IIA

P7669	66/609	Shot down by Bf 109s while escorting Blenheims on shipping attack off Gravelines, 29.4.41
P7670	66/111/CGS	SOC 2.11.44
P7671	66/152/610	Pilot blacked out during aerobatics; stalled and spun into ground, Winfield Farm, near Driffield, 27.10.41
P7672	91/501/306/Cv VA/ 12 Obs Sqn USAAC Eglinton/61 OTU	SOC 6.45
P7673	310/416/Cv ASR.IIC/ 277/7 PAFU/1 AGS/ 10 AGS	SOC 20.6.45
P7674	91/602/485/61 OTU/ 58 OTU/53 OTU	SOC 6.45
P7675	91/308/315/266/ 123/58 OTU	Dived into ground during combat practice, Thornhill, Stirling, 16.5.42
P7676	91/266/123/52 OTU	Hit water low flying over Severn, 11.9.42
P7677	91/501/Colerne/ CGS	Hit Wellington N2865 during practice attack 2m W of Huntingdon, 10.4.43; DBF
P7678	64/CGS	Dived into ground 2m WSW of Wisbech, Cambs., 9.4.43; cause not known
P7679	610/130/411	Ditched on patrol, 13.10.41
P7680	19/Middle Wallop/ 152	Shot down by Bf 109s while escorting Blenheims off Belgian coast, 24.10.41
P7681	222/501/52 OTU/ 53 OTU/TTC CF	SOC 8.3.45
P7682	222/452	Missing on sweep, presumed shot down by Bf 109s near Béthune, 9.8.41
P7683	603/111/123/58 OTU/ 56 OTU/58 OTU	Collided with P8387 in formation and crashed, Hammering Mere Farm, 19.8.43; DBF
P7684	610	Missing after interception of Do 215 off Isle of Wight, 15.4.41
P7685	610	Flew into hill in bad weather 2m NE of West Dean, Sussex, 23.3.41
P7686	19/603/152/266/ Cv VA/USAAC/ Eglinton/61 OTU	SOC 19.7.45
P7687	41/145/417/53 OTU/ 61 OTU/58 OTU/ 53 OTU	SOC 23.11.44
P7688	41/403/131/61 OTU/ 57 OTU	SOC 26.1.46
P7689	41/54	Abandoned near Maidstone, 12.3.41; cause not known
P7690	64/65/504/58 OTU/ AFDU/1687 Flt	SOC 2.45
P7691	609/56/66/130/152	Missing (Rotterdam) 28.8.41
P7692	74/485/Cv VA/ 603/315/81/164/ 602/USAAC/61 OTU	Flew into target and crashed, Prestatyn Beach, Flint, 26.7.43
P7693	91/19	Missing, pres shot down by Bf 109s off Walcheren, 12.8.41
P7694	65/616/411/340/ 53 OTU	SOC 5.45
P7695	64/131/61 OTU/58 OTU/1 TEU/5 PAFU	Engine cut; crashed on approach, Ternhill, 5.4.45
P7696*	611/308/234/457/ 61 OTU/57 OTU/ 17 SFTS/5 PAFU	Crashed on landing, Ternhill, 16.3.45
P7697	222/485/65	Missing from sweep, 21.8.41
P7698	611/308/416/58 OTU/57 OTU	NFT 2.6.44
P7699	222	Shot down by Ju 88 intruder over Coltishall, 4.5.41
P7730	65/616	Missing, presumed shot down by Bf 109s on sweep, 21.6.41
P7731	421 Flt/501	Missing on patrol, 6.8.41
P7732	65/616/19/331/ 58 OTU/Cv ASR.IIC/ 276/RAE	SOC 5.6.45
P7733	65	Shot down by Bf 109s on sweep off Cap Gris Nez, 5.2.41
P7734	66/609/71/504/ 58 OTU/Cv ASR.IIC/ 277	SOC 16.8.44
P7735	421 Flt/91	Destroyed on ground by Bf 109, Hawkinge, 4.2.41
P7736	65/616	Shot down on ground attack mission to Maupertus airfield, 24.4.41
P7737	610/145	Collided with P7493 over Tangmere, 21.5.41
P7738	41/54/71/401/316/ 306/52 OTU/ ADGB CS	Engine cut; crashed in forced landing, New House Farm, Denham, Bucks., 5.9.44
P7739	41/56/66/152/154/ 58 OTU/57 OTU/CGS	SOC 2.11.44
P7740	74	To 5 MU 6.6.42; NFT
P7741	74	Shot down by Bf 109 while escorting Blenheims over Boulogne, 2.2.41
P7742	603/111/145/61 OTU/ 53 OTU/61 OTU	SOC 21.11.44
P7743	66/118/403/54/403/ 457/61 OTU/52 OTU	Engine cut; bellylanded in field, Llandevenny, Mon., 13.2.42
P7744	66/118/403/54/403/ 122/74/350/57 OTU/ 61 OTU/57 OTU	SOC 28.4.45
P7745	66/118/313/306/ 308/58 OTU/FLS	SOC 10.44
P7746	303/403/54/403/ 131	Stalled avoiding high ground in snowstorm and abandoned, Rushton Cottage, The Wrekin, Salop., 7.12.41
P7747	64/417/53 OTU	SOC 10.44
P7748	64/66/130/152/ 58 OTU	Collided on night take-off with Lysanders P1665 and T1620, Balado Bridge, 31.5.43
P7749	603/111/306	Stalled in bad visibility and hit ground near Squires Gate, 5.12.41; DBF
P7750	603/111	Collided with P7848 in cloud on sweep and crashed, 23.7.41
P7751	64/72/74	Undershot night approach and hit pillbox, Acklington, 9.9.41; DBR
P7752	65/610	Shot down by Bf 109s over Channel, 5.3.41
P7753	65/616	Damaged by return fire from Ju 88 and abandoned near Littlehampton, Sussex, 5.5.41
P7754	65/616/19/331/ CGS/53 OTU	SOC 25.9.44
P7755	610/130/411	Missing on training flight, presumed ditched off Grimsby, Lincs., 29.7.41
P7756	54/403/54/403/ 457/CGS	SOC 19.11.44
P7757	234/66/Cv to VA/ 61 OTU	Stalled on take-off and spun into ground, Montford Bridge, 12.2.43
P7758	145/485	Crashed during low aerobatics, Leconfield, 18.6.41
P7759	65/616/24/412/ 310/331	Dived into sea 3m W of Brough Head, Orkneys, 16.3.42
P7770	64/611/58 OTU	Caught fire starting up, Balado Bridge, 4.8.42; DBR
P7771	616/19	Missing 6.8.41

69

P7772	64/611/52 OTU/53 OTU	SOC 17.10.45
P7773	145/485	Missing while escorting Stirlings to Mazingarbe, 11.7.41
P7774	611	Shot down by Bf 109s on ground attack mission to Vlissingen, 28.4.41
P7775	610/64/611/277/ 1696 Flt	SOC 7.12.44
P7776	611/71/403/457/ 58 OTU	Hit P8679 during mock attack and crashed near Dunfermline, Fife, 5.6.42
P7777	610/412/310/416/ 61 OTU/52 OTU/ 61 OTU	SOC 30.12.44
P7778	64	Missing from convoy patrol, 23.2.41; believed collided with P7852
P7779	234	Collided with P7317 over Channel, 13.5.41
P7780	222	Broke up in air near South-borough, Norfolk, 3.4.41
P7781	64/417/53 OTU	Crashed in sea 1m S of St.Donats, Glam., 21.5.42
P7782	74/602/412/310/ 416/53 OTU/57 OTU/ CGS	SOC 20.4.45
P7783	91	Damaged by Bf 109s N of Dover and abandoned, Little Mongeham, Kent, 4.4.41
P7784	64	Shot down on ground attack mission, Mardyck, 9.4.41
P7785	609	Damaged by Bf 109s and crashed near Hawkinge, 27.3.41
P7786	303/452/313/331/ 58 OTU/FAA	SOC 23.11.44
P7787	234/66	Missing while escorting Blenheims over Belgium, 12.8.41
P7788	222/485	Missing from escorting Blenheims to Le Trait, 12.8.41
P7789 _____	303/452/Cv VA/ Eglinton/Northolt/ 52 OTU/61 OTU	SOC 27.9.45
P7810	152/130/350/ Northolt	SOC 20.12.44
P7811	64/452/121/340	Bellylanded in error, Turn-house, 21.11.41; SOC 23.12.41
P7812	65/616	Damaged by Bf 109 and aband-oned off Isle of Wight, 21.4.41
P7813	19	Missing 27.6.41; presumed shot down by Bf 109
P7814	65/616/457/452/ 57 OTU/61 OTU	SOC 10.45
P7815	65/616	Crashed in forced landing near Bacton, Norfolk, 26.6.41
P7816	41	Dived into ground in haze on return from sweep, Ashford, Kent, 22.2.41
P7817	611	Shot down by Bf 109s while escorting convoy off Deal, 7.5.41
P7818	41/54/602/71/403/ 457/CGS/Cv ASR.IIC/ 277/CGS	SOC 4.11.43
P7819	303	Shot down by Bf 109s, Dungeness Lighthouse, 16.4.41
P7820	91/222/485/64/416/ 57 OTU/53 OTU	Collided with Wellington BJ819 and crashed, Sturton, Lincs., 22.5.44
P7821	303/152/Middle Wallop/66	Abandoned while escorting Blenheims to Bergen op Zoom, 20.8.41
P7822	145/485/19/331/ 58 OTU/53 OTU	Collided with X4067 during turn and crashed in sea off St.Athan, 15.2.43
P7823	54/504/152/504	Dived into ground, Rough-lean, near Lurgan, Co.Down, 7.1.42
P7824	603/111	Shot down escorting Blenheims over France, 19.8.41
P7825	145/403	Dived into ground out of cloud 1m NW of Cosford, 30.7.41
P7826	65/122/74/350/ Atcham/52 OTU/ 53 OTU	Collided with P7293 near Blyton and crashed, Kirton Lindsey, Lincs., 16.11.43
P7827	65/616/411/74/ 121/340/53 OTU	Hit by R6621 while parked, Llandow, 2.5.43
P7828	65/616/121/340/ 58 OTU	Collided with P8660 on take-off, Balado Bridge, 24.2.43
P7829	65/616/412/340/ 53 OTU	Dived into ground near St.Athan, 22.11.42
P7830	66/609/Middle Wallop/66/152/ 57 OTU	SOC 5.3.45
P7831	145/485	Abandoned 15m N of Cher-bourg, 24.7.41; cause not known
P7832	72/74/610/340/ 61 OTU/52 OTU/FAC Gosport/5 PAFU	SOC 28.6.45
P7833	54	Missing, believed after engine failure on patrol off Clacton, 20.4.41
P7834	66/609/313/417/ 52 OTU	Collided with P9562 during practice attack and crashed near Bear Inn, Cirencester, Glos., 10.9.42
P7835	66/609/118/308/315	Missing while escorting Blenheims over France, 24.7.41
P7836	65/616/52 OTU/ 277/57 OTU	Collided with P8071; crash-landed, Boulmer, 10.7.43; not repaired and SOC 26.1.45
P7837	616/412/310	Stalled and spun into ground 12m SE of Dyce, 19.11.41
P7838	611/602/122/277/ AEAF CF	SOC 5.6.45
P7839	74/308/315/610	Hit ground recovering from dive 1m NNW of Bewholme, near Catfoss, 3.10.41
P7840	64/340/53 OTU/CGS	SOC 2.11.44
P7841	65/616	Caught fire in dispersal pen, Tangmere, 5.3.41; DBF
P7842	66/118	Bellylanded in forced landing near Ibsley, 3.5.41; DBR
P7843	66/118/152/306/ 66	Collided with P8430 5m NW of the Lizard and crashed, 24.1.42
P7844	152/130/66/AAEE/ RAE	SOC 8.3.45
P7845	54/308	Missing escorting Stirlings to Lille, 8.7.41
P7846	616/Cv VA/54	Missing while escorting Blenheims to Ostend; presumed shot down by fighters 10m off Manston, 3.10.41
P7847	222	Broke up in air near Salhouse, 2m S of Wroxham, Norfolk, 24.3.41
P7848	603/111	Collided with P7750 while escorting Blenheims over France and crashed, 23.7.41
P7849	19/131/Cv VA/ 2 US/5 US	To USAAF 18.11.42
P7850	610/266/123/ 58 OTU/CGS	SOC 2.11.44
P7851	603/111/74/CGS/ 7 SFTS/1 AGS/10 AGS	SOC 21.5.45
P7852	64	Missing from convoy patrol, 23.2.41; believed collided with P7778

P7853	222/452/129/610/ 61 OTU/5 PAFU	SOC 28.6.45
P7854	74	Spun into ground during slow roll over Manston, 10.4.41
P7855	65/308/315/130/ Rotol/AFDU/61 OTU/ SHAEF CF/BAFO Comm Wing	SOC 12.12.45
P7856	65/616/Digby/310/ 416/61 OTU/57 OTU	NFT 9.3.44
P7857	222/2 FPP	Hit house in forced landing, Wilsbridge, Bristol, 8.3.42
P7858	303/452/313/611/340/ 57 OTU/Cv ASR.IIC/ 277/57 OTU	NFT 3.12.44
P7859	303	Shot down by Bf 109 over Le Touquet, 20.4.41
P7880	610/130/411/306	Engine cut; crashlanded 10m NE of Chester, 22.10.41; SOC 1.4.42
P7881	66/609/616	Missing escorting Blenheims over France, 24.7.41
P7882	152/130/134/312/ ECFS/53 OTU	Undershot landing and stalled into ground, Hibaldstow, 4.5.44; DBR
P7883	152/611/308/19/234/ 152/74/61 OTU/ 53 OTU	Flew into hill 4m NE of Chapel-en-le-Frith, Derby, 10.12.43
P7884	66/501/152/ Northolt/57 OTU	Collided with another Spitfire and crashed, 30.9.44
P7885	66/152/52 OTU/53 OTU	SOC 30.12.44
P7886	611/308/19/331/ 58 OTU/AFDU/ 1695 Flt	SOC 12.44
P7887	66/118/Middle Wallop/234/19	Stalled on take-off and undercarriage collapsed, Matlask, 4.9.41; DBF
P7888	421 Flt/91/308	Missing from escorting bombers to Hazebrouck, 12.7.41
P7889	234/66/19/52 OTU/ Cv ASR.IIC/277/ 61 OTU	Collided with P7855 over Hawarden and DBR, 27.7.43
P7890	19	Missing, presumed shot down by Bf 109s near St.Omer, 21.7.41
P7891	234/41/145/CGS/ 61 OTU	SOC 22.4.45
P7892	266/123/58 OTU	To Admiralty 7.8.43
P7893	152/308/401/316/ 133/57 OTU/61 OTU	SOC 30.10.44
P7894	65/122/61 OTU/ 52 OTU	Crashed in forced landing Keevil, 15.2.42
P7895*	65/72/74/57 OTU/ 53 OTU/7 PAFU/ 7 SFTS	Crashed on take-off, Peterborough, 8.3.45
P7896	64/340/53 OTU/ 61 OTU	Tyre burst on landing; swung and overturned, Rednal, 27.3.43
P7897	152/310/416/ 61 OTU	Engine caught fire; bellylanded in field, Pudleston, Herefordshire, 4.1.44
P7898	234/66/152/57 OTU	SOC 26.1.45
P7899*	222/308/123/57 OTU/ 61 OTU/17 SFTS/ 5 PAFU	SOC 28.6.45
P7900	266/130/350/SF Northolt/57 OTU/ 58 OTU/Heston/ 57 OTU	SOC 3.5.45
P7901	266/Middle Wallop/ 152	Shot down by AA fire from convoy off Cromer, Norfolk, 27.10.41
P7902	152/501/66/152/66/ 61 OTU/57 OTU	Collided with Hurricane AG111 during practice attack and crashed near Wooler, Northumberland, 5.5.43
P7903	152/CGS/53 OTU/ 52 OTU	Engine cut; bellylanded in field, Beckwith Farm, Framcote, Glos., 20.6.43
P7904	152/130	Missing escorting Blenheims to Ijmuiden, 21.8.41
P7905	152/403/457	Tyre burst on landing; swung and overturned, Andreas, 31.12.41
P7906	152/501/Cv VA/ 603/164/602/USAAF/ 61 OTU	Collided with X4606 and abandoned when engine caught fire, Burton, Salop., 8.8.44
P7907	222/616/234/19/152	Flew into water, Lough Foyle, 15.2.45
P7908	145/485/401/154/58 OTU/2 TEU/13 Gp CF	SOC 25.5.45
P7909	222/Coltishall/ 266/Cv VA	To Admiralty 4.9.42
P7910	152/41/145/340/ 53 OTU/52 OTU	Hit Master DL556 while landing and overturned, Aston Down, 13.1.43
P7911	66/118/403/54/403/ 122/154/58 OTU/ 277/57 OTU	SOC 9.3.45
P7912	64/19/234/131/ 61 OTU/52 OTU/ AFDU/1687 Flt	Ran short of fuel and overturned in forced landing, Wormegay, Norfolk, 16.7.44; DBR
P7913	66/118/CGS	Abandoned after engine fire, Middle Drove, Norfolk, 8.6.43
P7914	610/130/411/52 OTU/ Northolt	To 4366M 24.11.43
P7915	610/130/411/121/340/ 53 OTU/Cv ASR.IIC/ 277/53 OTU/CGS	SOC 2.4.45
P7916	145/485/130/133/ 134/57 OTU/52 OTU/ 58 OTU/FLS	SOC 26.1.45
P7917	64/609/403/54/ 403/457/58 OTU/ Cv ASR.IIC/277	SOC 16.8.44
P7918	54/412/310/416/ Cv ASR.IIC/277/ 57 OTU/52 OTU	Collided with Mustang AG489 and crashed 2m N of Nether Lyppiat, near Brimscombe, Glos., 4.7.43
P7919	611/308/315/123/ AFDU/1690 Flt	SOC 22.11.44
P7920	54/Cv VA/332/24/ Northolt/53 OTU/ 52 OTU	Undercarriage damaged on landing; overshot and bellylanded, Rednal, 21.9.44
P7921	19/AFDU/61 OTU/ 53 OTU	SOC 25.1.45
P7922	234	Damaged by Bf 109s and abandoned off Portland, 19.5.41
P7923	610/130/411/CGS	SOC 9.11.44
P7924	145/19	Crashlanded on return from sweep, Ashford, Kent, 7.8.41; DBR
P7925	234/152/66/58 OTU/ ADGB CF	SOC 4.1.45
P7926	610/130/411/121/ 340/53 OTU/ECFS	SOC 10.44
P7927	152/130/133/134/ 52 OTU/Northolt/ 53 OTU/61 OTU	SOC 20.12.44
P7928	74	Missing while escorting Blenheims, 6.5.41
P7929	222/Coltishall/19/ 331/58 OTU/53 OTU	SOC 30.12.44
P7960	6 FPP	Undershot landing and hit house, Meir, 9.2.41
P7961	145/Heston/FCCS	SOC 6.3.45
P7962	303	Damaged by Bf 109s and abandoned over Dover, 9.5.41
P7963	54/19/331/58 OTU/ 61 OTU	Hit farmhouse on take-off, Rednal, 8.9.42

P7964	610/130/411/Cv VA/ 145/134/133/134	To Admiralty 4.9.42; to 5262M 9.3.45
P7965*	72/74/Cv VA/USAAF Eglinton/61 OTU	SOC 19.7.45
P7966	616/412/154/ 61 OTU/52 OTU	Dived into storage shed, Quedgeley, Glos., 15.10.42
P7967	41	Abandoned with damaged undercarriage at night 11m SW of Catterick, 5.6.41
P7968	72/74/610/61 OTU/ 52 OTU	Engine cut; undershot belly- landing ½m SW of Nympsfield, Glos., 30.5.42; DBR
P7969	65/122/154/AFDU/ 52 OTU/CGS	SOC 29.11.44
P7970	91/485	Missing near Béthune while escorting Blenheims, 12.8.41
P7971	266/19	Undershot night approach and hit trees, Horstead Hall, 1m SW of Coltishall, 12.10.41
P7972	610/130	Dived into ground out of low cloud, St.Just, Cornwall, 3.7.41
P7973	222/452/313/154/ Cv V/57 OTU/61 OTU	To Australia 23.2.45; became museum aircraft in AWM
P7974	145/485/266/57 OTU/ CGS	Bellylanded while lost in bad visibility, Cottingham, near Hull, 3.4.44
P7975	145/485	Shot down in sea 10m SW of Boulogne while escorting Blenheims to Hazebrouck, 23.6.41
P7976	54/111/74/350/Atcham/ 52 OTU/61 OTU	SOC 23.11.44
P7977	145/485	Missing, presumed shot down by Bf 109s escorting Blenheims near Gosney, 19.8.41
P7978	64/411/Digby/ 58 OTU	Collided with X4914 and crashed, Sauchie, near Alloa, Clackmannan, 17.6.43
P7979	54/602/54/411/121/ 340/52 OTU/61 OTU	Dived into ground, Berriew, near Welshpool, Montgomery, 5.2.44
P7980	54/485/616	Missing escorting Blenheims to Hazebrouck, 3.7.41
P7981	41/145	Engine cut during loop; crash- landed, Burneston, Yorks., 10.8.41
P7982	64/416	Skidded into snow bank on take- off and undercarriage collapsed, Peterhead, 6.2.42; hit by Stirling N6086 on 7.2.42 and DBR
P7983	154/145/417/53 OTU	SOC 8.3.45
P7984*	222/616/234	Ran out of fuel on convoy patrol and engine cut; ditched 5m SW of Exmouth, Devon, 25.7.41
P7985	234/412/121/340/ 53 OTU	Dived into ground out of cloud, Digby, 15.6.43
P7986	145/485/1401 Flt/ 521/Cv VA/349/ 61 OTU	Collided with R6801 over Leicestershire and crashed, 3.10.43
P7987	234/71/401/317/ 133/310/134/57 OTU	SOC 3.5.45
P7988	152/111/131/61 OTU/ 57 OTU/53 OTU	SOC 9.10.45
P7989	303/154/310/416/ 53 OTU	SOC 8.1.46
P7990*	222/501/504/57 OTU	Crashed, Hawarden, 11.4.42; NFD
P7991	118/501/234/19/66	Crashed on approach, St.Merryn, 12.1.42
P7992	66/Middle Wallop/ 66/19/66/58 OTU	Undershot landing at Balado Bridge, 27.10.42
P7993	234/66/234/66/ 58 OTU/52 OTU/ 57 OTU	SOC 12.10.45
P7994	64/Drem/133/134/ Cv ASR.IIC/277	Missing, presumed shot down by flak off Boulogne, 25.11.43
P7995	64/66/234/91	Missing escorting Blenheims to Rotterdam, 28.8.41
P7996	152/501/152/66/ 53 OTU	SOC 8.3.45
P7997	152/501/152	Swung during heavy landing and tipped up, Fowlmere, 30.8.41; DBR
P7998	66/118/457/452/ 57 OTU/52 OTU/ 61 OTU/53 OTU/ 1687 Flt	SOC 1.45
P7999	152/501/130/66/ 313/66	Swung on take-off and crashed, Portreath, 18.3.42
P8010	266/123/CGS	Engine cut; bellylanded on Pandora Sands, 7m N of Kings Lynn, Norfolk, 6.7.43
P8011	234	Believed damaged in air raid, Warmwell, 1.4.41; to AST for repair 3.4.41 and SOC 2.5.41
P8012	66/65/412/61 OTU/ 58 OTU/53 OTU	SOC 14.8.44
P8013	65/57 OTU/ Cv ASR.IIC/276	SOC 25.7.44
P8014	266/65/122/154/ 61 OTU/53 OTU	SOC 25.8.45
P8015	Middle Wallop/234	Damaged by Bf 109s and ditched off Weymouth, 9.7.41
P8016	74/6 MU	Abandoned after control lost, Woodmansterne, Surrey, 4.3.41
P8017	19/403/Cv V/457/ 452/57 OTU	Engine cut; ditched 1m N of Boulmer, 5.1.44
P8018	74/145/417/CGS	SOC 2.11.44
P8019	610/1 Del Flt	Overshot landing in bad weather and hit houses, St.Eval, 19.6.41
P8020	41/145/610/350/ 53 OTU/Cv ASR.IIC/ 277	SOC 16.8,44
P8021	AAEE & R-R/CGS	SOC 2.11.44
P8022	266/485/306/303/308/ Cv ASR.IIC/277/ 5 PAFU/10 AGS	SOC 18.6.45
P8023	66/609/54/602/65/ 122/154/58 OTU	Engine lost power; bellylanded 3m SW of Balado Bridge, 24.10.43; DBR
P8024	152/111/130/61 OTU	Engine overheated; overshot forced landing and overturned, Whitchurch Heath, Salop., 1.2.43; DBR
P8025	145/485/306/ Northolt/61 OTU/ 58 OTU/53 OTU	SOC 23.11.44
P8026	234/Middle Wallop/ 501/19/152	Tyre burst on take-off; tipped up, Eglinton, 9.4.42; DBR
P8027	610	Missing while escorting Blenheims to Boulogne; presumed shot down by Bf 109s over Channel, 5.3.41
P8028	222	Collided with Spitfire P7908 during practice dogfight and crashed, Easton, Norfolk, 27.3.41
P8029	303	Shot down by flak attacking Berck airfield, 12.4.41
P8030	72/74/310/416/ 61 OTU/Cv ASR.IIC/ 277/61 OTU	SOC 30.12.44
P8031	64/485/71/303/306/ 308/52 OTU/Northolt/ 7 PAFU	SOC 11.5.45
P8032	152/501/152/234/ 19/66/Cv ASR.IIC/ 277	SOC 14.8.44
P8033	145/71/74/350/CGS	SOC 2.11.44

P8034	266	Left formation and dived into sea 10m SE of Dover, 4.6.41; cause not known
P8035	64/611/52 OTU/61 OTU/AFDU/1695 Flt/ 7 PAFU/1 AGS	SOC 29.6.45
P8036	234/501/152/Cv VA/1402 Flt/ATA	Undercarriage collapsed in heavy landing, 22.6.44; not repaired and SOC 16.8.44
P8037	234/501/130/152/ 61 OTU/CGS	Engine cut; bellylanded, Middle Green, 6m SW of Kings Lynn, Norfolk, 19.6.43
P8038	303/452/313/332/ USAAF/Cv VB/ 315/611/53 OTU	SOC 29.9.45
P8039	303	Shot down by Bf 109s off Dungeness, 16.4.41
P8040	303/452/313/350/ 57 OTU	Crashed in forced landing, Picton, Cheshire, 26.10.42
P8041	303/452/457/154	SOC 20.5.42
P8042*	72/74/53 OTU/CGS	SOC 2.11.44
P8043	41/504	Took off in coarse pitch and ran off runway, Kirkistown, 30.1.42; DBR
P8044	41/145	Control lost in cloud; dived into ground, Kirbymoorside, Yorks., 28.10.41
P8045	72/74	Spun into ground, Sarington Hall, Ouston, Northumberland, 2.8.41
P8046	74/234	Missing escorting Whirlwinds over Maupertus airfield, 26.8.41
P8047	74/602/313/417/ 61 OTU/AFDU/ SF Gosport/Davidstow Moor	SOC 11.10.44
P8048	64/CGS/Northolt	PSOC 21.6.47
P8049	41	Dived into ground out of cloud near Richmond, Yorks., 2.4.41
P8070	145/616	Missing, presumed shot down by Bf 109s while escorting Stirlings to Mazingarbe, 9.7.41
P8071	145/313/417/61 OTU/53 OTU/57 OTU	Spun into sea off Boulmer after collision, 10.7.43
P8072	66/130/66/152/ 53 OTU/Cv ASR.IIC/ 277/61 OTU	SOC 26.1.45
P8073	303/452/313/Cv VA/ 53 OTU/58 OTU	SOC 16.8.44
P8074	222/501/133	Abandoned out of fuel and crashed, Maladerrack, Eire, 30.11.41
P8075	91/222/501/504/ 58 OTU/61 OTU/ 58 OTU/2 TEU/ 53 OTU	SOC 8.3.45
P8076	152/130/411/121/ 340	Overshot landing at Drem and hit dispersal pen, 28.12.41
P8077	152/501/234/19/ 152	Spun into ground near Eglinton, 24.2.42
P8078	222/308/306/58 OTU	Engine cut; hit tree in forced landing 1m E of Milnathort, Kinross, 20.7.42
P8079	303/RAE/61 OTU/ Cv ASR.IIC/277/ 61 OTU	Collided with P7608 and crashed, Marshbrook, Salop., 27.4.44
P8080	602/71/401/61 OTU/ Digby/57 OTU	Spun into ground during practice dogfight, High House Farm, Alnwick, Northumberland, 1.3.43
P8081	222/452/312/58 OTU/ 53 OTU/1 AGS/10 AGS	SOC 21.5.45
P8082	41/122/154/52 OTU/276	SOC 25.7.44
P8083	AFDU/1687 Flt	SOC 3.45
P8084	64	Flew into ground in bad visibility on training flight 1¼m W of Kirknewton, 1.11.41
P8085	303/452	Shot down by intruder on night training near Somercotes, Lincs, 5.7.41
P8086	66/118/412/Northolt/ Eglinton/116/1402 Flt/8 OTU/61 OTU/ Cv VA/61 OTU	SOC 18.9.45
P8087	65/308/306/303/ 306/308/58 OTU/ CGS/53 OTU	SOC 18.5.45
P8088	66/118/152/19/ 61 OTU/CGS/61 OTU	Dived into ground, Lower Heath Common, Prees, Salop., 16.9.44; cause not known
P8089	66/118/313/306/ 308/350/58 OTU	Ran out of fuel and stalled on approach, Balado Bridge, 23.12.42
P8090	66/118/403/54/403/ 457/CGS/AFDU	To 4256M 28.10.43
P8091	72/74/350/Northolt/ AFDU/1690 Flt/ 7 PAFU	Blt as IIB. Undercarriage collapsed on landing, Castle Bromwich, 7.1.45; to 4936M 18.1.45
P8092	266/123/52 OTU/ AFDU	Preserved as museum aircraft
P8093	266/123/152 OTU	Stalled on approach and hit ground, Aston Down, 26.6.42
P8094	609/308	Missing escorting Blenheims to St.Omer/Longuenesse, 7.8.41
P8095	65/Cv VA/USAAF Eglinton/332/61 OTU	Hit tree in fog, Grub Street, Staffs., 16.4.44
P8096	266/123/CGS/ Cv ASR.IIC/277/ 53 OTU	SOC 6.11.45
P8097	152/66/130/123/66/ 61 OTU/CGS	SOC 14.8.44
P8098	609/Cv VA/130	Hit hut recovering from dive over Portreath, 11.10.41
P8099	303/452/313/Cv VA/ USAAF/RAE/61 OTU	Hit by Martinet EM646 while parked, Rednal, 23.10.44; not repaired and SOC 6.11.44
P8130	303/452	Crashed on take-off, Sutton Bridge, 11.6.41; DBR
P8131	Middle Wallop/66/ CGS/61 OTU/276/ Warmwell/276/ 5 PAFU/1 AGS/10 AGS	SOC 18.6.45
P8132	65/122/145/417/ 52 OTU/ADGB CS	SOC 8.3.45
P8133	266/121/340/53 OTU	Spun into ground 1m S of Llanbirt, Glam., 25.4.42
P8134	AAEE/58 OTU/53 OTU	SOC 14.12.45
P8135	66/145/306/308/222/ 64/611/57 OTU	Blt as IIB SOC 30.12.44
P8136	65/411/340/ 58 OTU/CGS	SOC 2.11.44
P8137	234	Missing from sweep over Cherbourg, 9.7.41
P8138	234/Middle Wallop/ 66/52 OTU/61 OTU/ 5 PAFU	SOC 28.6.45
P8139	56/66/130/66/57 OTU/ 52 OTU/13 OTU	Tipped up on take-off, Bicester, 10.6.44; DBR
P8140	74/611/308	Hit tree in forced landing short of fuel on return from sweep, Hawkhurst, Kent, 12.7.41
P8141	222/501/504/61 OTU/ 52 OTU/57 OTU	SOC 8.3.45
P8142	266/71/303/306/ 308/52 OTU/61 OTU	SOC 16.8.44
P8143	91/501	Hit balloon cable and crashed Bleasdon, near Weston-super-Mare, Somerset, 10.6.41

P8144	222/41/74/350/ 61 OTU/57 OTU	Collided with P7856 and crashed, Shilbottle, Northumberland, 7.5.43
P8145	616/412/310/416/ 61 OTU/52 OTU/ 57 OTU	NFT 12.11.43
P8146	72/74/350/57 OTU/ TTC CF	Blt as IIB SOC 10.44
P8147	65/306/308/350/52 OTU/ 5 PAFU/57 OTU/CGS	SOC 30.11.44
P8148	72/452/610/ 61 OTU/52 OTU	Collided with P8278 and abandoned over Weston-super-Mare, Somerset, 12.7.42
P8149*	72/74/350/ Northolt	SOC 1.7.45
P8160	65	Missing escorting Blenheims over France, 21.8.41
P8161	603/9 MU	Flew into ground in mist on ferry flight, Colne, Lancs., 14.5.41
P8162	41/416/61 OTU/CGS	SOC 2.11.44
P8163	41	Flew into high ground in cloud 5m S of Northallerton, Yorks., 1.6.41
P8164	65/72/19/234/131/ 57 OTU	SOC 30.12.44
P8165	65/504/57 OTU/CGS	SOC 2.11.44
P8166	72/64/19	Control lost in bad weather; flew into ground in bad visibility and skidded into wood near Langham, 5.9.41
P8167	266/Cv VA/610/133/ 601/421/164/602/ 61 OTU	SOC 15.12.44
P8168	41/145/417/53 OTU 5 PAFU/7 PAFU/ 7 SFTS	Crashed on landing, Peterborough, 6.5.45; DBR; NFD
P8169	71/401/64/611/ 52 OTU	Hit water in formation and crashlanded 2m ENE of Lydney, Glos., 14.5.42
P8170	266/452/610/61 OTU/ 53 OTU/61 OTU	SOC 16.8.44
P8171	41/145/19/61 OTU	Overturned in forced landing, 20.7.44 and SOC 16.8.44
P8172	610/130/411	Hit by flak off Le Touquet and abandoned off Dungeness, 27.9.41
P8173	266	Missing, presumed shot down by Bf 109s while escorting Blenheims to Mazingarbe, 3.7.41
P8174*	72/65/122/74/ 350/52 OTU/7 SFTS/ 7 PAFU/10 AGS	SOC 25.5.45
P8175	66/111/403/457/ 61 OTU/57 OTU	Engine lost power and cut on approach to forced landing near Huxley, Cheshire, 25.7.42
P8176	66/71/131/53 OTU/CGS	SOC 30.11.44
P8177	65/122/154/52 OTU/ Coningsby/1690 Flt	SOC 22.11.44
P8178	54	Missing in cloud while escorting Blenheims to Calais, 7.5.41; believed shot down by Bf 109 off Dunkerque
P8179	65/308/401/61 OTU/ Cv ASR.IIC/277/ FLS/12 Gp CF	SOC 14.6.45
P8180	65/122/131/57 OTU/ AFDU/1690 Flt/ 5 PAFU	To 4937M; SOC 10.7.45
P8181	65/64/611/61 OTU	Spun into ground in bad visibility near Hawarden, 10.7.42
P8182	66/118/152	Abandoned near Totnes, Devon, 10.6.41
P8183	74/602/71/306/308	Broke up in cloud and crashed ½m S of Lytham pier, Lancs., 21.12.41
P8184	66/118/74	Undercarriage jammed partly down; aircraft abandoned off Llanbedr, 10.10.41
P8185	266	Missing on sweep; presumed shot down by Bf 109s while escorting Blenheims, 27.6.41
P8186	64/145/417/53 OTU/ 58 OTU/53 OTU	SOC 22.4.45
P8187	266/123/58 OTU	Hit water low flying over Lake of Menteith, near Aberfoyle, Perthshire, 3.6.43
P8188	266	Damaged by Bf 109s near St. Omer while escorting Blenheims to Lille and presumed ditched in Channel, 27.6.41
P8189	66/303/306/65/616/132/ 52 OTU/AFDU/53 OTU	SOC 25.1.45
P8190	266/123/331/ 58 OTU	Engine caught fire; abandoned, Norman Law Farm, Fife, 11.9.42
P8191	41/401/317/133/134/ 53 OTU/61 OTU/CGS	Collided with bowser taxiing at Catfoss, 14.7.44; DBR
P8192	72/145/417/Colerne/ 53 OTU/57 OTU	Abandoned after engine fire near Shilbottle, Northumberland, 4.9.44
P8193	66/313/306/53 OTU/ 57 OTU	Hit tree low flying Houxty, near Bellingham, Northumberland, 26.4.44
P8194	91/234/Middle Wallop/ 66/152/66/57 OTU/ AAEE	Damaged 28.1.44; SOC 20.3.44
P8195	65/Cv VA/130/134/ 133/421/61 OTU	Undershot landing, stalled and undercarriage collapsed, Rednal, 21.3.44; DBR
P8196	54/91/501/133/134/ 57 OTU/53 OTU/MAP	Crashed on experimental take-off, Castle Bromwich, 12.6.45
P8197	65/122/61 OTU/ 57 OTU	Dived into ground after night take-off, Boulmer, 22.11.43; DBF
P8198	54/111	Shot down by Bf 109s on sweep over France, 9.8.41
P8199	74/331/58 OTU/CGS	SOC 12.9.44
P8200	72/74/350/52 OTU/ 53 OTU	SOC 26.1.45
P8201	41/145/417/58 OTU/ 53 OTU	SOC 8.3.45
P8202*	66/303/616/504/ 52 OTU/61 OTU	SOC 29.9.44
P8203	266/123/277/ Cv ASR.IIC/ 57 OTU/9 PAFU	Undershot landing at Ternhill, 24.5.45
P8204	118/Middle Wallop/ 130/19/66/152/AFDU/ 1695 Flt	SOC 14.12.44
P8205	66/303	Damaged by Bf 109s over Channel and crashlanded, Crowbridge, near Tonbridge, Kent, 4.6.41; DBR
P8206	41/306/308	Collided with P7745, Woodvale, 9.1.42
P8207*	72/74/122/132/ 52 OTU	SOC 25.1.45
P8208	303/1 CACF/ 1 CACU/52 OTU	Collided with P8207 during gunnery practice and crashed in River Severn, 26.1.43
P8209	152/501/504/ 58 OTU/57 OTU	SOC 9.3.45
P8230*	501/145/1 CACU/ AFDU/1687 Flt	SOC 1.45
P8231	72	Crashed in sea 4m N of Farne Is., 29.4.41; believed shot down by return fire from Ju 88

P8232*	222/308/65/616/ 1 CACU/276	Shot down over Channel by FW 190, 31.8.43
P8233	118/403/54/403/ 131/61 OTU/52 OTU	Hit tree low flying near Keevil, 25.6.43
P8234*	222/308/132/61 OTU/ AFDU/13 Gp CF	SOC 12.4.45
P8235	65/61 OTU/52 OTU/ 58 OTU/2 TEU/ 53 OTU	Engine cut; bellylanded in field ½m NW of Hibaldstow, 17.9.44
P8236	266/Cv VA/1402 Flt/ 8 OTU	SOC 17.4.45
P8237	118/603/Middle Wallop/152/Cv VA/ 61 OTU	Flew into high ground in bad visibility 1m N of Oswestry racecourse, Salop., 9.12.43
P8238*	72/417/53 OTU	Hit trees low flying near Skirlough, Yorks., 5.5.44
P8239	64/603/111/130/ Cv VA/53 OTU	Hit pole in forced landing while short of fuel in fog, Wenvoe, Glam., 31.3.43
P8240	152	Believed damaged in air raid, Portreath, 10.5.41; SOC 21.5.41
P8241	609/19/350/57 OTU/ 5 PAFU	SOC 28.6.45
P8242*	501/306/308/132/ 61 OTU	Collided with P8345 on take- off, Montford Bridge, 14.6.42
P8243	66/130/19	Missing, believed shot down attacking Bf 110s off Dutch coast, 29.8.41
P8244*	222	Missing while escorting Blenheims to Hazebrouck, 19.8.41
P8245	611	Dived into ground, Dengie Flat, Essex, 18.5.41
P8246	66/501/152/Cv VA/ 121/421	To Admiralty 7.9.42
P8247*	306/303/306	Shot down by Bf 109s on Blenheim escort over Northern France, 23.7.41
P8248	66/64/611/52 OTU/ 5 PAFU/7 SFTS/ 9 PAFU/10 AGS	SOC 13.6.45
P8249	91/501/133/134/ 57 OTU/53 OTU	Collided with K9951 on approach, Llandow, 27.5.42
P8250	145/234/412/310/ CGS/61 OTU	SOC 25.1.45
P8251	66/130/19/152/ 154/152/57 OTU	Tyre burst on landing; swung and DBR, Boulmer, 10.3.44
P8252*	72/74/122/AFDU	SOC 14.8.44
P8253	66/152/154/ Cv ASR.IIC/276	SOC 25.7.44
P8254	145	Shot down by Bf 109s while escorting Blenheims to Forêt de Guines, 18.6.41
P8255	66/130/19	Missing, believed shot down by Bf 110s off Dutch coast, 29.8.41
P8256	91/501/133/134/ 57 OTU	SOC 30.12.44
P8257*	72/74/122/132/ AFDU/Gosport/ 5 PAFU	Crashed on landing, Ternhill, 14.3.45
P8258	66/266/133/134/ 57 OTU/58 OTU/ 2 CTW/FLS	SOC 8.3.45
P8259	74/602/313/Cv VA/ 1406 Flt	Spun into ground during practice dogfight, Dunnet Head, Caithness, 23.2.43
P8260	66/234/152/AFDU/ 5 PAFU/1 AGS/10 AGS	SOC 21.5.45
P8261	74/122/154/61 OTU/ Cv ASR.IIC/277/ 5 PAFU	SOC 11.5.45
P8262	303/Cv VA/Northolt/ 1 CACU/AFDU	SOC 12.44

P8263	610/130/411	Damaged taxying at Edgehill, 29.9.41; NFT
P8264	609/452/131/ 61 OTU/ECFS	SOC 30.12.44
P8265*	610/1 CACU/ Cv ASR.IIC/276	SOC 25.7.44
P8266	609/616/234/152	Forcelanded while lost near Hougher, Co.Donegal, Eire, 10.1.42; interned
P8267	54/111/133/Interned in Eire/61 OTU	Spun into ground near Wrex- ham, Denbigh, 15.5.44
P8268	54/111/610/340/ 53 OTU/61 OTU	Collided with Wellington BK186 during fighter affiliation and crashed 1m S of Long Stretton, Salop., 14.5.43
P8269	65	Hit by Hurricane during practice attack and dived into ground, Alwalton, Hunts., 3.5.41
P8270	609/152/130/19/66	Missing on interception off Devon coast, 5.9.41; believed control lost in cloud
P8271	609/616/501/130/66/ Cv ASR.IIC/277/ 53 OTU/57 OTU	SOC 30.12.44
P8272	616	Missing, presumed shot down by Bf 109s while escorting Blenheims, 25.6.41
P8273	AAEE	Flew into ground during low aerobatics 1m N of Over Wallop, Hants., 3.7.41
P8274	74/313/53 OTU/ Cv ASR.IIC/277/ 53 OTU/5 PAFU	SOC 28.6.45
P8275	74/602/313/312/ 416/58 OTU	Hit tree low flying, Thornhill, Stirling, 14.11.42
P8276	74/616/411/121/ 340/58 OTU	Flew into high ground in mist Dollar Bank Farm, Clack- mannan, 16.1.43
P8277	64/66/19	Overshot landing and hit hedge, Matlask, 5.9.41
P8278	152/501/66/52 OTU/ 57 OTU/53 OTU	SOC 8.3.45
P8279	66/130/CGS/57 OTU	SOC 11.44
P8310	145	Missing escorting Blenheims to Marquise, 14.8.41
P8311	308	Missing escorting Blenheims to Hazebrouck, 29.8.41
P8312	501/52 OTU/RAFC	Collided with C-47A 42-24069 and abandoned 2m W of Navenby, Lincs., 27.10.43
P8313*	145/306/308	Missing from sweep to St.Omer, 22.7.41
P8314*	501/145	Missing on sweep; presumed shot down by Bf 109s, 26.6.41
P8315*	611	Stalled during flapless landing and undercarriage collapsed, Drem, 29.11.41
P8316*	222/64/54/CGS	Tyre burst on landing; swung and undercarriage collapsed, Catfoss, 9.8.44
P8317*	145/306/308/132/ 53 OTU/1 CACU/ AFDU/53 OTU	SOC 23.11.44
P8318*	145/306/308	Missing while escorting Stirlings to Lille, 19.7.41
P8319*	145/306/308/132/ 61 OTU/CGS	SOC 2.11.44
P8320*	222/AFDU	Engine lost power; overshot emergency landing and overturned, Kirmington, 5.2.44
P8321*	222/CACF/1 CACU	Hit by X4384 while parked, Detling, 14.7.42
P8322*	72/74/122/132/ 57 OTU/Cv ASR.IIC/ 277/61 OTU	SOC 27.9.45

Serial	Units	Fate
P8323*	145	Ran out of fuel and abandoned near Worthing, Sussex, 4.6.41
P8324	145/306/154/313/ 61 OTU/Cv VB/122/ 234/Cv ASR.IIC/277/ RAFC/5 PAFU/ 17 SFTS	SOC 19.7.46
P8325*	303/65/Digby/416/ 61 OTU/1 CACU/276	SOC 16.8.44
P8326*	145/306/308	Abandoned over Channel after escorting Blenheims to Hazebrouck, 19.8.41
P8327*	145/308	Missing from sweep to Hazebrouck, 24.7.41
P8328*	145	Shot down by Bf 109s while escorting Blenheims to Forêt de Guines, 18.6.41
P8329*	303	Overturned landing on soft ground, Martlesham Heath, 2.7.41; DBR
P8330*	303	Collided with Bf 109 while escorting Blenheims and crash-landed, Manston, 23.6.41; DBR
P8331*	303	Shot down by flak on ground attack mission to Hardelot, 27.6.41
P8332*	222	To RCAF 1.4.42; preserved
P8333*	303/124/54/1 AACU	Flew into ground crossing coast in bad visibility, Church Hunton, Kent, 9.11.42
P8334*	303	Missing 23.7.41
P8335*	303	Shot down in Channel by Bf 109s while escorting Blenheims to Comines, 28.6.41
P8336*	303/57 OTU/53 OTU/ CGS	Ran out of fuel and engine cut; bellylanded E of Catfoss, 25.9.44
P8337*	222/Coltishall/132/ 53 OTU/58 OTU/ 2 CTW/61 OTU	Engine cut; bellylanded in field, Cheshire, 4.6.44.
P8338*	303/312/132/52 OTU/ 53 OTU	SOC 8.3.45
P8339*	145/Cv VB/121	Damaged by flak attacking flak ship and crashed in sea off Haamstede, 21.9.42
P8340*	124/54/FIU/52 OTU/ 61 OTU	Damaged aircraft on landing; overshot and bellylanded, Rednal, 25.8.44
P8341*	145/306/308/132/ 61 OTU/1 CACU/ 53 OTU	SOC 23.10.43
P8342*	145/306/57 OTU/ 61 OTU	SOC 25.4.46
P8343*	222/132/57 OTU	SOC 30.12.44
P8344*	145/266/65/616/54/ 57 OTU	SOC 30.12.44
P8345*	222/64/611/61 OTU	Ran out of fuel; bellylanded and overturned, Rednal, 26.3.43; DBR
P8346*	303	Missing, presumed shot down by Bf 109s while escorting Blenheims to Comines, 28.6.41
P8347*	222/266/65/616/312	SOC 10.44
P8348	222/416/FIU/ Cv VB/52 OTU/53 OTU	SOC 25.9.45
P8349	66/130/53 OTU/ 61 OTU	SOC 27.9.45
P8360	303/403/457/412/ 57 OTU	Collided with P8362 near Eshott, 27.2.43
P8361	303/452	Shot down by Bf 109s near Béthune, 9.8.41
P8362	66/266/57 OTU	Collided with P8360 near Eshott, 27.2.43
P8363	74	Abandoned on patrol, 16.5.41; NFD
P8364	74	Missing while escorting Blenheims to Gravelines, 6.5.41
P8365	54/64/610/611/ 52 OTU/57 OTU	SOC 29.12.44
P8366	66/19/234/133/134/ 53 OTU	Collided with P8249 during combat practice near Minehead, Somerset., 8.4.42
P8367	616/485/313/306/ 308/53 OTU/52 OTU/ 53 OTU	Engine cut; bellylanded, Gray-ingham Grange Farm, near Kirton-in-Lindsey, 5.1.44
P8368	118	Collided with P8376 during attack practice and abandoned near Fordingbridge, Hants., 30.6.41
P8369	609/616/Digby/130/ 310/416/61 OTU/ 13 OTU/ATA	Engine cut; bellylanded near Cullen, Banff, 27.10.44; DBR
P8370	66/130	Shot down by Bf 109s while escorting Blenheims to Ijmuiden, 21.8.41
P8371	601/610/130/452/ 411/131/57 OTU/ 53 OTU	SOC 25.1.45
P8372*	145/306/308/ 1 CACU/53 OTU	SOC 23.11.44
P8373	74/403/54/403/ 53 OTU/FAA/57 OTU	SOC 30.12.44
P8374*	610	Missing escorting Blenheims to Chocques, 10.7.41
P8375	602/71/Cv ASR.IIC/ 277/53 OTU	SOC 9.10.45
P8376	118	Collided with P8368 during attack practice and abandoned near Fordingbridge, Hants., 30.6.41
P8377	118/403/54/403/122/ 74/350/52 OTU	Spun into ground, Stow-on-the-Wold, Glos., 10.8.42
P8378	152	Undershot landing, Swanton Morley and hit bowser, 21.10.41
P8379	452/313/312/416/CGS	SOC 2.11..44
P8380	74/403/54/403/ 457/53 OTU	Flew into ground in bad visibility, Cymmer, S.Wales 15.8.42
P8381	609/452/129/ 61 OTU/52 OTU	Crashed on approach, Babdown Farm, 14.10.42
P8382*	303/65/616/54/ AFDU	Hit obstruction on take-off, Duxford, 20.5.43; DBR
P8383*	222/308	Hit by flak near Fruges and abandoned while escorting Blenheims to Mazingarbe, 4.9.41
P8384	611/308/19	Abandoned at low altitude in bad weather, Manor Farm, Wood Norton, Norfolk, 2.11.41
P8385*	303/306/65/616/ 133/134/AFDU/ 61 OTU	SOC 23.11.44
P8386	616	Missing, presumed shot down by Bf 109s while escorting Stirlings to Mazingarbe, 9.7.41
P8387	611/308/315/266/ 123/58 OTU	Collided with P7683 and crashed, Garter Clasher Farm, Stirlingshire, 19.8.43
P8388	74/152/12 OTU/ 58 OTU/2 TEU/ 1690 Flt	Engine ran rough and damaged bearers, 10.11.44; SOC 1.12.44
P8389*	610/130/616/315/ 1 CACF/61 OTU/ 59 OTU/61 OTU	SOC 12.44
P8390	303/74/122/132/ 416/61 OTU/57 OTU	Taxied into bowser, Eshott, 13.8.43; DBR
P8391	412/310/416/61 OTU	SOC 16.8.44
P8392	616/71/401/57 OTU/ 61 OTU/CGS	SOC 30.11.44

P8393	234/308/401/302/ 133/134	Crashed in sea off Rathlin Island, 6.1.42
P8394	74/152/58 OTU	Crashed at Gate Hill, near Stirling, 29.1.43; cause not known
P8395	234	Missing, presumed shot down by Bf 109s while escorting ASR launch in Channel, 17.7.41
P8396	74/602/71/401/308/ 306/53 OTU	Collided with X4067 over St. Hilary, Glam., 16.1.43
P8397	616/Digby/310/416/ 58 OTU/RAE	SOC 16.8.44
P8398	610/CACF/1 CACU/ AFDU/58 OTU/ 61 OTU	SOC 14.8.44
P8399	616/610	Missing from sweep, 28.6.41
P8420	66/130/52 OTU/ Northolt	SOC 1.45
P8421	74/19/57 OTU	SOC 1.6.45
P8422	609/266/123/66/ 416/61 OTU/RAE/ 58 OTU/1 TEU/ 5 PAFU	SOC 28.6.45
P8423	74/602/71/401/64/ 130/133/134/53 OTU/ 52 OTU/53 OTU/ 58 OTU/FLS	SOC 16.8.44
P8424	65/122/154/ 58 OTU/FLS	SOC 8.3.45
P8425	611/308/403/54/ 403/457/CGS/61 OTU	SOC 12.44
P8426	54/602/313/61 OTU/ 52 OTU/58 OTU/ 2 TEU/61 OTU	SOC 12.44
P8427	64/611/52 OTU/ 57 OTU	SOC 25.4.46
P8428	603/111	Shot down escorting Blenheims over France, 19.8.41
P8429	609/152/130/ 61 OTU	Collided with P7921 during formation practice and lost tail; crashed 1m W of Montford Bridge, 8.4.43
P8430	609/616/234/66	Collided with P7843 5m NW of The Lizard, Cornwall, 24.1.42
P8431	1406 Flt/Cv ASR.IIC/ 277/57 OTU/53 OTU	SOC 12.44
P8432	234/19/66/53 OTU/ 57 OTU/277/AEAF CF	SOC 4.1.45
P8433	152/61 OTU/52 OTU	SOC 30.12.44
P8434	616	Spun into ground on approach 1m NW of Bognor, 21.7.41
P8435	234/SF Middle Wallop/ 66	Missing while escorting Blenheims to Bergen op Zoom, 20.8.41
P8436	602/71/401/Northolt/ Cv VA/Bovingdon/ 67th Obs Gp US	SOC 12.10.45
P8437	266/123/58 OTU/ 52 OTU/57 OTU/CGS	SOC 2.11.44
P8438	616/Cv VA/145/ 134/133	Collided with P8595 and crashed, Epworth, Lincs., 3.4.42
P8439	234/91	Damaged by flak escorting Blenheims to Rotterdam and crashlanded, 28.8.41
P8440	1402 Flt/AFDU/ 1690 Flt	SOC 22.11.44
P8441	RAE/277/61 OTU/ 13 OTU	SOC 30.12.44
P8442	234/19/66/152/ 61 OTU/57 OTU/ 61 OTU	SOC 30.12.44
P8443	66/57 OTU/61 OTU	Abandoned out of control after aileron jammed, Meadow Tarn, near Baschurch, Salop., 2.6.44
P8444	152/131/52 OTU/CGS	SOC 12.44
P8445	308/122/131	Bounced on landing, swung and undercarriage leg collapsed, Merston, 19.5.42; DBR
P8446	152	Missing in Antwerp area while Providing return cover for Blenheim raid on Cologne, 12.8.41
P8447*	306/65/616/133/ 134/53 OTU	Hit tree low flying, Cowley Farm, Llancarfan, Glam., 9.2.43; DBF
P8448	152	Engine cut in circuit; crash-landed, Eglinton, 15.2.42
P8449	234/91	Crashed in sea, 29.8.41; NFD
P8460	19/74	Dived into sea out of cloud ½m off Fairbourne, Merioneth, 30.11.41
P8461	303/306	Shot down by Bf 109s escorting Blenheims over France, 23.7.41
P8462	303/306	Missing while escorting Hampdens to St.Omer, 14.8.41
P8463	303/81	Flew into high ground in cloud near Stanhope, Co.Durham, 27.3.42
P8464*	610/616/315/266/ 124/54/1 CACU/ 61 OTU	SOC 20.12.44
P8465*	303/306	Ran out of fuel; hit poles in forced landing, Richmond Park, Surrey, 23.7.41
P8466*	306	Missing from escorting Hampdens to St.Omer, 14.8.41
P8467*	118/132/57 OTU	Engine overheated; crashlanded in field, West Thurston, North-umberland, 8.3.43
P8468	64/611/61 OTU/ 52 OTU/AFDU	Collided with P8440 over New-market airfield and crashed, 15.2.43
P8469*	111/130/133/57 OTU	SOC 12.12.44
P8470*	485	Missing from escorting Stirlings to Lens, 8.7.41; presumed shot down by Bf 109s off Gravelines
P8471*	266	Hit hangar on take-off, Collyweston, 31.8.41
P8472	602/412/310/416/ 61 OTU	Engine cut; bellylanded, Ellesmere, Salop., 2.9.42
P8473*	306	Missing from escorting Hampdens to St.Omer, 14.8.41
P8474*	222	Shot down by Bf 109s while escorting Blenheims on shipping attack off Boulogne, 18.7.41
P8475	145/308/61 OTU/ 53 OTU	SOC 8.3.45
P8476*	306/CACF/1 CACU/ AFDU/1690 Flt	NFT 5.3.44
P8477	65/122/154/61 OTU/ CGS	SOC 11.9.44
P8478	602	Missing, presumed shot down by Bf 109s near Lille, 21.7.41
P8479	74/62 OTU/ Cv ASR.IIC/277/ 61 OTU	SOC 14.8.44
P8500	616	Damaged by Bf 109s and crash-landed on beach, Dunkerque, after escorting Stirlings to Lille, 6.7.41
P8501*	306/65/616/52 OTU/ 53 OTU/CGS	SOC 2.11.44
P8502	303	Missing while escorting Stirlings to Lille, 8.7.41; presumed shot down by fighters
P8503*	222/315/266/124/ 54/55 OTU/AFDU/ 1690 Flt	SOC 4.12.44

P8504*	610	Missing, presumed shot down by Bf 109s near Gravelines after escorting Stirlings to Lille, 8.7.41
P8505*	222/266/65/616/54/ 61 OTU	Collided with P8195 and crashed, Bowmere Heath, Salop., 12.6.43
P8506*	610/616/315	Missing, presumed shot down by Bf 109s while escorting Stirlings to Mazingarbe, 9.8.41
P8507*	303/306	Missing, presumed shot down by Bf 109s while escorting Blenheims to Hazebrouck, 29.8.41
P8508	501/417/53 OTU	Crashed in sea 5m SE of Porthcawl, Glam., 10.9.42
P8509*	266/Cv ASR.IIC/ 277/61 OTU	Crashed after collision near Rednal, 7.4.44
P8510	501/152/61 OTU	SOC 28.12.44
P8511*	118	Shot down by flak attacking convoy off Barfleur, 1.9.41
P8512	152	Missing while escorting Hampdens to Brest, 24.7.41
P8513	66/CGS/7 PAFU/ 10 AGS	SOC 21.5.45
P8514	1406 Flt/53 OTU/ 5 PAFU	SOC 28.6.45
P8515	266/123/61 OTU	SOC 27.9.45
P8516*	118	Flew into hills in cloud, Holworth Farm, near Overmoigne, Dorset, 4.8.41
P8517	222/Cv VB/315/317	Missing 29.7.42
P8518*	303/306/308/132/ 58 OTU/1 CACU/ 61 OTU	SOC 26.1.45
P8519*	306/308	Missing from sweep to St. Omer, 17.7.42
P8520*	610	Missing escorting Stirlings to Chocques, 10.7.41
P8521*	610/124/54/ Cv ASR.IIC/276	SOC 25.7.44
P8522*	303/65/616/611/ 1 CACF/61 OTU	SOC 26.1.45
P8523*	610	Missing escorting Stirlings to Chocques, 10.7.41
P8524*	303/306	Missing, presumed shot down by Bf 109s near St.Omer while escorting Blenheims, 16.8.41
P8525	Northolt/308	Missing escorting Blenheims to Lille, 2.7.41
P8526*	610/306	Engine cut on approach to Northolt; crashlanded, Eastcote, Middlesex, 19.8.41
P8527*	610/616/315/266/ 124/53 OTU	Dived into ground 1m SE of Pontypool Road, Glam., 24.8.42
P8528	308/315/130/133/ 134/53 OTU/134/ 57 OTU	Hit HT cables low flying and crashed, Weldon Bridge, Northumberland, 9.4.43
P8529*	118/132/58 OTU	Control lost in cloud; dived into ground, Slamannan, Stirling-shire, 8.4.43
P8530*	145/124/54/61 OTU	Collided with P8268 and crashed, Bowmere Heath, Salop., 10.9.42
P8531*	Northolt/1 CACU	Stalled off turn and spun into ground, Camer Farm, Graves-end, Kent, 23.6.42
P8532	92	Built as Mk.VA. Missing 26.6.41
P8533*	610/222/145/154/ 132/53 OTU	SOC 12.44
P8534*	610/616/1 CACF/ 1 CACU/58 OTU/ 61 OTU	SOC 25.7.44
P8535*	118/124/54/ 58 OTU/61 OTU	SOC 30.12.44
P8536*	145	Missing escorting Blenheims to Lille, 2.7.41; presumed shot down by Bf 109s
P8537	92/313	Built as Mk.VB; to Admiralty 18.9.42
P8538	92/1 FPP	Built as Mk.VB; hit barrack block on attempted overshoot and crashed, Biggin Hill, 26.6.41
P8539	611	Built as Mk.VB. Shot down by Bf 109s near Lille while escorting Stirlings to Chocques, 10.7.41
P8540*	616/315/132/52 OTU/13 Gp CF	SOC 16.8.44
P8541*	64/222	Missing from escorting Hampdens to St.Omer, 12.8.41
P8542	610	Built as Mk.VB. Missing escorting Blenheims to Arques, 13.10.41
P8543*	308/132/3 SGR/ 1 CACF/57 OTU	Tyre burst on take-off and undercarriage collapsed, Eshott, 27.8.44; DBR
P8544*	72	Hit by flak near St.Omer and ditched in Channel, 17.7.41
P8545*	610/616/315/Cv VB/ 72/350/315/611	Shot down by flak attacking ships off Hoorn, 23.8.43
P8546	403/54/403/131	Lost power; stalled on approach and dived into ground, Tryddyn, near Wrexham, 23.10.41
P8547*	308/132/57 OTU/ 58 OTU/2 TEU	Engine cut; crashlanded, Sheardale, near Dollar, Clackmannan, 23.12.43; DBR
P8548*	64 or 222/145/ 1 CACU	Collided with AD388 during practice attack and crashed, Yew Tree Farm, Frinsted, near Sittingbourne, Kent, 14.4.43
P8549*	303/Cv VB/350/ 401/402/416/341/ FLS	Bomb exploded in air over Gofinch Ranges, Northumber-land, 9.3.44
P8560	74/72	Built as Mk.VB. Missing, presumed shot down by Bf 109s near Mardyck, 27.9.41
P8561	611/132/308/402/ 19/65/130/26	Built as Mk.VB; Missing on gunfire spotting sortie, 23.6.44
P8562*	610/AFDU/1687 Flt	SOC 2.45
P8563*	315/308/81	Flew into high ground near Stanhope, Co.Durham, 26.3.42
P8564	609/317	Built as Mk.VB; crashed, 7.3.42; NFD
P8565*	118/124/54/ Cv ASR.IIC/276/ 5 PAFU	SOC 6.7.45
P8566	266	Shot down by Bf 109s near Hazebrouck while escorting Blenheims, 3.7.41
P8567*	303/65/616/611/ 58 OTU/57 OTU	Engine cut; bellylanded on approach to Eshott, West Moor Farm, 9.9.44
P8568*	118/132/53 OTU/ 61 OTU	SOC 23.11.44
P8569*	118/124/54/61 OTU	Engine cut; wing hit ground in forced landing and wings torn off, Myddle, Salop., 23.1.43
P8570*	65/616/312/417/ 58 OTU/53 OTU	SOC 30.12.44
P8571	412/416/58 OTU/ FLS/CFE	SOC 26.3.44
P8572	602/71	Hit ground recovering from dive near Ongar, Essex, 9.8.41
P8573	308	Missing from sweep to St. Omer, 7.8.41

Serial	Units	Fate
P8574*	602/313/52 OTU	Hit HT cables on low flying exercise and crashed, Slimbridge, Glos., 7.3.43
P8575*	222/145/154/53 OTU	SOC 24.5.45
P8576*	308/65/616/504	Abandoned after glycol leak over Irish Sea west of Isle of Man, 9.2.42
P8577	602/111/403/610/ 61 OTU	Engine cut; bellylanded, Haughton, Salop., 12.7.42; DBR
P8578	74	Built as Mk.VB; SOC 14.7.41
P8579	303/54/53 OTU/ 61 OTU	SOC 30.9.44
P8580*	118/315/118/132	Swung on landing and overturned, Skeabrae, 24.2.42; DBR
P8581	611	Built as Mk.VB. Missing while escorting Blenheims to Hazebrouck, 14.7.41
P8582*	610/616/315/118/ 132/58 OTU	Flew into sea during gunnery exercise 5m NE of Dunbar, E.Lothian, 5.5.43
P8583	234/19/66/CGS	Collided with Hampden P2067 and crashed, Crowland, Lincs., 31.8.42
P8584*	118/124/54/ Cv ASR.IIC/276	SOC 16.8.44
P8585	74/609/603/52 FG USAAC/118/64/ 17 SFTS/5 PAFU/ 17 SFTS	Built as Mk.VB. Crashed in forced landing near Manby, 24.1.46
P8586*	616/412	Collided with Hampden AD939 over Waddington, 31.8.41
P8587*	303/306/132/57 OTU	Flew into hill in low cloud, Scald Hill, Dunsdale, Northumberland, 25.3.43
P8588*	610/616/315/118/ 132	Engine cut; crashlanded, Pitluarg, Aberdeenshire, 21.10.41
P8589*	118/65/616/121	Undercarriage collapsed on landing, Southend, 28.7.42; NFT
P8590*	306/308	Missing from sweep to St. Omer, 22.7.41
P8591*	222/132/52 OTU/ CGS/53 OTU	SOC 9.44
P8592*	222/132/53 OTU	Collided with P7504 and crashed near Cowbridge, Glam., 5.7.42
P8593*	222/64/611/54/ 58 OTU/CGS	Throttle jammed closed; overshot forced landing, Weel Carr, near Beverley, Yorks., 25.6.44
P8594	41/145/57 OTU/CGS	SOC 5.7.45
P8595	66/133	Collided with P8438 and crashed, Epworth, Lancs., 3.4.42
P8596	303	Missing escorting Blenheims to Lille, 2.7.41
P8597	266/123/61 OTU/CGS	SOC 14.11.44
P8598	485/313/312/416/ 58 OTU/53 OTU	SOC 30.12.44
P8599	64	Collided with another Spitfire during practice dogfight and abandoned near Clifton Hall, West Lothian, 27.9.41
P8600	72	Built as Mk.VB. Missing from sweep to Fruges; presumed shot down by Bf 109s near Gravelines, 10.7.41
P8601*	74	Crashed during formation practice, 17.9.41; NFD
P8602*	118/132/57 OTU	Engine cut; crashed in forced landing, Kyloe, Northumberland, 6.11.43
P8603	611/603	Built as Mk.VB. Missing from escorting Hurricanes to Hesdin, 8.12.41; presumed shot down by Bf 109s near Le Tréport
P8604	72	Built as Mk.VB. Missing from sweep to Fruges; presumed shot down by Bf 109s near Gravelines, 10.7.41
P8605	452/71/61 OTU/ 58 OTU	Hit X4682 while landing, Grangemouth, 12.11.42; DBR
P8606	609/316	Built as Mk.VB. Shot down by FW 190 15m NE of Calais, 4.4.42
P8607	611/64/124/41	Built as Mk.VB. Dived into ground near Weston Patrick, Basingstoke, Hants., 15.8.42
P8608	266/123/57 OTU	SOC 20.12.44
P8609	74/72	Built as Mk.VB. Ran out of fuel on returned from sweep and abandoned 3m off Ramsgate, 27.8.41
P8640	609/92/610/High Ercall/308/302/416/ 186/130/1 AGS	Built as Mk.VB; SOC 10.9.45
P8641*	303/1 CACU/53 OTU	Hit by P7378 awaiting take-off, Llandow, 4.4.43; DBF
P8642*	303/145/53 OTU/ 58 OTU/61 OTU	SOC 14.8.44
P8643*	222/266/1 CACU/ 61 OTU	SOC 30.12.44
P8644*	222/315/266/124/54/ 58 OTU	Lost wing during steep turn ½m SW of Bogside, Clackmannan, 18.6.42
P8645*	222/Cv VB/452	Ditched off North Foreland on return from sweep to Lille, 8.11.41
P8646*	616/331/58 OTU/ 5 PAFU/RAFC/ 17 SFTS	SOC 4.11.44
P8647*	145/306/308/65/ 616/312/132/61 OTU	Swung on landing and overturned, Eshott, 5.2.44
P8648*	610/315/266/124/54/ 58 OTU/61 OTU/CGS	SOC 2.11.44
P8649*	222/308/65/616/ 132/58 OTU/2 TEU/ 61 OTU	SOC 20.12.44
P8650*	616/610/118/132/ 416/61 OTU/2 TEU	Hit trees low flying and crashed near Angus, 29.12.43
P8651	616	Damaged by Bf 109s and abandoned while escorting Stirlings to Lille, 5.7.41
P8652	308/401/610/350/ 52 OTU/53 OTU/ 7 PAFU/1 AGS	SOC 29.7.45
P8653*	54/AFDU/57 OTU	Took off in coarse pitch; hit ground and overturned, Eshott, 2.2.44
P8654	609	Damaged by Bf 109s and hit cliffs near Ramsgate, 11.6.41
P8655*	145/306/308/124/ 54/61 OTU	SOC 26.1.44
P8656	234	Engine cut; bellylanded, West Knighton, Dorset, 14.7.41
P8657	152/411/121/340/ 58 OTU/61 OTU	To 4431M 6.12.43
P8658*	616/610	Engine cut on return from sweep; hit hedge and overturned in forced landing 3m E of Heathfield, Kent, 14.7.41
P8659	234/19/152/61 OTU/ 7 SFTS/1 AGS/10 AGS	SOC 21.5.45
P8660*	610/118/124/54/ 58 OTU/CGS	Hit by P7524 while parked. Catfoss, 26.9.44; DBR
P8661*	308/315/610/123/ 3 Del Flt	Crashed in bad weather near Llanfair, Anglesey, 24.11.41

P8662*	118/61 OTU/	
	1 CACU/53 OTU	SOC 8.3.45
P8663	616/411/CGS/61 OTU	SOC 29.3.45
P8664	501/504/58 OTU	Collided with Whitley LA847 during fighter affiliation and crashed in Spey Bay, 14.6.43
P8665*	610/616/315/266/	Crashed after control lost
	65/616/133/134/	in cloud 4m N of Ruthin,
	61 OTU	Denbigh, 26.1.44
P8666*	610/616/315/266/	Ran out of fuel while on
	65/616/504	baulked approach; bellylanded and hit bank near Kirkistown, 14.1.42
P8667	19/313/417/61 OTU	Engine cut on take-off; crash-
	Cv ASR.IIC/276/	landed and overturned 1m W of
	11 APC	Fairwood Common, 7.11.43
P8668	234/19	Missing, believed shot down by Bf 110s off Dutch coast, 29.8.41
P8669*	303	Sent for repair 4.8.41; NFT
P8670*	610/616/315	Crashed in forced landing near Wattisham, 9.8.41
P8671*	118/132/57 OTU	Engine cut; crashlanded, Goswick Sands, Northumber-land, 6.4.43; overtaken by tide
P8672*	303	Shot down by Bf 109s while escorting Blenheims to St.Omer, 25.6.41
P8673*	118/154/132/52	
	OTU/58 OTU/53 OTU	SOC 20.12.44
P8674	412/310/416/58 OTU/	Shot down in sea by FW 190s
	Cv ASR.IIC/276	10m N of Sept Iles, Brittany, on ASR flight, 7.6.43
P8675*	118/124/AFDU	Undercarriage leg collapsed on landing, Dalton, 1.10.43; DBR
P8676*	145/306/308	Dived into ground 1m NW of Ruislip, Middlesex, 9.8.41; cause not known
P8677*	118/124/54/61 OTU	SOC 29.9.44
P8678	452/129/610	Flew into ground in low cloud 3m N of Scarborough, Yorks., 4.10.41; DBF
P8679	19/504/58 OTU	Hit by P7776 during practice attack and crashed, Dunferm-line, Fife, 5.6.42
P8690*	610/616	Missing, presumed shot down by Bf 109s while escorting Stirlings, 21.7.41
P8691*	72/74/416/58 OTU/	
	1 CACU/61 OTU	SOC 26.1.45
P8692*	222/152/53 OTU	Missing, presumed crashed in sea, 3.11.42
P8693*	118/124/61 OTU/	Hit factory chimney and
	58 OTU	crashed, Kirriemuir, Angus, 18.10.43
P8694*	306/308/65/616/	Flew into ground, while low
	611/58 OTU	flying, West Haugh, Stirling-shire, 2.7.43
P8695	152/611/AFDU/	
	1687 Flt	SOC 20.8.45
P8696*	610/616/315	Missing, presumed shot down by Bf 109s on sweep, 9.8.41
P8697*	118/124/54	Stalled and crashed in circuit, Castletown, 28.1.42
P8698	308	Missing from sweep to St. Omer, 17.7.41
P8699	609/111	Built as Mk.VB. Missing after attacking Do 217s off Dieppe, 19.8.42
P8700	54/92/72/154/313/	Built as Mk.VB;
	66/306/302/316/504/	To 5517M 7.45
	129/57 OTU/577	
P8701*	303/65/616	Missing from sweep, 8.11.41
P8702	71/401/74/350	SOC 9.1.42

P8703	452	Built as Mk.VB. Missing while escorting Blenheims to Rouen, 18.9.41; presumed shot down by Bf 109s
P8704	64/611/52 OTU/	
	53 OTU/ECFS/5 PAFU	SOC 28.6.45
P8705	118/124/54/58 OTU/	
	61 OTU	SOC 9.10.45
P8706	19/234/Cv VA/72/	Stalled on approach and hit
	332/164	ground, Skeabrae, 8.7.42

P8707 to P8724 All built as Mk.VB

P8707	616/610/331	To Admiralty 21.2.44
P8708	266/Atcham/111/	Converted to Seafire 6.43;
	Fowlmere/312	To Admiralty 9.11.43
P8709	AGME/AAEE/234/587	SOC 25.10.45
P8710	616/610/129	Engine seized; crashed in forced landing 5m NE of Brighton, Sussex, 10.4.42; DBR
P8711	452	Lost 18.2.42; NFD
P8712	145	Shot down by Bf 109s near Le Touquet, 23.7.41
P8713	72	Missing escorting Blenheims to Hazebrouck, 29.8.41
P8714	234	Missing while escorting Blenheims to Le Havre, 15.10.41
P8715	19/416/411	Damaged by Bf 109 during ground attack mission and abandoned off Cherbourg, 14.4.43
P8716	452	Collided with another Spitfire during dummy attack, 7.9.41
P8717	452	Missing escorting Blenheims to Gosney, 19.8.41
P8718	602/485/504/313/	To France 19.1.45
	315/11 FU	
P8719	602	Missing from escorting Blenheims to St.Omer, 7.8.41
P8720	603/332/501	Engine caught fire; crashlanded, Cloughley Golf Course, Co. Down, 26.2.43
P8721	610	Missing, presumed shot down by Bf 109s near Le Touquet, 21.8.41
P8722	602	Engine cut on return from ground attack mission to Le Tréport; ditched in Channel, 2.1.42
P8723	602	Crashed in sea while escorting minesweepers in Channel, 25.1.42
P8724	602	Crashed 4.4.42; NFD
P8725*	222/Cv VB/302	Spun into ground, Fairmile, Henley-on-Thames, Oxon., 29.5.42
P8726	403/54/403	Missing escorting Blenheims to Lille, 27.8.41
P8727	CGS/Cv ASR.IIC/276	Sold 24.7.46; to G-AHZI
P8728	222/145	Engine cut on night take-off; stalled and dived into ground, Catterick, 19.10.41
P8729	19/331	Engine cut; bellylanded, Cleat Farm, Kirkwall, Orkneys, 10.1.42

P8740 to 8799: All built as Mk.VB

P8740	54/403	Missing escorting Blenheims to Chocques, 21.8.41
P8741	74/501/72/5 US	Collided with BL688 in form-
	501	ation near Portaferry, Co. Down, 12.4.43
P8742	610/302/403/401/	Hit wall on take-off from
	416/412/317	wrong runway, Perranporth, 7.7.43

Above: Whirlwind I P7110 on a test flight before delivery

Below: A well-known shot of P3395 of No.1 Squadron in its dispersal pen

Above: Anson I R3373 with the Royal Canadian Air Force

Below: Vega Gull P1751 in the pre-war markings of No. 24 Squadron

P8743	611/64	Bellylanded at Southend, 24.3.42
P8744	54/403/72/152/165	Missing 6.1.44
P8745	609	Damaged by Bf 109 while escorting Blenheims to St.Omer and abandoned, 16.8.41
P8746	611/64/Hornchurch/ 308	Collided with W3774 during formation practice and crashed, Stockwell Farm, Yorks., 14.5.43
P8747	92/Colerne/Fairwood Common/Angle/453/ 341/52 OTU/FLS/63	Hit by flak off Cherbourg and abandoned, 8.6.44
P8748	615/610/129/602/164/ 341/340/303/ 3501 GSU	Hit trees during aerobatics near Luton, Beds., 17.6.44
P8749	610/129/610	Crashed in sea off Scarborough, Yorks., 16.3.42
P8750	72/401	Damaged by Bf 109s 20m NW of Le Havre and abandoned, 1.5.42
P8751	72/416/186	Missing on night training flight, 14.3.44
P8752	610	Missing, presumed shot down by Bf 109s near Le Touquet, 21.8.41
P8753	609/303/118/RAE/ 316/63/41 OTU/ 58 OTU/61 OTU	SOC 22.6.45
P8754	54	Damaged by Bf 109s and abandoned near Gravelines after escorting Stirlings to Lille, 11.7.41
P8755	616/610/616/65/129/222	To USSR 25.11.42
P8756	611	Missing, presumed shot down by Bf 109s near St.Omer while escorting Blenheims, 7.8.41
P8757	72/154	Collided with BM453 during formation landing, Hornchurch, 29.6.42; DBR
P8758	133/306/316/306/ 402/316/63/1665 HCU	SOC 12.12.45
P8759	145/41/421/401/403	Hit tree during practice attack on troops, Kenley, 11.2.43; NFT
———		
P8780	611/222	Missing, presumed shot down by FW 190s while escorting Bostons to Abbeville, 30.4.42
P8781	616/610/AAEE/RAE/ Davidstow Moor/ 269/Lagens	SOC 28.3.46
P8782	145/41/308/504/ 313/118	To Armée de l'Air, 9.4.45
P8783	72/401	To USSR 23.11.42
P8784	92/603/332/403/ Cv to PR XIII	To Admiralty 3.3.44
P8785	266/154/602/504	Collided with BL887 during practice attack and crashed 1½m from Hatton, Aberdeen, 28.12.43
P8786	485/603	Missing while escorting Hurricanes to Hesdin, 8.12.41; believed shot down by Bf 109s near Le Tréport
P8787	602	Missing escorting Hampdens to Abbeville, 20.9.41
P8788	152/402/1656 CU	To Portugal 22.8.47
P8789	118/65	Engine cut on sweep; abandoned over Channel, 1.6.42
P8790	602	Missing while escorting Blenheims to Gosnay, 21.9.41; presumed shot down by Bf 109s
P8791	602/411/242/133/ 336/131/310/313/ 67 Obs Gp US/290	To Portugal 12.11.47

P8792	54/403/54/124	Engine cut after take-off; crashed and overturned 1½m S of Biggin Hill, 3.4.42
P8793	603	Missing while escorting Blenheims over France, 16.8.41
P8794	121	Missing from escorting Bostons to Le Havre, 4.5.42
P8795	610/129	Damaged by FW 190s and abandoned off Le Touquet, 30.4.42
P8796	603	Crashed in sea at night 1m off Newburgh, Aberdeenshire, 18.12.41; cause not known
P8797	54/124	Missing from sweep to St.Omer, 13.3.42
P8798	611/Eglinton/ 2 Ph Sq US/61 OTU	SOC 27.9.45
P8799	602/118/234/81/41/ 91/501/129/63	Engine cut; hit tree in forced landing, Crays Hill, Essex, 13.11.44

*   *   *   *   *   *   *   *   *   *

P8804		Heston T.1/37 to Contract No. 678258/37

*   *   *   *   *   *   *   *   *   *

10 Hawker Hurricane Is delivered in July 1940 to replace L1759 - L1763 and L1878 to L1882 from Hawker, Kingston, to Contract No. 527112/36

P8809	310	Crashed on approach to Wattisham on return from patrol, Sudbury, Suffolk, 1.11.40
P8810	232/MSFU/9 PAFU/ ECFS/7 PAFU	SOC 17.12.44
P8811	310	Damaged by return fire from Bf 110 and abandoned near Chelmsford, Essex, 3.9.40
P8812	73	Shot down by Bf 109s over Isle of Sheppey; abandoned and crashed, Ludgate, Kent, 23.9.40
P8813	302/422 Flt/96/ 87/55 OTU	Flew into hills in bad visibility on navex, Bewcastle Fells, Cumberland, 26.2.43
P8814	310	Shot down by Bf 109s while attacking Do 17s and abandoned near Hornchurch, 31.8.40
P8815	-	Diverted to SAAF
P8816	501/145	Shot down by Bf 109s near West Wittering, Sussex, 7.11.40
P8817	-	To SAAF
P8818	601	Shot down by Bf 109s over Tunbridge Wells and crashed, Southborough, Kent, 6.9.40

*   *   *   *   *   *   *   *   *   *

150 Airspeed Oxford Is and IIs delivered between February and July 1940 by Airspeed, Portsmouth, to Contract No. 777546/38

Mk.I: P8822-P8830; P8855-P8916; P8995-P9046.
Mk.II: P8831-P8854; P8917-P8994.

P8822	14 FTS/14 PAFU/ ECFS/11 PAFU	SOC 16.7.44
P8823	14 FTS	SOC 6.3.41
P8824	5 FTS/4 FTS/ 70 OTU/EACF	SOC 1.10.43
P8825	RAFC/5 FTS/3 FTS/ 3 PAFU/21 PAFU	SOC 25.11.44
P8826	RAFC/5 FTS/3 FTS/ 3 PAFU/20 PAFU	Spun into ground near Islip, Oxon., 20.2.44

P8827	RAFC/5 FTS/2 FTS/ RAFC/1623 Flt/691/ 18 PAFU/3 FIS	SOC 18.1.47
P8828	5 FTS/RAFC	Hit tree in forced landing at night in bad weather near Ripon, Yorks., 9.10.40
P8829	RAFC	Wing hit wall low flying; crashed 1m W of S.Rauceby, Lincs., 24.9.40
P8830	3 FTS/15 FTS	Lost height on approach and hit ground, Weston-on-the-Green, 17.1.42; DBF
P8831	CFS/3 FIS/60 OTU	Hit hangar on overshoot and crashed, High Ercall, 21.3.44
P8832	24/MCS	Ambulance; SOC 24.6.48
P8833	24/MCS	Ambulance; SOC 3.2.41
P8834	CFS/7 FIS/20 PAFU	Swung while taxying and hit hangar, Kidlington, 28.3.43; to GI airframe
P8835 to P8868	-	To RNZAF as NZ1291-1310;
P8891 to P8897	-	1251-1271 respectively
P8898	2 FTS/12 FTS/3 FTS/ 3 PAFU/21 PAFU	SOC 22.7.46
P8899	2 FTS/1447 Flt/ 3 FIS	Engine cut on approach; belly- landed, Lulsgate Bottom, 14.11.44
P8900	2 FTS/14 FTS	DBR in heavy landing, Lyneham, 26.1.42
P8901 to P8904	-	To RNZAF as NZ1275-1278
P8905	2 FTS/15 PAFU/ 18 PAFU/14 PAFU/ 7 PAFU	SOC 14.2.46
P8906	2 FTS/2 PAFU/ 15 PAFU/21 PAFU	SOC 3.7.45
P8907 to P8909	-	To RNZAF as NZ1281-1283
P8910	2 FTS/6 AACU	To KLM 12.1.46
P8911	2 FTS/2 PAFU/6 PAFU/ 3 GTS/186/286/ 20 PAFU/7 PAFU/ 5 SFTS/7 SFTS	Undershot landing at night and overturned, Sutton Bridge, 7.1.45
P8912 to P8916	-	To RNZAF as NZ1286-1290
P8917	CFS/3 FIS/11 PAFU/ 21 OAFU	To USAAF 1.3.44
P8918	CFS/2 CFS/2 AGS/ 151/157	Swung on landing and hit excavator, Sydenham, 30.4.44
P8919	CFS/9 OTU/11 PAFU/ N.Weald	SOC 23.4.45
P8920	CFS/3 FIS/1530 Flt/ 1st BAD USAAF	SS 23.7.47
P8921	CFS/7 FIS/3 FIS/ 271/Llandow/3 OAPU Acclimatisation Flt	SS 18.3.49
P8922	2 FTS	Destroyed in air raid, Brize Norton, 16.8.40
P8923	2 FTS/1481 Flt/ 301 FTU/1 FU/525	Undercarriage retracted accidentally on ground, Lyneham, 15.6.44
P8924	2 FTS	Undershot night landing and hit haystack, Brize Norton, 30.7.40
P8925	11 FTS/2 FIS/1 FU	To RDAF 12.12.46
P8926	11 FTS/11 PAFU/ 83 OTU	Overshot forced landing in snowstorm and overturned, Woodseaves, Salop., 13.11.43
P8927	11 FTS	Spun into ground 3m NE of Shawbury, 11.7.40
P8928	11 FTS/Dalcross/ 18 PAFU	To Admiralty 27.2.44
P8929	11 FTS/2 FIS	Engine cut; lost height, hit water and crashlanded, Claudy Wood, Forres, Moray, 29.1.42
P8930	11 FTS	Ran into wreck of N4779 on landing, Shawbury, 26.7.41
P8931	11 FTS/3 FTS/ 3 PAFU/M.Mowbray	To USAAF 7.7.44
P8964	11 FTS/16 PFTS/ SF Oakington	SOC 30.6.49
P8965	11 FTS	Engine cut; dived into ground after control lost in turn near Shawbury, 30.3.41
P8966	14 FTS/12 PAFU/ 15 PAFU	SOC 8.6.50
P8967	14 FTS	Failed to take-off at night and hit hedge, Cranfield, 4.9.40
P8968	14 FTS/6 FTS/ 7 AACU/6 PAFU	Collided with HN724 and crashed, Macaroni Down Farm, near Bibury, Glos., 14.6.43; DBF
P8969	3 FTS/11 FTS/ 11 PAFU	SOC 30.6.49
P8970	11 FTS/2 FIS/116	
P8971	2 FTS/14 FTS/ 14 PAFU	Engine cut on approach; belly- landed ½m E of Ossington, 8.3.42
P8972	2 FIS	Flew into trees during low flying exercise and crashed, Downie Park, Angus, 10.11.44
P8973	11 FTS/11 PAFU	Hit hill low flying and belly- landed, Eaton Constantine, Salop., 17.2.43
P8974	CFS/3 FIS/ECFS	SOC 12.4.45
P8975	CFS/7 FIS/3 FIS/ Topcliffe/1659 CU	Hit by Halifax R9382 while parked, Topcliffe, 28.2.44
P8976	CFS/9 FTS/Swinderby/ 1485 Flt/6 PAFU/ Waddington/Strubby/ E. Kirkby	SOC 8.6.50
P8977	14 FTS/11 FTS/11 PAFU	To USAAF 29.1.44
P8978	14 FTS/12 FTS/5 OTU/Turnberry/Full Sutton/10 AFTS	SS 13.1.56
P8979	14 FTS/11 FTS/ 11 PAFU	SOC 11.8.43
P8980	14 FTS	Engine cut; lost height and side- slipped into ground 2m NE of Lyneham, 23.11.41
P8981	RAFC/1 Cam Unit/ 667/285	SOC 8.1.45
P8982	RAFC/15 FTS/68 15 PAFU/68	Engine cut on take-off; swung and hit hedge, Wilts., 27.4.44
P8983	15 FTS/2 FTS	Destroyed in air raid, Brize Norton, 16.8.40
P8984	15 FTS/2 FTS	Destroyed in air raid, Brize Norton, 16.8.40
P8985	2 FTS	Destroyed in air raid, Brize Norton, 16.8.40
P8986	2 FTS/15 FTS/ 2 FTS	Destroyed in air raid, Brize Norton, 16.8.40
P8987	2 FTS/15 FTS/2 FTS	Engine cut; hit hedge in forced landing near Brize Norton, 7.7.41
P8988	2 FTS/15 FTS/ 3 FTS/2 FIS	Collided with Valentia K3601 and crashed near Cranwell, 4.2.41
P8989	2 FTS/15 FTS/ 2 FTS	Destroyed in air raid, Brize Norton, 16.8.40
P8990	15 FTS/3 FTS	Hit tree low flying and crashed, Oversley, near Alcester, Warks., 17.8.41
P8991	RAFC/3 FTS/3 PAFU	SOC 29.12.42
P8992	RAFC/3 PAFU	To USAAF 1.12.43
P8993	RAFC	Stalled and hit ground after night take-off, Barkston LG, 19.8.40
P8994	RAFC/15 PAFU/264	SOC 25.11.44

P8995	2 FIS/2 CFS/1 FIS/ 8 FTS	SS 21.2.56
P8996	14 FTS/3 GTS/BOAC	SOC 6.1.44
P8997	2 FTS	Undershot landing at night, hit wall and overturned 1m SW of Akeman Street, 8.12.41
P8998	3 FTS/3 PAFU/ 16 PFTS/3 FIS	SOC 28.1.47
P9020	3 FTS/15 FTS	Swung on take-off, rolled and crashed, Kidlington, 16.6.41; DBR
P9021	3 FTS	Stalled in forced landing while lost and dived into ground, Salperton, Glos., 29.9.40; DBF
P9022	3 FTS/2 FTS/2 PAFU/ 3 GTS/16 PFTS/616/ 62 Gp CF	SS 14.6.49
P9023	3 FTS/3 PAFU/ 21 PAFU	Propellers hit ground on take-off; bellylanded, Seighford, 15.3.45
P9024	14 FTS/14 PAFU	To 3152M 17.7.42
P9025	2 FTS	SOC 4.3.42
P9026	15 FTS/15 PAFU	To RDAF 31.10.46 as 239
P9027	54 OTU/151	SOC 12.1.45
P9028	CFS/7 FIS	Flew into ground on low flying exercise near Everleigh, Wilts., 31.8.42
P9029	3 FTS/15 FTS/ 15 PAFU/3 FIS	SOC 15.1.47
P9030	2 FIS/2 CFS/ 18 PAFU/14 PAFU	SOC 30.8.44
P9031	14 FTS/2 CFS/12 FTS/ 3 FTS/16 FTS/Mepal/ 16 RFS/5 RFS	SOC 24.3.54
P9032	2 CFS/18 PAFU/ 14 PAFU	SOC 10.9.44
P9033	3 FTS/3 PAFU/ 11 PAFU	SOC 30.1.45
P9034	RAFC/15 PAFU	Ran away unmanned and hit N3572, Ramsbury, 19.2.43
P9035	RAFC	Crashed 6.12.40; NFD
P9036	2 FTS	Hit tree and crashed in forced landing while lost ½m E of Kingston Bagpuize, 9.1.42
P9037	14 FTS/14 PAFU/ 3 PAFU	SOC 7.9.44
P9038	2 FTS/6 FTS/6 PAFU/21 PAFU	SOC 23.8.44
P9039	2 FTS	Collided with Anson N9821 near Little Rissington, 20.9.40
P9040	54 OTU	Swung on landing and over-turned, Church Fenton, 7.7.41
P9041	54 OTU/15 FTS/2 FTS/ 1 GTS/RAFC/6 AACU/ 577	Flew into hill in box valley in bad weather 6½m NW of Thirsk, Yorks., 21.12.43; DBR
P9042	54 OTU/61 OTU	SOC 12.5.44
P9043	15 FTS	Flew into ground on night take-off, Weston-on-the-Green, 21.4.41
P9044	RAFC	Stalled in forced landing while lost, Wigsley, 9.11.41
P9045	-	To RNZAF but lost at sea en route 8.40
P9046	-	To RNZAF as NZ1247

*   *   *   *   *   *   *   *   *   *

100 Westland Lysander IIs delivered between November 1939 and April 1940 by Westland, Yeovil, to Contract No. 981730/39

P9051	71 OTU/267/173	Hit shelter on take-off and over-turned, Heliopolis, 27.11.42
P9052	451/WDCF	SOC 1.12.43
P9053	71 OTU	
P9054	ME	SOC 28.8.41
P9055	WDCF	Taxied into slit trench in sand storm, LG.75, 30.10.41; SOC 1.2.42
P9056	13/231	Abandoned after supply container jammed in tailplane 3m W of Bushmills, Ulster, 20.11.40
P9057	16/3 AACU	Swung on landing and under-carriage collapsed, Dum Dum, 28.3.43
P9058	16/28	SOC 17.6.42
P9059	16/13/6 AACU/ 9 Gp ASR & TTF	To FFAF 10.1.42
P9060	614/241/6 AACU/ Cv TT/288/1487 Flt/ 60 OTU/132 OTU/ 3 APS	To 3952M 21.11.43
P9061	4/1 SAC/41 OTU/ 6 AACU/Cv TT/ 56 OTU	SOC 1.3.44
P9062	4/CF India/CF Dum Dum/211 Gp CF	Ran out of fuel and overturned in forced landing in Hooghly River, 16.11.42
P9063	4	Missing 12.5.40
P9064	4	Shot down by Do 17 on take-off, Clairmarais, 21.5.40
P9065	416 Flt/231/ 6 AACU/Cv TT	To 3945M 14.7.43
P9066	ME	SOC 22.4.41
P9067	26/268/20	SOC 31.7.44
P9068	13/7 AACU	Forcelanded in bad weather on hillside and undercarriage coll-apsed, Warsop, Notts., 17.12.40
P9069	267	SOC 1.11.43
P9070	2/28	Undershot landing in dust storm and undercarriage torn off, Ranchi, 10.6.42
P9071	WDCF	Tail hit obstruction landing at Mersa Matruh, 26.11.41; DBR
P9072	1 SAC	Hit hill low flying near Dinton, Wilts., 25.2.41
P9073	73/6	Lost in action, 13.12.41; NFD
P9074	234 Wg	SOC 1.5.43
P9075	13/231/221 Gp CF/28	Engine cut; crashlanded at Detta Khel and destroyed by tribes-men, 28.7.42
P9076	614/1 SAC/20	SOC 31.7.44
P9077	16/7 AACU/13 Gp TTF/289/1429 Flt/ 60 OTU/3 APC	To 4004M 2.8.43
P9078	613/1 SAC	To FFAF 10.1.42
P9079	613/1 SAC/1480 Flt	To 3935M 22.7.42
P9080	26	Destroyed in air raid, West Malling, 18.8.40
P9095	110 RCAF/614/231/ 241/India	SOC 31.7.44
P9096	416 Flt/231/116	To 3934M 7.43
P9097	416 Flt/231	Engine cut; hit wall in forced landing, Castlewellan, Co. Down, 11.7.40
P9098	416 Flt/231	Damaged in gale, Newtownards, 21.11.40; not repaired and SOC 14.6.41
P9099	614/6 AACU/7 AACU/ 13 Gp TTF/289/Cv TT/ 41 OTU	Lost at sea en route to Middle East 8.1.43
P9100	614/8 AACU/12 Gp TTF/288/Cv TT/ 1487 Flt/41 OTU/ 1489 Flt	SOC 27.9.43
P9101	4/26/1 SAC/221 Gp CF	Swung on landing and under-carriage collapsed, Dum Dum, 19.4.42
P9102	-	To FFAF 24.8.40
P9103	-	To FFAF 24.8.40

P9104	110 RCAF/613/13 Gp TTF/289/1489 Flt/ 16 APC	SOC 16.1.44
P9105	RAE/3 RS/516	Tested Stieger high lift wing at RAE; to 3924M 25.7.43
P9106	204 Gp CF	SOC 1.5.43
P9107	81/26/268/20	SOC 31.7.44
P9108	4/16/1 SAC/41 OTU/ Cv TT	To 3943M 7.43
P9109	Cv Mk.III/231	Overshot forced landing in bad weather, Vearney, near Portaferry, Co.Down, 15.3.42
P9110	Cv Mk.III/16/Cv TT/ 1489 Flt/1487 Flt	SOC 3.7.43
P9111	Cv Mk.III/1 AACU/ 24/TFU/116/Cv TT/ 6 AAPC/1630 Flt/289	SOC 25.1.44
P9112	Cv Mk.III/1 AGS/ 1 AOS/1 OAFU	SOC 23.11.43
P9113	Cv Mk.III/110 RCAF/ 9 AGS/Cv TT/9 AOS/ 2 AGS	SOC 28.9.43
P9114	Cv Mk.III/110 RCAF	Crashed in forced landing while lost near Tunbridge Wells, Kent, 25.11.40
P9115	Cv Mk.III/Cv TT/ 10 AGS/1481 Flt	SOC 23.7.43
P9116	Cv Mk.III/110 RCAF/ 24/Northolt/CGS	
P9117	Cv Mk.III/Cv TT/ 5 AOS	SOC 6.10.44
P9118	Cv Mk.III/1 AOS	Engine cut; overturned in forced landing, Innerswell, Wigtown, 28.4.43
P9119	Cv Mk.III/4	Hit wall in forced landing in bad weather, Wath-on-Dearne, Yorks., 16.1.41
P9120	RAE/613/India	NFT
P9121	614/4 IAF	Engine lost power on take-off; crashed on approach to forced landing, Kohat, 21.4.42
P9122	Cv Mk.III/6 OTU/ 42 OTU/2/Cv TT	To USAAF 3.43
P9123	Cv Mk.III/110 RCAF/ 225/21 OTU/19 OTU	SOC 9.2.44
P9124	208/WDCF	Hit railway embankment on take-off, Maaten Bagush, 20.12.41
P9125	Cv Mk.III/110 RCAF/ 400/1 AOS/Cv to TT/ 7 OTU/1 APC	Hit hill in bad weather, White Abbey, Co.Antrim, 17.3.43
P9126	Cv Mk.III/2 AGS/ 2 AOS	SOC 24.1.44
P9127	26/16	Shot down by Spitfires near Dunkerque, 31.5.40
P9128	Cv Mk.III/110 RCAF/ Cv TT/20 OTU	SOC 23.10.43
P9129	Cv Mk.III/18 Gp TTF/ Leuchars/16 Gp APC/ 161	Missing on SOE mission, 1.8.44
P9130	Cv Mk.III/26/6 AACU	SOC 9.2.44
P9131	26/7 AACU/4 IAF	SOC 1.8.42
P9132	26/268/231/India	SOC 9.8.42
P9133	Cv Mk.III/225/4 AOS	SOC 16.11.43
P9134	-	To FFAF 8.7.41
P9135	26/1 SAC	Stalled on landing, Old Sarum, 19.2.41; DBR
P9136	Cv Mk.III/2 AGS	Stalled on take-off due to incorrect trim, Dalcross, 13.10.41
P9137	28	SOC 30.8.45
P9138	28/20	Tyre burst on landing on rough strip and undercarriage collapsed, Kyanktaw, 19.1.43; abandoned
P9139	28	
P9140	4/241/6 AACU/7 AACU/13 Gp AAC Flt	Bounced on landing and undercarriage collapsed, Turnhouse, 28.10.41
P9176	613/1 SAC/2 IAF/ 1 ATU	SOC 31.7.44
P9177	613/268/5/4 IAF/ 221 Gp CF	SOC 31.7.44
P9178	28	SOC 27.1.44
P9179	301 MU	Ran out of fuel and crashed in forced landing near Goth Rehri, India, 6.8.42
P9180	1 ATU	SOC 31.12.43
P9181	ME	To FFAF 10.1.42
P9182	208	Swung on landing and undercarriage collapsed, Tmimi, 18.12.41
P9183	8 AACU/Pembrey/ 10 Gp AAC Flt	Tyre burst on take-off; swung and undercarriage collapsed, Staverton, 7.11.41
P9184	4/231/ME	To FFAF 10.1.42
P9185	3 RAAF	DBR in air raid, Abu Sueir, 12.8.41
P9186	614	Collided with N1251 and crashed near Dysart, Fife, 10.8.40
P9187	8 AACU/11 Gp AAC Flt/Cv to TT/289/ 54 OTU/58 OTU	To 3888M 30.6.43
P9188	6	Hit cairn landing in desert near Mersa Matruh, 9.2.41; DBR
P9189	237	Shot down on reconnaissance near Amba Alagi, Ethiopia, 15.5.41
P9190	3 RAAF	SOC 3.7.42
P9191	267	SOC 6.45
P9192	ME	Lost 15.4.41; NFD
P9193	28	Swung on landing and undercarriage leg collapsed, Ranchi, 11.6.42
P9194	614/2 IAF	Undershot landing and tail knocked off; overturned, Yeravda, 28.3.42
P9195	-	Destroyed on evacuation, El Adem, 22.4.41
P9196	1 AGS(I)	
P9197	6	To FFAF
P9198	204 Gp CF	Undershot landing and hit truck, Gerawla, 17.7.41
P9199	6	Overshot landing and hit hedge, Ramleh, 19.12.40

*   *   *   *   *   *   *   *   *   *

32 Wellington IAs delivered between January and April 1939 by Vickers, Weybridge to Contract No.549268/36

P9205	9	Crashed in circuit on night training flight, Troston, Suffolk, 22.7.40
P9206	NZ Flt/20 OTU	Wingtip hit ground on landing in bad weather, Lossiemouth, 29.12.40
P9207	NZ Flt/38/ 115/218	One flap retracted; dived into ground on take-off, 4m N of Marham, 15.1.41
P9208	RAE	DBF in air raid, Exeter, 5.4.41
P9209	NZ Flt/75/311/ 57/CGS/FE	SOC 19.11.44
P9210	NZ Flt/75/RAE	Destroyed on trials flight by satisfactory working of weapon under test; crashed, Pawlett Ham, Somerset, 24.3.42
P9211	AAEE/20 OTU	To 3340M

Serial	Units	Fate
P9212	NZ Flt/311	Engine cut; hit tree in attempted forced landing 1m NW of Honington, 16.4.41
P9213	214/37	Shot down by fighters, Stavanger, 30.4.40
P9214	214/15 OTU/301/ CCDU/TRE/TFU/ MAEE/Cv XV	SOC 27.2.45
P9215	214/37	Shot down by fighters, Stavanger, 30.4.40
P9216	214/37/11 OTU/ 305/27 OTU	Undercarriage collapsed on landing, Lichfield, 27.9.41
P9217	214/37/11 OTU/ 16 OTU/26 OTU	SOC 20.6.43
P9218	214/149	Missing (Aalborg airfield) 22.4.40
P9219	99	Ran out of fuel in bad weather and crashed in forced landing on return from sweep, Walsoken, near Wisbech, Lincs., 21.2.40
P9220	38/1 AAS/CGS	SOC 15.1.44
P9221	99/18 OTU	Undershot in snowstorm and hit crane, Bramcote, 3.2.41
P9222	99/20 OTU/214/ 3 Gp TF/AGME/ CCDU/FE	SOC 29.6.45
P9223	Cv DWI/1 GRU/ 3 GRU/221/CCTDU/ 1417 Flt/172	Lost propeller on approach and overshot landing, Sywell, 20.12.42
P9224	149/115/311/ Czech TU/5 Gp TF/ Bassingbourn/ 5 Gp TF	To 3645M 3.43
P9225	149	Hit by AA from Dunkerque on return from reconnaissance and abandoned near Hondeschoote, 24.3.40
P9226	38/115/311/ 12 OTU	Overshot landing and hit hedge, Chipping Warden, 26.9.41
P9227	38/115	Missing from intruder to Bremen, 18.7.40
P9228	9/RAE/300/22 OTU/ 300/5 Gp TF/ 1483 Flt/1 AAS/ CGS	Collided with Spitfire P7530 and crashed near Lakenheath, 13.8.43
P9229	115/12 OTU	Hit by X9621 while parked, Benson, 27.9.41; DBF
P9230	115/311/CGS	Caught fire running up, Sutton Bridge, 27.6.42
P9231	9/1 AAS/303 FTU/ 3 OADU/1 OADU/ 303 FTU/1 OADU/FE	Cv XV; NFT 22.6.44
P9232	9	Hit by flak en route to attack road and rail targets at Duisburg and crashed, Simonshaven, Neth., 6.6.40
P9233	99/214/RAE/93/ SDF/AAEE/7 OTU	To 3440M 17.11.42
P9234	149/99	Missing (Stavanger) 18.4.40
P9235	38/115/311/ RAE/1 AAS	Flew into hill after take-off 2m SE of Louth, Lincs., 7.9.42
P9236	115	Flash bomb exploded while being loaded, Marham, 11.7.40; DBF

*   *   *   *   *   *   *   *   *   *

**50 Wellington ICs delivered in March and April 1940 by Vickers,
Weybridge to Contract No.549268/36**

Serial	Units	Fate
P9237	RAE & Mkrs/AFEE	Cv XVI; SOC 11.8.44

Serial	Units	Fate
P9238	Mkrs & AAEE/ 25 OTU	Prototype Mk.III; to 3410M 10.42
P9239	9/214/22 OTU/ 29 OTU	
P9240	149/99/21 OTU	To 3101M 7.42 Flew into ground 1m S of Brigg, Lincs., 27.1.43
P9241	149/99	Ran out of fuel and abandoned over Thetford, Norfolk, 30.5.40, but pilot crashlanded aircraft, Kilverstone Hall, on return from St.Omer
P9242	99	Missing from intruder over NW Germany, 19.9.40
P9243	99	Missing (Wilhelmshaven) 14.10.40
P9244	149	Hit radio mast on approach and crashed on return from Gelsenkirchen, Mildenhall, 12.8.40
P9245	149	Ditched off Clacton, Essex, on return from Boulogne, 9.9.40
P9246	149	Shot down by Bf 110s on anti-shipping sweep off Stavanger, 12.4.40
P9247	149	Flew into ground in low cloud near Digby returning from Hannover, 12.2.41
P9248	149	Missing (Cologne) 18.4.41
P9249	38	Engine cut on ferry flight; bellylanded and hit water tank, Marham, 18.6.40
P9250	38	Tyre burst on take-off for ferry flight, swung and undercarriage collapsed, Heliopolis, 6.2.42; DBF
_____		
P9265	38	Set on fire during strafing attack, Luqa, 25.11.40
P9266	149	Shot down by Bf 110s on anti-shipping sweep off Stavanger, 12.4.40
P9267	149	Stalled on attempted overshoot on training flight and hit ground, Mildenhall, 4.4.41
P9268	149	Overshot landing into bomb dump, Mildenhall, 17.12.40 on return from Mannheim
P9269	38	Missing from sweep off Stavanger, 12.4.40; presumed shot down by fighters
P9270	149	Wing hit trees on approach, spun into ground on return from raid on troop concentrations, Barton Mills, Suffolk, 24.5.40
P9271	115/12 STT/ 11 STT	To 3255M 17.7.42
P9272	99/149	Missing (Kiel) 28.8.40
P9273	99/149	Missing (Grevenbroich) 10.10.40
P9274	99	Engine cut; hit trees on take-off and crashed during emergency landing on return from Dortmund, Cambridge, 26.7.40
P9275	99	Missing (Dortmund) 26.7.40
P9276	99	Crashed in The Wash on return from Stavanger, 1.5.40
P9277	99/OADF/ 15 OTU/ME	Ditched on ferry flight, 8.7.41
P9278	9	Hit tree in forced landing in bad visibility, Toddington, Beds., on return from Kiel, 16.10.40
P9279	99/22 OTU	Missing 1.7.42

P9280	99/75/40/4 BATF/ 40/1429 Flt/ 30 OTU/11 OTU	SOC 25.5.43
P9281	99	Shot down by night fighter during raid on Düsseldorf, 12.6.41
P9282	99	Ran out of fuel returning from St.Omer and abandoned, Chrishall, Essex, 30.5.40
P9283	9/115	Engine cut; hit obstruction in forced landing, Booton, near Reepham, Norfolk, 27.10.40 on return from Gelsenkirchen
P9284	115/38/115	Shot down by flak, Stavanger, 11.4.40
P9285	115/38/115/ 27 OTU	Missing on navex, presumed ditched, 16.7.42
P9286	38/115	Shot down by night fighter 6m SSW of Medemblik on return from Hamburg, 17.11.40
P9287	38	Missing (Berlin) 8.10.40
P9288	37	Missing from attack on enemy columns near Nieuport, 1.6.40
P9289	149/18 OTU/15 OTU/ 304/20 OTU/21 OTU/ Cv XVI/303 FTU/ 2 OADU/FE	SOC 26.4.45
P9290	38/115/12 OTU	To 3322M 8.42
P9291	38/115/218/148/ 2 METS/SRF	
P9292	38/115/75	Ditched on return from Emden, 24.10.40
P9293	38	Ditched returning from Tobruk, 7.1.41
P9294	38/148/37/ 108/2 METS	Crashed in forced landing 5m NW of Suez, 11.5.42
P9295	38/1 AAS	SOC 11.8.44
P9296	38/115/218/11 OTU	To 3321M 13.8.42
P9297	38/115	Damaged by flak attacking Meuse bridges and crash-landed near Poix-Terron, Ardennes, 22.5.40
P9298	115	Missing from attacks on roads between Cambrai and St. Quentin, 21.5.40; crashed near Antwerp
P9299	115/38/115/218/ Czech TU/1429 Flt	Flew into dead-end valley in bad weather and crashed, 6.4.42
P9300	115/12 OTU	Dived into ground on over-shoot, Mount Farm, 18.4.41

*   *   *   *   *   *   *   *   *   *

183 Supermarine Spitfire Is delivered between January and August 1940 by Supermarine, Southampton, to Contract No. 980385/39

P9305	19	Shot down by Bf 109s near Dunkerque, 26.5.40
P9306	74/131/52 OTU/ 61 OTU	To Museum of Science, Chicago, 9.44
P9307	PDU/Cv PR.III/PRU/ 1 PRU	Missing from PR mission to Brest, 10.4.41
P9308	PDU	Missing from PR mission to Hamburg, 19.5.40
P9309	PDU/PRU/308/ Baginton/52 OTU	Lost wing and crashed near Yatesbury, 10.5.42
P9310	PDU/PRU/Cv PR.F later PR.VI/8 OTU	Missing on training flight, 1.10.42

P9311	249/610/602/ 61 OTU/73 OTU	Collided on take-off with Kittyhawk AK727, Abu Sueir, 22.10.43
P9312	266	Shot down by Bf 109s and abandoned near Canterbury, 16.8.40
P9313	PDU/PRU	Missing from PR sortie along French coast, 9.11.40
P9314	41	Missing 22.6.40
P9315	RAE/PDU/PRU/ 3 PRU	Engine cut on approach; under-carriage collapsed in heavy landing, Benson, 5.11.40
P9316	92/66	Shot down by Bf 109s; abandoned and crashed, Purleigh, Essex, 4.9.40
P9317	222	Missing from patrol over Dunkerque, 1.6.40; recovered by enemy
P9318	222/234/58 OTU/ 53 OTU/61 OTU/ 58 OTU/1 TEU	SOC 15.4.45
P9319	234/129/61 OTU	Taxied into tractor, Rednal, 4.6.42; to 3143M 2.7.42
P9320	234/58 OTU	Missing on low flying exercise, 31.10.41; presumed flew into hills
P9321	234/74	Forcelanded at Calais/Marck and abandoned, 24.5.40
P9322	609/61 OTU/ 53 OTU	Broke up in air near Llanishen, Cardiff, 15.9.42
P9323	222	Shot down by Bf 109s; abandoned and crashed, Minster, Isle of Sheppey, Kent, 30.8.40
P9324	222/41	Shot down by Bf 109 near Bulphan, Essex, 15.9.40
P9325	222/122/61 OTU	To Admiralty 4.7.43
P9326	222/54/57 OTU/ 52 OTU/Atcham/ 53 OTU	Control lost during roll; spun into ground ½m E of Navenby, Lincs., 16.5.43; DBF
P9327	152/7 OTU	Dived into ground near Abergele, Denbigh, 12.10.40; cause not known
P9328	602/222/Cv PR.V/140	SOC 14.3.45
P9329	257/1 OTU/7 OTU/ 65/Atcham/61 OTU	Crashed into hill in bad visibility 4m E of Church Stretton, Salop., 20.1.43
P9330	257/610	Overturned on landing on boggy ground, Hooton Park, 7.11.40; DBR
P9331	212	Abandoned in France, 6.40
P9332	249/7 OTU/57 OTU/ 61 OTU/1 CACF/ 1 CACU/53 OTU	To 3595M 2.3.43
P9333	266	Shot down in sea off Portsmouth, 12.8.40; NFD
P9334	41/122/57 OTU/ 73 OTU	SOC 27.7.44
P9335	249/7 OTU/41/611/ 485/57 OTU/61 OTU/ 57 OTU/61 OTU/ 53 OTU	SOC 8.44
P9336	249/74	Damaged by Bf 109s and abandoned; crashed, Buckland Mill, near Dover, 28.7.40
P9337	222	Shot down by Bf 109, Tenterden, Kent, 31.8.40
P9338	72	Left formation and crashed, Capel-le-Ferne, near Folkestone, Kent, 12.10.40; cause not known
<u>P9339</u>	222	Shot down by Bf 109 on patrol over Dunkerque, 1.6.40
P9360	222	Destroyed in air raid, Hornchurch, 31.8.40
P9361	222/5 OTU/7 OTU/ 58 OTU/57 OTU	SOC 6.3.45

Serial	Units	Fate
P9362	222/3 FPP/66/ 57 OTU/1 PRU	SOC 6.1.45
P9363	234	Damaged by Bf 109s and abandoned near Twyford, Hants., 15.8.40
P9364	222	Missing on interception, 27.9.40; believed aircraft crashed near Hollingbourne, Kent
P9365	234	Undershot landing at night, St. Eval, 31.7.40
P9366	234	Overshot landing on return from night patrol, St.Eval, 6.8.40
P9367	92/54/57 OTU/ Cv VA/316/306/81/ 165/167/ATA	SOC 6.6.45
P9368	92/616/72/111/132/ 52 OTU/132/52 OTU/ 53 OTU/52 OTU/ 57 OTU	To Admiralty 14.6.44
P9369	92/64	Damaged by Bf 109 and crash-landed, Capel-le-Ferne, Kent, 8.8.40; DBR
P9370	92	Shot down by Bf 109s near Dunkerque, 23.5.40
P9371	92/132/58 OTU/ 53 OTU/2 TEU/ 53 OTU	SOC 6.45
P9372	92	Shot down by Bf 109 and abandoned over Biggin Hill, 9.9.40
P9373	92	Missing, presumed shot down by Bf 110s near Dunkerque, 23.5.40
P9374	92	Damaged by Bf 109s and force-landed near Calais, 24.5.40
P9375	222/53 OTU	Abandoned in spin 1m E of Gatwick, 4.6.41
P9376	222/72/57 OTU/ 52 OTU/53 OTU	To 4606M 3.44
P9377	222	Damaged by Bf 109s and crash-landed on beach 9m N of Dunkerque, 1.6.40; destroyed by pilot
P9378	222	Believed hit by own AA; pilot blown out of cockpit; crashed, Boughton Monchelsea, Kent, 4.9.40
P9379	54/74	Shot down by Bf 109s off Folkestone, Kent, 31.7.40
P9380	249/65/74/222/53 OTU/1 AAS/53 OTU	Overshot landing, Hibaldstow, 8.3.44
P9381	249/602	Damaged by Bf 109s near Dorchester and abandoned, Galton Heath, Dorset, 25.8.40
P9382	PRU	Landed at Dyce on return from PR mission, 25.7.40; shown as DBR by enemy action
P9383	616/53 OTU	Crashed at Colwinston, Glam., 9.7.41
P9384	PDU/RAE/PRU	Missing on ferry flight, Heston-Wick, 17.10.40
P9385	PDU/PRU/Cv PR.F later PR.VI/1 PRU/ 8 OTU	SOC 7.44
P9386	Airspeed/257/7 OTU/ 19/152/58 OTU/ 52 OTU/57 OTU	Dived into ground, East Lothian, 5.5.41
P9387	54/122/53 OTU	SOC 20.5.42
P9388	54	Shot down by Bf 109s while escorting Swordfish off Calais, 25.5.40
P9389	54	Damaged by Bf 109s and abandoned; crashed, School Lane, Kingsdown, Kent, 24.8.40
P9390	54	Damaged by Bf 109s near Deal, 7.7.40; to 2111M 22.10.40
P9391	238/7 OTU/19/152	Pilot thrown out of aircraft, crashed 2m E of Dorchester, Dorset, 11.10.40
P9392	212	Missing on reconnaissance flight, 19.6.40
P9393	74	Shot down by Bf 109 and abandoned; crashed in sea off Dover, 11.8.40
P9394	212/603/41/ 57 OTU/52 OTU	SOC 16.8.44
P9395	257/1 OTU/7 OTU	Crashed 11.10.40; NFD
P9396	212/PRU/1 PRU	Missing from PR mission to Brest, 10.4.41
P9397	222/57 OTU/Cv VA/ 130/134/133/421/601	To Admiralty 8.9.42
P9398	64/74	Shot down by Bf 109 in Folkestone Harbour, 31.7.40
P9399	64/74	Crashlanded during cloud-flying exercise, Lympne, 1.6.40; to 2137M 22.10.40
P9420	222	Damaged by cannon shell on night interception; crashlanded near Hemswell, 26.6.40
P9421	64	Shot down by Bf 109s off Dover, 25.7.40
P9422	7 OTU/19	Shot down by Bf 109, Birling, Kent, 5.9.40
P9423	249/602	Damaged by return fire from Ju 88 near Westhampnett; abandoned and crashed, North Berstead, Sussex, 19.8.40
P9424	249/266/72/123/ 58 OTU	Crashed 23.12.41; NFD
P9425	CFS/AAEE/CFS/ 58 OTU/2 CTW/ 1 TEU/53 OTU	SOC 20.11.44
P9426	PDU/RAE/PRU	Took off with mechanic on tail; stalled and crashed, Heston, 21.11.40
P9427	609/74/41/152	Missing, presumed shot down by Bf 109s off Needles, Isle of Wight, 28.11.40
P9428	41	Believed collided with R6635 during attack on Do 17s and crashed, North Benfleet, Essex, 5.9.40
P9429	41/74/41/611/303/ 306/61 OTU/57 OTU/ 58 OTU	Took off in coarse pitch; stalled and dived into ground, Grangemouth, 29.6.43; DBF
P9430	41	Damaged by Bf 109s and crash-landed near Rayleigh, Essex, 7.9.40; DBF
P9431	66/7 OTU/19	Damaged by Bf 109s and crashlanded, Duxford, 15.9.40
P9432	66/152/64/Kenley/ 53 OTU/73 OTU/ 74 OTU	Stalled on approach; hit rocks and overturned, Aqir, 2.8.43
P9433	92/610/131/52 OTU/ 57 OTU	To Admiralty 9.7.43
P9434	92/222/57 OTU	Spun into ground, Picton, Cheshire, 6.12.41
P9435	65	Damaged attacking Do 17s near Calais and crashlanded on beach, 28.5.40
P9436	65/57 OTU	Engine cut; overturned in forced landing, Caerwys racecourse, Flint, 10.7.41
P9437	65	Shot down by AA near Calais, 26.5.40
P9438	72	Damaged by Bf 109 off Dungeness and abandoned near New Romney, Kent, 31.8.40

P9439	72/610/602/61 OTU	Overturned in forced landing, while lost, Brook Nest Farm, Stevenage, Herts., 21.11.41; DBR
P9440	152/603/61 OTU/ 19/331/58 OTU/ 61 OTU/57 OTU	SOC 3.5.45
P9441	74	Missing 24.5.40
P9442	152/602/52 OTU/ 61 OTU	SOC 29.12.41
P9443	222	Damaged by Bf 109s and crash-landed near Sittingbourne, Kent, 30.8.40
P9444	RAE/72/58 OTU/ 61 OTU/53 OTU	To Science Museum 8.44
P9445	92/5 OTU/7 OTU/ 53 OTU	Crashed in sea off Southern-down, Glam., 5.10.41
P9446	54/602/234/ 57 OTU/52 OTU	Engine failed and cockpit filled with smoke; abandoned over Sapperton, Glos., 6.2.43
P9447	64/222/41	Shot down by Bf 109s, Preston Hill, near Maidstone, Kent, 11.10.40
P9448	RAE/72/53 OTU/ Cv VA/81	Swung on landing and over-turned, Ouston, 7.2.42
P9449	64	Shot down by Bf 109s, Hailsham, Sussex, 22.10.40; to 2119M
P9450	64	Shot down by Bf 109 on patrol, Brenley, Kent, 5.12.40
P9451	610	Crashed at Eglingham, North-umberland, 11.12.40; NFD
P9452	610	Shot down by Bf 109 off Calais, 18.7.40
P9453	PDU/PRU	Missing on low altitude reconnaissance of Belgian coast, 14.9.40
P9454	92/65	Abandoned after catching fire, Mayfield, Sussex, and crashed, Tolhurst Farm, Ticehurst, 1.12.40
P9455	54	Missing from patrol over Calais, 24.5.40
P9456	152	Shot down by Ju 88 near St. Catherines, Isle of Wight, and crashed in sea, 12.8.40
P9457	72	Shot down by Bf 109 near Staplehurst, Kent, 31.8.40
P9458	72	Shot down by Bf 109, Pluckley, Kent, 1.9.40
P9459	603/53 OTU	Crashed in sea, 29.10.41; NFD
P9460	72/61 OTU	To 3593M 3.43
P9461	602	Wing hit ground in night landing in mist, Drem, 1.8.40; DBR
P9462	5 OTU/7 OTU/41/ 92/53 OTU	Ran short of fuel while lost; bellylanded near Weston Zoyland, 10.9.41; DBR
P9463	603/152	Shot down near Portsmouth, 25.9.40; NFD
P9464	238/92	Shot down by Bf 109, Smeeth, Kent, 11.9.40
P9465	74/7 OTU/54/ 58 OTU/131	SOC 19.12.41
P9466	234	Shot down by Bf 109s, St.Mary Cray, Kent, 7.9.40
P9467	609	Damaged by Bf 109s and abandoned over Thames Estuary, 7.9.40
P9468	249/234/57 OTU/ 53 OTU	Engine cut; abandoned 3m N of Widecombe, Devon, 16.8.42
P9469	602/222	Damaged by return fire from bombers and abandoned, Saleshurst, Kent, 7.10.40
P9490	7 OTU/61 OTU/ 53 OTU/RAFC	Dived into ground 1m E of Desborough, 10.1.44
P9491	249/234/602/234/ 58 OTU/53 OTU	Flew into mountain in cloud 2½m SSW of Tonpentre, Glam., 3.1.42
P9492	74/222	Damaged by Bf 109 and crash-landed near Denham, Bucks., 30.9.40; DBR
P9493	249/234	Flew into ground on night patrol, Porthtowan, Cornwall, 25.7.40
P9494	249/234/61 OTU/ 57 OTU	Collided with X4270 near Hawarden, 14.3.42
P9495	610	Damaged by Bf 109s over Romney Marsh, 12.8.40 and SOC on return
P9496	610	Damaged by Bf 109s; aband-oned and crashed, Paddleworth, Kent, 26.8.40
P9497	5 OTU/7 OTU/ 58 OTU	Spun into ground during aerobatics near Bannockburn, Stirlingshire, 2.10.41
P9498	610	Hit tractor on take-off and crashed into pillbox, Gravesend, 29.6.40
P9499	5 OTU/603/266/111/ 58 OTU/52 OTU/ 61 OTU	Engine cut; undercarriage collapsed in forced landing, Rednal, 5.8.43
P9500	5 OTU/41/122/ 53 OTU	Collided with AR240 and belly-landed near Cowbridge, Glam. 15.3.42
P9501	5 OTU/7 OTU/57 OTU/ 129/58 OTU/52 OTU/ 2 TEU/1 TEU	SOC 18.8.44
P9502	610	Control lost during combat practice; dived into ground, Titsey Park, Kent, 12.7.40
P9503	257/610/609	Damaged by return fire from bomber and abandoned 1m S of Upavon, 27.10.40
P9504	1 AAS	To 2728M 9.41
P9505	249/222/234/266/ 111/57 OTU/58 OTU/ Cv PR.IV/140	SOC 27.2.45
P9506	249/54	Crashed in forced landing, S. Ellerton, 10.2.41
P9507	249/64	Missing on reconnaissance near Rouen, 5.7.40
P9508	249/234/123	Lost at sea en route to ME, 8.1.43
P9509	19/152/58 OTU/ 53 OTU	Ran out of fuel on approach and crashlanded 1m S of Llandow, 2.4.42
P9510	249/602/61 OTU/ 52 OTU/17 SFTS	SOC 8.3.45
P9511	249/610	Shot down by Bf 109s and hit house, Stelling Minnis, Kent, 28.8.40
P9512	249/610/41	Engine cut after take-off; crashlanded, Globe Road, Hornchurch, 12.10.40
P9513	249/92/152/58 OTU/ 452/313/61 OTU/ 53 OTU	Hit by N3247 while parked Llandow, 12.4.42; DBR
P9514	5 OTU	Hit wall on take-off, Aston Down, 16.5.40
P9515	5 OTU/602/610/53 OTU/52 OTU/58 OTU/ 1 TEU/66/53 OTU	SOC 6.45
P9516	5 OTU/65/222/132	Flew into ground in bad weather, Tillymaud Farm, Longhaven, Aberdeen, 29.11.41
P9517	5 OTU	Crashed in forced landing near Leominster, Hereford, 21.5.40
P9518	5 OTU/Cv PR.VII/ 1 PRU/8 OTU	Engine cut; overshot forced landing near Fraserburgh, 26.12.43

Spitfire I

P9519	7 OTU/234/66/64/ 303/412/58 OTU	SOC 12.7.44
P9540	257/61 OTU/Cv VA/ 121/164/602/61 OTU/ Northolt/52 OTU/61 OTU/1 TEU/61 OTU	SOC 12.44
P9541	257/7 OTU/57 OTU/ 52 OTU	Caught fire in air and aband- oned, Heycombe, Bath, 8.4.43
P9542	257/7 OTU/222/ 92/308/Baginton/ 52 OTU/58 OTU/ 57 OTU	SOC 9.44
P9543	257/7 OTU/152/ 58 OTU/3 SGR	Undercarriage jammed; stalled while bellylanding, Squires Gate, 21.3.42
P9544	257/1 OTU/92/ Baginton/52 OTU	To Portugal 25.9.43
P9545	257/610/64/58 OTU/ 132/58 OTU	Collided with N3100 near Abernethy, Perthshire, 21.4.42
P9546	257/7 OTU/457/ 58 OTU/52 OTU	Broke up in air 1m SSW of Dymock, Glos., 11.2.42
P9547	54/74	Shot down by Bf 109s near Dover, 28.7.40
P9548	92	Abandoned on night patrol 1m SW of Blaxall, Suffolk, 27.8.40
P9549	54/53 OTU	Flew into hill in bad visibility near Trebanog, 21.11.41
P9550	PDU/PRU/1 PRU/ 1401 Flt/Cv VA/ 1401 Flt	Missing on met flight, 7.11.41
P9551	PRU	Hit by flak on PR mission to Genoa and abandoned, Viareggio, 2.2.41
P9552	PRU/1 PRU	Missing from PR mission to Stettin, 10.5.41
P9553	603	Damaged by Bf 109s and aband- oned near Croydon, Surrey, 2.10.40
P9554	64	Damaged by Bf 109 and aband- oned near Waldron, Sussex, 16.8.40
P9555	64/303/58 OTU	Crashed after collision near Airdrie, Lanarkshire, 26.4.42
P9556	64/53 OTU/Cv VA	To Admiralty 4.9.42
P9557	64/57 OTU/73 OTU	SOC 27.7.44
P9558	54	Engine cut; abandoned 2m SW of Catterick, 25.10.40
P9559	54/57 OTU	Collided with Spitfire N3066 and crashed Kimmel Park, Bodelwyddan, Flint, 2.11.41
P9560	54	Dived into ground near Bolton- on-Swale, Kent, 7.9.40; cause not known
P9561	PRU	Missing from PR sortie to Ostend, 16.2.41
P9562	65/CGS/52 OTU/ 58 OTU/1 TEU	SOC 6.3.45
P9563	64/53 OTU/Cv VA/ 332/164	Stalled off turn and dived into ground, Skeabrae, 23.8.42
P9564	64	Crashed 4m N of Leconfield, 30.9.40; NFD
P9565	AAEE/SD Flt/61 OTU/ 59 OTU/61 OTU/1 PRU/ 542/140/542/8 OTU	SOC 25.8.44
P9566	-	To Turkey direct as N22; returned as HK854
P9567	-	To Turkey direct as N23 returned as HK856
P9568 to P9584	-	Cancelled

Note: P9553 - P9567 built for Turkey but only P9566 and P9567 delivered

*   *   *   *   *   *   *   *   *   *

**Two D.H.89As purchased from Airwork in September 1939 to
Contract No. 978450/39**

P9588	2 EWS/2 SS	Sold to Allied Airways 30.4.43
P9589	2 EWS/1 SS/15 Gp CF	Sold 25.11.46

*   *   *   *   *   *   *   *   *   *

**Martin-Baker MB.2 prototype ex G-AEZD delivered in June
1939 by Martin-Baker to Contract No. 982598/39**

P9594	AAEE/AFDU/Mkrs	Retd to Martin-Baker Aircraft Co.

*   *   *   *   *   *   *   *   *   *

**12 Short Sunderland Is delivered between September 1939 and
April 1940 by Short Bros., Rochester, to Contract No.
B985038/39**

P9600	210/10 RAAF/ 228/4 OTU	SOC 11.12.46
P9601	10 RAAF	Destroyed in air raid, Mount Batten, 28.11.40
P9602	210/10 RAAF	Overshot on landing at night and ran aground on Lismore Island, Oban, 2.9.40
P9603	10 RAAF	Crashed on landing, Pembroke Dock, 24.6.41
P9604	10 RAAF/MAEE/ 4 OTU	Crashed into hangar, Wig Bay, 11.6.42
P9605	10 RAAF/4 OTU	SOC 10.5.44
P9606	10 RAAF/201/4 OTU	SOC 10.5.44
P9620	204	Ran short of fuel and ditched at night in bad weather in Atlantic; wrecked, 29.10.40
P9621	228/201	Forcelanded in bad weather and ran aground, Scalasaig Bay, Colonsay, 9.10.40; DBR
P9622	228/201	Flew into hill while lost, Dunnet Head, Caithness, 29.10.40; DBF
P9623	210/95	Forcelanded on ferry flight and interned in Portugal, 14.2.41
P9624	210	Crashed on landing, Oban, 15.3.41

*   *   *   *   *   *   *   *   *   *

**Consolidated 28-5 delivered in July 1939 by Consolidated
Aircraft, San Diego, to Contract No. B988730/39**

P9630	MAEE/228/240/ MAEE/210/MAEE	Swung during heavy landing and sank, Dumbarton, 10.2.40

*   *   *   *   *   *   *   *   *   *

**Cierva C-40 delivered by Cierva Autogyro Co., Feltham, to
Contract No. 968954/38**

P9635	-	Allotted but not delivered
P9636	74 Wg/1447 Flt/529	SOC 7.9.44

*   *   *   *   *   *   *   *   *   *

P9642 - P9691; P9709 - P9748; P9787 - P9836; P9847 - P9891; P9909 - P9943; P9957 - P9986	Fairey Barracudas delivered direct to Admiralty to Contract No. 993331/39

*   *   *   *   *   *   *   *   *   *

10 Airspeed Oxford Is delivered abroad

P9990 to P9999	-	Diverted before delivery

*   *   *   *   *   *   *   *   *   *

Above: Three Wellington Is of No.311 (Czech) Squadron with R1410 in the foreground

Below: Halifax II R9441 at Boscombe Down in February 1942

Spitfire VBs of No. 92 Squadron, R6923 in the foreground

550 Wellington ICs delivered between August 1940 and May 1941 by Vickers, Chester to Contract No. 992424/39

R1000	20 OTU/7 OTU/ 6 OTU	Overshot flapless landing and undercarriage collapsed, Silloth, 3.6.43; to 3737M
R1001	20 OTU	Hit by Z8841 while parked, Lossiemouth, 1.3.42
R1002	304	Engine cut returning from Bremen; crashed in forced landing in wood near Langham, 15.7.41
R1003	304/27 OTU/ 105 OTU	SOC 15.8.44
R1004	115	Ran out of fuel in fog returning from Bremen and abandoned; crashed in Histon Road, Cambridge, 12.2.41
R1005	20 OTU	Flew into sea after baulked approach, Lossiemouth, 4.2.41
R1006	301/21 OTU/18 OTU	Caught fire on ground, Bramcote, 2.2.42
R1007	40	Missing (Kiel) 8.4.41
R1008	218	Missing (Hannover) 15.8.41
R1009	218	Damaged by Ju 88 and crash-landed, Red Lodge, 2m S of Swaffham, Norfolk, on return from Düsseldorf, 25.2.41; DBR
R1010	18 OTU/15 OTU/ 23 OTU/105 OTU	SOC 18.7.44
R1011	BDU/23 OTU/ 28 OTU	Flew into high ground in cloud, Low Moors, Douston, Derby, 30.1.43
R1012	11 OTU	Lost prop; other engine cut; crashlanded at Hunsdon, 14.9.41
R1013	40	Shot down by night fighter on return from Berlin, Cloppenburg, 13.3.41
R1014	304	Crashed after take-off due to incorrect trim, Bleasby, Notts., 6.2.41
R1015	311	Missing (Hamburg) 16.9.41; crashed 10m ESE of Lingen-Ems
R1016	305/150	Missing (Hannover) 15.8.41; crashed in Ijsselmeer near Workum
R1017	305	Collided with Oxford over Elton, Notts., and lost tail, 12.6.41
R1018	38/148	SOC 27.7.44
R1019	305/12 OTU/27 OTU/ 14 OTU/11 OTU	SOC 5.3.44
R1020	37/75	Flaps jammed up on training flight; overshot landing, skidded and hit tender, Feltwell, 18.11.40
R1021	311/7 OTU	Crashed in forced landing while lost on navex, near Cork, Eire, 26.9.42
R1022	311/11 OTU	Overshot flapless landing at Bassingbourn, 16.6.41
R1023	9/12 OTU/15 OTU	To 3453M 29.11.42
R1024	149	Missing (Hannover) 13.8.41; crashed in sea off Sylt
R1025	218/16 OTU/ 11 OTU	Crashed on approach, Westcott, 13.3.43
R1026	301	Engine caught fire and prop fell off; lost height and hit trees on return from Bremen, Winkburn, Notts., 23.6.41; DBR
R1027	20 OTU/12 OTU	Engine cut on overshoot; swung and hit tree, Chipping Warden, 14.2.42
R1028	21 OTU	Engine cut; crashed on approach, Little Rissington, 8.10.43; DBF

Serial	Units	Remarks
R1029	OADF/15 OTU/ OADF/70/108	Engine cut; bellylanded on return from Sidi Barrani, Amriya, 29.6.42
R1030	40	Engine cut; ditched 10m off Harwich on return from Ostend, 3.9.41
R1031	21 OTU	Stalled after take-off with full flap from Edgehill, Lower Brailes, Warks., 24.10.41
R1032	214/21 OTU/ Cv XVI/242	SOC 30.4.46
R1033	115/38/37/38	Missing (Derna) 14.4.41
R1034	311/115/38/ 115/22 OTU	To 3055M c 5.42
R1035	300	Hit ground on attempted overshoot 1m WSW of Swinderby, 28.12.40, on return from Antwerp
R1036	311/22 OTU	Flew into trees on overshoot, Stratford, 29.6.42
R1037	12 OTU	Control lost after overshoot; hit ground in turn, Chipping Warden, 20.10.41
R1038	75	Missing (Kiel) 12.9.41
R1039	20 OTU/16 OTU/ 30 OTU/14 OTU	SOC 8.4.44
R1040	57/9	Shot down by night fighter near Maastricht en route to Cologne, 8.7.41
R1041	103/15 OTU/21 OTU	SOC 22.3.44
R1042	150/29 OTU/ 105 OTU	SOC 15.9.44
R1043	103	Engine cut; hit trees in forced landing at night, Manor Farm, Mudford, Somerset, 30.3.41, on return from Brest; DBF
R1044	150	Flew into Colborough Hill in cloud, Halstead, Leics., 28.5.41 on return from Boulogne
R1045	149	Missing (Wilhelmshaven) 22.2.41
R1046	214/311	Missing (Bremen) 21.10.41; crashed 4m S of Schiermonnikoog
R1047	301/17 OTU/21 OTU	Lost prop and hit tree on overshoot 1m S of Edgehill, 6.2.42
R1048	22 OTU/14 OTU/ 1 AAS	SOC 28.6.44
R1049	221	Damaged by intruder over Langham and crashed, Westgate, Norfolk, 10.4.41
R1060	20 OTU/105 OTU	SOC 21.2.44
R1061	300/103	Ditched in Heligoland Bight on return from Lubeck, 29.3.42
R1062	BDU/23 OTU	Sank back on overshoot and bellylanded, Pershore, 13.7.42
R1063	115	Shot down by night fighter in sea off Schiermonnikoog on return from Münster, 7.7.41
R1064	301/304	Missing (Ostend) 17.12.41; presumed ditched
R1065	301/11 OTU	Missing (Cologne) 31.5.42
R1066	SF Stradishall/ Wyton/15/40	Shot down by CR.42 night fighter, Ottaviano, during raid on Naples, 6.12.41
R1067	OADF/15 OTU/37	Ditched off Sollum returning from Benghazi, 1.8.41
R1068	21 OTU	Flew into hill in cloud near Morfa Towyn, Merioneth, 17.8.41
R1069	21 OTU	SOC 14.7.48
R1070	-	To 3269M 17.7.42
R1071	21 OTU/15 OTU/ 12 OTU	Hit hangar on approach and crashed, Chipping Warden, 24.10.41
R1072	21 OTU/11 OTU/ 21 OTU/18 OTU/ 105 OTU	SOC 21.7.44
R1073	11 OTU/25 OTU	Dived into ground near Lindholme, 11.6.42; cause not known
R1074	1 OTU/3 OTU	To 3360M 12.41
R1075	16 OTU	Hit balloon cables and crashed, Erdington, Birmingham, 7.8.42
R1076	12 OTU	Engine cut on take-off; crashlanded, Benson, 4.5.41
R1077	25 OTU/30 OTU/ 16 OTU/14 OTU/ 104 OTU	To 3679M 27.4.42
R1078	25 OTU/11 OTU	Shot down by night fighter near Rheine during raid on Bremen, 26.6.42
R1079	11 OTU	To 4807M 31.5.44
R1080	SF Stradishall/ Wyton/9/15 OTU	Forcelanded in France on ferry flight to Gibraltar, 27.4.41
R1081	11 OTU/105 OTU	SOC 18.7.44
R1082	21 OTU	Engine cut; stalled on approach and spun into ground ½m N of Wellesbourne Mountford, 13.2.42
R1083	21 OTU	To 3327M 15.8.42
R1084	115	Damaged by Do 17Z near Swaffham on return from Hannover; crashlanded at Narborough, Norfolk, 11.2.41
R1085	21 OTU	Lost prop; stalled in attempted forced landing, Woolerton, Salop., 14.4.42
R1086	12 OTU/20 OTU/ 2 OTU	Crashlanded with engine fire, Southwick, Hants., 1.1.44; DBF
R1087	23 OTU	To 3346M 23.8.42
R1088	101	Ran out of fuel and crashlanded, Park Farm, Brabourne, Kent, 3.8.41 on return from Hamburg; DBF
R1089	20 OTU/21 OTU/ Cv XVI	SOC 14.8.44
R1090	21 OTU/18 OTU/ 15 OTU/105 OTU	SOC 15.8.44
R1091	11 OTU/17 OTU	To 3685M 4.42
R1092	70	SOC 27.7.44
R1093	20 OTU	Flew into hill in cloud on navex near Carn Garbh, Helmsdale, Caithness, 30.7.41
R1094	115/Well Flt	Lost height after take-off and hit ground, Luqa, 4.11.40
R1095	75/37	Bomb exploded while aircraft parked, LG.09, 27.9.41
R1096	9	Engine cut after being shot at by convoy; overshot forced landing, hit ditch and undercarriage collapsed 2m N of Woodbridge, Suffolk, on return from Rotterdam, 11.2.41
R1097	20 OTU	Lost power on attempted overshoot; bellylanded, Lossiemouth, 6.8.42
R1098	Stradishall/Wyton/ 15 OTU/108	Swung on take-off for Heraklion and undercarriage collapsed, LG.09, 20.3.42; DBR

R1099	93/SDF/18 OTU/	
	105 OTU	SOC 9.8.44
R1135	218	Missing (Emden) 16.11.41
R1136	214/27 OTU	DBR 29.8.41; NFD
R1137	311/SFP	Engine cut; bellylanded and hit hedge, Earls Barton, Northants., 19.12.40
R1138	18 OTU	Lost height and hit tree, Ullesthorpe, Leics., 23.10.41
R1139	OADF/15 OTU/38	Missing (Benghazi) 13.11.41
R1140	25 OTU/Exeter/	
	103/14 OTU	SOC 21.3.46
R1141	15 OTU	Engine cut; undershot approach, Harwell, 7.7.42
R1142	21 OTU	Stalled on overshoot and crashed 2m E of Edgehill, 21.5.42
R1143	25 OTU/15 OTU/	
	21 OTU	SOC 12.3.44
R1144	11 OTU/Cv XVI/	Branch from tree fell on
	18 MU	aircraft during gale, Lennox-love SLG, 17.11.44; not repaired
R1145	27 OTU	Crashed on landing in error on Bramcote decoy site, 9.8.41
R1146	21 OTU	Hit tree after night take-off, Edgehill, 4.10.41
R1147	-	To 2853M 4.41
R1148	11 OTU	Crashed near Spalding at night, Lincs., 25.7.41; cause not known
R1149	11 OTU	Stalled on approach in bad visibility, Bassingbourn, 15.11.41
R1150	-	To 3266M 7.42
R1151	25 OTU	Crashed on overshoot, Bircotes, 25.5.42; to 3239M
R1152	Hendon/221/21 OTU	Shot down in error near Verwood, Hants., 16.8.43
R1153	18 OTU/20 OTU	Missing, presumed ditched, 12.5.43
R1154	20 OTU/21 OTU	SOC 12.6.44
R1155	20 OTU	Dived into sea at night 4m N of Kingston, Moray, 25.3.41
R1156	3 FPP	Engine cut; stalled in circuit at Llandow and hit pole, Llysworney, Glam., 12.10.40
R1157	20 OTU/16 OTU/	
	28 OTU/105 OTU	SOC 25.6.44
R1158	18 OTU/27 OTU	Caught fire during refuelling, Lichfield, 22.5.42
R1159	149	Hit tree descending in mist and crashlanded on return from Cologne, Peaseland Green, Suffolk, 20.3.41
R1160	18 OTU/ATA/	
	105 OTU	SOC 15.9.44
R1161	75/311/105 OTU	SOC 22.6.44
R1162	75/27 OTU	Missing (Bremen) 26.6.42
R1163	15/75/103/	Missing presumed ditched,
	16 0TU/11 OTU	20.11.42
R1164	20 OTU	Flew into ground in cloud on ferry flight, Kirkbride - Lossiemouth, 3m ENE of Largs, Ayrshire, 25.1.41
R1165	18 OTU/21 OTU	SOC 14.7.48
R1166	40	Hit by flak and under-carriage jammed; overshot landing and hit hut on return from Berlin, Alconbury, 24.3.41
R1167	40	Missing (Hannover) 16.5.41
R1168	40/156/20 OTU	Flew into hill at night, Simsharnie, Morayshire, 2.4.42
R1169	15/20 OTU/28 OTU	SOC 29.1.44
R1170	20 OTU	Flew into sea in rainstorm 5m NW of Lossiemouth, 30.7.41
R1171	20 OTU	Engine cut; stalled on overshoot, Lossiemouth, 21.9.41
R1172	20 OTU/11 OTU/	
	Cv XVI/232	SOC 6.4.46
R1173	51 MU	Abandoned on ferry flight in bad weather over Alford, Lincs., 29.12.42
R1174	18 OTU/11 OTU	Dived into ground out of cloud, Morvil Mountain, Fishguard, Pembs., 29.12.42
R1175	9/15 OTU	SOC 7.2.44
R1176	99	Shot down in sea by flak, Kiel, 26.11.40
R1177	75	Engine cut; abandoned over Sible Hedingham, Suffolk, on return from Frankfurt, 29.9.41
R1178	300	Ditched 9m NE of Cromer on return from Hamburg, 26.7.41
R1179	115/15 OTU	Engine cut; crashed in forced landing ½m S of Chislehampton, Oxon., 13.4.42
R1180	38	Swung on landing and under-carriage collapsed, Luqa, 27.8.41; DBR
R1181	99/149	Lost height on take-off, Mildenhall; hit trees and cottage, Holmsey Green, Suffolk, 10.4.41
R1182	38/40	Ditched 15m N of Gozo on return from Elmas, 10.11.42
R1183	218/18 OTU/	Crashed on take-off,
	27 OTU/28 OTU	Castle Donington, 16.3.44
R1184	300	Missing (Cologne) 11.7.41
R1210	218	Abandoned short of fuel in bad visibility on return from Bremen over Tebay, West-moreland, 12.2.41
R1211	300/21 OTU	Hit trees at night 1m N of Edgehill, 21.11.42
R1212	304	Control lost on overshoot on return from night navex, Flintham Woods, near Syer-ston, 15.4.41
R1213	305/103	Struck by lightning during raid on Mannheim and crashed near Vlissingen, Neth., 29.8.41
R1214	305	Shot down by night fighter, Budel, Noord Brabant, on return from Emden, 3.5.41
R1215	304	Missing (Mannheim) 8.11.41
R1216	150/23 OTU/	Caught fire running up,
	27 OTU/28 OTU	Wymeswold, 22.5.43
R1217	103	Hit by flak; engine caught fire returning from Duisburg, 17.10.41; classed DBR after return
R1218	15	Abandoned out of fuel and crashed, Sand Hutton, Yorks., 25.4.41, on return from Kiel
R1219	115/101	Ditched off Blankerberge on return from Cologne, 11.10.41
R1220	Mkrs & AAEE	Blt as Mk.IV; retained as test aircraft and crashed on test flight, Addlestone, Surrey

R1221	115	Hit tree on approach descending in fog on return from Brest, East Winch, Norfolk, 23.2.41; DBF
R1222	15/115	Shot down by night fighter 2m NE of Weert, Neth. on return from Duisburg, 16.7.41; crashed at Neder-weert, Limburg
R1223	214/23 OTU/28 OTU	Crashed on overshoot, Wymeswold, 6.12.42
R1224	12 OTU/15 OTU/ 26 OTU/14 OTU/ 28 OTU	SOC 31.3.44
R1225	311/9/1505 Flt/ 20 OTU/11 OTU	SOC 5.3.44
R1226	214	Shot down by night fighter, Breezand, Neth., during raid on Hamburg, 9.5.41
R1227	301	Missing, presumed ditched, after raid on Bremen, 9.5.41
R1228	305/311/21 OTU	SOC 1.4.44
R1229	149	Bounced on landing, stalled and crashed on return from Emden, Mildenhall, 1.4.41
R1230	304	Shot down by night fighter near Kessel during raid on Essen, 11.4.42
R1231	221/3 OTU/1417 Flt/ 3 Gp TF/172/ATA	SOC 19.11.44
R1232	304/18 OTU/ 21 OTU/1443 Flt	Hit tree on overshoot, Moreton-in-Marsh, 31.8.42
R1233	12 OTU	Engine cut; lost height and crashlanded ½m E of Chipping Warden, 22.9.41
R1234	12 OTU/103	Lost prop; spun into ground after take-off en route to Cologne, Kirmington, 31.5.42
R1235	301/18 OTU/22 OTU	Missing (Cologne) 31.5.42
R1236	301/18 OTU/16 OTU/ 25 OTU/28 OTU/ 22 OTU/14 OTU	SOC 8.4.44
R1237	75/21 OTU	Hit trees on night approach, Moreton-in-Marsh, 25.9.41
R1238	115	Stalled on landing and hit obstruction on return from Bremen, Finningley, 12.2.41
R1239	214/40/20 OTU/ 11 OTU	SOC 12.4.45
R1240	15/40/57/40/ 1429 Flt/27 OTU/ 14 OTU	SOC 30.4.44
R1241	15 OTU/21 OTU/ 105 OTU	SOC 15.8.44
R1242	15 OTU/21 OTU	Crashed on overshoot, Moreton-in-Marsh, 5.5.43
R1243	15 OTU	Flew into sea in fog 1½m E of Criccieth Castle, Caernarvon, 26.3.41
R1244	9	Engine cut; crashed in forced landing at Misérieux, Ain, in Vichy France on return from Turin, 12.1.41 and interned
R1245	93/RAE/304/ 105 OTU	SOC 15.9.44
R1246	SF Stradishall	Missing on ferry flight to Middle East, 11.12.40
R1247	148	Destroyed in air raid, Luqa, 26.2.41
R1248	70	Sank back on take-off and hit ground, LG.16, 23.5.41
R1249	148	Engine caught fire; crash-landed at Kabrit, 21.9.41
R1250	ME	Missing on ferry flight, 11.12.40
R1251	148	Engine cut; lost height and bellylanded near Sollum, 6.4.41; destroyed by crew
R1252	18 OTU/15 OTU/ 11 OTU/17 OTU	To 3684M 8.42
R1253	1503 Flt	To 2829M 17.12.41
R1254	11 OTU/1 AAS	To 3657M 11.42
R1265	18 OTU/15 OTU	SOC 19.11.44
R1266	18 OTU/23 OTU	Missing (Essen) 2.6.42; crashed, Kerkdriel, Neth.
R1267	9	Overshot landing into bomb dump after losing hydraulics on return from Boulogne, Honington, 17.5.41
R1268	304	Engine cut on training flight; hit trees on hill in bad visibility, Edmondsley, Durham, 14.12.40
R1269	115/1429 Flt/ 22 OTU/26 OTU/ 28 OTU	Engine lost power on over-shoot; swung and crash-landed, Castle Donington, 24.2.44
R1270	20 OTU	To 3326M 8.42
R1271	57	Engine caught fire returning from Berlin; ditched off Lincolnshire coast, 21.9.41
R1272	20 OTU	Flew into hill on night navex 3m SE of Cabrach, Banff, 4.8.42
R1273	300	Swung on take-off for Berlin and hit hedge, Langham, 23.3.41; DBR
R1274	301/103/11 OTU/ 14 OTU	SOC 8.4.44
R1275	221/15 OTU	Missing from leaflet drop over Northern France, 14.10.41; crashed near Evreux
R1276	221/3 OTU/15 OTU	SOC 12.6.44
R1277	221/1 OTU/ 3 OTU/7 OTU	SOC 13.3.44
R1278	221/1 OTU/3 OTU	Hit ground on attempted overshoot, Skellingthorpe, 18.11.41
R1279	15/9	Missing after engine failure over Alps on return from Genoa, 29.9.41
R1280	15/115	Lost prop; engine cut in circuit; crashed ½m N of Oakington on return from Brest, 4.5.41
R1281	57/9	Missing (Emden) 27.4.41; crashed at Ommen, Neth.
R1282	12 OTU/26 OTU 28 OTU	Crashed on take-off, Harwell, 31.5.43
R1283	12 OTU/27 OTU	Engine cut; hit tree in forced landing 2m N of Chetwynd, 15.12.41
R1284	12 OTU/9/23 OTU	Flew into ground after night take-off, Pershore, 2.7.42
R1285	12 OTU	Engine cut; spun into ground, Watlington, Oxon., 28.2.41
R1286	9/15 OTU	Engine cut; flew into ground 6m NE of Pontrydfendaid, Aberystwyth, Cardigan, 13.6.41
R1287	9/18 OTU	Hit bowser on take-off, Bramcote, 25.3.42
R1288	9	Ran out of fuel and ditched off Spurn Head on return from Cologne, 2.3.41
R1289	RAE/OADF/70	SOC 23.12.44
R1290	RAE/37	Collided with wreck of Well-ington N2855 on take-off, Fuka, 3.5.41; DBF

Serial	Units	Fate
R1291	15 OTU	Hit hedge in forced landing when lost in bad weather near Bletchley, Bucks., 5.1.41
R1292	11 OTU	Engine cut; stalled and crashed in forced landing, West Wendy, Cambs., 21.6.41
R1293	99/22 OTU/21 OTU	Engine cut on take-off; crashlanded, Enstone, 15.11.43
R1294	149	Lost wing fabric on air test; stalled off turn on approach and crashed, Mildenhall, 16.12.40
R1295	12 OTU/22 OTU/ 14 OTU	SOC 7.8.44
R1296	11 OTU	SOC 30.6.44
R1297	11 OTU/21 OTU/ 29 OTU/16 OTU	Hit by flak and abandoned, Düsseldorf, 11.9.42
R1298	18 OTU	Hit balloon cable on navex and crashed near Middlewich, Cheshire, 4.2.41
R1299	18 OTU/15 OTU/ 11 OTU	Control lost on approach 2m SW of Cranfield, 29.5.41
R1320	18 OTU	Destroyed in air raid, Bramcote, 13.3.41
R1321	214/3 Gp TF	Crashed on take-off, Langham, 30.6.41
R1322	305/TFU/305	Shot down by night fighter in Ijsselmeer 8m SW of Lemmer during raid on Bremen, 9.5.41
R1323	40	Shot down by flak off Hellevoetsluis, Neth., en route to Düsseldorf, 12.6.41
R1324	12 OTU/28 OTU	Missing on ASR search; presumed ditched in North Sea, 13.6.43
R1325	15 OTU/12 OTU/ 27 OTU/20 OTU/ 15 OTU	Crashed in circuit, Hampstead Norris, 23.9.43
R1326	218	Shot down by Bf 110 2m SW of Medemblik, Neth. on return from Bremen, 13.3.41
R1327	300/18 OTU/ 11 OTU/18 OTU/ 15 OTU	SOC 12.3.44
R1328	12 OTU/218/ 214/40	Engine cut on return from Frankfurt, 13.9.41; presumed ditched in North Sea
R1329	12 OTU/18 OTU/ 23 OTU/21 OTU	Crashed in forced landing, Wattisham, Suffolk, 9.3.42; DBR
R1330	40	Missing (Hamburg) 12.5.41
R1331	40	Flew into hillside near Combe Martin, North Devon, on return from Berlin, 18.4.41
R1332	12 OTU/99/115	Engine caught fire on return from Emden, 27.9.41; presumed ditched off Friesians
R1333	99	Hit Devil's Dyke on take-off en route for Mannheim, Newmarket, 18.12.40
R1334	15 OTU/11 OTU	Collided with Ju 88C over Ashwell, Cambs., 22.7.41
R1335	12 OTU/9	Damaged by night fighter and crashed 8m NNW of Hasselt on return from Cologne, 28.3.41
R1336	11 OTU	Swung on take-off and undercarriage collapsed, Steeple Morden, 21.6.42; DBR
R1337	11 OTU	Missing, presumed ditched, on navex, 18.8.41
R1338	40/101/25 OTU/ 14 OTU/105 OTU	To 3681M 27.4.43
R1339	149/218	Ditched in North Sea on return from Kiel, 21.6.41
R1340	12 OTU	Swung on take-off, swung and hit tree, Chipping Warden, 17.1.42
R1341	9	Shot down 15m NE of Verden during raid on Hannover, 13.8.41
R1342	214/23 OTU	Control column jammed; wing hit ground on overshoot, Pershore, 15.3.42
R1343	149	Missing (Brest) 2.7.41
R1344	300/103/21 OTU	Caught fire in air and crashed, Compton Wyngates, Warks., 20.12.42
R1345	12 OTU/21 OTU	Missing on night navex, 18.8.42
R1346	218/16 OTU	Both engines cut; ditched 3m off Holland-on-Sea, Essex, on return from Düsseldorf, 10.9.42
R1347	300/103/21 OTU	SOC 27.3.44
R1348	301	Overshot landing and hit X3163 on return from Osnabrück, Swinderby, 13.6.41
R1349	301/12 OTU	Missing (Bremen) 26.6.42; presumed ditched on return
R1365	301	Shot down by night fighter off Terschelling on return from Bremen, 19.6.41
R1366	301/27 OTU	Lost power on landing and hit hangar; crashed on attempted overshoot, Lichfield, 19.7.41
R1367	20 OTU	Stalled in circuit at night and crashed 1½m SE of Lossiemouth, 14.2.41
R1368	218	Abandoned out of fuel on return from Brest 2m W of King's Lynn, Norfolk, 23.4.41
R1369	57	Ditched off Friesians on return from Kiel, 25.7.41
R1370	93/RAE/93 16 OTU/105 OTU	Swung on take-off after tyre burst; engine caught fire, Bramcote, 29.5.44
R1371	311	Missing (Hannover) 20.7.41; crashed in Waddenzee
R1372	99	Missing (Bremen) 26.6.41
R1373	301	Missing (Bremen) 30.6.41
R1374	150	Shot down by flak near Nantes during raid on St.Nazaire, 8.5.41
R1375	150/25 OTU	Undershot landing and undercarriage collapsed, Bircotes, 12.6.42
R1376	214/18 OTU/ 11 OTU	SOC 5.3.44
R1377	20 OTU	Overshot and crashlanded in bad visibility, Lossiemouth, 28.5.42
R1378	311	Engine cut; bellylanded at East Wretham, 18.3.41 on return from Bremen
R1379	115	Shot down by night fighter near Tonning, Germany, on return from Kiel, 10.5.41
R1380	214	Shot down by night fighter, Kiel, 8.4.41
R1381	148	Destroyed in air raid, Luqa, 26.2.41
R1382	148	Destroyed in air raid, Luqa, 26.2.41
R1383	148	Destroyed in air raid, Luqa, 26.2.41

R1384	148	Destroyed in air raid, Luqa, 26.2.41
R1385	ME	SOC 13.2.41; believed DBR in air raid on ferry flight
R1386	148	Engine jammed on full throttle; overshot night landing into depression, Luqa, 5.2.41
R1387	148/37	Shot down by CR.42s, Tirana, 16.3.41
R1388	OADF	SOC 1.4.41 at RAF Newton
R1389	27 OTU/25 OTU/ 30 OTU/16 OTU	Missing 9.10.42
R1390	301	Blt as Mk.IV. Missing (Emden) 7.6.42; crashed off Borkum
R1391	149/15 OTU	Engine cut; overshot landing, and undercarriage collapsed, Hampstead Norris, 8.12.41
R1392	304	Hit by flak, Boulogne, and crashed 1½m S of Brightling, Sussex, 28.5.41
R1393	103	Hit by flak and ditched 5m off Orfordness, Suffolk, returning from Essen, 26.3.42
R1394	150	Missing (Hannover) 15.8.41
R1395	103	Missing (Hamburg) 16.1.42
R1396	103	Missing (Turin) 11.9.41
R1397	103	Missing (Brest) 25.7.41
R1398	20 OTU/14 OTU	SOC 14.5.44
R1399	20 OTU/11 OTU	SOC 5.3.44
R1400	218/22 OTU/ 105 OTU	SOC 31.8.44
R1401	218/27 OTU/12 OTU/ 23 OTU/14 OTU	Crashed on landing, Cottesmore, 1.10.42; DBR
R1402	214/20 OTU/12 OTU	To 3390M 28.9.42
R1403	214/15 OTU/ 27 OTU/6 OTU	Crashed in forced landing, Eaglescliffe, Co.Durham, 20.11.42
R1404	11 OTU	Destroyed when N2912 was shot down and fell on R1404, Bassingbourn, 24.4.41
R1405	15 OTU/11 OTU	Stalled on night approach and hit ground ½m W of Bassingbourn, 3.6.41
R1406	40	Missing (Cologne) 27.6.41; found crashed 4m NW of Eeklo, Belgium
R1407	99/11 OTU	Bellylanded in error at night, Steeple Morden, 17.8.42
R1408	149	Missing (Brest) 2.7.41; crashed at Plouzane, Finistère
R1409	305/15 OTU/75/ 1505 Flt/21 OTU/ Cv XVI/303 FTU/ 1 OADU/FE	SOC 14.6.45
R1410	311/12 OTU	Crashed off Friesians on return from Bremen, 26.6.42
R1411	99	Shot down by Ju 88 on approach to Mildenhall and crashed, Beck Row, Suffolk, 1.9.41 on return from Cologne
R1412	150/21 OTU/ 6 OTU/103 OTU	SOC 1.6.44
R1413	304	Missing, presumed ditched, on anti-submarine patrol, 16.10.42
R1414	150/23 OTU	Bellylanded in error at Pershore, 12.7.42; DBF
R1435	150	Shot down by night fighter near Westhever, Neth., on return from Hamburg, 11.5.41
R1436	15/218/20 OTU/ 14 OTU	SOC 12.3.44
R1437	57	Missing (Vegesack) 10.4.41; crashed near Bremen
R1438	40	Stalled in cloud in circuit, Alconbury, 3.6.41 on return from Düsseldorf
R1439	149	Shot down by flak, Kiel, 16.4.41
R1440	99	Shot down by night fighter in Ijsselmeer off Urk on return from Vegesack, 10.4.41
R1441	311/57	Hit trees on approach in bad visibility, East Wretham, 28.3.41 on return from Cologne
R1442	218	Missing (Brest) 11.4.41; presumed ditched
R1443	304	Shot down by flak in Channel during raid on Le Havre, 7.5.41
R1444	150/26 OTU/21 OTU/ 15 OTU/21 OTU	SOC 23.3.44
R1445	103/11 OTU	Engine cut on take-off; stalled and hit houses in Ashwell, Steeple Morden, 28.6.42
R1446	103/23 OTU/ 15 OTU/21 OTU	SOC 12.3.44
R1447	214	Crashlanded, Bergen-op-Zoom, on return from Mannheim, 10.5.41
R1448	218/20 OTU	Engine cut; caught fire in air and wing detached, Elgin, 6.8.42
R1449	149/20 OTU	Engine cut on take-off; stalled and hit ground, Lossiemouth, 22.2.42
R1450	109/26 OTU/ 16 OTU/25 OTU	Shot down by night fighter over Schleswig during raid on Hamburg, 29.7.42
R1451	311/18 OTU/ 11 OTU	Crashed at Watlington, Oxon., 2.9.43; NFD
R1452	103	Overshot landing and hit obstruction, Newton, 21.3.41, on return from Lorient
R1453	5 BATF/26 OTU/ 16 OTU/28 OTU	SOC 25.4.44
R1454	25 OTU	Swung on landing and skidded into trees, Finningley, 11.6.42
R1455	9	Missing (Kiel) 20.8.41; crashed in sea 1m S of Hojer Sluse, Denmark
R1456	40/1503 Flt/16 OTU/ 26 OTU/11 OTU	SOC 20.6.44
R1457	75/40/156/22 OTU/ 105 OTU	SOC 17.6.44
R1458	28 OTU/1 AAS	SOC 24.6.44
R1459	301/103/29 OTU	Lost height after take-off from North Luffenham for Bremen and crashlanded 6m E of Oakham, Rutland, 13.9.42
R1460	109/27 OTU	Bounced on landing, swung off runway, hit trench and undercarriage collapsed, Lichfield, 11.9.41
R1461	40	Crashed in sea during raid on Hamburg, 12.5.41; believed shot down by night fighter
R1462	57/214	Crashed near Hamburg during raid, 12.5.41; NFD
R1463	150	Flew into hill descending in cloud on return from intruder mission 4m NE of Beverley, Yorks., 22.2.42
R1464	15/40	Shot down by night fighter, Meerloo, 10m NNW of Venlo en route to Düsseldorf, 12.6.41

R1465	214/22 OTU	Flew into high ground in cloud on night navex 4m S of Tal-y-Bont, Brecknock, 6.7.42
R1466	311/75/15 OTU	Flew into ground at night, Moss Hill, Berks., 29.11.42
R1467	103/20 OTU	Caught fire starting up, Elgin, 7.7.42; DBR
R1468	115	Flew into ground on approach in heavy rain, West Raynham, 28.8.41, on return from Mannheim; DBF
R1469	149/115/150/7 OTU	SOC 5.10.43
R1470	115	Shot down in The Wash by Ju 88 on return from Brest, and crashed on mudflats off Terrington St. Clement, Norfolk, 4.4.41
R1471	115	Missing (Mannheim) 6.8.41
R1472	99/22 OTU	Overshot landing and hit hedge, Wellesbourne Mountford, 27.3.42
R1473	304	Hit by flak during raid on Bremen and crashed, Plantlünne, 9.5.41
R1474	115/149	Shot down by Ju 88, Beck Row, Mildenhall, on return from Bremen, 18.3.41
——		
R1490	458/301/142/ 18 OTU/301/305/ 104 OTU/14 PAFU	Blt as Mk.IV To 4745M 28.3.44
R1491	150/15 OTU	Caught fire in air and crashed, Llanfilin, Denbigh, 25.1.43
R1492	301	Shot down by night fighter 11m NNE of Emmen, Neth, on return from Bremen, 4.7.41
R1493	40	Ran out of fuel and ditched in English Channel returning from Bordeaux/Mérignac, 11.4.41
R1494	103	Engine cut; believed ditched 50m off Cromer on return from Hannover, 16.5.41, but may be aircraft crashed 5m E of Veendam, Neth.
R1495	150	Missing (Hamburg) 17.7.41
R1496	218	SOC 19.11.44
R1497	218/311	To 4261M 29.10.43
R1498	15/1504 Flt/ 22 OTU	To 3357M 9.9.42 at 81 OTU
R1499	9	Crashlanded in belief that fuel had run out, Honington, 8.9.41 on return from Berlin
R1500	115	Missing (Hannover) 15.8.41; ditched in North Sea
R1501	115	Sank back on take-off for Cologne and skidded on belly, Marham, 27.6.41; DBF
R1502	115	Damaged by night fighter on return from Bremen and abandoned 3m S of Medemblik 14.7.41
R1503	99	Flew into trees on take-off 1½m ENE of Waterbeach, 12.8.41, en route for Boulogne
R1504	25 OTU/304/7 OTU	Both engines cut due to fuel being cut off in error; ditched 2m N of Downhill, Co.Derry, 30.10.41
R1505	115/101/214/ 22 OTU	Lost prop and abandoned at night near Cranwell, 10.8.42
R1506	149	Shot down by night fighter off Heligoland on return from Hamburg, 9.5.41
R1507	218	Missing, presumed ditched, returning from Kiel, 26.4.41
R1508	57/20 OTU/ 27 OTU/21 OTU	Engine caught fire; abandoned near Beaconsfield, Bucks., 7.8.43
R1509	115	Damaged by flak and night fighter, Hamburg, and abandoned near Bremervorde, 30.6.41
R1510	300	Blt as Mk.IV. Engine cut in circuit; crashlanded 1m E of Kirton-in-Lindsey, 24.9.41
R1511	218	Missing (Bordeaux) 11.10.41
R1512	149	Missing (Hamburg) 11.5.41
R1513	9	Missing (Kiel) 13.8.41; crashed in River Weser
R1514	149/16 OTU/ 28 OTU	SOC 5.7.44
R1515	AAEE/104 OTU	Blt as Mk.IV. Crashed on take-off, Mullaghmore, 20.12.43
R1516	311	Shot down in error by night fighter near Mere, Somerset, 2.7.41, returning from Cherbourg
R1517	115	Engine cut after take-off from Marham on air test; crashlanded at Palgrave Farm, Sporle, Norfolk, 17.6.41; DBF
R1518	75	Ran out of fuel on return from Berlin; abandoned 3m SSW of North Walsham, Norfolk, 21.9.41
R1519	99	Ditched 30m off Portland on return from Brest, 4.1.42
R1520	301/305/301/ 305/104 OTU	Blt as Mk.IV. Flew into hill in cloud 2m S of Dundrod, Co.Antrim, 31.12.43
R1521	25 OTU/30 OTU/ 28 OTU/Cv XVI/ 242	SOC 30.4.46
R1522	22 OTU/14 OTU	Crashed on take-off, Cottesmore, 6.12.42
R1523	3 PRU/311/ 20 OTU/21 OTU	SOC 21.3.46
R1524	149	Missing (Mannheim) 6.8.41; crashed at St. Martens-Voeren, Liège.
R1525	301/305/104 OTU	Blt as Mk.IV; to 4592M 3.44
R1526	10 BATF/3 OTU/ 27 OTU	Missing (Düsseldorf) 1.8.42
R1527	1504 Flt/22 OTU	SOC 6.4.43
R1528	3 BATF/1503 Flt/ 20 OTU/15 OTU	SOC 12.2.44
R1529	9 BATF/3 OTU/ 1508 Flt/3 OTU/ 105 OTU	SOC 17.6.44
R1530	ATA/460/305/ 104 OTU	Blt as Mk.IV; SOC 8.3.44
R1531	1504 Flt/27 OTU/ 303 FTU/7 OTU/ Cv XVI/303 FTU/ FE	NFT 6.7.44 on arrival
R1532	311/27 OTU/28 OTU	SOC 11.12.43
R1533	20 OTU/7 OTU	Swung on night landing, hit flares and caught fire, Limavady, 31.8.42
R1534	109/21 OTU	Caught fire in air and abandoned, Upper Talwedd, Radnor, 20.12.42
R1535	301	Blt as Mk.IV. Damaged by night fighter and crashed on return from minelaying, Dunmoor Hill, near Wooler, Northumberland, 9.1.43

R1536	218	Shot down by night fighter 6m NW of Roermond en route to Duisburg, 16.7.41
R1537	99	Shot down by flak, Cologne, 20.6.41
R1538	103/18 OTU/ 27 OTU/28 OTU	Flew into ground in bad visibility near Stoke-on-Trent, Staffs., 30.1.43
R1539	103	Ran out of fuel and crashed in forced landing in fog, Holbeach, Lincs., on return from Frankfurt, 21.9.41
R1585	301	Blt as Mk.IV. Hit by flak while minelaying and crashed 7m NNE of Rodekro, Denmark, 12.10.42
R1586	22 OTU	Engine cut; stalled in circuit and crashed at Loxley, near Wellesbourne Mountford, 26.6.41
R1587	149	Collided with Hurricane V7225 4m NW of Ely, Cambs., 17.5.41
R1588	103/156/22 OTU	Missing (Bremen) 14.9.42; presumed ditched on return
R1589	75/57	Flew into ground in bad weather, Larman's Fen, Southery, near Feltwell on return from Essen, 4.7.41
R1590	301	Blt as Mk.IV. Shot down by night fighter off Ijmuiden during raid on Essen, 27.3.42
R1591	9/3 Gp TF/ 1483 Flt/15 OTU/ 21 OTU	SOC 20.3.44
R1592	305/301/150/57/ 22 OTU/11 OTU/ 14 OTU	SOC 6.7.44
R1593	149/1483 Flt/ 15 OTU/21 OTU	SOC 28.3.45
R1594	218/311	DBR by fire, Marham 27.6.41; cause unknown; possibly air raid
R1595	15 OTU/16 OTU	To 3080M 5.42
R1596	15/218	SOC 1.7.44
R1597	218/23 OTU	Flew into cu-nim cloud and crashed on fire near Llangammarch Wells, Brecon, 8.4.42
R1598	311/3 OTU	Crashed on overshoot, Cranwell, 23.1.43
R1599	311	Shot down by night fighter, Baexem, 5m ESE of Weert, Neth. during raid on Berlin, 18.4.41
R1600	17 OTU/11 OTU/ 311/Cv XVI/232	SOC 30.4.46
R1601	218/1505 Flt/ 16 OTU/21 OTU	Crashed on landing, Honiley, 3.3.43
R1602	304	Hit by another aircraft after landing, Oakington, on return from Essen, 10.3.42
R1603	22 OTU/14 OTU	Crashed in forced landing, Harlaxton, 17.12.42
R1604	214	Missing (Mannheim) 30.8.41; crashed near Vlissingen, possibly due to lightning strike (see also R1213)
R1605	57/1503 Flt/16 OTU/ 21 OTU/15 OTU/ 28 OTU/Cv XVI	SOC 27.12.45
R1606	150	Missing (Mannheim) 8.11.41; presumed ditched off Dutch coast
R1607	15 OTU	Flew into hill at night, Hampstead Norris, 15.12.41
R1608	57	Missing (Kiel) 25.6.41; believed crashed in Kiel Fjord
R1609	214	Missing (Emden) 25.6.41
R1610	300	Blt as Mk.IV. Engines lost power on take-off for training flight; crashlanded, Hemswell, 7.5.42
R1611	214	Hit trees low flying and hit dyke in attempted forced landing, Manea Station, Cambs., 4.6.41
R1612	15 OTU/1 AAS	SOC 1.11.44
R1613	214	Shot down by night fighter, Brookstreek, near Quackenbrück on return from Bremen, 15.7.41
R1614	214	Missing (Bremen) 15.7.41; presumed ditched on return flight
R1615	301	Shot down by flak near Turnhout, Belgium, en route to Essen, 2.6.42
R1616	301/27 OTU/22 OTU	Shot down by night fighter, Biervliet, Neth., on return from Düsseldorf, 11.9.42
R1617	300/103	Shot down by intruder on return from Bremen near Elsham Wolds, 3.7.42
R1618	23 OTU	Engine cut on take-off; swung off runway and stalled, Defford, 27.4.42
R1619	301	Damaged in heavy landing and caught fire, Swinderby, 26.4.41
R1620	300/104 OTU	Blt as Mk.IV; to 4583M 26.2.44
R1621	214/22 OTU/ 26 OTU/14 OTU	SOC 29.4.44
R1622	20 OTU	Grazed hangar on take-off and crashed in sea, Lossiemouth, 23.8.41
R1623	214/7 OTU	SOC 17.3.44
R1624	57	Missing (Duisburg) 16.7.41; crashed near Hamont, Belgium
R1625	Rotol/AAEE	Blt as Mk.IV; SOC 17.3.44
R1626	23 OTU/105 OTU	SOC 1.7.44
R1627	149	Missing (Emden) 16.11.41
R1628	AAEE/RAE/26 OTU	Crashed in forced landing 1½m E of Buckingham, 9.4.43
R1629	149/RAE/TFU/ 105 OTU	Hit by R1412 landing at Bramcote, 24.9.43
R1640	300	Engine cut; ditched 40m E of Grimsby on return from Bremen, 30.6.41
R1641	300	Undercarriage raised prematurely; sank back, caught fire and blew up, Hemswell, 18.8.41, en route to Duisburg
R1642	300	Missing (Bremen) 4.7.41
R1643	40/99/11 OTU	SOC 5.11.44
R1644	150	Shot down by flak 4m NNW of Venlo on return from Düsseldorf, 27.6.41
R1645	27 OTU/30 OTU/ 28 OTU	SOC 25.4.44
R1646	20 OTU	Flew into mountain near Braemar, Aberdeenshire, 19.1.42
R1647	40/27 OTU/ 15 OTU	SOC 12.3.44
R1648	75	Ditched in North Sea on return from Mannheim, 7.8.41
R1649	1505 Flt/21 OTU/ Cv XVI/242	SOC 6.5.46

Above: Lancaster R5609 OF-S of No.97 Squadron at Boscombe Down for trials

Below: The reason was these large A.S.V. aerials

101

Above: Beaufighter R2274 was converted to a Mk.V by the addition of a Boulton Paul four-gun turret

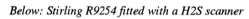

Below: Stirling R9254 fitted with a H2S scanner

R1650	301/460	Blt as Mk.IV; to 3667M 21.4.43
R1651	23 OTU/28 OTU	SOC 12.4.44
R1652	9 BATF/3 OTU/ 105 OTU	SOC 15.9.44
R1653	20 OTU/105 OTU	SOC 24.7.44
R1654	22 OTU	Control lost in cloud; dived into ground 1m W of Cornwell, Oxon., 14.10.41
R1655	DH/RAE/TFU/ 460/142/18 OTU/ 104 OTU	Blt as Mk.IV SOC 7.2.44
R1656	15 OTU/16 OTU	To 3081M 5.42 at 16 OTU
R1657	12 OTU/23 OTU/304	To 3465M 20.12.42
R1658	12 OTU/22 OTU	Missing (Bremen) 14.9.42
R1659	15 OTU/22 OTU/ 3 OTU/303 FTU/ 1 OADU/1331 CU	SOC 11.6.45
R1660	304/15 OTU	To 4195M 5.10.43
R1661	11 OTU	Undershot landing at night, Waddington, 25.4.42
R1662	23 OTU	Both engines cut; hit tree in forced landing 3m N of Bawtry, Notts., 27.6.41
R1663	23 OTU/21 OTU/ 105 OTU	To 4415M 12.43
R1664	20 OTU	Engine cut; crashed in forced landing 1m W of Kingston, Moray, 18.6.41
R1665	20 OTU	Flew into hill at night after take-off 1½m SW of Elgin, 25.8.41
R1666	10 BATF/3 OTU/ 27 OTU/28 OTU	SOC 25.4.44
R1667	305/301/103 21 OTU	Crashed at Park Drain, Yorks., 15.10.42; NFD
R1668	20 OTU/21 OTU/ 23 OTU	SOC 10.8.44
R1669	20 OTU/14 OTU	Swung and dived into ground on approach, Husbands Bosworth, 27.3.44; DBF
R1695	458/460	Blt as Mk.IV. Engines lost power; ditched 13m N of Cromer, Norfolk, on return from Düsseldorf, 11.9.42
R1696	305	Shot down by night fighter 4m WSW of Einkuisen, Neth. en route to Bremen, 19.6.41
R1697	305/304/ 30 OTU/28 OTU	SOC 31.3.46
R1698	105/21 OTU	SOC 1.6.44
R1699	105/101	Missing (Turin) 11.9.41; believed crashed near Epernay
R1700	101/18 OTU/ 27 OTU/28 OTU/ Cv XVI/232	SOC 26.4.46
R1701	101	Missing (Berlin) 8.11.41; presumed ditched off Dutch coast
R1702	101	Shot down by Bf 109, Brest, 24.7.41
R1703	101	Missing (Cologne) 31.8.41; crashed at Genk, Belgium
R1704	304	Dived into sea, St.Brides Bay, Pembs., 15.10.42
R1705	300	Blt as Mk.IV. Missing (Mannheim) 8.11.41
R1706	57	Run into by another aircraft, Marham, 21.9.41, after returning from Frankfurt
R1707	11 OTU/9/57/ 40/156/20 OTU	Crashed on night navex near Morpeth, Northumberland, 2.6.43
R1708	25 OTU	Shot down by intruder, Misson, Yorks., 13.6.41

R1709	25 OTU/23 OTU/ 14 OTU	SOC 4.5.44
R1710	22 OTU/26 OTU/ 16 OTU/11 OTU/ Cv XVI/232	SOC 6.5.46
R1711	22 OTU/28 OTU/ Cv XVI	SOC 27.11.45
R1712	RAE/214	Hit by flak over Münster en route to Berlin and crash-landed at Manston, 21.9.41
R1713	115/218	Missing (Kiel) 21.6.41; presumed ditched
R1714	22 OTU	Missing (Cologne) 31.5.42
R1715	300/104 OTU	Blt as Mk.IV; SOC 1.4.44
R1716	150/304	Missing from anti-sub patrol, 1.11.42
R1717	214	Ditched off Dunkerque on return from Frankfurt, 3.9.41
R1718	311	Shot down by night fighter in Ijsselmeer off Takozijl on return from Hamburg, 17.7.41
R1719	11 OTU/218/ 22 OTU	Abandoned after engine cut 1m S of Yattendon, Berks., 13.3.42
R1720	11 OTU/12 OTU/ 14 OTU/Cv XVI/242	SOC 6.5.46
R1721	22 OTU/115	Engine cut; second lost power in circuit; hit tree and crashed, Marham, 13.6.41 on return from Hamm
R1722	11 OTU/9/57	Engine cut due to shortage of fuel; hit tree in forced landing 2m S of Berners Heath, Suffolk, 27.10.41 on return from Hamburg
R1723	11 OTU	Flaps jammed up; overshot landing at Steeple Morden, 14.6.41
R1724	27 OTU/WTU/ ASRTU	SOC 5.3.44
R1725	300	Blt as Mk.IV Missing (Essen) 9.6.42
R1726	218	Missing (Brest) 24.7.41; crashed in sea off Brest peninsula
R1727	22 OTU/26 OTU/ 28 OTU	SOC 12.4.44
R1728	11 OTU	Missing over North Sea, possibly due to enemy aircraft, 18.6.41
R1729	11 OTU	Crashed on take-off, Oakley, 25.5.43
R1757	9/57	Missing (Nürnberg) 12.10.41; crashed near Blenkenham, Neth.
R1758	9	Shot down by Bf 109s off Zeebrugge during shipping reconnaissance off French and Belgian coast, 9.6.41
R1759	214	Missing (Hamburg) 16.1.42; presumed ditched in North Sea
R1760	103/20 OTU	Engine cut; lost height and ditched 1m off Cruden Bay, Aberdeenshire, 1.4.42
R1761	304	Engine cut on approach from navex; overshot to avoid workmen and hit trees, Madley, 19.8.41
R1762	103/305	Missing (Osnabrück) 10.7.41
R1763	9/57/18 OTU/ 105 OTU	SOC 1.7.44
R1764	9/15 OTU	Tyre burst on take-off; swung and undercarriage collapsed, Hampstead Norris, 18.11.41

R1765	458	Blt as Mk.IV. Hit by flak; ran out of fuel; abandoned and crashed at Tunnel Hill, near Aldershot, Hants., on return from Le Havre, 23.10.41
R1766	25 OTU/18 OTU/ 23 OTU/30 OTU/ 28 OTU	SOC 31.3.44
R1767	25 OTU	Dived into ground at night 1m NE of Chatteris, Cambs., 10.9.41
R1768	25 OTU/26 OTU/ 11 OTU	SOC 1.7.44
R1769	11 OTU/15 OTU	Engine cut; stalled on overshoot and hit building, Mount Farm, 9.12.41
R1770	40	Missing (Osnabrück) 10.7.41
R1771	75/311/1429 Flt/ 311/1429 Flt/ 6 OTU/3 OTU	SOC 28.1.44
R1772	115	Missing (Kiel) 8.9.41
R1773	22 OTU	Engine cut; lost height and hit tree ½m S of Great Coxwell, Berks., 8.4.42
R1774	25 OTU/28 OTU/ 22 OTU/1443 Flt/ 28 OTU	SOC 30.3.44
R1775	458	Blt as Mk.IV Missing (Emden) 16.11.41
R1776	22 OTU/20 OTU/ 11 OTU/16 OTU	To 3972M 21.7.43
R1777	311/21 OTU	Crashed on landing, Chipping Norton, 8.11.42
R1778	101	Ditched 40m WSW of Esbjerg returning from Hamburg, 30.11.41
R1779	17 OTU/18 OTU/ 21 OTU/29 OTU/ 20 OTU	Crashed in forced landing, Binn Hill, Garmouth, Moray, 4.4.43
R1780	101/11 OTU	Caught fire on ground, Westcott, 29.6.43
R1781	101/12 OTU/ 28 OTU/105 OTU	SOC 9.7.44
R1782	22 OTU	Sank back on take-off and hit ground, Stratford, 30.6.42; DBF
R1783	15 OTU	Missing from leaflet drop over Northern France, 15.10.41; crashed at Barville, Eure
R1784	RAE/214	Missing (Berlin) 8.9.41
R1785	458	Blt as Mk.IV; hit by flak and crashed during raid on Cherbourg, 9.1.42
R1786	15 OTU/25 OTU/ 28 OTU	Crashed on overshoot, Wymeswold, 28.11.42
R1787	15 OTU/14 OTU	SOC 7.2.44
R1788	20 OTU/11 OTU	SOC 20.3.44
R1789	214	Missing (Hanau) 2.4.42; crashed 6m WNW of Ludwigshafen
R1790	20 OTU/11 OTU	Hit trees after take-off and crashed, Wootton Underwood, Bucks., 27.10.43
R1791	15 OTU	Shot down by night fighter near Charleroi on return from Cologne, 31.5.42
R1792	75/57	Flew into ground after take-off, Feltwell, 13.9.41 en route to Brest
R1793	15 OTU/40/ 1503 Flt	SOC 19.11.44
R1794	57	Missing (Bremen) 28.6.41
R1795	458/300/104 OTU	Blt as Mk.IV. Swung on landing and undercarriage collapsed, Nutts Corner, 18.1.44
R1796	301/17 OTU/301/ 18 OTU/20 OTU/ 14 OTU	SOC 6.7.44
R1797	17 OTU/12 OTU/ 109/1474 Flt/ 14 OTU	SS 21.3.46
R1798	115	Shot down by night fighter 2m NE of Drachter, Neth. on return from Berlin, 8.9.41
R1799	57/1503 Flt/ 1483 Flt/15 OTU	Crashed on overshoot, Yeovilton, 23.1.43
R1800	101	Shot down by night fighter in Ijsselmeer on return from Hamburg, 3.8.41
R1801	101/419/12 OTU/ 28 OTU	Crashed at Woodhouse Eaves, Leics., 7.10.42
R1802	149/311	Ditched en route to Kiel 80m ENE of Cromer, Norfolk, 13.3.42
R1803	23 OTU	Engine cut; flew into hill while overshooting Pershore, 25.1.42
R1804	311	Swung on take-off for air test and hit steamroller, East Wretham, 19.7.41
R1805	115	Both engines cut in circuit, Marham, on return from Hamburg, 30.6.41
R1806	27 OTU	DBF in accident, 10.8.41; NFD

* * * * * * * * * *

Two Supermarine 322 prototypes under Contract No.B976687/39 to Specification S.24/37
Numbers duplicated two below

R1810	Mkrs	Both retained
R1815	Mkrs	by makers

* * * * * * * * * *

145 Miles Magister Is delivered by Philips & Powis, Woodley, between September 1939 and January 1940 to Contract No.778435/38

R1810	79/Croydon/152/ 2 Del Flt	Sold 20.5.46
R1811	SF Northolt/145/2 FIS	Engine cut; crashlanded on hill, Carnbeg, Kincardine, 15.5.42; DBF
R1812	SF Northolt	Stalled and spun into ground, Polehill Farm, Hillingdon, Middx., 12.5.40
R1813	24 EFTS	Stalled at low altitude and wing hit ground, Streatley, Beds., 10.2.41
R1814	24 EFTS/21 EFTS	SOC 25.2.44
R1815	236/612/SF Sumburgh/ ATA	Sold 12.6.46; became LV-XPZ
R1816	236	Spun into ground off stall turn, Clopton, Suffolk, 13.12.39
R1817	266/10 OTU/22 OTU	Flew originally as U-0258. Engine cut; undercarriage collapsed in forced landing in ploughed field, Henley-in-Arden, Warks., 30.3.42
R1818	24 EFTS/RAE	Stalled on landing and hit ground, Farnborough, 17.9.46; DBR
R1819	Waddington/409/ 148 Wg/409	Sold 26.2.48; became G-AKMR
R1820	24 EFTS	Hit HT cables low flying near Shillington, Beds., 24.5.41
R1821	39 MU/Colerne CF	Sold 23.5.47

Serial	Units	Fate
R1822	SF Northolt/Bally-halbert/133/134/3 Del Flt	Dived into ground during roll, Burgess Farm, near High Ercall, 26.5.42
R1823	ATA	To 4514M 1.2.44
R1824	242/219/264/16 EFTS/11 FTS/5 FIS/16 PFTS/11 EFTS	Sold 16.2.49; became G-ALIP
R1825	87/151	Sold 23.4.46; became G-AITN
R1826	39 MU CF/5 EFTS/16 EFTS/ECFS	Sold to Eire as 126, 27.5.46
R1827	242/222	Hit tree low flying, Ashwell, Berks., 17.2.40
R1828	242/219/600/ATA	Sold 27.5.46 to Argentina
R1829	235/SF St.Eval	Damaged in air raid, St.Eval, 17.5.41; SOC 31.5.41
R1830	235/6 CPF/SF St.Eval	Spun into sea during aerobatics off Mawgan Porth, Cornwall, 2.6.40
R1831	253/15 EFTS/29 EFTS	Sold 29.5.46; became G-AHKP
R1832	248/SF Dyce/248	Hit ground during low aerobatics, Sumburgh, 28.8.40
R1833	235/2 FIS/9 PAFU/ECFS	SOC 14.11.44
R1834	253/614/15 EFTS/21 EFTS/FTC CF	Sold to Eire 7.11.44 as 138
R1835	248/16 Gp CF/125/302/534	Flown by makers as U-0257
R1836	253/5 OTU/15 EFTS/21 EFTS/FTC CF	SOC 25.5.44
R1837	248/15 EFTS/54 OTU	SOC 25.2.44
R1838	266/5 OTU/316	Hit balloon cable in bad visibility and crashed, Malpass Road, Newport, Mon., 2.6.41
R1839	266/151	Sold 6.6.46; became G-AIYB
R1840	15 EFTS	SOC 20.12.40
R1841	15 EFTS/29 EFTS	Sold 25.11.46; became G-AITO
R1842	8 EFTS/10 FIS/ATA	Sold 25.11.46; became G-AITX
R1843	15 EFTS	Engine cut; ditched in Solway Firth 3m S of Gretna, Dumfries, 16.1.41; towed ashore but DBR; to 2517M
R1844	15 EFTS/29 EFTS/21 EFTS/7 FIS	Failed to recover from spin; dived into ground, Woodborough, Wilts.,18.10.43
R1845	15 EFTS	To Turkey 13.6.43
R1846	15 EFTS/60 OTU/ATA	Sold 3.6.46 to Argentina
R1847	8 EFTS/29 EFTS/3 GTS/3 AGS	Sold 2.12.46; became F-BDPN
R1848	15 EFTS	Overshot landing and hit fence, Kirkpatrick RLG, 8.7.41
R1849	15 EFTS/21 EFTS	To 4096M 9.43
R1850	15 EFTS	Failed to take-off due to frost on wings; hit hangar, Kingstown, 26.10.40
R1851	15 EFTS	Dived into ground during searchlight exercise, Gates Hill, Cumberland, 11.6.42
R1852	15 EFTS	Stalled and spun into ground, Burnfoot, 18.5.41
R1853	15 EFTS/ECFS/11 AGS	Sold 10.3.47 to Thailand
R1854	15 EFTS/21 EFTS	SOC 25.2.44
R1855	15 EFTS/ATA	To 4483M 21.1.44
R1856	8 EFTS	SOC 6.4.40
R1857	MAP at DH	Sold 18.6.46 to Argentina
R1858	Stoke Orchard/225/15 EFTS/21 EFTS/FTTC	Hit trees and crashed, Babington Hall, Glos., 16.7.44
R1859	24 EFTS/60 OTU/132 OTU/E.Fortune	Sold 1.1.48; became G-AKRK
R1875	Tangmere/219/ECFS	Hit tree on low level navex and crashed near Hullavington, 30.3.44; DBF
R1876	24 EFTS/2 FIS	Sold 1.1.48; became G-AKRJ
R1877	225/SF Kenley/9 FTS/16 EFTS	Dived into ground at night, Etwall, Derbyshire, 1.9.42; cause not known
R1878	504	Damaged in air raid, Exeter, 6.4.41; SOC 17.4.41 as BER
R1879	F-B FTS/ATA TU	SOC 30.11.44
R1880	202 Gp CF/39	Engine cut; undercarriage collapsed in forced landing on rough ground 3m NW of Goubrine North, 18.5.43; DBR
R1881	37	Engine cut; hit rock and undercarriage collapsed in forced landing in desert 25m from Suez, 13.2.41
R1882	204 Gp CF/173/267/216 Gp CF/CF Levant	SOC 1.2.44
R1883	103 MU	
R1884	204 Gp CF/WDCF/E Med CF	NFT 2.44
R1885	TURP/1 GRU/234 Wg	SOC 31.5.45
R1886	ME	SOC 29.6.44
R1887	Northolt/16 EFTS/ATA	Hit tree on approach and crashed, Thame, 19.10.43
R1888	5 EFTS/16 EFTS/5 FIS/6 FIS/32 MU	Sold 8.1.48; became G-AKRU
R1889	Northolt/24/15 EFTS/21 EFTS	Hit railway signal and stalled while low flying near Taplow, Berks., 3.7.42
R1890	St.Eval	Destroyed in air raid, St.Eval, 22.8.40
R1891	15 EFTS/8 EFTS	Stalled on approach and dived into ground, Woodley, 10.11.40
R1892	Northolt/Kenley/485/616/485	Crashed on take-off from field, Marston Moretaine, Beds., 11.10.42
R1893	8 EFTS/15 EFTS/21 EFTS/8 EFTS/10 FIS/7 FIS/CFS/11 RFS	Sold 15.2.49; became G-ALHA
R1894	Abingdon/AASF	Abandoned in France 5.40
R1895	218/8 EFTS/16 EFTS	Sold 1.4.46 to Argentina
R1896	FIU	Sold 30.5.46 to Argentina
R1897	Hucknall/18 OTU/24 EFTS	Damaged 6.8.41; SOC 22.9.41
R1898	24 EFTS/2 FIS/ATA	Sold 29.11.46; became G-AITW
R1899	ATA TU	Engine cut; tipped up in forced landing in cornfield, White Hill Farm, Stopsley, Beds., 20.6.42
R1900	8 EFTS/10 FIS	Stalled at low altitude during practice forced landing and crashed, Ipsden, Oxon., 17.2.43
R1901	15 EFTS/21 EFTS/Broadwell	Sold 22.9.47 to Thailand
R1902	15 EFTS	Stalled during loop and abandoned in spin 1m N of Enfield, Middx., 18.5.41
R1903	MAP at Fairey	Sold 12.6.46; became LV-XQR
R1904	15 EFTS	Failed to become airborne due to frost and hit house, Kingstown, 26.10.40
R1905	15 EFTS	Stalled and spun into ground on approach, Burnfoot LG, 24.7.41
R1906	8 EFTS/10 FIS	Stalled off turn and spun into ground, Buckshill, near Woodley, 14.11.44
R1907	8 EFTS/ECFS/ME	To Turkey 13.6.43
R1908	8 EFTS/ECFS/AFDU	To 4676M 16.3.44
R1909	8 EFTS	Stalled off turn and dived into ground, Chobham Common, Surrey, 24.7.41
R1910	21 AD	Abandoned in France 6.40
R1911	21 AD	Abandoned in France 6.40
R1912	310/533/ME	SOC 26.4.45

R1913	24 EFTS/8 EFTS/	
	10 FIS/FTCCF/ATA	Sold 10.3.47 to Thailand
R1914	604/SF Middle Wallop/	
	604/137	Sold 30.5.46; became G-AHUJ
R1915	600/602/SF Ayr/602/	
	SF Redhill	To Turkey 13.6.43
R1916	152	DBR in air raid, Warmwell, 1.4.41
R1917	500/SF Detling	Stalled in forced landing and hit trees, Ightham, Kent, 8.11.40; presumed engine failure
R1918	302/SF Kenley/SF Martlesham Heath/ 312/5 EFTS/CFS/ ECFS/16 PFTS	SOC 2.7.46
R1919	SF Leuchars/ SF Turnhouse/ SF Exeter/308	Crashed in forced landing while lost in bad visibility 2m NE of Ormesby, Norfolk, 21.1.43
R1920	SF Martlesham Heath/ 601/ATA	Hit cable during forced landing practice and crashed near Barton-in-the-Clay, 29.11.42; DBF
R1921	15 EFTS/Hucknall/ PEFTS/11 EFTS	Dived into ground, Kinalty Farm, near Kirriemuir, Angus, 16.4.42; presumed spun at low altitude
R1922	15 EFTS/Hucknall/ PEFTS/11 EFTS	Sold 10.1.49
R1923	15 EFTS/Hucknall/ PEFTS	Collided with R1921 taxying at Hucknall, 2.2.41; DBR
R1924	15 EFTS	SOC 10.2.41
R1940	ME	
R1941	6/259 Wg	SOC 26.4.45
R1942	WDCF	Demolished on evacuation, El Aden, 22.4.41
R1943	318	Stalled on take-off and crashed, Ismailia, 24.11.43
R1944	WDCF	Destroyed 6.5.41 on evacuation?
R1945	70/148/173	SOC 31.5.45
R1946	202 Gp CF/WDCF	Destroyed on evacuation of airfield, 21.4.41
R1947	70/WDCF	Hit obstruction on take-off, Kolundia, 29.11.42; DBR
R1948	FAA/CF Levant	SOC 29.3.45
R1949	70	SOC 26.4.45
R1950	151/Andover	Sold 18.4.46; became G-AHNW
R1951	15 EFTS/29 EFTS/ 5 GTS	DBR in heavy landing, Shobdon, 5.5.43
R1952	SD Flt St.Athan/ME	SOC 31.12.46
R1953	267	Stalled avoiding dispersed aircraft and wing hit ground, Heliopolis, 21.11.40
R1954	267/CF Levant/ 75 OTU	SOC 31.5.45
R1955	24 EFTS/42 OTU/ 60 OTU	Engine cut; stalled and spun into ground 5m E of Stoke Orchard, 20.1.44
R1956	253/2 EFTS/6 FIS	Swung on take-off and hit gunpost, Worcester, 15.7.42
R1957	5 EFTS	Forcelanded in bad weather; hit obstruction on take-off and crashed, Ashby-de-la-Zouche, Leics., 29.5.41
R1958	16 EFTS/2 OAFU	Sold 7.6.46 to Argentina
R1959	Doncaster/15 EFTS/ 29 EFTS	Spun into ground during spinning practice, Charlton, near Malmesbury, Wilts., 20.8.42
R1960	24 EFTS/2 FIS	Dived into ground, Fordoun, Angus, 10.4.42
R1961	17 OTU/1 OTU/ 15 EFTS/21 EFTS/ 8 AGS/418/2 Gp CF/ 418	Sold 10.3.47; became G-AJSF

R1962	5 EFTS/81/1 Del Flt	Sold 10.3.47; became G-AJGL
R1963	5 EFTS/24 EFTS/ ECFS/9 PAFU/ECFS/ 3 FIS/7 EFTS/ 11 EFTS/11 RFS	Sold 4.10.48; became G-AJCM
R1964	5 EFTS/ECFS/ 9 PAFU/ECFS	SOC 3.8.44
R1965	5 EFTS	Bounced on landing and hit trees on attempted overshoot, Meir, 11.7.40
R1966	15 EFTS	Control lost in cloud; spun into Solway Firth off Drumburgh, Cumberland, 27.3.41
R1967	15 EFTS/29 EFTS/ 21 EFTS	SOC 25.2.44
R1968	15 EFTS	Flaps raised on overshoot; stalled and crashed, Kingstown, 25.7.41
R1969	15 EFTS	Undershot approach and hit ground, Kingstown, 2.7.40
R1970	15 EFTS/21 EFTS/ 2 FIS	Sold 10.3.47; became G-AJGK
R1971	274	Crashed in desert near Sidi Barrani, 20.5.41
R1972	CF Levant	Hit tree low flying and crashed 1m N of Petah Tiqva, 23.6.41
R1973	2 French Ftr Flt	Engine cut; spun into ground in forced landing, Hywilla Road, near Haifa, 30.9.40
R1974	274/WDCF	Hit by Blenheim V5514 while parked, Burg-el-Arab, 10.5.41
R1975	SF St.Athan/87/ 1 Del Flt	Sold 11.9.46; became OY-DNI
R1976	8 EFTS/15 EFTS/ 605/229	Sold 19.3.47; became G-AKAU
R1977	9 Gp CF/131	Collided on take-off with Spitfire, Ternhill, 27.9.41
R1978	Ibsley/118/51 OTU	Sold 18.4.46; became G-AHNV
R1979	F-B FTS/19	Flew into ground after control lost at low altitude near Redruth, Cornwall, 23.7.42
R1980	F-BFTS/24 EFTS/ 2 FIS	To 4318M 11.11.43
R1981	F-BFTS/60 OTU	Swung on landing at night and hit flare, Macmerry, 21.9.41; DBR
R1982	9 Gp CF/1 AACU/91/ 531/ATA	Sold 30.5.46 to Argentina
R1983	8 EFTS/4 FIS/22 EFTS	Sold 10.3.47 to Thailand
R1984	MAP at Miles/F-B FTS	Dived into ground near Odiham, 17.12.40

*   *   *   *   *   *   *   *   *   *

**47 Westland Lysander IIs delivered between April and June 1940
by Westlands, Yeovil, to Contract No. 994551/39**

R1987	267	Engine cut; landed on beach and swung into sea 15m NW of Gaza, 29.8.41
R1988	237/WDCF	Undercarriage collapsed while landing in Western Desert, 6.7.42
R1989	2/268/1 IAF	Undershot landing, hit bund and overturned, Peshawar, 20.12.41
R1990	4/1 SAC/41 OTU/Cv TT/ 53 OTU/1490 Flt/ 1487 Flt/1498 Flt	SOC 15.11.43
R1991	614/13/6 AACU/20	Engine cut; overturned in forced landing 3m W of Jamshedpur, 19.7.42; DBF
R1992	267/WDCF	Ran out of fuel while lost between Maaten Bagush and Siwa and crashed in forced landing in desert, 1.4.42

R1993	267/6/MECF/ CUWD	Crashed in forced landing in sandstorm, Western Desert, 16.10.42
R1994	267	
R1995	237	SOC 29.3.45
R1996	6	Overshot landing in sandstorm, Tobruk, 13.4.41; DBF
R1997	2/268	Flew into ground in bad visibility, Dullington, Cambs., 18.12.40
R1998	613/1 SAC/41 OTU/ Cv TT/1489 Flt/ 16 APC/14 APC	SOC 26.2.44
R1999	225/241/8 AACU	SOC 23.8.43
R2000	2/6 AACU	Hit balloon cable in bad visibility and crashed, Runcorn, Cheshire, 14.1.41
R2001	2/6 AACU/9 Gp TF/ Cv TT/1492 Flt/ 3 RAFRS/1 RAFRS	SOC 30.6.43
R2002	231	Stalled on landing and undercarriage collapsed, Newtownards, 24.12.40
R2003	613/1 SAC/41 OTU/ ATA/Cv TT	To 3936M 17.7.43
R2004	613/4 IAF/CF Dum Dum/CF Bengal	Swung on take-off into drain and undercarriage collapsed, Jorhat, 8.12.42
R2005	613/1 SAC	To FFAF 3.11.41
R2006	225/239/4 IAF/ 1 AGS(I)	SOC 31.7.44
R2007	225/13/2/7 AACU/ 239/1 IAF/ 2 IAF/151 OTU	Bounced on landing and undercarriage collapsed, Risalpur, 16.3.43
R2008	225/1 SAC	Hit tree in forced landing while lost, Hungerford, Berks., 11.5.41
R2009	2/268	Stalled on landing, Bury St.Edmunds, 2.11.40; DBR
R2010	2/1 SAC/41 OTU/ 1482 Flt/24 OTU	To 3930M 20.7.43
R2025	4/241	Failed to become airborne and hit barrels, Inverness, 24.9.40; DBR
R2026	4/241/28/20	Swung on landing, Maungdaw, 30.1.43; DBR
R2027	13/7 AACU/ 11 Gp AACF	Overshot landing in heavy rain and hit dispersal pen, Croydon, 7.6.41
R2028	13/231	DBR in gale, Newtownards, 21.11.40
R2029	26/India	SOC 16.10.44
R2030	26	Hit trees recovering from dive near Stradishall, 24.8.40
R2031	4	Crashed in forced landing in bad weather 5m S of Scarborough, Yorks., 16.7.40
R2032	4	Overshot forced landing while lost on navex and hit wall, Cockermouth, Cumb., 1.8.40
R2033	13/1 IAF	Swung on landing and undercarriage collapsed, Peshawar, 16.1.42
R2034	13/8 AACU/11 Gp AACF/287/1489 Flt/ 16 APC	SOC 12.1.44
R2035	13/1 SAC/41 OTU	Ran out of fuel in bad weather on navex; crashed in forced landing 7m NW of Hay, Herefordshire, 21.10.41
R2036	-	To FFAF
R2037	ME	
R2038	237	Engine cut on take-off; hit tree, Agordat, 10.2.41; DBF
R2039	-	To FFAF

R2040	-	To FFAF
R2041	ME	
R2042	4/8 AACU/ 10 Gp AACF/ 286/2 AAPC	SOC 12.1.44
R2043	-	To FFAF 4.8.40
R2044	ME	SOC 13.2.41
R2045	-	To FFAF 24.8.40
R2046	-	To FFAF 24.8.40
R2047	-	To National Steel Car Corp., Canada as pattern aircraft; became RCAF 700

*   *   *   *   *   *   *   *   *   *   *

11 Bristol Beaufighter prototypes and early production aircraft delivered between April and December 1940 by Bristols, Filton, to Contract No. 983771/39

R2052	AAEE & Mkrs	Prototype Mk.I; DBR 23.2.41
R2053	AAEE & Mkrs	Prototype Mk.I; SOC 4.11.40
R2054	AAEE & Mkrs/604	Prototype Mk.I. Stalled on approach at night and spun into ground 1m NE of Middle Wallop, 6.2.41
R2055	Mkrs/RAE/FIU/ AGME/AAEE	Prototype Mk.I; SOC 1.42
R2056	AFDU/25/604/25	Mk.I; crashed in forced landing after collision near Wittering 1.4.42
R2057	AFDU/25/AAEE/Mkrs/ AAEE & Mkrs	Mk.I; SOC 1.1.45
R2058	R-R & Mkrs/ AAEE/RAE	Prototype Mk.II; to 3344M 23.9.42
R2059	SD Flt/FIU/SD Flt/ 51 OTU	Mk.I; SOC 28.8.45
R2060	Mkrs, AAEE & RAE/GRU	Mk.I; to 3401M 7.10.42 at 51 OTU
R2061	R-R & AAEE	Prototype Mk.II; to 3599M 19.2.43
R2062	R-R	Prototype Mk.II; destroyed in air raid, Hucknall, 27.9.40

*   *   *   *   *   *   *   *   *   *

139 Bristol Beaufighter IFs delivered between July 1940 and March 1941 by Bristols, Filton, to Contract No. 983771/39

R2063	RAE/Mkrs/AAEE/ 219/54 OTU/51 OTU	Swung and hit earth mound on take-off, Cranfield, 24.12.42
R2064	-	DBR 11.9.40; NFD
R2065	600/219	Hit trees descending out of cloud, Balcombe Place, Sussex, 31.10.40
R2066	FIU/SD Flt/RAE	To 3432M 13.11.42
R2067	25	Missing from night patrol, 15.9.40
R2068	25	Presumed ditched in fog 5m off Brighton, Sussex, 21.11.40
R2069	25/68/256/51 OTU	Control lost during dummy attack on B-17; crashed at Easton Maudit, Northants., 24.3.44
R2070	219/600/219	Stalled on approach to Tangmere and dived into ground, Eastergate, Sussex, 21.3.41
R2071	600/219	Crashed at Church Street, Edenbridge, Kent, 13.11.40; possibly shot down by another night fighter
R2072	29/600/219	Skidded and overshot landing, Redhill, 15.10.40
R2073	604	Flew into hill in cloud on air firing exercise 10m W of Swanage, Dorset, 29.5.41

R2074	600/219	Dived into ground, Slindon, Sussex, 8.2.41; presumed loss of control in cloud on GCI exercise	R2123	605/219	Hit landing light on approach on return from patrol and under-carriage leg collapsed on landing, Tangmere, 11.4.41; DBR
R2075	600/219	Overshot landing and ran into filled-in bomb crater; under-carriage collapsed, Kenley, 21.10.40; DBR	R2124	-	Destroyed in air raid, Filton, 13.10.40
R2076	600/219/285/ Woodvale	SOC 21.4.45	R2125	RAE/FIU/RAE	To 4402M 11.43
R2077	23/29/23/604/25/ 141/153	To 3442M 8.9.42 at 51 OTU	R2126	219/604	Engine cut on take-off; crash-landed, Middle Wallop, 24.12.41; DBR
R2078	AAEE/FIU/ ECFS	To 4521M 5.2.44	R2127	219	Collided with R2083 during AI exercise and abandoned near Brighton, 30.4.41
R2079	600/219	Abandoned out of fuel after radio failure in fog, Woking, Surrey, 14.10.40	R2128	29/256/51 OTU	Engine cut on approach; hit trees and crashed, Cranfield, 17.3.44
R2080	25/51 OTU	Hit balloon, caught fire and crashed near Kingsdown, Kent, 18.7.44	R2129	25/51 OTU	Crashed after control lost at night, Meadow Farm, Beds., 15.2.44
R2081	25/604/25/ 51 OTU	SOC 23.4.45	R2130	Mkrs	Cv Mk.VI prototype; SOC 26.9.44
R2082	25/51 OTU	SOC 28.2.46	R2131	219	Stalled after take-off and dived into ground, Merston, Sussex, 28.10.41
R2083	600/219	Collided with R2127 during AI practice and abandoned near Brighton, 30.4.41			
R2084	219	Stalled and spun into ground on approach to Kenley, Riddles-down, 15.11.40	R2132	604/219/ 51 OTU	SOC 25.10.45
			R2133	600/68	Engine lost power on take-off; yawed and dived into ground, Shawbury, 7.8.41
R2085	604	Engine cut in circuit on return from patrol; flew into ground near Kings Sambourne, Hants., 27.6.41; DBF	R2134	604/219/68/256/ 51 OTU/AAEE	SOC 7.1.48
			R2135	219	Abandoned over sea 3m S of Brighton, Sussex, 16.12.41
R2086	219/54 OTU/51 OTU/ CGS	SOC 27.12.45	R2136	604	Engine caught fire on overshoot; bellylanded, Colerne, 17.4.42; DBF
R2087	604	Abandoned after engine failure at night on patrol 5m NE of Stratford-on-Avon, Warks., 17.1.41	R2137	604/25/288/51 OTU	SOC 27.12.45
			R2138	29/604	Dived into ground, Mullion, Cornwall, 11.1.43; presumed control lost descending in cloud
R2088	604/600/68/51 OTU	SOC 13.6.45	R2139	604/68/TFU/68/ 51 OTU	Undershot approach and hit obstruction, Cranfield, 21.1.44
R2089	51 MU	Both engines cut after take-off due to shortage of fuel; hit huts during forced landing, Lichfield, 12.1.41	R2140	29	Abandoned after engine cut Potterhanworth, Lincs., 28.11.40
R2090	600/219/51 OTU/ 54 OTU	SOC 29.11.45	R2141	29	Flew into ground at night, Staplehurst, Kent, 21.7.41; cause not known
R2091	25/604/68/ 604/256/169	SOC 27.12.45	R2142	604	To 3155M 3.7.42 at 9 OTU
R2092	25/604/51 OTU	SOC 30.8.45	R2143	235/604/51 OTU	SOC 7.6.45
R2093	29	Hit Defiant on take-off, 18.8.41; DBF	R2144	29	Undershot and hit tree on approach; engine caught fire; crashlanded ½m SE of West Malling, 23.12.41
R2094	29/406/141/153	SOC 2.7.45			
R2095	29/51 OTU	SOC 7.45	R2145	25/604/25	Swung on landing and under-carriage collapsed, Bally-halbert, 29.1.42; not repaired and to 3156M 3.7.42
R2096	219	Stalled on approach to Debden and spun into ground, Smiths Green Farm, 17.12.40			
R2097	219/54 OTU/51 OTU	Engine cut; bellylanded but hit tree, Milton Keynes, Bucks., 30.11.42	R2146	FIU/604/219/25/ 239/515	SOC 16.7.45
			R2147	FIU	Overshot landing and skidded into ditch, Shoreham, 9.12.40
R2098	25/604/68/51 OTU	Spun into ground during single-engined flying, Putnoe Wood, near Bedford, 15.4.43	R2148	29/141/219/68	Control lost in cloud; spun into ground, Cromer, Norfolk, 14.6.43; DBF
R2099	23/604/SD Flt/604/ 600/68	Crashed near Poynton Green, Salop., 23.10.41, at night; NFD	R2149	25/604/141/51 OTU	SOC 28.3.46
R2100	219/51 OTU	SOC 29.11.45	R2150	29	Dived into ground, Scopwick, Lincs., 15.2.41; presumed control lost on approach
R2101	25/604	Damaged by return fire from He 111; caught fire and aband-oned off Bournemouth, 7.5.41			
R2120	219	Engine cut; abandoned after control problems, Partridge Green, Sussex, 13.2.41	R2151	25/23/25/219/ FIU/51 OTU	SOC 22.5.45
R2121	604/600/141	Engine cut on take-off; swung and undercarriage collapsed, Ayr, 17.9.41	R2152	252/272/2 OTU	Flew into high ground at night, Vara Moor, 3m S of Broughton, Yorks., 28.4.43
R2122	25/51 OTU	SOC 13.6.45			

R2153	235/252/272/2 OTU	To synthetic trainer 10.41
R2154	219	Hit high ground on night approach, Fontwell, 3m NE of Tangmere, 15.12.41; DBF
R2155	219	Overshot landing in bad weather on return from night patrol and hit hedge, Tangmere 19.1.41; DBR
R2156	25	Damaged by enemy aircraft and crashed on landing, Wittering, 17.5.41
R2157	25	Missing on night patrol, 6.8.41
R2158	604/600	Both engines cut; ditched off Prestwick, 13.3.41; to 2552M
R2159	604/29/256/19 MU	Destroyed in hangar fire, St.Athan, 3.2.44
R2180	29/141/153/29/51 OTU	Engine lost power; lost height and bellylanded near Elstow, Beds., 23.12.44
R2181	25/51 OTU	SOC 29.11.45
R2182	29	Undercarriage collapsed on landing, Wellingore, 6.3.41; DBR
R2183	29	Flew into high ground in bad visibility, Boxley Grange, Kent, 21.11.41
R2184	600/29	Crashed in sea on night patrol 3m SE of Brightlingsea, Essex, 21.5.43; cause not known
R2185	600/89/68/51 OTU	Engine cut on practice over-shoot; crashlanded, Twinwood Farm, 15.5.43; not repaired; to 4035M 11.8.43
R2186	FIU	Hit hut on approach and crash-landed, Ford 3.1.41; DBR
R2187	604/51 OTU	Hit truck crossing flare path on take-off and undercarriage torn off, Cranfield, 16.7.44
R2188	600/604/51 OTU	Tyre burst on take-off; swung and undercarriage raised to stop, Cranfield, 8.7.43; DBR
R2189	FIU/219/51 OTU	To 4600M 27.2.44
R2190	604	Overshot landing and skidded, West Malling, 5.6.41; to 2769M 10.41
R2191	25/600/68/219/60 OTU/51 OTU	SOC 28.3.46
R2192	29/51 OTU	SOC 10.8.45; 4095M NTU
R2193	29	Flew into ground in steep turn, Aylsford Hills, Chatham, Kent, 3.3.42
R2194	25	Damaged 22.2.41; to 2550M 5.4.41
R2195	FIU/SD Flt/FIU/SD Flt/TFU/604/51 OTU	Bellylanded after engine cut on take-off from Cranfield, Stagsden, Beds., 18.9.43; DBF
R2196	29/51 OTU	SOC 31.1.46
R2197	25	Lost power on overshoot; stalled and undercarriage collapsed, Wittering, 28.3.42; DBF
R2198	252/3 OTU/272/2 OTU	Bounced on landing and flew into ground, Driffield, 4.4.42
R2199	252/272/2 OTU/51 OTU/577	SOC 30.5.46
R2200	600/68/153/29/CGS	SOC 24.4.45
R2201	FIU/51 OTU	SOC 29.11.45
R2202	219/60 OTU/51 OTU	To 4599M 1.3.44
R2203	604	Engine cut; swung on approach and wing hit ground; under-carriage collapsed, Middle Wallop, 11.12.41; DBR
R2204	219/60 OTU/51 OTU	Crashlanded after engine fire, Cranfield, 5.12.42; DBF
R2205	25	Abandoned after engine failure on patrol over North Sea, 8.9.42

R2206	25	Overshot flare path and hit hedge, Wittering, 22.3.41; DBR
R2207	604/256/51 OTU	SOC 17.5.46
R2208	604/51 OTU	SOC 28.4.45
R2209	25	Undershot approach and hit wall and ditch, Wittering, 18.5.41
R2240	29	Engine cut; cartwheeled in forced landing, Dickens Street, East Fixley, Kent, 22.6.41; DBF
R2241	219/RAE	Engine cut after escorting SOE Hudson to S.W. France; abandoned off Les Sables d'Olonne, Vendée, 3.9.44
R2242	29	SOC 26.3.41
R2243	604/FIU	Hit by Lancaster ND632 while parked, Ford, 26.8.44; DBF
R2244	Mkrs/FIU/604/410/219/410	To 3859M 6.43
R2245	29	Damaged by return fire from bomber and crashed on approach, West Malling, 11.5.41; DBF
R2246	29/51 OTU	SOC 30.8.45
R2247	25/256/51 OTU	SOC 25.4.46
R2248	29/68/141	Hit hill on overshoot, Arundel Park, Sussex, 10.2.43
R2249	29/54 OTU/51 OTU	Engine cut on approach; crash-landed, Cranfield, 29.11.43
R2250	29/51 OTU	SOC 29.11.45
R2251	25/51 OTU	SOC 30.8.45
R2252	604/153/62 OTU/51 OTU	Collided with Dominie X7450 on approach and crashed, Cranfield, 11.11.43; DBF
R2253	219/51 OTU	To 4570M 24.2.44
R2254	25	Shot down by Beaufighter X7941 in error off Bridlington, Yorks., 23.7.42
R2255	25	Overshot flapless landing on return from patrol, Wittering, 14.3.41; later destroyed in air raid
R2256	600/68/256	Throttle jammed on approach; hit top of Wellington X3926 and cartwheeled, Squires Gate, 1.6.42; DBF
R2257	25/604/29	Dived into ground during attack on ground target, Leysdown ranges, Kent, 7.7.42
R2258	604/1 BDU	SOC 14.6.45
R2259	604	Abandoned out of fuel on patrol in fog 6m SW of Hungerford, Berks., 5.4.41
R2260	29/51 OTU	SOC 23.4.45
R2261	68/256/51 OTU	SOC 21.4.45
R2262	29	Engine cut; forcelanded in orchard 2m SW of West Malling, 19.6.41
R2263	25	Undercarriage leg jammed up; DBR on landing, Wittering, 10.5.41
R2264	68	Engine cut on patrol; crash-landed 2m S of Shrewsbury, Salop., 7.7.41
R2265	29	Undercarriage raised too soon on take-off; crashlanded, Wellingore, 29.4.41
R2266	46	SOC 1.1.44
R2267	29/219	Stalled on approach to Tang-mere and spun into ground, Boxgrove, Sussex, 5.6.42; DBF
R2268	Mkrs & AAEE/235/Mkrs & RAE	SOC 6.2.45

R2269	252/143/235	Ditched off Egersund while escorting Beauforts, 17.5.42	R2318	600/125	Broke up in air during aerobatics and crashed, Park Mill, Glam., 17.6.42
			R2319	307/60 OTU/132 OTU	SOC 23.3.44
* * * * * * * * *			R2320	409/54 OTU/63 OTU	SOC 28.6.45
			R2321	409/54 OTU/51 OTU	To 4806M 16.6.44 at 51 OTU; 4810M NTU

150 Bristol Beaufighter IIFs delivered between March and August 1941 by Bristols, Filton, to Contract No.983771/39

R2270	Mkrs/AAEE/RAE/ 604/406	SOC 15.2.44	R2322	307/96/60 OTU/ 132 OTU	To 3960M 13.7.43
R2271	30 MU	Dived into ground out of cloud, Bagillt, Flint, 26.4.41	R2323	600	Abandoned in bad visibility 12m E of Corsham, Wilts., 20.9.41
R2272	600/ECDU/11 OTU	SOC 15.1.45	R2324	32 MU	Broke up in dive during AI trials, Llanbethery, Glam., 29.5.41; cause not known
R2273	600	SOC 21.6.41			
R2274	AAEE/FIU/406	Cv to Mk.V with turret; SOC 25.2.43	R2325	600/125/456/ 54 OTU	SOC 26.2.45
R2275	600	Engine cut on interception; flew into sea 18m NW of Lands End, Cornwall, 1.12.41	R2326	600/60 OTU/ 132 OTU	SOC 7.6.44
			R2327	600/125/54 OTU	SOC 3.9.44
R2276	600/255/409/ 60 OTU/132 OTU	SOC 7.6.44	R2328	406/60 OTU/132 OTU	To 3683M 5.5.43 at 1 AAS
			R2329	Mkrs/AAEE	To Admiralty 26.7.43
R2277	604/25/600/125/ 54 OTU	SOC 25.10.45	R2330	600/125/63 OTU	SOC 7.6.44
			R2331	409/60 OTU/132 OTU	To 4171M 11.9.43
R2278	600/60 OTU/132 OTU/ ECFS/132 OTU	Hit trees on overshoot and crashed, East Fortune, 14.6.43; DBF	R2332	409/54 OTU	SOC 3.6.44
			R2333	255	Caught fire in air and abandoned 10m NW of Cromer, 28.2.42; possibly damaged by return fire from enemy aircraft
R2279	600/307/96/60 OTU/ 132 OTU/63 OTU	SOC 28.6.45			
R2280	600	Landed with undercarriage unlocked, Colerne, 14.7.41; DBR	R2334	456	Bounced on landing, only one engine responded for overshoot, swung and cartwheeled, Valley, 18.11.41
R2281	406	Engine cut on take-off for air test; hit hut, Acklington, 6.1.42			
R2282	600/125	SOC 27.9.45	R2335	FIU	Undercarriage jammed up and control lost while attempting to free it; dived into ground 4m W of Ford, 4.9.41
R2283	406/60 OTU/132 OTU	Engine cut on overshoot; dived into ground, East Fortune, 28.5.43; DBF			
			R2336	406	To Admiralty 21.4.43
R2284	600	To Admiralty 3.7.43	R2337	600/125	Spun into ground after take-off, Colerne, 16.5.42; DBF
R2300	600	Control lost; crashed in sea after night take-off, Predannack, 22.8.41	R2338	406/54 OTU	SOC 28.3.46
			R2339	406/409/54 OTU	Lost power on attempted overshoot; wing hit ground, crash-landed, Charterhall, 17.9.43
R2301	307	To Admiralty 11.12.43			
R2302	600/125	SOC 28.6.45	R2340	406/132 OTU	Swung on overshoot to avoid hangar, East Fortune; stalled and crashed, Prestonkirk, 17.5.43
R2303	54 OTU	Hit by V8165 while parked, Charterhall, 14.6.43			
R2304	255/410/63 OTU	Abandoned after engine fire and crashed, Shepherds Patch, near Slimbridge, Glos., 1.1.44	R2341	456/60 OTU/ 54 OTU	Hit hill in cloud, Whitelee Farm, near Lauder, Berwickshire, 1.2.44; presumed due to loss of control
R2305	600	SOC 25.10.45			
R2306	600	Cv to Mk V second prototype; spun into ground on night flying test, Holly Bush Farm, Acton Turville, Glos., 28.9.41	R2342	409/54 OTU	To 3860M 16.6.43
			R2343	456/54 OTU	SOC 21.10.44
			R2344	456/54 OTU	Engine lost power on attempted overshoot at night; swung and hit tree, Winfield, 2.1.43
R2307	406/63 OTU	To 4176M 18.4.44			
R2308	255/410/54 OTU	To 3861M 16.6.43	R2345	406	To 3350M 29.8.42
R2309	255	Hit trees on approach at night and crashed, Coltishall, 13.12.41	R2346	406/54 OTU/ 132 OTU/63 OTU	SOC 28.6.45
			R2347	TFU/RAE	SOC 25.4.46
R2310	255/600/125/63 OTU	SOC 29.11.45	R2348	406/63 OTU	SOC 5.10.44
R2311	AAEE/RAE/AAEE	To Admiralty 26.7.43	R2349	406/54 OTU	To synthetic trainer 9.41 at 54 OTU
R2312	600	Missing from interception off Cornwall, 15.12.41; presumed damaged by return fire from He 111 and ditched			
			R2370	255/54 OTU	SOC 27.9.45
R2313	54 OTU	Control lost in bad weather; dived into ground, Greenwood, near Reston, Berwick, 24.10.42	R2371	456/132 OTU	SOC 7.6.44
			R2372	456/RAE	SOC 26.9.44
R2314	54 OTU	To Bristols 2.2.45; NFT	R2373	TFU/63 OTU	SOC 13.9.44
R2315	307	Engine cut on take-off; crash-landed, Exeter, 30.8.41; DBF	R2374	600/125	SOC 28.6.45
R2316	21 MU	To Bristols 15.1.42 and SOC 4.2.42	R2375	RAE/FIU/219/ 409/54 OTU	Stalled off turn and dived into ground on approach 2m S of Winfield, 17.2.44
R2317	600	Spun into ground while attempting aerobatics, Goonhilly Downs, Mullion, Cornwall, 12.7.41; DBF	R2376	600/125/54 OTU	SOC 30.8.44
			R2377	255	Crashed in sea off Happisborough, Norfolk, 16.10.41; cause not known

R2378	406/54 OTU	Collided with T3359 and crashed near Polworth, Berwickshire, 13.11.42
R2379	54 OTU/307	Engine cut on approach to Exeter; crashlanded, Broad Clyst, 3.2.42
R2380	406/63 OTU	SOC 27.9.45
R2381	456	Swung on take-off and hit sand-dunes, Valley, 3.5.42
R2382	456/54 OTU	SOC 3.6.44
R2383	125/54 OTU	SOC 25.5.44
R2384	406/8 OTU/ 132 OTU/63 OTU	SOC 19.5.44
R2385	Mkrs/406	SOC 4.9.45
R2386	406/60 OTU/ 132 OTU	To 4190M 27.9.43
R2387	406/54 OTU	Bounced on landing, stalled and cartwheeled, Winfield, 6.3.43
R2388	406/54 OTU	SOC 25.5.44
R2389	406	To Admiralty 14.12.43
R2390	FIU/307/96	SOC 25.4.46
R2391	RAE	Became static test aircraft
R2392	307/63 OTU	SOC 28.6.45
R2393	32 MU	Stalled on approach and hit ground, St.Athan, 23.11.41
R2394	456/63 OTU	Swung on take-off and hit T3052, Honiley, 23.12.43
R2395	456/132 OTU	To 3788M 7.6.43
R2396	600/125/ 54 OTU	SOC 26.2.45
R2397	255/96/63 OTU	SOC 25.10.45
R2398	255	Engine cut at low altitude; control lost and dived into ground, Hevingham, Norfolk, 8.12.41
R2399	255/54 OTU	SOC 7.6.44
R2400	255/60 OTU 132 OTU	SOC 19.5.44
R2401	255/60 OTU/132 OTU/618/54 OTU	Hit by 13092 while parked, Charterhall, 2.6.44
R2402	255/410/54 OTU	SOC 6.7.44
R2403	255	Engine cut; control lost on approach to Coltishall and spun into ground, Sco Ruston, 22.8.41; DBF
R2404	406	Overshot landing on one engine and undercarriage raised to stop, Acklington, 8.12.41; not repaired and SOC 14.5.42
R2430	255/63 OTU	SOC 5.10.44
R2431	255/54 OTU	SOC 12.7.45
R2432	255	Damaged by enemy action, 20.9.41; SOC 14.5.42
R2433	255/54 OTU	SOC 24.8.44
R2434	54 OTU	SOC 14.2.45
R2435	406	Lost control of elevators on test flight; bellylanded at Acklington, 14.11.41
R2436	255/307/96/60 OTU	To 4021M 7.8.43
R2437	54 OTU	Engine cut; crashlanded in field near Duns, Berwickshire, 19.10.42
R2438	307	To Admiralty 1.5.43
R2439	409	Crashed in circuit 1½m NE of Coleby Grange, 11.1.42
R2440	54 OTU/307/409/ 54 OTU	Flew into ground in bad weather 1m SE of Duns, Berwickshire, 23.7.42; DBF
R2441	307/96/60 OTU/ 132 OTU	SOC 27.9.45
R2442	54 OTU/307	Flew into high ground in bad visibility, Hameldown Moor, near Widecombe, Devon, 27.9.41

R2443	307/60 OTU/ 132 OTU/235	SOC 26.7.45
R2444	307/54 OTU	Bounced on landing, stalled and hit ground, Church Fenton, 18.2.42
R2445	307	Hit tree low flying over Exeter, airfield, 14.2.42
R2446	307	Both engines cut on approach to Exeter; crashlanded, Honiton Clyst, 13.2.42
R2447	307	Caught fire refuelling at Exeter, 23.3.42
R2448	406/255	Control lost on approach to flarepath on return from patrol; crashlanded, Cowstock, Norfolk, 15.1.42
R2449	307	Engine cut after take-off from Exeter; lost height and hit trees and crashed, Exminster, Devon, 3.4.42; DBF
R2450	307	Overshot flapless landing and undercarriage raised to stop, Exeter, 26.3.42; not repaired; to 3351M 29.8.42
R2451	600/125	SOC 28.6.45
R2452	307/409/54 OTU	Dived into sea on GCI practice off St.Abb's Head, Berwick-shire, 30.3.44; cause not known
R2453	307/600/60 OTU/ 63 OTU	SOC 31.5.45
R2454	FIU/157/132 OTU	SOC 25.10.45
R2455	54 OTU	Undercarriage collapsed in heavy landing, Charterhall, 8.6.43
R2456	54 OTU	Bounced on landing, hit ground and cartwheeled, Charterhall, 18.2.43
R2457	307	Flew into sea on night patrol 1m S of Beer Head, Devon, 12.4.42
R2458	307/96/60 OTU/ 132 OTU/618	SOC 25.10.45
R2459	409/60 OTU/ 132 OTU/235	To 3789M 5.7.43
R2460	255	Swung on take-off and hit building materials, Shawbury, 2.4.42; DBF
R2461	406/60 OTU/ 132 OTU/63 OTU	Dived into ground in bad weather at night, Astwood Bank, Redditch, Worcs., 15.11.43; cause not known
R2462	409	To Admiralty 22.4.43
R2463	307	Overshot flapless landing and hit obstruction, Exeter, 9.12.41; DBR
R2464	409/54 OTU	SOC 23.8.44
R2465	409/60 OTU/ 132 OTU	SOC 9.6.44
R2466	409/60 OTU/ 132 OTU/54 OTU	SOC 14.2.45
R2467	409/54 OTU	SOC 15.3.45
R2468	409	Hit obstruction in night landing Coleby Grange, 16.12.41; not repaired and SOC 14.5.42
R2469	409	Undercarriage jammed on take-off; stalled at low altitude and hit ground, Metheringham, Lincs., 2.9.41; DBF
R2470	255/3 Del Flt	Swung on take-off and wing hit ground, High Ercall, 28.8.42
R2471	409	Overshot landing into ditch, Coleby Grange, 11.11.41; not repaired and SOC 14.5.42
R2472	409/54 OTU	Wing hit ground on take-off; cartwheeled, Winfield, 24.6.42; DBF

R2473	406	Flew into ground on approach at night 3m SW of Acklington, 14.9.41
R2474	456	Stalled off turn and spun into sea on approach, Valley, 5.1.42
R2475	409	Stalled and dived into ground recovering from dive, Potter-hanworth, Lincs., 19.1.42
R2476	409/456	Port flap failed on approach to Valley; banked into sea, Trewan Sands, 5.1.42
R2477	FIU/600/301 FTU	SOC 28.6.45
R2478	406/54 OTU	Damaged and SOC 21.4.43
R2479	409	Swung on approach when prop went into fine pitch; crash-landed, Holdingham, Lincs., 3.6.42

* * * * * * * * * *

Three de Havilland Rapides delivered in July 1939 by de Havilland, Hatfield, to Contract No.981944/39

R2485	2 EWS	SOC 12.9.42
R2486	RAE/2 EWS/2 SS/ATA/ CCCF/RAFNI CF	Sold 25.8.47; to G-AKJY
R2487	RAE/2 EWS/Halton/ 59 OTU/FLS/AAEE	Sold 30.3.50; to G-ALHZ

* * * * * * * * * *

Martin-Baker M.B.3 prototype to Spec. F.18/39 delivered by Martin-Baker, Denham, to Contract No.1165/39

R2492	Mkrs	FF 3.8.42; crashed on test flight when engine cut on take-off, Wing, 12.9.42

* * * * * * * * * *

Martin-Baker M.B.5 prototype to Spec. F.18/39 delivered by Martin-Baker, Denham, to Contract No.1165/39

R2496	Mkrs & AAEE	FF 23.5.44; retained by mkrs

* * * * * * * * * *

R2500	Cancelled Martin-Baker F.18/34 to Contract No.1165/39
R2505, R2506	Beauforts to Contract No. 552915/36 to replace aircraft converted to Beaufighters. Not built

* * * * * * * * * *

de Havilland Hertfordshire prototype delivered in June 1940 by de Havilland, Hatfield, to Contract No.97/39, later amended to B.8999/39, and 40 cancelled production aircraft

R2510	24	Lost speed after take-off from Hendon; dropped wing and hit ground, Woodlands Way, Mill Hill, Middlesex, 23.10.40
R2511 to R2529	-	Cancelled
R2550 to R2560	-	Cancelled

* * * * * * * * * *

68 Westland Lysander Is delivered between May and July 1940 by Westland, Yeovil, to Contract No.981730/39

R2572	613/Cv TT/4 AGS	Replaced diversion to Egypt; SOC 23.8.43
R2575	613/Cv TT/4 AGS	Bounced on landing and over-turned, Morpeth, 30.5.42; DBR
R2576	613/Cv TT/4 AGS	SOC 10.11.43
R2577	613	To 3203M 17.7.42
R2578	613/Cv TT/4 AGS/ Weston Zoyland	SOC 25.8.43
R2579	613	To 3205M 17.7.42
R2580	613	To 3233M 17.7.42
R2581	613/Cv TT/4 AGS/ 4 AOS	To 3920M 14.5.44
R2582	613/81 Gp AACF/ 52 OTU/Cv TT/ 52 OTU/55 OTU	SOC 23.7.43
R2583	81 Gp AACF/116	To 3918M 17.7.43
R2584	4 STT	To 3204M 17.7.42
R2585	1 AACU/7 AACU/ 4 AGS/W Zoyland	SOC 27.11.43
R2586	10 OTU/Abingdon	SOC 12.6.43
R2587	1 AACU/1 TTU	SOC 21.11.43
R2588	1 AACU/7 AACU/ Cv TT	To 3942M 22.7.43
R2589	1 AACU/Cv TT/4 AOS	Engine cut while towing target; crashlanded in field, Glenluce, Wigtownshire, 15.3.43; DBR
R2590	1 AACU/7 AACU/4/ 1498 Flt/1487 Flt	SOC 24.9.43
R2591	1 AACU/6 AACU/ Cv TT	SOC 30.7.43
R2592	-	To 3217M 17.7.42
R2593	Cv TT/4 AGS	To 3916M 22.7.43
R2594	Cv TT/4 AGS/4 AOS	To 3913M 6.7.43
R2595	-	To 3232M 17.7.42
R2596	-	To 3070M 5.3.42
R2597	Cv TT/4 AGS/5 AOS	To 3886M 30.6.43
R2598	Cv TT/8 AGS/4 AGS/ 4 AOS/W.Zoyland	Engine cut; hit pole in forced landing and undercarriage coll-apsed, Chevington, North-umberland, 29.6.43; not repaired and SOC 22.11.43
R2599	-	To 3265M 17.9.42
R2600	-	Lost at sea en route to Middle East, 5.9.42
R2612	239 Wg	SOC 8.4.43
R2613	AAEE	SOC 9.7.44
R2614	14 Gp CF/58 OTU	SOC 12.8.43
R2615	3 SGR	To 3919M 22.7.43
R2616	3 SGR	To 3923M 6.7.43
R2617	-	To 3245M 17.7.42
R2618	-	To 3246M 17.7.42
R2619	1 Gp CF	To 3912M 6.7.43
R2620	Mildenhall/Newmarket/ 1483 Flt/3 Gp AACF/ Cv TT/1483 Flt/ 1484 Flt	To 3921M 23.7.43
R2621	4 AGS/7 AGS	SOC 14.9.43
R2622	24/510	To 3941M 28.7.43
R2623	-	To 3176M 18.3.41
R2624	613/FFAF	Engine cut while low flying; stalled and hit ground 2m S of S Warnborough, Hants., 15.8.40
R2625	13/419 Flt/138	
R2626	13/419 Flt/138/ 161/4 AGS/7 AGS	To 3940M 15.7.43
R2627	13/4 Gp CF	To 3922M 6.7.43
R2628	SF Northolt/SF Reyk-javik/SF Kaldadarnes/ SF Reykjavik	NFT
R2629	2 STT	To 3177M 17.7.42
R2630	10 OTU/82 Gp AACF/ 57 OTU/ATA/1487 Flt	Engine cut while towing drogue; ditched in St. Ives Bay, Cornwall, 7.3.43
R2631	Mkrs & AAEE/WDCF	SOC 1.5.43

R2632	4 Gp CF/58 OTU/	
	Cv TT/4 AGS/7 AGS/	
	Weston Zoyland	SOC 13.8.43
R2633	-	Lost at sea en route to
		Middle East, 5.9.42
R2634	24/510	SOC 30.7.43
R2635	24/510	To 3917M 28.7.43
R2636	12 FTS/5 Gp CF/	
	12 FTS/1660 CU/	
	5 Gp CF	SOC 1.8.44
R2637	-	To 3189M 17.7.42
R2638	285/Cv TT/	
	1488 Flt/17 APC	SOC 2.11.43
R2639	3 RAFRS/1 RAFRS/	
	3 AAPC TTF/679	SOC 2.4.44
R2640	148/WDCF	SOC 29.3.45
R2641	237/WDCF	Missed runway landing in dust
		storm and lost tailwheel,
		Gambut, 13.5.42; abandoned on
		evacuation of airfield
R2642	208/3 RAAF/237	Crashed on landing,
		Msus, 24.12.41; NFD
R2643	208	SOC 31.12.42
R2644	267/WDCF	Caught fire on ground,
		Al Maoui, Tunisia, 23.4.43
R2645	71 OTU	Hit ground while message
		dropping, Ismailia, 25.9.41
R2646	ME	Damaged and SOC 15.9.41
R2647	WDCF	Crashed near Thalata, 14.12.41;
		DBF; NFD
R2648	451/CF Lydda/	
	Levant CF/WDCF	SOC 22.2.45
R2649	ME	SOC 3.7.42
R2650	-	Diverted to REAF
R2651	2/CV TT/5 AOS	SOC 15.9.43
R2652	2/Cv TT/9 AOS	SOC 25.8.43

*   *   *   *   *   *   *   *   *   *

R2659	Stirling for cannon trials to Contract No. 2596/39
R2665	Halifax for cannon trials to Contract No. 10713/39
R2671	Manchester for cannon trials to Contract No. 7625/39

*   *   *   *   *   *   *   *   *   *

Stearman Hammond Model Y delivered in June 1939 from KLM to Contract No.987931/39

R2676	RAE	SOC 3.2.42

*   *   *   *   *   *   *   *   *   *

Ten Hawker Hurricane Is delivered in July 1940 by Hawker, Kingston, to Contract No.527112/36

R2680	238/56 OTU/32/	Engine cut; crashlanded 2m N
	183/55 OTU	of Dumfries, 19.4.43; DBF
R2681	238/59 OTU/5 FTS/	
	56 OTU/Catterick	SOC 27.11.44
R2682	238	Shot down by return fire from
		Ju 88s, Lydd, Kent, 11.9.40
R2683	145	Damaged by Bf 109s and crash-
		landed on Isle of Wight,
		7.11.40; cv to Mk.II BV163
R2684	302/46/121/52 OTU/	Hit tree low flying ½m S of
	59 OTU	Appleby, Cumb., 5.7.42; DBF
R2685	302/303/52 OTU/1 AAS	SOC 24.2.45
R2686	56/253	Shot down by Bf 109 near
		Ashford, Kent, 20.9.40
R2687	87/302	Dived into ground during
		practice dogfight near Arundel,
		Sussex, 20.2.41; cause not
		known

R2688	303/258/615/56 OTU	SOC 9.12.44
R2689	56/249	SOC 1.12.40
R2690 to		Cancelled Hurricanes to
R2693	-	Contract 751458/38

*   *   *   *   *   *   *   *   *   *

Five Wellington Is delivered in August 1939 by Vickers, Weybridge, to Contract No.549268/36 replace L4312-L4316

R2699	214	Crashed on approach on
		training flight, Methwold,
		13.12.39
R2700	AMDP/CC Pool/	
	2 GRU/3 GRU/	
	PRU/15 OTU/221	To 2776M 23.10.41
R2701	99/RAE/2 GRU/RAE	Cv D.W.I.; SOC 20.11.40
R2702	99/15 OTU/27 OTU	To 3155M 22.6.42
R2703	SD Flt Boscombe	
	Down/AAEE/15 OTU	To 3292M 20.7.42

*   *   *   *   *   *   *   *   *   *

R2710-R2720;	Cancelled Lerwicks to Contract
R2740-R2759	No. B993201/39

*   *   *   *   *   *   *   *   *   *

Three D.H. Flamingos delivered by de Havilland, Hatfield, to Contract No.8999/39

R2764	24	Crashed at Gt. Ouseburn.
		Yorks., 30.4.42; NFD
R2765	AAEE/24/MCS	SOC 15.11.44
R2766	Kings Flt/24/MCS	Ex G-AGCC; to Admiralty
		10.3.45

*   *   *   *   *   *   *   *   *   *

30 Bristol Blenheim IVs delivered in June and July 1940 by Avro, Chadderton, to Contract No. 588371/36

R2770	14	NFT 9.8.40
R2771	53	Lost height in circuit in bad
		visibility on return from sweep
		and flew into ground, Manston,
		5.10.40; DBR
R2772	82	Shot down by flak, Aalborg,
		13.8.40
R2773	53	Shot down by Bf 109 during
		attack on destroyer, Brest,
		4.1.41
R2774	236	Missing on bomber escort to
		Cherbourg, 1.8.40
R2775	236/2 OTU/220/	
	301 FTU/1 OADU	To Portugal 1.9.43
R2776	236	Destroyed in air raid,
		St.Eval, 21.8.40
R2777	236	Hit building material on night
		take-off and undercarriage
		collapsed, Carew Cheriton,
		30.7.40
R2778	55/1 METS	To 4027M 8.43
R2779	254	Engine cut while escorting
		DC-2; lost height and hit sea
		attempting to ditch in fog near
		Lundy Island, 4.5.42
R2780	11	Swung on landing and under-
		carriage collapsed, Almyros,
		29.3.41; abandoned in Greece
		5.41
R2781	17 OTU/54 OTU/	
	301 FTU/1 OADU	To Portugal 1.9.43
R2782	235/143/489/143	To Admiralty 23.3.44

R2783	59	Shot down by Bf 109 during reconnaissance, Lorient, 23.11.40
R2784	82/21	Shot down by flak 1m NW of Leiden during attack on power station, 14.4.41
R2785	59/105/88/105/ 21/1442 Flt/ OADU/ME	NFT
R2786	15	Missing (Ostend) 13.9.40
R2787	40/139/110	Hit tree on take-off for shipping sweep, Wattisham, 18.4.41
R2788	101	Missing (Boulogne) 9.9.40
R2789	1 OTU	Engine cut on approach; stalled and hit ground, Prestwick, 10.10.40; DBF
R2790	-	To FFAF 23.12.40
R2791	15/139	Hit by flak on shipping sweep and crashed into ship off Texel, 25.5.41
R2792	17 OTU	Flew into wood in bad visibility on night navex, Eriswell, Suffolk, 26.11.40; DBF
R2793	40/139	Mistook position of airfield at night and stalled on overshoot, Radwinter, Essex, 23.12.40, returning from Ostend; DBF
R2794	59	Flew into ground at night in bad visibility 1½m NW of Littlehampton, Sussex, 28.8.40, on return from Caen
R2795	59	Missing (Caen) 19.8.40
R2796	15/21	Missing from an intruder operation over N.France, 20.11.40
R2797	236/42 OTU	Hit trees on night approach and crashed, Tidworth, Wilts., 5.6.42
R2798	236/5 OTU	SOC 23.5.44
R2799	236	Hit parked Blenheims during take-off in snow, St.Eval, 21.2.41; DBR

*   *   *   *   *   *   *   *   *   *

R2800-R2805; R2825-R2864; R2877-R2926; R2939-R2963; R2995-R3040; R3076-R3128; R3140-R3144		Cancelled Avro-built Blenheim IVs to Contract No. 588371/36

*   *   *   *   *   *   *   *   *   *

100 Wellington ICs delivered between April and June 1940 by Vickers, Weybridge, to Contract No.B3913/39

R3150	115/37/149/37	Missing (Bitterfeld) 30.9.40; believed shot down over Osnabrück
R3151	115/20 OTU	Flew into in sea 4m NNE of Buckie, Banff, 17.5.41; cause not known
R3152	115	Missing from attack on roads between Compiègne and St.Omer, 21.5.40; crashed near Le Havre
R3153	115/218	Hit by landing aircraft, Marham, 16.9.41; DBF
R3154	115	Flew into ground in low cloud, Lastingham, Yorks., 1.5.40 on return from Stavanger
R3155	115/AAEE	SOC 4.8.44; 4818M NTU
R3156	115/75	To 2185M 24.8.40

R3157	115/75	Shot down by flak 3m NNW of Tournai on return from reconnaissance to Dinant, 22.5.40
R3158	115/75	Crashed on landing in mist, Manston, on return from Reisholz, 22.10.40
R3159	115/75	Undershot and hit trees on return after abandoning raid on Soest, East Wretham, 2.9.40
R3160	115/149	Missing (Le Havre) 19.9.40
R3161	9/149/23 OTU/ 28 OTU	To 3867M 17.6.43
R3162	38	Crashed at Veurne, Belgium, on return from Dixmude, 31.5.40
R3163	149	Missing (Schwartzwald) 6.9.40
R3164	149	Missing (Hanau) 29.9.40
R3165	149/75	Missing (Gelsenkirchen/Horst) 21.7.40
R3166	75/311/21 OTU	To synthetic trainer at 28 OTU; to 3154M 2.7.42
R3167	75/99	Abandoned in bad weather over Hampton, Middlesex, on return from Berlin, 14.11.40
R3168	75	Ran out of fuel and crashed, Simonsbath, Devon, on return from Leipzig, 30.9.40
R3169	75/57/75	Hit balloon cable and crashed in Humber near Trinity Sands on return from Hamburg, 7.5.41
R3170	99	Shot down by flak near Haarlem during raid on Schiphol, 6.7.40
R3171	214/75	Missing (Duisburg) 16.7.41; presumed ditched off Dutch coast
R3172	148/75/11 OTU/ 18 OTU/11 OTU	SOC 1.11.44
R3173	148/9/18 OTU	To 2648M
R3174	148/149	Missing (Kolcda) 17.8.40
R3175	148/149	Missing (Boulogne) 9.9.40
R3176	75	Engine cut; bellylanded and hit ridge, Barton Mills, Suffolk, on return from Horst, 4.8.40
R3177	311	Lost 28.10.40; not mentioned in 311 Sqn ORB and NFD
R3178	214/11 OTU	Hydraulics failed; flaps jammed up; overshot runway and hit wall, Bassingbourn, 19.6.41
R3179	37/	Missing 17.11.40
R3195	115/37/75/57/ 21 OTU/30 OTU	To 3163M 15.7.42
R3196	99	Ran out of fuel in bad visibility and abandoned 3m E of Thetford on return from attack on troop concentrations near St.Omer, 30.5.40
R3197	99/12 OTU/ 15 OTU/22 OTU	SOC 30.9.42
R3198	38/115/22 OTU	Engine cut; crashed off turn in circuit, Wellesbourne Mountford, 28.4.42
R3199	99	Shot down by flak, Wolfenbuttel, during raid on Berlin, 10.4.41
R3200	37/99	Hit by flak over Ruhr and engine cut; ditched 30m off Great Yarmouth, 20.6.40

R3201	99/21 OTU/15 OTU	Stalled on approach, hit trees and crashed, Hampstead Norris, 3.11.41
R3202	115	Ditched off Rottumeroog, Friesians on return from Hamburg, 3.8.40
R3203	99/OADF	Flaps jammed up; overshot landing into sea, Gibraltar, 2.5.41
R3204	9	To 3207M 17.7.42
R3205	15 OTU	Missing, presumed ditched, on navex, 18.10.41
R3206	149/311/1429 Flt/ 27 OTU/14 OTU	SOC 8.4.44
R3207	11 OTU	To 3345M 23.8.42
R3208	214	Missing, presumed ditched, (Hamburg) 9.5.41
R3209	214	Missing (Düsseldorf) 8.12.40, Believed ditched off Calais
R3210	37	Missing (Gelsenkirchen) 21.7.40
R3211	37/75	Missing (Hamm) 30.12.40
R3212	149/300/18 OTU/ 21 OTU/304	To 4428M 5.12.43
R3213	38/115	Shot down by flak, Am Falkenburg, during raid on Hamburg, 17.11.40
R3214	99/18 OTU/11 OTU	To 3473M 25.12.42
R3215	103/18 OTU/304/ WTU/ASRTU	SOC 29.6.44
R3216	75/9/18 OTU	Stalled on landing, bounced and swung off runway, Bitteswell, 29.9.41; DBF
R3217	214/99/FPP/SFS/ FTU/Cv XVI/303 FTU/1 OADU/FE	SOC 26.4.45
R3218	75/311/1429 Flt	
R3219	38	Missing (Leipzig) 1.10.40
R3220	9	Missing (Düsseldorf) 8.12.40; crashed near Ostend
R3221	Cv III/Mkrs & AAEE/ 310 FTU/301 FTU	SOC 19.11.44
R3222	99	Missing (Bremen) 20.10.41
R3223	20 OTU	Bounced on landing and stalled on overshoot, Lossiemouth, 31.10.40
R3224	37/75/22 OTU/ 25 OTU/16 OTU	To 2988M c 3.42
R3225	18 OTU/11 OTU/ Cv XVI/232	SOC 6.5.46
R3226	-	To 3179M 17.7.42
R3227	11 OTU	Shot down by intruder on approach, Bassingbourn, 7.5.41
R3228	99	To 3173M 17.7.42
R3229	11 OTU/22 OTU	Flaps jammed; overshot landing into railway embankment, Stratford, 13.2.42
R3230	311/9/22 OTU/ 20 OTU	Crashed on take-off, Lossiemouth, 26.10.42
R3231	37/75/57/11 OTU/ 29 OTU	To 3104M 15.5.42
R3232	115/214/3 Gp TF/ 1483 Flt/15 OTU/ 20 OTU	Control lost; crashed near Auchtermuchty, Kinross, 5.1.43
R3233	214/1503 Flt/ 16 OTU	To 3304M 31.7.43
R3234	311/1429 Flt/ 15 OTU/Cv XVI/232	SOC 6.5.46
R3235	75	Crashed near Amsterdam on return from Gotha, 26.7.40
R3236	37	Missing (Bremen) 7.7.40; believed ditched off Friesians
R3237	1429 Flt Cv XVI/5 FPP	Bellylanded due to bad weather, Cumberland, 1.2.45
R3238	115	Ran out of fuel on return from Bremen; abandoned in fog near Wicken Bonhunt, Essex, 12.2.41
R3239	37/75/37	Engine cut in circuit; lost height and crashlanded, Kephissia, near Athens, 7.3.41; not repaired before evacuation
——		
R3275	37/75/57/ 12 OTU/28 OTU	SOC 14.8.44
R3276	115	Engine cut; hit trees in forced landing, Corpusty, Norfolk, on return from Mannheim, 23.8.40
R3277	311/75/12 OTU/ 28 OTU/1 AAS	SOC 17.11.45
R3278	115/148	Damaged in air raid, Luqa, 9.1.41 and SOC 18.1.41 as DBR
R3279	115	Damaged by flak and dived into sea off Teignmouth, Devon, returning from Brest, 3.3.41
R3280	Mildenhall/149/ 18 OTU	Missing, presumed ditched in Irish Sea on night navex, 11.9.42
R3281	37/ATA	SOC 29.11.45
R3282	9	Ran out of fuel and crashed in sea off Lowestoft, Suffolk, on return from Berlin, 2.10.40
R3283	9	To 3185M 17.7.42
R3284	37/75/11 OTU	To 3990M 21.7.43
R3285	149/17 OTU/ 18 OTU/21 OTU	SOC 14.8.44
R3286	9/Czech TU/ 1429 Flt/29 OTU/ 25 OTU/11 OTU	SOC 22.6.44
R3287	99	To 3235M 17.7.42
R3288	150	Flew into mountainside while descending in cloud, Moel Farlwyd, 2m W of Blaenau Ffestiniog, Merioneth, on return from Lorient, 21.3.41
R3289	99	Missing (Ruhr) 7.11.40; believed shot down by intruder off Felixstowe
R3290	-	To 3219M 17.7.42
R3291	115/38	SOC 1.5.41 in Middle East; reason not known; may have been abandoned in Greece
R3292	115	Shot down by night fighter on return from Osnabrück, 1.10.40
R3293	38/OADF/15 OTU	Crashed in sea on ferry flight near Kalafrana, 16.6.41
R3294	15 OTU/23 OTU	To 3329M 15.8.42
R3295	99/101	Ran out of fuel and crash-landed, Schiermonnikoog, returning from Hamburg, 1.12.41
R3296	9/12 OTU	Stalled overshooting Benson and spun into ground, Drayton St.Leonard, Oxon., 19.6.41
R3297	75/57/25 OTU/ 30 OTU/11 OTU/ 105 OTU	SOC 8.7.44
R3298	Mkrs & AAEE/TFU/ Bristols	Mk.V prototype; SOC 5.3.43
R3299	Mkrs & AAEE	Mk.V prototype; to 3504M 16.1.43

*   *   *   *   *   *   *   *   *   *

Serial	Units	Fate
R3303	-	To RCAF 28.2.40 as 6014
R3304	10 OTU	Engine cut on navex; ditched in Irish Sea, 1.10.40
R3305	48	Wing hit ground in turn in bad visibility on beach, Hoylake, Cheshire, 1.1.41
R3306	10 OTU	Hit trees recovering from dive during army co-operation exercise and crashed, Tilehurst Camp, Berks., 27.7.41
R3307	-	To RCAF 28.2.40 as 6015
R3308	48/15 Gp CF/ ATA	SOC 23.5.44
R3309	-	To RCAF 28.2.40 as 6011
R3310	14 OTU/25 OTU/ 14 OTU	Abandoned in bad weather on night navex ½m W of Sutton St.James, Lincs., 3.10.41
R3311	-	To SAAF 11.3.40 as 1106
R3312	206/500	To SAAF 27.9.41 as 3133
R3313	11 AONS/BATDU/ RAE/WIDU/109/ 16 OTU/29 OTU/ 6 PAFU/10 RS	SOC 25.10.45
R3314	-	To SAAF 11.3.40 as 1107
R3315	-	To SAAF 15.3.40 as 1116
R3316	608/10 OTU	SOC 19.10.44
R3317	-	To SAAF 15.3.40 as 1114
R3318	48/6 OTU/ 5 AOS/7 OAFU	SS 25.5.60
R3319	-	To SAAF 15.3.40 as 1115
R3320	A-S/3 PAFU/1 AGS/ 3 PAFU/ATA	SS 21.3.49
R3321	-	To RCAF 30.11.40 as 6266
R3322	-	To RCAF 7.3.40 as 6024
R3323	48/1 OTU/ATA/	SOC 15.12.44
R3324	-	To RCAF 17.3.40 as 6023
R3325	10 OTU/2 OAFU/ 2 AOS/SPTU/19 PAFU/ 2 AGS/25 EFTS/SFC	SOC 20.2.45
R3326	-	To SAAF 3.1.41 as 1198
R3327	-	To RCAF 16.3.40 as 6020
R3328	612/2 OTU/42 OTU/ 7 AOS/5 PAFU/ 3 OAFU	SOC 26.7.46
R3329	4 FP/ATA	SS 28.7.47
R3330	-	To RCAF 16.3.40 as 6021
R3331	48/16 OTU	Engine cut on navex; wing hit ground in forced landing, Cotton Hall Farm, Denbigh, 21.2.41
R3332	-	To RCAF 16.3.40 as 6022
R3333	612	Ran out of fuel and ditched on convoy escort 25m NE of Tiumpan Head, Lewis, 6.9.40
R3334	4 FPP	To RAAF 31.3.40
R3335	502/48	Engine cut on take-off; stalled and crashed in garden, Anderson Road, Goathill, Stornoway, 16.12.41
R3336	4 FPP/8 FPP/ 10 OAFU/3 OAFU/ 10 OAFU	Collided with DJ335 and spun into Solway Firth 2m SW of Southerness Point, Dumfries, 27.6.44
R3337	-	To RAAF 31.3.40
R3338	6 FTS 32 OTU	To Canada 1.6.41 SOC 30.8.44
R3339	-	To RAAF 1.6.41
R3340	98/4 FPP/ATA	SOC 2.9.48
R3341	4 FPP	Hit by Battle L5452 while parked, Pouan LG, France, 8.5.40; DBR
R3342	-	To RAAF 31.3.40
R3343	2 FPP/4 FPP/7 FPP/ SFPP/4 AOS/ATA	SOC 18.9.44
R3344	4 FPP/11 SFF/ SFPP/3 RS/62 OTU/ 63 OTU/7 OAFU	SOC 31.12.45
R3345	-	To SAAF 19.7.40 as 1105
R3346	217/2 OTU/ 6 AOS/2 OAFU	Flew into sea on night approach 5m W of Millom, 13.4.44
R3347	9 AONS/2 SGR	To SAAF 26.5.41 as 1220
R3348	-	To RCAF 12.3.40 as 6025
R3349	500	SOC 27.8.40
R3350	500	To Canada 17.7.41
	33 ANS	SOC 22.1.45
R3351	-	To RCAF 12.3.40 as 6026
R3368	500/3 SGR/10 OAFU/ 3 SGR/10 OAFU/ 10 ANS/2 FP	Undercarriage collapsed while taxying at Portsmouth, 5.9.46
R3369	48/3 OTU/51 OTU/ 60 OTU/ATA	SOC 5.11.47
R3370	-	To RCAF 14.3.40 as 6027
R3371	15 OTU/10 OTU/ 1443 Flt/6 OTU/ 24 OTU/19 OTU/ATA	SOC 30.1.47
R3372	98 31 ANS	To Canada 14.12.40 SOC 8.10.46
R3373	-	To RCAF 14.3.40 as 6028
R3374	15 OTU/19 OTU/ S of ASR	SS 25.5.50
R3375	98/ATA/SPTU	SS 25.7.47
R3376	-	To RCAF 14.3.40 as 6029
R3377	31 ANS	To Canada 14.12.40 SOC 22.1.45
R3378	-	To RAAF 18.7.40
R3379	-	To SAAF 2.40 as 1124
R3380	17 OTU	To RCAF 1.8.41
R3381	17 OTU/3 AOS/ 3 OAFU	Overshot landing into ditch, Halfpenny Green, 15.3.44
R3382	-	To SAAF 30.3.40 as 1109
R3383	17 OTU 32 OTU	To Canada 4.4.41 SOC 22.1.45
R3384	20 OTU	Ran short of fuel on night navex and abandoned over Rose Valley, near Kinloss, 4.5.41
R3385	-	To SAAF 30.3.40 as 1108
R3386	14 OTU	Hit by Hampden P1289 taking off from Cottesmore, 15.7.41
R3387	500/7 AONS	To SAAF 26.9.41 as 1216
R3388	-	To SAAF 30.3.40 as 1118
R3389	500	Undershot night landing, hit trees, caught fire and bomb exploded, Detling, 31.5.40
R3390	-	To RCAF 6.5.41
R3391	-	To SAAF 1.4.40 as 1117
R3392	19 OTU/2 AOS/ 2 OAFU/7 AOS	Turned off runway after landing from night navex and ran into ditch, Bishops Court, 18.9.43
R3393	12 OTU/11 OTU/ 14 PAFU/ATA	SOC 5.11.47
R3394	-	To RCAF 1.4.40 as 6033
R3395	24	Used as VIP transport; to SAAF 15.1.41 as 1201
R3396	500	Lost at sea in *Murkon* en route to SAAF 30.9.41
R3397	-	To RCAF 1.4.40 as 6032
R3398	185/14 OTU	Crashed in forced landing, Castle Bytham, 6m NE of Cottesmore, 24.11.40
R3399	185/14 OTU/4 FPP/ ATA	SS 31.3.49
R3400	-	To RCAF 1.4.40 as 6030
R3401	18 OTU	To RCAF 12.3.41
R3402	18 OTU	Crashed on take off, Staverton, 10.12.40
R3403	-	To RCAF 4.4.40 as 6031
R3404	608	To RCAF 28.5.41
R3405	18 OTU/12 OTU/ 10 OTU	SOC 19.10.44

R3406	-	To RCAF 4.4.40 as 6034
R3407	SGR	To SAAF 16.11.40 as 3159
R3408	18 OTU	Hit balloon cable on night navex and crashed ¼m NNW of Stoke House, Walsgrave, Warks., 23.4.41
R3409	612/1 OTU/1 AOS	Iced up on navex and abandoned, Brant Fell, Cautley Crag, near Sedbergh, Westmoreland, 7.1.42
R3410	18 OTU/22 OTU/ 3 PAFU/7 AGS/ 3 OAFU/5 AOS	Engine cut after take off; crashlanded and hit bank, Ballyn, 2m W of Jurby, 27.8.43
R3411	4 FPP	Attacked on ground by enemy aircraft and burnt out, Amiens, 18.5.40
R3412	10 FTS	Destroyed in air raid, Ternhill, 16.10.40
R3413	612	To RCAF 4.3.41
R3429	TFU/Netheravon/295/ ATA/48MU CF	SOC 13.11.47
R3430	4 FPP/SFS/ 2 OAFU/1 OAFU	SOC 19.8.44
R3431	6 FTS	To Canada 1.6.41
	32 OTU	Crashed on search ½m W of Walker's Hook, BC, 17.12.42
R3432	2 SAN/1 BAS/2 AOS/ 2 OAFU	Flew into hill in bad visibility, Mullaghouyr, near Laxey, Isle of Man, 16.12.42
R3433	TFU/5 FTS	SOC 6.2.45
R3434	500	To RCAF 28.5.41
R3435	500	Stalled at low altitude in thick fog on patrol; crashed at Walcot, near Diss, Norfolk, 19.11.40
R3436	24	Hit HT cables in forced landing Wheatsheaf Lane, Barnet, Herts., 23.11.40
R3437	12 OTU/10 OTU/ 20 OTU	Stalled at low altitude in snow storm near Stonewall Farm, 3m E of Banff, 15.5.41; DBF
R3438	24	To Canada 12.4.41
	31 BGS	SOC 28.7.44
R3439	19 MU	SOC 12.9.40
R3440	24	To RCAF 16.3.41 in *Horda* but lost en route
R3441	2 SGR/SGR	To SAAF 18.11.40 as 1190
R3442	500	To RCAF 11.4.41
R3443	10 FTS/6 AONS/ 9 OAFU/7 AGS/ 6 OAFU/7 OAFU/ 22 FTS/66 Gp CF	SOC 5.11.48
R3444	-	To RCAF 8.4.40 as 6035
R3445	14 OTU/29 OTU/ 26 OTU/3 OTU/ 12 RS/7 OTU/ 14 RS	SOC 19.9.44
R3446	-	To RCAF 8.4.40 as 6036
R3447	10 FTS	To Canada 11.4.41
	31 GRS	SOC 16.8.46
R3448	-	To RCAF 8.4.40 as 6037
R3449	10 FTS	Destroyed in air raid, Ternhill 16.10.40
R3450	-	To RCAF 8.4.40 as 6038
R3451	-	To RCAF 30.11.40 as 6274
R3452	-	To SAAF 18.4.40 as 1121
R3453	-	To RAAF 1.4.40
R3454	-	To SAAF 16.4.40 as 1120
R3455	-	To RAAF 5.4.40
R3456	-	To RAAF 3.4.40
R3457	-	To RAAF 5.4.40
R3458	-	To SAAF 16.4.40 as 1122
R3459	1 FPP/ATA	SOC 3.8.45
R3460	-	To SAAF 16.4.40 as 1119
R3461	16 OTU	To SAAF 27.7.41 as 3141

R3462	16 OTU/26 OTU/ 6 OAFU/S of ASR	SOC 3.5.45
R3463	16 OTU	To Canada 12.8.41
	33 ANS	SOC 22.1.45
R3464	-	To SAAF 15.4.40 as 1123
R3465	16 OTU/18 OTU/ 10 OTU/24 OTU/ 42 OTU	SOC 26.3.45
R3466	-	To SAAF 16.4.40 as 1112
R3467	16 OTU	To Admiralty
R3468	-	To SAAF 15.4.40 as 1110
R3469	-	To SAAF 18.4.40 as 1111
R3470	-	To RCAF 18.4.40 as 6044
R3471	-	To RCAF 17.4.40 as 6045
R3472	-	To RCAF 18.4.40 as 6041
R3473	-	To RCAF 18.4.40 as 6042
R3474	-	To RAAF 22.4.40
R3475	-	To RAAF 22.4.40
R3476	-	To RCAF 29.4.40 as 6047
R3512	-	To RAAF 24.4.40
R3513	-	To RCAF 25.4.40 as 6039
R3514	-	To RCAF 18.4.40 as 6043
R3515	-	To RCAF 13.5.40 as 6046
R3516	-	To RAAF 22.4.40
R3517	-	To RCAF 13.4.40 as 6050
R3518	-	To RAAF 22.4.40
R3519	-	To RCAF 13.5.40 as 6051
R3520	-	To RAAF 2.5.40
R3521	-	To RAAF 8.4.40
R3522	-	To RCAF 29.4.40 as 6048
R3523	-	To RCAF 9.5.40 as 6052
R3524	-	To RAAF 8.4.40
R3525	-	To RCAF 2.5.40
R3526	-	To RCAF 25.4.40 as 6040
R3527	-	To RCAF 13.5.40 as 6049
R3528 to R3531	-	To RAAF 13.5.40
R3532	-	To RAAF 29.4.40
R3533	-	To RCAF 13.5.40 as 6054
R3534	-	To RCAF 9.5.40 as 6055
R3535	-	To RCAF 9.5.40 as 6053
R3536	-	To RCAF 13.5.40 as 6056
R3537	-	To RAAF 29.4.40
R3538	-	To RCAF 13.5.40 as 6057
R3539 to R3543	-	To RAAF 13.5.40
R3544	-	To RAAF 16.5.40
R3545	-	To RAAF 13.5.40
R3546	-	To RCAF 13.5.40 as 6058
R3547	-	To RCAF 13.5.40 as 6059
R3548 to R3551	-	To RAAF 30.6.40
R3552 to R3558	-	To RAAF 16.5.40
R3559 to R3561	-	To RAAF 22.5.40
R3581 to R3583	-	To RAAF 22.5.40
R3584	WIDU/109/1 BAS/ 3 AOS/7 OTU	SOC 19.4.45
R3585	-	To SAAF 3.1.41 as 3113
R3586	WIDU/109/1 BAS/ 3 AOS/3 OAFU/ 16 PFTS	SOC 30.8.44
R3587	14 OTU/1 FIS/ 18 PAFU/7 PAFU	SS 8.2.49

*   *   *   *   *   *   *   *   *   *

250 Bristol Blenheim IVs delivered between March and June 1940 by Rootes to Contract No. 1485/39

R3590	59/18	Crashlanded on return from reconnaissance, Vaucogne, Aube, 11.5.40

117

Serial	Units	Fate
R3591	57/17 OTU	Engine cut on take-off; crash-landed 1m W of Upwood, 11.9.42
R3592	57/5 BGS/5 AOS	Engine cut; lost height and crashed in forced landing on sands in Duddon Estuary near Millom, 27.7.42; DBF
R3593	2 FP/ME	Lost 26.11.40; NFD
R3594	57/15/114	Hit tree on approach to Horsham St. Faith and crashed returning from Cologne, Old Catton, Norfolk, 27.11.40
R3595	57	Presumed lost in France 5.40
R3596	53	Damaged by ground fire near Arras and crashed on landing, Hawkinge, 22.5.40
R3597	114/218	Flew into ground on low flying exercise, Harrold, Beds., 13.7.42
R3598	57/18	Missing from reconnaissance of Channel Ports, 23.5.40; believed crashed near Abbeville
R3599	105/21/13 OTU	Stalled in cloud and spun; abandoned and crashed, Green Lane, Trowbridge, Wilts., 24.5.42
R3600	PDU/110	Missing from attack on convoy off Dutch coast, 6.5.41
R3601	RAE/SDF/TFU/13 OTU/17 OTU/13 OTU	To Admiralty 8.2.44
R3602	PDU/53	Damaged by Bf 109 6.6.40 and abandoned at Rouen/Boos
R3603	40/15	Missing (Sterkadeholten) 18.7.40
R3604	40/15/82	Shot down by ships' flak off Den Helder, 20.3.41
R3605	53/2 OTU/13 OTU	Raised flaps on overshoot and sank into ground 1m NE of Catfoss, 30.6.41
R3606	105/107	Shot down by fighters, Amiens, 10.7.40
R3607	59/57/40/18/13 OTU	Overturned in forced landing when lost on navex in bad visibility, Ratby, Leics., 13.3.42
R3608	57/11	Engine cut on landing while avoiding another aircraft, Haifa, 15.6.41
R3609	40	Missing (Chartres airfield) 15.8.40
R3610	PDU/107	Lost 12.6.41; NFD
R3611	40/139/17 OTU	Engine cut on take-off; stalled and spun in to ground, Alconbury, 17.6.42
R3612	PDU/40	Missing (Ostend) 9.9.40
R3613	114/59	Crashed at Dussen, Belgium, on reconnaissance, 26.5.40
R3614	40/15	Engine cut on return from attack on Aa canal; control lost and spun into ground near Alconbury, 24.5.40
R3615	114/107/13 OTU/79 Wg/77 Wg/79 Wg/76 Wg/528/527	SOC 6.3.45
R3616	107	Damaged by Bf 110 over Acquigny after attacking bridge at Vernon and crashed, Caugé, Eure, 13.6.40
R3617	101/2 Gp TF/51 OTU	Shot down by intruder at night, Sherington, Bucks., 13.10.41
R3618	101/82	Crashed 2m NW of Poix after attacking enemy troops near Abbeville, 8.6.40
R3619	101/82	Damaged by Bf 109 during abortive raid on Bremen and crashed near Wittenhoek, Texel, 29.7.40
R3620	35/17 OTU/18/114	Missing from night intruder sortie to Bonn in support of raid on Essen, 2.6.42
R3621	35/17 OTU	Engine cut on take-off from Upwood; swung and flew into ground, Bury, Hunts., 3.9.40
R3622	254	Missing on sweep to Stavanger and Bergen, 25.6.40
R3623	254/51 OTU/301 FTU/1 OADU	To Portugal 17.9.42
R3624	254	Hit by AA fire and ditched off Goodwins, 29.5.40
R3625	248	Collided with Blenheim and dived into sea on shipping patrol off Wick, 13.12.40
R3626	248	Missing from reconnaissance to Norwegian coast, 1.10.40
R3627	254	Lost 12.6.40; NFD
R3628	254	Lost prop and crashlanded at Scatsta, 29.4.40; DBR
R3629	254	Damaged by Hurricane on convoy escort and undercarriage collapsed on landing, Montrose, 2.10.40; destroyed in air raid, 25.10.40
R3630	254	Shot down by Bf 109s over Goodwin Sands, 1.6.40
R3631	Andover/59	Missing from shipping sweep off Channel Ports, 21.8.41
R3632	Andover	DBR in air raid, Andover, 13.8.40
R3633	53	Presumed lost in France 6.40
R3634	53	Bellylanded near Rosières in fog while lost on return from night reconnaissance over Germany, 9.5.40
R3635	59	Missing (Cherbourg) 20.9.40
R3636	21	Engine exploded after take-off from Bodney for Wilhelmshaven; spun into ground 1m W of Garboldisham, Norfolk, 18.3.41; DBF
R3637	59	Blew up at night near Ludlow, Salop., 10.7.40
R3638	53/57/59/2 OTU/42 OTU	SOC 5.2.45
R3639	59	Crashed on landing, Thorney Island, 23.7.40
R3660	53/55	Crashed near El Alamein on return from night raid, 29.10.41
R3661	53	Shot down by Bf 109 in Scheldt during raid on Vlissingen, 18.7.40
R3662	18	Missing from night intruder over N.France, 6.7.40
R3663	18	Crashed on landing returning from Nordenham, Great Massingham, 2.9.40
R3664	59	Shot down by flak 15m S of Dunkerque, 28.5.40
R3665	AASF/Thorney Island	Ditched 14.7.40; NFD
R3666	57/218/18	Shot down on shipping sweep by Bf 110s off Kamperduin, 23.7.41
R3667	57	SOC 14.10.40
R3668	59/1 AGS	SOC 23.1.44
R3669	18/105/17 OTU	Engine cut; crashed in forced landing near Wellingore, 8.7.42
R3670	82/110	Shot down by flak near Amiens, 8.6.40

R3671	139	Missing from anti-shipping sweep, 14.10.40	R3701	82	Shot down by Bf 109 off Dutch coast on intruder to Amsterdam area, 13.7.40
R3672	114	Overshot landing from training flight on to railway line and overturned, Oulton, 11.12.40; DBR	R3702	59	Missing from reconnaissance mission, 21.5.40
R3673	139/218/21	Overshot landing and hit trees, Bodney, 24.3.41, on return from Hannover	R3703	53	Damaged by fighters and abandoned over St.Margarets, Kent, 27.5.40
R3674	21	Crashed 5m W of Pont-Audemar, Eure, during attack on enemy troops, 11.6.40	R3704	15/139/226	Shot down by fighters off Le Havre on shipping sweep, 14.7.41
R3675	21/17 OTU	Engine cut after take-off; stalled and crashed, Upwood, 9.12.41; DBF	R3705	139/13 OTU	Engine cut on take-off from Bicester; lost height and crash-landed, Bucknell, 29.11.40
R3676	21	Missing (Forêt de Gault) 13.6.40; crashed, St.Hilliers (Seine-et-Marne)	R3706	15	Hit by flak during attack on enemy columns near Montreuil and crashlanded near Etaples, 20.5.40
R3677	53	Destroyed in air raid, Detling, 13.8.40	R3707	82/105	Shot down by Bf 109 after attack on convoy off Ameland, 25.5.41
R3678	53/59/2 OTU/ 107/114	SOC 15.5.44	R3708	82/21/57/13/244	SOC 1.8.43
R3679	53/RAE/53	Presumed Blenheim DBR in air raid, Bircham Newton, 16.2.41	R3709	82	Shot down attacking dumps near Abbeville, Lamotte-Buleux, Somme, 8.6.40
R3680	Mkrs/57	Engine cut; overshot landing at Dyce, 4.7.40	R3730	82	Missing from reconnaissance off Dutch and Belgian coast, 8.9.40
R3681	110/5 AOS/1 AAS	SOC 16.4.44			
R3682	40/57/105	Overshot landing; swung and undercarriage collapsed, Swanton Morley, 23.3.41	R3731	82	Shot down by Bf 109, Austerlitz near Utrecht, during intruder over NW Germany, 27.6.40
R3683	40/107	Hit by flak, Gravelines, and overturned on landing, Wattisham, 2.6.40	R3732	18/82/21	Missing (Stavanger) 9.7.40
			R3733	18/W.Raynham/ Thorney Island/ ME/India	SOC 1.1.47
R3684	110/17 OTU/13 OTU	SOC 7.3.44			
R3685	40/107	Shot down by flak, Poix, during attack on Forêt de Boray, 9.6.40	R3734	18/17 OTU	Engine cut; lost height and crashlanded 3m W of Whittlesey ranges, Hunts., 29.8.41
R3686	107	Hit by flak attacking troops near Abbeville and crashlanded, Longueville-sur-Scie, Seine-Maritime, 7.6.40	R3735	53	Lost in France 6.40
			R3736	110	Flew into sea at night in the Wash returning from intruder operation and crashlanded, Wattisham, 24.7.40
R3687	21	Hit trees and crashed in return from Hamburg, Longfield, Kent, 16.11.40	R3737	107	Both engines cut returning from night intruder; crashlanded 5m W of Stowmarket, Suffolk, 15.11.40
R3688	105/107	Shot down by Bf 110 on return from Soest, Willemsoord, Neth., 23.6.40;	R3738	110	Shot down by Bf 109s in sea off Voorne during raid on Vlissingen airfield, 20.7.40
R3689	2 SAC/40/101/60	Tyre burst on take-off, Dum Dum, 24.10.42	R3739	107	Missing (Forêt de Boray) 8.6.40
R3690	RAE/82	Missing (French airfields) 11.7.40	R3740	107	Shot down by flak from convoy off Farsund, Norway, 18.4.41
R3691	2 SAC/53	Missing from reconnaissance over N.France, 23.5.40	R3741	110/18	Shot down by flak during attack on shipping off Tréguier, Côtes-du-Nord, 7.5.41
R3692	2 SAC/40	Crashlanded near St.Valery after attacking enemy columns near Abbeville, 6.6.40	R3742	21	Missing (Merville) 14.6.40; presumed shot down by Bf 109s
R3693	2 SAC/40	Shot down by flak 5m SW of Dreux while attacking troops in Somme area, 14.6.40	R3743	40/114	Flew into sea in flat calm on low-level bombing practice; bellylanded at North Wootton, Norfolk, 8.8.41
R3694	2 SAC/59	Missing (Cherbourg) 17.7.40			
R3695	2 SAC/59/1 OTU/ 2 OTU/235/254/ 143	To Admiralty 6.1.44	R3744	40/110/114	Engine cut on take-off from Horsham St.Faith for Mannheim; lost height and bellylanded, Sprowston, Norfolk, 16.12.40
R3696	2 SAC/59	Lost in France 6.40			
R3697	2 SAC/59	Wing hit ground in circuit; crashed 1m N of Eastchurch, 4.6.40; DBF	R3745	AAEE/40/3 OTU/ 51 OTU/13 OTU	Overshot flapless landing, Bicester, 22.4.43; DBR
R3698	139/Mkrs/ 13 Gp AACF	Engine cut on take-off; swung into soft ground and under-carriage collapsed, Aston Down, 4.9.41	R3746	110/15	Crashlanded after raid on Poix, 2m SSW of Gamaches, Seine Maritime, 8.6.40
R3699	53	Became uncontrollable on patrol and abandoned near Tonbridge, Kent, 21.10.40	R3747	110/15	Shot down, Malleville-les-Grès, Seine Maritime, en route to Le Bourget, 12.6.40
R3700	53	Missing on reconnaissance, 27.5.40			

R3748	110	Crashed off Haamstede, Neth. after attack on Bernburg airfield, 24.7.40
R3749	110	DBR in air raid, Wattisham, 27.10.40
R3750	57	Shot down by fighters, Stavanger, 9.7.40
R3751	57/13 OTU	Control lost in cloud; dived into ground, Shillingford, Devon, 3.3.41; DBF
R3752	57/18/101/54 OTU	Iced up; lost height and flew into ground 3m E of Church Fenton, 8.1.42
R3753	114	Shot down by Bf 109 off De Kooy on intruder mission to Dortmund, 10.11.40
R3754	82	Missing (Abbeville) 8.6.40
R3755	82/21	Missing from anti-shipping sweep, 5.9.40
R3756	82	Missing (Amsterdam) 13.7.40
R3757	139/21	Lost height after take-off on night training flight; hit ground and blew up, Bodney, 5.11.40
R3758	82/21/614	Overshot landing; hit ditch and overturned, Odiham, 29.8.42
R3759	82	Overshot at night in heavy rain and hit pillbox, Hendon, 9.6.40
R3760	AAEE/21/3 OTU/ 54 OTU	Hit tree on approach at night, and crashlanded, Church Fenton, 13.12.41
R3761	82/21/13 OTU	Engine cut on take-off from Bicester; lost height and crashed at Stratton Audley, Oxon., 28.9.42; DBF
R3762	82/72 OTU	Engine cut; bellylanded, Kosti, 5.4.42; believed not repaired and SOC 31.8.42
R3763	40	Shot down by flak during attack on Eelde airfield, 26.7.40
R3764	15	Damaged by Bf 109 during attack on Vlissingen airfield after aborting raid on Paderborn and abandoned off Breskens, 30.7.40
R3765	82	Ditched near Outer Dowsing lightship when lost and low on fuel on return from Hamm, 11.11.40
R3766	15/114/1 AGS	Engine cut; crashed in forced landing, Fairwood Common, 21.8.43
R3767	15/82	Shot down by Bf 109s off Heligoland, 26.8.41
R3768	15	Missing (Lannion) 12.8.40; crashed, Fermanville, Manche
R3769	15	Crashed on return from intruder mission to St.Omer and blew up, Latimer, 3m SSE of Kettering, 4.9.40
R3770	15	Missing (Forêt de Guines) 16.8.40
R3771	15	Control lost during fighter affiliation; dived into ground Norbury, Salop., 4.8.40
R3772	110/17 OTU	Stalled on landing and undercarriage leg collapsed, Warboys, 30.3.42
R3773	110	Flew into ground at night, Offton, Suffolk, 31.8.40, on return from Emden
R3774	110	Missing (St.Omer) 27.5.40
R3775	110	Missing (St.Inglevert) 10.8.40; crashed, Lihen-lès-Guines, Pas de Calais
R3776	110	Shot down by Bf 109 off Dutch coast on return from Soest, 26.6.40
R3777	15/45/607	SOC 17.7.44
R3778	40	Shot down by Bf 109 on photographic reconnaissance over Boulogne area, 27.6.40
R3779	53	Shot down by Bf 109s on shipping strike off Calais, 9.9.40
R3800	82	Shot down, Aalborg, 13.8.40
R3801	18/101/107	Missing (Westerland) 30.6.41; crashed in sea off Sylt
R3802	82	Shot down, Aalborg, 13.8.40
R3803	101/82/21	Missing (Kiel Canal) 30.7.41
R3804	114	Missing (Soest) 5.7.40
R3805	114/13 OTU/ 114/13 OTU	Both engines cut in Finmere circuit; stalled and spun into ground, Sherswell Park, 17.7.41
R3806	114/57/107/114	Lost power on take-off; hit tree and crashed, Thornaby, 19.4.41; DBF
R3807	110	DBR in air raid, Wattisham, 27.10.40
R3808	82/13 OTU/54 OTU	Control lost on night overshoot; stalled and crashed, Church Fenton, 26.3.42; DBF
R3809	114	Missing (Boulogne) 26.9.40; presumed ditched in Channel
R3810	107	Shot down by flak attacking troop columns, La Mare (sic), 12.6.40
R3811	40	Missing from night intruder to Querqueville/Maupertus airfields, 26.8.40
R3812	82	Stalled on landing at night and undercarriage collapsed, Bodney, 4.3.41
R3813	114/13 OTU/ 21/114	Lost height and crashed after engine caught fire on exercise, Lacha Lane, Chester, 3.8.42
R3814	40/110/17 OTU	Flew into sea 17.9.41; cause not known
R3815	107	Shot down by fighters, Amiens, 10.7.40
R3816	107	Elevator trim tabs jammed; stalled after take-off and crashlanded, Manston, 7.8.41
R3817	59	Missing on reconnaissance mission, 19.6.40
R3818	59	Missing on reconnaissance mission, 19.6.40
R3819	53	Destroyed in air raid, Detling, 13.8.40
R3820	21	Stalled during dummy attack on another aircraft and spun into sea 1m N of Lossiemouth, 23.7.40
R3821	82	Shot down, Aalborg, 13.8.40
R3822	21	Missing (Stavanger) 9.7.40
R3823	107	Shot down by flak, Wittes, Pas de Calais, after attack on Merville, 30.6.40
R3824	107	Hit parked aircraft on landing at night, Wattisham, 4.9.40 on return from Mardyck
R3825	57/107/1416 Flt/ 140	SOC 24.5.44
R3826	235/254	Missing from patrol, 24.6.40
R3827	235/254	Crashed on take-off, Wick, 4.3.41
R3828	107/110	Damaged by flak and crashlanded, Wattisham, on return from reconnaissance to Munster, 26.6.40; DBR

Above: Lysander II of No. 225 Squadron picking up a message

Below: Another of No. 225's Lysanders, R1999

121

Above: Lancaster R5852, OL-Y of No. 83 Squadron

Below: Lancaster R5727, fitted with a ventral turret, in Canada

122

R3829	82	Shot down, Aalborg, 13.8.40	R3879	2 OTU/13/Blen Flt/42 OTU	SOC 21.1.44	
R3830	57/101/82/17 OTU/ 301 FTU/1 OADU	To Portugal 1.9.43	R3880	59	Missing from reconnaissance mission, 31.8.40	
R3831	107/110	DBR in air raid, Wattisham, 11.11.40	R3881	59	Hit HT pole in low cloud and crashed, Titterstone Quarry, Clee Hill, Ludlow, Salop., 10.7.40	
R3832	57/110	Lost power after take-off from Horsham St.Faith and crash-landed, Costessey Hall, 14.3.41; DBF	R3882	59/57	Stalled and dived into ground on approach from night navex, Bog-o-Mayne, near Elgin, Moray, 4.9.40	
R3833	59/5 AOS	Engine cut; lost height and ditched in Irish Sea between Jurby and Rhyl, 15.11.42	R3883	59/57/8/55/ WDCF/14/4 METS	SOC 1.12.43	
R3834	2 SAC/6 OTU/ 42 OTU	Tyre burst on take-off; swung and undercarriage collapsed; engine caught fire, Thruxton, 6.7.42; DBR	R3884	114/21	Shot down by ship's flak on shipping sweep off Texel, 31.3.41	
R3835	59	Destroyed in air raid, Manston, 16.8.40	R3885	139	Engine failed on ferry flight; lost height and ditched off Gibraltar, 11.5.41	
R3836	53	Shot down by ships' flak off Ballum, Ameland during raid on barges at Haarlem, 25.7.40	R3886	236	Engine cut; crashed in forced landing after hitting HT cables, Carnanton, Cornwall, 4.11.40; DBR	
R3837	59/17 OTU/114	Shot down by Bf 110 on night intruder mission to Venlo, Schandeloo, Neth., 26.7.42	R3887	254	Stalled on approach, Sumburgh, 22.7.40; DBF	
R3838	105/13 OTU	Missing on navex over North Sea, presumably ditched off Lincolnshire coast, 31.3.42	R3888	254	To Admiralty 16.3.43	
			R3889	57/59	Missing (Lorient) 26.11.40	
R3839	272/254	Flew into Ridgeway after night take-off for convoy escort from Carew Cheriton, 5.3.42	R3890	57/59/75 Wg/70 Wg	Skidded on wet grass on landing and overshot; hit house, Inverness, 17.11.42	
R3840	1 CACU/3 FPP	Hit balloon cable and crashed near Birmingham, 28.10.40	R3891	114/13 OTU	SOC 27.2.44	
R3841	18	Missing from attack on enemy shipping off Camaret, Finistère, 15.4.41	R3892	139/114	Shot down by Bf 109, Middenbeemster, Neth., on return from Bremen/Oslebshausen, 19.8.40	
R3842	18	Stalled and spun into ground during formation practice 3m SW of Gt. Massingham, 19.7.40	R3893	40	Shot down by flak, Eletôt, Seine Maritime, during attack on enemy troops near St.Valery, 12.6.40	
R3843	18	Flew into bomb bursts of another aircraft while attacking convoy off Zandvoort, 20.9.41	R3894	15/8	Undercarriage jammed up; bellylanded, Khormaksar, 10.9.41; NFT	
R3844	59/105/88/105/ 21/14/162	SOC 1.2.44	R3895	114	Missing (Aalborg) 31.7.40	
R3845	101/Lorraine/ 13(H)	Overshot landing and overturned, Gaza East, 6.11.42	R3896	15	Crashed near Bruges on photographic reconnaissance of Ghent area, 7.7.40	
R3846	101	Hit by flak, Wilhelmshaven, and believed crashed off Texel, 19.3.41	R3897	114	Shot down by flak attacking Gilze-Rijen airfield and crashed, De Moer, 31.12.40	
R3847	59/57	Shot down by fighters, Stavanger, 9.7.40	R3898	114	Shot down by Bf 109s during attack on Haamstede airfield, 1.8.40	
R3848	57/13 OTU	Engine cut; lost height and second engine failed; crash-landed, Brook Farm, Moorhouse, Notts., 29.6.42; DBF	R3899	40/14/11	SOC 30.4.44	
R3849	53	Destroyed in air raid, Detling, 13.8.40	R3900	21	Shot down by ship's flak on shipping sweep off Texel, 3.3.41	
R3870	107	Hit by flak, Merville, and crashed, Ecques, Pas de Calais, 30.6.40	R3901	139/13(H)/ 52/454	Undercarriage retracted after landing, Qaiyara, 25.11.42; DBR	
R3871	107/225/13/42 OTU	To Admiralty 13.4.44	R3902	139/13 OTU	Engine cut on take-off; ran into hedge attempting to stop, Bicester, 2.11.42; DBR	
R3872	21/11	NFT				
R3873	107	Shot down by flak on shipping strike off Farsund, Norway, 18.4.41	R3903	139	Shot down by Bf 109 during attack on De Kooy off Bergen aan Zee, 4.6.41	
R3874	110/13 OTU	Engine cut after take-off from Bicester; hit tree and crashed, Stoke Littlewood, 6.11.42	R3904	15/82	Shot down, Aalborg, 13.8.40	
			R3905	15/139/110	Shot down by ships' flak attacking convoy off Westkapelle, Walcheren, 12.4.41	
R3875	21/17 OTU	Spun into ground on navex, Cressage, Salop., 7.9.41; DBF; presumed control lost in cloud	R3906	139/110/17 OTU/ 13 OTU	SOC 27.2.44	
R3876	21	Missing (Stavanger) 9.7.40	R3907	139/105/88/13 OTU	Engine cut; stalled and dived into ground out of cloud, Stert, near Devizes, Wilts., 29.1.42; DBF	
R3877	-	To FFAF 10.40				
R3878	236	Shot down by Bf 109 on reconnaissance off Brest, 21.12.40				

R3908	139/9 AOS/9 OAFU	SOC 5.2.44
R3909	53/235	Hit pole on night approach in bad weather and crashed, Dyce, 5.9.41
R3910	21/82	Missing from airfield attacks on Cherbourg and Guernsey, 10.8.40
R3911	53/Manston/11	Missing from attack on Japanese carrier force off Ceylon, 9.4.42
R3912	139/13 OTU	Dived into ground out of cloud 1½m W of Pawlett, Somerset, 5.7.42
R3913	82	Missing (Aalborg) 13.8.40
R3914	82/21	Flew into hill returning from Cologne and blew up, Middleton in Teesdale, Co. Durham, 26.11.40
R3915	82	Missing from reconnaissance off Dutch and Belgian coast 8.9.40
R3916	107	Shot down by fighters, Amiens, 10.7.40
R3917	113	SOC 14.2.41
R3918	ME	Lost in Greece 5.41
R3919	55/113/152 OTU	Undershot landing and hit wires, Peshawar, 28.6.43; DBR

*   *   *   *   *   *   *   *   *   *

100 Fairey Battle Is delivered between October 1939 and May 1940 by Austin Motor Co. to Contract No. 2580/39

R3922	-	To RCAF 27.10.40 as 1744
R3923	-	To RCAF 27.10.40 as 1770
R3924	-	To RAAF 18.8.40
R3925	-	To RAAF 2.11.40
R3926	-	To RCAF 27.10.40 as 1777
R3927	-	To RAAF 18.9.40
R3928	-	To RAAF 27.10.40
R3929	-	To RAAF 1.11.40
R3930	-	To RCAF 27.10.40 as 1751
R3931	-	To RAAF 14.11.40
R3932	-	To RCAF 27.10.40 as 1823
R3933	-	To RCAF 27.10.40 as 1775
R3934	-	To RAAF 18.8.40
R3935	-	To RCAF 6.9.40 as 1701
R3936	-	To RAAF 19.9.40
R3937	-	To RCAF 27.10.40 as 1745
R3938	-	To SAAF 19.7.40 as 926
R3939	-	To RAAF 19.9.40
R3940	-	To RCAF 22.10.40 as 1732
R3941	-	To RCAF 28.11.40 as 1836
R3942	-	To RCAF 26.9.40 as 1711
R3943	-	To RCAF 28.11.40 as 1793
R3944	-	To RAAF 19.8.40
R3945	-	To SAAF 19.7.40 as 927
R3946	-	To RCAF 22.10.40 as 1728
R3947	-	To RCAF 11.3.41 as 1923
R3948	-	To RAAF 15.1.41
R3949	-	To RAAF 24.3.41
R3950	-	To RCAF 7.3.41 as 1899
R3951	-	To RAAF 24.3.41
R3952	-	To RCAF 7.2.41 as 1845
R3953	-	To RCAF 1.2.41 as 1929
R3954	-	To RAAF 4.6.41
R3955	-	To RCAF 28.11.40 as 1828
R3956	-	To RAAF 15.1.41
R3957	-	To RAAF 15.1.41
R3958	-	To RCAF 3.12.40
R3959	-	To RCAF 8.10.40
R3960	-	To RCAF 21.10.40
R3961	-	To RCAF 4.5.41
R3962	-	To Canada 28.12.40
	31 SFTS	SOC 4.11.44

R3963	-	To RCAF 28.12.40
R3964	-	To RCAF 28.12.40
R3965	-	To RCAF 26.10.40
R3966	-	To RCAF 29.12.40
R3967	-	To RCAF 26.10.40
R3968	-	To RCAF 23.2.41 as 1882
R3969	-	To Canada 28.12.40
	31 SFTS	Flew into boat house, Seeleys Bay, Lake Ontario, 9.6.41
R3970	-	To RCAF 11.12.40 as 1838
R3971	-	To RCAF 18.12.40 as 1819
R3990	-	To RCAF 28.10.40
R3991	-	To Canada 28.10.40
	31 SFTS	SOC 7.3.45
R3992	-	To Canada 28.10.40
	31 BGS	SOC 1.5.44
R3993	-	To Canada 20.3.41
	31 BGS	SOC 1.5.44
R3992	-	To RCAF 23.10.40
R3993	-	To RCAF 20.3.41
R3994	-	To RCAF 23.10.40
R3995	-	To Canada 31.3.41
	31 SFTS	SOC 17.6.46
R3996	-	To RCAF 31.3.41
R3997	-	To RCAF 31.3.41
R3998	-	To Canada 15.3.41
	31 BGS	SOC 4.11.44
R3999	-	To RCAF 5.12.40 as 1784
R4000	-	To RCAF 24.8.40
R4001	-	To RCAF 11.6.41 as 1999
R4002	-	To RAAF 11.3.41
R4003	-	To SAAF 5.41 as 933
R4004	-	To SAAF 5.41 as 931
R4005	-	To RCAF 1.11.40 as 1756
R4006	-	To RAAF 14.11.40
R4007	-	To RCAF 2.3.41 as 1880
R4008	-	To RAAF 14.11.40
R4009	-	To RAAF 14.11.40
R4010	-	To RCAF 7.2.41 as 1846
R4011	-	To RCAF 3.12.40 as 1786
R4012	-	To RAAF 14.11.40
R4013	-	To Canada 8.10.40
	31 SFTS	SOC 4.11.44
R4014	-	To RCAF 1.10.40
R4015	-	To Canada 1.12.40
	31 SFTS	SOC 4.11.44
R4016	-	To RCAF 26.10.40
R4017	-	To RCAF 21.10.40
R4018	-	To RCAF 3.10.40
R4019	-	To RAAF 15.1.41
R4035	-	To RCAF 5.12.40 as 1783
R4036	-	To RCAF 15.11.40 as 1739
R4037	-	To RCAF 8.10.40
R4038	-	To RCAF 5.12.40 as 1785
R4039	-	To Canada 18.12.40
	31 SFTS	SOC 1.3.44
R4040	-	To RCAF 5.12.40 as 1788
R4041	-	To Canada 24.8.40
	31 SFTS	To GI as A165 18.7.42
R4042	-	To RCAF 3.11.40
R4043	-	To RCAF 12.10.40
R4044	-	To RCAF 15.11.40 as 1740
R4045	-	To RCAF 28.11.40 as 1822
R4046	-	To RCAF 21.10.40 as 1822
R4047	-	To RCAF 28.11.40 as 1835
R4048	-	To RCAF 28.11.40 as 1792
R4049	-	To RAAF 2.11.40
R4050	-	To RCAF 28.12.40
R4051	-	To RCAF 3.10.40
R4052	-	To Canada 24.8.40
R4053	-	To Canada 21.10.40
	31 SFTS	SOC 4.11.44
R4054	-	To RCAF 3.12.40 as 1787

*   *   *   *   *   *   *   *   *   *   *

Lockheed Hudson I delivered in July 1940 by Lockheed Aircraft, Burbank, to Contract No.791587/38, to replace N7260

R4059	220	Swung on take-off and under-carriage collapsed, Wick, 5.7.41; DBF

* * * * * * * * * *

R4060, R4061		Percival Q.6s to Contract No.965632/38 cancelled

* * * * * * * * * *

Six Airspeed Oxford Is delivered in July and August 1940 by Airspeed, Portsmouth, to Contract No.777546/38

R4062 to R4064	-	To RNZAF 23.8.40 but lost at sea en route, 31.8.40
R4065	-	To RNZAF 30.8.40 as NZ1248
R4066	- 21 SFTS	To S.Rhodesia 12.8.40; SOC 2.7.45
R4067	- 21 SFTS	To S.Rhodesia 29.8.40; SOC 31.3.44

* * * * * * * * * *

Miles Falcon delivered in November 1939 by Philips & Powis, Woodley, to Contract No.8425/39

R4071	RAE/FRL/RAE	Ex PH-EAD for spoiler tests; sold 29.1.46; became G-AGZX

* * * * * * * * * *

100 Hawker Hurricane Is delivered in July and August 1940 by Gloster Aircraft, Hucclecote, to Contract No.19773/39

R4074	151/46	Shot down by fighters, Newchurch, Kent, 22.10.40
R4075	1	Shot down by enemy aircraft off Harwich, 15.8.40
R4076	3/17/331/56 OTU/ 2 TEU	SOC 6.6.44
R4077	3/Sumburgh/17	To Admiralty 22.12.41
R4078	3/Sumburgh/17	To Admiralty 12.12.41
R4079	3/245	Dived into ground during practice dogfight near Cushendall, Co.Antrim, 30.11.40
R4080	59 flight OTU	Crashed on training flight near Crosby, 11.11.41
R4081	32/253/303/71/ 56 OTU	Cv to Mk.II DR358, 8.41
R4082	-	To SAAF 20.8.40
R4083	-	To SAAF 20.8.40
R4084	310	Collided with P3888 and abandoned, Purley Way, Wallington, Surrey, 9.9.40
R4085	310	Damaged by fighters and abandoned ½m S of Billericay, Essex, 15.9.40
R4086	213/111/59 OTU	Crashed after collision near Crosby, 20.12.41
R4087	310	Damaged by fighters and abandoned near Chatham; crashed, Pitsea, Essex, 15.9.40
R4088	257/55 OTU	Missing on training flight, 16.7.41
R4089	310	To 4504M 1.2.44
R4090	4 FPP	Abandoned after engine failure on ferry flight, Rora Moss, Longside, Aberdeenshire, 1.8.40
R4091	17/308/401/56 OTU	Cv to Mk.II DR373, 9.41
R4092	601	Shot down off Portland Bill, Dorset, 11.8.40
R4093	56	Shot down by Bf 110 off Sheerness, Kent, 13.8.40
R4094	253/257	Missing from interception off St. Catherines Point, Isle of Wight, 8.8.40
R4095	302/MSFU	To Admiralty 30.3.42
R4096	111	Shot down by enemy aircraft near Martlesham Heath, 26.8.40
R4097	238	Shot down in sea 2m E of Weymouth, Dorset, 11.8.40
R4098	232/59 OTU	Abandoned in bad visibility, Barnglieshead Farm, near Dumfries, 17.3.42
R4099	213/238/59 OTU	Engine cut on take-off; stalled and spun into ground 1m E of Crosby, 25.8.41; DBF
R4100	303/59 OTU	SOC 18.6.41
R4101	501/306/52 OTU	DBR in accident, 3.8.41; NFD
R4102	43	Damaged by return fire from He 111s and crashlanded, Milland, Sussex, 13.8.40
R4103	2 SAAF/73 OTU/ Aden Def Flt	SOC 1.12.43
R4104	2 SAAF	To SAAF as 296
R4105	501/605/245	To Admiralty 4.41
R4106	32	Damaged by Bf 109 and abandoned, Chartham Hatch, Kent, 18.8.40
R4107	43/1 RCAF/55 OTU/ 316/87/55 OTU	Engine cut; crashlanded near Annan, 28.6.43
R4108	43	Damaged by enemy aircraft and crashed in forced landing, Tangmere, 12.8.40; later destroyed in air raid, 16.8.40
R4109	43/1 RCAF/213	Crashed after collision with Hurricane V6697 during practice dogfight near Castletown, 18.3.41
R4110	43	Destroyed in air raid, Tangmere, 16.8.40
R4111	615	Damaged by Bf 109 and abandoned off Herne Bay, Kent, 26.8.40
R4112	111/229/601/59 OTU	Hit trees in forced landing in bad weather 1½m E of Heathergill, Dumfries, 13.8.41; DBF
R4113	8 FTS/56 OTU/India	SOC 28.9.44
R4114	56/249	Shot down by Bf 109s, Hollingbourne, Kent, 7.9.40
R4115	242/111/59 OTU	Engine cut due to fuel mismanagement; crashed in attempted forced landing, Sleinsford, Northumberland, 23.9.42
R4116	615	Hit by return fire from Do 17 and crashlanded, Throwley, Kent, 28.8.40
R4117	56	Damaged by Bf 109s over Thames Estuary and abandoned, Herne Bay, Kent, 28.8.40
R4118	605/111/59 OTU/ 56 OTU/India	To GI airframe 4.10.44
R4119	615/5 FTS	To 3452M 24.11.42
R4120	501/601/501	Overshot forced landing in bad visibility and hit wall, Winfrith, Dorset, 30.4.41
R4121	615	Damaged by Bf 109s and abandoned off Sheerness, Kent, 26.8.40
R4122	32/315/303/55 OTU/ 239/56 OTU/2 TEU	SOC 7.6.44; 2687M NTU
R4123	317/55 OTU	Hit by P2906 while parked, Usworth, 9.3.42; DBR
R4171	1 RCAF	Shot down during interception near West Malling, 1.9.40

R4172	111	Shot down by Bf 109 off Folkestone, Kent, 4.9.40
R4173	303	Shot down by Bf 109, Roding Road, Loughton, Essex, 7.9.40
R4174	17	SOC 1.10.40; NFD
R4175	303	Crashed on patrol, Ewell, Surrey, 6.10.40; cause not known
R4176	145	Shot down by enemy aircraft S of Isle of Wight, 12.8.40
R4177	145/MSFU	To RCAF 4.6.42
R4178	303/504/249/316	To Admiralty 23.10.41
R4179	303/8 FTS/32 MU	Engine cut on approach; force-landed with undercarriage unlocked, St. Athan, 18.7.44
R4180	145	Shot down by enemy aircraft S of Isle of Wight, 12.8.40
R4181	151	Missing from interception over Chelmsford, Essex; presumed crashed off Essex coast, 18.8.40
R4182	151	NFT 28.8.40; SOC 21.9.40
R4183	151/52 OTU	Collided with W9149 during combat practice and crashed, 3.8.41
R4184	151	Dived into ground after night take-off, Digby, 26.10.40
R4185	151	Forcelanded while lost in bad visibility after interception near Biscathorpe, Lincs., 16.9.40
R4186	615	Destroyed in air raid, Kenley, 18.8.40
R4187	111	Shot down by AA while attacking Do 17s over Kenley, 18.8.40
R4188	111/238/59 OTU	Engine cut; bellylanded, Cornhill-on-Tweed, Northumberland, 5.5.43; DBR
R4189	257/601/607	Shot down by Bf 109 off Selsey, Sussex, 28.9.40
R4190	257/46/257/46	Flew into ground on patrol, Endery Farm, Asterby, Lincs., 22.2.41
R4191	145/601	Missing, presumed shot down by Bf 109s off Sussex coast, 18.8.40
R4192	615/317/71 OTU	SOC 28.8.44
R4193	111	Collided with Do 17 during attack and crashed, Collier Street, Kent, 15.8.40
R4194	615/9 FTS	SOC 22.12.41
R4195	111/257	Shot down by AA while attacking Bf 109s and crashed ½m S of Lydd, Kent, 22.10.40
R4196	56/43/17/55 OTU	SOC 13.7.42 for spares
R4197	56	Shot down by Bf 109s, Colchester, Essex, 31.8.40
R4198	56	Damaged over Thames Estuary, believed by Spitfire, and abandoned, 28.8.40
R4199	17	Shot down by Bf 110 off Portland, 25.8.40
<u>R4200</u>	32/315/303/55 OTU/ ME	SOC 1.4.44
R4213	151	Shot down by enemy aircraft, Epping Green, Essex, 30.8.40
R4214	601	To Admiralty 18.3.42
R4215	601	Shot down by enemy aircraft over Thames Estuary, 4.9.40
R4216	32/317/59 OTU/ 56 OTU/2 TEU	Engine cut due to fuel mismanagement; crashed in attempted forced landing, Dunbog, Fife, 27.3.44
R4217	303/56 OTU/55 OTU	Flew into Southwaite Head, Dockray, Cumberland, descending in cloud, 20.7.42

R4218	145/601	Damaged by Bf 110 and crash-landed near Axminster, Dorset, 7.10.40; cv to Mk.II BV155 during repair
R4219	501	Shot down by Bf 109s near Biggin Hill and crashed, East Seal, Kent, 18.8.40
R4220	615/402/52 OTU/ 56 OTU	Dived into ground during aerobatics, Clushford Toll, Fife, 27.4.42; presumed loss of control
R4221	615	Damaged by Bf 109 and crash-landed near Orpington, Kent, 18.8.40
R4222	501/245/8 FTS	To 2872M 3.11.41
R4223	501	Damaged by Bf 109s near Hawkinge and abandoned off Folkestone, Kent, 29.8.40
R4224	145/17	Damaged by Bf 110 and crashlanded near North Weald, 3.9.40
R4225	145/43	Engine cut on patrol; belly-landed, Hazeldene, Co. Durham 10.11.40
R4226	111	To Admiralty 20.7.41
R4227	145/43	Engine cut on convoy patrol; abandoned 1m off May Island, Firth of Forth, 15.12.40
R4228	111/87/1449 Flt	Ditched after engine cut 4m SW of St.Agnes, Cornwall, 1.11.42
R4229	56/249	Damaged by Bf 109s and abandoned near Maidstone, Kent, 6.9.40
R4230	56/249	Damaged by Bf 109s and abandoned over Maidstone, Kent, 7.9.40
R4231	43/56 OTU/9 Gp CF/ Netheravon/38 Gp CF	SOC 20.12.44
R4232	56/238/59 OTU/ 55 OTU	Dived into hill in cloud 2m S of Langholm, Dumfries, 6.12.42

*   *   *   *   *   *   *   *   *   *

R4236 and R4239	Vickers Type 432s to Specification F.22/39 under Contract No.17894/39 not built
R4243 - R4283; R4296 - R4325; R4345 - R4384; R4400 - R4445; R4460 - R4479; R4499 - R4521	200 cancelled Westland Whirlwinds to Contract No.20186/39
R4525 - R4554; R4572 - R4611; R4630 - R4649; R4670 - R4694; R4710 - R4744	Allotted to 150 cancelled Fairey-built Avro Manchesters

*   *   *   *   *   *   *   *   *   *

400 de Havilland Tiger Moth IIs delivered between December 1939 and May 1940 by de Havilland, Hatfield, to Contract No.20916/39

R4748	1 EFTS/26 EFTS/ 28 EFTS	Overturned by gust on landing, Penkridge, 4.12.44
R4749	10 EFTS/2/GPEU	SOC 3.1.45
R4750	1 EFTS/1 AACU/ 1607 Flt/595/631/ 2 STT	Sold 9.5.46; became G-AHLB
R4751	1 EFTS/28 EFTS	Sold 27.3.51
R4752	10 EFTS/10 FIS/RAE	To 6049M 9.8.46
R4753	1 EFTS/21 EFTS/ 10 FIS	SOC 14.7.44

Serial	Units	Fate
R4754	1 EFTS/29 EFTS/ 19 FTS/3 EFTS	Sold 16.9.48
R4755	-	To SAAF 19.3.40
R4756	-	To SAAF 19.3.40
R4757	2 EFTS/4 EFTS	Sold 29.3.51; became G-AMTU
R4758	10 EFTS/8 EFTS/ 26 EFTS/SF Halton	Sold 24.5.55; became EI-AHB
R4759	9 EFTS/8 RFS/25 RFS/ 2 RFS/2 GS/1 GU	Sold 6.11.53; became G-ANKN
R4760	10 EFTS/AAEE/ 4 EFTS/2 GU	SOC 14.5.53
R4761	- 25 EFTS	To S.Rhodesia 7.2.40 Undershot landing and overturned, Belvedere, 29.12.41; to GI airframe 0012M
R4762	13 EFTS/9 EFTS/ 29 EFTS	SS 30.3.50
R4763	4 EFTS	To BOAC as 6083M 16.8.46; later became G-ALOX
R4764	4 EFTS/7 EFTS/ 4 EFTS/18 EFTS/ 101 GOTU/29 EFTS	SS 30.3.50
R4765	3 EFTS/18 RFS/ 19 RFS/HCCS/ HC Exam Unit	Sold 18.10.54; became G-AOIP
R4766	1 PFTS/1 EFTS/ 29 EFTS	To 5902M 28.3.46
R4767	17 EFTS/15 EFTS	SS 30.3.50
R4768	13 EFTS/13 EFTS/ 21 EFTS	To SAAF 20.3.43 as No.4636
R4769	1 PFTS/25 PEFTS	To R.Neth AF 28.8.46
R4770	11 EFTS/7 EFTS/ 10 FIS/4 EFTS/4 RFS	Sold 12.5.49; became G-ALVP
R4771	PEFTS/1 PFTS/ 14 EFTS	To Belgian AF 1.4.46
R4772	6 EFTS	Stalled on to runway on landing, Denton, 21.6.45; DBR
R4773	6 EFTS/14 EFTS/ 16 EFTS	Engine cut on approach to forced landing, stalled and crashed in field, Church Greasley, near Derby, 6.7.45
R4774	14 EFTS	SOC 8.6.50
R4775	1 PFTS/25 PEFTS/ SF Rivenhall/SF Gosfield	Sold 24.4.46
R4776	7 EFTS/20 EFTS/ 4 EFTS/12 RFS	Sold 4.11.53; became G-ASSC
R4777	2 EFTS/4 EFTS	Sold 5.4.51
R4778	13 EFTS/16 OTU/ 22 EFTS/4 FIS/ 22 EFTS/21 EFTS	Sold 2.11.48; became G-AMEE
R4779	2 EFTS/19	SOC 25.9.45
R4780	10 EFTS/21 EFTS	Overturned on landing, Denham, 29.4.44; DBR
R4781	- 25 EFTS	To S.Rhodesia 7.2.40 SOC 13.3.46
R4782	14 EFTS	SS 30.3.50
R4783	10 EFTS/15 EFTS/ 1333 TSTU/Netheravon	Sold 24.2.49; became G-AMDL
R4784	26	Flew into HT cables 1m S of Three Bridges Stn., Sussex, 24.12.40; DBF
R4785	1 EFTS/13 EFTS/ 21 EFTS/7 EFTS/ 3 EFTS/3 EFTS/ 6 FTS	Damaged 27.1.49; sold 2.5.49 as wreck
R4786	- 27 EFTS	To S.Rhodesia 12.1.40 SOC 13.10.43
R4787	- 27 EFTS	To S.Rhodesia 12.1.40 NFT
R4788	-	To S.Rhodesia 12.1.40 SOC 17.10.45
R4789	-	To S.Rhodesia 7.2.40 SOC 14.7.44
R4790	- 27 EFTS	To S.Rhodesia 7.2.40 SOC 31.3.42
R4791	- 27 EFTS	To S.Rhodesia 12.1.40 Spun into ground on approach, Whites Run LG, 23.5.41; DBF
R4892	- 25 EFTS	To S.Rhodesia 7.2.40 SOC 2.11.45
R4793	- 28 EFTS	To S.Rhodesia 12.1.40 Hit ground recovering from spin, Mount Hampden, 13.2.42
R4794	- 25 EFTS/28 EFTS	To S.Rhodesia 7.2.40 Damaged 9.9.41; NFT
R4795	-	To S.Rhodesia 7.2.40 SOC 2.11.45
R4796	-	To S.Rhodesia 7.2.40 SOC 6.3.43
R4797	- 25 EFTS	To S.Rhodesia 7.2.40 SOC 31.5.46
R4810	- 25 EFTS	To S.Rhodesia 7.2.40 Stalled after take-off and hit trees, Hanyani Road LG, 23.5.42; DBR
R4811	- 25 EFTS	To S.Rhodesia 7.2.40 To SAAF 3.3.44
R4812	- 28 EFTS	To S.Rhodesia 7.2.40 SOC 9.8.44
R4813	- 25 EFTS	To S.Rhodesia 7.2.40 SOC 6.4.43
R4814	- 25 EFTS	To S.Rhodesia 12.1.40 SOC 31.12.44
R4815	- 27 EFTS	To S.Rhodesia 12.1.40 SOC 8.8.45
R4816	-	To S.Rhodesia 12.1.40 SOC 18.10.45
R4817	- 25 EFTS	To S.Rhodesia 12.1.40 To SAAF 31.5.44
R4818	-	To S.Rhodesia 12.1.40 To SAAF 3.3.44
R4819	- 25 EFTS	To S.Rhodesia 12.1.40 SOC 17.10.45
R4820	- 25 EFTS	To S.Rhodesia 12.1.40 Engine cut after take-off; stalled and dived into ground, Belvedere, 20.5.41; DBF
R4821	- 25 EFTS/27 EFTS	To S.Rhodesia 12.1.40 Stalled off climbing turn and hit ground, Whites Run LG, 21.4.41
R4822	- 25 EFTS	To S.Rhodesia 12.1.40 SOC 13.10.43
R4823	-	To S.Rhodesia 12.1.40 To SAAF 3.3.44
R4824	- 25 EFTS	To S.Rhodesia 12.1.40 To SAAF 31.5.44
R4825	- 25 EFTS	To S.Rhodesia 12.1.40 Spun into ground, Tynewald South, 20.6.40; DBF
R4826	-	To S.Rhodesia 12.1.40 To SAAF 3.3.44
R4827	- 25 EFTS	To S.Rhodesia 12.1.40 Stalled and spun into ground, Salisbury, 11.6.41
R4828	- 25 EFTS	To S.Rhodesia 12.1.40 SOC 13.10.41
R4829	- -	To S.Rhodesia 7.2.40 to SAAF 3.3.44
R4830	- 25 EFTS	To S.Rhodesia 7.2.40 SOC 17.10.45
R4831	- 28 EFTS/25 EFTS	To S.Rhodesia 7.2.40 SOC 9.2.43
R4832	4 EFTS/7 EFTS/ 4 EFTS/13 EFTS/ 21 EFTS	Stalled on approach and hit ground, Booker, 18.2.42
R4833	3 EFTS/7 FTS/ Wattisham	Sold 5.10.54; became G-AOEV
R4834	13 EFTS/21 EFTS	DBR in heavy landing, Booker, 24.5.44

Serial	Units	Fate
R4835 to R4844	-	To RAAF 6.2.40
R4845	14 EFTS/18 EFTS/18 RFS/22 RFS/14 RFS	Sold 18.9.53
R4846	4 EFTS/7 EFTS/4 EFTS	SS 28.3.50
R4847	11 EFTS/7 EFTS/26 EFTS	Sold 31.3.51
R4848	Ratcliffe/CLE/AFEE/14 EFTS/25 RFS/2 GS/1 GU	Sold 18.2.54
R4849	13 EFTS/21 EFTS/28 EFTS	Stalled at low altitude while lost in haze and crashed near Chetwynd, 28.11.45
R4850	4 EFTS/7 EFTS/4 EFTS	Hit water and overturned in Humber while low flying near Saltmarsh, Yorks., 30.6.44
R4851	14 EFTS/8 RFS/11 RFS/Newton/SLAW	SOC 13.7.53; later to G-APTI
R4852	7 EFTS	To Admiralty 11.12.46
R4853	14 EFTS	Collided with R4967 and crashed, Stag House Farm, Market Bosworth, Leics., 8.6.43
R4854	6 EFTS/4 EFTS	SS 28.3.50
R4855	22 EFTS/21 EFTS/29 EFTS	SS 30.3.50
R4856	Ternhill/15 EFTS/19 FTS/22 EFTS/22 RFS/9 RFS	Stalled during turn and dived into ground 1m E of Thorne Moorlands, Yorks., 20.4.51
R4857	13 EFTS	Spun into ground near Twyford, Berks., 30.8.40
R4858	268/GPEU/4 GTS/ORTU	Stalled while low flying and crashed ½m S of Netheravon, 18.7.44
R4859	26/18 EFTS	SOC 27.12.44
R4875	14 EFTS	To R Neth AF 22.7.46 as A-17
R4876	22 EFTS	Sold 31.3.51; became G-AMMG
R4877	13 EFTS/1 PFTS/25 PEFTS/276/18 EFTS/18 RFS	Sold 24.10.50; to G-AMGB
R4878	1 EFTS/28 EFTS/19 FTS/6 RFS	Sold 4.11.53; became G-AOBP
R4879	-	To RAAF 6.3.40
R4880	-	To RAAF 6.3.40
R4881	-	To RAAF 6.3.40
R4882 to R4891	-	To RAAF 20.3.40
R4892	-	To RAAF 6.3.40
R4893	-	To RAAF 6.3.40
R4894	10 EFTS	Spun in on ground in circuit 1m S of Stoke Orchard, 23.5.42
R4895	9 EFTS/28 EFTS/25 RFS/MUAS	Sold 4.11.53; became G-AOAF
R4896	18 EFTS/18 RFS/19 RFS	Sold 5.10.53; became G-AOJK
R4897	9 EFTS/29 EFTS	Sold 25.9.53; became G-ANDC
R4898	16 OTU/1 EFTS/7 EFTS	To Admiralty 11.12.46
R4899	1 EFTS/18 EFTS/26 EFTS/4 EFTS	Sold 9.3.50; became G-AJXT
R4900	7 EFTS	SOC 16.12.41 on overhaul
R4901	Leeming/Defford	SOC 19.10.44
R4902	16 OTU/19 EFTS	Stalled off turn on approach to forced landing while lost and spun into ground, Hamilton Gardens, Scraptoft, Leics., 12.12.41
R4903	22 EFTS	Hit fire tender recovering from dive while low flying, Bottisham, 10.5.41
R4904	10 EFTS/15 EFTS/22 SFTS	Damaged 13.5.49 and SOC
R4905	7 EFTS	Sold 25.9.53; became G-ANFJ
R4906	7 EFTS/130	Engine cut due to fuel shortage; crashed in attempted forced landing, Seddlescombe, Sussex, 25.8.44
R4907	3 FPP/ATA/14 EFTS	Sold 2.9.53; became G-ANCS
R4908	- / 27 EFTS	To S.Rhodesia 12.1.40 / Stalled on take-off and hit tree, Filabusi, 8.9.41
R4909	- / 25 EFTS	To S.Rhodesia 12.1.40 / to SAAF 31.5.44
R4910	- / 25 EFTS/27 EFTS	To S.Rhodesia 12.1.40 / Damaged 14.7.41; NFD
R4911	- / 26 EFTS	To S.Rhodesia 12.1.40 / SOC 17.10.45
R4912	- / 26 EFTS	To S.Rhodesia 12.1.40 / SOC 17.10.45
R4913	- / 25 EFTS	To S.Rhodesia 12.1.40 / SOC 9.2.43
R4914	- / 25 EFTS	To S.Rhodesia 12.1.40 / To SAAF 13.3.44
R4915	- / 26 EFTS	To S.Rhodesia 12.1.40 / SOC 7.5.43
R4916	- / 25 EFTS	To S.Rhodesia 12.1.40 / SOC 2.11.45
R4917	-	To S.Rhodesia 12.1.40 / To SAAF 14.6.44
R4918	1 EFTS/21 EFTS/105 OTU/1381 TCU	To Admiralty 15.10.46
R4919	1 EFTS/25 PEFTS	Engine cut; stalled in forced landing and hit ground, Annesley Park, Notts., 13.2.42
R4920	1 EFTS	Hit HT cables in haze and dived into ground, Brickenden Bury, Herts., 22.10.40; DBF
R4921	9 EFTS	Engine shut down and would not restart; crashlanded 1m NE of Ansty, 29.5.43
R4922	7 EFTS/6 FTS	Sold 26.1.50; became G-APAO
R4923	1 EFTS/25 PEFTS/21 EFTS	Stalled on approach to practice forced landing while avoiding cables, Meadle, near Princes Risborough, Bucks., 7.11.49; DBR
R4924	10 EFTS/10 FIS/7 FIS/CFS	To 6488M 17.11.47
R4940	3 EFTS	Spun in on approach, Watchfield, 21.12.40
R4941	13 EFTS/21 EFTS/15 EFTS/2 GTS/10 FIS/19 FTS/3 EFTS/7 FTS	To 6727M 9.2.50
R4942	3 EFTS/21 EFTS	SOC 13.3.45
R4943	4 EFTS/7 EFTS/4 EFTS	Damaged 16.4.41; NFD
R4944	4 EFTS/17 EFTS/16 EFTS/Oldenburg	Sold 24.5.55; became EI-AHC
R4945	DH/3 EFTS/6 FTS/Lakenheath	To 6864M 6.51
R4946	4 EFTS/7 EFTS/4 EFTS/19 EFTS/24 EFTS	To R.Neth AF 12.2.47 as A-44
R4947	SD Flt/93/FEE/TFU	Controls jammed; dived into trees 1m NE of Bransgore, Hants., 26.5.42
R4948	4 EFTS/7 EFTS/4 EFTS/4 FIS/22 EFTS	Collided with N9434 on approach, Cambridge, 18.2.45
R4949	14 EFTS	To R.Neth AF 22.7.46 as A-35
R4950	Benson/17 EFTS/28 EFTS/Oakington/Hemswell/Kirton/2 GS	Sold 2.3.54; became G-ANPC
R4951	6 EFTS/9 RFS	Engine cut; overturned in forced landing, Eastoft, Yorks., 30.7.51; DBR

R4952	110 RCAF/400	Collided in haze with Tomahawk AH747 in circuit and broke up, Odiham, 8.2.42
R4953	17 EFTS	Dived into ground off turn, North Witham, 26.3.41; DBF
R4954	4 EFTS/14 EFTS/ Kinloss/LAS/Colerne	Sold 8.3.54; became G-ANOU
R4955	13 EFTS/21 EFTS	Spun into ground 1m W of Postcombe, Oxon., 21.6.41
R4956	14 EFTS/664/7 FTS	Sold 2.4.54; became G-ANOI
R4957	Benson/17 EFTS/ 15 EFTS/2 GTS/ 11 EFTS	SS 29.12.49
R4958	16/116/544/Benson/ 15 RFS	Sold 28.10.53; became G-ANME
R4959	16 OTU/1 EFTS/ 26 EFTS/15 RFS	Sold 4.11.53; became G-ARAZ
R4960	112 RCAF/402/ 18 EFTS	Sold 12.10.53; became G-ANDP
R4961	4 EFTS/2 CU	Sold 12.10.53; became G-APJP
R4962	22 EFTS	Shot down by enemy aircraft near Caxton Gibbet, 16.7.41
R4963	13 EFTS/21 EFTS	To SAAF 20.3.43 as No.4640
R4964	9 EFTS/11 RS	SS 30.3.50
R4965	19 EFTS/15 EFTS/ 22 SFTS	Tipped up in long grass during practice forced landing, Knapthorpe Manor Farm, 1m S of Caunton, Notts., 16.6.49
R4966	13 EFTS/21 EFTS	To S.Rhodesia 17.3.43 SOC 2.11.45
R4967	14 EFTS/21 EFTS	DBR in heavy landing, Denham, 2.5.44
R4968	2 EFTS	Damaged 3.4.41 and SOC
R4969	3 FPP/ATA/21 EFTS	Sold 29.3.51
R4970	112 RCAF	Hit HT wires and crashed, High Post,3.9.40
R4971	10 EFTS/3 EFTS/ 22 EFTS/22 RFS/ 18 RFS	SOC 4.2.48
R4972	CFS/4 EFTS/3 EFTS/ 5 RFS/Hemswell	Sold 7.10.54; became G-AOIR
R4973	TFPP/3 FPP/RAFC/ SF Halton/1 STT/ SF Halton/1 EFTS/ 1 RFS	Sold 20.10.50; became G-AMFF
R4974	16 OTU/19 EFTS/ 15 EFTS/3 RFS/ 61 Gp CF/226 OCU	Sold 1.9.54; became G-ANTL
R4975	9 EFTS/4 EFTS/ 4 RFS/2 RFS/7 RFS/ 2 RFS/22 RFS/2 AGS	Sold 24.10.53
R4976	231	Engine cut on take-off; overturned, Ballyhalbert, 20.3.42
R4977	-	To RNZAF 1.3.40 as NZ885
R4978	-	To RNZAF 1.3.40 as NZ879
R4979	-	To RNZAF 1.3.40 as NZ883
R4980	-	To RNZAF 1.3.40 as NZ882
R4981	-	To RNZAF 1.3.40 as NZ884
R4982	-	To RNZAF 1.3.40 as NZ878
R4983	-	To RNZAF 1.3.40 as NZ897
R4984	-	To RNZAF 1.3.40 as NZ896
R4985	-	To RNZAF 1.3.40 as NZ887
R4986	-	To RNZAF 1.3.40 as NZ890
R4987	-	To RNZAF 1.3.40 as NZ886
R4988	-	To RNZAF 1.3.40 as NZ891
R4989	-	To RNZAF 1.3.40 as NZ888
R5005	-	To RNZAF 1.3.40 as NZ889
R5006	-	To RNZAF 1.3.40 as NZ899
R5007	-	To RNZAF 1.3.40 as NZ898
R5008	-	To RNZAF 1.3.40 as NZ654
R5009	-	To RNZAF 1.3.40 as NZ651
R5010	-	To RNZAF 1.3.40 as NZ893
R5011	-	To RNZAF 1.3.40 as NZ892
R5012	10 EFTS/9 EFTS/CNS	SOC 22.5.45
R5013	1 AACU/1608 Flt/288	SOC 24.8.44
R5014	18 EFTS/6 FTS/ Hemswell	Sold 25.6.54; became G-ANSM
R5015	18 EFTS/16	Sold 5.4.51
R5016	6 EFTS/6 RFS	Sold 6.10.53; became G-ANES
R5017	CFF	Lost in France 6.40
R5018	18 EFTS/20 EFTS/ 21 EFTS/63 Gp CF	Sold 29.10.53; became G-ANED
R5019	18 EFTS/18 RFS/ 19 RFS/10 RFS	To 7042M 22.8.53
R5020	CFF/17/7 EFTS	Overshot forced landing while lost and hit trees 4m E of Lutterworth, Leics., 23.6.41
R5021	PDU	Pres. lost in France 5.40
R5022	14 EFTS	To 5435M 4.8.45
R5023	Wolverhampton/ 14 EFTS/19 EFTS/ 24 EFTS/28 EFTS/ 29 EFTS/Hull UAS/ 5 RFS/23 RFS/11 RFS/ 64 Gp CF/Leconfield	Sold 1.4.54; became G-AOGY
R5024	14 EFTS/101 GOTU/ 2 GTS/ATA	SOC 30.11.44
R5025	14 EFTS/17 EFTS/ 6 EFTS/10 FIS/ 11 EFTS	Sold 5.4.51
R5026	14 EFTS	SOC 25.5.50
R5027	14 EFTS	Sideslipped into ground, Nether Whitacre, Warks., 3.4.44
R5028	Wolverhampton/ 7 EFTS/93/1458 Flt/ 537/118/132/504/310	SOC 19.10.44
R5029	14 EFTS/1 AACU/ 101 GOTU	Engine cut; dived into ground recovering from spin, Innsworth, Glos., 14.6.42; DBF
R5030	14 EFTS	SOC 25.5.50
R5031	Wolverhampton/ 7 EFTS	Abandoned after controls jammed, Ellistown, Leics., 19.6.41
R5032	CFF	Lost in France 6.40
R5033	PDU/4 EFTS	SS 28.3.50
R5034	18 EFTS	Stalled at low altitude in slipstream and hit ground near Fairoaks, 28.5.43
R5035	PDU/22 EFTS	Sold 29.3.51
R5036	PDU	Pres. lost in France 5.40
R5037	6 EFTS/11 RFS	To 6832M 15.1.51
R5038	10 EFTS/16 EFTS/ 16 RFS/RAFC	Sold 23.2.49; became G-AMDM
R5039	7 EFTS	Stalled in forced landing while lost and hit dyke, Waltham-on-the-Wolds, Leics., 16.12.40; DBF
R5040	22 EFTS	Hit hedge on take-off from forced landing, Uttoxeter Racecourse, Staffs., 30.5.43
R5041	22 EFTS/1 EFTS/ 16 EFTS/SF Uetersen	Sold 8.8.53; became G-AODS
R5042	6 EFTS/3 RFS/ 14 RFS	Sold 7.10.53; became G-ANEM
R5043	112 RCAF/17 EFTS/ 15 PEFTS/22 SFTS	Stalled on take-off from practice forced landing and dived into ground, Ossington, 4.12.48
R5044	18 EFTS 33 FIS	To S.Rhodesia 7.3.43 Engine cut after roll; hit ant hill in forced landing and undercarriage torn off near Moffat, 28.12.44; not repaired and SOC 5.4.45
R5057	22 EFTS/25 PEFTS/ 29 EFTS	SOC 5.6.50
R5058	18 EFTS	Spun into ground off climbing turn, Chobham Common, Surrey, 1.6.41

Serial	Units	Fate
R5059	13 EFTS/21 EFTS/ 17 EFTS/Coltishall/ 278/Bradwell Bay	SS 28.3.50
R5060	14 EFTS	SS 30.3.50
R5061	6 EFTS	SOC 8.6.50
R5062	6 EFTS/3 EFTS	Spun into ground near Lechlade, Glos., 26.3.41
R5063	6 EFTS/4 EFTS	To R.Neth AF 12.2.47 as A-43
R5064	2 EFTS	Flew into trees on hill in cloud and stalled into ground, Birdlip, Glos., 13.12.40
R5065	6 EFTS	Sold 26.1.50; became G-ANEI
R5066	2 EFTS/652	Crashed on overshoot, Charity Farm, Brinckley, Cambs., 31.7.42
R5067	-	To RNZAF 29.3.40 as NZ877
R5068	-	To RNZAF 29.3.40 as NZ876
R5069	-	To RNZAF 29.3.40 as NZ880
R5070	-	To RNZAF 14.5.40 as NZ895
R5071	-	To RNZAF 14.5.40 as NZ894
R5072	-	To RNZAF 14.5.40 as NZ652
R5073	-	To RNZAF 14.5.40 as NZ650
R5074	-	To RNZAF 14.5.40 as NZ653
R5075	-	To RNZAF 14.5.40 as NZ900
R5076	-	To RNZAF 29.3.40 as NZ881
R5077	MSFU	Spun into ground while low flying, Haddon Lane, Burton Wirrall, Cheshire, 10.9.41
R5078	2 EFTS/6 FIS/ 2 EFTS	SOC 18.3.46
R5079	54 OTU/22 EFTS/ 5 FIS/29 EFTS/ Netheravon	Sold 10.1.51
R5080	2 EFTS/6 FIS	Hit trees low flying when neither pilot in control, Kinnersley, Worcs., 10.2.42
R5081	13 EFTS/4 EFTS/ 21 EFTS/2 TAF CS	Hit by NL970 while parked, Yazagyo, 6.11.44; DBR
R5082	54 OTU/1 EFTS/ 4 FTS	Bounced on landing and lost wheel, Heany, SR, 2.7.51; DBR
R5083	3 EFTS/22 FTS/7 FTS/ 21 EFTS/7 FTS/2 GS/ 1 GU	Sold 18.11.53
R5084	13 EFTS/21 EFTS/ 1 EFTS/1 SFTS(I)	NFT
R5085	3 EFTS	Hit hedge in practice forced landing and overturned, Bush Barn LG, Buckland, 21.7.44
R5086	13 EFTS/21 EFTS/ Stornoway/16 EFTS/ 2 GU	Sold 4.11.53; became G-APIH
R5100	13 EFTS/16 OTU	To SAAF 20.3.43 as No.4641
R5101	13 EFTS/21 EFTS/ 28 EFTS	Collided with BB816 and crashed, Watling Street, Staffs., 21.1.43
R5102	13 EFTS/17 EFTS/ 28 EFTS/25 RFS	Hit tree low flying on navex near Newport, Salop., 24.10.48
R5103	13 EFTS/1 AACU/ 1620 Flt/22 EFTS/ 1 EFTS/1 RFS/ 17 RFS/1 RFS	Sold 18.11.53
R5104	CFS/4 EFTS	Sold 31.3.51
R5105	13 EFTS/21 EFTS	To SAAF 20.3.43 as No.4642
R5106	13 EFTS/11 EFTS/ PAU/Cv to Queen Bee/ PAU	SOC 29.10.45
R5107	CFS/4 EFTS/Turnhouse/ 11 EFTS/11 RFS/ AUAS/QUAS	Swung on landing and over- turned, Sydenham, 28.11.49; not repaired and sold 4.5.50
R5108	CFS/4 EFTS/2 GU	Sold 4.11.53
R5109	7 EFTS/19 EFTS/ 24 EFTS	Sold 31.3.51
R5110	6 EFTS/3 EFTS/ 8 EFTS/8 RFS/ OUAS	Sold 29.3.51
R5111	6 EFTS/3 EFTS/ 24 EFTS/15 EFTS	Sold 31.3.51
R5112	14 EFTS/28 EFTS	Swung on landing and hit hut, Wolverhampton, 18.7.45; DBR
R5113	6 EFTS/5 RFS/ 23 RFS/7 RFS	Sold 6.11.53; became G-ANKO
R5114	1 EFTS/29 EFTS/ 15 RFS	To 7043M 20.8.53
R5115	6 EFTS/6 RFS/OUAS/ 5 RFS/Llandow	Sold 21.3.55; became G-ANZR
R5116	6 EFTS/3 EFTS	Overshot landing and hit building, Caxton Gibbet, 4.7.44; DBR
R5117	1 EFTS/Shorts	Sold 18.10.46; became G-AIXL
R5118	6 EFTS/6 RFS/14 RFS/ 2 GS/1 GU	Sold 18.11.53; became G-ANLA
R5119	6 MU	Engine cut on ferry flight; overturned in forced landing on sandbank off River Nith, Solway Firth, 24.5.41
R5120	10 EFTS/19 EFTS/ 24 EFTS/24 RFS/ 8 RFS/2 RFS/ 22 RFS/62 Gp CF/ 81 Gp CF	Sold 6.11.53; became G-ANHI
R5121	ITS(O)/1 SFTS(I)	Spun into ground during instrument flying 10m S of Ambala, 9.2.42
R5122	10 EFTS	Stalled at low altitude and hit ground near Brean, Somerset, 20.6.41
R5123	17 EFTS/6 FIS/ 17 EFTS/28 EFTS/ 25 RFS	Hit tree low flying near Stafford, 30.11.52
R5124	10 EFTS/3 EFTS/ 25 RFS/2 RFS/ 2 GS/1 GU	Sold 6.11.53; became G-ANKP
R5125	1 SFTS(I)	
R5126	1 SFTS(I)	
R5127	10 EFTS	Spun into ground 1m W of Kingston Seymour, Somerset, 28.3.41
R5128	17 EFTS	Bounced on landing, stalled and dived into ground, Sibson, 21.8.41
R5129	10 EFTS/AAEE/ DH/654	Sold 6.9.46; became G-AINW
R5130	3 FPP/ATA/8 FIS/ 5 RFS/23 RFS/ Hull UAS/11 RFS/ 63 Gp CF	Sold 4.11.53; became G-APOV
R5131	2 EFTS/4 EFTS/AFS Malaya/Mal Aux AF	Engine cut on take-off; over- turned in forced landing 3½m S of Tengah, 20.6.53; DBR
R5132	18 EFTS	Undershot landing and wing hit tree; stalled into ground, Fairoaks, 11.10.40
R5133	12 FTS/CF Grantham/ 12 PAFU/ECFS/7 FTS	To 6726M 9.2.50
R5134	2 EFTS/6 FIS/2 EFTS/ 2 FTS	SOC 8.6.50
R5135	54 OTU/Andover/ 15 PAFU	SOC 23.9.44
R5136	54 OTU/16 EFTS/ CFS/7 FTS/30 MU/ SF Sealand	Sold 30.6.54; became G-APAP
R5137	19 EFTS/24 EFTS/ 3 EFTS/Southampton UAS/8 EFTS/8 RFS/ 14 RFS/2 GS/1 GU	Sold 4.11.53
R5138	13 EFTS/1 PFTS/ 25 PEFTS	To Burmese AF 12.1.48
R5139	13 EFTS/21 EFTS/ 3 EFTS/22 FTS/ 7 FTS/2 GS/1 GU	Sold 18.11.53

R5140	CFS/4 EFTS/ 21 EFTS/6 EFTS/ 10 FIS/7 FIS/ CFS	Sold 8.4.48; became G-AKYR
R5141	3 EFTS	Crashed after control lost over Berkshire, 6.4.45
R5142	13 EFTS/21 EFTS	To Admiralty 11.1.43
R5143	7 EFTS/15 EFTS	Hit tree in forced landing when short of fuel in bad weather 3m W of Bellingham, Northumberland, 12.4.43
R5144	13 EFTS/21 EFTS	To Admiralty 11.1.43
R5145	13 EFTS/21 EFTS/ 18 EFTS	Sold 5.4.51
R5146	3 EFTS/9 RFS/22 RFS/ 62 Gp CF/81 Gp CF/ Colerne CS	Sold 18.11.53; became G-ANNF
R5147	13 EFTS/Cv to Queen Bee/PAU	Hit mast in pilotless landing, Manorbier, 30.7.43
R5148	3 EFTS	Overturned by gust on take-off, Haldon, 11.2.45
R5149	7 EFTS	To Admiralty 11.11.46
R5170	17 EFTS/116/15 EFTS	Sold 30.3.51
R5171	19 EFTS/24 EFTS	To R.Hellenic AF 28.9.49
R5172	9 EFTS/15 EFTS/ 22 SFTS/SF W.Malling	Sold 18.8.54; became G-AOIS
R5173	9 EFTS	Hit tree on night approach, Southam, 23.11.41
R5174	9 EFTS/22 EFTS/ 22 Gp CF	Sold 13.7.54; became G-ANRI
R5175	13 EFTS/21 EFTS/ 16 EFTS/SF Dyce/ SF Kinloss	Sold 24.5.55; became EI-AHD
R5176	9 EFTS/ATA/25 EFTS	Sold 11.2.49; became G-ALFG
R5177	239/1 EFTS/3 EFTS/ 18 EFTS/18 RFS	Damaged on ground, 16.1.49, and sold 30.8.49 as wreck
R5178	14 EFTS	Stalled during practice forced landing and hit ground, Knowle LG, 24.4.41
R5179	22 EFTS/25 EFTS	Sold 16.4.46; became G-AHLP
R5180	10 EFTS/16 EFTS	SS 30.3.50
R5181 to R5186	-	To RAAF 31.5.40
R5187	22 EFTS/22 RFS/ 25 RFS	SS 28.3.50
R5188	22 EFTS	DBF in accident, 11.6.41; NFD
R5189	22 EFTS	Hit pole during low flying training, Baldock Station, Herts., 30.7.40
R5190	16 OTU/22 EFTS	Hit trees on night approach, near Long Stowe, Cambs., 19.12.41; DBF
R5191	CLS/CLE/GTS/ 2 EFTS	To SAAF 20.3.43 as No.4637
R5192	22 EFTS/13 OTU/ SF Horsham/105/ 81 OTU/28 OTU	Sold to RPAF 24.5.48
R5193	9 EFTS	Spun into ground off turn 1½m NE of Anstey, Warks., 7.7.41
R5194	9 EFTS	Overstressed and wings folded during aerobatics, Harborough Magna, Warks., 20.4.41
R5195	7 EFTS	Engine cut during attempted forced landing while lost in bad weather; stalled and crashed, Nailstone, Leics., 8.1.41; DBR
R5196	22 EFTS/15 EFTS	SS 29.12.49
R5197	-	To Admiralty 15.1.43
R5198	-	To Admiralty 15.1.43
R5199	2 EFTS/6 FIS/2 EFTS	To 5428M 18.7.45
R5200	2 EFTS/6 FIS/ 4 EFTS/4 RFS	SOC 8.6.50
R5201	6 EFTS/3 EFTS	Hit hut on take-off, Shellingford, 23.11.43
R5202	6 EFTS	SOC 25.5.50
R5203	2 EFTS/6 FIS/ 2 EFTS	Stalled during low aerobatics and dived into ground near Overbury, Glos., 22.3.43
R5204	6 EFTS/4 EFTS/6 FIS	Hit HT wires and crashed on barn, Stoulton Bridge, Worcester, 13.4.42
R5205	2 EFTS/25 EFTS	SOC 8.3.45
R5206	6 EFTS/2 GU/7 FTS	Sold 10.5.54; became VH-AHT
R5207	Wolverhampton/ 7 EFTS	Sold 5.4.51
R5208	7 EFTS/13 OTU/ 26 OTU	Sold 6.11.53
R5209	7 EFTS/7 RFS/ 25 RFS	SS 28.3.50
R5210	7 EFTS/29 MU	Hit wires recovering from spin and crashed, Rowton Hall, Salop., 18.10.42
R5211	22 EFTS/4 FIS/ 22 EFTS/6 FTS/ SF Llanbedr/SF Valley	Stalled and dived into ground during aerobatics 2m NNE of Llanbedr, 30.9.49
R5212	22 EFTS/4 FIS	Stalled while low flying and crashed, Wicken Fen, Cambs., 8.7.42
R5213	239	Ran away and hit blister hangar, Gatwick, 4.3.42; DBR
R5214	7 EFTS	To Admiralty 11.12.46
R5215	4/17 EFTS/4 STT/ 1 RS/21 EFTS	SOC 20.5.45
R5216	14 EFTS/20 EFTS/ 11 EFTS/10 FIS/ 22 EFTS/SF Sylt	Sold 7.10.55; became G-AOED
R5217	16/1424 Flt	To S.Rhodesia 17.3.43 Sold 12.3.47
R5218	10 EFTS/3 EFTS	Engine cut during aerobatics; overturned in forced landing, Little Hinton, Wilts., 22.6.44; DBF
R5219	10 EFTS/3 EFTS/ 6 FTS	Sold 9.6.49; became G-ALUC
R5236	SF Filton/17 EFTS/ 28 EFTS/170/SF Middle Wallop	Sold 25.8.47; became G-AKGT
R5237	17 EFTS/28 EFTS/ 25 RFS	Sold 4.11.53; became G-ANRA
R5238	17 EFTS/1 AACU/ 1621 Flt/285	Sold 24.10.53; became G-ANRZ
R5239	10 EFTS/7 EFTS/2 GU	Sold 3.9.53; became G-ANVV
R5240	17 EFTS/28 EFTS/ 3 EFTS/28 EFTS/ 25 RFS/3 EFTS/2 FTS	SOC 25.5.50
R5241	10 EFTS/16 EFTS/ Dyce	Hit by T7737 while parked, Dyce, 1.7.52; DBR
R5242	10 EFTS/21 EFTS	To R.Neth AF 12.2.47 as A-38
R5243	16 OTU/1 EFTS/ 21 EFTS/9 RFS/ 10 RFS/19 RFS	Sold 18.11.53; became G-ANNH
R5244	16 OTU/24 EFTS/ 24 RFS	SOC 8.2.49
R5245	10 EFTS/1485 Flt/ 1690 Flt	To 4934M 12.44
R5246	10 EFTS/3 EFTS	Sold 30.3.51; became G-AMIV
R5247	16 OTU/19 EFTS	Stalled on approach and dived into ground, Little Sutton, 16.11.41
R5248	16 OTU/19 EFTS	Sideslipped into ground while demonstrating forced landings near Bagillt, Flint, 11.8.41; DBR
R5249	16 OTU/22 EFTS	SS 28.3.50
R5250	16 OTU/19 EFTS/ 24 EFTS/Schwechat	Sold 8.8.55; became G-AODT
R5251	16 OTU/19 EFTS/ 24 EFTS/24 RFS/ 17 RFS/1 RFS/SF Honiley/SF Oakington	Sold 1.4.54; became G-ANXT

R5252	16 OTU/93/51 OTU/ AFDU/501	Engine cut; hit hedge in forced landing, E.Newlands Farm, Essex, 6.10.44
R5253	54 OTU/4 EFTS	Hit slipstream on take-off and blown into ground, Brough, 17.6.43
R5254	1 EFTS/7 EFTS	SS 29.12.49
R5255	1 EFTS/15 EFTS/ 15 PAFU/14 EFTS	Spun into ground in bad weather on navex near Blockley, Glos., 31.5.44
R5256 to R5265	-	To RAAF 31.5.40

*   *   *   *   *   *   *   *   *   *

Weir W.6 helicopter for research purposes from G & J Weir, Glasgow, to Contract No.968953/38

R5269	Mkrs	Not delivered to RAF

*   *   *   *   *   *   *   *   *   *

R5273-R5320; R5339-R5380; R5397-R5426; R5448-R5477	Cancelled Armstrong Whitworth Manchesters to Contract No. 982865/39:

*   *   *   *   *   *   *   *   *   *

200 Lancaster Is delivered between February and July 1942 by Avro, Manchester, to Contract No.982866/39

R5482	97/101	Undercarriage collapsed in heavy landing from air test, Holme, 20.12.42
R5483	97/1654 CU/622	Missing (Berlin) 21.1.44
R5484	44/83	Two engines cut; crashed on return from Plzen, Pontavert, Aisne, 17.4.43
R5485	109/TFU/1654 CU/ 1657 CU/467	Missing (Révigny) 19.7.44
R5486	97	Swung on landing from navex and undercarriage collapsed; caught fire, Finningley, 23.3.42
R5487	97	Missing (Hamburg) 27.7.42; presumed ditched on return
R5488	97/61	Missing (minelaying off Denmark) 4.7.42; presumed ditched on return
R5489	44	Control lost on approach to Waddington on training flight; crashed, Branston, Lincs., 16.8.42; DBF
R5490	97/1654 CU/622/15	SS 24.1.48
R5491	44/61/61 CF/ 1656 CU	Tyre burst on landing; swung and undercarriage collapsed, Lindholme, 27.5.43; DBR
R5492	44/44 CF/44/106/ 1661 CU	Dived into ground at night ½m SW of Exeter, 3.9.43; presumed loss of control
R5493	44	Missing (minelaying off Lorient) 25.3.42
R5494	44/OADU	Swung on three-engined landing and undercarriage leg collapsed, Gibraltar, 7.7.42; DBF
R5495	44/97	Missing (Essen) 9.6.42
R5496	44/97	Missing (Bremen) 5.9.42
R5497	44/97	Missing (Neustadt) 18.12.42
R5498	207	Ran out of fuel on exercise and both starboard engines cut on night approach; crashed on boundary, Bottesford, 8.4.42; DBF
R5499	207	Missing (minelaying in Kattegat) 11.8.42
R5500	207/460/1656 CU/ 1667 CU/1 LFS	To 4902M 10.44
R5501	207	Collided with Master DK973 on training flight and crashed, Canwick Hill, ½m E of Bracebridge Heath, Lincs, 28.3.42; DBF
R5502	97/207 CF/97	Shot down by night fighter 4½m NW of Binche, Belgium on return from Nürnberg, 29.8.42
R5503	207/207 CF/1660 CU/50/1664 CU/ 1651 CU	To 5452M 7.45
R5504	207/1660 CU	Swung on landing and undercarriage collapsed, Swinderby, 30.3.43; to 3881M 6.43
R5505	207/61/ECFS/CRD	SOC 15.1.47
R5506	44	Shot down by fighters near Ormes, Eure, en route to Augsburg, 17.4.42
R5507	207/97 CF/1660 CU/101/1656 CU/ 1 LFS/1668 CU/ 1660 CU	SOC 2.11.45
R5508	44/97 CF/1660 CU/15	SOC 15.1.47
R5509	207	Missing (minelaying in Baltic) 17.8.42
R5510	44	Hit by flak, Augsburg, and crashed 3m W of target, 17.4.42
R5511	61/1654 CU/1656 CU	To 3606M 2.43
R5512	97	Hit by flak and crashed en route to Duisburg, Volewijks Park, Amsterdam, 21.12.42
R5513	97	Shot down by flak, Augsburg, 17.4.42
R5514	44/156/1654 CU/ 622/3 LFS/90	SS 20.11.46
R5515	44	Overshot approach on training flight, bounced on landing and stalled into ground, Waddington, 6.6.42
R5516	44	Missing (Essen) 6.6.42
R5517	61	Missing (Emden) 23.6.42
R5537	97	Shot down by night fighter, Westmalle, Belgium, on return from Frankfurt, 25.8.42
R5538	97/1660 CU	To 3481M 1.43
R5539	AAEE	Top skin panel detached from wing; dived out of cloud and broke up during recovery near Malmesbury, Wilts., 18.4.42
R5540	61/44 CF/1661 CU	Bounced on landing, stalled and crashed, Winthorpe, 28.1.43; DBF
R5541	97	Engine cut on training flight; lost height and crashed in field 4m E of Wragby, Lincs., 30.4.42
R5542	44/44 CF/106 CF/ 83/1667 CU/3 LFS/ 1660 CU/1661 CU	SOC 29.10.45
R5543	61	Missing from attack on tanker *Corunna* off North coast of Spain, 20.8.42
R5544	61	Missing (Essen) 2.6.42; crashed near target
R5545	61	Overshot landing from training flight, swung and undercarriage collapsed, North Luffenham, 1.5.42

R5546	AAEE/50	Missing (Nürnberg) 31.3.44; shot down by night fighter
R5547	44/1654 CU/1661 CU	Swung on landing and under-carriage leg collapsed, Balderton, 8.9.43; DBR
R5548	97	Photoflash exploded on ground, Woodhall Spa, 28.12.42; DBR
R5549	207/1661 CU/12/ 1667 CU/1 LFS/ 1656 CU	SOC 3.11.44
R5550	207	Hit by L7385 while parked, Bottesford, 6.8.42; DBF
R5551	97/106	Shot down by night fighter near Arnhem on return from Oberhausen, 15.6.43
R5552	97/166	Crashed at Middelharnis, Over-flakee, on return from Frankfurt, 21.12.43
R5553	97	Flaps jammed up returning from Stuttgart; overshot landing at Woodhall Spa, 5.5.42
R5554	44	Missing (Munich) 20.9.42; crashed at Berlaimont, Nord.
R5555	44	Missing (Warnemünde) 9.5.42; crashed 5m WNW of Rostock
R5556	44/44 CF/1661 CU	Destroyed by fire on ground, 13.3.43
R5557	44	Missing (Warnemünde) 9.5.42
R5558	97	Ditched on return from Duisburg 3m off Wells-next-the-Sea, Norfolk, 14.7.42;
R5559	97/1662 CU	To 3605M 2.43
R5560	61/1654 CU	Landed heavily and tail unit distorted, Wigsley, 7.11.42; to 3471M 1.43
R5561	61	Missing (Cologne) 31.5.42; crashed at Niederaussem
R5562	61	Missing (Essen) 3.6.42; crashed near Rees
R5563	61	Missing from attack on tanker *Corunna* off north coast of Spain, 19.8.42
R5564	83	Missing (Essen) 2.6.42
R5565	83/NTU/61	Missing (Magdeburg) 22.1.44
R5566	83 CF/83	Missing (Genoa) 7.11.42; believed crashed off Corsica
R5567	83 CF/83	Caught fire on ground, Wyton, 25.9.42; probably due to faulty heater lamp
R5568	44	Missing (Warnemünde) 9.5.42; crashed 4½m WNW of Rostock
R5569	97	Dived into ground on over-shoot on training flight, Brattleby, Lincs., 14.11.42
R5570	83/207	Missing (Turin) 9.12.42; crashed near Milan
R5571	97	Missing (Essen) 2.6.42
R5572	97/106	Crashed 5m SSE of Zutphen on return from Gelsenkirchen, 26.6.43
R5573	106	Crashed at Oupeye, Liège, during raid on Cologne, 9.7.43
R5574	106	Missing (Munich) 22.12.42; crashed at Beaufort-en-Argonne, Meuse; believed shot down by night fighter
R5575	97/106 CF/97	Crashed in Waddenzee on return from Berlin, 18.1.43
R5576	106	Engine cut on take-off for bombing practice; swung, stalled and spun into ground, Coningsby, 21.7.42; DBF

R5603	44	Missing (Essen) 5.8.42
R5604	97/106	Missing (Düsseldorf) 1.8.42; crashed 5m WNW of Cologne
R5605	61	Missing from attack on tanker *Corunna* off North coast of Spain, 19.8.42
R5606	Mkrs/AFEE	To 4130M 9.43
R5607	97/RAE/97	Missing (Essen) 13.3.43; crashed 4m NNE of Dorsten
R5608	106	Missing (minelaying off Gironde) 26.7.42
R5609	97/TFU/AAEE/ 97/106/1 LFS/ 1662 CU	To 5288M 7.45
R5610	83	Shot down by night fighter 4m SSW of Herentals, Belgium, on return from Frankfurt, 25.8.42
R5611	RAE/106	Shot down by night fighter en route to Plzen, Rossum, Overijssel, 14.5.43
R5612	97/RAE/97/ 106/ETPS	SS 22.5.47
R5613	61	Shot down by night fighter 9m SE of Brussels on return from Essen, 3.6.42
R5614	97/106	Bounced on landing and crashed on attempted over-shoot, Syerston, 1.8.43; DBF
R5615	61	Missing (Bremen) 28.6.42
R5616	207	Missing (minelaying off Swinemunde) 17.8.42; crash-ed in sea off Mano, Denmark
R5617	207	Flew into high ground at night during night navex, Standon Hill, Tavistock, S.Devon, 24.5.42
R5618	61/1654 CU	SOC 15.5.47
R5619	83	Missing (Duisburg) 26.7.42
R5620	83	Missing (Bremen) 26.6.42; crashed at Winkelsett
R5621	83	Shot down by flak ship while minelaying off Swindemünde, 12.6.42
R5622	83	Missing (Plzen) 17.4.43; crashed at Dobrany, Cz.
R5623	83	Missing (Frankfurt) 25.8.42; blew up 8½m SSW of Fulda
R5624	44/1661 CU	SOC 15.5.47
R5625	83/50/83/622	Missing (Lisieux) 9.7.44
R5626	83/50/83	Shot down during raid on Essen, 4.4.43
R5627	61	Shot down by night fighter, Bad Zwischenahn airfield, during raid on Bremen, 4.6.42
R5628	207	Missing (minelaying in Kattegat) 10.9.42
R5629	83	Shot down during raid on Dortmund, 5.5.43
R5630	83	Missing (Berlin) 18.1.43
R5631	44/106 CF/1660 CU/ 3 LFS/90	To 5052M 2.45
R5632	207	Missing (Duisburg) 24.7.42; ditched in North Sea
R5633	207	Missing (Mainz) 13.8.42
R5634	97/1667 CU	SOC 15.5.47
R5635	207/1661 CU	To 3508M 2.43
R5636	83	Missing (minelaying off Friesians) 12.6.42
R5637	97/106	Missing (Düsseldorf) 28.1.43; crashed 4m SW of Roermond
R5638	106	Crashed in centre of city during raid on Düsseldorf, 11.9.42
R5639	50	Missing (Osnabrück) 18.8.42

Serial	Units	Fate
R5640	83	Missing (Essen) 9.6.42; crashed 8m ESE of Wesel
R5658	49/1654 CU/1668 CU/5 LFS	SOC 22.5.47
R5659	83	Missing (Essen) 9.6.42; crashed at Vardingholt
R5660	AFEE/50 CF/1654 CU	Engine cut; overshot landing and hit gunpost, Wigsley, 29.10.42
R5661	61	Crashed in sea attacking tanker *Corunna* off North coast of Spain, 19.8.42
R5662	61	Missing (Frankfurt) 25.8.42; crashed 4m SW of Cologne
R5663	61	Hit by flak and crashed off Helsingor, Sweden, while minelaying in Oresund, 4.7.42
R5664	44/OADU/44	Engine cut on return from Kassel; overshot landing and crashlanded in field, Waddington, 28.8.42
R5665	44/106	Shot down by night fighter on return from Remscheid, 31.7.43
R5666	44	Missing (Nienburg) 18.12.42; crashed near Bramsche
R5667	83/1656 CU/1657 CU	Crashed on landing, Lindholme, 19.8.43
R5668	106/207/BDU/1661 CU/5 LFS	To 4901M 10.44
R5669	83/44	Missing (Berlin) 24.12.43
R5670	83	Stalled after overshoot and dived into ground in circuit on return from Genoa, Mildenhall, 7.11.42; DBF
R5671	83/NTU/1656 CU/1 LFS/EANS	SOC 15.1.47
R5672	97/1656 CU/1 LFS	Dived into ground near Caistor, Lincs., 8.4.44; cause not known
R5673	83	Missing (Genoa) 7.11.42
R5674	207/103/1662 CU/3 LFS	Collided with R5846 and crashed near Hockwold, Suffolk, 18.12.44
R5675	97	Shot down by night fighter 9m E of Alkmaar, Neth., on return from Bremen, 28.6.42
R5676	106/106 CF/1660 CU	Overstressed and broke up in air, Sturton-by-Stow, Lincs., 12.2.43
R5677	106	Missing (Wuppertal) 30.5.43
R5678	106	Missing (Düsseldorf) 16.8.42
R5679	61	Crashed and blew up, Gronhoj, Denmark, after minelaying off Rostock, 25.9.43
R5680	106	Shot down by night fighter near Apeldoorn during raid on Essen, 15.1.43
R5681	106	Missing (Essen) 17.9.42; crashed near Datteln
R5682	61	Hit by flak during raid on Bremen and shot down by night fighter 5½m SE of Leeuwarden, Neth., 5.9.42
R5683	106	Blew up over The Wash 4m ENE of Boston en route to Duisburg, 25.7.42; cause not known
R5684	106	Crashed in sea off Coxyde, Belgium, on return from Frankfurt, 25.8.42
R5685	50/44/50/460/1667 CU	Yawed on approach and crashed 1m E of Faldingworth, 30.9.43; DBF
R5686	207/83	Ditched off Dutch coast on return from Münster, 12.6.43
R5687	50/44/50	Shot down by flak over Bremerhaven during raid on Hamburg, 28.7.43
R5688	50/12	Ditched in North Sea 60m E of North Foreland returning from Bochum, 14.5.43
R5689	50	Two engines cut on approach; crashlanded, Thurlby, Lincs., on return from minelaying, 19.9.42
R5690	50/50 CF/1654 CU/3 LFS	SOC 18.10.46
R5691	50	Presumed ditched on return from day raid on Milan, 24.10.42
R5692	RAE/1667 CU/15/75/90/3 LFS/5 LFS	SOC 15.5.47
R5693	207	SOC 15.5.47
R5694	1 OADU/207	Flew into high ground in bad weather returning from day raid on Bad Zwischenahn, Easton, Lincs., 25.11.42; DBF
R5695	207	Missing from day raid on Haselunne, 25.11.42
R5696	97	Missing from day raid on Danzig, 11.7.42
R5697	44/106	Missing (Duisburg) 21.12.42; crashed en route at Monnickendam, Neth.
R5698	149/1654 CU	Collided with JB132 near Southwell, Notts, 1.9.43
R5699	61	Undershot approach due to down-draught and crashlanded, Syerston, 21.12.42, after aborting raid on Munich
R5700	106/9	Crashed at Bad Münder-am-Deister during raid on Hannover, 23.9.43
R5701	97	Missing (Aachen) 6.10.42
R5702	50/106/460/100/625	Missing (Berlin) 16.2.44
R5703	61	Dinghy inflated in air and tangled in tail unit; dived into ground after take-off for Wismar 1m NE of Gunthorpe, Notts., 1.10.42; DBF
———		
R5724	61	Damaged by flak and fighters near Viborg while minelaying and bellylanded, Wittering, 25.9.42
R5725	50	Missing (Düsseldorf), 11.9.42
R5726	50/44/100/1662 CU/5 LFS	Control lost in cloud; broke up and dived into ground, Brenston, Notts., 4.4.44
R5727	44	To Canada as pattern aircraft, 11.42; became CF-CMS
R5728	50	Shot down by night fighter 4m NE of Soignies, Belgium, during raid on Saarbrücken, 30.7.42
R5729	44	Missing (Braunschweig) 15.1.44
R5730	1654 CU/5 LFS/1656 CU	SOC 29.1.47
R5731	106	Missing (Hamburg) 4.3.43; believed aircraft crashed 4m WNW of Hohenlockstedt
R5732	44	Engine cut on three-engined approach after aborting raid on Mainz; turned and dived into ground, Waddington, 12.8.42
R5733	50/44/1654 CU/3 LFS/6 LFS/231	SS 7.5.47
R5734	1654 CU/61	Missing (Nürnberg) 31.3.44
R5735	50	Missing (Düsseldorf) 16.8.42
R5736	1654 CU/207/1660 CU	Flew into hill in bad visibility, Llangernyw, Denbigh, 6.7.43

Lancaster I

R5737	61	Missing (Saarbrücken) 30.7.42; crashed 2m NNW of Vouziers, Ardennes
R5738	97	Shot down by night fighter 5m WSW of Venlo during raid on Essen, 10.1.43
R5739	1654 CU/15/622/15	Missing (Leipzig) 20.2.44
R5740	44	Missing (Gelsenkirchen) 26.6.43
R5741	97	Missing (Saarbrücken) 2.9.42; presumed ditched on return
R5742	61	Missing (Nürnberg) 29.8.42
R5743	83	Missing (Wilhelmshaven) 20.2.43; presumed crashed in sea
R5744	49/9	Crashed at Rheingönheim during raid on Mannheim, 6.9.43
R5745	207/460	Damaged by explosion of DV172; caught fire and blew up, Binbrook, 3.7.43
R5746	50	Missing (Le Havre) 12.8.42
R5747	50/1654 CU/50/ 1654 CU	SOC 20.4.45
R5748	106	Shot down by night fighter 3m NW of Drachten, Neth., on return from Hamburg, 27.7.42
R5749	106	Shot down during raid on Essen, 13.3.43
R5750	106	Missing (Wilhelmshaven) 19.2.43; presumed crashed in sea
R5751	49/57/1661 CU/ 1 LFS/1656 CU/ 1662 CU/1668 CU	To 5257M 6.45
R5752	49	Hit by flak, Duisburg, and two engines cut; hit trees and crashlanded 2m NW of Martlesham Heath, 7.9.42; DBR
R5753	50	Undercarriage leg collapsed in heavy landing from training flight, Skellingthorpe, 17.11.42; DBR
R5754	83	Missing in bad weather en route to Berlin, 30.3.43; presumed ditched
R5755	207	Shot down by night fighter in Ijsselmeer near Medemblik on return from Bremen, 5.9.42
R5756	207/1667 CU/ 1651 CU/1660 CU/ 1661 CU	SOC 17.10.45
R5757	49/156/61/ 1661 CU/5 LFS	SOC 15.1.47
R5758	207/97 CF/1660 CU	Engine cut on take-off; swung and hit drain, Swinderby, 3.5.43
R5759	61	Missing (Wismar) 2.10.43; crashed 2½m S of Rostock
R5760	207	Missing (Mainz) 13.8.42
R5761	207	Shot down by night fighter, Altforst, Neth., on return from Essen, 6.8.42
R5762	49	Hit by flak en route to Duisburg and crashlanded on sand dunes S of Ijmuiden, 21.12.42
R5763	49	Shot down by night fighter 7½m SE of Huy, Belgium on return from Karlsruhe, 3.9.42

* * * * * * * * *

R5768	Mkrs/83/1656 CU/ 1660 CU	SOC 19.11.43
R5769	25 OTU/106/50/9/ 9 CF/1661 CU	SOC 2.9.43
R5770	25 OTU/106/ 1660 CU	Engine cut on take-off; swung and undercarriage raised to stop, Swinderby, 4.7.43
R5771	25 OTU/83/49/420/ 57/50 CF/1654 CU	To 3746M at 2 AGS 27.5.43
R5772	25 OTU/49/83 CF/ 1654 CU	Engine cut after take-off and caught fire; crashlanded 1m NE of Wigsley, 26.1.43
R5773	RAE/TDU	To 3892M at Jurby 6.43
R5774	TDU	To 3890M 30.6.43
R5775	49/83 CF/1654 CU/ 1660 CU	To 4281M 22.9.43
R5776	1654 CU/408/ 1654 CU	To 3745M at 1 AGS 14.5.43
R5777	1654 CU	SOC 4.11.43
R5778	207/50	Hit by flak and engine cut, Warnemünde, 9.5.42; SOC on return as BER
R5779	83	Missing (Essen) 9.3.42
R5780	83/106/49/57/ 1656 CU	Hit tree low flying 2m ENE of Lichfield and dived into ground, 19.10.42; DBF
R5781	83	Missing (Lubeck) 29.3.42
R5782	207/50	Missing (Hamburg) 18.4.42
R5783	97	Ran out of fuel returning from Brest and crashed in forced landing, Friskney, Lincs., 21.10.41
R5784	61/50/9/57/ 1485 Flt/1660 CU	To 3984M at 9 OAFU 20.7.43
R5785	61	Hit by flak during raid on Le Havre and ditched off Sussex coast, 11.4.42
R5786	61/50/50 CF/1654 CU	SOC 1.4.43
R5787	61	Hit by flak during raid on Brest and crashlanded, St-Renan, Finistère, 1.2.42
R5788	207/83/49/ 1660 CU	To 3983M at 1 OAFU 30.7.43
R5789	61	Engine caught fire en route to Cherbourg; lost height and hit trees in forced landing, Wiltshire Cross, Tidworth, Wilts., 9.1.42
R5790	207/83/49/ 44 CF/1661 CU	To 3774M 5.43
R5791	207/1485 Flt/ 1654 CU	To 4001M 26.7.43
R5792	97	Collided with Hurricane V6864 on training flight and crashed, Walpole St. Andrew, Norfolk, 24.11.41
R5793	25 OTU/49/83/ 1656 CU	SOC 26.5.43
R5794	25 OTU/49	Engine cut en route to Essen; shot down by night fighter, Voorheide, Belgium, 2.6.42
R5795	97	Shot down by Bf 109s 4m off Brest, 18.12.41
R5796	61/207/106/ 57/50 CF/ 1654 CU/1660 CU	SOC 19.11.43
R5797	Mkrs	To 3778M 5.6.43
R5829	25 OTU/1654 CU	SOC 15.7.43
R5830	AAEE/83/1656 CU	SOC 16.11.43
R5831	83	Hit balloon cable on return from Essen and crashed, Warden Point, Isle of Sheppey, 26.3.42

R5832	61/61 CF/1660 CU/ 1661 CU	3744M NTU; SOC 30.4.43
R5833	207/83/50	Missing (minelaying) 6.6.42
R5834	61	Hit by flak over Bremen and engine failed; ran out of fuel, bellylanded and hit ditch, Loddon, Norfolk, 11.2.42
R5835	207/83/49/408/ 1654 CU/1661 CU	SOC 6.10.43
R5836	83/49/49 CF/ 1661 CU	Stalled on landing and undercarriage collapsed, Scampton, 1.12.42
R5837	83	Hit by flak en route to leaflet drop over Paris and ditched off Manston, 9.4.42
R5838	83/9/9 CF/ 1661 CU	Engine cut; undercarriage collapsed landing at Wickenby, 12.3.42
R5839	106/49/1458 CU/ 1661 CU	SOC 18.10.43
R5840	106	Missing (minelaying) 3.5.42; crashed off Pellworm
R5841	106/1660 CU	Engine caught fire; crashed in forced landing, Swinderby, 11.4.43; DBF

*　*　*　*　*　*　*　*　*　*

**57 Lancaster Is delivered between January and September 1942
by Metropolitan-Vickers, Manchester, to Contract No.982866/39**

R5842	Mkrs/61/44/44 CF/44/ 49 CF/1661 CU/5 LFS	SOC 24.4.46
R5843	61/50 CF/1654 CU	Crashed near Wittmund on return from Berlin, 18.1.43
R5844	61/97 CF/106 CF/106	Missing (Essen) 2.6.42
R5845	61/97 CF/1660 CU/ 3 LFS/90/1656 CU/ 1667 CU	SOC 14.9.45
R5846	61/44 CF/1661 CU/ 1668 CU/1654 CU/15/ 622/75/5 LFS/3 LFS	Collided with R5674 and crashed near Hockwold, Suffolk, 18.12.44
R5847	Mkrs/207	Shot down by night fighter, Zwiggelte, Neth., on return from Bremen, 4.6.42
R5848	207/106 CF/1660 CU	Swung on take-off and under- carriage collapsed, Swinderby, 10.4.43
R5849	R-R & AAEE	Caught fire in air near Hucknall, 11.6.43
R5850	83/49 CF/1661 CU	Engine lost power; overshot landing, Winthorpe, 19.1.43; DBF
R5851	207/50/1654 CU/ 1668 CU/1 LFS	Crashed on three-engined overshoot, Syerston, 13.3.44
R5852	207/83 CF/1654 CU	Overshot landing, swung and undercarriage collapsed, Condover, 9.9.42; DBF
R5853	97 CF/61 CF/1660 CU/ 576/1 LFS/1667 CU/ 1651 CU	SOC 4.10.45
R5854	106/97/1660 CU/ 1668 CU	To 4864M 8.46
R5855	83/49 CF/1661 CU/ 5 LFS/6 LFS/ 231 OCU	SS 4.3.49
R5856	83/1660 CU/61	Missing (St.Leu d'Esserent) 8.7.44
R5857	83	Engines cut after take-off for transit flight; crashlanded, Starvegut Farm, near Milden- hall, 7.11.42
R5858	44	Two engines failed on convoy escort 200m NW of Ireland; ditched, 14.6.42

R5859	61	Hit trees on approach and crashlanded on return from Mannheim, Bodney, 7.12.42
R5860	207	All engines cut; wing caught fire; ditched in North Sea 90m off Humber returning from Emden, 21.6.42
R5861	106	Missing (Wilhelmshaven) 9.7.42; believed shot down by night fighter off Ameland
R5862	44/1660 CU/166	Missing (Berlin) 21.1.44
R5863	44/207	Crashed while practising three-engined overshoots, Normanton, Notts., 19.8.42
R5864	106/61	Incendiaries caught fire during bomb loading and 4,000 lb bomb blew up, Syerston, 8.12.44
R5865	207/57/1661 CU/ 1668 CU	To 4950M 12.44
R5866	61/1654 CU/1667 CU/ 1 LFS/300/1 LFS	Undercarriage collapsed on starting engines, Hemswell, 25.9.44
R5867	207	Missing (Duisburg) 24.7.42; crashed near Krefeld
R5868	83/467	Preserved 22.2.56 for RAF Museum
R5888	61	Missing (Düsseldorf) 11.9.42
R5889	49/97/1661 CU	Tyre burst on take-off and caught fire on landing, Winthorpe, 9.7.43; DBF
R5890	49	Missing (Essen), 17.9.42
R5891	1654 CU	Overshot landing at Wigsley, 23.7.42; DBR
R5892	49/1661 CU	Ditched after explosion in wing off St Albans Head, Dorset, 21.2.43
R5893	1654 CU/1667 CU/ 1 LFS	SOC 15.5.47
R5894	49/9/57	Hit HT cables and crashed 3m SSE of Scampton, 2.3.43, on return from Berlin
R5895	97 CF/1660 CU/207	Missing (Magdeburg) 22.1.44
R5896	49/1660 CU/15	SOC 7.4.44
R5897	49	Missing (Nürnberg) 29.8.42
R5898	49/44	Shot down by night fighter 3m NNE of Oss, Neth., on return from Duisburg, 10.4.43
R5899	106	Hit by flak while minelaying off Danzig and ditched, 19.9.42
R5900	106	Damaged by flak and under- carriage collapsed on landing, Syerston, 18.1.43, on return from Berlin
R5901	106/44	Crashed at Bissendorf during raid on Hannover, 19.10.43
R5902	50	Missing (Wismar) 13.10.42
R5903	44	Missing (Osnabrück) 7.10.42; crashed 7½m SE of Meppen
R5904	9/9 CF/1661 CU/15	Missing (Homberg) 21.7.44
R5905	44	Abandoned after raid on Wismar and crashed 2½m SSW of Ulfborg, Denmark, 24.9.42
R5906	106 CF/15/622/3 LFS	SS 22.5.47
R5907	83 CF/9	Hit by flak during raid on Wismar and crashed, Wendorf 24.9.42
R5908	207/49 CF/1661 CU	Undercarriage collapsed in heavy landing, Scampton, 27.11.42
R5909	50	Blew up and crashed in Baltic off Hyllekrog, Lolland, on return from Wismar, 24.9.42

R5910	61/106/1654 CU/	
	5 LFS	To 4948M 12.44
R5911	83	Missing (Kiel) 14.10.42
R5912	49/156/NTU/1668 CU	To 4949M 12.44
R5913	83	Crashed near La Baule during raid on St. Nazaire, 1.3.43
R5914	106	Shot down by night fighter, Poelkapelle, Belgium, on return from Munich, 22.12.42
R5915	9/97/1660 CU/622	Missing (Berlin) 21.1.44
R5916	9	Collided with W4265 over Waddington, 8.11.42, on return from Genoa
R5917	9/97/1660 CU	Flaps jammed; overshot landing and undercarriage collapsed, Swinderby, 18.5.43

*   *   *   *   *   *   *   *   *

14 de Havilland Dominie Is delivered between September and December 1939 by D.H. Hatfield to Contract No.21547/39

R5921	EWS/2 EWS/34 Wg/ 2/Hartfordbridge/ Old Sarum/12 PAFU/ 16 FU	Sold 10.3.47; became G-AJKX
R5922	2 EWS/2 SS/Halton/ 2 Dly Flt/1 Dly Flt/ Redhill/12 FU	Sold 9.12.47; became G-AKNV
R5923	2 EWS/2 SS	Swung on take-off and hit fence, Yatesbury, 22.4.41; DBR
R5924	2 EWS/2 SS/7 AGS/ Croydon/2 SS/ Halton	Sold 8.47; became G-AKFO
R5925	2 EWS/24/MCS	SOC 31.12.45
R5926	2 EWS	Sold 21.10.42; to G-AGFU
R5927	2 EWS/2 SS	Hit balloon cable and crashed in flames, Horton, Bucks., 14.2.42
R5928	2 EWS/1 SS/Abbots-inch/1680 Flt	Overshot forced landing in snowstorm, Carrick Knowe Golf Course, Corstorphine, Edinburgh, 1.3.41
R5929	2 EWS/2 SS	Stalled off turn while low flying and crashed, Easton Hill, near Bishops Cannings, Wilts., 27.5.41
R5930	2 EWS/1 SS/2 SS/ 2 RS/57 OTU/56 OTU/ 58 OTU/60 OTU/ 13 OTU	Sold 9.1.47; to G-AIUO
R5931	2 EWS/24/MoS/ SF Halton	Sold 15.12.47; became G-AKOO
R5932	2 EWS/83 Gp CF/ 3 Dly Flt/13 Gp CF/ 15 Gp CF	Sold 9.12.47; to G-AKNW
R5933	2 EWS/BW Flt/2 RS/ 54 OTU	Sold 9.12.47; to G-AKNY
R5934	2 EWS/BW Flt/526/ 527/RWE	Sold 25.8.47; became G-AKSH

*   *   *   *   *   *   *   *   *

200 Airspeed Oxford Is and IIs delivered between July and November 1940 by Airspeed, Portsmouth, to Contract No. B19646/35

R5938	-	To S.Rhodesia 29.7.40;
	21 SFTS	SOC 5.1.45
R5939	-	To S.Rhodesia 29.7.40
	21 SFTS	SOC 2.7.45
R5940	-	To S.Rhodesia 29.7.40
	21 SFTS	SOC 2.11.45
R5941	-	To S.Rhodesia 29.7.40
	22 SFTS/21 SFTS	Bounced on landing and under-carriage collapsed, Thornhill, 12.7.41; DBR
R5942	RAFC	Dived into ground in snow-storm, Great Gonerby, Lincs., 29.10.41
R5943	RAFC	Engine cut; lost height and hit tree in forced landing, Sud-brook, near Ancaster, Lincs., 13.12.41
R5944	-	To 2388M 26.10.40
R5945	RAFC/14 FTS/ 14 PAFU	Engines cut due to fuel starvation; hit HT cables in attempted forced landing and crashed, Kneesall, Notts., 8.10.42
R5946	15 FTS/RAFC/ 15 PAFU/18 PAFU/ Waddington	SOC 9.7.46
R5947	RAFC/12 FTS/ 20 PAFU	SOC 12.5.44
R5948	RAFC/2 CFS/6 FTS/ 16 PFTS/16 PAFU/ 2 PAFU/301 FTU/ 304 FTU	SOC 30.6.50
R5949	RAFC/12 FTS/14 PAFU/ 48/Llandow/Down Ampney/11 FU/16 FU	SOC 27.1.47
R5950	2 FTS	Collided with Wallace K6030 over Cranwell and crashed, 4.10.40
R5951	2 FIS/2 CFS/ 18 PAFU/2 FIS	SOC 13.11.44
R5952	2 FIS/2 CFS/ 18 PAFU/17 SFTS/ 21 PAFU	Sold 23.6.49
R5953	2 FIS/14 FTS/ 14 PAFU	To 3959M 14.7.43
R5954	2 FIS/2 CFS	Swung on night take-off, hit tree and flew into ground, Fulbeck, 25.11.40
R5955	3 FTS/6 PAFU/3 FIS/ Hartfordbridge/140/ 8 OTU/E.Fortune	Sold 23.6.49
R5956	2 FIS/2 CFS/1 FIS	Dived into ground during low level aerobatics, Debdale Woods, Warks., 5.6.42
R5957	2 FIS/14 FTS	Turned after night take-off and flew into ground 1m N of Sibson, 27.2.41
R5958	15 FTS	Hit tree and crashed low flying 2m E of Kidlington, 31.3.41
R5959	PFTS/16 PFTS	SOC 21.3.55
R5960	15 FTS/15 PAFU/ 295/81 OTU	Undercarriage retracted in error after landing, Sleap, 28.2.45; DBR
R5961	15 FTS/15 PAFU/ 6 PAFU/15 PAFU	To 4197M 8.6.45
R5962	-	To S.Rhodesia 19.8.40;
	21 SFTS/	SOC 5.4.45
R5963	-	To S.Rhodesia 19.8.40;
	21 SFTS/23 SFTS	SOC 5.4.45
R5964	-	To S.Rhodesia 19.8.40;
	21 SFTS	SOC 30.9.44
R5965	-	To S.Rhodesia 19.8.40
	ITS Kumalo/21 SFTS	SOC 17.10.45
R5966	-	To S.Rhodesia 2.9.40;
	21 SFTS	SOC 5.3.45
R5967	-	To S.Rhodesia 2.9.40;
	21 SFTS	SOC 1.3.43
R5968	-	To S.Rhodesia 2.9.40;
	21 SFTS/23 SFTS	SOC 5.2.45
R5969	-	To S.Rhodesia 2.9.40;
	21 SFTS	SOC 15.10.41

R5970	- 21 SFTS	To S.Rhodesia 2.9.40; SOC 29.2.44	
R5971	- 21 SFTS/23 SFTS	To S.Rhodesia 2.9.40; Vibrated after take-off and bellylanded, Heany, 12.10.42; DBF	
R5972	15 FTS/3 FTS/ 3 PAFU/150 Wg/ 116/FCCS	SOC 19.4.45	
R5973	15 FTS/15 PAFU	Sold 25.1.47; became G-AJGE	
R5974	15 FTS/2 FIS/ 116/86	To R.Hellenic AF 25.4.47	
R5975	PFTS/16 PFTS/ 14 FTS/14 PAFU	SOC 24.4.44	
R5976 to R5978	-	To S.Rhodesia 7.9.40 but lost at sea en route	
R5979	- 21 SFTS	To S.Rhodesia 7.9.40 SOC 1.3.43	
R5992	- 21 SFTS	To S.Rhodesia 2.9.40; SOC 5.4.45	
R5993	- 21 SFTS	To S.Rhodesia 2.9.40; SOC 4.8.45	
R5994	- 21 SFTS	To S.Rhodesia 21.9.40; SOC 1.3.43	
R5995	- 21 SFTS	To S.Rhodesia 16.9.40; Engine cut; lost height and over- turned in forced landing near Bulawayo, 1.1.42; DBR	
R5996	-	To S.Rhodesia 22.10.40 but lost at sea en route	
R5997	- 21 SFTS	To S.Rhodesia 22.10.40; Damaged by bird strike; hit ditch in forced landing, Westacre, 24.4.42; DBR	
R5998	- 21 SFTS	To S.Rhodesia 8.40; SOC 4.11.44	
R5999	- 21 FTS/23 SFTS	To S.Rhodesia 16.9.40; Crashed, Sauerdale, SR, 30.10.44	
R6000	- 21 SFTS/23 SFTS/ CFS	To S.Rhodesia 22.10.40; SOC 4.8.45	
R6001	-	Lost at sea en route to S.Rhodesia	
R6002	- 21 SFTS	To S.Rhodesia 12.10.40; SOC 2.11.45	
R6003	-	To S.Rhodesia 16.9.40; SOC 4.8.45	
R6004	- 21 SFTS/CFS	To S.Rhodesia 12.10.40; SOC 4.8.45	
R6005	- 21 SFTS	To S.Rhodesia 11.10.40; SOC 6.9.44	
R6006	-	To RNZAF 25.10.40 as NZ1249	
R6007	-	To RNZAF 11.10.40 as NZ1250	
R6008	-	To RNZAF 11.10.40 as NZ1256	
R6009	- 21 SFTS/23 SFTS	To S.Rhodesia 12.10.40; SOC 30.9.44	
R6010	-	To SAAF 28.10.40 as No.1977	
R6011	-	To SAAF 28.10.40 as No.1918	
R6012	-	Both lost at sea	
R6013	-	en route to SAAF	
R6014	-	To SAAF 1.11.40 as No.1916	
R6015	15 FTS/15 PAFU/ 3 FIS/85/219/ 488/219/488	SOC 8.3.45	
R6016	15 FTS/6 FTS/ 6 PAFU/1483 Flt/ St.Athan	SOC 3.5.44	
R6017	14 FTS/3 FTS	Stalled on night overshoot and crashed, Bibury, 8.12.41; DBF	
R6018	15 FTS/11 FTS/ 11 PAFU/ATTDU	SOC 13.4.48	
R6019	15 FTS/4 FPP	Flew into hill in bad visibility on ferry flight from Prestwick to Kidlington, Brynford, near Holywell, Flint, 4.11.40	
R6020	3 FTS/14 FTS	DBF 13.4.41; NFD	
R6021	2 FIS/2 CFS/1 FIS/ 18 PAFU	SOC 8.6.50	
R6022	2 CFS	Collided on take-off with N4766, Church Lawford, 4.1.42; DBR	
R6023	RAFC/1483 Flt/ 3 PAFU/Halton	To Belgian AF 29.9.47	
R6024	2 FIS/1 FIS/18 PAFU/ GCA Wg Yatesbury/ 488/604/264/410	SOC 17.9.45	
R6025	RAFC/301 FTU/ 304 FTU/12 FU	SOC 15.5.45	
R6026	2 FTS/2 FIS/ 1 RFTS/2 FIS/ 10 RFS/3 CAACU	Sold 30.7.56	
R6027	14 FTS/16 PFTS/ 5 BATF/1654 CU/ 1485 Flt/RAFC/ 88/487/16/268	SOC 2.4.46	
R6028	3 FTS/16 PFTS/ 21 EFTS/GCA Wg Yatesbury/85 Gp CS	SOC 1.5.45	
R6029	2 FIS/2 CFS/18 PAFU	Sold 18.2.47; became G-AJLR	
R6030	14 FTS/14 PAFU/ 3 FIS/EFS/BBU/8 FIS	SS 15.1.54	
R6031	6 FTS/6 PAFU	SOC 25.9.44	
R6032	2 FTS/3 FTS/ 3 PAFU/3 FIS	SOC 12.5.44	
R6033	14 FTS/14 PAFU	SOC 24.2.43	
R6034	2 FIS/2 CFS/ 1 FIS/18 PAFU/ USAAF	SOC 26.6.44	
R6035	2 FTS/15 FTS/ 15 PAFU	Engine cut after take-off; crash- landed, Manor Farm, Brimpton, Berks., 16.6.43; DBF	
R6036	14 FTS/7 FIS/ 82 OTU/1695 Flt	SOC 28.3.48	
R6037	14 FTS/16 PFTS/ 14 PAFU	SOC 14.3.44	
R6038	15 FTS/15 PAFU	Engine lost power in practice forced landing; crashlanded and hit fence near Kingsclere, Hants., 21.5.43	
———			
R6050	15 FTS/15 PAFU	SOC 23.3.44	
R6051	2 CFS/14 FTS/ 14 PAFU/38 Gp CF/ 224	SOC 5.11.45	
R6052	15 FTS/14 FTS/ 16 PFTS/11 PAFU	SOC 30.1.46	
R6053	15 FTS/15 PAFU/ 18 PAFU/1 BAS/ 15 PAFU/Woolfox Lodge	To R.Hellenic AF 17.4.47	
R6054	15 FTS/15 PAFU/ 13 Gp CF/Church Fenton	SOC 7.8.47	
R6055	14 FTS/14 PAFU/ Halton	SOC 25.4.45	
R6056	2 FIS/2 CFS/ 14 FTS/15 FTS	Flew into ground 12m S of Tetbury, Glos., 25.8.41	
R6057	14 FTS/14 PAFU	Flew into ground in turn on navex near Horsham St.Faith, 29.4.42	
R6058	11 FTS/2 CFS/ 116/AEAF CF	SOC 5.12.44	
R6059	2 FIS/2 CFS/1 FIS	Bounced on landing and crashed on attempted overshoot, Warwick RLG, 4.8.42	
———			
R6070	15 FTS/12 FTS/ 14 PAFU	SOC 21.8.45	

R6071	14 FTS/14 PAFU/ 18 PAFU	SOC 9.8.44
R6072	15 FTS/3 FTS	Crashed in night landing, South Cerney, 25.10.41
R6073	15 FTS/3 FTS	Undercarriage collapsed in heavy landing at night, Bibury, 20.8.41
R6074	2 FIS/2 CFS/1 FIS/ 18 PAFU/Lissett	Engine cut after take-off; force- landed in field near Carnaby, 12.11.45; DBR
R6075	15 FTS/2 PAFU	Collided with V3585 after take- off from Akeman Street, 23.6.42
R6076	2 FIS/2 CFS/6 PAFU	SOC 14.3.45
R6077	1 PFTS/16 PFTS/ 11 PAFU/Reid & Sigrist	SOC 24.10.44
R6078	1 PFTS/16 PFTS	DBR 10.9.41; NFD
R6079	3 FTS/3 PAFU/418	SOC 7.9.44
R6080	3 FTS/3 PAFU/25	SOC 6.8.44
R6081	1 PFTS/16 PFTS/ 15 PAFU	Hit tree in forced landing while lost in bad weather; dived into ground, South Anston, Yorks., 27.9.42
R6082	RAFC	Overshot forced landing and hit HT cables while lost on navex, Morton, Derbyshire, 31.3.41
R6083	RAFC/Abingdon/ Driffield/Lissett/ Burn/N.Coates/ 16 Gp CF/21 PAFU/ 2 PRFU/1 PRFU	To 6600M 1.10.48
R6084	235/1 PFTS/16 PFTS/ ATA	SOC 10.9.45
R6085	14 FTS/16 PFTS/ 11 PAFU/320/2 Gp CF	SOC 5.12.44
R6086	3 FTS/5 OTU/ 131 OTU/544	SOC 25.9.45
R6087	14 FTS	Overturned in forced landing while lost at night, Hemingford Abbots, Hunts., 16.4.41
R6088	2 FIS/2 CFS/3 PAFU	Sold 18.8.50
R6089	2 FTS/1483 Flt/ 1 RFTS/2 FIS	Stalled and spun into ground near Lunen, Angus, 16.2.43
R6090	3 FTS/9 PAFU/ 14 PAFU/ECFS/ 16 PFTS	SOC 13.5.44
R6091	2 FIS/2 CFS/ATA	To R.Danish AF 26.3.47 as 241
R6092	2 CFS	Spun into ground off turn, Stock Park, Shuckborough, Warks., 26.6.41
R6093	14 FTS/42 OTU/ USAAF	SOC 7.3.45
R6094	14 FTS/14 PAFU	SOC 30.3.43
R6095	14 FTS	Crashed on formation take-off, Cranfield, 13.4.41
R6096	15 FTS/15 PAFU	To 4059M 31.1.44
R6097	RAFC/15 PAFU	Engine cut; crashlanded, Preston Farm, Ramsbury, Wilts., 4.7.43
R6098	3 FTS/3 PAFU/ SF Halton/3 FIS/ SF Halton/SF Linton,	Undercarriage collapsed while starting engine, Linton- on-Ouse, 10.8.44; DBR
R6099	2 FTS/2 PAFU/ 11 PAFU/21 PAFU	SOC 14.8.43
R6100	2 FTS/6 FTS	Hit balloon cable on navex and crashed, Sullivan Road, Stoke, Coventry, 7.10.41
R6101	-	To SAAF 12.10.40
R6102	-	To SAAF 12.10.40
R6103	-	To SAAF 12.10.40 as No.1902
R6104	-	To SAAF 22.10.40
R6105	15 FTS	Abandoned due to fog during night flying training 5m W of Woodstock, Oxon., 4.6.41

R6106	15 FTS/15 PAFU/ 3 FIS	To Belgian AF 17.12.46 as O-14
R6107	2 CFS	Shot down by intruder on night flying exercise, Fulbeck, 26.2.41
R6108	2 CFS/18 PAFU	Undershot night approach and flew into ground ½m S of Snitterfield, 14.12.43
R6109	-	To SAAF 21.10.40
R6110	-	To SAAF 1.11.40 as No.1915
R6111	-	To SAAF 1.11.40 as No.1917
R6112	-	To SAAF 1.11.40 as No.1911
R6113	3 FTS/14 FTS/ 14 PAFU	To USAAF 10.11.43
R6114	3 FTS	Control lost on overshoot; flew into ground 1m N of Bibury LG, 3.6.41
R6129	2 FTS/1 PFTS/ 16 PFTS	Abandoned in bad weather near Retford, Notts., 16.11.41
R6130	2 CFS/16 PFTS/ Melbourne/1527 Flt	SOC 8.6.50
R6131	-	To SAAF 11.11.40
R6132	-	To SAAF 23.10.40 as No.1927
R6133	12 FTS/14 PAFU	To Belgian AF 26.7.47 as O-18
R6134	-	To SAAF 29.10.40
R6135	-	To SAAF 30.10.40
R6136	-	Lost at sea en route to RNZAF
R6137	-	To SAAF 11.11.40 as No.1913
R6138	-	To SAAF 11.11.40
R6139	21 SFTS	To S.Rhodesia 11.40; SOC 6.45
R6140	-	To RAAF 29.11.40
R6141	RAFC	Engine cut on night take-off; flew into ground 1m E of Barkston LG, 21.6.41
R6142	RAFC/15 PAFU/ 3 FIS	To USAAF 23.12.43
R6143	2 FTS/3 PAFU	SOC 15.11.43
R6144	2 FIS/RAFC/2 FIS	
R6145	2 FTS/1 FIS/ 18 PAFU	Dived into ground on overshoot, Bretford, near Rugby, Warks., 22.11.42
R6146	2 FTS/3 FIS/ 20 PAFU/85 Gp CS	
R6147	1 PFTS/16 PFTS/ 2 PAFU/3 PAFU/ 256/4 Dly Flt/ 85 Gp CS	Destroyed in air raid, Melsbroek, 1.1.45
R6148	1 PFTS/16 PFTS/ 20 PAFU	Hit tree during low flying exercise and crashed near Steeple Claydon, Bucks., 5.4.44; DBR
R6149	23 SFTS	To S.Rhodesia 11.40; Damaged 11.41; NFT
R6150	-	To S.Rhodesia 11.40 NFT
R6151	-	To RAAF 29.11.40
R6152	-	To RAAF 29.11.40
R6153	15 FTS	Hit pile of rubble in forced landing while lost on navex and swung into ditch, Grafton Underwood, 15.6.41
R6154	15 FTS	Collided with another aircraft over Weston-on-the-Green, 27.5.41
R6155	15 FTS/15 PAFU	Flew into high ground in bad weather, Upsall, near Thirsk, Yorks., 5.8.42
R6156	15 FTS	Shot down by enemy aircraft 1m N of Tackley, Oxon., 13.8.41
R6157	2 FIS/2 CFS/ 18 PAFU/Blakehill Farm	SOC 5.3.45

R6158	15 FTS	Took off at night with wrong mixture setting; failed to climb and hit poles, Weston-on-the-Green, 21.3.41; DBF
R6159	15 FTS/15 PAFU	SOC 28.6.43
R6160	12 FTS/3 FTS/ 3 PAFU/Northolt/ 4 Dly Flt	SOC 13.3.45
R6161	15 FTS/2 FIS/ATA/ 100 Gp CF/4 RS	To Burmese AF 18.11.48
R6162	11 FTS/11 PAFU	Hit by W6637 while dispersed, Bridleway Gate, 31.5.42
R6163	2 FIS/2 CFS/ 42 OTU/Netheravon/ 38 Gp CF/311	Overshot landing and hit fence, Dyce, 15.11.44
R6177	11 FTS	SOC 11.7.43
R6178	11 FTS/11 PAFU	Taxied into LB427 at night, Shawbury, 27.6.43; DBR
R6179	15 FTS/Sydenham/ USAAF	Flew into hill in Ulster, 31.2.42; NFD
R6180	15 FTS/2 FIS	To Admiralty 12.9.42
R6181	15 FTS/18 PAFU	SOC 27.12.44
R6182 to R6184	-	To RAAF 11.40
R6185	- 23 SFTS	To S Rhodesia 29.11.40
R6186	- 23 SFTS/2 CAOS/ 21 SFTS	To S.Rhodesia 11.40; SOC 31.12.43
R6187	- 21 SFTS/23 SFTS	To S Rhodesia 11.40; Damaged 2 7.41; NFT
R6188	- 21 SFTS/23 SFTS	To S.Rhodesia 11.40; Collided with V3320 near Heany, 27.1.45
R6189	-	To SAAF 7.1.41
R6190	-	To RAAF 29.11.40
R6191	-	To RAAF 29.11.40
R6192	-	To SAAF 7.1.41
R6193	-	To RAAF 18.12.40
R6194	-	To RAAF 18.12.40
R6195	-	Both lost at sea en route
R6196	-	to S.Rhodesia 1.41

*   *   *   *   *   *   *   *   *   *

150 Airspeed Oxford Is (R6236-R6248; R6263-R6299; R6317-R6341) and Oxford IIs, (remainder) delivered between May and August 1940 by De Havilland, Hatfield, to Contract No. B20356/39

R6211	-	To RNZAF 16.5.40 as NZ1258
R6212	-	To RNZAF 26.7.40 as NZ1262
R6213	-	To RNZAF 26.7.40 as NZ1266
R6214	-	To RNZAF 26.7.40 as NZ1272
R6215	-	To RNZAF 24.5.40 as NZ1273
R6216	-	To RNZAF 26.7.40 as NZ1274
R6217	-	To RNZAF 24.5.40 as NZ1276
R6218	-	To RNZAF 26.7.40 as NZ1278
R6219	-	To RNZAF 21.8.40 as NZ1279
R6220	-	To RNZAF 21.8.40 as NZ1280
R6221	-	To RNZAF 24.5.40 as NZ1281
R6222	-	To RNZAF 21.8.40 as NZ1282
R6223	-	To RNZAF 21.8.40 as NZ1283
R6224	-	To RNZAF 21.8.40 as NZ1284
R6225	-	To RNZAF 21.8.40 as NZ1285
R6226	-	DBR 30.12.40; NFD
R6227	14 FTS/14 PAFU/ 83 OTU	SOC 8.7.44
R6228	CFS/3 FIS/14 PAFU/ Northolt	DBR 2.10.44; NFD
R6229	CFS/6 FTS	Stalled on landing and hit ground, Little Rissington, 1.5.41; DBF
R6230	CFS/3 FIS	To Admiralty 22.2.44
R6231	14 FTS/6 FTS/7 FIS/ Pershore/1 FU/140	SOC 24.5.46
R6232	14 FTS/14 PAFU	SOC 15.12.42
R6233	14 FTS	Flew into ground in bad visibility, Bozeat, Northants., 17.10.40
R6234	14 FTS/15 FTS/ 11 FTS/6 FTS/ 6 PAFU/18 PAFU	SOC 19.5.44
R6235	14 FTS/1 PFTS/ 16 PFTS/20 PAFU	SOC 24.7.44
R6236	14 FTS	Collided with L4642 over Milton Keynes, Bucks., 3.12.40
R6237	14 FTS/3 FTS	To Admiralty 30.7.43
R6238	11 FTS	Undercarriage collapsed in heavy landing at night, Shawbury, 15.6.41
R6239	11 FTS/11 PAFU/ 3 PAFU	SOC 4.4.45
R6240	11 FTS/11 PAFU/ 3 PAFU	Wing dropped on approach; dived into ground, South Cerney, 25.11.43
R6241	15 FTS/RAFC/ 15 PAFU/7 AACU/ 3 PAFU	SOC 23.9.44
R6242	2 FTS/RAFC/17 SFTS/ 15 PAFU/20 PAFU	SOC 14.3.44
R6243	15 FTS/15 PAFU/ 18 PAFU	SOC 28.12.43
R6244	3 FTS/2 FIS/11 PAFU	SOC 6.1.45
R6245	3 FTS	Hit hedge on night take-off and crashed, Bibury, 8.8.40
R6246	11 FTS	Engine cut; hit cottage in attempted forced landing and crashed, Muckley Corner, near Lichfield, Staffs., 8.6.40
R6247	15 FTS/RAFC/ 6 FTS/3 FTS/ 3 PAFU/14 PAFU	SOC 30.8.44
R6248	CFS/7 FIS/ 15 PAFU/502/ 1 CAACU/24 RFS	To 7282M 9.55
R6263	3 FTS/3 GTS/ 11 PAFU/7 FTS/ 3 FIS/7 FIS	Sold 23.6.49
R6264	RAFC/3 FTS/6 FTS/ 6 PAFU	SOC 20.5.44
R6265	RAFC/14 PAFU/ 12 PAFU/6 PAFU	SOC 12.4.46
R6266	15 FTS	Hit N4580 on take-off, Chipping Norton, 3.7.40
R6267	3 FTS/3 PAFU/3 FIS	SOC 22.8.45
R6268	3 FTS/1447 Flt/10 RS	To 4344M 18.11.43
R6269	3 FTS/15 FTS/ 15 PAFU/3 FIS	To R.Neth AF 27.8.46
R6270	3 FTS/7 FIS	SOC 5.6.47
R6271	3 FTS/42 OTU	Hit HT cables and crashed near Holbourne, Derbyshire, 21.5.43; DBF
R6272	3 FTS/8 AACU/ 14 PAFU	SOC 22.6.50
R6273	3 FTS/2 PAFU/ECFS/ 6 AACU/Tempsford	SOC 14.11.44
R6274	3 FTS/2 FTS/3 FIS/ 2 FIS/14 PAFU	SOC 22.6.50
R6275	RAFC	Landed down-wind, braked and overturned, Barkston LG, 8.6.40
R6276	RAFC/2 FTS/ 2 PAFU/5 GTS/ 4 GTS	SOC 12.5.44
R6277	3 FTS/15 FTS/ 15 PAFU	SOC 22.11.43
R6278	3 FTS/14 FTS/ 14 PAFU	SOC 10.6.43

Above: Wellington R1090, ED-K of No.21 OTU, crashlanded at Moreton-in-Marsh

Below: R2510, the prototype Hertfordshire

Above: Beaufighter I R2192, PN-B of No.252 Squadron

Below: Magister I R1823 of No.87 Squadron at Debden in 1940

R6279	11 FTS/11 PAFU/	
	3 PAFU	To 5487M 26.7.45
R6280	3 FTS/11 FTS/	Hit tree during practice
	11 PAFU/15 PAFU	approach and crashed, Horton
		Court, Chipping Sodbury, Glos.
		25.7.44
R6281	11 FTS/6 FTS/	
	11 PAFU/3 PAFU	SOC 18.1.45
R6282	11 FTS/4 AOS/1 FIS/	
	3 FIS/14 PAFU	SOC 30.8.44
R6283	11 FTS	Collided with Oxford after
		landing, Shawbury, 26.5.41
R6284	11 FTS/2 CFS/	
	18 PAFU/3 FIS/	
	3 PAFU/16 PFTS	SOC 20.10.44
R6285	11 FTS/2 FIS/	
	2 CFS/2 AGS/	
	12 PAFU/3 FIS/	
	20 PAFU/7 PAFU/	
	SF Acklington	SOC 20.10.54
R6286	11 FTS/11 PAFU	Hit HT cables over Severn and
		crashed, Utoxeter, Salop.,
		4.2.43
R6287	11 FTS	Dived into ground in circuit at
		night, Shawbury, 9.12.40
R6288	2 FTS	SOC 5.5.42
R6289	14 FTS/16 PFTS/	
	RAFC	DBR 20.7.43; NFD
R6290	14 FTS	Raised flaps too soon on night
		overshoot and sank into ground,
		Cranfield, 26.11.40
R6291	11 FTS/11 PAFU	SOC 11.10.44
R6292	11 FTS/2 CFS/	
	20 PAFU	SOC 3.3.44
R6293	11 FTS	SOC 8.4.43
R6294	11 FTS/3 PAFU/	
	20 PAFU/3 PAFU	SOC 25.4.45
R6295	11 FTS/2 CFS/	
	18 PAFU	SOC 3.3.44
R6296	11 FTS	Hit tree on take-off from
		forced landing, Bredenbury,
		4m NW of Bromyard, Hereford,
		9.1.41
R6297	2 FTS/RAFC/	
	18 PAFU	SOC 13.7.45
R6298	2 FTS/8 AACU/	Swung on landing and over-
	21 PAFU	turned, Peplow, 13.2.45
R6299	2 FTS	SOC 5.9.40
R6317	2 FTS/15 FTS/	
	15 PAFU	SOC 3.1.44
R6318	2 FTS/6 PAFU/	
	18 PAFU	SOC 23.5.46
R6319	3 FTS/6 AACU/	
	14 PAFU	SOC 19.5.44
R6320	3 FTS	Bounced on landing, wing hit
		ground and undercarriage coll-
		apsed, Bibury, 20.7.40
R6321	14 FTS/3 FTS	Collided with W6555 while
		changing formation over South
		Cerney, 22.5.42
R6322	3 FTS	Engine cut on take-off; hit
		hedge, stalled and crashed,
		South Cerney, 18.12.41; DBR
R6323	14 FTS/6 FTS/	Ran into BM839 taxiing at
	7 AACU/287/	Snaith, 11.2.46; later
	11 Gp CF/1508 Acclim	DBF during road transit,
	Flt	10.3.46
R6324	RAFC/6 PAFU/	
	18 PAFU	SOC 22.9.44
R6325	14 FTS	Stalled during single-engined
		practice landing and hit ground,
		Cranfield, 4.9.40
R6326	11 FTS	Undershot night approach and
		hit tree, Shawbury, 8.10.40
R6327	11 FTS/16 PFTS	SOC 22.10.44

R6328	11 FTS/11 PAFU/	
	10 RS/16 PAFU	SOC 21.6.44
R6329	11 FTS/2 FIS/410	Flew into high ground in
		fog on ferry flight, Wrotham
		Camp, Kent, 21.12.44
R6330	3 FTS/3 GTS/	
	2 FIS/14 OAFU	SOC 18.10.45
R6331	3 FTS	SOC 20.8.40
R6332	3 FTS	Control lost in turn after night
		take-off from Bibury; dived into
		ground, Broadfield, Glos.,
		6.8.40
R6333	14 FTS	Overshot night landing,
		Cranfield, 4.4.41; DBR
R6334	3 FTS/11 PAFU	DBR 11.12.44
R6335	14 FTS/2 FTS/	
	8 AACU/587	SOC 19.5.44
R6336	14 FTS/14 PAFU	SOC 8.12.42
R6337	2 FTS/7 FIS	Sold 23.6.49
R6338	2 FTS/6 PAFU/	
	12 PAFU/11 PAFU	SOC 8.11.43
R6339	2 FTS	Stalled off turn at low altitude
		and crashed, Akeman Street,
		22.9.40
R6340	14 FTS/2 CFS/	
	18 PAFU/SF Spilsby/	
	SF E.Kirkby	SOC 2.1.46
R6341	2 FTS/15 FTS/2 FTS/	
	2 PAFU/10 RS	SOC 24.7.44
R6342	RAFC	Stalled on take-off avoiding
		another aircraft and hit ground,
		Cranwell, 17.5.41
R6343	2 FIS/2 CFS/11 FTS/	
	Dalcross/11 FTS/	
	11 PAFU/Chedburgh	Sold 3.11.49
R6344	2 FTS/2 FIS/	
	1483 Flt/116	SOC 20.11.44
R6345	2 FTS/14 FTS/	
	14 PAFU/3 PAFU/	
	TFU/233/512/	
	Bradwell/Kemble	To 5087M 31.3.45
R6346	15 FTS/12 FTS/	
	14 PAFU/Market	
	Harborough/Chedburgh	SOC 19.9.55
R6347	15 FTS/15 PAFU/	
	9 OTU/1 OTU/	
	489/455	SOC 25.6.44
R6348	15 FTS	Hit truck on landing on flare
		path, Kidlington, 17.2.42; DBR
R6349	15 FTS/15 PAFU	Collided with P8982 on
		approach in bad visibility,
		Kirmington, 16.7.42
R6350	15 FTS/7 FIS/Coltis-	
	hall/613/Coltishall	SOC 28.12.45
R6351	RAFC	Swung on landing, hit flare
		and tipped up, Barkston LG,
		14.2.41; DBF
R6352	2 FTS/1530 Flt/299/	
	42 OTU/Shepherds	
	Grove/42 OTU	SOC 14.3.45
R6353	2 FTS/3 PAFU/233/	
	107 OTU/1508 Flt/	
	304	SOC 27.11.47
R6354	2 FTS/Halton/	
	400/613	SOC 26.8.44
R6355	RAFC/3 PAFU/	
	8 OTU/132 OTU/	
	8 OTU	SOC 18.12.45
R6356	2 FTS	Bounced on landing and under-
		carriage collapsed, Brize
		Norton, 19.8.41
R6357	2 FTS	Engine cut on low flying
		exercise; hit trees and crashed,
		Tadpole Bridge, 2½m S of
		Bampton, Oxon., 29.12.40

<u>R6358</u>	RAFC/15 FTS/ 15 PAFU/18 PAFU	To USAAF 27.2.44
R6371	2 FIS/2 CFS/ 18 PAFU	To Admiralty 22.2.44
R6372	2 FIS/RAFC/2 CFS	Hit tree after take-off, Fulbeck, 23.4.41
R6373	2 FIS/2 CFS/14 FTS/ 14 PAFU/11 PAFU/ 2 FIS/502	SS 27.3.50
R6374	4 FPP/15 FTS/ 15 PAFU/1484 Flt/ 20 PAFU	SOC 2.6.44
R6375	4 FPP/RAFC	DBR 5.6.41; NFD
R6376	RAFC/15 FTS/ RAFC/15 FTS/ 15 PAFU/12 PAFU/ 21 PAFU	SOC 25.11.44
R6377	15 FTS	
R6378	15 FTS/15 PAFU	Overshot landing and flew into ground on attempted overshoot, Sherburn-in-Elmet, 27.5.42
R6379	15 FTS/15 PAFU	Control lost after night take-off; dived into ground, Leconfield, 6.9.42
R6380	15 FTS/2 FIS/ 21 PAFU	SOC 3.7.45
R6381	15 FTS	Failed to climb on take-off; hit trees and crashed, Glympton Heath, 4m N of Woodstock, Oxon., 8.7.41; DBF
R6382	15 FTS/2 FIS/15 PAFU/83 Gp CF/ Redhill/Kenley/587	SOC 19.5.44
R6383	15 FTS/15 PAFU/ 18 PAFU/Kenley/ 587/Wombleton/ 1666 HCU	SS 14.2.49
R6384	PFTS/16 PFTS	Undershot flarepath and hit hedge, Sibson, 14.4.42; DBR
R6385	15 FTS/1 PFTS/ 16 PFTS/1 FU/ 16 PAFU/116	SOC 19.10.44
R6386	15 FTS/15 PAFU/ 18 PAFU	To R.Norwegian AF 4.6.47 as V-AG
R6387	15 FTS/2 FIS/3 FIS	SS 3.2.56
R6388	15 FTS/15 PAFU	Dived into ground near Ramsbury, 7.6.43; cause not known
R6389	15 FTS/15 PAFU/ RAFC/17 SFTS	Lost nacelle fairing and control lost; dived into ground, Pytchley Lodge, Northants., 8.8.44
R6390	15 FTS/2 FIS/ 7 AACU	Engine cut; hit trees and bridge during attempted forced landing on Nuneaton-Coventry road, 28.2.43; DBF
R6391	15 FTS/6 FTS/ ATA/39 MU	SS 4.9.47
R6392	15 FTS/2 FIS/AST	SOC 16.9.44
R6393	15 FTS/14 FTS	Overshot landing into fence, Wanborough LG, 10.9.41; DBR
R6394	2 FTS/RAFC	Engine cut on night take-off; hit tree and crashed ½m SW of Fulbeck, 24.11.41
R6395	2 FTS/2 PAFU/289/ 409/410/409	Collided with vehicle while taxying, Twente, 9.6.45
R6396	2 FTS	Hit tree on night approach and crashed, Southrop, 25.8.41
R6397	2 FTS/2 PAFU	To USAAF 20.11.43
R6398	2 FTS	Hit tree on overshoot at night and crashed, Southrop, 2.10.41
R6399	2 FTS/14 FTS/ 14 PAFU	SOC 21.1.43
R6400	RAFC	Crashed in forced landing, Upper Team, Staffs., 9.1.41

R6401	RAFC/12 FTS/ 16 PFTS/2 PAFU/ 3 PAFU/263	To US Navy 14.4.44
R6402	2 FIS	Hit trees on night approach, Fulbeck, 9.11.40
R6403	11 FTS/2 CFS/ 12 FTS/2 CFS/ 18 PAFU	SS 3.11.49
R6416 - R6439		Cancelled Oxfords
R6453 - R6478		from Philips & Powis
R6490 - R6539		to Contract B20357/39

*   *   *   *   *   *   *   *   *

Nine Supermarine Walrus Is transferred from Admiralty
from batch R6543 to R6591 to Contract B21120/39

R6543	ASR Flt ME	SOC 31.1.46
R6546	281	Crashed on take-off 3½m E of Warkworth, Northumberland, 20.5.43
R6547	293	Unable to take-off in choppy seas after picking up pilot; abandoned and later foundered 50m SE of Venice, 10.12.44
R6548	275/278	Sold 12.3.47
R6549	293	Hit by Kittyhawk EX591 while parked, Fano, 29.11.44
R6552	ASR Flt ME	SOC 27.6.46
R6584	8 ARD SAAF	SOC 11.4.46
R6588	ASR Flt ME	SOC 29.2.44
R6590	275	Damaged on take-off; aband- oned and sank 2m N of Cairnlyn Bay, Anglesey, 7.5.43

*   *   *   *   *   *   *   *   *

450 Supermarine Spitfire Is delivered between May 1940 and April 1941 by Supermarine, Southampton, to Contract No. B19713/39. Many converted to later marks as shown

R6595	PDU/610	Damaged by Bf 109 over Folkestone and crashed on approach, Hawkinge, 26.8.40; DBF
R6596	92/222/131/52 OTU/ 57 OTU	Collided with X4595 and crash- landed near Brunton, 17.3.44
R6597	92/41/152	Shot down by Bf 109, Arne, near Wareham, Dorset, 28.11.40
R6598	PDU/PRU	Missing from PR mission to Ostend, 23.2.41
R6599	238/7 OTU/610	Damaged 12.10.40; SOC 25.10.40
R6600	238/602/152/ 58 OTU/57 OTU	Engine cut; hit trees in forced landing ¼m NE of Easthouse, Warkworth, Northumberland, 22.12.43
R6601	238/602/610/57 OTU	Overshot approach to Hawarden, lost power due to glycol leak and crashed, Ledsham, 10.7.41
R6602	238/65/PRU/1 PRU/ 53 OTU/Cv VA/ 52 FG/61 OTU	Collided with X4821 and crashed, Bangor, Flint, 6.5.44
R6603	238/74/66	Shot down by enemy aircraft, Denge Wood, Petham, Kent, 18.9.40
R6604	238/7 OTU/41/54/41/ 452/313/61 OTU	To Admiralty 11.5.43
R6605	238/7 OTU/41	Damaged by Bf 109s and abandoned, 14.9.40; NFD
R6606	238/74/61 OTU/ 53 OTU/58 OTU	Flew into Westcairn Hill in cloud, Midlothian, 17.2.43

R6607	238/7 OTU/152	Flew into ground in bad visibility, Winfrith, Dorset, 18.10.40
R6608	238/152/58 OTU/ 61 OTU	Undercarriage collapsed in heavy landing, Heston, 11.10.41
R6609	65	Shot down by Bf 109s near Folkestone, Kent, 7.7.40
R6610	238/7 OTU/65/41/ 1416 Flt/140	Missing on tactical reconnaissance mission to Port-en-Bessin, 24.11.41
R6611	238/7 OTU/41/616/ 56/308/403/52 OTU/ 61 OTU	Dived into ground during aerobatics, Waterbury, Oxon., 16.9.41
R6612	238/7 OTU/41/610/ 602/57 OTU/412/ 53 OTU	Caught fire on approach and crashlanded in field, Llandow, 13.2.42
R6613	238/92	Shot down by Bf 109s over Folkestone, Kent, 11.9.40
R6614	19/152	Damaged by Bf 109s and abandoned off Dorset coast, 11.8.40
R6615	65	Shot down by Bf 109s near Folkestone, Kent, 7.7.40
R6616	92	Collided with X4038 during attack on Do 17 and crashed, Portslade, Sussex, 10.10.40
R6617	65	Caught fire after take-off and abandoned near Rochford, 7.8.40
R6618	65	Destroyed by Bf 109s on ground, Manston, 16.8.40
R6619	65/603/41/111	Collided with another Spitfire and crashed near Aberdeen, 8.5.41
R6620	65/152/58 OTU/Cv VA/ 58 OTU/57 OTU	To Admiralty 24.7.43
R6621	610/234/53 OTU/ 61 OTU/CGS/53 OTU	SOC 8.3.45
R6622	92	Shot down by Bf 109s, Hesketh Park, Dartford, Kent, 27.9.40
R6623	19/64/41/452/313/ 81/165/52 FG/61 OTU	Collided with N3364 and crashed 1m W of Bellatyne, Salop., 22.4.44
R6624	92	Damaged by Bf 109s and abandoned, Sole Street House, Faversham, Kent, 14.9.40
R6625	19/7 OTU/19	Dived into ground while on patrol, Horndon-on-the-Hill, Essex, 14.9.40
R6626	603/266/111/58/ Benson	To Portuguese AF 14.8.43
R6627	19/234/602/124/ 52 OTU/58 OTU/ 1 TEU	SOC 18.8.44
R6628	222	Shot down by Bf 109, Bishopsbourne, Kent, 30.8.40
R6629	610/313/58 OTU/ 57 OTU	To Admiralty 15.1.44
R6630	610	Shot down by Bf 109s off Calais, 11.8.40
R6631	609	Shot down by Bf 109 on interception off Isle of Wight, 28.11.40
R6632	616/132/52 OTU/ 12 Gp CF/Digby/ 53 OTU/1 TEU	SOC 26.4.45
R6633	616	Damaged by Bf 109s and crashlanded, Adisham, Kent, 26.8.40
R6634	609	Damaged by return fire from Ju 88 and abandoned 5m off Swanage, Dorset, 18.7.40
R6635	41	Collided with P9428 during attack on Do 17s and crashed, North Benfleet, Essex, 5.9.40
R6636	609	Damaged by return fire from Ju 88 and forcelanded on Studland beach, Dorset, 18.7.40; overtaken by tide and DBR; to 2139M
R6637	609	Missing from interception off Portland Bill, 9.7.40
R6638	611/222/123/58 OTU	Engine overheated; bellylanded in field and hit bank near Ladybank, Fife, 29.7.42
R6639	5 OTU/64/53 OTU	Overturned in forced landing while lost after radio failed, Lulworth, Dorset, 10.9.41
R6640	5 OTU	Caught fire and crashlanded at Kemble, 1.7.40
R6641	5 OTU/610/ 53 OTU/57 OTU	SOC 18.4.45
R6642	92	Shot down by Bf 109s over Thames Estuary, 15.10.40
R6643	5 OTU/64/152/ 58 OTU	Missing on training flight, 10.4.41; not found
R6644	5 OTU/616/65/308	Caught fire and abandoned, Madresfield, near Gt.Malvern, Worcs., 11.5.41
R6683	5 OTU/64	Crashed in sea on patrol off Flamborough Head, Yorks., 6.10.40
R6684	5 OTU/222/53 OTU/ Cv II/64/611/52 OTU/ 57 OTU/53 OTU/ 5 PAFU	SOC 16.5.45
R6685	222/Hornchurch/132	Crashed after collision, Hormond Hill, Strichen, Aberdeen, 18.9.41
R6686	5 OTU/610/58 OTU/ 57 OTU	Collided with Wellington L7818 and crashed, Cold Ashton, Glos., 8.4.42
R6687	19/7 OTU/61 OTU/ 57 OTU	Engine cut in circuit; crashed on approach and overturned, Eshott, 24.5.44
R6688	19	Stalled off turn and dived into ground, Balsham Linton, Cambs., 13.7.40
R6689	66	Damaged by Bf 109s over Ashford, Kent, and abandoned, 4.9.40
R6690	609	Shot down by Bf 110 near Kenley, 15.9.40
R6691	609/616/65/602/ 58 OTU	Collided with AR246 and crashed, Letham Moss, Stirlingshire, 18.3.43
R6692	609	Overstressed attacking Ju 88 12.8.40 and SOC
R6693	610	Stalled on approach and dived into ground, Hawkinge, 25.7.40; DBF
R6694	610/485/52 OTU/ 61 OTU/42 OTU	SOC 18.12.44
R6695	610	Shot down by Bf 109, Hawkinge, 22.8.40
R6696	616	Dived into ground during night flying training near Lockington, E.Yorks., 7.8.40
R6697	64/41/485	To 2842M 3.12.41
R6698	616/61 OTU/57 OTU	Engine caught fire; hit fire tender on landing, Eshott, 9.6.43
R6699	609/54/41/313/ 61 OTU	Broke up in spin near Heston, 24.12.41
R6700	64/303/R-R/Mkrs	SOC 10.8.42
R6701	616	Damaged by Bf 109s over Dover and abandoned off Dungeness, Kent, 26.8.40
R6702	616/41/222/616	Shot down by Bf 109s near Throwley, Kent, 27.9.40

R6703	92	Damaged by return fire from Ju 88 over Solent and crashlanded, Norton, Selsey Bill, Sussex, 19.8.40; DBF
R6704	616/72/124/58 OTU	To Admiralty 5.9.42
R6705	54	Shot down by Bf 109 near Manston, 9.7.40
R6706	74/609/66/57 OTU/ 53 OTU	Aileron failed; spun into ground, Barrow-on-Humber, Lincs., 22.8.43
R6707	54	Shot down by Bf 109s over convoy off Dover, 25.7.40
R6708	54	Shot down by Bf 109s off Deal, Kent, 22.8.40
R6709	54/41/452/313	Missing escorting Blenheims to Comines, 26.6.41
R6710	54/266/72/61 OTU/ 17 SFTS	SOC 28.10.44
R6711	54	Shot down near Deal, Kent, 7.7.40
R6712	65/53 OTU	DBR in ground collision, Heston, 11.5.41
R6713	65	Crashed during patrol, Westbere, Kent, 18.8.40; cause not known
R6714	65	Dived into ground near Auchtermuchty, Fife, 16.10.40; DBF
R6715	66	Shot down by return fire from Do 17 20m E of Aldeburgh, Suffolk, 20.8.40
R6716	74/66/129/61 OTU/ 53 OTU	To Admiralty 14.9.43
R6717	603	Crashed in forced landing while lost in bad visibility near Inkhorn, Aberdeen, 2.8.40; DBR
R6718	RAE/CGS/Mkrs/ 52 OTU/140/ 2 TEU/1 TEU	SOC 6.3.45
R6719	222/132/52 OTU/ 61 OTU	SOC 5.5.45
R6720	222/Cv VA/53 OTU/ 130/134/133/134/ 133/116/288	To 5425M 4.7.45
R6721	603/72/92	Crashed in forced landing 3m SW of Leatherhead, Surrey, 27.10.40; DBR
R6722	Folland/Cv VA/54/124/ 81/164/167	To Admiralty 9.9.42
R6751	603	Shot down by Bf 109s off Dover, 28.8.40
R6752	603/266/72/ 57 OTU/58 OTU/ 61 OTU/57 OTU	SOC 12.8.44
R6753	603	Damaged by Bf 109s and abandoned near New Romney, Kent, 29.8.40
R6754	603/66/57 OTU	Crashed on landing, Hawarden, 11.11.40; to 2419M
R6755	603/41	Damaged by Bf 109s and abandoned, East Malling, Kent, 27.9.40
R6756	41	Shot down by Bf 109s near Dover, 8.9.40
R6757	74/41/74	Shot down by Bf 110s 30m E of Harwich, Essex, 11.8.40
R6758	616	Shot down by Bf 109s near Dungeness, Kent, 26.8.40
R6759	74/611/57 OTU/ Cv VA/41/81/165/167	To Admiralty 6.9.42
R6760	7 OTU/92/234/ 58 OTU	Dived into ground, Strathalan Camp, Auchterarder, Perthshire, 20.10.41; cause not known
R6761	19/AFDU/92/Cv VA/ 92	Missing, presumed shot down by Bf 109s on convoy patrol, 23.6.41
R6762	7 OTU/266/222/ 53 OTU/52 OTU/ 57 OTU	Collided with P-47 and crashed near Eshott, 12.4.44
R6763	152/64/303/ 58 OTU/53 OTU	SOC 16.8.44
R6764	152/234	DBR in accident, 7.11.40; NFD
R6765	610/41/611/485/ 61 OTU	Crashed after collision in cloud near Heston, 20.10.41
R6766	65	Abandoned during night flying training and crashed, Eastry, Kent, 13.8.40
R6767	64/92	Shot down during interception, 27.9.40; location unclear
R6768	266	Shot down by Bf 109s near Eastry, Kent, 16.8.40
R6769	609/64/57 OTU/ 61 OTU	Crashed while low flying, Hatton, Cheshire, 3.10.43; presumed due to high speed stall
R6770	19/AAEE/92/Cv VA/ 74/Cv IX/310/306	Missing for ground attack mission near St.Omer, 22.8.42
R6771	74/66/92/131/ 52 OTU/MSFU/ 58 OTU/53 OTU	To 33 MU 17.8.44 and SOC
R6772	74/222	Damaged by Bf 109s and abandoned, Challock, Kent, 18.9.40
R6773	74/222/57 OTU/303	SOC 19.12.41
R6774	MAP Hatfield	To 3597M 3.43
R6775	65/54/41/61 OTU/ 58 OTU/1 TEU	SOC 15.8.44
R6776	19/AAEE/AFDU/ Cv VA/AFDU/92/ 316/306	Damaged by Bf 109s on ground, Bolt Head, 1.5.42; not repaired
R6777	65/616/72/92/145/ AFDU/152/Hucknall/ 57 OTU/53 OTU	Broke up in air and crashed, Blackhill, Glam., 8.7.42
R6778	19/616	Damaged by return fire from Do 17 over Kenley, 1.9.40, and SOC as DBR
R6779	74/66	Shot down by Bf 109s, Bayford Marshes, Upchurch, Kent, 8.10.40
R6780	74/602/152/58 OTU	Dived into ground near Callander, Perthshire, 4.9.41
R6799	65	Stalled on take-off at night and hit ground, Rochford, 2.8.40; DBF
R6800	66	Shot down by Bf 109, Crockham Hill, Sevenoaks, Kent, 17.10.40
R6801	152/609/152/Cv VA/ 53 OTU/332/164/ 61 OTU	Collided with P7986 during combat practice over Leicestershire, 3.10.43
R6802	610	Shot down by Bf 109s off Dungeness, Kent, 16.8.40
R6803	65/53 OTU	DBR in accident 10.10.41; NFD
R6804	PDU/PRU/1 PRU	Missing from PR mission to Trondheim, 27.7.41
R6805	PDU/PRU/1 PRU	Missing from PR mission over Ruhr, 3.5.41
R6806	610/132/52 OTU/ 58 OTU/1 TEU	SOC 23.3.45
R6807	610/263	Stalled in Biggin Hill circuit and spun into ground, Skid House, Tatsfield, Kent, 13.7.40
R6808	603	Destroyed in air raid, Hornchurch, 31.8.40
R6809	19/222/Cv VA/AFDU/ 91/302/222/64/118/ 350/CGS	SOC 4.9.45
R6810	152	Shot down by Bf 109s off Portland, 25.8.40

Serial	Units	Fate
R6811	152	Shot down by Bf 109s, Bestwall, near Langton Matravers, Dorset, 8.8.40
R6812	54	Damaged by Bf 109 over Margate; stalled on approach to Manston and crashed near Old Charles Inn, Margate, Kent, 24.7.40
R6813	64/61 OTU/57 OTU	Collided with R7067 1m SE of Morpeth, 7.7.43
R6814	54	Engine caught fire; abandoned near Leeming and crashed, Burniston, 24.10.40
R6815	54/122/53 OTU	Engine caught fire; belly-landed, Tintern, Monmouth, 4.6.42
R6816	54	Shot down near Dover, 25.7.40
R6817	Eastleigh/53 OTU/ Cv VA/521	Engine cut; crashlanded and overturned, Coltishall, 11.11.42; DBF
R6818	65	Damaged by Bf 109 over Thames Estuary and crash-landed, Havengore Island, Foulness, Essex, 20.8.40; to 2481M
R6829	152/57 OTU	Collided with R7062 and crashed, Queensferry, Cheshire, 13.2.42
R6830	74/4 FPP	Engine cut; overshot forced landing into hedge, Stapleford Abbots, Essex, 13.8.40; DBF
R6831	152	Damaged by return fire from He 111s and crashed 8m off Portland, 27.8.40
R6832	54	Damaged by another Spitfire in dogfight with Bf 109s and abandoned; crashed at Frid Wood, Stockbury, Kent, 28.8.40
R6833	19/AFDU/92/Cv VA/ 92/72/312	Abandoned in bad visibility near Aberystwyth, Cardigan, 24.1.42
R6834	602/54/57 OTU	Flew into mountain in cloud near Blaenau Ffestiniog, Caernarvon, 26.5.41
R6835	603/457/53 OTU/ SF Atcham/61 OTU	To Admiralty 17.5.43
R6836	603/266/61 OTU	Crashed during low aerobatics, Southall, Middlesex, 22.8.41
R6837	222/65/145/118/66/ 501/53 OTU/61 OTU/ 58 OTU/1 TEU/ 57 OTU	SOC 9.2.45
R6838	611/92	Damaged by Bf 109s and crash-landed on mudflats off Allhallows, Essex, 15.10.40
R6839	74/602	Missing from patrol, 26.10.40
R6840	74/222/CGS/73 OTU	SOC 27.7.44
R6879	PRU/1 PRU	Missing 13.9.40
R6880	152/4 FPP	Hit balloon cable and crashed, Brockworth, Glos., 13.8.40
R6881	266/72/57 OTU	To Admiralty 12.5.43
R6882	19/7 OTU/AFDU/ Cv VA/AFDU/92/ 609	Broke up in air and abandoned 2½m NE of East Stoke, Notts., 10.1.42
R6883	118/53 OTU/57 OTU	Collided with K9953 during practice dogfight near Alnwick, 7.10.43; landed safely but NFT and presumed SOC as BER
R6884	65/41	Damaged by Bf 109s over West Malling and abandoned, Mereworth, Kent, 27.9.40
R6885	41	Damaged by Bf 109 and abandoned over Thames Estuary, 5.9.40
R6886	65/122/58 OTU/ 3 SGR/8 OTU	Engine caught fire; abandoned, Newton Moor, Inverness, 5.11.42
R6887	41/485/57 OTU/ Cv VA/41/81/ 165/167	To Admiralty 31.8.42
R6888	19/7 OTU/AFDU/92/ Cv VA/High Ercall/ 302/308/130/222/611	Missing from patrol over Normandy; presumed shot down by Bf 109s, 14.6.44
R6889	19/152/AFDU/19/ Cv VA/AAEE	To 3650M 2.4.43
R6890	19/7 OTU/Cv VA/92/ 616/403/121/316/ 306/312/444/ 58 OTU/53 OTU	SOC 13.10.45
R6891	610	Lost control and abandoned 2m NE of Edlingham, Northumberland, 19.11.40
R6892	54/41/452/57 OTU	Caught fire and crashed, Queensferry, Cheshire, 13.2.42
R6893	54/41	Engine cut on take-off; crash-landed among obstructions, Catterick, 21.3.41
R6894	RAE/Cv to PR.I/PRU	Shot down by Bf 109s near Canterbury on return from PR mission to Kiel, 8.10.40
R6895	54/53 OTU/58 OTU/ 57 OTU/Atcham/287/ 61 OTU/57 OTU	SOC 6.3.45
R6896	234	Missing from patrol, 2.9.40;
R6897	19/Cv VA/AFDU/92/ 234/310/332/411	Collided with AB847 during practice dogfight and crashed, Orby, Lincs., 28.1.43
R6898	54/41/452/313/ 61 OTU	Hit tree and crashed, Bramley, Hants., 8.12.41
R6899	54	Crashed during practice dogfight near Catterick, 3.2.41
R6900	Cv to PR.C/RAE/ PRU/Cv to PR.IV/ 1 PRU/8 OTU	SOC 15.3.45
R6901	54	Missing off Flamborough Head, 9.9.40; believed lost due to radio failure and ditched
R6902	Cv to PR.F/PDU/ Cv to PR.VI/3 PRU/ 1 PRU/8 OTU	SOC 22.3.45
R6903	Cv to PR/RAE/PRU/ 1 PRU/3 PRU/1 PRU	Missing from PR mission to La Pallice, 21.7.41
R6904	19/Northolt/19/92/ Cv to VA/616/65/41/ 121/306	Missing from ground attack mission near St.Omer, 22.8.42
R6905	Cv to PR.D/PDU/ 1 PRU/Cv to PR.VI/ 1401 Flt/521/8 OTU	SOC 22.3.45
R6906	Cv to PR/PDU/PRU	Shot down by Bf 109 over Boulogne, 18.1.41
R6907	152	Dived into ground near Blandford, Dorset, 29.11.40; believed due to anoxia
R6908	RR/19/Cv V/92	Lost 9.5.41; NFD
R6909	152/Cv to PR.III and PR.VI/1401 Flt	Damaged in accident 6.11.41; SOC 15.1.42
R6910	152/65/145/118/ Cv to PR.VII/1 PRU/ 140/8 OTU	SOC 22.4.45
R6911	19/7 OTU/Cv VA/ 52 OTU	Lost at sea in *Peter Maersk* west of Azores en route to ME, 7.12.42
R6912	19	Damaged by enemy aircraft; overturned on landing, Duxford, 31.8.40; DBF
R6913	54/234/58 OTU/ Cv VA/52 OTU/ 61 OTU/Northolt/ 52 OTU/61 OTU	SOC 6.11.44

R6914	54/611/485/123/ 53 OTU/61 OTU	To 4525M 7.2.44
R6915	609/61 OTU/57 OTU	To IWM and preserved
R6916	72/222/53 OTU/ 61 OTU/53 OTU/ 73 OTU	SOC 27.7.44
R6917	19/7 OTU/Cv VA/ 74/609/122	Swung on landing and over-turned on soft snow, Scorton, 10.3.42
R6918	610	Missing from patrol off Calais, 11.8.40
R6919	19/AFDU/92/Cv VA/ 92/316/41	Engine cut; crashlanded on approach, Penrhos, 26.10.42
R6920	266/58 OTU	To Portuguese AF 27.11.42
R6921	611/7 OTU/131/ 52 OTU	Ran out of fuel while lost in bad weather and crashlanded, Cheddar Head Farm, Wells, Somerset, 23.11.41
R6922	609/92	Missing 19.10.40; found crashed, Tuesnoad Farm, Smarden, Kent
R6923	19/92	Shot down by Bf 109 on bomber escort off Dover, 21.6.41
R6924	19/7 OTU/AFDU/92/ 504/58 OTU/53 OTU	Swung after night landing and hit steamroller, Fairwood Common, 26.1.43
R6925	266/66	Damaged by fighters and abandoned over Thames Estuary, 18.9.40
R6926	616	Damaged by Bf 109s over Dover and abandoned, Running-hill, Elham, Kent, 23.8.40
R6927	266/66/57 OTU/ 61 OTU	Stalled on landing and under-carriage collapsed, Heston, 3.10.41; DBR
R6928	72	Destroyed in air raid, Biggin Hill, 31.8.40
R6957	234/57 OTU/Cv VA/ 332/164/602/349/ 61 OTU	SOC 27.9.45
R6958	19	Damaged by enemy aircraft and abandoned over Thames Estuary, 31.8.40
R6959	234/58 OTU/132/ 52 OTU/61 OTU/ 58 OTU/1 TEU 2 TEU	SOC 18.8.44
R6960	Cv VA/AFDU/92/91/ 234/316/306/453/ 341/FLS/2 TEU/ 57 OTU	Undercarriage collapsed on landing in snowstorm, Boulmer, 6.12.44
R6961	609/66/53 OTU/ 61 OTU/53 OTU	SOC 6.3.45
R6962	54/74	Shot down by Bf 110s 30m E of Harwich, Essex, 11.8.40
R6963	616/65/308/57 OTU/ Atcham/61 OTU/ 53 OTU/1 TEU	SOC 27.8.44
R6964	152/58 OTU/Cv PR.V/Cv PR/VII/ 1 PRU/541	Missing 7.12.42
R6965	92/611/602/610/ 53 OTU/61 OTU/278	SOC 5.3.45
R6966	616	Shot down by Bf 109s near Canterbury, Kent, 25.8.40
R6967	234	Damaged by Bf 109 and abandoned near Widley, Hants., 16.8.40
R6968	152/58 OTU/Cv to PR/ 1 PRU/8 OTU/58 OTU	Control lost in bad weather; crashed, Avonbridge, Stirling-shire, 25.2.43
R6969	54/602/610/122/ 53 OTU	Spun into ground during aerobatics, Aberthaw, Glam., 7.12.41
R6970	610/57 OTU/52 OTU	To Admiralty 9.9.42

R6971	610/72	Damaged by Bf 110s and abandoned, Hartfield, Sussex, 4.9.40
R6972	64/303/58 OTU/ 57 OTU/1 PRU/ 53 OTU	To Admiralty 2.7.43
R6973	54/57 OTU/131	To 2683M 20.9.41
R6974	54/124	Engine cut; ditched off Duncansby Head, Caithness, 18.7.41
R6975	64/303/58 OTU/ 131/52 OTU/ 61 OTU	SOC 9.2.45
R6976	610/53 OTU/61 OTU/ 57 OTU	SOC 25.5.45
R6977	609/64/303/412/ 58 OTU	To Admiralty 26.5.43
R6978	611/65	Missing from interception of Ju 88 off Selsey Bill, 12.12.40; possibly collided with R6982
R6979	609/66/501/ 53 OTU/61 OTU/ 57 OTU	SOC 6.3.45
R6980	616/65/308/52 OTU/ 61 OTU	Engine cut; crashlanded, 2m S of Rednal, 14.7.42
R6981	72/54	Damaged by Bf 109s; abandoned and crashed, Godmersham, Kent, 15.8.40
R6982	54/74/65	Missing from interception of Ju 88 off Selsey Bill, 12.12.40; possibly collided with R6978
R6983	74/234/58 OTU	Broke formation and descended in cloud; flew into Bengengie Hill, 3m NW of Alva, Clack-mannan, 26.9.41
R6984	54/74/616/65/308/ 403/52 OTU/61 OTU	Engine caught fire; abandoned near Harmondsworth, Middle-sex, 9.9.41
R6985	234	Shot down by Bf 109s off Swanage, Dorset, 15.8.40
R6986	609/611/485/131/ 1 PRU/8 OTU/53 OTU	SOC 6.3.45
R6987	65/132	To Portuguese AF 7.1.43
R6988	234	Shot down by Bf 109s, Bournemouth, 15.8.40
R6989	603/61 OTU/57 OTU	Crashed in forced landing near Holywell, Flint, 15.8.42
R6990	64	Shot down by Bf 109s off Dungeness, Kent, 15.8.40
R6991	64/266/58 OTU/ 61 OTU	Collided with X4834 during formation change and lost tail; abandoned near Bolesworth, Cheshire, 26.6.42
R6992	64/53 OTU/Cv VA/ 1402 Flt	Abandoned after instrument failure 3½m W of Ennyvale, Co. Tyrone, 20.9.42
R6993	610/602/57 OTU/303/ 57 OTU/High Ercall/ 61 OTU	To Admiralty 19.5.43
R6994	152	Shot down by Bf 109s off Portland, Dorset, 25.8.40
R6995	64	Hit by cannon shell on interception, 9.8.40; NFT
R6996	610/64/303/58 OTU/ 53 OTU	To Admiralty 15.1.44
R7015	54	Damaged by Bf 109s and crash-landed, Hythe, Kent, 15.8.40
R7016	152	Missing from patrol over Channel, 23.9.40
R7017	54/245/234/53 OTU	DBR 1.9.41; NFD
R7018	616/57 OTU	Crashed near Wrexham, 22.8.41; DBF; NFD
R7019	54/603	Damaged by return fire from Do 17 and abandoned, Chartway Street, Kent, 15.9.40

R7020	609/603/266/ Cv to PR/3 SGR/ 8 OTU/57 OTU	Hit HT cable low flying and overturned in forced landing 2m N of Netherwitton, Northumberland, 14.3.44
R7021	54/603	Shot down by Bf 109, Addington Park, near West Malling, 29.8.40
R7022	266/72/53 OTU/ Cv VA/332/164/602/ 349/61 OTU	Dived into ground near Montford Bridge, 16.3.44
R7023	Mkrs/61 OTU	To Admiralty 7.9.42
R7024	66/57 OTU	Collided with R7138 and crashed 2m W of Malpas, Cheshire, 20.10.42
R7025	611/485/123	Lost at sea en route to Middle East, 8.1.43
R7026	303/58 OTU/ 52 OTU/58 OTU/ 1 TEU/57 OTU	SOC 26.8.44
R7027	123	To Portuguese AF 7.1.43
R7028	RAE/Cv G/1416 Flt/ RAE/Cv PR.VII/140	SOC 10.9.43
R7029	Cv PR.IV/1 PRU	Dived into ground, Cockley Green, Oxon., 27.4.42
R7030	Cv PR.IV/RAE/ 1 PRU/8 OTU	SOC 3.7.44
R7031	Cv PR.IV/Heston Acft/1 PRU/8 OTU	SOC 4.4.45
R7032	Cv PR.IV/RAE/ 1 PRU/8 OTU	SOC 6.3.45
R7033	Cv PR.IV/1 PRU	Pilot thrown out of aircraft in turbulence near Bishops Stortford, Herts., 5.10.41
R7034	Cv PR.IV/RAE & AAEE	SOC 1.4.50
R7035	Cv PR.IV/1 PRU	Missing from PR mission to Stavanger, 18.3.42
R7036	Cv PR.IV/1 PRU	Missing from PR mission to Bremerhaven, 12.4.42
R7037	Cv PR.IV/1 PRU	Missing from PR mission, Cherbourg - Le Havre, 3.6.42
R7038	Cv PR.IV/1 PRU	Missing from PR mission to Wilhelmshaven, 16.9.42
R7039	Cv PR.IV/1 PRU	Missing from PR mission over French/Spanish frontier, 10.9.41
R7040	Cv PR.IV/1 PRU	Missing from PR mission to Brest, 2.12.41
R7041	Cv PR.IV/1 PRU/ Benson/541	Missing on PR mission to Kristiansand, 12.1.43
R7042	Cv PR.IV/1 PRU/541	Dived into ground near Turweston, 16.2.43; cause not known
R7043	Cv PR.IV/1 PRU	Missing from PR mission to Kiel, 30.9.41
R7044	Cv PR.IV/1 PRU/541	Missing on PR mission to Stadlandet, 13.1.43
R7055	Cv PR.V/1 PRU	Lost power on overshoot and ditched, Gibraltar, 15.4.42
R7056	Cv PR.V/1 PRU	Missing from PR mission to Trondheim, 10.4.42
R7057	501/53 OTU	Flew into mountain near Glyn Neath, Glam., 12.8.41
R7058	308/403/57 OTU	Engine cut during aerobatics; bellylanded, Belton Farm, Whitchurch, Salop, 18.11.41; to 2877M
R7059	1416 Flt/Cv PR.VII/ 1 PRU/8 OTU	Engine caught fire; crashed Newton Farm, near Laurencekirk, Kincardine, 25.7.43
R7060	313/61 OTU/Cv VA/ 332/164/61 OTU	SOC 18.12.44
R7061	485/52 OTU	Hit hill on take-off from Aston Down, France Lynch, Glos., 18.12.41
R7062	308/403/57 OTU	Collided with R6829 and crashed, Rhosemor, Flint, 12.12.41
R7063	53 OTU/61 OTU/ 52 OTU/57 OTU	Spun into ground near Morpeth, 11.10.43; presumed pilot blacked out in turn
R7064	411/52 OTU	Lost cowling in spin crashlanded and hit fence 3m SE of Aston Down, 25.3.42; DBR
R7065	403/53 OTU/ 61 OTU/57 OTU	Collided with Beaufort W6540 near Rothbury, Northumberland, 19.6.44
R7066	403/52 OTU/61 OTU	Crashed in forced landing near Heston, 11.8.41
R7067	53 OTU/303/306/308/ 57 OTU/53 OTU	SOC 11.8.44
R7068	403/52 OTU	DBR in accident, 25.11.41; NFD
R7069	72/111/58 OTU/ 61 OTU/58 OTU/ 1 TEU	SOC 6.3.45
R7070	Cv to PR.I/PRU/ 1 PRU	Missing from PR mission to Brest, 25.5.41; believed ditched on return
R7071	602/61 OTU	To Portuguese AF 14.9.43
R7072	124/53 OTU	Lost at sea en route to Middle East, 8.1.43
R7073	123/58 OTU	Collided with X4905 and crashed near Falkirk, Stirlingshire, 17.4.42
R7074	124	Spun into sea during practice dogfight off Dunnet Head, Caithness, 27.7.41
R7114	1 PRU/52 OTU	Hit by R6806 after landing, Aston Down, 12.4.42; DBR
R7115	122	Dived into ground ½m W of Catterick Camp, Yorks., 19.9.41
R7116	1416 Flt/Cv to PR.VII/ 1416 Flt/140	Missing 8.11.42; NFD
R7117	1 PRU/313/57 OTU	SOC 9.8.44
R7118	1 PRU/AFDU/61 OTU	To 4519M 15.3.45
R7119	132/52 OTU	To Admiralty 9.9.42
R7120	RAE & AAEE/Cv to PR.VI	To 3566M 7.3.43
R7121	RAE/57 OTU	Engine caught fire; forcelanded, Eshott, 19.5.43; SOC as DBR
R7122	123	Hit X4596 on landing, Turnhouse, 9.7.41
R7123	132	To Portugal 20.1.43
R7124	132/53 OTU	Crashed while low flying over Severn near Newnham, Glos., 24.4.42
R7125	123/61 OTU	To Admiralty 19.5.43
R7126	411/57 OTU	Control lost in snow storm; hit tree and blew up, Park Gate Road, Chester, 7.12.41
R7127	411/54/Cv VA/332/ 164/602/61 OTU	Collided with X4173 and crashed near Rednal, 12.9.43
R7128	Cv PR.III/1 PRU/ 3 SGR	Overshot landing and hit obstruction, Squires Gate, 22.4.42; DBR
R7129	308/403/52 OTU/ 61 OTU	Collided with R7150 near Heston, 21.8.41
R7130	124/Cv PR.VII/140	SOC 6.3.45
R7131	124/340/52 OTU/ 1 PRU/8 OTU/ Benson/8 OTU	SOC 19.5.45
R7132	124/123/58 OTU/ 73 OTU	SOC 1.3.44
R7133	129	Dived into ground, Sledmere, Yorks., 10.8.41
R7134	124/52 OTU/57 OTU/ 61 OTU/58 OTU/ 2 CTW/1 TEU	SOC 1.9.44

R7135	124/52 OTU	Crashed in Severn while low flying, Oldbury Sands, near Chepstow, Mon., 8.2.42
R7136	124/340/52 OTU	To Admiralty 5.9.42
R7137	129/610	Engine cut on take-off; overshot runway and overturned, Leconfield, 2.9.41
R7138	122/57 OTU	Tyre burst on landing; swung and tipped up, Eshott, 19.10.43
R7139	Cv G & PR.IV/ 1416 Flt/140/ 1 PRU/543/8 OTU	SOC 6.3.45
R7140	308/403/57 OTU	Crashed near Chester, 7.12.41; NFD
R7141	501/Baginton/ 52 OTU/61 OTU	SOC 22.3.45
R7142	Cv PR.I/RAE/ 1416 Flt/Cv PR.V/ 1 PRU/Cv PR IV/140	Broke up in dive and crashed 3m E of Corfe, Dorset, 16.12.41
R7143	Cv PR.IV/RAE/ 1416 Flt/140/ Cv PR.VII/Benson	To RCAF 16.1.43
R7144	132/52 OTU/ 58 OTU/2 TEU	Collided with P9371 and crashed ¼m NW of Cuthmuir, Kinross, 18.12.43
R7145	132/3 SGR/8 OTU/ 58 OTU	To Admiralty 4.9.42
R7146	Cv PR.III/1 PRU/ 3 SGR/8 OTU/52 OTU	To Portuguese AF 14.8.43
R7147	Cv to PR.III/1 PRU/ Halton/8th BC Benson	To USAAC 14.8.42
R7148	Westlands/131/52 OTU	Engine cut on navex; belly-landed 3½m SW of Shaftesbury, Dorset, 25.2.42
R7149	122/57 OTU/58 OTU	Ran out of fuel; stalled on emergency approach and hit ground, Leuchars, 24.9.43
R7150	308/403/52 OTU/ 61 OTU	Collided with R7129 near Heston, 21.8.41
R7151	123/58 OTU/61 OTU/ 52 OTU/58 OTU/ 1 TEU	SOC 11.8.44
R7152	123/58 OTU/61 OTU/ 73 OTU	Engine cut; forcelanded 7m from Abu Sueir, 10.11.43
R7153	411/129/58 OTU/ 1 TEU	SOC 18.8.44
R7154	124	Engine cut; crashlanded, Sandwood Bay, Sutherland, 30.9.41; DBR
R7155	-	To 12 MU 1.3.41; NFT
R7156	124	DBR in accident 27.8.41; no record after 15.8.41 with 124 Sqn
R7157	124/52 OTU	Dived into ground near Quedgeley, Glos., 26.9.42
R7158	92/315/402/312/129/ 316/416/421/340/ FLS/57 OTU	SOC 17.4.45
R7159	411/53 OTU	To Portuguese AF 27.11.42
R7160	452/313/61 OTU/ 57 OTU	To Admiralty 5.9.42
R7161	92/Cv VB/315	Taxied into AB217, Northolt, 13.3.42; NFT
R7162	411/303/306/61 OTU/ 53 OTU	SOC 11.8.44
R7163	452/313	Dived into ground, Uckerby, Yorks., 27.5.41; cause not known
R7192	Cv VB/92/111	Collided with BL429 during take-off, Debden, 14.3.42
R7193	313/57 OTU	To Admiralty 7.9.42
R7194	129/Cv VA/145/ 136/133/134/133/611/ 421/61 OTU	Crashed on landing at night; overturned, Montford Bridge, 15.4.44
R7195	92/Cv VB/129/66/501	NFT 14.1.42
R7196	412/Cv VA/145/134/ 133/134/133/601/ 52 FG/2 US/52 OTU/ 61 OTU	SOC 3.6.45
R7197	66/501/412/ Cv PR.VII/1 PRU/140	SOC 27.2.45
R7198	412/Cv PR.V/1 PRU/ 8 OTU	Flew into mountain in Skye, 19.6.43
R7199	24/510/MCS	SOC 10.12.44
R7200	124/340/52 OTU	To Admiralty 4.7.43
R7201	123/58 OTU/1 TEU/ 57 OTU	To 33 MU 24.8.44 and SOC
R7202	122/53 OTU/57 OTU	Flew into hill on navex, Darden Hill, near Upper Rothbury, Northumberland, 3.2.43
R7203	123/58 OTU/57 OTU	SOC 17.8.44
R7204	123/58 OTU	Lost at sea en route to Middle East, 8.1.43
R7205	452/313/Cv VA/1401 Flt/521/61 OTU/ATA	SOC 10.7.45
R7206	131/52 OTU	Collided with X4932, 6.2.42; SOC 20.5.42
R7207	RAE	Blt as Mk.VB; to Admiralty 18.9.42
R7208	611	Blt as Mk.VA. Missing escorting Stirlings to Lille, 11.7.41
R7209	611	Blt as Mk.VA. Missing escorting Blenheims to Desvres, 22.6.41
R7210	145/41	Missing, believed shot down near Hazebrouck, 12.8.41
R7211	Cv to PR.IV/Cv PR.VII/ 1 PRU/541/TDU	SOC 15.3.45
R7212	132/52 OTU	Engine cut on take-off from Aston Down; hit wall in forced landing, Gatcombe Park, Minchinhampton, 16.12.41
R7213	611/145/41	Mk VA. Engine cut on patrol; stalled avoiding beach obstacles and crashed in sea 1m W of Bognor Regis, Sussex, 23.11.41
R7214	132/Lee/73 OTU	SOC 27.7.44
R7215	132/52 OTU	Lost at sea en route to Middle East, 8.1.43
R7216	132/58 OTU	Overshot landing with flaps up, Grangemouth, 21.3.42; DBR
R7217	611/41	Mk.VA. Shot down by Bf 109s near Armentières, 18.8.41
R7218	611/145	Mk.VA. Missing escorting Stirlings to Lille, 8.7.41
R7219	92/74/72	Mk VA. Shot down by fighters escorting Blenheims to Hazebrouck, 14.7.41
R7220	54/403/54/74/332/164/ 602/82 FG/349/ 58 OTU/61 OTU	Mk VA; To 5586M for transfer to Armée de l'Air 27.2.46
R7221	603	Missing, presumed shot down by Bf 109s near Hazebrouck while escorting Blenheims, 27.9.41
R7222	54	Shot down by Bf 109s escorting Stirlings to Lille, 5.7.41
R7223	64/603/41	Ditched in Channel on return from sweep, 27.8.41
R7224	91/609/603/416/ 93/306/302/2 FP	Undercarriage leg collapsed on landing, Weston-super-Mare, 28.12.43; to 4406M 12.43
R7225	54	Missing while escorting Stirlings to Arques, 12.7.41
R7226	64/603	Flew into Auchterhouse Hill, Angus, in bad visibility, 1.1.42
R7227	64/603	Shot down by Bf 109s 15m E of Gravelines while escorting Blenheims, 23.7.41

R7228	74/72	Wheels prematurely raised on take-off; hit ground and crash-landed ½m SW of Valley, 26.8.41	R7276	91		Dived into sea while escorting Walrus on ASR practice off Dungeness, 9.9.41; cause not known
R7229	64/603/315/81/ 165/167/61 OTU	SOC 19.1.45	R7277	611		Missing from escorting Stirlings to Lille, 8.7.41
R7230	611/603//602/81	Skidded on snow on landing and undercarriage collapsed, Ouston, 14.1.42; DBR	R7278	74		Missing on sweep, presumed shot down by Bf 109 off Cap Gris Nez, 17.6.41
R7231	611/332/164	To Admiralty 7.9.43	R7279	54/403		Missing from escorting bombers to Chocques, 21.8.41
R7250*	132/52 OTU	Stalled on landing and under-carriage collapsed; overturned, Aston Down, 18.3.42	R7290	91		Shot down by Bf 109 while escorting ASR launch off Calais, 1.10.41
R7251*	411/CF Colerne/ 55 OTU	SOC 27.9.45	R7291	611/145/41		Missing, believed shot down by Bf 109s near Béthune, 18.8.41
R7252*	411/53 OTU/61 OTU	SOC 30.12.44	R7292	91/71/308 US/91/ 306/345		SOC 8.12.44
R7253	611/145	Stalled while searching from crashed aircraft and spun into ground, Shripney, Sussex, 21.7.41	R7293	64/603/611		Shot down by Bf 109s near St. Omer while escorting Blenheims to Hazebrouck, 3.7.41
R7254	611/41/81/165	Abandoned 2m off Ailsa Craig, Firth of Clyde, 20.5.42	R7294	91		Set on fire by strafing Bf 109, Hawkinge, 5.5.41
R7255	611/145/41	Shot down on sweep near Le Havre, 28.8.41	R7295	54		Damaged by Bf 109s and abandoned off Folkestone, 16.6.41
R7256	54/403/54/AFDU/ 130/601/2 US/ 5 US/61 OTU	SOC 6.11.44	R7296	91/611/64/317/41		Flew into Taren Hendre Mountain, near Towyn, Meri-oneth, 22.10.42
R7257*	411/57 OTU	Engine caught fire; crashlanded in field and hit tree, Alston Street, Crewe, Ches., 29.5.42	R7297	54/41/81/165/5 US/ Eglinton/Bovingdon/ 61 OTU		SOC 19.3.45
R7258	54/41	Shot down by Bf 109s off Boulogne while escorting Blenheims to Arcques, 13.10.41	R7298	610/72/309 US/ 153 US/131/310/ 313/FLS/1 TEU/ FLS/61 OTU		Flew into ground on night training flight, Redwood Farm, Salop., 8.11.44
R7259	54	Shot down by fighters while escorting Blenheims near Hazebrouck, 25.6.41	R7299	64/603		Damaged by flak and crash-landed, Bomford Bridge, near Canterbury, 8.7.41; DBF
R7260	54/403	Engine cut; abandoned off Dover on return from sweep, 9.8.41	R7300	64/603		Damaged by Bf 109 near Cassel and ditched 2m off Dover, 21.8.41
R7261	2 US/5 US/61 OTU	SOC 10.9.45	R7301	54/403/54/72		To Admiralty 1.9.42
R7262	132/331/Mkrs/ WL 122 Wg/57 OTU	NFT 2.45	R7302	54/124/81/165/164/ 602/14 Gp CF/ 52 OTU/61 OTU		SOC 17.12.44
R7263	611/145	Missing from escorting Stirlings to Lille, 8.7.41	R7303	54		Missing from sweep to St. Omer, 22.7.41
R7264	54	Collided with another Spitfire while attacking Bf 109 near Hardelot, 14.7.41	R7304	611/145/41		Shot down by Bf 109s near St.Omer while escorting Blenheims, 27.8.41
R7265	91/72/313/403	Spiralled into ground 3m E of Barnard Castle, Yorks., 24.9.42	R7305	54/603		To Admiralty 4.9.42
R7266	54/403	Missing on sweep over Pas de Calais, 9.8.41	R7306	611/145/AAEE/RAE/ 52 OTU/FLS/57 OTU		SOC 29.11.45
R7267	54/41/332/164	Controls faulty on air test; hit wires and bellylanded in field, Sapiston Mill, Dounby, Orkneys, 15.6.42; DBR	R7307	611/145/41		Shot down by Bf 109s near Le Tréport while escorting Blen-heims to Le Trait, 31.8.41
R7268	54	Missing, presumably shot down by Bf 109s near Hazebrouck, 23.7.41	R7308	54/124/81/165/167/ Cv PR.VII/8 OTU/Cv PR.XIII/400/83 GSU		SOC 28.3.45
R7269	54	Missing, believed shot down by Bf 109s off Cap Gris Nez while escorting Stirlings to Mazingarbe, 9.7.41	R7309	611/145		Shot down escorting Stirlings to Mazingarbe by Bf 109s near Boulogne, 9.7.41
R7270	603	SOC 30.6.41	R7333	64/603		Missing from escorting Hurricanes to Hesdin, 8.12.41; presumed shot down by Bf 109s near Le Tréport
R7271	611/145/41/65/133	To Admiralty 2.9.42				
R7272	64/603	Missing from sweep to Pont-a-Vendin, 30.6.41	R7334	91/501/118		Control lost in cloud; dived into ground, Alderholt Park, near Fordingbridge, Hants., 13.6.42
R7273	54/403	Ran out of fuel and abandoned over sea after escorting Blenheims to St.Omer, 27.8.41	R7335	64/603/401/332/164/ Cv PR.VII/8 OTU/ Cv PR.XIII		To Admiralty 3.3.44
R7274	611/145/41	Missing 12.8.41; no record in 41 Sqn ORB	R7336	91/41/401/41/131/ 610/340		Collided with Martlet FN246 on approach, Ayr, 25.8.43
R7275	54	Damaged by Bf 109 and engine cut; abandoned over Strait of Dover, 4.6.41				

Serial	Units	Fate
R7337	Mkrs/AAEE/452/602/131	Landed with undercarriage unlocked, Llanbedr, 5.5.42
R7338	91	Abandoned out of control in cloud, Sneeth, Kent, 17.3.42
R7339	64/603	Missing from escorting Blenheims to Abbeville near St.Omer, 4.7.41
R7340	91	Missing from shipping reconnaissance off Le Touquet, 1.7.41
R7341	603	Engine cut; ditched off North Foreland, Kent, 23.7.41
R7342	54/Cv VA/403	Missing from escorting Blenheims to Gosney, 19.8.41
R7343	611/54/403/54/124/134/133/134/52 FG/61 OTU	Spun into ground while joining formation 2m S of Ford, Salop., 13.5.44
R7344	91/308	Missing from escorting Blenheims to Hazebrouck, 19.8.42
R7345	64/603	Damaged by Bf 109 and crash-landed on Goodwin Sands, 21.6.41
R7346	92	Missing escorting Blenheims to Lille, 18.8.41
R7347	-	Delivered to USA
R7348	91/457/452/93/165/308/315	Throttle control jammed; crash-landed, Heston, 3.2.44
R7349	611	Shot down by Bf 109s escorting Blenheims to Chocques, 24.6.41
R7350	145/41/71/603/332/12 Gp CF/Digby/61 OTU	SOC 12.10.44

Note: From R7219 onwards, all airframes were converted during completion to Mark VAs apart from those shown * which remained Mark Is.

*   *   *   *   *   *   *   *   *   *

100 Fairey Battle Trainers delivered between May and November 1940 by Faireys, Heaton Chapel, to Contract No. B15547/39

Serial	Units	Fate
R7356	12 FTS/1 FTS	Lost height in turn at night and hit ground 2m E of Shrewton, 15.12.41
R7357	12 FTS	DBR 30.12.40; believed DBR in air raid, Cambridge
R7358	-	To SAAF 19.6.40 as 921
R7359	-	To SAAF 19.6.40 as 917
R7360	11 FTS	To RCAF 21.12.40
R7361	12 FTS/16 PFTS/3 AGS	SOC 21.1.44
R7362	12 FTS/16 PFTS/3 AGS	SOC 14.7.44
R7363	12 FTS	Shot down by enemy aircraft 3m S of Grantham, 18.5.41
R7364	12 FTS/7 FTS/12 FTS/16 PFTS/3 AGS	SOC 8.44
R7365	12 FTS/7 FTS/1 FTS	To RCAF 11.6.41 as 2003
R7366	12 FTS/1 FTS/4/2 AACU/3 AGS	SOC 30.6.43; 3903M NTU
R7367	12 FTS/7 FTS/2 BGS/2 AOS/1 FTS/3 AGS	SOC 30.6.43
R7368	12 FTS/7 FTS/1 FTS/8 BGS/27 MU	SOC 7.12.44
R7369	12 FTS/16 PFTS	SOC 22.9.43
R7370	12 FTS	To RCAF 8.1.41
R7371	5 BGS/CFE/2 BGS/2 AOS/38 MU	SOC 28.12.44
R7372	7 OTU/3 FPP/ATA	SOC 12.7.44
R7373	7 OTU/12 OTU	To RCAF 10.4.41
R7374	7 OTU	To RCAF 1.4.41
R7375	7 OTU/1 FTS/3 AGS	To 2485M 10.12.43
R7376	7 OTU/1 FTS/3 AGS	SOC 23.8.44
R7377	6 OTU/1 FTS	To RAAF 7.4.41
R7378	6 OTU/12 OTU/2 BGS/4 AOS/2 AGS/1609 Flt/1606 Flt	To 3909M 15.7.43
R7379	6 OTU/12 OTU/ATA/3 AGS	SOC 14.7.44
R7380	6 OTU/12 OTU/PRU	To RAAF 9.6.41
R7381	6 OTU/12 OTU/2 BGS/2 AOS/2 AGS/231/ATA	SOC 8.7.44
R7382	CFE/2 BGS/2 AOS	SOC 4.7.44
R7383	15 EFTS/1 PFTS/16 PFTS	SOC 28.3.46
R7384	-	To RCAF 21.12.40
R7385	7 FTS/1 FTS	To RAAF 7.4.42
R7399	303/308/317/52 OTU	SOC 30.6.43
R7400	15 EFTS/1 PFTS/16 PFTS	SOC 14.9.43
R7401	301/2 BGS/2 AOS/2 OAFU/3 AGS	SOC 21.1.44
R7402	300/1 FTS	To SAAF 20.3.42 as 1034
R7403	-	To RCAF 8.10.40
R7404	-	To RCAF 3.10.40
R7405	-	To RCAF 1.10.40
R7406	12 OTU/16 PFTS/3 AGS/ATA	SOC 17.5.44
R7407	12 OTU/16 PFTS	Lost in accident, 25.11.41; NFD
R7408	-	To RCAF 1.10.40
R7409	312/96	
R7410	306/316/2 AGS	Engine cut; hit HT wires in forced landing, Dalcross, 20.10.42; DBR
R7411	307	Lost glycol when believed hit by ground fire and abandoned 5m E of Goole, Yorks., 30.10.40
R7412	-	To Canada 1.4.41
	31 BGS	SOC 1.5.44
R7413	-	To RCAF 3.10.41
R7414	-	To RCAF 1.12.40
R7415	-	To RCAF 1.10.40
R7416	-	To RCAF 12.10.40
R7417	-	To RCAF 8.10.40
R7418	-	To Canada 21.10.40
	31 SFTS	Abandoned on navex and crashed, Watertown, NY, 21.12.40
R7419	-	To Canada 28.12.40
	31 SFTS	SOC 5.6.41
R7420	-	To RCAF 28.12.40
R7421	-	To RCAF 21.10.40
R7422	-	To RCAF 1.12.40
R7423	-	To Canada 3.11.40
	31 SFTS	SOC 11.1.43
R7424	-	To RCAF 16.11.40
R7425 to		
R7427	-	To RCAF 28.12.40
R7428	-	To RCAF 3.11.40
R7429	-	To RCAF 3.12.40
R7430	-	To RCAF 21.10.40
R7431 to		
R7433	-	To RCAF 16.11.40
R7434	-	To RCAF 21.10.40
R7435	-	To RCAF 21.10.40
R7436	-	To RCAF 3.11.40
R7437	-	To RCAF 16.11.40
R7438	-	To RCAF 26.10.40
R7439	-	To RCAF 26.10.40
R7440	-	To RCAF 21.10.40
R7441	-	To RCAF 23.10.40
R7442	-	To RCAF 16.11.40
R7443	-	To RCAF 16.11.40
R7444	-	To Canada 21.10.40
	31 SFTS	SOC 4.11.44

R7445	-	To RCAF 16.11.40
R7446	-	To RCAF 28.12.40
R7447	-	To RCAF 16.11.40
R7448	-	To RCAF 16.11.40
R7461	-	To Canada 16.11.40
	31 SFTS	SOC 11.7.41
R7462	-	To Canada 28.12.40
	31 SFTS	SOC 1.5.44
R7463	-	To RCAF 28.12.40
R7464	-	To RCAF 16.11.40
R7465 to		
R7467	-	To RCAF 28.12.40
R7468	-	To RCAF 21.2.41
R7469	-	To RCAF 8.1.41
R7470	-	To RCAF 10.3.41
R7471	-	To RCAF 10.3.41
R7472	1 FTS	Crashed after control lost in fog after take-off from Shrewton, 27.3.41
R7473	-	To RCAF 21.12.40
R7474	-	To Canada 5.1.41
	31 SFTS	DBR 14.7.41; NFD
R7475	-	To RCAF 5.1.41
R7476	-	To RCAF 5.1.41
R7477	16 PFTS/1600 Flt	SOC 14.7.44
R7478	-	To SAAF 2.41 as No.945
R7479	-	To RCAF 10.4.41
R7480	-	To RCAF 31.5.41

*   *   *   *   *   *   *   *   *   *

50 Percival Proctor Is and IIIs delivered in January and February 1941 by F. Hills & Sons to Contract No. B5153/39 Mark IIIs from R7530

R7485	2 SS/BW Flt/1 EFTS/ 4 RS	Sold 15.5.46; became G-AHMU
R7486	2 SS/11 Gp CF	Sold 10.5.46; became G-AHNB·
R7487	2 SS/1 RS	To 4809M
R7488	2 SS/BW Flt/2 SS/ BW Flt/2 RS/CF White Waltham	Sold 10.9.46; became G-AIHB·
R7489	2 SS/1 RS	Sold 5.9.46; became G-AIKK
R7490	ATA/SF Hucknall/ 12 Gp CF/SF Digby/ 12 Gp CF	Sold 30.1.46; became G-AHES
R7491	ATA/SF Abingdon/ 1 RS/ECFS	Sold 24.6.46; became G-AHVD
R7492	24/USAAC/510/ 1 EFTS	Sold 25.2.46; became G-AHFZ
R7493	2 SS/BW Flt/MCS	Sold 5.9.46; became G-AIEB
R7494	2 SS/SF Henlow/MCS	Sold 28.6.46; became G-AHVA
R7495	24 EFTS/24/510	Sold 13.9.46; became G-AIHF
R7496	1 EFTS/25 OTU/ SF Lindholme/1 Gp CF	Sold 28.5.46; became G-AHNF
R7497	4 SS/4 RS/Yatesbury	Sold 17.6.46; became G-AHVE
R7498	2 SS/BW Flt/4 RS	SOC 14.9.44
R7499	2 SS/BW Flt/2 RS/ 1st BAD Grove/ 38 Gp CF	Sold 18.11.46; became G-AIXP
R7520	1 EFTS/8th AFSC/ MCS	SOC 10.9.45
R7521	2 SS/BW Flt	Sold 18.1.46; became G-AHEU
R7522	2 SS	Spun into ground off turn, Highway Farm, near Calne, Wilts., 24.4.42
R7523	2 SS/BW Flt/85 Gp CF	SOC 21.9.45
R7524	1 EFTS/Chivenor	Sold 30.10.46; became G-AIWA
R7525	1 EFTS/CF Woodley/ 8 Gp CF	Sold 1.5.46; became G-AHKW
R7526	2 SS	Ran into P62S7 while taxying, Yatesbury, 31.8.42

R7527	2 SS	Hit tree and dived into ground, Langley Barrell, near Chippenham, Wilts., 13.9.42
R7528	1 EFTS/24/SF Halton	Sold 13.5.46; became G-AHMT
R7529	1 EFTS/CGS	Sold 4.2.46; became G-AHEV
R7530	1 SS	Lost wing taking avoiding action and crashed, Sudbrook, Lincs., 22.10.41
R7531	1 SS/4 SS/2 SS/2 RS	Hit house low flying, Nutley, Surrey, 10.9.43
R7532	1 SS/1 RS/CF Redhill	Sold 9.9.46; became G-AIKJ
R7533	1 SS/1 RS	To USAAF 12.12.43
R7534	1 SS/1 RS/2 TAF CS/ 87 Gp CF	Sold 5.1.49
R7535	1 SS/9th AF/12 Gp CF/ SF Northolt/12 Gp CF	Sold 25.3.48; became G-AKWP
R7536	4 SS/2 SS/4 RS/4 RS/ 84 Gp CF	Engine cut; crashlanded near Ypres, Belgium, 4.10.44
R7537	4 SS/2 SS/4 SS/4 RS/ MCCF/2 Gp CS	SOC 14.11.46
R7538	4 SS/Yatesbury/4 RS	To RNZAF 9.11.44
R7539	4 SS/2 SS/4 SS/516/ 44 Gp CF	Sold 8.4.48; became G-AKWJ
R7559	4 SS/25 Gp CF/Tern-hill/22 Gp CF/White Waltham/5 Gp CF	Sold 24.2.49; became G-AMAL
R7560	4 SS	Overturned in forced landing while lost in bad visibility, Rankswood House, Worcester, 3.11.42
R7561	4 SS/4 RS	To USAAF 9.10.43
R7562	4 SS/4 RS	Sold 9.12.48
R7563	4 SS/2 SS/4 SS/4 RS/ TTCCF/85th Base Gp USAAF/ASWDU	SOC 31.12.48
R7564	4 SS/4 RS	Engine cut; hit hedge in forced landing, Peggs Farm, 2m N of Ledbury, Hereford, 21.1.43
R7565	4 SS/2 SS/4 SS/4 RS/ 23 Gp CF/27 Gp CF	Sold 5.1.49
R7566	4 SS/2 SS/4 SS/4 RS/ Halton/St.Athan/ TTCCF	Sold 22.3.51
R7567	4 SS/4 RS/110 Wg/ 147/St.Mawgan	Sold 22.9.48; became G-ALFF
R7568	4 SS/4 RS/FTCCF/ 84 Gp CF	Overshot forced landing in bad visibility and hit fence, Corby, Northants., 24.12.44
R7569	4 SS/2 SS/4 SS/4 RS/ 510/MCS	Sold 26.5.48
R7570	4 SS/2 SS/4 SS 4 RS/SF Castletown	Engine cut; ditched near Lybster, Caithness, 10.3.44
R7571	4 SS/4 RS/83 Gp CF/ 2 TAF CS	SOC 27.4.45
R7572	4 SS/SF Hurn/ SF Rivenhall	Swung on landing and under-carriage collapsed, Harwell, 2.10.45
R7573	4 SS/2 SS/4 SS/4 RS/ 51 Gp/CF Yeadon/ 21 Gp CF	SOC 8.1.47

*   *   *   *   *   *   *   *   *   *

250 Hawker Typhoon IAs and IBs delivered between December 1941 and July 1942 by Gloster Aircraft to Contract No. 12148/39

R7576	RAE/56/RAE	To 4638M 24.9.43
R7577	Mkrs & AAEE	SOC 2.12.43
R7578	Mkrs & Napiers	SOC 31.3.43
R7579	CFE/Mkrs	SOC 1.4.43
R7580	AFDU/56/59 OTU	Spun into ground 2m E of Milfield, 13.6.43
R7581	AFDU/609	To 3514M 14.3.43
R7582	56	To 4633M 24.9.43

Serial	Units	Fate
R7583	56	To 4637M 24.9.43
R7584	56	To 3517M 14.3.43
R7585	56	Hit tractor on overshoot, Matlask, 24.8.42
R7586	56	To 3521M 15.5.43
R7587	56	To 3518M 15.5.43
R7588	56	SOC 8.6.43
R7589	56/266/181/RAE	SOC 8.11.43
R7590	266/8 MU	Undercarriage retracted on landing, Little Rissington, 22.6.42
R7591	56/59 OTU/FLS	SOC 30.5.44
R7592	56	Dived into ground near East Harling, Norfolk, 1.11.41; presumed due to carbon monoxide fumes
R7593	56	SOC 11.12.42
R7594	56	To 3527M 25.5.43
R7595	56/AFDU/609/RAE/3 TEU	To 5443M 18.7.45
R7596	56	To Hawkers as instr. airframe 1.7.42
R7597	56	SOC 20.2.46
R7598	56	To synthetic trainer 8.10.42
R7599	56	SOC 5.6.43; 3511M NTU
R7613	56	SOC 8.6.43; 3516M NTU
R7614	AAEE	SOC 17.6.43
R7615	56/56 OTU	To 4175M 14.9.43
R7616	56	To 3520M 14.7.43
R7617	AAEE/Mkrs/RAE	SOC 30.9.44
R7618	266	Flew into ground in bad visibility ½m N of Welney, Cambs., 13.6.42
R7619	266	SOC 17.6.43
R7620	56/DH	SOC 1.4.45
R7621	56/182/59 OTU	Crashed on landing, Milfield, 17.6.43; DBR
R7622	266	SOC 9.4.43
R7623	266	To 3519M 10.4.43
R7624	266/Duxford/609/182/198/1 ADF	Engine cut; crashlanded 1m W of Ouston, 2.5.43; DBR
R7625	-	Crashed before delivery, 27.3.42
R7626	266	To 3515M 26.8.43
R7627	266/181/193	SOC 12.1.44
R7628	609	Bellylanded at Duxford, 10.6.42
R7629	56/182	Overshot landing at Martlesham Heath, 30.9.42
R7630	266/FIU/609/3/59 OTU	Crashed on landing, Milfield, 26.6.43
R7631	266/486/181/183	To 4639M 24.9.43
R7632	-	SOC 2.4.43
R7633	56	Engine cut; bellylanded, Oulton, 27.8.42
R7634	266	SOC 29.11.45
R7635	266	SOC 8.6.43; 3512M NTU
R7636	266	To 3513M 22.4.43
R7637	266	Spun into ground near Duxford, 8.3.42
R7638	Napiers & Mkrs	To 4568M 23.2.44
R7639	266/RR	To 3700M 26.5.43
R7640	609	SOC 9.4.43
R7641	56/266	To 3523M 16.3.43
R7642	266	SOC 17.6.43
R7643	56/Napier	SOC 30.10.43
R7644	56	Tail broke off in dive near Spalding, Lincs., 18.8.42
R7645	266	Abandoned after engine failure 25m off Cherbourg, 15.9.42
R7646	Mkrs/56/Mkrs & AAEE	SOC 9.6.46
R7647	609	Engine cut; abandoned near Ely, Cambs., 29.5.42
R7648	56	SOC 8.5.43
R7649	266/181/183/3/59 OTU	SOC 12.1.44
R7650	-	Not assembled; to spares
R7651	609/FIU/193/55 OTU	SOC 26.9.46
R7652	56	Undercarriage collapsed on landing, Matlask, 20.9.42
R7653	56/182/198	Crashed in forced landing, Acklington, 26.2.43
R7654	266	Flew into ground out of cloud Gt.Casterton, Rutland, 24.4.42
R7655	266	Engine cut; crashed in forced landing near Duxford, 4.6.42
R7672	266	Engine cut on landing, Duxford, 29.6.42
R7673	AAEE	To 4632M 24.9.43
R7674	266	SOC 20.2.46
R7675	56	SOC 20.2.46
R7676	266/181	Spun into ground, Duxford, 27.9.42
R7677	609/182	SOC 13.8.43
R7678	56	Shot down by Spitfires off Dover, 1.6.42
R7679	56	SOC 10.6.43
R7680	609/56	SOC 30.8.43
R7681	609/182/197/55 OTU	SOC 18.2.46
R7682	56	Taxied into Spitfire BM268, Westhampnett, 5.6.42; DBR
R7683	56/182/59 OTU	SOC 31.7.46
R7684	56/Duxford/193	SOC 20.10.43
R7685	Glosters	To 4567M 23.2.44
R7686	266	Engine cut; ditched 15m E of Torquay, Devon, 3.2.43
R7687	266	Control lost in cloud; crashed near Rufus Stone, Hants., 28.11.42
R7688	609/182/195	SOC 11.1.44
R7689	266/609	Shot down by FW 190 off Ramsgate, 15.12.42
R7690	609/198	SOC 10.8.43
R7691	609/182	Tyre burst on take-off, Martlesham Heath, 13.11.42
R7692	Mkrs	Broke up in air and crashed near Staines, Middlesex, 11.8.42
R7693	-	Not assembled; to spares
R7694	56/Napier	Crashed on test flight, 26.8.42
R7695	266	Broke up in air, Glanvilles Wooton, Dorset, 24.10.42
R7696	266/181/198/181/59 OTU	SOC 20.7.44
R7697	Napiers	SOC 7.5.45
R7698	609/Duxford/198	SOC 11.1.44
R7699	-	To 4250M 27.10.43
R7700	AAEE & Mkrs	To 4645M 4.44
R7701	-	To 3524M 16.3.43
R7702	56	Engine cut; undercarriage collapsed on landing, Matlask, 4.11.42
R7703	609	SOC 12.3.43
R7704	266	To 5198M 7.4.45
R7705	-	Not assembled; to spares
R7706	609/182/197/59 OTU	SOC 15.12.43
R7707	266	SOC 20.2.46
R7708	609	Hit by own AA and abandoned, Pegwell Bay, Kent, 31.10.42
R7709	-	To 4286M 3.11.43
R7710	609	Collided with R7817 on take-off, Duxford, 26.6.42
R7711	56	Crashed on landing, Coltishall, 1.10.42
R7712	Napiers	Retained by makers as test a/c
R7713	609	SOC 23.6.43
R7714	56	Shot down by fighters off Ijmuiden, 10.4.43
R7715	266	Engine cut on approach; bellylanded, Exeter, 13.2.43
R7716	-	To 4289M 3.11.43

Serial	Unit	Remarks
R7717	-	SOC 16.7.43
R7718	-	SOC 27.7.43
R7719	-	SOC 25.7.43
R7720	-	SOC 16.7.43
R7721	-	To 3525M 16.3.43
R7738	-	SOC 8.6.43
R7739	56	Dived into ground recovering from spin 3m E of Oulton, 12.4.43
R7740 to R7751	-	All SOC 8.6.43
R7752	609/56	SOC 25.8.43
R7753	-	SOC 8.6.43
R7754	-	To 3723M 16.8.43
R7755	-	To 3726M 5.6.43
R7756	-	SOC 23.7.43
R7757	-	SOC 28.7.43
R7758	-	To 3724M 26.6.43
R7759	-	SOC 8.6.43
R7760	-	To 4272M 2.11.43
R7761	-	SOC 8.6.43
R7762	-	To 3722M 4.8.43
R7763	-	SOC 23.7.43
R7764	-	To 4274M 2.11.43
R7765	-	To 3728M 26.7.43
R7766	486	To 4270M 2.11.43
R7767	-	To 4276M 2.11.43
R7768	-	To 3727M 6.6.43
R7769	-	To 3725M 8.7.43
R7770	-	SOC 15.7.43
R7771	Napiers & Mkrs/182	Damaged by flak and crash-landed near Lohne, 28.2.45
R7772	-	To 3729M 30.7.43
R7773	-	SOC 15.7.43
R7774	-	To 3710M 27.5.43
R7775	-	To 3529M 12.4.43
R7792	-	To 3528M 4.5.43
R7793	-	To 3716M 2.6.43
R7794	-	To 3714M 2.6.43
R7795	-	SOC 1.7.43
R7796	-	SOC 10.7.43
R7797	-	To 3522M 15.5.43
R7798	-	To 3711M 6.7.43
R7799	-	SOC 1.7.43
R7800	266	SOC 10.6.43
R7801	-	To 3706M 17.8.43
R7802	-	To 3531M 17.4.43
R7803	-	SOC 26.6.43
R7804	-	To 3530M 3.3.43
R7805	-	To 3713M 16.6.43
R7806	-	To 3718M 3.8.43
R7807	-	To 3712M 2.6.43
R7808	-	To 3719M 30.7.43
R7809	-	SOC 30.6.43
R7810	-	SOC 28.2.43
R7811	-	SOC 21.12.42
R7812	-	SOC 29.11.45
R7913	266	Missing from patrol over Dieppe, 19.8.42
R7814	266	Collided with Spitfire, Warmwell, 16.9.42; DBR
R7815	266	Shot down by Spitfires 20m S of Dungeness 19.8.42
R7816	609	Engine cut; crashlanded, Catwater Farm, Cambridge, 30.7.42
R7817	609	Collided with R7710 on take-off, Duxford, 26.6.42; DBR
R7818	609	Flew into Dover balloon barrage and crashed, 5.11.42
R7819	266	Engine cut; bellylanded, Warmwell, 8.11.42
R7820	266/247	Shot down by flak near Vimoutiers, 18.8.44
R7821	266	Dived into ground, Morebath, Bampton, Devon, 2.2.43
R7822	266/3 TEU	Caught fire and crashed, Low Newton, Northumberland, 5.6.44
R7823	56	Crashed in forced landing, Matlask, 24.4.43
R7824	56	SOC 20.2.46
R7825	56/181/184	SOC 15.11.45
R7826	56	To 4644M 3.44
R7827	-	To 3526M 5.43
R7828	-	To 4287M 11.43
R7829	266	Engine cut; bellylanded, Exeter, 19.6.43
R7845	609	SOC 16.12.43
R7846	56	Abandoned in spin, Fordham, Suffolk, 8.12.42
R7847	266	Engine cut; undershot landing at Ibsley, 15.9.42
R7848	-	SOC 20.1.44
R7849	609/56	SOC 16.9.43
R7850	Napiers	SOC 9.7.44
R7851	1	To 4338M 11.43
R7852	-	Not assembled; to spares
R7853	56	Hit by fire from Spitfire and abandoned 10m off Dungeness, 30.7.42
R7854	56	Lost tail during aerobatics near Brinton, Norfolk, 17.1.43
R7855	609	Crashed on landing, Manston, 16.4.43
R7856	1	Spun into ground 3m NW of Tangmere, 23.8.43
R7857	-	SOC 10.7.43
R7858	-	SOC 22.7.43
R7859	-	SOC 25.7.43
R7860	-	To 4284M 11.43
R7861	1	Missing 21.10.42; presumed collided with R7867 4m off Amble, Northumberland,
R7862	1	Engine cut; crashlanded near Charterhall, 21.11.42
R7863	1	Missing 19.5.43
R7864	1	Engine cut; crashlanded, Danehills, Sussex, 13.2.43
R7865	1	SOC 20.2.46
R7866	486	Engine cut; crashlanded, Durrington, Sussex, 24.11.42
R7867	1	Missing off Amble, Northumberland, 21.10.42; see R7861
R7868	1	Hit by R8630 while parked, Acklington, 9.11.42; DBR
R7869	56/183/3	SOC 3.8.43
R7870	-	To 3707M 6.43
R7871	-	To 4273M 11.43
R7872	609	Shot down by FW 190s off Cap Gris Nez, 14.2.43
R7873	-	SOC 26.6.43
R7874	-	To 3715M 6.43
R7875	-	To 3717M 7.43
R7876	1	Missing, believed shot down by FW 190s 40m S of Beachy Head, 29.3.43
R7877	1	To 4339M 11.43
R7878	-	To 3721M 7.43
R7879	257	SOC 31.10.43
R7880	609/245	Tyre burst on take-off, Lydd, 24.9.43; DBR
R7881	RAE/FIU/3 TEU	SOC 16.9.45
R7882	266	Crashed on landing, Exeter, 5.4.43
R7883	609	Bellylanded at Duxford, 1.8.42; to spares
R7884	-	SOC 8.6.43

R7885	-	SOC 14.7.43
R7886	-	SOC 8.6.43
R7887	-	SOC 8.6.43
R7888	-	
R7889	181/55 OTU	SOC 21.6.47
R7890	-	To 3720M 6.43
R7913	-	SOC 21.6.47
R7914	182/195	SOC 11.1.44
R7915	266	Engine cut; ditched 25m SE of Start Point, Devon, 17.6.43
R7916	-	To 4283M 11.43
R7917	-	SOC 14.7.43
R7918	-	Not assembled; to spares
R7919	1	Damaged by FW 190s and crashlanded, Lympne, 16.6.43; DBR
R7920	-	To 4275M 11.43
R7921	1	SOC 19.2.44
R7922	1	SOC 11.1.44
R7923	1	SOC 11.1.44

*   *   *   *   *   *   *   *   *   *

Two Hawker Tornado prototypes delivered in July 1941 by Hawker, Kingston and Avro, Woodford respectively, to Contract No. 12148/39

R7936	Mkrs, RR and AAEE	SOC 7.4.44
R7937	-	Cancelled
R7938	Mkrs & RR	Retained as test aircraft

R7939 - R7975; R7992 - R8036;		
R8048 - R8091; R8106 - R8150;		198 cancelled Tornados
R8172 - R8197		

*   *   *   *   *   *   *   *   *   *

265 Hawker Typhoon IAs (first five aircraft) and IBs delivered between March and November 1942 to Contract No. 12148/39. First 15 built by Hawkers, Langley, remainder by Glosters

R8198	Mkrs/DH	SOC 27.6.43
R8199	56	Shot down by Spitfires off Dover, 1.6.42
R8200	56	SOC 16.11.45
R8220	56/609	SOC 11.1.44
R8221	609/182	Hit balloon cable and force-landed 4m S of Salisbury, Wilts., 13.2.43
R8222	609	To 4400M 3.12.43
R8223	56	SOC 11.1.44
R8224	56/609	Overstressed during aerobatics, Lympne, 13.9.43; SOC
R8225	193	SOC 12.1.44
R8226	18 MU	Engine cut; crashlanded, Craigs Marsh, Dumfries, 15.1.43
R8227	197/486	Hit by DN559 while parked, Tangmere, 23.5.43
R8228	-	SOC 26.9.46
R8229	181	SOC 3.9.46
R8230	245	Hit by flak and crashlanded near Loningen, 11.4.45
R8231	-	SOC 26.9.46

Production by Glosters

R8630	1	SOC 22.9.43
R8631	1	To 4336M 18.11.43
R8632	257	SOC 11.8.43
R8633	257	Lost tail and crashed 2½ SW of High Ercall, 29.7.42
R8634	1	Engine cut; crashlanded, Pevensey, Sussex, 28.4.43

R8635/G	RAE & Mkrs	Engine cut; crashlanded on Meadfoot Beach, Torquay, 21.5.43
R8636	257/245	SOC 18.10.46
R8637	257	Overshot landing at Zeals, 24.1.43
R8638	257/266	Engine lost power; hit obstruction on runway during forced landing, Portreath, 30.7.43
R8639	257	SOC 11.8.43
R8640	-	To 4271M 2.11.43
R8641	-	SOC 8.6.43
R8642	257	SOC 27.7.43
R8643	-	SOC 8.6.43
R8644	-	SOC 8.6.43
R8645	-	To 4268M 2.11.43
R8646	-	To 4277M 24.10.43
R8647	-	Not assembled; to spares
R8648	-	To 3709M 9.7.43
R8649	-	To 3708M 23.7.43
R8650	257	Crashed in forced landing 2m NW of Linstead, Hants., 29.11.42
R8651	193	SOC 12.1.44
R8652	257/59 OTU	Bellylanded, Rearsby, 15.8.43
R8653	257	SOC 13.8.43
R8654	257/247	SOC 11.9.43
R8655	257	SOC 29.11.45
R8656	257	SOC 22.9.43
R8657	-	To 4269M 2.11.43
R8658	257	SOC 19.9.43
R8659	257	To 4249M 27.10.43
R8660	186/195	SOC 12.7.44
R8661	257/59 OTU	Blt as Mk.IA; SOC 9.7.44
R8662	-	To 3705M 8.43
R8663	257	Engine cut; crashlanded, Chilframe, Dorset, 15.12.42
R8680	257	SOC 17.9.43
R8681	486	SOC 19.7.43
R8682	486	Tyre burst on take-off; swung and hit Lancaster R5665, Tangmere, 24.2.43
R8683	486	Missing, presumed ditched near le Havre, 2.10.42
R8684	486	SOC 19.2.44
R8685	257	To 4643M 20.9.43
R8686	-	Not assembled; to spares
R8687	Duxford/247/245/ 175/184/245	SOC 15.11.45
R8688	RAE/247	Shot down by P-47, 3m SW of Ewijk, Neth. 14.1.45
R8689	-	To 4642M 20.9.43
R8690	1	Engine cut; crashlanded 4m NE of Longtown, 5.9.42
R8691	257	SOC 23.9.43
R8692	486	SOC 9.7.43
R8693	RAE/266/247	SOC 25.10.45
R8694	266	SS 13.3.47
R8695	-	To 4252M 27.10.43
R8696	486/168	SOC 27.8.46
R8697	486	Collided on ground with DN611, Tangmere, 3.8.43
R8698	486	Engine caught fire; crashed in Battle, Sussex, 16.10.42
R8699	486	SOC 3.9.43
R8700	486	SOC 19.7.43
R8701	486	Dived into sea 6m SE of Selsey Bill, Sussex, 31.0.42
R8702	193	SOC 12.1.44
R8703	257	SOC 11.9.43
R8704	486	SOC 19.2.44
R8705	59 OTU	SS 13.3.47
R8706	486	Engine cut; crashlanded, Sidlesham, Sussex, 1.3.43

Serial	Units	Fate
R8707	Duxford/198	To 3701M 26.5.43
R8708	1	To 4337M 18.11.43
R8709	Duxford/198/59 OTU	Engine cut on take-off, Milfield, 20.5.43
R8710	Duxford/257	SOC 23.9.43
R8711	257	Hit radar tower on approach, Bolt Head, 29.9.42
R8712	486	SOC 18.12.43
R8713	Duxford	SOC 2.9.43
R8714	-	To 4288M 3.11.43
R8715	Duxford/609/56	To 4341M 18.11.43
R8716	-	To 3875M 24.6.43
R8717	-	SOC 24.6.43
R8718	-	SOC 21.7.43
R8719	-	SOC 30.6.43
R8720	9 FPP	Landed down-wind and hit another aircraft, Brockworth, 29.8.42; DBR
R8721	56	Crashed on landing, Matlask, 2.5.43; SOC 24.6.43
R8722	-	SOC 8.7.43
R8737	-	To 4110M 31.8.43
R8738	-	To 3874M 23.6.43
R8739	-	SOC 24.6.43
R8740	-	To 4285M 11.11.43
R8741	-	SOC 24.6.43
R8742	181	Engine cut; bellylanded, Cheddington, 9.3.43; SOC 24.6.43
R8743	266	Engine cut; ditched 15m SE of Torquay, Devon, 20.2.43
R8744	486	Ran out of fuel and crashlanded, Tarring Neville, Sussex, 14.3.43
R8745	56	SOC 30.4.46
R8746	181	SS 13.3.47
R8747	-	To 3873M 23.6.43
R8748	-	To 4253M 27.10.43
R8749	-	SOC 11.10.43
R8750	-	SOC 23.7.43
R8751	-	SOC 24.6.43
R8752	1	Hit by flak and bellylanded, Lympne, 2.6.43
R8753	-	SOC 13.7.43
R8754	-	To 3873M 24.6.43
R8755	-	SOC 3.7.43
R8756	-	SOC 17.6.43
R8757	-	SOC 21.7.43
R8758	-	SOC 3.7.43
R8759	-	SOC 16.4.43
R8760	195	Compressed air bottle exploded in flight; airframe DBR, 25.2.43
R8761	-	SOC 8.7.43
R8762	Mkrs & AAEE/ Napier	SOC 8.10.43
R8763	-	SOC 11.6.43
R8764	-	To 3698M 27.5.43
R8765	-	To 3692M 18.6.43
R8766	-	To 3695M 16.6.43
R8767	266	Spun into sea during dogfight with FW 190s, Guipavas, 15.8.43
R8768	257/486	SOC 7.7.43
R8769	-	SOC 17.6.43
R8770	-	SOC 11.10.43
R8771	-	SOC 11.10.43
R8772	181/266	Throttle jammed; crashlanded, Whimple, Devon, 28.2.43
R8773	-	SOC 30.6.43
R8774	-	SOC 13.7.43
R8775	-	To 4251M 27.10.43
R8776	-	SOC 11.10.43
R8777	-	SOC 13.7.43
R8778	-	SOC 23.7.43
R8779	-	SOC 13.7.43
R8780	-	To 3702M 21.5.43
R8781	486/609/195/164/266	SOC 10.9.46
R8799	182/56/182/56	Engine cut; dived into sea 40m E of Gt. Yarmouth, 10.4.43
R8800	486	Shot down by return fire from Do 217 10m SE of Shoreham, 18.12.42
R8801	486	Crashlanded, Tangmere, 31.10.42; to spares
R8802	181/266	Crashlanded between Etaples and Guincamp, 11.1.43; believed hit by flak
R8803	Napier/266	SOC 16.9.46
R8804	266	Hit by flak and ditched off St Brieuc, 9.7.43
R8805	-	To 3704M 21.5.43
R8806	-	To 3696M 16.6.44
R8807	-	Not assembled; to spares
R8808	-	To 3699M 27.5.43
R8809	Mkrs & AAEE	Engine cut; crashlanded, Oatlands Hill, 17.5.43; retained by Hawkers
R8810	609	Engine cut; crashlanded near Deal, Kent, 9.3.43; SOC 24.6.43
R8811	266	Damaged by Spitfires and abandoned 4½ ESE of Exeter, 17.4.43
R8812	609	Flew into hill in bad visibility near Battle, Sussex, 23.10.42
R8813	266	SOC 4.10.43
R8814	486	Engine cut; spun into ground, Willesborough, Kent, 25.10.42
R8815	609	Engine cut; crashlanded, Swingate, Kent, 18.1.43; SOC 17.6.43
R8816	486	Crashed on take-off while avoiding another Typhoon, Tangmere, 24.2.43
R8817	-	To 3703M 22.5.43
R8818	-	To 3693M 15.5.43
R8819	Duxford/195	SOC 12.1.44
R8820	-	SOC 10.6.43
R8821	-	SOC 11.6.43
R8822	56	Collided with DN433 and crashed near Blickling, Norfolk, 20.1.43
R8823	266	Overshot landing at Warmwell, 27.10.42
R8824	56	SOC 11.1.44
R8825	56	Hit by pieces of DN265 and forcelanded, Barton Lamas, Norfolk, 28.4.43
R8826	182/609/601/609	SOC 20.9.45
R8827	56	SOC 22.10.43
R8828	181/Snailwell/181	SOC 22.9.43
R8829	181	SOC 28.6.43
R8830	181	SOC 17.7.43
R8831	-	To 3694M 14.6.43
R8832	257	SOC 11.8.43
R8833	181	Shot down by Bf 109 off Pas de Calais, 30.7.43
R8834	182	Shot down by flak, Triqueville, Eure, 16.4.43
R8835	181/3	Shot down by FW 190s SSW of Abbeville, 18.5.43
R8836	181	SOC 14.10.43
R8837	609	Crashed in sea 15m S of South Foreland, Kent, 23.12.42
R8838	609	Shot down by FW 190s near Dixmude, 7.2.43
R8839	182	Tyre burst on take-off, Ridgewell, 22.1.43; DBR
R8840	181/164/198	SOC 10.9.46

157

R8841	609/247	SOC 20.8.43
R8842	182	Engine cut; crashlanded 2m SW of Andover, 6.3.43; SOC 10.6.43
R8843	486/184/175/181	Damaged by flak and crashlanded near Goch, 29.9.44
R8844	245/247	SOC 11.1.44
R8845	609	Shot down by P-47s near Doullens, 21.12.43
R8861	266	Flew into sea 3m S of Bolt Head, Devon, 15.4.43; cause not known
R8862	182/181	SOC 4.9.43
R8863	181/182	SOC 4.9.43
R8864	266	Crashed in night landing, Warmwell, 12.10.42
R8865	56	Hit by flak and crashlanded, Kijksduin, near The Hague, 13.1.43
R8866	181/3/181	Missing on sweep to Poix, 15.7.43
R8867	181/247/198/247/ 59 OTU	Tyre burst on take-off, Milfield, 18.4.43; DBR
R8868	181	SOC 21.7.44
R8869	-	SOC 10.6.43
R8870	-	To 3697M 17.6.43
R8871	181	SOC 17.5.43
R8872	257	Engine cut; crashlanded in circuit, Exeter, 22.12.42
R8873	56	Engine cut; crashlanded 2m SW of Matlask, 27.4.43; SOC 24.6.43
R8874	609	SOC 29.11.45
R8875	181	Tyre burst on take-off; belly-landed, Detling, 25.9.43; to spares
R8876	56	Hit by flak over The Hague and crashed near Haarlem, 13.1.43
R8877	181	Engine cut; crashlanded near Appledram, 2.6.43
R8878	266/59 OTU/FLS	SOC 19.9.46
R8879	181/3	Shot down by FW 190s near Poix, 18.5.43
R8880	181	Missing in sea fog off Huik van Holland, 19.2.43
R8881	486	Damaged by flak and crashlanded, Selsey Bill, Sussex, 16.4.43; SOC 24.6.43
R8882	1/3 TEU/54 OTU	SOC 28.6.45
R8883	609	Dived into sea 3m ESE of Dover, 30.4.43; cause not known
R8884	183/175	SOC 16.8.43
R8885	183/197/486	SOC 11.1.44
R8886	183/197/486	SOC 9.2.45
R8887	-	To 4640M 24.9.43
R8888	609	Engine cut; crashlanded near Manston, 29.3.43
R8889	AAEE & Mkrs	SOC 17.6.43
R8890	193	SOC 12.1.44
R8891	Mkrs & AAEE	Tropical trials in Middle East; crashlanded 28m E of Cairo, 7.8.44; DBR
R8892	182	SOC 15.8.43
R8893	182	Crashed while attacking MT in Forêt d'Hardelot, 28.4.43
R8894	198	Hit by flak off Boulogne and presumed ditched, 10.2.44
R8895	181/3	Engine cut; ditched after take-off, Bradwell Bay, 22.3.44
R8896	181	SOC 4.9.43
R8897	439/83 GSU	Broke up in air near Milford, Surrey, 28.8.44
R8898	609	SOC 17.6.43
R8899	609/56	SOC 24.8.43
R8900	198/181	SOC 6.7.44
R8923	257/263	Collided with MN769 over S. Oostburg, Belgium, 14.10.44
R8924	182	Shot down by flak near Hesdin, 25.4.43
R8925	Mkrs	To 3486M 3.1.43
R8926	3/3 TEU/183/164	To 5870M 15.3.46
R8927	181/182	Missing from sweep to Amiens, 19.8.43
R8928	182	Tyre burst on take-off; belly-landed, Manston, 13.6.43
R8929	181	SOC 11.8.43
R8930	182	Hit by flak; crashlanded near Fairlop, 18.4.43
R8931	182	Overshot landing and hit trench, Appledram, 26.6.43
R8932	181/247	Forcelanded after engine cut, Achmer, 17.4.45; not repaired
R8933	183/175	SOC 16.8.43
R8934	266	SOC 3.10.43
R8935	198	Engine cut; crashlanded near Radcliffe, Northumberland, 11.3.43
R8936	266/486	SOC 4.10.43
R8937	266	Engine cut; crashlanded 1½m N of Topsham, Devon, 30.4.43
R8938	195	SOC 11.7.44
R8939	198/266	To 4641M 24.9.43
R8940	609/56	SOC 28.8.43
R8941	486	Crashed on landing, Tangmere, 8.1.43
R8942	1	Collided with DN615 in cloud and crashed near Benenden, Kent, 6.3.43
R8943	RAE/DH/175/247	SOC 15.8.46
R8944	183	Ditched out of fuel off Cherbourg, 14.5.43
R8945	182	SOC 21.8.43
R8946	3	Shot down by FW 190s during attack on convoy off Huik van Holland, 1.7.43
R8947	182/181	SOC 3.8.43
R8966	182/198	Hit by flak and abandoned near B.7, Normandy, 18.8.44
R8967	FLS	Engine cut; crashlanded near Lowick, Northumberland, 30.9.44
R8968	55 OTU/3 TEU	SOC 14.6.45
R8969	164	To 5871M 15.3.46; NTU
R8970	136 Wg/183	Shot down by Bf 109s near Le Neubourg, Eure, 17.8.44
R8971	438/439	Flew into hill near New Cumnock, Ayrshire, 20.2.44
R8972	609	Shot down by flak near Hottot, 11.7.44
R8973	183	Shot down by Bf 109s near Caen, 6.6.44
R8974	182	SOC 18.8.43
R8975	182	SOC 25.8.43
R8976	181/183/175	SOC 2.8.43
R8977	181/3/609	SOC 9.8.46
R8978	183/175	SOC 17.8.43
R8979	183/3	Shot down by flak near Matigny, 18.5.43
R8980	257	SOC 20.9.43
R8981	182	Hit by flak and crashlanded near Ford, 13.5.43

*   *   *   *   *   *   *   *   *   *

Lockheed 12A purchased in November 1939 from Brian Allen under Contract No. 794774/38

R8987	RAE	Ex G-AEMZ. Crashed on landing, Farnborough, 15.4.42

Serial	Units	Fate
R8991 to R8999	-	Diverted to Finland
R9000	-	To R Egyptian AF
R9001	110 RCAF/400/ 1488 Flt/43 OTU/ 1488 Flt	Engine cut; forcelanded on mud-flats, Ray Sand, Essex, 29.6.43
R9002	110 RCAF/400/116/ 1447 Flt/4 OTU/ 8 OTU/3 OTU/4 OTU	SOC 10.9.43
R9003	110 RCAF/Cv TT/ 2 AOS/7 AGS	SOC 6.1.44
R9004	110 RCAF	Lost height after night take-off and flew into ground 2m W of Odiham, 23.1.41; DBF
R9005	110 RCAF/400/ Cv TT/7 AGS	SOC 31.5.43
R9006	110 RCAF/400/ 9 Gp TTF/1486 Flt	SOC 19.6.43
R9007	110 RCAF/400/ Cv TT/CGS	SOC 24.2.44
R9008	110 RCAF/400/ Cv TT/13 Gp TTF/ 1490 Flt/14 APC	SOC 25.2.44
R9009	110 RCAF/400/ Cv TT/CGS/148	Swung on landing and under-carriage collapsed 10m SW of Udine and blown up by enemy troops, 23.4.45
R9010	1424 Flt/Old Sarum	SOC 26.2.44
R9011	1424 Flt/43 OTU	To USAAF 13.6.43
R9012	4/Cv TT/9 AOS	SOC 9.2.44
R9013	4/Cv TT/14 OTU/ ME	SOC 30.11.44
R9014	16	Engine cut; forcelanded in ploughed field and hit ditch, Sutton Mallet, Somerset 25.4.41
R9015	16	Dived into ground, Broadwindsor, Dorset, 16.12.40; presumed control lost in cloud
R9016	16/Cv TT/7 OTU/ 4 APC	DBR 23.7.43; NFD
R9017	16/Cv TT/1 AGS/ 1447 Flt/3 OTU	SOC 15.6.43
R9018	16/58 OTU/Cv TT/ 21 OTU	SOC 20.7.43
R9019	16/Cv TT/FAA/12 FU	Swung on landing and under-carriage collapsed, Blida, 9.7.45; DBR
R9020	2	Bounced on landing, stalled and undercarriage collapsed, Sawbridgeworth 21.6.41
R9021	614/Cv TT/1 AGS	SOC 24.5.43
R9022	614/2 AGS/5 AOS/ Cv TT/4 AOS/WDCF/ WACF/ME	SOC 31.5.45
R9023	Cv TT/5 AOS/ME/ WA/ME	SOC 31.5.45
R9024	614/1 AOS/Cv TT/ 1 AOS	SOC 17.12.43
R9025	614/Cv TT/5 Gp TTF/ 20 OTU/11 OTU	SOC 23.10.43
R9026	4/Cv TT/8 AGS	SOC 23.10.43
R9027	Mkrs/419 Flt	Hit anti-invasion obstructions in forced landing, Connel, Argyll, 21.10.40
R9028	4/Cv TT/5 AOS/CGS	SOC 16.1.44
R9029	4/Cv TT/41 OTU	Failed to recover from dive during evasive action practice, Salisbury Plain, 20.3.42; DBF
R9030	4/Cv TT/23 OTU	SOC 14.6.43
R9056	4	Lost height in turn and hit ground on coastal reconnaissance mission, Carlton, Yorks., 7.10.40
R9057	4/Cv TT/5 AGS	SOC 9.4.44
R9058	16/2 OTU/1 OTU/ 6 OTU	SOC 6.7.43
R9059	16/Cv TT/4 AOS/ 4 AGS/5 AOS	SOC 18.10.43
R9060	16/26	Hit balloon cable and crashed ½m N of Eastleigh Station, Hants., 5.3.41; DBF
R9061	Cv TT/8 AGS	SOC 26.10.43
R9062	Cv TT/2 AGS	SOC 1.9.43
R9063	13	Undershot approach and hit trees, Hooton Park, 17.12.40
R9064	225/1492 Flt/Cv TT/ 1492 Flt/1497 Flt/ 18 APC	SOC 14.12.43
R9065	225/Cv TT/7 AGS	SOC 14.9.43
R9066	231/Cv TT/55 OTU	SOC 4.7.43
R9067	Cv TT/9 AGS/9 OAFU	SOC 25.8.43
R9068	614/Cv TT/2 AGS/ 1492 Flt/3 RAFRS/ 1 RAFRS/3 RAFRS/ 1627 Flt/56 OTU	SOC 26.2.44
R9069	614/Cv TT/8 AGS	SOC 27.6.43
R9070	614/Cv TT/4 AOS/ 4 AGS	SOC 30.6.43
R9071	614/Cv TT/1 AOS/ 7 AGS	SOC 23.1.44
R9072	1 AOS	Stalled on take-off and dived into ground due to incorrect trimming, Wigtown, 30.11.41
R9073	Cv TT/61 OTU/ME/ WA/ME	SOC 31.5.45
R9074	225/Cv TT/1 AAS	Overshot down-wind landing and swung to avoid hedge, Waddington 6.7.43
R9075	4/Cv 11/17 OTU/ 24 OTU/17 OTU	DBR 23.7.43
R9076	225	Engine cut on ASR search; ditched 2m W of Linney Head, Pembs., 29.4.41
R9077	4	Took off with incorrect trim; stalled and spun into ground, Thornaby, 21.9.40
R9078	4/Cv TT/3 Gp TTF/ 1483 Flt/1488 Flt/ 17 APC	SOC 25.10.43
R9079	4	Shot down by Bf 109 on ASR flight over Channel, 15.11.40
R9100	4	Hit by Whitley while parked, Clifton, 23.12.40; DBR
R9101	16	Overshot landing at Roborough, 1.11.40
R9102	16	Got into flat spin and hit ground 3m E of Roborough, 28.12.40
R9103	225/Cv TT/5 AOS	SOC 24.12.43
R9104	16/26/Cv TT/9 AGS/ 9 OAFU	SOC 25.8.43
R9105	26/1416 Flt/140/ Cv TT/30 OTU	SOC 23.10.43
R9106	161	Stalled on landing and hit ground, Tempsford, 16.5.43; DBF
R9107	16/Cv TT/42 OTU/ 4 AAPC/1628 Flt	Overshot landing into fence, Towyn, 5.8.43
R9108	16/26/Cv TT/ 4 AOS	To 3943M 7.7.43
R9109	231/Cv TT/1481 Flt/ 24 OTU	SOC 20.10.43
R9110	1 AGS	SOC 23.10.43
R9111	1 AOS/7 AGS/Cv TT/ 7 AGS	SOC 31.5.43
R9112	241/414/Cv TT/ 1494 Flt	SOC 26.9.43
R9113	1 AOS/7 AGS/Cv TT/ 7 AGS/1488 Flt	SOC 14.10.43
R9114	1 AGS/Cv TT/1 AGS	SOC 21.10.43

Lysander III

Serial	Units	Fate
R9115	SF Coningsby/20 OTU/ 1481 Flt/1494 Flt	Engine cut; DBR in heavy landing, Ballyhalbert, 16.11.43
R9116	110 RCAF/1 AOS/ Cv TT/1 OAFU/CNS	SOC 25.10.43
R9117	110 RCAF/2 OTU/ 1 OTU/6 OTU/ Cv to LR/161	SOC 25.9.45
R9118	4/CGS	SOC 16.1.44
R9119	110 RCAF/400/ Cv TT/9 OAFU	SOC 24.9.43
R9120	110 RCAF/19 OTU	Reduction gear lost; hit concrete blocks in forced landing on beach, Findhorn Bay, Moray, 16.3.42
R9121	225/9 AGS/Cv TT/ 9 AGS/2 AGS	SOC 26.10.43
R9122	225/Cv TT/RAE	To Admiralty 20.3.42
R9123	225/19 OTU/Cv TT/ 28 OTU	SOC 18.10.43
R9124	4/Cv TT/10 AGS/ 1 OAFU	SOC 19.11.43
R9125	225/Cv TT/CGS/ 7 OTU/CNS/161	
R9126	Cv TT/2 AGS	SOC 14.10.43
R9127	225	Hit wall in forced landing in bad weather near Tiverton, Devon, 9.11.40
R9128	225	Stalled on take-off due to wrong tail trim and spun into ground, Old Sarum, 21.10.40
R9129	225/Cv TT/ 12 Gp TTF/1489 Flt/ 56 OTU	Hit by Hurricane W9171 while parked, Kinnell, 12.10.42
R9130	225/9 AGS/9 OAFU	DBR 23.8.43; NFD
R9131	614/Cv TT/5 Gp TTF/ CGS	SOC 16.1.44
R9132	231	SOC 15.7.43
R9133	614/Cv TT/1 AGS/ RAE/1 AGS/4 AOS	SOC 25.8.43
R9134	309	Crashed on landing, Dumfries, 6.2.41
R9135	13/Cv TT/55 OTU	SOC 11.8.43

*   *   *   *   *   *   *   *   *   *

Parnall Hendy Heck III to Spec. T.1/37 delivered in June 1941 by Parnall & Co to Contract No. 23979/39

Serial	Unit	Fate
R9138	24	Ex G-AFKF; to 3600M 5.3.43

*   *   *   *   *   *   *   *   *   *

150 Short Stirling Is delivered between January 1942 and January 1943 by Short Bros., Rochester, to Contract No.763825/38 and Short Bros & Harland, Belfast, to Contract No. 774677/38 (from R9295 as Series II)

Serial	Unit	Fate
R9141	214/1651 CU	Swung on take-off and undercarriage collapsed, Waterbeach, 18.9.43
R9142	149/1657 CU	Swung on take-off and undercarriage leg collapsed, Waterbeach, 24.9.43
R9143	214/7/149/1665 CU	SOC 14.1.45
R9144	15/1657 CU/1665 CU	SOC 14.1.45
R9145	214	Hit by flak during raid on Berlin and crashed, Königreich, 4m NNE of Buxtehude, 2.3.43
R9146	214	Shot down by night fighter near Oss, Neth. returning from Cologne, 16.10.42
R9147	7/1651 CU	SOC 3.9.44
R9148	214/1651 CU/	
R9149	7	Shot down by night fighter en route to Munich, Elan, Ardennes, 10.3.43
R9150	7	Shot down by night fighter on return from Turin, Pécy, Seine-et-Marne, 30.11.42;
R9151	15	Damaged by flak, Osnabrück, and crashlanded, Docking, 18.8.42
R9152	214/1651 CU/ 1653 CU	SOC 1.8.44
R9153	15	Missing (Nürnberg) 29.8.42; crashed at Mesmont, Ardennes
R9154	7	Missing (Duisburg) 7.8.42; crashed at Hüthum-Emmerich
R9155	214	Missing (Kassel) 28.8.42; crashed at Issum
R9156	7/1665 CU/1653 CU	SOC 19.7.45
R9157	1651 CU	SOC 19.7.45
R9158	7	Ran short of fuel on return from Nürnberg; overshot landing and hit hangar, Manston, 29.8.42; DBR
R9159	218/1651 CU	Engine cut on landing; swung and hit building, Wratting Common, 28.11.43
R9160	218	Shot down by night fighter off Dutch coast on return from Kassel, 28.8.42;
R9161	149	Shot down by night fighter, Regniowez, Ardennes, on return from Saarbrücken, 29.7.42
R9162	149	Missing (minelaying in Kattegat) 11.8.42; presumed ditched
R9163	149/214	Abandoned short of fuel on returning from minelaying off Gironde 4m N of Alton, Hants., 18.2.43
R9164	149	Shot down by night fighter on return from Essen, Tongrinne, Belgium, 17.9.42;
R9165	214	Swung on landing, Chedburgh, 21.11.42 on return from Turin
R9166	214	Missing (Bremen) 14.9.42; crashed at Barrien
R9167	149	Shot down by night fighter en route to Krefeld, Kronenburg, Neth., 3.10.42
R9168	15	Shot down by night fighter 5m SW of Epe, Neth. during raid on Diepholz airfield, 17.12.42
R9169	7	Missing (Hamburg) 10.11.42
R9170	149	Shot down by night fighter on return from Düsseldorf near Oud Beyerland, Neth., 11.9.42
R9184	218	Crashed in sea off Dieppe on return from Genoa, 24.10.42
R9185	218	Missing (minelaying off Gironde) 7.11.42; crashed 12m W of St.Brieuc, Côtes-du-Nord
R9186	214/1651 CU	SOC 1.8.44
R9187	218	Missing (Vegesack) 24.9.42; believed shot down by night fighter
R9188	Mkrs & RAE	Mk.III; to 3970M 7.43
R9189	218	Swung and undercarriage collapsed on take-off for St.Nazaire, Downham Market, 28.2.43; DBR
R9190	218	Shot down by night fighter while minelaying off Swinemünde, 12.10.42; crashed off Sio Island, near Rudkobing
R9191	214/1651 CU/	

Serial	Units	Fate
R9192	7/15/1657 CU	Collided with Wellington X3637 in cloud over Suffolk, 6.11.43; DBR
R9193	7/15/1651 CU	Bounced on landing, swung and tailwheel collapsed, Wratting Common, 5.7.44; DBR
R9194	7/214	Hit by flak on return from Turin and crashed, Couvron-et-Aumencourt, Aisne, 29.11.42
R9195	15/1657 CU/ 1653 CU	Tyre burst on take-off and wheel detached in flight; bellylanded at Woodbridge, 14.5.44
R9196	218/1651 CU/ 1665 CU	SOC 14.1.45
R9197	214	Shot down by night fighter, Leusden, 3m SSE of Amersfoort, Neth. on return from Hamburg, 4.2.43
R9198	214/90/1665 CU/ 1657 CU/1665 CU	Swung and undercarriage collapsed on take-off, Woolfox Lodge, 26.6.43
R9199	214/7	Missing (Duisburg) 9.4.43
R9200	214/149/75/214	SOC 19.7.45
R9201	15	Missing (minelaying in Gironde) 7.11.42; crashed at St.André-des-Eaux, Côtes-du-Nord
R9202	149	Missing (Turin) 30.11.42; crashed at Irasco-Finerola, Italy
R9203	149/218/214	To 4240M 10.43; 4258M NTU
R9241	7 CF/218	Engine caught fire after take-off for Milan; broke up and crashed Cattawade, Suffolk, 24.10.42
R9242	149/214	Shot down by night fighter, Heerlerheide, Limburg, during raid on Bochum, 14.5.43
R9243	75/1651 CU	Swung on take-off and undercarriage collapsed, Waterbeach, 6.8.44
R9244	218/1651 CU	Undercarriage leg collapsed on landing, Wratting Common, 10.5.44; DBR
R9245	75	Hit Devil's Dyke on take-off for minelaying off Bordeaux and spun into ground, Newmarket, 16.12.42
R9246	75	Bellylanded in bad weather during air firing exercise near Holme, Hunts., 24.11.42
R9247	75	Missing (Fallersleben) 18.12.42; crashed at Vechta airfield
R9248	75	Damaged by flak, Lorient, crashed at St. Thégonnec, Finistère, 24.1.43
R9249	TFU/1657 CU	Crashed on three-engined approach in bad weather, Chipping Warden, 22.10.43
R9250	75	Shot down by night fighter on return from Hamburg, Ingen, Neth. 4.2.43
R9251	7/1657 CU/ 1651 CU	SOC 19.7.45
R9252	TFU/7/NTU/ 1651 CU	SOC 15.8.44
R9253	149	Missing (minelaying off Warnemünde) 9.12.42; crashed at Westermarsch
R9254	AAEE/214/1653 CU	Swung and undercarriage collapsed on take-off, Chedburgh, 13.8.44
R9255	TFU/7	Engine hit by flak, Berlin; swung on landing and undercarriage collapsed, Oakington, 28.3.43; DBR
R9256	90/1651 CU/	
R9257	TFU/7/1657 CU/214	Swung on take-off for Turin and undercarriage collapsed, Chedburgh, 12.8.43; DBR
R9258	7/214	Crashed at Bemerode during raid on Hannover) 23.9.43
R9259	7	Shot down by night fighter on return from Mannheim, Savenière, Belgium, 7.12.42;
R9260	TFU/7	Lost power on take-off for Hamburg; undercarriage collapsed in heavy landing, Oakington, 3.8.43
R9261	7	Shot down by night fighter in Musholm Bugt 7m WNW of Slagelse, Denmark, on return from Stettin, 21.4.43
R9262	7	Shot down by night fighter on return from Munich, Seraincourt, Ardennes, 22.12.42
R9263	TFU/7	Shot down by night fighter near Akkerwoude, Friesland, on return from Bocholt, 1.5.43
R9264	7	Shot down by night fighter, Hendrik-Ido-Ambacht, Neth., on return from Cologne, 3.2.43
R9265	149	Broke up in air recovering from dive on air test and crashed near Great Gransden, Beds., 19.12.42
R9266	TFU/7	Shot down by flak 3m W of Neuss during raid on Krefeld, 22.6.43
R9267	7	Bellylanded after engine failure on training flight, Hatley St.George, Cambs., 12.6.43
R9268	15/1665 CU	SOC 14.1.45
R9269	NTU/214/1659 CU/ 1657 CU/1653 CU	Undercarriage collapsed on landing, Chedburgh, 30.6.44
R9270	TFU/7	Crashed at Les Souhesmes, Meuse on return from Nürnberg, 9.3.43
R9271	149/90	Missing (Essen) 6.3.43; crashed 1m E of Sankt Peter
R9272	TFU/7	Shot down by night fighter 5m WSW of Tilburg on return from Krefeld, 22.6.43
R9273	TFU/7/1657 CU	Wing hit hut on approach; crashlanded, Stradishall, 9.5.44
R9274	15	Shot down by night fighter near Nijmegen on return from Hamburg, 4.2.43
R9275	TFU/7	Missing (Frankfurt) 11.4.43; crashed at Koerich, 10m WNW of Luxembourg
R9276	149/90	Shot down by night fighter in sea during raid on Wilhelmshaven, 20.2.43
R9277	7/NTU/214/BDU/ 1657 CU	Lost aileron control; overshot landing and undercarriage collapsed, Stradishall, 11.2.44
R9278	TFU/7	Shot down by night fighter, St-Souplet, Nord, on return from Stuttgart, 15.4.43
R9279	15	Missing (Cologne) 27.2.43; presumed ditched on return
R9280	7/BDU/1653 CU	Engine lost power; swung on take-off and wing torn off, Chedburgh, 22.3.44
R9281	7	Ditched off Dutch coast on return from Elberfeld, 25.6.43
R9282	214	Shot down by night fighter on return from Hamburg, Benschop, Utrecht, 4.2.43
R9283	7/214/1657 CU	SOC 26.6.44

R9284	7/214/1651 CU	SOC 15.8.44
Stirling I		

R9285	214/1665 CU	SOC 14.1.45
R9286	7	Damaged by flak and ditched on return from Münster, 12.6.43
R9287	149/218/1651 CU/ 1653 CU	SOC 15.8.44
R9288	7/214	Swung on take-off for Boulogne and hit bomb dump, Chedburgh, 8.9.43
9289	7/214	Swung on take-off for SOE mission and undercarriage collapsed, Tempsford, 10.12.43
R9290	75	Missing (minelaying in Fehmarn Channel) 29.4.43; crashed in sea off Lolland, Denmark

Built at Belfast from this point

R9295	7/149 CF	Damaged during raid on Essen; overshot landing and hit trees, Hollywell Row, Mildenhall, 11.3.42
R9296	7/149/149 CF/ 1657 CU	Swung on take-off and undercarriage collapsed, Stradishall, 22.7.43
R9297	7/218/7/7 CF/ 1657 CU	SOC 19.7.45
R9298	218/7/218/7/1657 CU/ AFEE/1657 CU	Shot down by intruder on approach, Shepherds Grove, and hit LK506, 29.5.44
R9299	149/149 CF	Caught fire in air and spun into ground 2m SW of Newmarket, 16.7.42
R9300	7/7 CF/1657 CU	Engine cut; swung on landing and undercarriage collapsed, Stradishall, 18.8.43
R9301	7/7 CF/7/1657 CU	Swung on take-off and under-carriage collapsed, Stradishall, 21.5.43
R9302	15/15 CF/1651 CU/ 1655 CU	SOC 14.1.45
R9303	15/214/214 CF/ 101 CF/218 CF/ 1657 CU/1665 CU	SOC 14.1.45
R9304	15/1651 CU	Tyre burst on landing; swung and undercarriage collapsed, Waterbeach, 28.2.43
R9305	7	Missing (Lubeck) 29.3.42; crashed at Ahrensburg
R9306	149/7/7 CF/90	Two engines failed on return from Lorient; flew into Bold Barrow Hill, Blandford, Dorset, 16.2.43
R9307	149	Swung on take-off for Le Havre and undercarriage collapsed, Lakenheath, 22.4.42
R9308	15	Damaged by Ju 88 during raid on Vegesack; overshot landing, Waterbeach, 20.7.42
R9309	Mkrs & AAEE	Cv to Mk.III. Engine caught fire; abandoned over Porton, Wilts., 6.9.42
R9310	15/149	Missing (minelaying in Baltic) 18.5.42; shot down by flak in sea off Asnaes, Denmark
R9311	15/218	Lost wheel on take-off; bellylanded on return from Cologne, Marham, 31.5.42
R9312	15	Missing (minelaying off Bayonne) 17.10.42; crashed at Pont du Cens, Nantes
R9313	15/218	Damaged by Hurricane on return from leaflet drop on Laon; caught fire and crashed, Lurgashall, 8m N of Petworth, Sussex, 5.5.42

Stirling I

R9314	15/149	Collided with Bf 110 5m W of Turnhout on return from Essen and ditched off Kent coast, 6.6.42
R9315	15/1657 CU	Swung and undercarriage collapsed on landing, Stradishall, 9.9.43
R9316	214/75	Damaged by flak, Lorient, and abandoned, Plouay, 10m NNE of Lorient, 14.2.43
R9317	214	Engine cut on approach; overshot landing after aborting raid on Bremen, Stradishall, 4.6.42; DBR
R9318	15	Missing (Essen) 17.9.42; believed crashed near Amsterdam
R9319	15/214	Engine cut after take-off for Emden; collided with R9350 on emergency landing, Stradishall, 20.6.42
R9320	149	Missing (minelaying in Baltic) 18.5.42; shot down by flak S of Lolland, Denmark
R9321	149	Shot down by night fighter, Wanheimerort, 4m S of Duisburg, during raid on Essen, 6.6.42
R9322	214/1521 BATF	Bomb dropped off on ground, Stradishall, 3.6.42; DBF
R9323	214/1665 CU	SOC 16.5.44
R9324	7	Shot down by night fighter on return from Essen, St.Remy-du-Nord, 17.6.42
R9325	214	Engine cut on approach on return from Cologne; swung and crashlanded, Stradishall, 31.5.42
R9326	214	Missing (minelaying off Friesians) 12.6.42; crashed off Memmert
R9327	RAE/149	Crashed at Obbekaer, 4m ENE of Ribe, Denmark during raid on Kiel, 5.4.43
R9328	7	Missing (Hamburg) 27.7.42; crashed in Elbe at Brunsbüttel-koog
R9329	214/149	Flew into high ground on return from minelaying off Lorient, Gibhill Forestry, Cornwood, S. Devon, 21.8.42
R9330	149	Lost power on take-off for Bremen; swung and under-carriage collapsed, Lakenheath, 29.6.42
R9331	7	Overshot landing from training flight, Waterbeach, 14.7.42; DBR
R9332	218/218 CF	Undercarriage collapsed on attempted overshoot, Marham, 31.7.42
R9333	218	Hit by flak during raid on Essen and crashed, Essen-Kray, 6.3.43
R9334	149	Flew into ground on overshoot on training flight, Lakenheath village, 3.1.43
R9349	218/90	Blew up near Clos sous les Bois, near Avranche, Manche, on return from St.Nazaire, 1.3.43
R9350	214	Shot down by night fighter on return from Essen, Bomal, Belgium, 17.9.42
R9351	15	Hit by flak off Korsor while minelaying in Great Belt and

crashed off Nyborg, 19.9.42

Serial	Units	Fate
R9352	15	Missing (Emden) 20.6.42; crashed at Siemolten
R9353	15/1657 CU	Bounced on landing and dived into ground on attempted overshoot, Stradishall, 20.4.44
R9354	218	Undercarriage collapsed in heavy landing on return from Hamburg, Downham Market, 27.7.42
R9355	214	Hit by flak, Frankfurt, and engine fell out; crashlanded at Manston, 9.9.42; DBR
R9356	214	Missing (Munich) 20.9.42; crashed at Hader
R9357	218/218 CF	Explosion caused loss of three engines; ditched in North Sea on return from Düsseldorf, 10.9.42
R9358	149/214	Hit tree after take-off for Munich 1m NW of Chedburgh, 9.3.43

* * * * * * * * * *

100 Handley Page Halifax IIs delivered between October 1941 and March 1942 by Handley Page, Radlett, to Contract No. 692649/37

Serial	Units	Fate
R9363	78/405 CF/408 CF/1659 CU	Hit by LL464 at dispersal, Topcliffe, 16.9.44; not repaired and SOC 28.9.44
R9364	35/76/78	Hit by flak and spun into sea off Dutch coast during raid on Essen, 2.6.42
R9365	10/76 CF/76	Shot down by night fighter on return from Essen, Rubrouck, Nord, 17.9.42
R9366	10/76 CF/76/1658 CU	Tyre burst on take-off; swung on landing and undercarriage collapsed, Riccall, 18.10.42; to 3413M
R9367	10/Hx CF/35/1652 CU/1658 CU	Tyre burst on landing; swung and undercarriage collapsed, Riccall, 17.8.43
R9368	10/1652 CU/78/405 CF/1659 CU	Tyre burst on take-off; swung on landing and undercarriage collapsed, Topcliffe, 23.3.44
R9369	10/78 CF/405 CF/1659 CU	Undercarriage not locked down and retracted on landing, Leeming, 15.1.43
R9370	10/35 CF/1658 CU	Wheel ran into hole and undercarriage collapsed while taxying, Riccall, 23.2.44
R9371	10	Brakes failed on ferry flight; overshot landing and hit hangar, Lossiemouth, 9.3.42; DBF
R9372	35/1652 CU	Engine cut over target; shot down by Bf 110, Ijmuiden, on return from Essen, 2.6.42
R9373	10/76/78/1658 CU	Landed with undercarriage up in error, Riccall, 4.2.43
R9374	10	Hit by flak over Brest and damaged by Bf 109; ditched 80m S of The Lizard, Cornwall, 30.12.41
R9375	76/78/Mkrs & AAEE	To 4751M 25.3.44; 4471M NTU
R9376	10/138/10/10 CF/10	Lost prop, crashlanded and undercarriage torn off near Melbourne, 14.11.42
R9377	35/1652 CU	Swung on landing at night and undercarriage collapsed, Marston Moor, 24.6.42
R9378	102/78/76 CF	Caught fire when incendiaries fell off rack, Middleton St.
R9379	76/103 CF	Stalled and spun in on approach, Elsham Wolds, 1.8.42; presumed engine lost power and control lost
R9380	102/103 CF/1656 CU	Tyre burst on take-off; swung and undercarriage collapsed on landing, Lindholme, 2.8.43; DBR
R9381	1652 CU/35/35 CF/1652 CU/1658 CU	To 4351M 23.11.43
R9382	10/76 CF/408 CF/1659 CU	Swung on landing, Topcliffe, 3.3.44; DBR
R9383	102/10	Hit trees on hill on return from Saarbrücken; abandoned and crashed, West End Village, 5m NE of Ilkley, Yorks., 20.9.42
R9384	102/76/10/1659 CU	Engine lost power on take-off; turned and dived into ground 2m SW of Topcliffe, 23.4.44
R9385	76/RAE	SOC 1.8.44
R9386	35/76/78/405 CF/1659 CU	Engine cut; would not climb on overshoot, hit trees and cartwheeled 1m SE of Topcliffe, 18.1.44
R9387	AAEE/10/76 CF/1658 CU	Tyre burst on night landing and undercarriage collapsed, Riccall, 13.8.43
R9388	102/158 CF/1658 CF	Stalled on three-engined overshoot, Riccall, and dived into ground, Cawood, 2.1.43; DBF
R9389	102/1427 Flt/1652 CU	SOC 1.11.45
R9390	102/460 CF/103 CF/1656 CU/1662 CU/Blyton	SOC 1.2.45
R9391	102/76/78	Ditched in North Sea on return from Hamburg, 4.5.42
R9392	35/10/10 CF/1658 CU	Swung on landing and undercarriage collapsed, Melbourne, 5.3.43
R9418	102/1658 CU/1669 CU	SOC 1.11.45
R9419	102/1427 Flt/102 CF	Bounced on landing, Topcliffe, overshot, lost height and hit house near Thirsk, 11.7.42; DBF
R9420	76/78/405 CF/1659 CU	Control lost in steep turn; spun into ground, Linton Woods, near Millbridge, Surrey, 24.7.43; DBF
R9421	102/10/10 CF	Undercarriage failed to lower; bellylanded at Linton-on-Ouse, 17.11.42
R9422	35/1652 CU/35/103/1656 CU	SOC 26.11.43
R9423	102/102 CF/1652 CU	Swung on landing and undercarriage collapsed, Marston Moor, 12.7.43
R9424	102/1652 CU	SOC 2.12.43
R9425	35/35 CF	Hydraulics failed during three-engined overshoot exercise; undercarriage and flaps stayed down; crashlanded, Newton-on-Ouse, Yorks., 16.4.42
R9426	102/102 CF/1652 CU	Swung and undercarriage collapsed on landing, Pocklington, 2.3.43; DBR
R9427	76/78	Swung on landing in cross-wind on ferry flight, Pocklington, 23.4.42; DBR
R9428	35/10/10 CF/1658 CU/1661 CU/1662 CU	To 4867M 8.44; 4869M NTU
R9429	102 CF/460/1658 CU	Swung on take-off and hit gunpost, Riccall, 9.12.43
R9430	10 CF/76 CF/78 CF/	

Serial	Units	Notes
R9431	1652 CU	Engine caught fire; crashlanded at Marston Moor, 16.4.42
R9432	1652 CU	To 3956M 1.7.43
R9433	1652 CU	Sideslipped into ground after control difficulties 5m SW of Malton, Yorks., 31.10.42
R9434	76/78/1652 CU/ 1658 CU/158 CF/ 1674 CU	SOC 21.6.44
R9435	Mkrs/1656 CU	Swung on landing and undercarriage collapsed, Lindholme, 31.3.44
R9436	Mkrs & AAEE	To 4204M 10.43
R9437	78/405 CF/1659 CU/ 1668 CU/1656 CU	Engine cut on take-off; turned and crashlanded on to dispersal, Lindholme, 29.4.44
R9438	35	Missing from attack on *Tirpitz* in Asenfjord, 31.3.42
R9439	35	Missing (Emden) 7.6.42
R9440	35	Engine cut on night training flight; overshot landing in haze, Linton-on-Ouse, 13.3.42; DBR
R9441	35/102/1652 CU	Engine lost power on take-off and wrong prop feathered; crashlanded, Marston Moor, 4.4.43; DBF
R9442	35/102	Shot down by night fighter, Corbais, Belgium, returning from Saarbrücken, 30.7.42
R9443	Mkrs & AAEE/ AFEE	To 4167M 11.9.43
R9444	35	Damaged by flak, Essen, and shot down by night fighter, 2.6.42
R9445	35	Damaged by flak, Billancourt, and crashlanded, Oakington, 3.3.42; DBR
R9446	35/102	Missing (Bremen) 25.6.42; presumed ditched on return
R9447	76/78	Missing (Flensburg) 24.9.42
R9448	35/405 CF/1659 CU	Dived into ground while flying on two engines, Crockey Hill, Escrick, Yorks., 18.4.43; presumed loss of control
R9449	35/102	Swung on landing on return from Frankfurt and hit W1239, Pocklington, 9.9.42
R9450	35	Crashed in sea on return from Essen 30m off Mablethorpe, Lincs., 10.3.42; cause not known
R9451	76	Missing (Hamburg) 4.5.42; crashed at Ottensen
R9452	76	Swung and hit obstruction on take-off for Essen; abandoned and crashed, 2m SSW of Filey, Yorks., 13.4.42
R9453	76	Presumed ran out of fuel and crashed in sea 16m S of Sumburgh, Shetlands, on return from attack on *Tirpitz*, 31.3.42
R9454	76/78/78 CF/1658 CU	SOC 31.5.44
R9455	76/78/78 CF/ 1658 CU	Engine overheated; lost height and crashlanded on flooded ground near Selby, Yorks., 3.2.42
R9456	76	Missing (Warnemünde) 9.5.42; crashed near Rostock
R9457	76	Shot down by night fighter near St. Maartenvlotbrug, Neth., on return from Bremen, 4.6.42;
R9482	76	Engine cut; stalled and dived into ground after take-off for air test, Middleton St.George,
R9483	35/405 CF/1659 CU	SOC 30.8.44
R9484	76	Missing (Essen) 11.4.42; crashed 3m N of Recklinghausen
R9485	76/76 CF	Hit by flak, Hamburg, and crashlanded near Buxtehüde, 27.7.42;
R9486	76/1652 CU/76/78/ 78 CF/502/1 OTU/ 518/517	SOC 16.6.44
R9487	76	Hit by by flak and crashed 3m NNW of Gelsenkirchen during raid on Essen 12.4.42
R9488	35/102	Stalled off turn and spun into ground on air test near Baldersby, Yorks., 14.4.42; DBF
R9489	35	Engine caught fire on air test; stalled and crashed, Catterton, near Tadcaster, Yorks., 21.7.42
R9490	Mkrs & TFU	To 4455M 15.1.44
R9491	10/102	Missing (Essen) 3.6.42; believed ditched off Harwich
R9492	10	Ran out of fuel on return from Dortmund and abandoned in spiral dive 3m S of Hindhead, Surrey, 15.4.42
R9493	10/35 CF/1651 CU/ 1652 CU	Engine cut on take-off; swung and undercarriage collapsed, Marston Moor, 2.12.42
R9494	35/102/1652 CU	Swung on landing and undercarriage leg collapsed, Marston Moor, 22.6.44
R9495	10/102	Missing (Bochum) 6.8.42; crashed 9m N of Eindhoven
R9496	35	Shot down by flak during attack on *Tirpitz* in Asenfjord, 31.3.42
R9497	10/102/1658 CU	Collided with DG420 near Copmanthorpe, Yorks., 19.8.43
R9498	10/102/102 CF/ 1652 CU/1662 CU	SOC 13.7.44
R9528	10/102	Shot down by flak during raid on Dunkerque, 29.4.42
R9529	10/102	SOC 30.6.42
R9530	102	Shot down by night fighter 40m W of Walcheren en route to Essen, 16.6.42
R9531	102/1658 CU	Stalled at low altitude off turn and hit ground near Scunthorpe, Lincs., 5.12.42; DBF
R9532	102	Damaged by flak, Essen, and control lost on approach, Dalton, 3.6.42
R8533	102/102 CF/1652 CU	SOC 18.9.44
R9534	AAEE/RAE	Mk.III prototype; to 4813M 14.6.44
R9535 and R9536		To English Electric as pattern aircraft
R9537	-	To London Passenger Transport Board as pattern aircraft
R9538	-	
R9539	-	Supplied as components
R9540	-	Supplied as components

* * * * * * * * * *

20 de Havilland Dominie Is delivered between January and August 1940 by D.H. Hatfield to Contract No. 26448/39

Serial	Units	Notes
R9545	2 EWS/ATA/AAEE	Hit by bowser, Boscombe Down, 17.12.47 and DBR
R9546	2 EWS/ATA/Mkrs	Sold 19.12.47; became G-AKOK
R9547	2 EWS/2 BWF/	

	1680 Flt	SOC 1.12.45

R9548	2 EWS/2 SS/Halton	Sold 11.3.48: became G-AKVU
R9549	24	To SAAF 1.2.43 as No.1363
R9550	ATA/RAE/Hendon	Sold 27.5.46; became G-AHPT
R9551	1 Cam Flt/1 Cam Unit	SOC 14.4.41
R9552	1 Cam Flt/Halton/	
	1 ADF/1 Cam Unit/	
	58 OTU/57 OTU/	Sold 15.12.47; became
	13 Gp CF/1 FU	G-AKRO
R9553	FPP/10 FPP/FTU/24	Engine cut on take-off; overturned in forced landing, Rednal, 27.4.43
R9554	7 FPP/5 FPP/	
	SF Northolt/2 Dly Flt/	
	SF Gatwick/SF Redhill	Sold 11.3.48; became G-AKTZ
R9555	7 FPP/2 FPP/2/	
	4 Dly Flt	SOC 13.3.46
R9556	7 FPP/ATA/24/4 RS	Sold 27.5.48; became G-ALAS
R9557	3 FPP	SOC 11.1.45
R9558	3 FPP/Vickers	Retained by Vickers, High Post, 4.46 as G-AHJA
R9559	3 FPP/Halton/TTCCF/	
	Staff College/RCCS	Sold 31.5.47; became G-AKED
R9560	SFPP/ATA/SF Sealand	Sold 11.3.48; became G-AKUB
R9561	7 FPP/SFP	Engine cut on take-off; swung into fence, Prestwick, 22.2.41
R9562	4/SF Northolt/MCS/	
	Halton	Sold 15.12.47; became G-AKSF
R9563	-	To Admiralty 29.8.40
R9564	3 FPP/SF Kenley/	
	SF Gatwick	Sold 9.12.47; became G-AKOB

*   *   *   *   *   *   *   *   *   *

300 Avro Anson Is delivered between July and September 1940 by Avro, Yeadon, to Contract No. B32842/39

R9567	5 AONS	To SAAF 14.9.40 as 1139
R9568	608	To RCAF 1.6.41
R9569	-	To SAAF 6.8.40 as 1128
R9570	17 OTU	To SAAF 23.6.41 as 3119
R9571	-	To SAAF 6.8.40 as 1129
R9572	-	To SAAF 6.8.40 as 1130
R9573	-	To SAAF 6.8.40 as 1131
R9574	-	To SAAF 6.8.40 as 1132
R9575	-	To SAAF 6.8.40 as 1133
R9576	19 OTU/7 AOS	SOC 4.5.45
R9577	608	To RCAF 28.5.41
R9578	17 OTU/25 OTU/	
	16 OTU/26 OTU/	
	5 AOS	To 4183M 4.10.43
R9579	300/20 OTU	Engine cut on night navex; ditched 10m NE of Lossiemouth, 15.8.42
R9580	301/20 OTU/2 AOS/	
	2 OAFU/11 RS	SOC 30.1.46
R9581	48	To S Rhodesia 20.4.41
	24 CAOS/24 BGNS	Crashed at Gutu, SR, 4.2.44
R9582	20 OTU/2 OAFU/	
	17 PAFU	SOC 17.5.44
R9583	20 OTU	Flew into high ground in cloud on night navex, Carnan-tri-tighearnan, Nairn, 27.7.40
R9584	20 OTU	Dived into hills on navex, Glen Avon, 6m SW of Tomintoul, Aberdeen, 7.8.41; cause not known
R9585	20 OTU	Collided with Master N7931 and crashed, Huntley Farm, near Stracathro, 17.12.41
R9586	4 FPP/ATA	SOC 16.3.45
R9587	3 SGR/26 OTU/	
	5 AOS/3 SGR	SOC 9.3.45
R9588 to		
R9591	-	To RCAF 6.5.41

R9592	19 OTU/10 RS	To 4939M 2.12.44

R9593	19 OTU/ATA	SS 15.1.51
R9594	19 OTU/ATA	To R.Neth AF 26.8.46 as D-5
R9595	2 AONS/6 AONS/	
	6 AOS/6 OAFU	SOC 13.6.45
R9596	2 AONS/4 AONS/	
	1 AOS/1 OAFU	SOC 30.6.44
R9597	2 AONS/2 SAN/	Undercarriage jammed; belly-landed, Llandwrog, 20.4.45;
	1 AONS/9 AOS/	not repaired and SOC 2.7.45
	9 OAFU	To RCAF 9.5.41
R9598	48	To RCAF 9.5.41
R9599	217	To SAAF 10.8.41 as 3145
R9600	311	To RCAF 12.3.41
R9601	4 FPP	
R9602	14 OTU/2 AOS/	
	9 OAFU/2 OAFU/	
	7 AOS	SOC 4.7.44
R9603	14 OTU/25 OTU/	
	14 OTU/2 AOS/	
	2 OAFU	SOC 3.1.46
R9604	14 OTU/25 OTU	Flew into hill, South Barrule,
	14 OTU/4 AOS	Isle of Man, 3.5.43
R9605	14 OTU/25 OTU/	
	5 PAFU/3 AOS/	To Belgian AF 12.6.47 as
	3 AGS/SPTU	NA.12
R9606	14 OTU/29 OTU	SOC 5.5.44
R9607	14 OTU/5 AOS/	
	AN&BS/16 PFTS/	
	1 OAFU/1 BAS	SOC 11.2.47
R9608	14 OTU	Overshot night landing and ran into boundary fence, Cottesmore, 13.8.42
R9609	14 OTU	To Canada 15.7.41
	32 OTU	SOC 23.1.45
R9610	20 OTU/2 OAFU/ATA	SOC 8.7.44
R9611	11 OTU/21 OTU	Ran out of fuel while lost on night navex and abandoned 1m from Nant-y-Bwch Station, near Tredegar, Monmouth, 26.4.41
R9627	20 OTU	To RCAF 29.7.41 as 6874
R9628	217/3 OTU/5 OTU	Missing on ferry flight in bad weather, Long Kesh to Turnberry, 28.1.43; presumed ditched
R9629	48/ATA/3 AOS/	
	3 OAFU	SOC 6.1.45
R9630	502/2 SGR/3 SGR	To RCAF 29.7.41 as 6875
R9631	502/2 SGR	To Canada 7.2.41
	33 SFTS	SOC 17.6.43
R9632	500/1 OTU/6 OTU/	
	12 RS/1 OAFU	SOC 28.1.47
R9633	500	To RCAF 12.3.41
R9634	1 OTU/3 OTU/5 OTU/	
	3 OTU/USAAF	SOC 5.6.45
R9635	1 OTU	To RCAF 4.3.41
R9636	1 OTU/17 PAFU/	
	15 PAFU	SOC 12.7.44
R9637	1 AONS/6 AONS	To RCAF 22.7.41
R9638	1 AONS/6 AONS/	Ran out of fuel on overshoot,
	6 AOS/SPTU	Cark, and crashlanded on Applebury Hill, Lancs., 23.2.44
R9639	6 AONS/1 AONS/	Engine cut on navex; lost
	9 AONS/9 AOS/	height and crashlanded in field,
	9 OAFU	Ouston Farm, Tetchill, Ellesmere, Salop., 22.8.42
R9640	6 AONS/1 AONS/	Flew into hill in cloud on navex,
	9 AOS/SPTU	Park Llewellen Farm, east side of North Barrule, Isle of Man, 17.7.42
R9641	10 FTS/11 FTS	To Canada 15.7.41
	31 ANS	SOC 5.6.44
R9642	10 FTS	To SAAF 14.1.41 as 3116
R9643	16 OTU/25 OTU/	Engine cut; crashlanded on
	17 OTU	rising ground at Weston Subedge, near Evesham,

Worcs., 18.6.41

Llandilo, Carmarthen, 13.11.43

Anson I

Anson I

Serial	Units	Remarks
R9644	14 OTU/2 AOS/ 10 AOS/10 OAFU	Hit by N5247 while taxying at Dumfries, 6.8.44; DBR
R9645	14 OTU/1 AOS/ 1 OAFU	Hit tree on overshoot and crashed 1m N of Bladnoch, Wigtown, 17.9.41
R9646	14 OTU/ATA 1 AOS/ATA	SOC 18.1.45
R9647	14 OTU/29 OTU/ 26 OTU/11 OTU/ 13 OTU/81 OTU/ 13 OTU/81 OTU/ FPU/4 OAFU	SOC 10.7.45
R9648	311/27 OTU/4 AOS/ SDU/10 OAFU/ 6 PAFU/20 MU/2 FP	SS 21.2.49
R9649	311	Caught fire when Very pistol accidentally discharged; crashed, Elton, near Peterborough, Northants., 1.10.40; DBR
R9650	500/11 OTU/6 PAFU/ 5 PAFU/62 OTU/ 54 OTU	SOC 17.1.46
R9651	2 SGR	To RCAF 4.3.41
R9652	16 OTU	Engine cut; lost height and hit ditch while bellylanding 12m W of Banbury, Oxon., 18.6.41; DBR
R9653	16 OTU	SOC 15.4.41
R9654	2 AONS/6 FTS	To SAAF 10.7.41 as 3130
R9655	ATA/4 AOS/4 OAFU/ 7 AOS/ATA/3 FP	SS 25.5.50
R9656	ATA/7 OTU/12 RS/ 10 RS	SOC 4.10.46
R9657	ATA/2 AOS/ATA	Crashed 23.5.44; NFD
R9658	ATA	Crashed 8.7.40; NFD
R9659	ATA//5 AOS/SFC	SOC 25.6.44
R9660	4 FPP/6 AONS/6 AOS/ 7 AOS/7 OAFU	SOC 13.3.44
R9661	4 FPP/ATA/5 AOS/ 2 OAFU/10 RS	SOC 19.2.45
R9662	4 FPP/7 FPP/27 OTU/ 81 OTU	SOC 10.10.45
R9663	20 OTU	Flew into hill in cloud on night navex, Bridge of Buchat, Aberdeen, 24.8.40
R9664	500 31 GRS	To Canada 4.3.41 SOC 16.8.46
R9665	48/3 OTU	Both engines cut on navex; wing struck pole in forced landing on Q-site at Cranford, Northants., 23.12.42
R9666	500	To RCAF 28.5.41
R9667	500/3 SGR/1 OTU/ 3 SGR/ATA/5 FP/ 66 Gp CF	SS 30.12.49
R9668	-	To RCAF 16.9.40
R9669	-	To RCAF 16.9.40
R9670	- 32 OTU	To Canada 16.9.40 SOC 21.7.44
R9685 to R9686	-	To RCAF 16.9.40
R9687	608/6 OTU/2 RS/ 83 Gp CS/85 Gp CS	SS 25.7.47
R9688	6 FTS	To RCAF 11.6.41
R9689	608/3 OTU/ 5 OTU/AAEE/5 OTU	Engine cut off Larne; ditched and towed by tug into Ferris Bay, Co.Antrim, 19.10.42
R9690	14 OTU/3 OTU/ 5 OTU/10 RS/ATA	SOC 8.7.44
R9691	16 OTU	To RCAF 22.9.41
R9692	14 OTU	To RCAF 12.8.41
R9693	16 OTU/29 OTU/ 6 PAFU/SPTU	Bellylanded in bad weather while lost, Golden Grove,
R9694	16 OTU	Ran short of fuel on night navex; abandoned in bad visibility and crashed, Grove Farm, Aston, Ivinghoe, Bucks., 28.9.41
R9695	2 AONS/1 AONS/ 1 BAS/2 SAN/RN/ 7 OAFU	Sold 4.12.46; became G-AIXV
R9696	2 SGR	To RCAF 7.2.41
R9697	6 FTS	To SAAF 10.7.41 as 3155
R9698	500	Lost height on approach to flare path on return from convoy patrol and flew into hillside, Detling, 23.2.41
R9699	500/13 OTU/500 25 OTU	Swung on night take-off, Finningley and hit Wellington DV494, 4.9.42
R9700	-	To RCAF 16.9.40
R9701	6 AONS/217	Engine cut; lost height and ditched 5m NE of Trevose Head, Cornwall, 21.11.40
R9702	16 OTU/1 OTU/ 3 OTU/12 RS	SOC 30.5.44
R9703	18 OTU	To RCAF 31.12.41
R9704	18 OTU/11 OTU/ 7 OTU/7 AOS/ 8 OAFU	NFT
R9705	18 OTU/304/18 OTU/ 2 AOS/2 OAFU	Engine lost power; abandoned on night navex in bad weather and crashed, Brown Moor, Hoddam Castle, near Ecclefechen, Dumfries, 22.5.42
R9706	18 OTU/12 OTU/ 1 OTU/6 OTU/ 7 AOS/7 ANS	SOC 28.3.46
R9707	18 OTU/22 OTU/ 7 AOS/10 OAFU/ 1 FU	To RHAF 13.5.47
R9708	18 OTU	Collided with R9709 and crashed, Wolvey, Warks., 4.10.41
R9709	18 OTU/12 OTU/ 9 OAFU/1 OAFU/ CNS/4 AGS/10 RS	SS 21.2.49
R9710	1 CACU/5 AOS/ 3 SGR/64 Gp CF	SS 30.12.49
R9711	44/10 FTS/6 AONS	To SAAF 10.10.41 as 315
R9712	-	To RCAF 20.12.40 but lost at sea en route, 19.1.41
R9713	-	To SAAF 8.2.41 as 1197
R9714	- 31 ANS	To Canada 22.12.40 SOC 22.1.45
R9715	- 31 ANS	To Canada 14.12.40 Engine cut; DBR in forced landing near London, Ont., 28.3.41; to GI airframe A138
R9716	17 OTU/29 OTU/ 6 PAFU/SPTU	SOC 18.10.45
R9717	17 OTU/29 OTU/ 6 PAFU/1 OAFU/ 1 FU	To Armée de l'Air 31.3.47
R9718	14 OTU/5 AOS/ 62 OTU/1 BAS/SFC	SS 3.9.47
R9719	ATA/11 PAFU	Engine cut; damaged in forced landing, Calveley, 27.2.45; SOC as BER
R9720	- 31 ANS	To Canada 16.9.40 Hit tree in forced landing in fog, Kincardine, Ont., 25.3.43
R9721	10 OTU/2 OAFU/ 5 AOS/3 OAFU	SOC 13.10.44
R9722	-	To RCAF 16.9.40
R9723	-	To RCAF 24.9.40
R9724	-	To SAAF 5.10.40 as 1167

Serial	Units	Fate
R9725	-	To RCAF 16.9.40
R9739	-	To RCAF 16.9.40
R9740	-	To RCAF 26.9.40
R9741	11 OTU / 31 GRS	To Canada 11.4.41 / SOC 22.1.45
R9742	-	To RCAF 30.11.40 as 6273
R9743	-	To RAAF 4.11.40
R9744	-	To RCAF 4.11.40 as 6237
R9745	-	To SAAF 18.12.40 as 120
R9746	-	To RCAF 21.9.40 as 6113
R9747	-	To SAAF 3.12.40
R9748	14 OTU/2 AOS/ 27 OTU/81 OTU	SOC 5.6.45
R9749	14 OTU	Engine cut on night navex; lost height and crashlanded, West-woodside, near Haxey, Lincs., 28.2.41
R9750	14 OTU	To RCAF 5.41
R9751	15 OTU/20 OTU/ 27 OTU/81 OTU	SOC 22.4.45
R9752	14 OTU	Ditched after engine failed 3m SE of Burrow Head, Wigtown, 24.8.40
R9753	14 OTU/2 FIS	SOC 28.5.45
R9754	14 OTU/17 OTU 9 OAFU/7 AOS	SOC 16.8.44
R9755	13 OTU/16 OTU/ 12 OTU/1 OAFU	SOC 27.9.45
R9756	13 OTU/1 AOS/ 1 OAFU	Ditched in bad weather while lost on night navex off Point of Ayre, Isle of Man, 5.11.42
R9757	ATA/1 FU	To Armée de l'Air 25.6.46
R9758	6 AONS/1 AOS/ 1 OAFU/9 OAFU/ 12 PAFU/1 AGS/ 14 PAFU	SOC 24.8.44
R9759	13 OTU/16 OTU	SOC 2.6.44
R9760	17 OTU/6 AOS/ 10 OAFU/10 ANS	SS 31.3.49
R9761	ATA	SOC 22.7.41
R9762	ATA	SS 5.11.46
R9763	4 FPP/ATA/3 RS/SF East Fortune/62 OTU	SOC 15.12.44
R9764	4 FPP/6 AONS/6 AOS/ 6 OAFU/7 AOS	SOC 1.9.44
R9765	4 FPP	SOC 12.11.40
R9766	16 OTU/10 OTU/ 2 OAFU/4 AOS/ 4 OAFU/1 OAFU	SOC 1.3.45
R9767	6 AONS	To SAAF 10.10.41 as 3157
R9768	6 AONS	To RCAF 30.7.41
R9769	HQ FPP/19 OTU/ 3 AOS/3 OAFU	SS 25.7.47
R9770	6 AONS/6 AOS/ 6 OAFU	SOC 9.7.44
R9771	4 FPP	To RCAF 16.3.41
R9772	6 FTS	To SAAF 26.7.41 as 3167
R9773	608/3 OTU	To RCAF 12.9.41 as 3542
R9774	1 AONS/19 OTU	Engine cut; lost height and hit telephone wires in forced landing, Tobermory, Mull, 31.8.41; DBR
R9775	608	To RCAF 28.5.41
R9776	1 AONS/2 OTU/ 20 OTU/19 OTU/ 10 OTU	SOC 11.9.44
R9777	608/3 OTU/5 OTU/ 7 OTU/3 SGR	SOC 28.9.44
R9778	608	To RCAF 28.5.41
R9779	2 AONS/6 FTS	To RCAF 5.41
R9780	2 AONS/2 SAN/ 1 BAS/2 AOS/ 2 OAFU	Broke up in air and dived into ground on navex, Whitehaven, Cumberland, 14.10.43
R9781	2 AONS/6 FTS/ 2 SAN/4 AOS/2 SAN/	
R9798	6 FTS	To RCAF 28.5.41
R9799	6 FTS	To SAAF 10.8.41 as 3172
R9800	6 FTS / 33 SFTS	To Canada 26.4.41 / SOC 16.2.45
R9801	48/6 OTU/FAA Gosport/6 OTU	SOC 28.9.44
R9802	6 FTS	To SAAF 7.2.41
R9803	6 FTS	To SAAF 20.6.41 as 1212
R9804	15 OTU/Thornaby/ 3 RS/62 OTU/7 AOS/ 7 OAFU	SOC 8.2.45
R9805	15 OTU/22 OTU/ 9 OAFU/11 PAFU/ 24 OTU	Overshot landing, Leamington Spa, 29.5.44
R9806	15 OTU/7 PAFU	SOC 4.9.44
R9807	15 OTU/3 AOS/6 AOS/ 3 PAFU	Crashed 11.11.45
R9808	102/612/3 OTU/ 5 OTU/10 RS/8 OTU/ SF Sumburgh	Overshot landing and swung into ditch, Vaagar, Faroes, 26.6.44; DBR
R9809	11 OTU/21 OTU/ PRU/FPU/7 ANS/ 1 RFS/7 RFS/2 RFS	SS 16.1.51
R9810	11 OTU	Undershot landing and hit hedge, Bassingbourn, 17.10.41
R9811	15 OTU/7 AOS/ 10 OAFU	SOC 14.1.45
R9812	BATDU/WIDU/109/ 1473 Flt/ROS Flt/ 1473 Flt/19 OTU/ 23 OTU/4 OAFU/ 20 PAFU/1 FU	To Armée de l'Air 28.6.46
R9813	BATDU/WIDU/109	Swung on landing, Boscombe Down and hit Spitfires P8036 and R7337, 24.7.41
R9814	BATDU/WIDU/ 1473 Flt/6 PAFU/ 12 PAFU	SOC 22.8.45
R9815	BATDU	Flew into ground in blind landing at night in fog and undercarriage collapsed, Boscombe Down, 5.9.40; DBF
R9816	A-S/AAEE/RAE/ Avro/AAEE	Testbed for Wright R-975-E for Mk.IV. To RCAF 19.3.42 as 10257
R9817	608	Engine lost power on patrol; lost height and ditched 3m off Collieston, Aberdeen, 7.3.41
R9818	608	To RCAF 27.4.41
R9819	608	To RCAF 28.5.41
R9820	-	To RCAF 16.9.40
R9821	-	To RCAF 16.9.40
R9822	-	To SAAF 5.10.40 as 1157
R9823	-	To RCAF 16.9.40
R9824	6 FTS/3 OTU/5 OTU/ 3 OTU/7 OAFU	SS 28.1.47
R9825	612/1 OTU/ 5 AOS/ATA	SOC 18.11.44
R9826	321	To RCAF 29.4.41
R9827	321/320/1 OTU	SOC 31.5.42
R9828	BATDU/1 BAS/ 3 AOS/3 OAFU	SOC 15.2.45
R9829	BATDU/1 BAS/ 3 AOS/3 OAFU	SOC 18.4.44
R9830	BATDU/1 BAS/ 3 AOS/3 OAFU/ SFC/BAS	SOC 1.1.45
R9831 to R9836	-	To RCAF 3.8.40 as 6063 to 9068
R9837	BATDU/1 BAS/ 3 AOS/SPTU/SFC/ 7 FIS/3 OAFU	SOC 1.6.45
R9838	-	To SAAF 15.10.40 as 1152
R9839	-	To SAAF 22.10.40 as 1171

8 OAFU/ATA   SOC 19.8.46

R9840	-	To SAAF 22.10.40 as 1168

R9841	-	To SAAF 22.10.40 as 1169
R9842	-	To SAAF 15.10.40 as 1153
R9843	-	To RCAF 17.8.40 as 6134
R9844	-	To RCAF 17.8.40 as 6146
R9845	-	To RCAF 17.8.40 as 6135
R9846	-	To RCAF 24.8.40 as 6147
R9864	RAE	SOC 4.6.46
R9865	-	To RCAF 19.9.40 as 6136
R9866	-	To RCAF 19.9.40 as 6148
R9867	-	To RCAF 19.9.40 as 6137
R9868	-	To RCAF 19.9.40 as 6149
R9869	-	To RCAF 3.8.40 as 6060
R9870	-	To RCAF 3.8.40 as 6061
R9871	-	To RCAF 3.8.40 as 6069
R9872	-	To RCAF 3.8.40 as 6070
R9873	-	To RCAF 3.8.40 as 6062
R9874	-	To RCAF 7.8.40 as 6071
R9875	-	To RCAF 7.8.40 as 6072
R9876	-	To RCAF 7.8.40 as 6073
R9877	-	To RCAF 9.8.40 as 6076
R9878	-	To RCAF 9.8.40 as 6077
R9879	-	To RCAF 9.8.40 as 6078
R9880	-	To RCAF 9.8.40 as 6079
R9881	-	To RCAF 13.8.40 as 6080
R9882	-	To RCAF 13.8.40 as 6081
R9883 to		
R9888	-	To RCAF 23.8.40
R9889	-	To RCAF 9.8.40 as 6074
R9890 to		
R9893	-	To RCAF 23.8.40 as 6084
R9894	-	To RAAF 12.9.40
R9895	-	To RCAF 9.8.40 as 6090
R9896	-	To RAAF 10.8.40
R9897	-	To RAAF 10.8.40
R9898	-	To RAAF 12.9.40
R9899	-	To RAAF 12.9.40
R9928	-	To RAAF 12.9.40
R9929	-	To RCAF 17.8.40 as 6108
R9930	-	To RCAF 17.8.40 as 6109
R9931	-	To RCAF 17.8.40 as 6099
R9932	-	To RCAF 6.9.40 as 6110
R9933	-	To RCAF 6.9.40 as 6111
R9934	-	To RCAF 6.9.40 as 6104
R9935	-	To RCAF 23.8.40
R9936	-	To RCAF 23.8.40
R9937	-	To RCAF 5.9.40 as 6095
R9938	-	To RCAF 5.9.40 as 6096
R9939	-	To RCAF 17.8.40 as 6082
R9940	-	To RCAF 17.8.40 as 6097
R9941	-	To RCAF 17.8.40 as 6083
R9942	-	To RCAF 17.8.40 as 6098
R9943	-	To RCAF 17.8.40 as 6088
R9944	-	To RCAF 17.8.40 as 6089
R9945	-	To RCAF 17.8.40 as 6093
R9946	-	To RCAF 17.8.40 as 6094
R9947	-	To RCAF 17 17.8.40 as 6123
R9948	-	To RCAF 17.8.40 as 6124
R9949	-	To RCAF 31.8.40 as 6091
R9950	-	To RCAF 31.8.40 as 6092
R9951	-	To RCAF 19.9.40 as 6138
R9952	-	To RCAF 19.9.40 as 6150
R9953	-	To RCAF 19.9.40 as 6105
R9954	-	To RCAF 6.9.40 as 6101
R9955	-	To RCAF 16.9.40 as 6127

R9956	-	To RCAF 21.9.40 as 6117
R9957	-	To RCAF 16.9.40 as 6128
R9958	-	To RCAF 21.9.40 as 6118
R9959	-	To RCAF 6.9.40 as 6106
R9960	-	To RCAF 6.9.40 as 6100
R9961	-	To RCAF 6.9.40 as 6102
R9962	-	To RCAF 6.9.40 as 6107
R9963	-	To RCAF 16.9.40 as 6125
R9964	-	To RCAF 16.9.40 as 6126
R9965	-	To RCAF 21.9.40 as 6119
R9966	-	To RCAF 21.9.40 as 6120
R9967	-	To RCAF 21.9.40 as 6121
R9968	-	To RCAF 26.9.40 as 6165
R9969	-	To RCAF 19.9.40 as 6129

* * * * * * * * * *

300 Airspeed Oxford Is and IIs delivered by Airspeed, Portsmouth, under Contract No. B19646/39 as follows:

R9974 - T1047	Oxford Is in November and December 1940
T1048 - T1111	Oxford IIs in December 1940 and January 1941
T1112 - T1186	Oxford Is in February 1941 and March 1941
T1187 - T1263	Oxford IIs in February 1941
T1264 - T1332	Oxford Is in February and March 1941
T1333 - T1404	Oxford IIs in March and April 1941

R9974	-	To S.Rhodesia 11.40;
	23 SFTS	NFT 6.2.43
R9975	-	To S.Rhodesia 30.12.40;
	23 SFTS	SOC 12.7.43
R9976	-	To S.Rhodesia 12.40;
	21 SFTS	SOC 5.11.45
R9977	-	To S.Rhodesia 30.12.40;
	22 SFTS/23 SFTS	SOC 4.8.45
R9978	1 PFTS/16 PFTS/	
	2 PAFU/3 PAFU	To 5488M 26.7.45
R9979	-	To RAAF 13.12.40
R9980	12 PAFU/3 FIS	SOC 3.6.53
R9981	-	To S.Rhodesia 6.2.41;
	23 SFTS	Braked on landing and over-turned, Heany, 25.2.42; DBR
R9982	-	To S.Rhodesia 11.40;
	23 SFTS	Flew into ground after night take-off 1m E of Heany, 19.8.41
R9983	15 FTS/15 PAFU	Wing dropped on take-off; undercarriage raised to stop, Worcester, 16.5.43
R9984	-	To S.Rhodesia 6.2.41;
	23 SFTS	DBR in crash, 25.5.44; SOC 11.8.44
R9985	-	To RAAF 13.12.40
R9986	-	To S.Rhodesia 11.40;
	23 SFTS/20 SFTS	Engine cut on take-off; hit wires and crashed, 2.6.41
R9987	-	To S.Rhodesia 11.40;
	23 SFTS	Engine cut on take-off; belly-landed,, Denyer LG, 19.9.42
R9988	-	To RAAF 13.12.40

Continued at T1001

Presentation Aircraft

Spitfires

24 Pagarnas No.1	P7820	Black Velvet	P8380
24 Pagarnas No.2	P7821	Bolsover I	R7261
Absque labore nihil (Darwen)	R7219	Bolsover II	R7276
Accrington, Church, Oswaldtwistle	R7154	Bombay Gymkhana I	R7273
Ad Morem Villae de Poole	R7126	Bombay Gymkhana II	R7275
Ada	P8742	Bongie	P8197
Afrikander	P8674	Bon-Accord	P8171
Aitch-Aitch	R7299	Borneo N.E.I.	P8238
Ajax	R7337	Boron	P8536
Aldergrove	P7843	Borough of Colwyn Bay	P8529
Aldershot (ex-The Cat)	P8136	Borough of Lambeth	P8088
Alton & District	P8173	Borough of Morley	P8658
Altrincham	R7158	Borough of Wanstead and Woodford	P8789
Ambala I	R6720	Bostonian, The	P8390
Amboina	P8516	Bow Street Home Guard	P7744
Antrim	P7828	B.R.C. Stafford	R7229
Ariel	P8647	B.R.C. Stafford II	R7263
Arkwright	R6722	Bredbury and Romiley	P8526
Armagh	P7849	Brenda	R7230
Assam One Lakhimpur	P8167	Brentwood	P7743
Assam II Lakhimpur	P8168	Bridgwater	R7163
Assam III Lakhimpur	P8169	Bristol Air Raid Warden	R7260
Assam IV Lakhimpur	P8170	Bristol Civil Defender	R7194
Assam V Lakhimpur	P8548	Brit, The	R7062
Assam VI Lakhimpur	P8543	British and Friends ex-Japan, The	P7914
Auckland I, Waiuku	P8786	British Glues and Chemicals Ltd	P8479
Aurangabad	P7445	British & Friends ex-Japan	P8348
Bali	P8367	Bromley	R7262
Balikpapan	P8340	Brycheiniog	R7264
Ballymena	P7835	Burdwan	P8013
Balmer Lawrie	P8422	Burnley District	R7271
Baltic Exchange I	P8174	Buxton	P8660
Baltic Exchange II	P8175	Bydand	P8172
Banda	P8333	Byng of Vimy	R7133
Bandoeng	P8338	Cable Queen	P8178
Bangor	P7842	Caernarvonshire	P8690
Banka	P8363	Caithness	R7057
Bankline	P7740	Camborne-Redruth	P8671
Bansi	P8523	Cambridgeshire	P7736
Barty	P8387	Canadian Scot - Fort William	P8463
Batavia	P8330	Caput inter nibila condit (Gateshead)	R7123
Batley	R7214	Cardiff I	P8438
Bawco	P7919	Cardiff I	P8673
B.B.&.C.I. Railway I	R7156	Cardiff II	P8672
B.B.&.C.I. Railway II	R7145	Cardiff III	P8678
Bechuana	P8517	Cat, The, later Aldershot	P8136
Belfast	P7684	Cawn Crete	P8382
Benoni	P8399	Celebes	P8375
Bermuda I	P8507	Ceram	P8342
Bermuda II	P8396	Ceredigion I (Aberystwyth)	P8691
Bermuda III	P8649	Ceredigion II (Aberystwyth)	P8676
Bermuda IV	P8504	Cheeping Wycombe	P8398
Besoeki	P8376	Chelmsford	R7065
Beverley & District	R7267	Cheshunt and Waltham	P8397
Bhavnagar	P8741	Chittagong II	P8190
Bidar	P7449	Chittagong I?	P8189
Bingley (U.D.C.)	P8665	Chorley & District	P8593
Birkenhead	R7278	City of Birmingham I	P7910
Black Horse, The	P8148	City of Birmingham II	P7911
Black Vanities	P8373	City of Birmingham III	P7912

City of Birmingham IV	P7913	Dursley & District	P8679
City of Bradford I	P7746	East India Fund Flight	R6766
City of Bradford II	P7747	Eastern Bengal Railway	P7855
City of Bradford III	P7748	Eastern Bengal Railway II	P7856
City of Bradford IV	P7749	Edglets	R7061
City of Bradford V	P7750	Elland	P8092
City of Bradford VI	P7751	Enfield Spitfire	P8278
City of Bradford VII	P8383	Enfield Spitfire	P8098
City of Bundaberg & District	P8576	Enniskillen	P7832
City of Coventry I	P7490	Eric	P7739
City of Coventry II	P7491	Erimus (Middlesbrough)	R7122
City of Coventry III	P7492	Ever Ready	P7921
City of Derry	P7839	Fairwarp	P7735
City of Exeter, Devon Squadron	P7964	Fashion Flier	P7741
City of Leicester Flight,		F.E.F.	P8465
City of Leicester I	P8563	Fei-yue	P8384
City of Leicester Flight,		Fermanagh	P7838
City of Leicester II	P8565	First Canadian Division	P8044
City of Leicester Flight,		First City of London Textile	P8662
City of Leicester III	P8657	Flint	P8654
City of Liverpool I	R7209	Flores	P8336
City of Liverpool II	R7206	Folkestone & Hythe	P8467
City of Liverpool III	R7208	Foremost	R7277
City of Liverpool IV	R7210	Foxhunter, The	P7493
City of Norwich	P8147	Frimley and Camberley	P8429
City of Nottingham	P7738	Frome & District	R7200
City of Oxford	P7915	Galleywood	R7066
City of Stoke-on-Trent I	P8568	Garfield Weston I	P8074
City of Stoke-on-Trent II	P8580	Garfield Weston II	P8075
City of St.Albans	P8144	Garfield Weston III	P8078
City of Worcester I	P8045	Garfield Weston IV	P8081
City of Worcester II	P8046	Garfield Weston V	P8083
Clan, the	P8530	Garfield Weston VI	P8084
Cliftononian	P8675	Garfield Weston VII	P8085
Colchester & District	P8677	Garfield Weston VIII	P8086
Corn Exchange	P8096	Gateshead	R7125
Cornwall	P8669	Gaumont British	P8645
Counter Attack	P8448	Gaumont British I	P8652
Courageous	P8642	Gaumont British II	P8653
Covent Garden	P8146	George Parbury, Leicester, The	P8538
Crisps	P8692	G.H.	R7272
Crosby I	P8439	Gibraltar	P8394
Crosby II	P8440	Gillingham	P7734
Cuba	P8666	Gold Coast I	P8194
Cuba II	P8668	Gold Coast II	P8195
Cuba III	P8667	Gold Coast III	P8196
Dacca	P8743	Gosport	R7153
Dart Valley, The	P8599	Grahame Heath	P7883
Dauntless, The	R7135	Grahame Heath	R6759
Defendamus (Taunton)	P8650	Grainger Weston	P8393
Delhi I	P8601	Grebbeberg	P8693
Delhi II	P8606	Grimsby I	R7265
Dereham and District Spitfire	P7897	Grimsby II	R7231
Derrick	R7294	Guildford I	P7625
Devon Squadron	P7928	Guildford II	P7733
Dewsbury	R7250	Gulbarga	P7446
Digboi - Assam	P8191	Halesowen	R7344
Dilwar	P8696	Halifax I	P8097
D.M.L. Overdale	P7814	Halifax II	P8093
Doningtonian	R7290	Halifax III	P8095
Down	P7823	Harlandic	P7685
D.S.& G. Worth Valley	R7063	Harry Livingstone, Leicester, The	P8532
D.S.&.G. Worth Valley	P8162	Hasarde, The	P8506
Dulvercombe	P8374	Hastings	R7067
Dumfriesshire	P7960	Hawick "Teribus"	R7128
Dunedin	P7822	Heart of England I, The	P8502

Heart of England II, The	P8609	Magnet	P8392
Heart of England III, The	P8544	Mah-tal	R7339
Hecla	P8513	Makassar	P8589
Hemel Hempstead	P7772	Malang	P8602
Hereward the Wake	P7926	Malverns, The	P8047
Hereward the Wake	P8039	Man & Metal	P7922
Hexham & District	R7343	Mandot	P7293
H.H. the Nawab of Bahawalpur	P7745	Manxman	P7966
Hinckley	P7916	Margaret Helen	P8643
Hissar I Punjab	P8024	Marlborough/Westland/Nelson	P8025
Holmewood I	R7195	Mauritius I	P8524
Holmewood II	R7196	Mauritius II	P8527
Hominis Vis	R7336	Medan	P8343
Hooghly	P7894	Megapi	P8372
Horwich	P8080	Melton Mowbray and District	P8522
Hunter	P8534	Mendip Spitfire, The	P8520
Huntly, Cock o' the North	P8644	Mercury	R7064
Hyderabad	P7372	M.E.S.	P8444
Ideal	P8090	Metabox	P8389
Ideal	R7297	Middelburg	P8595
Impregnable	P8385	Mid-Ulster	P7834
Indian Posts	P8547	Mindapore	P8132
Indian Telegraphs	P8445	Miners of Durham I	P8089
Indian Telegraphs II	P8545	Miners of Durham II	P8091
Industria (West Hartlepool)	R7132	Molukken	P8443
Inspiration	P7962	Mombasa	R7161
Jamshedpur Golmuri II	R7266	Montague Bee	P8179
Jamshedpur Golmuri II	R7269	Morishabad	P8570
Jamshedpur Golmuri III	P8604	Morvi I	P8435
Jason	R7069	Morvi II	P8436
Java	P8327	Mountains o'Mourne, The	P7840
Jersey I	P7610	Mymensingh I	P8437
Jessore	P7895	Mymensingh II	P8424
J.G. (also Stamford)	P8505	N.A.B.	R7340
Jubilee (Richmond)	P8347	Nabha I	P8603
Kalahari	P8461	Nabha II	P8584
Kamba Mam	R7152	Nabha III	P8518
Kambu-meru	R7159	Nadia	P7676
Katwijk	P8597	Nae Bother	R7270
Kerr	P8209	N.E.M.	P7742
Kidderminster, Bewdley & Stourport	P8048	Newbury I	R7292
Kikuyu-embu	R7155	Newbury II	R7296
King's Messenger	R7279	Newfoundland I	P7844
Kirby, The	R7333	Newfoundland II	P7845
Kirby II, The	R7335	Newfoundland III	P7846
Kirkcaldy	R7302	Newtonia	P8655
Kiwi	P9398	Nippy	P8656
Krakatau	P8361	Norfolk Farmer, The	P8138
La Rosalinda	P8193	North Barrule IOM	R7131
Lady Linlithgow	P8600	North Borneo I	P8176
Lahore City	P7319	North Borneo III	P8186
Larne	P7841	North Borneo IV	P8187
Layland, Leeds City	P7983	North Borneo V	P8188
Leigh	P8525	North Borneo II	P8177
Lest we forget	R7201	North West Frontier II	P8512
Lewis and Harris Fighter	P8149	North West Frontier II	P8598
Leyland	P8161	North West Frontier III	P8515
Lombok	P8341	North West Frontier IV	P8695
London Stock Exchange	R7204	North West Frontier V	P8501
Londonderry	P7683	North West Surrey	P8641
L.T.R. Fighter	P8661	Northampton	P8041
Luton I	P8130	Northampton (County Borough)	P7918
Luton II	P8131	Nuflier	P8140
Mabel	P8145	Observer Corps	P7666
Mackinuous, India	P7494	Old Lady, The	P8509
Madura	P8339	Oldham	P8370

Oldham and Lees	P8379	Sind V	P7836
On Target	P8094	Sind VI	P7887
Onward	R7217	Sind VII	P7888
Orkney	P8344	Siwaboong	P8377
Ossett and Horbury Spitfire, The	P8346	Skyscraper Sheila	P8503
Otago I	P7626	Skysweeper	P8082
Otago II	P7674	S.M.Y.C.	R7160
Palembang	P8366	Soebang	P8332
Palembang Oeloe I	P8371	Soekaboemi	P8349
Palembang Oeloe II	P8607	Soerabaya	P8378
Pampero I	P7753	Southampton I	R7059
Pampero II	P7754	Southampton II	R7060
Pampero III	P7755	Southern Belle	R7157
Pampero IV	P7756	Southland II	P7970
Papyrus	R7338	Southport I	P8142
Pastures, The	R7295	Southport II	P8143
Pegasus	R7070	Spirit of Crewe	P8395
Pemba I	P7730	Spirit of Crewe II	P8425
Pemba II	P7731	Spirit of Leek, The	R7211
Perfect	R7334	Spirit of Redhill	P7621
Perseus	R7071	Spirit of Warrington I	P8797
Peterborough & District	R7192	Spirit of Warrington II	P8714
Picture Post	P8567	Stir-gar	P8562
P.J. Spitfire, The	P8160	Stockport	R7215
Portadown	P7833	Stourbridge	R7197
Preston & District I	R7202	Stroud	P8381
Preston & District II	R7207	St.Austell & District	R7116
Preston & District III	R7203	St.Helens	P8651
Pride of the Isle	P7969	St.Vincent	P8180
Provident	R7205	Sulhamstead	P8521
Puck	R7212	Sumatra	P8331
Pudukkattai Nagarathars	P8471	Sumbawa	P8329
Pulchritude et Salubritis (Bournemouth)	R7220	Sunderland I	R7072
Quthung	P8757	Sunderland II	R7073
Rainscombe	P7859	Sunderland III	R7074
Rajshahi	P7665	Sunderland IV	R7114
Red Rose, The	P7920	Surinam	P6364
Resurgam	P8279	Sutherland	R7028
Riouw	P8596	Swan, The	R7268
R.J.Mitchell	R7058	Swansea I	R7130
Robert Peel	P8139	Swansea III, Swansea Wales 1st Flight	R7134
Rochdale & District I	P8345	Tasmania I	P8181
Rochdale & District I	P8648	Tasmania II	P8142
Rochdale & District II	P8646	Tasmania III	P8183
Rotherham & District	R7298	Teling Tinggi	P8585
Rotterdam	P8365	Tippera	P7831
Rowley Regis	P7732	Toba	P8369
Rugby & District	P8141	Toby	R7162
Saddleworth	R7253	Township of Shipley	P8528
Sans Tache	R7293	Transkeian Territories I	P8184
Sarum and South Wilts Spitfire	P8137	Transkeian Territories II	P8185
Sayles	P7757	Transpitter, The	P8254
Scawfell	P8588	Transport Men-ace, The	P7929
Second City of London Textile	P8670	Tra-mor-Tramerion	R7136
Secundus Dubusque Rectus	R7129	Trustworthy	R7291
Semarang	P8335	Turris jehova fortissimo ets nomen	
Sherwood Forester	R7198	(Plymouth)	R7127
Sialkot I	P8277	Tyrone	P7686
Sialkot II	P8239	Tyrone	P7825
Sialkot II	P9397	Venture I	P7923
Sibayak	P8368	Venture II	P7924
Silver Snipe	R7193	Venture II	P8040
Sind I	P7826	Vetustas dignatatem generat	
Sind II	P7827	(East Retford & District)	R7218
Sind III (or Mysore)	P7829	Victor McLaglen, Seattle	R7151
Sind IV	P7830	Violetta	P8542

172

Waikato	P8022	Wonkers	P8744
Walsall I	R7143	Woolton	R7199
Walsall II	R7139	Woolwich	R7216
Warden of London, The	P7752	Worksop	P7737
West Riding	R7274	Worthing	R7068
Weston-super-Mare	P7925	Wulfrun	P8715
Who's a-fear'd	P8531	Zanzibar I	P7697
Winged Victory	P8200	Zanzibar II	P7698
Women of Bengal	P7892	Zanzibar III	P7699
Women of Bengal II	P7899	Zira	R7256

Other Types

Flamingo

Lady of Hendon	R2765

Oxford (Air ambulances presented by Girl Guides Association)

Florence Nightingale	P8832
Nurse Cavell	P8833

Stirling

East India III	R9295

Typhoon

Borough of Sutton and Cheam	R8199
Islands of Britain	R8200
Land Girl	R8224

Wellington

Ionides	R1288
The Broughton Wellington	R1333
Akyem Abuakwa	R1448
Sierra Leone I	R1452
The Broughton Wellington	R1516
British Guiana II	R1719
Jodhpur	R1721

Whirlwind

Bellows Argentina I	P7055
Pride of Yeovil	P7056
Bellows	P7094
Comrades in Arms	P7102
Bellows Argentina II	P7116
Bellows Argentina III	P7117
Bellows Argentina No.4	P7118
Bellows Argentina No.5	P7119
Bellows Argentina No.6	P7120
Bellows Argentina No.7	P7121
Bellows Uruguay	P7122

ABBREVIATIONS

AAC	Army Air Corps
AACF	Anti-aircraft Co-operation Flight
AACU	Anti-aircraft Co-operation Unit
AAEE	Aeroplane & Armament Experimental Establishment
AAF	Auxiliary Air Force
AAGS	Air Armament & Gas School
AAPC	Anti-aircraft Practice Camp
AAS	Air Armament School
AASF	Advanced Air Striking Force
AAU	Aircraft Acceptance Unit
ABGS(ME)	Air Bombing and Gunnery School (Middle East)
ACCCF	Army Co-operation Command Communications Flight
Acclim	Acclimatisation
ACDU	Army Co-operation Development Unit
ACSEA	Air Command South East Asia
AD	Aircraft Depot
ADF(U)	Aircraft Delivery Flight (Unit)
ADGB	Air Defence of Great Britain
ADLS	Air Delivery Letter Service
AEAF	Allied Expeditionary Air Forces
AF	Airfield (later Wing)
AFDU	Air Fighting Development Unit
AFE/AFEE	Airborne Forces (Experimental) Establishment
AFS/AFU	Advanced Flying School/Unit
AFS(ME)	Air Fighting School (Middle East)
AFS	Auxiliary Fighter Squadron, Singapore
AFTS/AFTU	Advance Flying Training School/Unit
AGME	Aircraft Gun Mounting Establishment
AGS	Air Gunnery School
AGS(ME/I)	Air Gunnery School (Middle East/India)
AHQ (I)	Air Headquarters (India)
AIEU	Armament and Instrument Experimental Unit
AIS	Air Interception School
AM	Air Ministry
AMDP	Air Member for Development & Production
AMSDU	Air Ministry Servicing Development Unit
ANBS	Air Navigation and Bombing School
ANS	Air Navigation School
AONS	Air Observers Navigation School
AOP(S)	Air Observation Post (School)
AOS	Air Observers School
AOTS	Aircrew Officers Training School
AP	Aircraft Park
APC(S)	Armament Practice Camp (Station)
APCS	Aden Protectorate Communications Squadron
ARD	Aircraft Repair Depot
ARU	Aircraft Repair Unit
A-S	Armstrong-Siddeley
ASRTU	Air-Sea Rescue Training Unit
AS&RU	Aircraft Salvage & Repair Unit
ASS	Air Signals School
AST	Air Service Training
ASWDU	Air-Sea Warfare Development Unit
ATA	Air Transport Auxiliary
ATDU	Air Torpedo Development Unit*
	* If transport aircraft involved, refers to Air Transport Development Unit
ATP	Advanced Training Pool
ATS	Armament Training Station
ATTDU	Air Transport Tactical Development Unit
ATU	Armament Training Unit (India)
AUAS	Aberdeen University Air Squadron
AW	Armstrong Whitworth
AWFCS	All-weather Fighter Conversion Squadron
BAC	Bristol Aircraft Company (until 1950s)
BAD	Base Aircraft Depot (USAAAF)
BADU	Blind, later, Beam Approach Development Unit
BAFF	British Air Forces in France
BAFO	British Air Forces of Occupation
BAFSEA	British Air Forces South-east Asia
BANS	Basic Air Navigation School
BARU	British Airways Repair Unit (ME)
BAS	Beam Approach School
BATDU	Blind Approach Training & Development Unit
BATF	Beam (originally Blind) Approach Training Flight
BBU	Bomb Ballistics Unit
BCCF(S)	Bomber Command Communications Flight (Squadron)
BCDU	Bomber Command Development Unit
BCIS	Bomber Command Instructors School
BDU	Bombing Development Unit
BEA	British European Airways
BFTS	Basic Flying Training School
BGS	Bombing & Gunnery School
BLEU	Blind Landing Experimental Unit
BOAC	British Overseas Airways Corporation
BP	Boulton Paul
BPC	British Purchasing Commission (in USA)
BSAA	British South American Airways
BSD/TU	Bomber Support Development/ Training Unit
BSTU	Bomber Support Training Unit
BTU	Bombing Trials Unit
BWF	Bristol Wireless Flight, Yatesbury
CA	Controller, Aircraft (Air Ministry)
CAACU	Civil Anti-aircraft Co-operation Unit
CACU/F	Coast Artillery Co-operation Unit/Flight
Cal Flt	Calibration Flight
Cam Flt/Unit	Camouflage Flt/Unit
CANS	Civil Air Navigation School
CATCS	Central Air Traffic Control School
CAW	College of Air Warfare
CBE	Central Bomber Establishment
CCCF(S)	Coastal Command Communications Flight (Squadron)
CCDU	Coastal Command Development Unit
CCF	Canadian Car & Foundry (Manufacturer)

CCF/U	Check & Conversion Flight/Unit	EWS	Electrical & Wireless School
CCGS	Coastal Command Gunnery School	FAA	Fleet Air Arm
CC(F)IS	Coastal Command (Flying) Instructors School	FATU	Fighter Affiliation Training Unit
		F-BFTS	France-Belgian Flying Training School
CCTDU	Coastal Command Tactical Development Unit	FBTS	Flying Boat Training Squadron
		FC	Ferry Control (numbered)
CFE	Central Fighter Establishment	FC	Fighter Command
CFF	Combined Forces in France	FCCS/F	Fighter Command Communications Squadron/ Flight
CF(S)	Communications Flight (Squadron)		
CF	Conversion Flight (number prefix)	FCIRS	Fighter Command Instrument Rating Squadron
CFCS	Central Fighter Control School		
CFE	Central Fighter Establishment	FCPU	Ferry Command Preparation Unit
CFS	Central Flying School	FCS	Fighter Control School
CFWD	Communications Flight Western Desert	FE	Far East
CGS	Central Gunnery School	FECS/F	Far East Communications Squadron/ Flight
CLE	Central Landing Establishment		
CLS	Central Landing School	FEE	Fighter Experimental Establishment
CNCS	Central Navigation and Control School	FETS	Far East Training Squadron
CNS	Central Navigation School	FF	Fighter Flight/Ferry Flight
COA	Cunliffe-Owen Aircraft	FFAF	Free French Air Force
CPE	Central Photographic Establishment	FG	Fighter Group (USAAF)
CPF	Coastal Patrol Flight	FIDS	Fighter Interception Development Squadron
CRD	Controller of Research & Development		
CRO	Civilian Repair Organisation	FIS	Flying Instructors School
CRS	Control and Reporting School	FIU	Fighter Interception Unit
CSDE	Central Servicing Development Establishment	Flot	Flottille
		FLS	Fighter Leaders School
CSE	Central Signals Establishment	Flt	Flight
CSF/S/U	Communications & Support Flight/ Squadron/Unit	FP/FPP(U)	Ferry Pool/Ferry Pilot Pool (Unit)
		FPU	Ferry Preparation Unit
CTTS	Communications & Target-towing Squadron	FPU	Film Production Unit
		FRD	Forward Repair Depot
CTU	Combat Training Unit	FR Flt	Fighter-reconnaissance Flight
CUAS	Cambridge University Air Squadron	FRL	Flight Refuelling Ltd
Cv	Converted	FRS	Flying Refresher School
CU	Communications Unit (unit prefixed)	FRU	Field Repair Unit
CU	Conversion Unit (numbered)	FTC	Flying Training Command
CUAS	Cambridge University Air Squadron	FTCCS	Flying Training Command Communications Squadron
CW	Communications Wing		
DAF	Desert Air Force	FTF/U	Ferry Training Flight/Unit
Del/Dly	Delivery	FTS	Flying Training School (prefixed S in wartime)
DFLS	Day Fighter Leaders School		
DGRD	Director General of Research & Development	FTU	Ferry Training Unit
		FU	Ferry Unit
DH	De Havilland	FWS	Fighter Weapons School
DTD	Director of Technical Development (AM)	GAL	General Aircraft Ltd
DUAS	Durham University Air Squadron	GATU	Ground Attack Training Unit
DWI	Directional Wireless Installation (Magnetic Minesweepers)	GC	Groupe de Chasse (e.g. GC.2/7)
		GCA	Ground Controlled Approach
EAAS	Empire Air Armament School	GCF	Gunnery Co-operation Flight
EAC	Eastern Air Command	GDGS	Ground Defence Gunners School
EACF	East Africa Communications Flight	GGS	Ground Gunners School
EANS	Empire Air Navigation School	GI	Ground Intructional
ECDU	Electronic Countermeasures Development Unit	GIS	Glider Instructors School
		GOTU	Glider Operational Training Unit
ECFS	Empire Central Flying School	Gp	Group
ECM	Electronic Countermeasures	GP	General Purpose
ECU	Electronic Countermeasures Unit	GPEU	Glider Pilots Exercise Unit
EEC	English Electric Company	GR&ANS	General Reconnaissance and Air Navigation School
EFS	Empire Flying School		
EFTS	Elementary Flying Training School	GRU	General Reconnaissance Unit (numbered 1 to 3)
ERFTS	Elementary & Reserve Flying Training School		
		GRU/F	Gunnery Research Unit/Flight
ERS	Empire Radio School	GS	Gliding School
ETPS	Empire Test Pilots School	GS	Grading School
EUAS	Edinburgh University Air Squadron	GSU	Group Support Unit

GTF	Gunnery Training Flight	OAPU	Overseas Aircraft Preparation Unit
GTS	Glider Training Squadron (no number)	OATS	Officers Advanced Training School
GTS	Glider Training School (numbered)	Obs	Observation (USAAF)
GU	Grading Unit	OCTU	Officer Cadet Training Unit
GUAS	Glasgow University Air Squadron	OCU	Operational Conversion Unit
HAD	Home Aircraft Depot	ORTU	Operational & Refresher Training Unit
HCCS	Home Command Communications Squadron	OTU	Operational Training Unit
		OUAS	Oxford University Air Squadron
HCEU	Home Command Examining Unit	PAFU	(Pilots) Advanced Flying Unit
HCU	Heavy Conversion Unit	PAS/U	Pilotless Aircraft Section/Unit
Hdlg Sqn	Handling Squadron	PDU	Photographic Development Unit
HFU	Home Ferry Unit	PEE	Proof & Experimental Establishment, Shoeburyness
HGCU	Heavy Glider Conversion Unit		
HGSU	Heavy Glider Servicing Unit	PEFTS	Polish Elementary Flying Training School
HGTU	Heavy Glider Training Unit	PFF	Pathfinder Force
HKAAF	Hong Kong Auxiliary Air Force	PFS	Parachute Flying Section
HP	Handley Page	PFTS	Polish Flying Training School
HUAS	Hull University Air Squadron	POTU	Polish Operational Training Unit
HxCF	Halifax Conversion Flight	PRDU/E	Photographic Reconnaissance Development Unit/Establishment
IAF	Indian Air Force		
JASS	Joint Anti-Submarine School	PRFU/S	Pilots Refresher Flying Unit/School
KAF	Kenya Air Force	PRRP	Pilots Reserve & Reinforcement Pool (Middle East)
KF	King's Flight		
LFS	Lancaster Finishing School	PRU	Photographic Reconnaissance Unit
MAAF	Mediterranean Allied Air Forces	PTS	Parachute Training School
MAC	Mediterranean Air Command	PTU	Parachute Test Unit
MACAF	Mediterranean Allied Coastal Air Forces	PTURP	Pilots Training Unit & Reinforcement Pool (see also TURP)
MAEE	Marine Aircraft Experimental Establishment		
		QB	Queen Bee
MAP	Ministry of Aircraft Production	QF	Queen's Flight
MATAF	Mediterranean Allied Tactical Air Forces	QUAS	Queen's University Air Squadron
MCA	Ministry of Civil Aviation	RAAF	Royal Australian Air Force
MCC&FF	Maintenance Command Communications and Ferry Flight	R&D	Research & Development
		RAE	Royal Aircraft Establishment
MCCS/F	Maintenance Command Communication Squadron/Flight	RAFC	Royal Air Force College
		RAFFC	Royal Air Force Flying College
MCS	Metropolitan Communications Squadron	RAFG	Royal Air Force Germany
MCU	Mosquito Conversion Unit	RAFM	RAF Mission
ME	Middle East	RAFNI	Royal Air Force Northern Ireland
MEAF	Middle East Air Force	RAFRS	Royal Air Force Regiment School
MECCS/U	Middle East Check & Conversion Squadron/Unit	RAFTC	Royal Air Force Technical College
		RATG/W	Rhodesia Air Training Group/Wing
MECGS	Middle East Central Gunnery School	RCAF	Royal Canadian Air Force
MECF/S	Middle East Communications Flight/Squadron	RCCS/F	Reserve Command Communications Squadron/Flight
MedME	Mediterranean and Middle East	RDAF	Royal Danish Air Force
MEFC	Middle East Ferry Control	RDFS	Radio Direction Finding School
METS	Middle East Training School	Rec	Reconnaissance
Mk	Mark	REAF	Royal Egyptian Air Force
Mkrs	Makers	RFS	Reserve Flying School
MoA	Ministry of Aviation	RFTS	Refresher Flying Training School
MoS	Ministry of Supply	RFU	Refresher Flying Unit
MSFU	Merchant Ship Fighter Unit	RHAF	Royal Hellenic Air Force
MTU	Mosquito Training Unit	RIAF	Royal Indian Air Force
MU	Maintenance Unit	RM	Royal Marines
MUAS	Manchester University Air Squadron	RMAF	Royal Malaysian Air Force
NA	North Africa	RMU	Radio Maintenance Unit
NAAF	Northwest African Air Forces	RN	Royal Navy
NACAF	Northwest African Coastal Air Force	RNAS	Royal Naval Air Station
NASAF	Northwest African Strategic Air Forces	RNethAF	Royal Netherlands Air Force
NATAF	Northwest African Tactical Air Forces	RNFS	Royal Navy Fighter Squadron (in ME)
Navex	Navigation exercise	RNorAF	Royal Norwegian Air Force
NTU	Navigation Training Unit, Pathfinder Force	RNZAF	Royal New Zealand Air Force
		RPAF	Royal Pakistan Air Force
OADF/U	Overseas Aircraft Delivery Flight/Unit	R-R	Rolls-Royce
OAFU	(Observers) Advanced Flying Unit	RRAF	Royal Rhodesian Air Force

RRE	Radar Research Establishment	TCCS/F	Transport Command Communications Squadron/Flight
RRFU	Radar Research Flying Unit	TCDU	Transport Command Development Unit
RS	Radio School	TCEU	Transport Command Examining Unit
RSU/RSS	Repair and Servicing Unit/Section	TCU	Transport Conversion Unit
RU	Repair Unit	TDU	Torpedo Development Unit
RWE	Radio Warfare Establishment	TEU	Tactical Exercise Unit
SAAF	South African Air Force	TF	Training Flight
SAC	School of Army Co-operation	TFPP	Training Ferry Pilots Pool
SAN	School of Air Navigation	TFS/F	Target Facilities Squadron/Flight
SAR	Search & Rescue	TFU	Telecommunications Flying Unit
SARTU/S	Search & Rescue Training Unit/Squadron	TRE	Telecommunications Research Establishment
S of AS	School of Air Support	TSCU	Transport Support Conversion Unit
S of AT	School of Air Transport	TSTU	Transport Support Training Unit
SATC	School of Air Traffic Control	TT	Target Towing
SD	Special Duties	TTC	Technical Training Command
SDF	Special Duties Flight	TTCCF	Technical Training Command Communications Flight
SDU	Signals Development Unit		
SF	Station Flight	TTF	Target Towing Flight
SFC	School of Flying Control	TTU	Torpedo Training Unit
SFF	Service Ferry Flight	TURP	Training Unit & Reserve Pool (ME)
SFPP	Service Ferry Pilots Pool	TWDU	Tactical Weapons Development Unit
SFTS	Service Flying Training School	UAS	University Air Squadron
SFU	Signals Flying Unit	ULAS	University of London Air Squadron
SGR	School of General Reconnaissance	USAAC/F	United States Army Air Corps/Forces
SGR&AN	School of General Reconnaissance and Air Navigation (India)	USN	United States Navy
		V-A	Vickers-Armstrongs
S&H	Short Bros. & Harland	WA	West Africa
SHAEF	Supreme Headquarters Allied Expeditionary Force	WDCF/U	Western Desert Communications Flight/Unit
Sigs	Signals	W(I)DU	Wireless (Intelligence) Development Unit
SIU	Signals Intelligence Unit	WEE	Winterisation Experimental Establishment
SLAIS	Specialised Low Attack Intructors School	Wg	Wing
SLAW	School of Land/Air Warfare	WL	Wing Leader
SLG	Satellite Landing Ground	WTU	Warwick Training Unit
SMR	School of Maritime Reconnaissance	YUAS	York University Air Squadron
SOE	Special Operations Executive		
S of P	School of Photography	**Fates:**	
SP	Staging Post		
SPTU	Staff Pilots Training Unit	BER	Beyond Economical Repair
Sqn	Squadron	BBOC	Brought back on charge
SRAF	Southern Rhodesian Air Force	BU	Broken up
SRF	Sea Rescue Flight	DBR	Damaged beyond repair
SS	Signals School	DBF	Destroyed by fire
SSVAF	Straits Settlements Volunteer Air Force	Exp	Flying hours expired
STT	School of Technical Training	NFD	No further data
SU	Support Unit	NFT	No further trace
TAF	Tactical Air Force	NT	No trace
TAFSU	Tactical Air Force Support Unit	NTU	Not taken up
TAMU	Transport Aircraft Modification Unit	ORB	Operations Record Book
TB	Torpedo-bomber	SOC	Struck off Charge
TC	Training Command (later Transport Command)	SS	Sold as scrap
		WFU	Withdrawn from Use
TCASF	Transport Command Air Support Flight		

Tiger Moth R5019 of No.18 Reserve Flying School

AIRCRAFT IN P and R SERIES

Airspeed Envoy	Communications	Small batch of civil light transports produced for communications plus one impressed aircraft for radio training
Airspeed Oxford	Trainer	Standard twin-engined trainer used mainly for pilot training. Some were used for communications. Many sent overseas for Empire Air Training Scheme.
Airspeed Queen Wasp	Target aircraft	Batch of radio controlled targets. Production cancelled after only a few had been built.
Armstrong Whitworth Albemarle	Glider tug and paratroop transport	Intended as a medium bomber for assembly by non-specialised constructors using quantities of non-strategic material. Not required as a bomber and converted to glider tugs and parachute troop transports.
Armstrong Whitworth Whitley	Night bomber	Batches of standard night bomber. Some used for anti-submarine patrols and others for parachute training.
Avro Anson	General reconnaissance	A small number of these P- and R-series aircraft went to operational and training squadrons but the majority were used as navigation and radio trainers. The ATA used this type as taxi aircraft to recover pilots after they had delivered aircraft.
Avro Lancaster	Heavy bomber	Early production batches laid down as Manchesters but completed as Lancasters
Avro Manchester	Heavy bomber	Final production batch, most of which was completed as Lancasters
Bristol Beaufighter	Night and long-range fighter	Twin-engined fighter used initially as night fighter but later aircraft delivered to Coastal Command as escort fighters and strike aircraft.

Bristol Blenheim	Light bomber and long-range fighter	Standard light bomber. Some delivered to Coastal Command for strike and escort duties. Replaced in Coastal Command by Beaufighters.
Cierva C-40A	Calibration	Civil Autogyro acquired for calibrating ground radar.
Consolidated 28-5	General Reconnaissance	Civil flying boat acquired for evaluation. Subsequently the type was purchased in military form as the Catalina
Curtiss Condor	Transport	Impressed twin-engined biplane airliners of US origin. Found unsuitable for military use.
de Havilland Dominie	Radio trainer and communications	Military production version of pre-war D.H.89 Rapide civil transport. Some civil D.H.89As were impressed for communications duties. Many sold to civilian use post-war.
de Havilland Flamingo	Transport	Impressed civil airliners from civil production line.
de Havilland Hertfordshire	Transport	Military version of Flamingo. Not produced in quantity because of pressing requirements for operational aircraft production.
de Havilland Hornet Moth	Communications	Light aircraft acquired for Admiralty.
de Havilland Queen Bee	Target aircraft	Batch of radio-controlled target aircraft.
de Havilland Tiger Moth	Primary trainer	Standard trainer for elementary flying training schools.
Fairey Barracuda	Torpedo-bomber	Prototype torpedo- and dive-bomber for FAA
Fairey Battle	Light bomber	Batches of obsolete light bomber. Many aircraft delivered as trainers (some with twin cockpits in place of glasshouse).
Fairey Swordfish	Torpedo-bomber	FAA biplane used in small numbers by RAF units
Folland 43/37	Testbed	Specially-designed aircraft capable of being fitted with a variety of engines without major modifications to act as flying testbeds.
General Aircraft GAL.38	Fleet spotter	Prototypes of four-engined slow-flying night reconnaissance aircraft for carrier use utilising an early form of stealth technology to shadow enemy ships.
Handley Page Halifax	Heavy bomber	Production batch of standard night bombers.
Handley Page Hampden	Medium bomber	Batches of standard Bomber Command aircraft. Some converted to torpedo-bombers
Hawker Hurricane	Fighter	Production batches of standard fighters. The Canadian Mk.X was the equivalent of the Mk.I
Hawker Tornado	Fighter	Prototypes of new single-seat fighter powered by unsuccessful Vulture engine. Production abandoned in favour of Typhoon.
Hawker Typhoon	Fighter	Early production batches which suffered from structural weakness in rear fuselage. Many were replaced in service by modified aircraft and reduced to components for spares. Some were not assembled and numbers were sent to Schools of Technical Training. Several losses were due to type's resemblance at a distance to FW 190.
Lockheed Hudson	General reconnaissance	Batch of US-built aircraft plus one aircraft delivered as replacement for undelivered Hudson from earlier batch. Some adapted as transports.

179

Lockheed 12A	Transport	Impressed civil aircraft for communications.
Martin-Baker M.B.2	Single-seat fighter	Prototype of pre-war fighter given RAF serial for trials.
Martin-Baker M.B.3/ M.B.5	Single-seat fighter	Prototype single-seat fighters of advanced design not placed in production.
Miles Falcon	Research	Purchased for spoiler tests.
Miles Magister	Trainer	Production batches of elementary trainers.
Miles M.15	Trainer	Prototype basic trainer. Not produced.
North American Harvard	Trainer	Batch of US-produced advanced trainers.
Parnall Hendy Heck III	Communications	Impressed light aircraft
Percival Proctor	Trainer and communications	Military production version of civil Vega Gull light aircraft used for radio training and communications.
Percival Q-6	Communications	Small batch of civil light transports, sometimes referred to as 'Petrels'.
Percival Vega Gull	Communications	Small batch of civil light aircraft acquired for light communications tasks.
Short Stirling	Heavy bomber	Production batch of standard heavy bombers.
Short Sunderland	General reconnaissance	Batch of standard long range patrol flying boats.
Stearman-Hammond V	Research	American twin-boom pusher light aircraft acquired for tricycle undercarriage trials.
Supermarine Spitfire	Fighter	Production batch of standard single-seat fighters. Early aircraft delivered during Battle of Britain, later aircraft converted to Mark Vs. Some converted to photographic reconnaissance aircraft; references to Marks III, IV, V, VI and VII in this volume relate to PR variants and are not in the standard mark progression, being conversion of Marks C, D, E, F and 0 to numbers. Only Mark IV was later an official mark number in normal sequence.
Supermarine Walrus	ASR amphibian	Royal Navy aircraft passed to RAF for air-sea rescue duties.
Supermarine 322	Torpedo-bomber	Prototypes of naval torpedo bomber; not produced in quantity.
Vickers Wellington	Heavy bomber	Production batches of standard night bomber. Some converted to D.W.I. minesweepers, others built as Mark IVs with Twin Wasp engines. A fair number were lost during the dangerous UK-Gibraltar-Malta-Egypt ferry flights due to lack of diversion airfields and enemy bombing at Malta.
Waco ZVN	Research	US light aircraft acquired for tricycle undercarriage trials.
Weir W.6	Experimental	Research helicopter built by G.&J.Weir. Flew in 1941.
Westland Lysander	Army Cooperation	Production batches of standard army cooperation aircraft. Many converted to target tugs and some for ASR and agent-dropping duties.
Westland Whirlwind	Single-seat fighter	Sole production batch of twin-engined fighters.

INDEX OF AIRCRAFT

Airspeed

Envoy	P5625-P5629
	P5778
Oxford	P1070-P1094
	P1800-P1849
	P1860-P1899
	P1920-P1969
	P1980-P2009
	P2030-P2059
	P6795-P6819
	P6831-P6880
	P8822-P8868
	P8891-P8931
	P8964-P8998
	P9020-P9046
	R4062-R4067
	R5938-R5979
	R5991-R6038
	R6050-R6059
	R6070-R6114
	R6129-R6163
	R6177-R6196
	R6211-R6248
	R6263-R6299
	R6317-R6358
	R6371-R6403
	R9974-R9988
Queen Wasp	P5441-P5445

Armstrong Whitworth

Albemarle	P1360-P1409
	P1430-P1479
	P1500-P1529
	P1550-P1569
	P1590-P1609
	P1620-P1659
Whitley V	P4930-P4974
	P4980-P5029
	P5040-P5065
	P5070-P5112

Avro

Anson	R3303-R3351
	R3368-R3413
	R3429-R3476
	R3512-R3561
	R3581-R3587
	R9567-R9611
	R9627-R9670
	R9685-R9725
	R9739-R9781
	R9798-R9846
	R9864-R9899
	R9928-R9969

Lancaster	R5482-R5517
	R5537-R5S76
	R5603-R5640
	R5658-R57O3
	R5724-R5763
	R5842-R5868
	R5888-R5917
Manchester	R5768-R5797
	R5829-R5841
	R8923-R8947

Bristol

Beaufighter	R2052-R2101
	R2120-R2159
	R2180-R2209
	R2240-R2284
	R2300-R2349
	R2370-R2404
	R2430-R2479
Blenheim	P4825-P4864
	P4898-P4927
	P6885-P6934
	P6950-P6961
	R277O-R2799
	R3590-R3639
	R3660-R37O9
	R3730-R3779
	R3800-R3849
	R3870-R3919

Cierva

C-40A	P9639

Consolidated

28-5	P9630

Curtiss

Condor	P6785-P6788

de Havilland

Dominie I	R2485-R2487
Falcon	R4071
Flamingo/	R251O
Hertfordshire	R2764-R2766
Hornet Moth	P6785-P6788
Queen Bee	P4677-P4716
	P4747-P4781
	P4788-P4822
	P5731-P5749
	P5767-P5775

Rapide	P1764-P1765
	P9588-P9589
	R5921-R5934
	R9545-R9564
Tiger Moth	R4748-R4797
	R4810-R4859
	R4875-R4924
	R4940-R4989
	R5005-R5044
	R5057-R5086
	R5100-R5149
	R5170-R5219
	R5236-R5265

Fairey

Barracuda	P1767; P1770
	P9647
Battle	P2155-P2204
	P2233-P2278
	P2300-P2336
	P2353-P2369
	P5228-P5252
	P5270-P5294
	P6480-P6509
	P6523-P6572
	P6596-P6645
	P6663-P6692
	P6718-P6737
	P6750-P6769
	R3922-R3971
	R3990-R4019
	R4035-R4054
	R7356-R7385
	R7399-R7448
	R7461-R7480
Swordfish	Between P3991 and P4279

Folland

43/37	P1774-P1785

General Aircraft

G.A.L.38	P1758, P1759

Handley Page

Halifax	R9363-R9392
	R9418-R9457
	R9482-R9498
	R9528-R9540
Hampden	P1145-P1189
	P1194-P1230
	P1233-P1261
	P1265-P1305
	P1309-P1356

Hampden (cont)	P2062-P2100		12A	R8987	**Supermarine**	
	P2110-P2145					
	P4285-P4324		**Martin-Baker**		Spitfire	P7280-P7329
	P4335-P4384					P7350-P7389
	P4389-P4418		M.B.2	P9594		P7420-P7449
	P5298-P5346					P7490-P7509
	P5386-P5400		M.B.3	R2492		P7520-P7569
	P5421-P5436					P7590-P7629
			M.B.5	R2496		P7660-P7699
Hawker						P7730-P7759
			Miles			P7770-P7789
Hurricane	P2535-P3584					P7810-P7859
	P2614-P2653		Magister	P2150		P7880-P7929
	P2672-P2701			P2374-P2410		P7960-P7999
	P2713-P2732			P2426-P2470		P8010-P8049
	P2751-P2770			P2493-P2510		P8070-P8099
	P2792-P2836			P6343-P6382		P8130-P8149
	P2854-P2888			P6396-P6424		P8160-P8209
	P2900-P2924			P6436-P6466		P8230-P8279
	P2946-P2995			R1810-R1859		P8310-P8349
	P3020-P3069			R1875-R1924		P8360-P8399
	P3080-P3124			R1940-R1984		P8420-P8449
	P3140-P3179					P8460-P8479
	P3200-P3234		M.15	P6326		P8500-P8549
	P3250-P3279					P8560-P8609
	P3300-P3324		**North American**			P8640-P8679
	P3345-P3364					P8690-P8729
	P3380-P3429		Harvard	P5783-P5982		P8740-P8759
	P3448-P3492					P8780-P8799
	P3515-P3554		**Parnall**			P9305-P9339
	P3574-P3684					P9360-P9399
	P3700-P3789		Hendy Heck III	R9138		PP9420-P9469
	P3802-P3836					P9490-P9519
	P3854-P3903					P9540-P9567
	P3920-P3944		**Percival**			R6595-R6644
	P3960-P3984					R6683-R6722
	P5170-P5209		Proctor	P5999-P6037		R6751-R6780
	P8809-P8818			P6050-P6079		R6799-R6818
	R2680-R2689			P6101-P6145		R6829-R6840
	R4074-R4123			P6166-P6200		R6879-R6928
	R4171-R4200			P6226-P6275		R6957-R6996
	R4213-R4232			P6301-P6322		R7015-R7044
Tornado	P5219, P5224			R7485-R7499		R7055-R7074
	R7936, R7938			R7520-R7539		R7114-R7163
				R7559-R7573		R7192-R7231
Typhoon	P5212, P5216					R7250-R7279
	R7576-R7599		Q-6	P5634-P5641		R7290-R7309
	R7613-R7655					R7333-R7250
	R7672-R7721		Vega Gull	P1749-P1754		
	R7738-R7775			P5986-P5993	Walrus	P5646-P5670
	R7792-R7829					P5696-P5720
	R7845-R7890					R6543
	R7913-R7923		**Short**			R6546-R6549
	R8198-R8200					R6552; R8584
	R8220-R8231		Stirling	R9141-R9170		R6588
	R8630-R8663			R9184-R9203		
	R8680-R8722			R9241-R9290	**Vickers**	
	R8737-R8781			R9295-R9334		
	R8799-R8845			R9349-R9358	Wellington	P2515-P2532
	R8861-R8900					P9205-P9237
	R8966-R8981		Sunderland	P9600-P9606		P9265-P9300
				P9620-P9624		R1000-R1049
Lockheed						R1060-R1099
			Stearman-Hammond			R1135-R1184
Hudson	P5116-P5165					R1210-R1254
	R4059		Y	R2676		R1265-R1299

Wellington (cont)	R1320-R1349	**Waco**		Lysander (cont)	P9095-P9140
	R1365-R1414				P9176-P9199
	R1435-R1474	ZVN	P6330		R1987-R2O10
	R1490-R1539				R2025-R2047
	R1585-R1629	**Weir**			R2572-R2600
	R1640-R1669				R2612-R2652
	R1695-R1729	W.6	R5269		R8991-R9030
	R1757-R1806				R9056-R9079
	R2699-R2703	**Westland**			R9100-R9135
	R3150-R3179				
	R3195-R3239	Lysander	P1665-P1699	Whirlwind	P6966-7015
	R3275-R3299		P1711-P1745		P7035-P7064
			P9051-P9080		P7089-P7122